"This timely book overruns with profound methods to : cated our lives to. From the basic idea of admitting you m seek out answers for the current elephants in the room – yo............realistic principles that can immediately be adopted into daily practice. A must read for all behavior analysts – new and old!"

— *R. Nicolle Carr, PhD, BCBA-D, LBA*

"The updated edition of *Understanding Ethics in Applied Behavior Analysis* teaches a nuanced, thoughtful approach to professional decision-making in real-world situations. Ethical behavior is not easy nor straightforward. Yet, this book's fresh approach inspires courage when facing complex dilemmas at work. Such difficulties become, instead, opportunities to collaborate and act on shared values. Readable and engaging, with examples brought to life by diverse experts in behavior analysis, this humble and caring text is a unique contribution to a complex topic."

— *Robyn M. Catagnus, EdD, BCBA-D, LBS*

"This book synthesizes concepts and terms in the new BACB® Ethics Code with existing ones for a more comprehensive and up-to-date view of ethical considerations. The authors apply the concepts in a thoughtful manner to the various facets of practice that all behavior analysts should read and become familiar with. This is a well-written book that addresses client rights, dignity, right to be free from aversive interventions, and informed choice, as integral aspects of the consent process. The section on ethical decision-making is particularly compelling and will serve as a very useful resource for behavior analysts. This book will serve as a much-needed resource on ethical practices for behavior analysts for years to come."

— *Michael Weinberg, PhD, LP, LABA, LBA, BCBA-D*

Understanding Ethics in Applied Behavior Analysis

This book provides the foundation for a lifelong journey of ethical practice in service for individuals with autism spectrum disorder and other developmental disabilities.

The second edition of *Understanding Ethics in Applied Behavior Analysis* includes an explanation of each element in the Ethics Code for Behavior Analysts, along with considerations for ethical practice and examples from the field. Professional behavior for the behavior analyst is also addressed when fulfilling roles as teacher, employee, manager, colleague, advocate, or member of a multidisciplinary team. This new edition expands on the first chapter's introduction of moral philosophy, adds a new chapter on ethical decision-making and core principles, and provides a study guide to assist those preparing for the Behavior Analyst Certification Board exams.

Drawing upon Beirne and Sadavoy's combined 40 years of clinical experience as well as the reflections of colleagues in the field, this is an indispensable guide to ethics for behavior analysis students.

Ann Beirne, MA, BCBA has worked as a clinician for over 20 years and has seen applications of applied behavior analysis across the lifespan and trained professionals on five continents to practice behavior analysis.

Jacob A. Sadavoy, MS, BCBA has passionately devoted over two decades in the application of the principles of applied behavior analysis in schools, centers, businesses, training institutions, and homes around the world.

Understanding Ethics in Applied Behavior Analysis

Practical Applications

Second Edition

Edited by Ann Beirne and Jacob A. Sadavoy

Routledge
Taylor & Francis Group

NEW YORK AND LONDON

Cover image: © Getty Images

Second edition published 2022
by Routledge
605 Third Avenue, New York, NY 10158

and by Routledge
4 Park Square, Milton Park, Abingdon, Oxon, OX14 4RN

Routledge is an imprint of the Taylor & Francis Group, an informa business

First edition published by Routledge 2019

Library of Congress Cataloging-in-Publication Data
Names: Beirne, Ann, editor. | Sadavoy, Jacob A., editor.
Title: Understanding ethics in applied behavior analysis : practical applications / edited by Ann Beirne and Jacob A. Sadavoy.
Description: Second edition. | New York, NY : Routledge, 2022. | Revision of: Understanding ethics in applied behavior analysis / Ann Beirne and Jacob A. Sadavoy. 2019. | Includes bibliographical references and index.
Identifiers: LCCN 2021024510 (print) | LCCN 2021024511 (ebook) | ISBN 9781032041360 (hardback) | ISBN 9781032041353 (paperback) | ISBN 9781003190707 (ebook)
Subjects: LCSH: Autism spectrum disorders. | Autism spectrum disorders—Diagnosis.
Classification: LCC RC570 .B44 2022 (print) | LCC RC570 (ebook) | DDC 616.85/88—dc23
LC record available at https://lccn.loc.gov/2021024510
LC ebook record available at https://lccn.loc.gov/2021024511

ISBN: 978-1-032-04136-0 (hbk)
ISBN: 978-1-032-04135-3 (pbk)
ISBN: 978-1-003-19070-7 (ebk)

DOI: 10.4324/9781003190707

Typeset in Times New Roman
by codeMantra

Contents

Preface

Why a Second Edition?

When the Behavior Analyst Certification Board® announced their revision of the ethical standards, we, like many other behavior analysts, waited with bated breath and no small amount of trepidation to see what the changes would be.

What we saw when we began diving into the Ethics Code® was a Code that represented the needs of the field that we wrote about so cautiously in our first edition. Issues such as diversity and self-care were coming to the forefront. Our core principles, including treatment of individuals with dignity, were now explicitly discussed. In addition, a new section on ethical decision-making was included, one that emphasized the importance of considering contextual variables.

In our combined 35 years of clinical experience, we have seen the growth and development of this field. Like many behavior analysts, we have sometimes been ahead of the cultural curve and at other times struggled to keep up. Now, as behavior analysts begin to grapple with new issues and in new ways, we believe that this represents an exciting opportunity – not only for us as individual professionals, but for the field as a whole.

Behavior analysis, as a practice, has existed for only a short time and has seen exponential growth in recent decades, which is projected to continue as we attempt to meet the growing need for services. The issues we grapple with today – the impact of neurodiversity, systemic racism and the underrepresentation of people of color in our field, the challenges of providing compassionate care while preventing burnout – are not the challenges of 20 years ago. The BACB® has responded, and as behavior analysts (and future behavior analysts) we must respond to them also.

In our first edition, we expressed a commitment to avoid the "one voice narrative." We sought to open wide the discussion surrounding ethics for behavior analysts and the challenges of maintaining high standards of ethics. In our discussions with other professionals, we have discovered that when asked, "What ethical issue is most important to you?" it is very rare to find two behavior analysts with the same answer. Individual experiences among professionals vary, but the necessity of elevating the voices of our colleagues and bringing ethical issues to light remains our commitment.

This Book and Your Ethics Study

When starting mentorship toward becoming board-certified, our first author was asked for goals for the supervision process, and said, "I don't want to be confounded by cases anymore. I want to know the answers." The mentor wisely said, "Well, I don't think I can do that for you." And he, of course, was exactly right. Looking back, mentorship cannot teach all the answers. We still do not have all the answers. That was not what that journey at the time was about, and as we continue the professional journey, knowing the answers still is not the goal. What was gained from the process was the ability to ask better questions.

This book also makes no promise to teach you all of the answers. You may feel a bit of conflict between the moral level of "goodness" and the ethical level. That is understandable and will likely continue throughout your career. And there may not be a clear, black-and-white answer to every ethical dilemma. If there were, we could certainly just hand you this book and send you on your way, ready to face any challenge with the right answer 100% of the time. We cannot give you the answers, but we can strive to help you to ask better questions.

We must acknowledge that ethical practice might be better described as a journey than a destination. To be a truly ethical practitioner is to consistently recognize the need to improve. Ethical practice is in a constant state of evolution and much of our behavior is appropriately shaped by others in the field, as well as related fields. This is why we have included "reflections" from relevant experts in issues ranging from staff training to functional assessments to moral philosophy. Many will offer opinions about the Ethics Code®, its importance, and its application to the daily realities of clinical practice. Some of these opinions may be different from yours, or even ours. Their viewpoints are included here not to dictate what your opinions should be, but to inform your own journey.

The chapters in Part 1 of this book include a review of a section of the Code, including an explanation of each element, some considerations when engaging in ethical practice, and examples from the field. In Part 2, we will explore the professional behavior of the behavior analyst and how to navigate the various professional environments in which we work, so that we can promote best practices and support lasting, meaningful behavior change. In Part 3, we have included essays on aspects of ethical practice from those within the field of behavior analysis as well as experts outside it.

Acknowledgments

Writing the second edition of this book was a bit less pressure but still a tremendous amount of work.

First and foremost, Jacob Sadavoy has been a champion. His patience and stick-to-it-tiveness got this done. I'm not sure what this would be without him. Definitely not a book, though.

Thank you to Routledge for taking a chance on this book the first time and for enthusiastically supporting our second edition.

When we first envisioned what this book would be, we knew we wanted to include as many voices as possible. All of the contributors who said "yes" did so with enthusiasm, and this would not be the same without them. You are all extraordinary.

A special note of appreciation should be extended to those contributors from outside the field of analysis, who volunteered their time and insight to a project whose scope was outside of their expertise. The fact that these professionals took an hour of their time to talk to me, have the call recorded and at the conclusion asked, "So what is this for again?" is compelling evidence of their generosity with their time and knowledge. Philip Zimbardo was ready, willing, and able to share his perspectives from outside the field. In an absolute Hail Mary pass of an email, I reached out to Todd May, who immediately returned the correspondence, sat down for an interview with me and was incredibly kind. Simply because, as he put it, "Not enough people want to talk about moral philosophy." I feel smarter just from having met him and honored that he took the time.

My parents were incredibly supportive throughout the entire writing process. They have been incredible cheerleaders when I needed it most.

I once heard that Leo Tolstoy's wife hand wrote six copies of *War and Peace* by candlelight each night after her children went to bed. If this is true, then my husband, David Freiman, earns only second place in the competition for long-suffering spouse of an author. David provided a patient ear for rants on ethics, proofread early drafts (as well as later ones) and even secured interviews. And moreover, he provided constant encouragement when I needed it most, and also when it was just nice to hear. He contributed wonderful ideas and barely ever said "I told you so" when he was right about them.

In the last edition, I wrote, "My children have shown extraordinary patience and enthusiasm for this project and for all the work it has necessitated." After a year of both Mom and Dad working from home, Mom also writing a book got old *real quick*. But still they never wavered in their support. You drive me forward every day.

Thank you especially to every child and family that has welcomed into your homes and your hearts and allowed me the privilege of working with you.

Ann Beirne

xiv   *Acknowledgments*

Our clinical skills are a sum of our clinical experiences which is why I recognize how fortunate I have been to have been blessed with gifted, impassioned, and inspired colleagues. Ann, your passion and dedication is infectious (you are also hilarious and I thoroughly appreciate our musical tangents). My parents, for instilling a sense of ethical behavior from Day 1 (the editing help was also appreciated). Our contributors, I am overjoyed to have your stories enrich this textbook. I am so grateful. My colleagues, who have led by example and sought to grow and learn alongside me, thank you. Lastly, my clients, whose desire to succeed and overcome daily obstacles has taught me about perseverance and teamwork. I am forever indebted to all of you.

J.A.S.

About Our Contributors

Dr. Matthew T. Brodhead

Matthew Brodhead is an assistant professor at Michigan State University and a Board-Certified Behavior Analyst-Doctoral. He examines behavioral determinants of response variability, choice, and independent social skills in children with autism. He is also interested in research and conceptual issues relating to the ethical and professional behavior of practicing behavior analysts. He is on the editorial boards of *The Analysis of Verbal Behavior, Behavior and Philosophy*, and the *Review Journal of Autism and Developmental Disorders*. Through workshops and consultation, he has established multiple school-based programs for children with autism, and he has provided training to teachers, related service providers, and behavior analysts throughout the United States.

Dr. Nasiah Cirincione-Ulezi

Nasiah Cirincione-Ulezi is the CEO and Founder of ULEZI, LLC. She is a Board-Certified Behavior Analyst and holds a doctorate degree in Education from Loyola University of Chicago. She holds a Master's degree in Special Education from the University of Illinois at Chicago and a Master's degree in Educational Leadership from the American College of Education. She completed advanced graduate studies in Infant and Toddler Studies at Erikson Institute in Chicago. Dr. Cirincione-Ulezi has worked in the field of Disability Services for more than 20 years, as a special educator, clinician, educational administrator and professor of education. She is deeply committed to using her skills and experience to uplift and transform the lives of the people she supports, in positive and meaningful ways.

Dr. Yulema Cruz

Yulema received an MS in Psychology with a concentration in ABA from Florida State University in 2006, and soon after became a BCBA. She received her PhD from Nova Southeastern University and is currently and assistant teaching professor at Rutgers University. Her academic interests include ethics and supervision in ABA, the latter of which is the topic of her dissertation. Aside from being an adjunct instructor for Purdue University Global and Florida *International* University, Yulema is also an ABA consultant, and supervisor. Additionally, she works in the development of supervision systems, and the dissemination of ABA to other countries and languages. As the President for FABA, she participated in the Program Committee, and co-chairs the Legislative and Political Action Committee.

Dr. Cheryl Davis

Cheryl Davis is a licensed and certified behavior analyst as well as a Special Education teacher who received her doctoral degree from Endicott College in Applied Behavior Analysis. Cheryl is a Professor of Practice at the Sage Colleges, as well as owner of 7 Dimensions Consulting, LLC. She received a Master of Science Degree in Intensive Special Education from Simmons College in Boston, MA after attending the University of Connecticut where she received a bachelor's degree in Human Development. Cheryl then pursued her BCBA, while working in a world renown ABA school. With over 20 years of experience working with children and families with autism, developmental disabilities, and related disorders, Cheryl specializes in effective programming for clients in need, online teaching, active responding, and skill acquisition. She has had experience as a teacher, job coach, home therapist, residential supervisor, public school consultant, staff trainer, and professor. Cheryl has extensive experience in developing training topics for both parents and teaching staff. She has provided professional development trainings to over 2,000 teaching staff.

Dr. Michael F. Dorsey

Dr. Dorsey is a Licensed Applied Behavior Analyst and professor of Education and the co-founder/director of the Institute for Behavioral Studies at Endicott College. Dr. Dorsey served as a member of the MABA Program Committee in 1975, and more recently as a member of the ABAI Accreditation Committee and as the Chair of the Practice Board. He is a licensed Psychologist and Board-Certified Behavior Analyst. Dr. Dorsey has served on the faculty of several prestigious universities, including the Johns Hopkins University School of Medicine. He has authored/co-authored many professional publications, including development of the Functional Analysis methodology. Dr. Dorsey has been a Gubernatorial appointee of the Developmental Disabilities Councils of both Florida and Massachusetts and chaired the Massachusetts MDDC Governmental Affairs Committee for over six years. In 1992 he served as a US representative to the First Papal Congress on Developmental Disabilities. Dr. Dorsey is a registered Lobbyist in Massachusetts and has co-authored several bills related to the practice of applied behavior analysis.

Dr. Ksenia Gatzunis

Dr. Ksenia Gatzunis is a doctoral-level Board-Certified Behavior Analyst (BCBA-D) whose primary work includes supervising graduate students who are pursuing certification with the Behavior Analyst Certification Board (BACB) and teaching Master's-level courses in applied behavior analysis. She has also provided clinical supervision to clinicians and trained practitioners in behavior analytic practices, both within the United States and internationally across several countries.

Dr. Peter F. Gerhardt

Dr. Gerhardt has more than 30 years' experience utilizing the principles of applied behavior analysis in support of individuals with autism spectrum disorders in educational, employment, residential and community-based settings. Dr. Gerhardt is the author or the coauthor of many articles and book chapters on the needs of adolescents and adults with ASDs and has presented nationally and internationally on this topic. Dr. Gerhardt is the founding chair of the Scientific Council for the Organization for Autism Research (OAR) and currently sits on numerous professional advisory boards including Behavior Analysis in Practice, the Cambridge Center for Behavioral Studies, the Association of Professional Behavior Analysts, and the Autism Society of America. He received his doctorate from Rutgers, the State University of New Jersey, Graduate School of Education.

Dr. Scott Herbst

Scott Herbst, PhD, BCBA, earned his doctorate at the University of Nevada, Reno where he focused on organizational behavior management (OBM), relational frame theory (RFT), and acceptance and commitment training (ACT). After six years as a professor at the Chicago School of Professional Psychology, he left to start SixFlex Training & Consulting, where he and his colleagues work with leaders and managers on applying RFT and ACT to team communication, performance management, coaching, and leadership. In addition to SixFlex, he is co-owner and Chief Programming Officer for Pivot 2 Inclusion, a firm that works with organizations to create workplaces where equity and inclusion are a natural part of doing business. He has numerous peer-reviewed and popular-press publications in the areas of organizational culture, leadership, stigma, and communication. He is currently on the editorial boards of the *Journal of Organizational Behavior Management* and *Behavior and Social Issues*, and a frequent guest reviewer for other publications. His mission in life is that people choose a purpose that inspires them and are energized and alive in the fulfillment of that purpose.

Joy Johnson, MEd, MS, BCBA, LBA

Joy is a BCBA/clinical manager for Signature Behavioral Health. She is a behavior analyst, inclusion specialist, and autism advocate who partners with organizations, individuals, and families to improve the lives of Autistic people. After spending years working in clinical settings, non-profits, and schools, her experience enables her to truly serve and represent Autistic community members in various contexts. She holds a Master's in education and a Master's in psychology with a specialization in ABA. In addition to her extensive education and professional experiences, she has a great deal personal experience. She is Autistic herself, which provides her with a unique perspective, knowledge, and source of passion.

Tamara S. Kasper

Tamara Kasper, MS, CCC-SLP, BCBA, has practiced for nearly 30 years, specializing in treatment of children with autism. Tamara has devoted her career to identifying and developing effective treatments to promote functional communication and social interaction skills. Under the mentorship of Dr. Vincent Carbone, Tamara became a Board-Certified Behavior Analyst. Tamara is a frequently invited international lecturer, directs the Center for Autism Treatment, and received the Wisconsin Speech-Language Pathology and Audiology Clinical Achievement Award.

Todd May

Todd has been teaching at Clemson University for nearly 30 years. For many of those years his area of specialization in philosophy was recent French thought, especially that of Michel Foucault and Gilles Deleuze. More recently he has turned his attention to broader life concerns: meaning in life, coping with suffering, acting with moral decency, and so on. He is the author of 16 books of philosophy. In addition to his academic work he teaches in a local prison and has organized both inside and outside the university, for instance opposing the university administration's public silence on such important issues as racism on campus and the Muslim ban.

May has published works on major poststructuralist philosophers and wrote books on more general topics accessible to the general reader, including *Death*; *Our Practices, Our Selves, or, What It Means to Be Human*; *Friendship in an Age of Economics: Resisting the Forces of Neoliberalism*; *A Significant Life: Human Meaning in a Silent Universe*; and *A Fragile Life: Accepting Our Vulnerability*.

May, along with Pamela Hieronymi, was a philosophical advisor to the NBC television show *The Good Place*.

Dr. Megan M. Miller

Dr. Megan Miller is the creator of the Do Better Movement and founder of the Do Better Collective. Megan earned her PhD in Special Education and Behavior Analysis at the Ohio State University in 2015. Dr. Miller's early training in behavior analysis occurred at the Cleveland Clinic Center for Autism as a volunteer/intern in 2003. Dr. Miller has taught courses in behavior analysis and special education as an adjunct professor for several universities. She has co-authored journal articles published in the *Journal of Developmental Physical Disability*, *Behavior Analysis in Practice*, and *Teaching Exceptional Children*. She also co-authored *The 7 Steps to Earning Instructional Control* with Robert Schramm, BCBA. Megan regularly presents to professional organizations around the globe as an invited speaker. In 2018, Dr. Miller started the #dobetter professional development movement to improve access to training in best practices in the field of behavior analysis via an online community, webinars, and a podcast.

Dr. Bobby Newman

Dr. Newman is a Board-Certified Behavior Analyst and Licensed Psychologist. Affectionately known as the Dark Overlord of ABA, Bobby is the first author on 13 books regarding behavior therapy, the philosophy of behaviorism, the autism spectrum disorders, utopian literature, and fitness. He has published over two dozen articles in professional journals, as well as numerous popular magazine articles and has hosted two series of radio call-in shows. Bobby is the past-president of the Association for Science in Autism Treatment and the New York State Association for Behavior Analysis. A popular speaker, Bobby also provides direct treatment, staff training and consultation around the world, and has been honored for this work by several parents and professional groups. He is the executive director of Clinical Services for Proud Moments. Bobby is also a certified personal trainer, obstacle course racer and marathoner and is an ambassador for the Great Sportsmanship Programme. Bobby teaches non-violent crisis intervention philosophy and techniques for agencies and families. Bobby was a final four finalist for the 2016 For Those Who Would Humanitarian Award.

Dr. Dana Reinecke

Dana Reinecke is a doctoral-level Board-Certified Behavior Analyst (BCBA-D) and a New York State Licensed Behavior Analyst (LBA). Dana is an assistant professor in the CASE program (Concentration in Autism and Special Education) with the Department of Special Education and Literacy at Long Island University Post. Dana provides training and consultation to school districts, private schools, agencies, and families for individuals with disabilities. She has presented original research and workshops on the treatment of autism and applications of ABA at regional, national, and international conferences. She has published her research in peer-reviewed journals, written chapters in published books, and co-edited books on ABA and Autism. Current areas of research include use of technology to support students with and without disabilities, self-management training of college students with disabilities, and online teaching strategies for effective college and graduate education. Dana is actively involved in the New York State Association for Behavior Analysis (NYSABA) and is currently serving as president-elect (2015–2016) and conference co-chair. She will become president of NYSABA in 2017.

Dr. Samantha (Russo) Volpe

Samantha Russo is the executive director of Enhanced Behavior Supports Program at Elwyn, an education, treatment, and support services institution for children and adults with autism, intellectual and developmental disabilities, and related behavioral health challenges. She received her board certification in behavior analysis (BCBA) in 2014 and holds a Pennsylvania teaching certificate. Samantha received her Master's in Applied Behavior Analysis from Temple University and her undergraduate degree in Special Education and Early Childhood Education from the University of Scranton. She completed her PhD in Applied Behavior Analysis from Endicott College.

Dr. Shane T. Spiker

Shane T. Spiker is a BCBA in Ormond Beach, Florida. Shane received his MS of Psychology in 2012, and in May 2019, he graduated with his PhD in Clinical Psychology with a concentration on instructional design from Walden University. He has worked in the field of behavior analysis for 12 years, with the majority of his experience with adults with autism and other disabilities. Shane specializes in working with teens and adults with dangerous problem behavior, sexual behavior challenges, and with medically complex individuals. Primarily, Shane serves as the director of Training and Dissemination at PBS Corp. He previously served as the vice president of the Sexual Behavior: Research and Practice SIG through ABAI. He is the author of *Anxiety Report*, a biographical accounting of a year in the life of a behavior analyst, and has written several articles on the subject of behavior analysis in practice. Additionally, he serves as a co-instructor at Florida Institute of Technology and Arizona State University, where he teaches graduate level coursework. Shane is a proud father and husband, loves a good bit of Vonnegut, and almost never turns down a fine cup of coffee.

Dr. Noor Y. Syed

Dr. Syed is currently with Lehigh University's Special Education Department as a Professor of Practice and clinical director for Lehigh University Autism Services. Previously, Dr. Syed was an assistant professor of Special Education at Manhattanville College. Dr. Syed has over ten years' experience in the field of applied behavior analysis, general and Special Education, autism, and developmental disabilities as a classroom teacher, Special Education Itinerant Teacher, ABA home-based therapist, and behavioral supervisor for center and home-based services. Dr. Syed has worked in early intervention, preschool, and school aged settings, as well as with adults.

Her research interests lie in verbal behavior, ethical practices in behavior analysis, and the implementation of behavior analysis to curriculum and teaching.

Alexandria Thomas

Alexandria Thomas is a recent Master's graduate in the Applied Behavior Analysis program at Michigan State University (MSU) under the leadership of Dr. Matthew Brodhead. She is currently pursuing to become a Board-Certified Behavior Analyst following graduation and currently works with an adult male to administer ABA treatment in the group home setting. She has worked to administer ABA treatment to clients of a variety of age groups (early intervention and adulthood) and settings (in-clinic, in-home, and via telehealth). She also has worked as a Program Coordinator through MSU's Spartan Caregiver Support organization to connect with families affected by autism to provide support and resources, especially for those whose services have been affected due to the pandemic. This was a free service to parents of children with autism in Michigan and took place over Zoom. She is especially interested in early intervention and transitioning clients out of ABA programs to residential settings while still incorporating principles of ABA for sustained changes over time.

Dr. Mary Jane Weiss

Dr. Weiss is a professor at Endicott College, where she directs the Master's Program in Autism and ABA and is a mentoring faculty member in the doctoral program in ABA. Dr. Weiss has worked in the field of ABA and Autism for over 30 years. She received her PhD in Clinical Psychology from Rutgers University in 1990 and she became a Board-Certified Behavior Analyst in 2000. She previously worked for 16 years at the Douglass Developmental Disabilities Center at Rutgers University, where she served as director of Research and Training and as clinical director. Her clinical and research interests center on defining best practice ABA techniques, exploring ways to enhance the ethical conduct of practitioners, evaluating the impact of ABA in learners with autism, teaching social skills to learners with autism, training staff to be optimally effective at instruction, and maximizing family members' expertise and adaptation. She serves on the Scientific Council of the Organization for Autism Research, is on the Professional Advisory Board of Autism New Jersey, is a regular reviewer for a variety of professional journals, and is a frequent member of service committees for the Behavior Analyst Certification Board. She is also a past-president of the Autism Special Interest Group of the Association for Behavior Analysis International, a former member of the Board of the Association for Professional Behavior Analysts, and a former vice president of the Board of Trustees for Autism New Jersey.

Dr. Merrill Winston

Dr. Winston is a Board-Certified Behavior Analyst who has worked in the field of Developmental Disabilities for over 20 years and has worked in small group homes, large residential facilities, secured facilities, family homes, and schools. Dr. Winston has worked with a broad population who exhibited behavior problems that ranged from mild to life-threatening. His particular areas of interest are crisis prevention and intervention, psychotropic medication usage with special populations, and the development and implementation of training programs designed to increase the skill levels of parents, professionals, teachers, and direct-care staff. Dr. Winston writes, "My goal when working with clients with behavior problems is not the simple reduction or elimination of the problem perse, instead I have a larger goal of defining and trying to manage and/or solve the problems faced by individuals with special needs and their families."

Dr. Philip Zimbardo

A professor emeritus at Stanford University and creator of the Stanford Prison Experiment, Dr. Zimbardo has spent over 50 years teaching and studying psychology. Dr. Zimbardo currently lectures worldwide and is actively working to promote his non-profit the Heroic Imagination Project (<ds>www.heroicimagination.org). He</ds> has written over 60 books and has over 600 publications; his current research looks at the psychology of heroism. He asks: "What pushes some people to become perpetrators of evil, while others act heroically on behalf of those in need?"

Prior to his heroism work, he served as president of the American Psychological Association and designed and narrated the award winning 26-part PBS series, *Discovering Psychology*. He has published more than 50 books and 400 professional and popular articles and chapters, among them: *Shyness*; *The Lucifer Effect*; *The Time Cure*; *The Time Parado*; and most recently, *Man, Interrupted*.

Michelle Lynn Zube

Michelle Zube is a Licensed (NYS), Board Certified Behavior Analyst and dual certified general and special education teacher in the state of New Jersey. She has developed programs for children both domestically and internationally for over 15 years and has consulted for school districts and businesses. Michelle is currently the Lead Behavior Analyst for Healthy Young Monds, LLC. She specializes in Acceptance and Commitment Training (ACT), Organizational and Behavior Management (OBM), and in transforming performance via coaching and mentoring. Michelle is also a co-editor for *A Scientific Framework for Compassion and Social Justice: Lessons in Applied Behavior Analysis* (Routledge, 2021).

Part 1

Ethics Code for Behavior Analysts

1.1   An Introduction to Studying Ethics

Before beginning a discussion of ethics for behavior analysts, it is important to talk about the value of discussing it in the first place. The Behavior Analyst Certification Board® requires that your coursework includes the study of professional and ethical practices according to the Ethics Code for Behavior Analysts®, which is certainly a good enough reason to study it.

It may be tempting, however, to simply assume that we can self-manage our own ethical practice without any outside guidance, letting our conscience be our guide. Sounds easy, right? What could go wrong? As it turns out, quite a lot can be wrong, particularly when working with vulnerable populations. The horrors of what took place at Willowbrook, an institution for individuals with developmental disabilities, are an example of what can happen when care of the vulnerable remains unchecked. In this institution, residents were egregiously neglected, left languishing in their own feces or urine, placed in solitary confinement, or subjected to other inhumane treatment. Budget cuts had devastated the staffing at Willowbrook, leaving up to 70 patients supervised by only two to three staff members (Bursztyn, 2007).

It would be easy, and even comforting, to dismiss those who worked at Willowbrook as anomalies – monsters who viewed those with disabilities as inherently less valuable, less worthy, and less deserving of basic human rights. However, characterizing the atrocities that occurred at Willowbrook as something that could never happen here or never happen under our watch allows us to distance ourselves from it too far easily. The fact is that many of these staff probably started off dedicated and well-meaning. They likely gained great personal satisfaction from their work, at least at first. Although we certainly have no clear data on this, one could guess that none of them set out to abuse the residents and it probably didn't happen overnight.

What happened was much more likely to have been a gradual change, a gradual descent toward this level of disregard and cruelty. This change could be described as what is metaphorically referred to as "boiling frog syndrome." In this legend, a frog placed in hot water will immediately jump out, but a frog placed in warm water with gradually increasing heat will boil alive, unaware of how dangerous their environment has become. While this may not be a factual account, it serves as a powerful metaphor. There are many examples of gradual changes being almost imperceptible and affecting our behavior in such subtle ways that we are often unaware of the process that created this situation – the intolerable becomes gradually tolerable, eventually being simply accepted as the way things are.

This is not how we often understand ethical violations, or those who make them. It is often our inclination to conceptualize those who behave in unethical ways as inherently lacking in morality, or perhaps tempted by great rewards, such as fame and fortune. As in Goethe's *Faust*, we expect that a bargain is struck with the devil, resulting in rewards

DOI: 10.4324/9781003190707-2

both grandiose and immediate. There may indeed be ethical violations that resemble this scenario, but there are a far greater number of violations that are the result of a slow degradation of our ethical stance over time. It is not one temptation, nor is it one decision, but many decisions over time.

When attempting to engage in ethical practice, it is essential to have a yardstick against which to measure ourselves. In the absence of that yardstick, we open the door for an erosion of our ethical foundation which can put practitioners in self-induced challenging situations or, worse yet, be a precursor for a second Willowbrook. Having a clear set of standards is simply the only way to avoid the lowering of our standards, one tiny bit at a time.

Incrementalism vs. Slippery Slope Fallacies

Ethical practice is often referred to as a "slippery slope." Where one misstep occurs, others are sure to follow. This is also described as *Incrementalism* – the process by which our ethical behavior gradually declines and our standards gradually lower.

This certainly appears to be logical and is a theory easily supported by the example of the conditions at Willowbrook. What began with good intentions did not suddenly burst into the horrific conditions for those residents, but rather developed over time. One questionable action led to another, then another, and another.

We must, however, guard against *slippery slope fallacies* in our approach to ethical practice. A slippery slope fallacy is considered an unsound argument in which, without sufficient evidence, it is assumed that one step will lead to several others. As practitioners of the science of behavior analysis, we must approach any assumption without evidence with a degree of caution, and slippery slope fallacies are not an exception to this rule.

The distinction between avoidance of the slippery slope of unethical behavior and engaging in slippery slope fallacies is far from straightforward. Though following rules may be considered simple, in this case that is not synonymous with "easy." All things being equal, an absolutist interpretation of the Code provides a clear path forward. However, in clinical services, all things are very rarely equal.

So what then would be the difference between incrementalism and a slippery slope fallacy? Like any logical fallacy, the slippery slope fallacy is an assumption made in the absence of evidence. Without such evidence, a determination cannot be made. In the case of incrementalism, however, there is a chain of events, one that can be monitored. This would be marked by a measurable change in behavior – a change in the standards of ethics.

The creation of a false dichotomy between "ethical" and "unethical" may not protect us against engaging in unethical practice. Rather, understanding that not every problem can lead to a clear, black-or-white solution liberates us to find the answers that fit. Often, a more holistic analysis, accounting for all of the factors that may affect our decisions, is necessary. Engaging in this thoughtful and conscientious decision-making is the cornerstone of ethical practice, but it represents a formidable challenge for the emergent (and often the seasoned) professional.

Ethics vs. Legality vs. Morals

Many people who begin studying ethics have a bit of confusion as to what exactly they are actually studying. There is a common misunderstanding of the nature of ethical rules for behavior analysts and their necessity in guiding practice. Which is, frankly, no surprise. "Ethics" is a word that is often used interchangeably with moral philosophy. There are countless books, articles, and lectures on the topic of ethics, the work of ancient and modern philosophers in this topic, and the nature of being a "good person." And the reason that all of these books, articles, and lectures exist is that the nature of what we call "good" is debatable. What does it mean to be good, or responsible, or ethical? As behavior analysts, our ethical obligations are not up for debate. They are spelled out in our Code, which is enforceable by the Behavior Analyst Certification Board®. The Ethics Code® is not a suggestion or a philosophy, it is instead a set of enforceable set of regulations. However, it is easy to become confused when behavior analytic guidelines are set forth that include language about "responsibility," "integrity," and "ethics." We are far more accustomed to thinking of these concepts as something every person determines somewhat for themselves within the greater context of society.

There are many behavior analysts who report that ethical violations tend to be those behaviors which are deliberate – those in which the actor knowingly engaged in unethical behavior for personal gain. They talk about behavior analysts who falsify billing, complete fraudulent forms, and exploit clients or their families, and other egregious violations. We are not naive enough to disagree that these violations exist, or indeed that they are more common than any of us would want to admit. However, there are other types of ethical violations that we see playing out frequently: the violations of people who "follow their hearts" rather than the Code.

When talking about ethics, it is preferable to begin with a discussion of the many facets of what we like to think of as being "good." Being a "good" person, and certainly a "good" behavior analyst involves responsible practice at three levels: legality, ethics, and morals. You can think of this as a ladder as the level of responsibility involved moves up into "good person," with each rung representing a different level of responsible practice.

Legality describes the level of responsibility involved in complying with the law. Not quite as simple as it sounds, this means being familiar with clients' rights under the law, familiar with requirements for mandated reporting, and a host of other crucially important areas. We might refer to this as the lowest standard of ethical behavior: refraining from behavior that will lead to being arrested or sued.

Ethics would be the next highest level on our ladder. Ethics involves following specific rules laid out by a governing body. In our case, this would be following the Ethics Code® set forth by the Behavior Analyst Certification Board®, referred to as the BACB®. It is not up to us as individual behavior analysts to decide what constitutes this Code – it has been laid out before us. While there might be some debate as to how to follow aspects of the Code in the way that benefits our clients, the Code itself is set. Compliance with it has little or nothing to do with following our hearts.

The highest rung on our metaphorical ladder would be *morality*. This is the level where we can look into the mirror and be happy with the person that we see. Have I done all the good that I can do? Have I left a legacy and will the world be better off because I was here? These are moral questions, and their answers can certainly influence the quality of our work. However, they are not necessarily questions of professional ethics.

If you are reading this and saying to yourself, "But I got into this field because I wanted to help people! Can't I be an ethical practitioner *and* a moral person?" the answer is "Yes, of course!" While it might seem a bit demoralizing to point out the difference between ethics and morals, this distinction can actually help us to become more ethical practitioners.

Practitioners will often say, "I am an ethical professional, no matter what the Code says. I follow my heart and I know what's right, I don't just follow some list of rules!" Unfortunately, these are the same professionals who, in an effort to "follow their hearts," create harmful multiple relationships, violate confidentiality by seeking out guidance involving specific clients on social media, or engage in practices without any scientific support. Understanding the difference between what we colloquially describe as "ethics" and what behavior analysts describe as "ethics" allows us to make a distinction between the actions that *feel* good – those things that make us proud to be moral people – and the actions that *are* good – those actions that are of the greatest benefit to our clients.

Ethical Philosophy and Ethical Practice

Though it is certainly appropriate to distinguish professional ethics from personal morals, it is also helpful to pause for a moment and examine the school of moral philosophy from which those personal morals may develop. Many of our ideas of right and wrong are aligned with our moral upbringing and history of reinforcement with making decisions about "right" and "wrong."

Deontological vs. Utilitarian Ethics

When it comes to ethical decision-making, two schools of thought from Western philosophy are relevant in considering the option before us. These schools of philosophy seek to answer essential questions. As explained in greater detail by Dr. Todd May in Part 3, these schools of philosophy provide a powerful framework to understand our approach to morality, as well as to our ethical practice as professionals.

Within a framework of *utilitarian philosophy*, morality is measured by the amount of "good" that one puts out into the world. It is the consequence of action that matters. One exercise in utilitarianism is known as "the trolley problem" (Thomson, 1976). This thought exercise, first developed by Phillippa Foot, presents a hypothetical scenario: you are the driver of a trolley, and the brakes fail. On the tracks ahead are five workers who will be run over and killed, unless you switch tracks. On the other track is one worker who will be killed. Do you switch tracks? Many of us, in a win for utilitarian philosophy, would switch tracks, saving the five by killing the one.

Utilitarianism has its drawbacks forever, and the trolley problem can illustrate these as well. Many of us would certainly switch tracks, saving five workers, but what if the scenario were different? Would we harvest the organs of one healthy person to save five others, a variation on the trolley problem suggested by Judith Jarvis Thomson? While many of us may say that these scenarios are different, a strict utilitarian would argue that the consequence is the same: the choice is between the one life and the five.

Deontological ethics, developed by Immanuel Kant, is a philosophical theory that prioritizes the intentions of actions rather than their effect. Within a deontological framework, it is the intentions of actions that are relevant. Acting with *intention toward* creating a better world is the ideal.

The advantage that these philosophies bring to our study of ethics is their focus on action. Within these theories, there is a focus on behavior. A utilitarian may focus on the question, "What behavior can I engage in to maximize the good in this outcome?" and a deontologist may ask, "With what intention should I respond?" Either approach, however, arrives at a behavioral response to a given situation and can therefore be useful in decision-making.

In a recent study published by the Journal of Applied Behavior Analysis, David Cox examined ethical decision-making (Cox, 2021). In this article he makes a distinction between two types of ethics: *descriptive ethics* and *normative ethics*. As described by Cox (2021), *descriptive ethics* is the study of beliefs about right and wrong and *normative ethics* refers to why these behaviors are considered right or wrong. In other words, Cox makes a distinction here as to what is considered ethical (*normative ethics*) and why it is considered ethical (*descriptive ethics*). Great variability was found in this way that subjects responded to various ethical scenarios. This is certainly one of the challenges of studying ethics in this format, given that these decisions can be contextually determined and informed by individual morality. Approaching these questions from a data-based viewpoint, however, is an exciting new development in our approach to ethical practice.

Care Ethics

Another school of thought has emerged from Carol Gilligan's theories on moral development (Gilligan, 1987). Gilligan developed the theory of *care ethics*. Within this philosophy, abstract principles of the outcomes of Actions or the intentions are of lesser value than the relationships that are developed. Morality centers around relationships rather than more individualistic principles, and those caring relationships extend out into the world.

As the field moves more toward compassionate practice, thanks to the work of Taylor, LeBlanc and Nosik (2019), as well as many others, *care ethics* becomes more relevant to our daily practice. Compassionate relationships can be the crux of our work – our most potent source of reinforcement and our guidance when making the difficult decision required of us. It is from the standpoint of that relationship that we answer the question, "How am I serving the needs of my clients?"

Absolute vs. Relative Ethics

It is also helpful to consider the concepts of absolute and relative ethics. Absolute ethics refers to the notion that there are universal truths within a greater moral code and that such truths remain unchanged. An ethicist who holds this view would maintain that unethical acts cannot be mitigated by any circumstance. Right is right and wrong is wrong, and this remains true regardless of context. Relative ethics, however, maintains that there are circumstances which alter whether or not an act would be considered ethical or unethical. In this view, context is essential to the determination of whether or not something is ethical. Our view of ethics may be affected by culture or upbringing, but may also be informed by more immediate circumstances as well. Stealing may be wrong, but stealing a loaf of bread for one's starving family is excusable, and would be considered ethical. Though our upbringing may inform the belief that lying and vandalism are wrong, very few of us would condemn the characters of *The Sound of Music* for doing exactly that, as they make their escape from the Nazis. Even the Ten Commandments of the Judeo-Christian tradition and the stories of the religious persons who upheld them seem to allow for the interpretation of relative ethics. Though the fifth commandment states, "Thou shalt not kill," St. Joan of Arc's holy work was in battle during the Hundred Years' War. Interpretation of Judeo-Christian and other religious texts involve volumes of work over decades and centuries. Even the most literal analysis requires adjustment for our modern times. Such general rules cannot account for all possible scenarios and greater analysis must be pursued. Though the Ten Commandments were offered on stone tablets, their interpretation is anything but written in stone.

Though philosophers may apply the philosophies of absolute and relative ethics primarily to our morality, they may also apply to our study of professional ethics. Rather than being informed by our culture, upbringing, and learning history, our ethics are determined by a governing body. In this case, the Behavior Analysts Certification Board® has outlined our ethical obligation in the Ethics Code®. This Code may be conceived as similar to the "rules" that we learn as part of moral upbringing – the commandments, so to speak, of our ethical practice.

There are several elements of the Ethics Code® which are *not* open to interpretation. Those which require us to be honest in our billing and documentation, to maintain confidentiality, and to use social media responsibly, for example, must be interpreted with an absolutist view. However, there are situations in which compliance with one Code element may conflict with compliance with another. Even in cases where the relevant Code element is clear, it may be difficult to discern a clear path forward.

The difficulty in complying with ethical requirements is often not in knowing the right thing to do. Commandments, whether they be religious dictates, rules, or the elements of the Ethics Code®, tell us in explicit detail what to do. The expectations for our behavior are abundantly clear. The difficulty, therefore, is instead in understanding *how to do it*. Balancing the client's needs, as well as their preferences, with our own need to comply with this Code is perhaps our greatest challenge, particularly in the provision of services to vulnerable populations. Navigating the challenges of ethical practice may also involve balancing the requirements of one Code element against that of another.

In cases where we must prioritize the various Code elements, there is value in a more relativist approach. Greater interpretation of the "right" way forward may be necessary if a clear path eludes us.

Works Cited

Bursztyn, A. (Ed.) (2007). *The Praeger handbook of special education*. Westport, CT: Greenwood Publishing Group.

Cox, D. J. (2021). Descriptive and normative ethical behavior appear to be functionally distinct. *Journal of Applied Behavior Analysis*, *54*(1), 168–191.

Gilligan, Carol (1987). Moral orientation and moral development. In Eva Feder Kittay & Diana T. Meyers (eds.), *Women and Moral Theory*. Rowman & Littlefield. pp. 19–23.

Taylor, B. A., LeBlanc, L. A., & Nosik, M. R. (2019). Compassionate care in behavior analytic treatment: Can outcomes be enhanced by attending to relationships with caregivers? *Behavior Analysis in Practice*, *12*(3), 654–666.

Thomson J. J. (1976). Killing, letting die, and the trolley problem. *The Monist*, *59*, 204–217.

1.2　Core Principles

Core Principles

Four foundational principles, which all behavior analysts should strive to embody, serve as the framework for the ethics standards. Behavior analysts should use these principles to interpret and apply the standards in the Code. The four core principles are that behavior analysts should: benefit others; treat others with compassion, dignity, and respect; behave with integrity; and ensure their own competence.

The Core Principles are a new distinction which were not explicitly highlighted in the Behavior Analyst Certification Board's Professional and Ethical Compliance Code for Behavior Analysts (BACB, 2014). They can be viewed as guiding values that behavior analysts should commit to continuously across all settings. One could make the argument that the behavior analyst's responsibility to colleagues, promoting an ethical culture, or the code element stipulating that behavior analysts do not engage in discriminatory practices subsumes some of these core principles. After all, an ethical culture would be integrous or there exists an incompatibility between an environment that is discriminatory while being respectful and compassionate. This code upgrade has come on the heels of seminal works in the field and discussions on limitations within our practice, specifically, within the realms of compassion (LeBlanc et al., 2019; Sadavoy & Zube, 2021; Taylor et al., 2018; Vilardaga, 2009), cultural responsiveness (Conners & Capell, 2020; Beaulieu et al, 2018; Fong et al., 2016, 2017; Fong & Tanaka, 2013; LeBlanc et al., 2020; Miller et al., 2019; Sadavoy & Zube, 2021), and simply the need to be more aware, thoughtful, and sensitive to the needs of stakeholders including clients, colleagues, and the organization as a whole (Callahan et al., 2019; Carr, 2020; Fuller & Fitter; 2020; Leaf et al., 2016; Neuringer, 1991; O'Leary et al., 2015; Turner et al., 2016).

The authors of this text are ecstatic at the opportunity to delve into an ethical discussion of each of these core principles as this new standard is critical for clinicians' effectiveness. It is not enough to simply discuss these principles in supervision or course sequences. First of all, we know that even the best analysts are not fully able to quantify their own performance accurately without measurement (Wolf, 1978). Beaulieu and colleagues (2016) demonstrated a competency bias in the realm of cultural responsiveness. They found that 92% of respondents to a survey (completed by 703 BCBAs or BCBA-Ds) believed they were either moderately comfortable or extremely comfortable working with individuals from diverse backgrounds despite the fact that 83% of them have had little to no ABA coursework on diversity. In another survey, related to a new core principle, notably compassion, LeBlanc and colleagues (2019) found that there was a desire for training on relationship building and compassionate care yet the majority of respondents indicated that they had received no explicit competency-based training or reading assignments in their coursework on either topic. Therefore, it is the recommendation of the authors of

DOI: 10.4324/9781003190707-3

this text to do more than read the seminal works mentioned earlier. A behavior analyst must be fluent and demonstrate these skills, generalized across environments and people. Secondly, it is imperative that the behavior analyst understands their scope of competence in order to responsibly treat clients within that scope and refer clients outside their scope (or gain competency) (Brodhead et al., 2018a). It is necessary for behavior analysts to develop competency assessments as well as measurements to support the acquisition of these skills and not presume skills are learned through readings, discussions, or observations (Falender & Shafranske, 2012; Kazemi et al., 2018; LeBlanc et al., 2020; Turner et al., 2016).

Lastly, it should be noted that other related helping professional codes have adopted and used guiding or core principles in their ethical and professional standards codes for many years. Some codes that contain similar core principles include: the American Psychological Association (2017), the Canadian Psychological Association (2017), American Speech-Language-Hearing Association (2016), and the National Association for Social Workers (2017). Table 1 highlights the different names given to the underlying philosophical basis for professional codes in related helping professions (APA, 2002/2017; ASHA 2016; CPA, 2017; Irwin et al., 2007; Reamer, 1998; Sinclair, 2017).

Organization	Year Introduced	Title of Principles	Names of Principles
Behavior Analysis Certification Board	2020	Core Principles	Benefit Others Treat Others with Compassion, Dignity, and Respect Behave with Integrity Ensure their Own Competence.
American Psychological Association	2002	General Principles	Beneficence and Nonmaleficence Fidelity and Responsibility Integrity Justice Respect for People's Rights and Dignity
Canadian Psychological Association	1986	Principles	Respect for the Dignity of Persons and Peoples Responsible Caring Integrity in Relationships Responsibility to Society
American Speech-Language-Hearing Association	1979	Principle of Ethics	Responsibility to Persons Served Professionally and to Research Participants, both Human and Animal Responsibility for One's Professional Competence Responsibility to the Public Responsibility for Professional Relationships
National Association of Social Workers	1996	Core Values of Service	Service Social Justice Dignity and Worth of the Person Importance of Human Relationships Integrity Competence

One of the barriers that may have delayed the incorporation of core principles in behavior analysis is an ingrained need to operationalize prior to implementation. This level of skepticism is of tremendous value because it ensures efficacy and quality of professional conduct and limits access to erroneous or potentially harmful applications of the science (Todd, 2019). However, Taylor and colleagues (2018) write, "behavior analysis has lagged in developing and delivering formal instruction in relationship skills as part of professional training, perhaps due to historical judgment of concepts such as empathy and compassion as too subjective to examine experimentally or teach" (p. 664). The challenges of measuring and operationally defining relationship skills or cultural responsiveness, compassion, or integrity should not limit the need to bring these critical skills to the forefront of training programs and supervisory oversight. There exists tremendous value for behavior analysts to have a deeper understanding of the philosophical underpinnings of other related fields in order to promote stronger collaborative relationships (LaFrance et al., 2019) but also provide an access to adopt best practices from other fields, that are aligned with a behavior analytic worldview, to optimize the best care available for clients.

Benefit Others

Behavior analysts work to maximize benefits and do no harm by:

• Protecting the welfare and rights of clients above all others
• Protecting the welfare and rights of other individuals with whom they interact in a professional capacity

Protecting the welfare and rights of clients above all others is a powerful statement and may seem straightforward; however, when pulled in multiple directions, it is paramount that behavior analysts remain client focused and ensure that the client's rights are protected and their dignity maintained. Complications can exist when another party is speaking to the rights of the client or if a third party wishes to proceed with an intervention which may conflict with the client's well-being. Rekers and Lovaas (1974), controversial and unethically disturbing work on the "Sissy Boy Experiment" was an attempt to use the principles of applied behavior analysis on a biologically male client who preferred to engage in activities that were deemed feminine. A punishment procedure was used to reduce the occurrences of these so-called feminine activities, while reinforcing specific activities that were labeled as masculine. Since the client was underage, the parents provided their consent to a treatment intervention that aligned with the proponents of conversion therapy, where the researchers attempted to alter the child's self-expression, identity, and freedoms. What was not taken into account were the participant's rights, self-expression, and choice.

It is critical to ensure that the clients' rights are being upheld before proceeding with an intervention. When developing or delivering interventions, it is important to ask oneself, "Are these behaviors that are being targeted socially significant and if so, to whom?" From the example above, it is the responsibility of the behavior analyst to go beyond consent. Clients who are unable to consent (whether it is because of their age or their capacity) should be offered a way to understand the behavior change program and give their assent or dissent (Roth-Cline & Nelson, 2013). A behavior analyst cannot assume a lack of capacity and being mindful of the client's participation is a way a behavior analyst can validate the client's dignity and privacy (De Lourdes Levy et al., 2003). The behavior analyst is responsible for acknowledging the assent or dissent of the client and, unless there is a safety or health concern, revisions should be considered so that the client is a willing participant in the intervention.

Informed consent should be the cornerstone of intervention (and research). Pritchett and colleagues (2020) reviewed behavior analytic literature and demonstrated that there existed an "absence of consent information in our studies [which] indicates that our procedures for obtaining consent and assent are not peer reviewed" (p. 21). One could extrapolate this finding into questioning whom the *maximizing benefit* is for. It is further complicated by a power imbalance between the professional and the client. The practitioner must be aware that prospective clients: may feel indebted (Fouka & Mantzorou, 2011), may fear negative repercussions for refusing to participate (LeBlanc et al., 2018), may feel there are insufficient alternatives, may have feelings of inadequacy, or feelings that subordinate their own participation at the expense of perceived lofty clinical expertise. As a result, when attempting to secure consent, context needs to be considered and addressed. To do so, behavior analytic services or interventions need to be explained, colloquially, to ensure that the client understands the potential risks as well as their rights. They may decide to opt out of services or a specific behavior plan. That decision has to be respected. It is the responsibility of the behavior analyst to support the client and ensure they are heard and appreciated even if their decision goes against the clinical judgment of the behavior analyst. Being proactive, honest, and explaining services and interventions is critical in making sure the client is an engaged and informed participant but it also ensures that the client is involved and the program is responsive to the environment (two criteria that lead to better clinical outcomes) (Williams, 2021).

• Focusing on the short- and long-term effects of their professional activities

This is a necessary distinction because it promotes thoroughness and thoughtfulness in service delivery. In a situation in which the behavior analyst is focused on the day-to-day targets and program objectives they may lose sight of the larger overarching goal of the behavior change program and miss environmental changes or shifts in the clients' priorities. A long-term goal for supervision is to provide oversight for the supervisee to gain the experience to be a competent, effective, compassionate, collaborative, and ethical BCBA. If supervision meetings solely address caseload and the behavior change program of clients, many skills needed to be an effective BCBA will be missed. Similarly, solely focusing on the long-term effects would also be an inadequate judgment regarding behavior changes since in many cases, that occurs gradually and over time, and requires measurement and observation. One cannot have a supervisee work at being competent, effective, compassionate, collaborative, and ethical without working through specific cases, analyzing data, communicating with team members, and demonstrating day-to-day problem solving. Another example is the responsibility associated with training. One could provide a training in an effort to disseminate the science of applied behavior analysis to a new audience; however, what effectiveness exists if there is no attention on long-term effects of the training (e.g. individualization of training, oversight of application of training procedures, behavior skills training, etc.)? More harm can be done for an attendee to say I attended a training in applied behavior analysis and it did not work or I tried it and it resulted in deleterious consequences. We must be conscious of our efforts in the present and anticipate negative unintended consequences in the future in order to mitigate potential harm to the best of our ability.

• Actively identifying and addressing the potential negative impacts of their own physical and mental health on their professional activities

With this Core Principle element, the BACB is essentially acknowledging the demands and challenges faced by ABA practitioners. "Burnout can be defined as a long-term reaction to occupational stress which involves, particularly, the helping professions" (Gabassi et al., 2002, p. 309). It can be characterized by emotional exhaustion, feelings of cynicism, and reduced personal accomplishment (Maslach et al., 1996). In a survey, Plantiveau and colleagues found that just under two thirds of newly minted BCBAs, working with the autistic population, were experiencing burnout (2018). This is a huge concern as many BCBAs have limited access and awareness of their self-care needs, as a means to combat burnout, coupled with a limited repertoire of skills related to compassionate care both outward to clients and inward to self (LeBlanc et al., 2019). As a result of both of these skill deficits, behavior analysts are vulnerable to burnout which is compounded by the lack of content on self-care featured in coursework or targeted in supervision. Awareness of burnout is important due to the negative impact it can have on decision-making and feelings of ineffectiveness (Fiebig et al., 2020). The BACB is imploring behavior analysts to *actively identify* their own physical and mental health in an effort to ensure effective decision-making when it comes to program decisions, communication with team members, and other professional activities. Sheer volume of work or intensity of caseload can contribute to burnout. If the demands exceed what is realistic or wanted for a work day, a byproduct of that disconnect could be resentment of tasks and feeling incomplete or ineffective. Thus, it is critical that behavior analysts are aware and thoughtful when it comes to caseload and work towards an optimal quantity that is ideally individualized based on comfort, scope, and effectiveness. It is equally critical that organizations reinforce their staff for engaging in self-care behaviors and seek to resolve (and not reinforce) situations in which staff members share feelings associated with burnout (e.g., daunting caseload, emotional exhaustion, inability to appreciate accomplishments, etc.). In fact, organizational leaders, supervisors, and professors should all feel a responsibility to model self-care behaviors and resist setting an example of work martyrdom as something that should be reinforced, healthy, or wanted. Research shows that workaholics report more interpersonal conflicts, poorer functioning outside work, and sleep-related challenges, than those that do not identify as workaholics (Andreassen, 2014). Yet, workaholism is still present, largely because it is reinforced as a desirable behavior in many North American communities. Additionally, through Acceptance and Commitment Training (ACTr), there exists an access to connect with your values and purpose, promote greater self-awareness, mindfulness, and flexibility, and an ability to move away from harmful thoughts related to burnout (e.g., a lack of personal accomplishment, feelings of inadequacy, or emotional exhaustion) (Dixon et al., 2020; Fiebig et al., 2020; Flaxman et al., 2013; Harrison, 2021; Hayes, 2020; Vilardaga, 2011). These are all skills that need to be taught and measured for new behavior analysts entering the field. It is also critical for those that are currently working in the field of behavior analysis to reflect on their self-care, ongoingly, to ensure their judgments and decisions are not impaired by fatigue or burnout. For more on self-care please reference the interview with Dr. Shane Spiker which appears later in this text.

- Actively identifying potential and actual conflicts of interest and working to resolve them in a manner that avoids or minimizes harm
- Actively identifying and addressing factors (e.g., personal, financial, institutional, political, religious, cultural) that might lead to conflicts of interest, misuse of their position, or negative impacts on their professional activities

It is critical to begin a client-behavior analytic relationship with a contract and firm guidelines as to roles and responsibilities including appropriate means of communication, an understanding of services, scope of practice, and general information about applied behavior analysis, as well as expectations for both parties in an effort to set the standards and foundation for a successful behavior analytic relationship. Having all of that in place does not protect the behavior analyst from finding themselves in a situation in which there can exist a conflict of interest but it does help and provides a resource if (or more likely when) confronted with a compromising situation. Ideally, these situations could be avoided altogether; however, that is unrealistic due to vulnerability of the client, intimacy of working one on one and, in some cases, in the home environment, while being a supportive, compassionate resource (which is not always present in the clients' community). For this reason, it is necessary for behavior analysts to be proactive in identifying potential conflicts of interests, in an attempt to address them before they are realized. In this case, when confronted with a situation that is uncomfortable (i.e., outside a familiar, typical behavior analytic client-analyst relationship) exploring that discomfort is taking steps to actively identify a potential conflict of interest.

Dr. Nicolle Carr discusses the challenges of working in rural communities in which there are very few service providers and there exists a friendly awareness of a large percentage of the population within the community (2021). This requires more thoughtful consideration as to which cases could be appropriate and which cases are not. In these situations, the potential for a conflict of interest or multiple relationships is more likely and a more thorough and comprehensive contract may be necessary.

The BACB also lists several factors that a behavior analyst must be mindful of in an effort to anticipate a conflict of interest, a misuse of role, or undermine the professional relationship. This requires an awareness of one's personal biases and how those biases may form preconceived stereotypical assumptions that may shroud one's ability to have the foundation of a professional-client or colleague relationship be one of respect, compassion, and appreciation. For example, if you have a strong political stance, would you be able to support a client who was an ardent supporter of the rival party? Are you comfortable with providing services to a family that is economically disadvantaged that may not have the resources you are accustomed to? With respect to supervision, are you able to invest the time in learning and collaborating thoroughly with someone from a foreign country in order to provide thoughtful individualized training or distance supervision that is appropriate to their culture and client's environment? If a supervisee approaches you for supervision and there exists a sexual attraction, will you be equipped to provide supervision devoid of inappropriate behavior? If there is an uncertainty upon taking on a client or supervisee, that uncertainty must be explored as it may be the beginnings of a conflict of interest, a misuse of position, or result in a negative impact on professional activities.

- Effectively and respectfully collaborating with others in the best interest of those with whom they work and always placing clients' interests first

A behavior analyst must be respectful, kind, and be aware that their behavior should not, under any circumstances, impede the well-being of another even when confronted with a different opinion or worldview. The behavior analyst must show a willingness to listen and understand that imposing an unpopular or unaligned view is likely going to result in ineffective dissemination (Carr, 2020). It is important to note that disagreements can and should arise. Thanks to skepticism and an inherent quest for truth, science is always evolving and it is critical that we continue to have conversations and debates around the best ways to intervene in an effort to design programs that maximize outcomes for our clients. Disagreements, skepticism, and debates should continue but they should occur from a place of being inquisitive and engaging empathically, and not from a place to "make wrong" expressed through vitriolic verbal behavior and at the expense of another's well-being. If the goal is to uphold the science or advocate for your client, the best way to accomplish both is to build relationships with those with differing points of view (Slim & Celiberti, 2021). LaFrance and colleagues (2019) state, "when mutual respect is realized, and when the common views and rationales of disciplines are familiar, real collaboration can occur"

(p. 721). They discuss the value of learning the scope of competence, perspective taking, and actively listening to maximize the effectiveness of collaborative efforts of multidisciplinary teams (LaFrance et al., 2019). It may shape the opposing viewpoint to align with yours or, perhaps, you will be enriched with a new perspective that was previously outside your learning history and personal biases. If one chooses not to make an effort to work collaboratively with other service professionals the outcome is often a negative rapport which leads to behavior interventions occurring in a silo and not generalized across your clients' environments. Furthermore, you are requiring more task demands on your client for having to case manage and coordinate service delivery which would be mitigated with healthy collaborative efforts.

Now, not all relationships are going to be fruitful. Some collaborators may have a negative opinion regarding applied behavior analysis or promoting treatments that are inappropriate for the client or, worse, pseudoscientific and not based on scientific evidence. For those that have a negative opinion regarding applied behavior analysis, there is more value in learning "why" than suggesting the individual with that opinion is wrong. The latter will not produce a positive outcome. The prior statement allows for a relationship to exist even with differing worldviews by allowing the behavior analyst to learn where the negative opinion originated (e.g., challenging collaboration in the past, misinformed reading material regarding the perils of applied behavior analysis, fear of something unfamiliar or new, etc.) and, with this knowledge, share the benefits and values of applied behavior analysis on an individual level. For those scenarios in which pseudoscientific interventions are recommended for a behavior analytic client, Matt Brodhead (2015) created a decision-making tree with an accompanying Checklist for Analyzing Proposed Treatments (CAPT) to help behavior analysis decide whether or not non-evidence-based interventions pose a safety concern or will interfere with behavior analytic services, respectively. In some situations, a behavior analytic relationship can coexist with non-behavior treatment; though it may not be ideal it may be in the client's best interest in an effort to foster a stronger working relationship with other professionals and clients (Brodhead, 2015). Healthy collaborative multidisciplinary teams are necessary to improve consumer outcomes (Hunt et al., 2003) and build therapeutic relationships (LaFrance et al., 2019; Taylor et al., 2018).

Treat Others with Compassion, Dignity, and Respect

Behavior analysts behave toward others with compassion, dignity, and respect by:

- Treating others equitably, regardless of factors such as age, disability, ethnicity, gender expression/identity, immigration status, marital/relationship status, national origin, race, religion, sexual orientation, socioeconomic status, or any other basis proscribed by law

In the preceding code, factors related to "persons' age, gender, race, culture, ethnicity, national origin, religion, sexual orientation, disability, language, or socioeconomic status" were mentioned with respect to either gaining adequate training and supervision oversight to effectively and efficiently provide service for different populations or around engaging in behaviors that will not demean, harass, or discriminate against individuals based on their identity (BACB, 2014, p. 5). Embedded as a core principle, the focus now is on behaviors related to compassion, dignity, and respect as opposed to abstaining from harassment or discrimination. An addition that needs to be highlighted, and celebrated, is the addition of gender expression and identity which is a necessary expansion of the narrow frame of gender, immigration status in recognition of the legal vulnerability of that marginalized group, as well as marital/relationship status. As this is a new addition to the code, it would be of value for practitioners to seek out training in an effort to better understand gender expression and identity as well as learn about the immigrant experience to better serve both these populations with compassion, dignity, and respect. Language is not in the list of factors; however, it is mentioned in section 2.08: Communicating About Services.

Another key distinction that should be highlighted is the concept of equitability and why that is superior to equality in relation to compassion, dignity, and respect. Treating everyone equally would be ignoring the systemic ways in which society reinforces some groups and punishes others. Li and colleagues (2019) found, "the mean salaries of men were 13%, 6%, and 15% greater than those of women at the assistant-, associate-, and full-professor levels, respectively" (p. 743). Equalizing salaries would be a great beginning (i.e., having all humans, regardless of gender, earning the same amount based on position). However, developing an equitable system, in which those who are marginalized gain access to the same resources and opportunities as cis men, would be both of value for the field and just. That would entail opportunities related to: professional recognition, professional organization leadership, invited presentation speakers, editorial board appointments, faculty hires, and publication trends commensurate with the gender distribution in the field (Nosik et al., 2019) with remuneration not based on gender. In Dr. Nasiah Cirincione-Ulezi's call-to-action (2020), the marginalization and underrepresentation of Black practitioners within the field of behavior analysis in leadership positions limits the growth and evolution of the field. The unfortunate reality is that cis men, who make up 12.83% of the field, are over-represented in positions of power and high rank within the field of behavior analysis (BACB, n.d.; Nosik & Grow, 2015) and until this changes, the field of ABA will continue to be limited by not having the enrichment of diverse opinions in positions of influence.

• Respecting others' privacy and confidentiality

Within the Code, privacy and confidentiality are paired with the verbs maintain and protect. Respect (as well as compassion) is a new addition, having previously not been featured in our ethics code, whereas dignity had been isolated, alongside welfare, for research participant protection (BACB, 2014; BACB, 2020). These three terms are now highlighted in our core principles and as such, should be a foundational element in our behavior towards clients, colleagues, and across all of our professional duties, and interactions with others as behavior analysts. Highlighting the need to be respectful with privacy and confidentiality is more involved than following Personal Information Protection and Electronic Documents Act (PIPEDA), Health Insurance Portability and Accountability Act (HIPAA), and General Data Protection Regulation (GDPR), maintaining records to board standards, or patient protection. ABA practitioners are required to be mindful of their environment and anticipate possible breaches of confidentiality. One should resist sending an email on public transportation because a passengers wandering eye may read something that should not be shared. A conversation at a café should be avoided because someone could overhear even if you are using initials. This can be even more complicated at your place of work when someone who is not a stakeholder seeks information. For example, if another teacher at a school asks a question about your client, sharing that information without client consent is a violation. Without written consent, you cannot share information to an extended family member who wants an update about your client if you are supporting behavior goals at a family event. In the community, you can't share information about your client to the server during your client's restaurant-related targets. As an ABA practitioner, you learn details about your client that cannot be shared out of respect for your client but also for your client's safety. Many practitioners work with clients who are vulnerable and sharing information, even inadvertently, could thrust your client into a harmful situation.

- Respecting and actively promoting clients' self-determination to the best of their abilities, particularly when providing services to vulnerable populations

This is such a critical new addition to the code and it is of great importance that it be written into the core principles, as it should be part of our philosophical approach towards clients. Dennis Reid and colleagues (2018) highlighted a few ways in which our verbal behavior can be aligned with demonstrating dignity and compassion toward our clients. They are as follows:

- Refrain from speaking about a person with a disability in the immediate presence of the individual without involving the person in the communication; attempt to speak about the person to another individual in a separate location or at least in a manner that is not likely to be apparent to the person who is the focus of the conversation
- Refer to the person, not a behavioral characteristic
- Avoid the potentially pejorative term low functioning; consider people-first language, such as someone with "more significant" or "more severe" disabilities
- Respect the adult status of the person; speaking about people in accordance with their age

(Reid et al., 2018, p. 74)

Ways in which we can be more effective working with adults with disabilities is to show them the same respect as we would a colleague or a friend. We would not walk ahead, talk down to, talk about in the presence of, or focus on the challenges of our friends and colleagues (Reid et al., 2018). For the same reason, we must be empathetic and show compassion and courtesy for adults with intellectual disability, some of whom are unable to tell us that they feel slighted by this oversight and disrespect.

The BACB® insists we go further and ensure self-determination is fostered. Self-determination, as a concept, gained prominence in the 1990s, and was centered around promoting autonomy and independence in which high levels of self-determination was thought to result in a better quality of life (i.e., improved relationships, job prospects, financial independence, and independent living) (Wehmeyer and Abery, 2013; Wehmeyer and Palmer, 2003; Wehmeyer and Schalock, 2001). Dr. Michael Wehmeyer's (1995) ARC Self-Determination Scale is a self-reporting assessment, containing 72 items divided into four main essential characteristics related to self-determination: autonomy, self-regulation, psychological empowerment, and self-realization. Peterson and colleagues (2020) noted the need to operationally define self-determination as it has been an abstract concept with a focus on an individual's agency when it comes to making decisions. The three concepts they isolate as encompassing self-determination are: choice, self-control, and self-management. These behaviors can be measured and promoted within a behavior analytic program. Choice needs to be available otherwise the client is passively participating in their own life and following the lead of whomever is making decisions for them. For self-control, understanding consequences of choices made based on informed decisions, may require accepting "larger delayed reinforcers," and overcoming impulsivity (Lerman et al., 2006). Finally, self-management is the ability to organize one's own behavior to access reinforcers and avoid punishers (Peterson et al., 2020). There exists an access to measure these three concepts in order to establish a behavior change program that promotes self-determination.

With all that being said, what determines "to the best of their abilities?" In the realm of respect, compassion, and dignity, the answer is subsumed in demonstrating thoughtfulness and care for the client. Dunning and colleagues (2016) define respect as the ability "to treat each other as individuals of goodwill and competence, even if they do not privately believe it" (p. 1). Presumed competence should be a foundation in which we serve clients to ensure that their abilities are not underestimated and that any challenges that arise in the behavior change program are a result of the program itself and not the fault of the client. It is essential that we train skills encompassing dignity, compassion, and respect to fluency. It is important that these skills be generalized across a variety of clients and settings to ensure that an assessment of "to the best of their abilities" is evolving and self-determination will be promoted in all facets of a client's life (and not in the facets of life the practitioner values or has familiarity).

- Acknowledging that personal choice in service delivery is important by providing clients and stakeholders with needed information to make informed choices about services

A behavior analyst is often confident that applied behavior analysis is the correct course of action; the therapy of choice. However, does that behavior analyst show respect, dignity, and compassion to a client who is unsure and considering non-behavior analytic services? In some situations, client resources (e.g., time and financial), training interest or availability, enthusiasm, or agreement could be a barrier limiting the fitness and ability to establish an applied behavior analytic program (Taylor and Fisher, 2010). Take for example a prospective client who is interested in doing Sensory Integration Therapy for their child with intellectual disabilities or a business committed to copying recommendations from a case study without completing an individualized needs assessment or an internal analysis as to how their organization runs. As a behavior analyst, in both cases, there would be a desire to support the client in making a different choice; an informed choice based on data, evidence, and science. Just as we would when conducting research, the behavior analyst must provide an accurate portrayal of service delivery and accept the client's decision as to whether they wish to participate. If they choose not to proceed with applied behavior analysis, that is a choice that must be respected and the client should be shown compassion as their interests come first (and not the interests of the behavior analyst). Imagine collaborating with a client who is not convinced that they selected the correct methodology for their needs. This partnership would likely be inefficient and buy-in would need to continually be established until the client chooses applied behavior analysis. If the client opts to use a different intervention when presented with all the information, the behavior analyst can take comfort in knowing that the choice was informed. That client may choose behavior analysis in the future, because a rapport of respect and compassion was shown by the behavior analyst.

Behave with Integrity

Behavior analysts fulfill responsibilities to their scientific and professional communities, to society in general, and to the communities they serve by:

- Behaving in an honest and trustworthy manner
- Not misrepresenting themselves, misrepresenting their work or others' work, or engaging in fraud
- Following through on obligations

Being honest and trustworthy, following through on commitments, and not misrepresenting yourself, your work, or the work of others is not about being good or just. Good, bad, right, or wrong are labels given to behavior but require context. Brodhead and colleagues (2018c) discuss deontology in which behaviors that are deemed as right or wrong are contingent on the context and function of the behavior. There exist certain contexts in which behaviors that may be deemed as wrong can be right and vice versa. They provide an example of lying to someone in an effort to maintain a surprise party that is being planned for them. Lying is deemed a negative, bad behavior, but in this context, lying, to maintain the secrecy of a surprise party, is good (Brodhead et al., 2018c; Fryling, 2016). Mayer and colleagues (1995) saw trust as a willingness of both parties in the relationship to accept risks and vulnerability largely based on perceived competence, integrity, and benevolence. The creation that can exist in a relationship in which trust, honesty, and consistency is evident would not be present in a relationship marred by doubts and uncertainty. The behavior analyst needs to alleviate concerns and provide an access to a fruitful professional relationship and one way to do so is by being true to their word.

- Holding themselves accountable for their work and the work of their supervisees and trainees, and correcting errors in a timely manner

The behavior change program is evaluated based on the data and social validity. A program's success can vary from being poor to excellent and, in both cases, there should be a commitment to do more, to do better as behavior change programs are dynamic and occur moment to moment, contingent on the environment. If the intervention is ineffective, owning and accepting the limitations of the program is of tremendous value because it provides an opportunity to make the necessary changes. One could opt to blame a member of a multidisciplinary team or the client themselves for the inadequacies but in doing so you are moving away from your commitment to change socially significant behavior. Instead, one could reassert their values and move towards their commitment to create a behavior change program that will produce positive outcomes (Tarbox et al., 2020).

- Being knowledgeable about and upholding BACB and other regulatory requirements

The behavior analyst must keep abreast of changes and advancements within the field and follow news from the BACB®, as oftentimes there may be updates that will concern the credentialed behavior analyst. Some ways to keep oneself updated are to read all newsletters from the BACB®, listen and follow their podcast *Inside the BACB*, and opt-in for email correspondence via your portal on the BACB website (BACB.com). This is the responsibility of each and every behavior analyst licensed by the BACB® and claiming not to be aware of changes is not integrous. Being a credentialed behavior analyst is an honor, and your behavior in respecting that honor is something to be valued.

- Actively working to create professional environments that uphold the core principles and standards of the Code
- Respectfully educating others about the ethics requirements of behavior analysts and the mechanisms for addressing professional misconduct

Similar to the previous code element 7.01, the behavior analyst has a responsibility to promote an ethical work culture and to ensure that those within the organization as well as stakeholders are aware of this code (BACB, 2014). Common attributes for ethically rich cultures would consist of organizations committed to analyzing the behavior of the organization and implementing changes based on that analysis in order to improve clinical processes, stakeholder engagement, employee satisfaction, and promoting a high level of autonomy and alignment. The organizational behaviors of the majority (macrobehaviors) make up macrocontingencies which have a cumulative effect on the organization as a whole (Glenn, 2004). By contrast, clinical programs that made less of an effort to promote a sound ethical culture were often more focused on getting more clients rather than clinical effectiveness, adversarial with parents, high rate of staff turnover, and poor communication. Similarly, these shared macrobehaviors within the workplace culture lead to macrocontingencies and also have a cumulative effect. When thinking of Sigrid Glenn's definition of interlocking behavioral contingencies, we might think of a tapestry. Each thread of the tapestry is pulled tightly and is weaved to fit with a neighboring thread. Upon each thread being in the correct place, you have a work of art. If we replace the threads with employees and tapestry with ethical culture one gets the idea of the role each employee plays in contributing to the ethical culture of the workplace. When the administration of a behavior analytic program does not operate in an ethical manner the loom is broken; the individual threads will not be able to be interwoven, and the art flawed. Thus, administration needs to lead by example. In order to do so they must provide a solid foundation. In addition to prioritizing clinical processes, stakeholder engagement, employee satisfaction, and promoting a high level of autonomy and alignment, the organization can also prompt an environment in which ethical conversations are generated to improve the organization's awareness and increase likelihood that decisions will be made with ethical considerations. This will strengthen the employees' sense of ethical conduct and promote alignment in the organization's behavioral contingencies.

Brodhead and colleagues (2018b) shared ways in which a prospective applicant could ask questions related to training, professional development, supervision, working within one's scope of competency, handling of confidential information, embracing collaborative efforts, and the company policies on cultural responsiveness. All of these questions will provide the applicant with information as to the ethical fortitude of an organization. Brodhead and colleagues (2018b) emphasized the importance of having organizational policies that align with the BACB® Ethics Code as a means to monitor and promote ethical behavior and ethical work culture. This obligation to promote an ethical culture relies heavily on the antecedents and consequences of the behavior we refer to as ethical or unethical. Is the environment one that encourages honesty, communication, and maintaining dignity of clients and others? Are staff encouraged to self-monitor their own ethical behavior? While the idea of promoting a culture may be somewhat elusive to us, the provision of contingencies that encourage and support behavior change is integral to our daily practice. It is essential that we remember that applied behavior analysis is a science. As such, it applies equally to all living things, whether we refer to clients, families, or staff. Contingencies, including the antecedents and consequent conditions in place, should aspire to promote an ethical culture within our workplaces including what to do when one witnesses a violation.

The BACB has documented the procedure and timeline for filing an alleged violation based on whether the perceived perpetrator is a BCBA/BCBA-D, RBT, infringement or misuse, self-report, or publicly available document (BACB, 2019). The flowchart is a fantastic resource that should be accessed, studied, and understood by all behavior analysts. The best protection a practitioner has against an ethical violation is documentation and case notes. The BACB® stresses the responsibility of the behavior analyst to address the individual directly before filing an alleged violation. It is commonplace to become impassioned in an ethical argument and, in some cases, the one filing the grievance may have been harmed in the claim. It is recommended to uphold the core principles and to approach the potential violator in a manner that is aligned with what the profession stands for; respect, compassion, and dignity. A resolution should be sought in this communication and the best way to do that is through an open dialogue in order to understand the other's perspective and listen from a place of empathy.

Ensure Their Competence

Behavior analysts ensure their competence by:

• Remaining within the profession's scope of practice

Brodhead and colleagues (2018c) write, "scope of practice refers to the range of activities in which members of a profession are authorized to engage, by virtue of holding a credential or license" (p. 425). Therefore, those credentialed with a BACB® are able to practice within the scope of practice as stipulated by the BACB®. For those that are duality certified, there would be other imposed restrictions based on the requirements for this other credentialing board. In some cases, one could be more limited in their scope of practice based on meeting the requirements of two credentialing boards instead of one. Imagine a Venn diagram in which one circle is the scope of practice for the BACB and the other circle is the scope of practice of state licensure. Your scope of practice would be the overlap between the two scopes of practice. Practicing outside of the overlap would be in violation of one (or both) of the credentialing boards. Ideally, if the state or provincial licensure is deemed necessary with a sufficient infrastructure to regulate, the guidelines would be aligned to the BACB (Green and Johnston, 2009).

• Remaining current and increasing their knowledge of best practices and advances in ABA and participating in professional development activities
• Remaining knowledgeable and current about interventions (including pseudoscience) that may exist in their practice areas and pose a risk of harm to clients

Remaining current is necessary for any field based in scientific methodology. As new discoveries are published, strategies that may have been learned in one's course sequence or during supervision may become obsolete. Further, one's program may lack efficacy or efficiency due to this oversight. A way to avoid this scenario is for a behavior analyst to contact the literature, ongoingly, and attend conferences and continuing education across a variety of topics to ensure that they are informed and that their clinical knowledge is up to date. Carr and Briggs (2010) provided tools to help behavior analysts access literature. They noted that barriers to accessing literature consist of: expense, overwhelmed by the sheer number of journals (how to discern quality), and time. They suggest that those facing these barriers consider free or inexpensive journals that may be available (one could also email the lead author in an effort to access a copy), highlight specific quality journals with a reputation of putting out sound, peer-reviewed articles, and to address concerns related to time; creating a social article club (if done with an ACE Provider, CEUs could be offered) or encouraging your workplace to support continuing education and offer opportunities to peruse literature during the work day. Leah Dunleavy (2014) had 24 occupational therapists complete a three-hour continuing education course on applied behavior analysis. She found gains in participants' self-efficacy, knowledge, and skill post-course and one month maintenance on behavioral concepts via a behavior analytic framework. However, "despite this increase, participants continued to implement sensory strategies to decrease challenging behaviors due to increased self-efficacy in using sensory strategies and the lack of support in implementing behavior techniques outside their session time" (p. 39). This finding, for behavior analysts, should have been expected, because they know that providing instruction and instruction alone is an ineffective model for training without modeling, rehearsal, and feedback (Alavosius & Sulzer-Azaroff, 1990; Parsons et al., 2013; Shook et al., 1978). Seeking out mentorship and supervision to learn a new skill is invaluable and should be accessed whenever possible (LeBlanc et al., 2020).

- Being aware of, working within, and continually evaluating the boundaries of their competence

Brodhead and colleagues (2018c) wrote that, "scope of competence refers to the range of professional activities of the individual practitioner that are performed at a level that is deemed proficient" (p. 425). For example, someone who has worked in changing organizational behaviors and cultures in an organizational behavior management capacity would not possess the scope of competence to be able to supervise an early intervention program if they have not received proper training and supervision on completing a behavior change program for early intervention clients. The Dunning-Kruger is our ability to label things we know (e.g., how to make a sandwich, definition of shaping, or the lyrics to *Bohemian Rhapsody*), label things that we know we don't know (e.g., the national anthem of Zambia, how to remove an appendix, or how to make a tourtiere), but we are unable to label things that we don't know we don't know. This blindspot provides us with a false sense of security which results in an overestimation of our own knowledge (Dunning, 2011). Brodhead and colleagues (2011c) created a table, the *Competence and Confidence Checklist*, to aid behavior analysts in self-assessing their abilities to perform competently with specific procedures and strategies, populations, and settings. A behavior analyst should be confident and comfortable creating a behavior change program for their client. If not, there could be a competency limitation and that must be explored.

- Working to continually increase their knowledge and skills related to cultural responsiveness and service delivery to diverse groups

Beaulieu and colleagues (2019) demonstrated with their questionnaire that the majority of behavior analysts polled have presumed competence when it comes to cultural responsiveness yet have minimal to no diversity training. Despite this dichotomy there exists a desire amongst behavior analysts to gain cultural responsiveness skills via diversity training (Fong et al., 2015). Studies have demonstrated an ability for practitioners to gain cultural responsiveness skills by focusing on and developing personal and interpersonal awareness and sensitivities, exposure and understanding of different cultures, and mastering effective skills for listening, speaking, and teaching (Cihon et al., 2018; Fong et al., 2016; Jernigan et al., 2016; Juarez et al., 2006). Many of these skills are subsumed in perspective taking and conveying empathy. Cultural responsiveness is essential for behavior analysts to practice across cultures effectively and to ensure the individualization of programming meets the environmental and social needs of the client. As such, it is paramount that supervisors demonstrate and train their supervisees to be culturally responsive and therefore possess the skills to enrich program targets and the clinical experience for clients of various cultural backgrounds. When developing a behavior change program, if the client's cultural needs and personal preferences are not taken into consideration, the behavior change program will be inefficient. For example, when working with a Muslim client, one might need to be familiar with teaching their client how to wash after using the toilet (istinja) or ensure that they have a clean, quiet space to pray with a mat five times a day. In some cultures, it is forbidden for individuals of opposite genders to touch and that includes high fives or handshakes. Also in many cultures it is customary to offer food to guests who enter the home; refusing to eat would be considered disrespectful and could potentially harm the client-therapist relationship (Beirne & Sadavoy, 2019).

It is important for practitioners to realize that without asking the right questions at intake, some clients may not be forthcoming with this crucial information. Therefore, it is essential that supervisees are taught to take culture into consideration when developing a program. Questions at intake that should be considered are: *what religious practices do you or anyone in your household practice regularly* (if religious practices are observed, asking follow up questions as to where and when and how to support the client in the participation of those customs should be discussed), *any specific rituals required for performing any personal care skill or daily living skill (such as: dressing, eating, cutting of hair or nails, and washing), gender preference, pronoun preferences, direct care staff considerations (clothing, scents, and are certain items not permitted in your home)*, and *what is socially significant to you and your family* (an ongoing question as social significance is not stagnant and the behavior change program must be essential to the client). Ignoring any of these identity markers will limit the effectiveness of the individualization of the behavior change program and supervisors must demonstrate and stress the importance of being culturally responsive as part of the supervisee's fieldwork experience. If working with transgender and gender-nonconforming (TGNC) clients or colleagues one might access Leland and Stockwell's (2019) TGNC-Affirming Clinical Skills Self-Assessment Tool to access any blindspot in an effort to promote inclusivity – both organizationally or individually (it should be noted that the practice of inclusivity should be sought regardless of whether you are working with a TGNC client or colleague). If ignored, if one assumes competence because "behavior is behavior," they would be at a huge risk of creating an environment that is neither supportive, encompassing, nor compassionate. In all cases, the behavior analysts have to look inward and assess their fitness in being able to provide service in an environment that may be uncomfortable when compared to other environments they frequent.

When working with cultures that are not your own, it is important that specific self-assessments be sought to help with cultivating affirming practices and learn of possible service delivery gaps based on cultural differences. Our second author states, "I am a white, middle socioeconomic class, male, immigrant, cishet. I can help organizational alignment, teach safety skills around the home, English verbal operants, or behavior skills training. I would be ill-equipped to teach menstrual care, behaviors associated with salat, Kinyarwanda verbal operants, suicidal ideation from identity marginalization, or teach clients who are black, brown, or indigenous how to respond to the police. I have had the privilege and honor of applying the principles of applied behavior analysis in fifteen different countries. In each of those countries, I recognize that I am ill-suited to provide therapy in that country and that the best clinicians are those that share the culture with their clients." Similarly, we would argue that each school, each classroom has its own culture and a behavior analyst would be wise to accept that they are a guest and as an outsider they must listen intently in an effort to learn about the culture and the environment in order to co-create a behavior change program through collaboration that is sensitive and informed by the client's environment.

Behavior analysts are *not* equipped to teach all behaviors in all scenarios; knowing what you can teach and what you can't requires thoughtful introspection, a commitment to continued culturally responsive learning, and an understanding of your competence, your client, and the environment.

Works Cited

Alavosius, M. P., & Sulzer-Azaroff, B. (1990). Acquisition and maintenance of health-care routines as a function of feedback density. *Journal of Applied Behavior Analysis, 23*(2), 151–162. https://doi.org/10.1901/jaba.1990.23-151.

American Psychological Association (APA). (2002). Ethical principles of psychologists and code of conduct. *American Psychologist, 57*, 1060–1073. 10.1037/0003–066X.57.12.1060.

American Psychological Association (APA). (2017). Ethical principles of psychologists and code of conduct (2002, amended effective June 1, 2010, and January 1, 2017). www.apa.org/ethics/code/index.html.

American Speech-Language-Hearing Association. (2016). Code of Ethics [Ethics]. www.asha.org/policy.

Andreassen C. S. (2014). Workaholism: an overview and current status of the research. *Journal of behavioral addictions*, *3*(1), 1–11. https://doi.org/10.1556/JBA.2.2013.017.

Beaulieu, L., Addington, J., & Almeida, D. (2018). Behavior analysts' training and practices regarding cultural diversity: the case for culturally competent care. *Behavior Analysis in Practice*, *12*(3), 557–575. https://doi.org/10.1007/s40617-018-00313-6.

Behavior Analyst Certification Board. (n.d.). BACB certificant data. Retrieved from www.bacb.com/BACB-certificant-data.

Behavior Analyst Certification Board. (2014). *Professional and Ethical Compliance Code for Behavior Analysts*. Littleton, CO: Author.

Behavior Analyst Certification Board. (2019, September 11). Reporting to the ethics department. BACB. www.bacb.com/ethics-information/reporting-to-ethics-department.

Behavior Analyst Certification Board. (2020). *Ethics Code for Behavior Analysts*. Littleton, CO: Author.

Brodhead, M. T. (2015). Maintaining professional relationships in an interdisciplinary setting: strategies for navigating nonbehavioral treatment recommendations for individuals with autism. *Behavior Analysis in Practice*, *8*(1), 70–78. https://doi.org/10.1007/s40617-015-0042-7.

Brodhead, M. T., Cox, D. J., & Quigley, S. P. (2018a). *Practical ethics for effective treatment of autism spectrum disorder*. Amsterdam: Academic Press.

Brodhead, M. T., Quigley, S. P., & Cox, D. J. (2018b). How to identify ethical practices in organizations prior to employment. *Behavior Analysis in Practice*, *11*(2), 165–173. https://doi.org/10.1007/s40617-018-0235-y.

Brodhead, M. T., Quigley, S. P., & Wilczynski, S. M. (2018c). A call for discussion about scope of competence in behavior analysis. *Behavior Analysis in Practice*, *11*(4), 424–435. https://doi.org/10.1007/s40617-018-00303-8

Callahan, K., Foxx, R. M., Swierczynski, A., Aerts, X., Mehta, S., McComb, M., Nichols, S. M., Segal, G., Donald, A., & Sharma, R. (2019). Behavioral artistry: examining the relationship between the interpersonal skills and effective practice repertoires of applied behavior analysis practitioners. *Journal of Autism and Developmental Disorders*, *49*(9), 3557–3570. https://doi.org/10.1007/s10803-019-04082-1.

Canadian Psychological Association. (2017). Canadian code of ethics for psychologists (4th ed.). https://cpa.ca/aboutcpa/committees/ethics/codeofethics.

Carr, J. E., & Briggs, A. M. (2010). Strategies for making regular contact with the scholarly literature. *Behavior Analysis in Practice*, *3*, 13–18. https://doi.org/10.1007/BF0339176.

Carr, R. N. (2020, February 10). *Board certified behavior A$$hole*. LinkedIn. www.linkedin.com/pulse/board-certified-behavior-ahole-r-nicolle-carr-ph-d-bcba-d-lba-ok.

Carr, R. N. (2021). Rural Access to Ethical and Appropriate Behavior Analytic Treatment in Schools. In Sadavoy, J. A. & Zube, M. L. (eds.), *A scientific framework for compassion and social justice: Lessons in applied behavior analysis* (pp. 247–251). Routledge.

Cihon, T., Artoni, V., Cavallini, F., & Corsano, P. (2018). Creating and sustaining an international collaboration in behavior analysis. *Behavior and Social Issues*, *27*, 71–90. https://doi.org/10.5210/bsi.v27i0.9135.

Cirincione-Ulezi, N. (2020). Black women and barriers to leadership in ABA. *Behavior Analysis in Practice*, *13*(4), 719–724. https://doi.org/10.1007/s40617-020-00444-9.

Conners, B. M., & Capell, S. T. (2020). *Multiculturalism and diversity in applied behavior analysis: bridging theory and application*. London: Routledge.

De Lourdes Levy, M., Larcher, V., & Kurz, R. (2003). Informed consent/assent in children. Statement of the ethics working group of the Confederation of European specialists in paediatrics (CESP). *European Journal of Pediatrics*, *162*(9), 629–633. https://doi.org/10.1007/s00431-003-1193-z.

Dixon, M. R., Hayes, S. C., Stanley, C., Law, S., & Al-Nasser, T. (2020). Is acceptance and commitment training or therapy (ACT) a method that applied behavior analysts can and should use? *The Psychological Record*, *70*(4), 559–579. https://doi.org/10.1007/s40732-020-00436-9.

Dunleavy, L. (2014). Evaluation of a continuing education course for occupational therapy practitioners on the use of applied behavior analysis. *Occupational Therapy in Health Care, 29*(1), 39–53. https://doi.org/10.3109/07380577.2014.950784.

Dunning, D. (2011). The Dunning-Kruger effect. *Advances in Experimental Social Psychology,* 247–296. https://doi.org/10.1016/b978-0-12-385522-0.00005-6.

Dunning, D., Fetchenhauer, D., & Schlösser, T. (2016). The psychology of respect: A case study of how behavioral norms regulate human action. In A. Elliot (Ed.), *Advances in motivation science* (Vol. 3, pp. 1–34). Elsevier. http://dx.doi.org/10.1016/bs.adms.2015.12.003

Gabassi, P. G., Cervai, S., Rozbowsky, P., Semeraro, A., & Gregori, D. (2002). Burnout syndrome in the helping professions. *Psychological Reports, 90*(1), 309–314. https://doi.org/10.2466/pr0.2002.90.1.309.

Falender, C. A., & Shafranske, E. P. (2012). The importance of competency-based clinical supervision and training in the twenty-first century: why bother? *Journal of Contemporary Psychotherapy, 42*(3), 129–137. https://doi.org/10.1007/s10879-011-9198-9.

Fiebig, J. H., Gould, E. R., Ming, S., & Watson, R. A. (2020). An invitation to act on the value of self-care: being a whole person in all that you do. *Behavior Analysis in Practice, 13*(3), 559–567. https://doi.org/10.1007/s40617-020-00442-x.

Flaxman, P. E., Bond, F. W., & Livheim, F. (2013). *The mindful and effective employee: An acceptance and commitment therapy training manual for improving well-being and performance.* Oakland, CA: New Harbinger Publications.

Fong, E. H., & Tanaka, S. (2013). Multicultural alliance of behavior analysis standards for cultural competence in behavior analysis. *International Journal of Behavioral Consultation and Therapy, 8*(2), 17–19. https://doi.org/10.1037/h0100970.

Fong, E. H., Catagnus, R. M., Brodhead, M. T., Quigley, S., & Field, S. (2016). Developing the cultural awareness skills of behavior analysts. *Behavior Analysis in Practice, 9*(1), 84–94. https://doi.org/10.1007/s40617-016-0111-6.

Fong, E. H., Ficklin, S., & Lee, H. Y. (2017). Increasing cultural understanding and diversity in applied behavior analysis. *Behavior Analysis: Research and Practice, 17*(2), 103–113. https://doi.org/10.1037/bar0000076.

Fouka, G., & Mantzorou, M. (2011). What are the major ethical issues in conducting research? Is there a conflict between the research ethics and the nature of nursing? *Health Science Journal, 5*(1), 3–14.

Fryling, M. J. (2016). A developmental-behavioral analysis of lying. *International Journal of Psychology & Psychological Therapy, 16*(1), 13–22.

Fuller, J. L., & Fitter, E. A. (2020). Mindful parenting: a behavioral tool for parent well-being. *Behavior Analysis in Practice, 13*, 767–771. https://doi.org/10.1007/s40617-020-00447-6.

Green, G., & Johnston, J. M. (2009). Licensing behavior analysts: risks and alternatives. *Behavior Analysis in Practice, 2*(1), 59–64. https://doi.org/10.1007/BF03391739.

Hayes, S. C. (2020). *A liberated mind: how to pivot toward what matters.* New York, NY: Avery.

Hunt, P., Soto, G., Maier, J., & Doering, K. (2003). Collaborative teaming to support students at risk and students with severe disabilities in general education classrooms. *Exceptional Children, 69*(3), 315–332. https://doi.org/10.1177/001440290306900304.

Irwin, D. L., Pannbacker, M., Powell, T. W., & Vekovius, G. T. (2007). *Ethics for speech-language pathologists and audiologists: An illustrative casebook.* Boston, MA: Thomson Delmar Learning.

Jernigan, V. B., Hearod, J. B., Tran, K., Norris, K. C., & Buchwald, D. (2016). An examination of cultural competence training in US medical education guided by the tool for assessing cultural competence training. *Journal of Health Disparities Research and Practice, 9*(3), 150–167.

Juarez, J. A., Marvel, K., Brezinski, K. L., Glazner, C., Towbin, M. M., & Lawton, S. (2006). Bridging the gap: a curriculum to teach residents cultural humility. *Family Medicine, 38*(2), 97–102.

Kazemi, E., Rice, B., & Adzhyan, P. (2018). *Fieldwork and supervision for behavior analysts: A handbook.* New York, NY: Springer.

LaFrance, D. L., Weiss, M. J., Kazemi, E., Gerenser, J., & Dobres, J. (2019). Multidisciplinary teaming: enhancing collaboration through increased understanding. *Behavior Analysis in Practice, 12*(3), 709–726. https://doi.org/10.1007/s40617-019-00331-y

Leaf, J. B., Leaf, R., McEachin, J., Taubman, M., Ala'i-Rosales, S., Ross, R. K., Smith, T., & Weiss, M. J. (2015). Applied behavior analysis is a science and, therefore, progressive. *Journal of Autism and Developmental Disorders, 46*(2), 720–731. https://doi.org/10.1007/s10803-015-2591-6.

LeBlanc, L. A., Nosik, M. R., & Petursdottir, A. (2018). Establishing consumer protections for research in human service agencies. *Behavior Analysis in Practice, 11*(4), 445–455. https://doi.org/10.1007/s40617-018-0206-3.

LeBlanc, L. A., Taylor, B. A., & Marchese, N. V. (2019). The training experiences of behavior analysts: compassionate care and therapeutic relationships with caregivers. *Behavior Analysis in Practice, 13*(2), 387–393. https://doi.org/10.1007/s40617-019-00368-z.

LeBlanc, L. A., Sellers T. P., & Ala'i S. (2020). *Building and sustaining meaningful and effective relationships as a supervisor and mentor*. New York, NY: Sloan Publishing.

LeBlanc, L., Gingles, D., & Byers, E. (2021). The role of compassion in social justice efforts. In J. A. Sadavoy & M. L. Zube (Eds.), *A scientific framework for compassion and social justice: lessons from applied behavior analysis*. London: Routledge.

Leland, W., & Stockwell, A. (2019). A self-assessment tool for cultivating affirming practices with transgender and gender-nonconforming (TGNC) clients, supervisees, students, and colleagues. *Behavior Analysis in Practice, 12*(4), 816–825. https://doi.org/10.1007/s40617-019-00375-0.

Lerman, D. C., Addison, L. R., & Kodak, T. (2006). A preliminary analysis of self-control with aversive events: the effects of task magnitude and delay on the choices of children with autism. *Journal of Applied Behavior Analysis*, 39, 227–232. https://doi.org/10.1901/jaba.2006.90-05.

Li, A., Gravina, N., Pritchard, J. K., & Poling, A. (2019). The gender pay gap for behavior analysis faculty. *Behavior Analysis in Practice, 12*(4), 743–746. https://doi.org/10.1007/s40617-019-00347-4.

Maslach, C., Jackson, S. E., & Leiter, M. P. (1996). MBI Maslach Burnout Inventory.

Mayer, R. C., Davis, J. H., & Schoorman, F. D. (1995). An integration model of organizational trust. *Academy of Management Review, 20*, 709–734.

Miller, K. L., Re Cruz, A., & Ala'i-Rosales, S. (2019). Inherent tensions and possibilities: behavior analysis and cultural responsiveness. *Behavior and Social Issues, 28*(1), 16–36. https://doi.org/10.1007/s42822-019-00010-1.

Neuringer A. (1991). Humble behaviorism. *The Behavior Analyst, 14*(1), 1–13. https://doi.org/10.1007/BF03392543.

Nosik, M. R., & Grow, L. L. (2015). Prominent women in behavior analysis: an introduction. *The Behavior Analyst, 38*(2), 225–227. https://doi.org/10.1007/s40614-015-0032-7.

Nosik, M. R., Luke, M. M., & Carr, J. E. (2019). Representation of women in behavior analysis: an empirical analysis. *Behavior Analysis: Research and Practice, 19*(2), 213–221. http://dx.doi.org/10.1037/bar0000118.

O'Leary, P. N., Miller, M. M., Olive, M. L., & Kelly, A. N. (2015). Blurred lines: ethical implications of social media for behavior analysts. *Behavior Analysis in Practice, 10*(1), 45–51. https://doi.org/10.1007/s40617-014-0033-0.

Parsons, M. B., Rollyson, J. H., & Reid, D. H. (2013). Teaching practitioners to conduct behavioral skills training: a pyramidal approach for training multiple human service staff. *Behavior Analysis in Practice, 6*(2), 4–16. https://doi.org/10.1007/BF03391798.

Peterson, S. M., Aljadeff-Abergel, E., Eldridge, R. R., VanderWeele, N. J., & Acker, N. S. (2020). Conceptualizing self-determination from a behavioral perspective: the role of choice, self-control, and self-management. *Journal of Behavioral Education*. https://doi.org/10.1007/s10864-020-09368-4.

Plantiveau, C., Dounavi, K., & Virués-Ortega, J. (2018). High levels of burnout among early-career board-certified behavior analysts with low collegial support in the work environment. *European Journal of Behavior Analysis, 19*(2), 195–207.

Pritchett, M., Ala'i, S., Re Cruz, A., & Cihon, T. (2020). Social justice is the spirit and aim of an applied science of human behavior: moving from colonial to participatory research practices. https://doi.org/10.31234/osf.io/t87p4.

Reamer, F. G. (1998). The evolution of social work ethics. *Social Work, 43*(6), 488–500. https://doi.org/10.1093/sw/43.6.488.

Rekers, G., & Lovaas, O. (1974). Behavioral treatment of deviant sex-role behaviors in a male child. *Journal of Applied Behavior Analysis*, 7, 173–190. https://doi.org/10.1901/jaba.1974.7-173.

Reid, D. H., Rosswurm, M., & Rotholz, D. A. (2017). No less worthy: recommendations for behavior analysts treating adults with intellectual and developmental disabilities with dignity. *Behavior Analysis in Practice, 11*(1), 71–79.

Roth-Cline, M., & Nelson, R. M. (2013). Parental permission and child assent in research on children. *The Yale Journal of Biology and Medicine, 86*(3), 291–301.

Sadavoy, J. A., & Zube, M. L. (2021). *A scientific framework for compassion and social justice: lessons in applied behavior analysis.* London: Routledge.

Shook, G. L., Johnson, C. M., & Uhlman, W. F. (1978). The effect of response effort reduction, instructions, group and individual feedback, and reinforcement on staff performance. *Journal of Organizational Behavior Management, 1*(3), 207–215. https://doi.org/10.1300/j075v01n03_05.

Sinclair, C. (2017). Ethics in psychology: recalling the past, acknowledging the present, and looking to the future. *Canadian Psychology/Psychologie canadienne, 58*(1), 20–29. https://doi.org/10.1037/cap0000086.

Slim, L., & Celiberti, D. (2021). Cultural considerations for delivering effective treatment. In Sadavoy, J. A. & Zube, M. L. (Eds.), *A scientific framework for compassion and social justice: Lessons in applied behavior analysis* (pp. 94–99). Routledge.

Tarbox, J., Szabo, T. G., & Aclan, M. (2020). Acceptance and commitment training within the scope of practice of applied behavior analysis. *Behavior Analysis in Practice.* Special issue. https://doi.org/10.1007/s40617-020-00466-3.

Taylor, B. A., & Fisher, J. (2010). Three important things to consider when starting intervention for a child diagnosed with autism. *Behavior Analysis in Practice, 3*(2), 52–53. https://doi.org/10.1007/BF03391765

Taylor, B. A., LeBlanc, L. A., & Nosik, M. R. (2018). Compassionate care in behavior analytic treatment: can outcomes be enhanced by attending to relationships with caregivers? *Behavior Analysis in Practice, 12*(3), 654–666. https://doi.org/10.1007/s40617-018-00289-3.

Todd, J. T. (2019). Some things you need to know to be a behavior analyst and other considerations: an informal recollection with examples. *European Journal of Behavior Analysis, 21*(1), 110–132. https://doi.org/10.1080/15021149.2019.1673622.

Turner, L. B., Fischer, A. J., & Luiselli, J. K. (2016). Towards a competency-based, ethical, and socially valid approach to the supervision of applied behavior analytic trainees. *Behavior Analysis in Practice, 9*(4), 287–298. https://doi.org/10.1007/s40617-016-0121-4.

Vilardaga, R. (2009). A Relational Frame Theory account of empathy. *International Journal of Behavioral Consultation and Therapy, 5*(2), 178–184. http://dx.doi.org/10.1037/h0100879.

Vilardaga, R., Luoma, J. B., Hayes, S. C., Pistorello, J., Levin, M. E., Hildebrandt, M. J., Kohlenberg, B., Roget, N. A., & Bond, F. (2011). Burnout among the addiction counseling workforce: the differential roles of mindfulness and values-based processes and work-site factors. *Journal of Substance Abuse Treatment, 40*(4), 323–335. https://doi.org/10.1016/j.jsat.2010.11.015.

Wehmeyer, M. L. (1995). *The Arc's Self-Determination Scale: Procedural Guidelines.*

Wehmeyer, M. L., & Abery, B. (2013). Self-determination and choice. *Intellectual and Developmental Disabilities, 51*(5), 399–411.

Wehmeyer, M. L., & Palmer, S. B. (2003). Adult outcomes for students with cognitive disabilities three-years after high school: the impact of self-determination. *Education and Training in Developmental Disabilities, 38*, 131–144.

Wehmeyer, M. L., & Schalock, R. L. (2001). Self-determination and quality of life: implications for special education services and supports. *Focus on Exceptional Children, 33*, 1.

Williams, C. M. (2021). Cultural responsiveness: the development and implications of cultural responsive practices to behavior change programs. In Sadavoy, J. A. & Zube, M. L. (Eds.), *A scientific framework for compassion and social justice: Lessons in applied behavior analysis* (pp. 84–93). Routledge.

Wolf, M. M. (1978). Social validity: the case for subjective measurement or how applied behavior analysis is finding its heart. *Journal of Applied Behavior Analysis, 11*(2), 203–214. https://doi.org/10.1901/jaba.1978.11-203.

1.3 Ethical Decision-Making

There has certainly been a great deal written and spoken of the unethical behavior analyst – the behavior analyst who bills fraudulently, who exploits the vulnerable clients they serve, takes advantage of students and supervisees, falsifies data, and ignores the Code either out of ignorance or apathy. To that behavior analyst, there is little that we can say. Certainly, a book about the importance of ethical behavior is a start. However, this content must be applied accurately and fluently for one to uphold the principles and responsibility of being a behavior analyst. It would be erroneous to think that any behavior analyst would practice ethically by going through the contents of this text, reviewing the Code, or by performing both tasks. We require constant feedback from clients and colleagues to ensure that we are being responsive. Further, with new code elements and updates via newsletters, a behavior analyst must accept that ethics is dynamic and with that comes the opportunity to welcome the ongoing challenge of building ethical skills.

After a thorough review of the Ethical Code for Behavior Analysts, you may be left with the question, "What now?" Knowing what to do is one thing, but deciding what to do in real-life situations may be quite another. There may be risks involved in any possible decision, there may be many parties with conflicting interests. In an ideal world, the solution to a problem would appear simple. But we do not live in an ideal world, and "simple" is very rarely the same as "easy".

Isaac Newton once wrote in a letter to a fellow scientist, "If I have seen further, it is by standing on the shoulders of giants." In any scientific field we rely on those who have come before us to pave the way that we walk on. Even for those of us who focus on clinical practice, those who have paved the way are essential to our practice. Several behavior analysts have taken a behavioral approach to ethical decision-making, task analyzing the necessary steps to identifying and addressing ethical violations and ensuring that our practice maintains high ethical standards. In this chapter, we will review some of these "giants" and their models for addressing ethical decision-making.

In this chapter we will review several models of ethical decision-making from some of these "giants" of the field. For each method, we will review a fictional scenario highlighting the use of that methodology to address the ethical concern.

BACB

Let us begin by going directly to the source. The Behavior Analyst Certification Board®, in the Ethics Code for Behavior Analysts®, has specified a recommended practice for implementing ethical practice and identifying and addressing potential violations.

DOI: 10.4324/9781003190707-4

Our Obligations

In the Code section titled, "Application of the Code," behavior analysts are encouraged to think analytically about ethical situations. This section states, "The standards included in the Code are not meant to be exhaustive, as it is impossible to predict every situation that might constitute an ethics violation" (BACB, 2021). The work of interpreting and responding to the complex interaction of different obligations and competing interests cannot be reduced to a simple list of directions.

Our obligations are not restricted to the exact phrasing of the Code. In addition, we must also follow our obligation under the law as well as licensing requirements specified by our state or other governing agencies. It is clarified with the Ethics Code, "in all instances of interpreting and applying the Code, behavior analysts should put compliance with the law and clients' interests first by actively working to maximize desired outcomes and minimize risk" (BACB, 2021).

Enforcement

The BACB also publishes a document on what happens next. How does the BACB® respond when a report is made?

The critical thing for any certificant to remember is that the BACB® is a non-profit organization that is committed to maintaining the quality of services for consumers. They accomplish this by establishing and enforcing standards. Ultimately, they want more BCBAs® providing high-quality service to anyone who needs them. They are not out to catch wrongdoers, their goal is to maintain the high-quality standards so that when someone seeks the services of a BCBA® they can be assured that they or their loved one will be in the care of someone who will look out for their safety and dignity.

That being said, it would be naive to assume that ethical violations do not happen and that the necessity of a system to enforce these standards is unnecessary.

The Code

What happens when a report is made?

Once a report is made the certificant and the person who made the report (referred to as the "notfier") will receive notice that a report has been made. A report must:

- *Be submitted against a certificant.* The BACB® can only respond to someone over whom they have some sort of authority.
- *Be submitted within six months of the violation.*
- *Be submitted in good faith.* Part of the review process includes determining if the report is some form of retaliation. Reports that do not appear to be submitted in good faith will be dismissed.
- *Have a valid signature.*
- *Include documentation.* This is why it is so critical to create and maintain documentation.

What sort of consequences may occur?

Once a case is evaluated it is routed either to *disciplinary review* or to *educational review*. An *educational review* will result in the person involved being asked to rectify the situation. Coaching can also be provided so that future ethics violations can be avoided.

A *disciplinary review* may involve different consequences. One might be asked to engage in professional development activities, pursue mentorship in the relevant area(s), submit some sort of product related to the violation, or to verify their competency to practice (for example, by reporting on treatment for a condition that affects ability to practice responsibly). In some cases there may be *sanctions* – immediate, severe consequences. These can include mandatory supervision, practice restrictions, or revocation, ineligibility, or suspension of certification.

What must be self-reported?

The BACB® requires not only that we monitor the ethical behavior of others, but also that we ensure that our own behavior is ethical as well. And this includes, if necessary, reporting to the BACB® ethical violations or incidents that may be cause for concern.

A great deal of confusion surrounds what sort of information must be self-reported. The BACB®, fortunately, has also provided some guidance for certificants in answering this as well. In their document *Considerations for Self-Reporting* (BACB, 2019), the BACB® outlines the questions that will determine whether a situation is one that requires reporting to the BACB®. By addressing factors such as the direct impact on the clients served, more complex cases such as reporting public health or safety violations become far more clear.

Decision-Making

The BACB® recommends the following steps to assess and respond to potential ethical violations.

1. *Clearly define the issue and consider potential risk of harm to relevant individuals.*
    The first phase of an ethical problem is often that sense of "this isn't right." Those alarm bells may go off for a variety of reasons, and not all indicate that an ethical issue is at play.
2. *Identify all relevant individuals.*
    Who are the people involved in this? Who is relevant and how? There may be many parties who may be involved, but this does not mean that all of them are relevant. A large company, for example, may have a CEO, a clinical director, and a supervisor who all to some extent oversee the work of the BCBAs who provide services. In some organizations, BCBAs may be pressured by those who lead the company to recommend excessive hours for their cases in order to meet an arbitrary standard rather than taking client needs into account. There may be school districts, teachers, classmates, and supervisors, and funders, all of whom may have a stake in the proposed outcome. While many parties may be tangentially involved, their involvement does not necessarily indicate relevance. The determination of relevance is restricted to those who are directly affected by the decision.
3. *Gather relevant supporting documentation and follow-up on second-hand information to confirm that there is an actual ethical concern.*
    In the words of W. Edwards Deming, "In God we trust. All others, bring data." As behavior analysts we value data in all things. Documentation of potential ethical issues is essential. If you suspect a possible ethical violation, begin to document any relevant information as soon as possible.

4. *Consider your personal learning history and biases in the context of the relevant individuals.*

   It is important to consider that our discomfort may be a product of our biases. Before moving any further, it is recommended that we pause and consider for a moment how much that discomfort is about the situation and how much is about our own perception of it.

5. *Identify the relevant core principles and Code standards.*

   What, if any, specific Code element is being violated? Is this an issue that involves a failure to meet our responsibility to our clients, to our supervisees, or a failure to uphold our core principles?

6. *Consult available resources (e.g. research, decision-making models, trusted colleagues).*

   A behavior analyst must respond to an ethical problem the way they would a clinical problem – by examining the relevant research and by consulting with experts. We are not expected to know everything. It is, however, our responsibility to seek out the knowledge that we lack.

7. *Develop several possible actions to reduce or remove risk of harm prioritizing the best interests of clients in accordance with the Code and applicable laws.*

   There is an ancient Arab proverb that states, "Trust in God but tie your camel." In other words, we may have all the confidence in the world that our first plan will work, but that does not mean we are excused from planning for other contingencies.

8. *Critically evaluate each possible action by considering its alignment with the "letter and spirit" of the Code, its potential impact on the client and stakeholders, the likelihood of it immediately resolving the ethical concern, as well as variable such as client preference, social acceptability, degree of restrictiveness, and likelihood of maintenance.*

   The actions taken must also reflect our commitment to the Code and its core principles. Do our actions reflect the ideals of benefiting others, treating others with compassion, dignity, and respect, behaving with dignity, and ensuring competence?

9. *Select the action that seems most likely to resolve the specific ethical concern and reduce the likelihood of similar issues arising in the future.*

   As behavior analysts we are concerned not only with what is happening in the moment but with future behavior. What solution will prevent this ethical issue from arising again?

10. *Take the selected action in collaboration with relevant individuals affected by the issue and document specific actions taken, agreed-upon next steps, names of relevant individuals, and due dates.*

    Perhaps the most important aspect of this step is "in collaboration with relevant individuals affected by the issue." Remember that you are not acting alone. As reviewed in Step 8, any actions or potential actions will affect others and they must have some involvement in the process.

11. *Evaluate the outcomes to ensure that the actions successfully addressed the issue.*

    Evaluation of the success of our intervention is a necessary step in our ethical response, just as it is with our clinical work. Understanding the success of our ethical interventions is critically important.

The Scenario

Sara was thrilled to begin her research assistantship at her graduate program, and particularly excited to be working with a very well known and well respected professor and BCBA-D. She was not the only woman in the program, but Sara still soon felt out of place and uncomfortable. Dr. Smith would frequently make jokes she found offensive and when she didn't laugh but tried to ignore it, he would say, "What's Stick-Up-Her-Ass-Sara grumbling about now?" She tried to talk to her colleagues but they told her to "lighten up" and "that's just how he is." They felt very lucky to be working there and said to her, "You don't seem to realize how much he has contributed to the field!" Other women didn't seem to mind being asked about their sex lives, but Sara found it inappropriate and asked him to stop, but he simply laughed. One day she wore one of her favorite sweaters, a gift from her mother, and he said, "Wow! That really hugs you in all the right places," and looked her up and down. Frustrated about what to do next, she said she was ill, went home, and threw the sweater in the trash.

The Process

Step 1. After giving it considerable thought and reading through the Ethics Code carefully, Sara determined that it was possible she was being harassed. This was harmful to her mental health and her productivity, but could also be harmful to her career in the long term.

Step 2. The people involved were the supervising professor and Sara. After careful consideration, Sara also decided that her colleagues who had witnessed these events could be considered involved, since they would also be affected by whatever action would be taken.

Step 3. Sara reviewed her notes from meetings and documented any time that her professor had made an inappropriate comment, along with her response. She made a file with any email "jokes," including an email chain in which several colleagues admonished her to "lighten up" and "get a sense of humor."

Step 4. In consideration of her biases, Sara could not be entirely sure that wasn't being, as her colleagues repeatedly told her, "uptight." Perhaps she didn't understand the workplace culture and maybe it wasn't for her. Perhaps she had inadvertently reinforced this behavior by wearing the wrong clothing or with a nervous smile. After further consideration, however, she realized that, regardless of whether or not her standards of humor were reasonable, she had asked him to stop and that request was ignored. She had made her discomfort clear and still the behavior continued.

Step 5. After a careful review of the Code, Sara concludes that she is being harassed in a clear violation of Code element 1.09, Nonharassment. In addition, she believes that Dr. Smith has failed to act with integrity or treat her with dignity according to the core principles.

Step 6. Sara reviews the university harassment policy and legal definitions of sexual harassment. All of her doubts are quickly resolved. She decides to call her advisor and ask what possible next steps to take. Her advisor offers some comfort and thanks her for coming forward. They discuss the process for making a report.

Step 7. Sara considers simply leaving the assistantship or trying yet again to address this with Dr. Smith directly. She reviews her documentation and sees that he has persisted with this behavior for a long time, and suddenly notices that another "uptight" grad student left last year. With all of the information available to her, Sara decides that she will make a report to the university and to the BACB(R).

Steps 8–10. Sara reviews the Code Enforcement Procedures and the university's harassment policies. She understands that there is substantial risk for Dr. Smith and her colleagues if any disciplinary action is taken. And if it is not, there could be consequences for her. Just as she is about to forget the whole thing, she gets a phone call from her best friend in the program. Great news! She might be accepted into Dr. Smith's assistantship also, wouldn't that be great? She knows at that point that Dr. Smith's behavior needs to stop, and whatever action is necessary to make that happen must be taken.

Thinking about the safety of her friend, Sara takes her sweater out of the trash, puts it back on and begins to type up the report.

Step 11. After Sara's report was submitted, several other women came forward, many of whom had quit positions or dropped classes taught by Dr. Smith. The university reprimanded him and reassigned many of his responsibilities. The BACB also restricted his practice so that he was no longer able to supervise. In Dr. Smith's lectures, he was noticeably more restrained. The university also hosted several talks on inclusion and anti-harassment efforts. There was a great deal of complaining, and several of Sara's colleagues said, "You can't even joke anymore." But there was also a great deal of discussion. Some of Sara's colleagues were upset at her, and blamed her for the disciplinary actions taken. But Sara felt much more confident without Dr. Smith, and it showed in her work.

Rosenberg and Schwartz (2019)

In Rosenberg and Schwartz's article a possible decision-making model for ethical issues is proposed. The goal is to provide a strategy for problem-solving and thus maintain a high standard for ethical behavior within the field. By answering this series of questions, Rosenberg and Schwartz encourage behavior analysts to engage in a process that will lead to consistent ethical practice.

Step 1. "Why does this trigger your ethical radar?" (Rosenberg & Schwartz, 2018).
The first sign of an ethical violation is often a feeling of discomfort – a "this isn't right" instinct. This "ethical radar," as Rosenberg and Schwartz refer to it, is that very first sign of trouble. We are encouraged to respond to it.

Step 2. Brainstorm possible solutions to the dilemma.
Think of ways to address the issue at hand and prevent exacerbating any potential violations. At this stage, any ideas are acceptable, you will be rejecting the bad ones later.

Step 3. Evaluate the pros and cons of these proposed solutions.
Now is the time that you evaluate your potential solutions. See which ones offer you the best chance of resolving the situation and preventing ethical violations or harm to those involved.

Step 4. Determine if you have found an acceptable solution (if no, return to Step 2).
Would any of these possible solutions resolve the situation in a way that meets both the letter and spirit of the Ethics Code and core principles? If not, it is back to the drawing board.

Step 5. Implement the solution and document.
Now it is time to put your solution into practice. Keep careful documentation of the actions you take. Make sure to include any relevant parties.

Step 6. Evaluate the effects.
As always we must make sure that your intervention was effective in resolving the issue.

The Scenario

Bill is a BCBA who works with several clients in a suburban area. One of his clients, Mikey, at age five, is the oldest of four siblings. His mother is a stay at home mom, his younger sister Jenny has cerebral palsy and he has infant twin brothers as well. They are struggling financially, since Mikey's father lost his job six months ago, but finally they have good news – he has found a great job! The bad news is it involves a lot of travel – two to three overnights a week. Mikey's mom asks Bill to babysit, since he and Mikey get along so well. She feels uncomfortable having "just any old person" in her home, given her children's needs, but she is overwhelmed. She reports that she and her husband sometimes have to sleep in shifts in order to keep up with the children and she does not know what else to do.

The Process

Step 1. Bill's "ethical radar" is sounding off at this point. He is extremely uncomfortable at being asked to babysit, as he knows that this would be the start of a multiple relationship – a "commingling of two or more of a behavior analyst's roles" (BACB, 2021). To do so would complicate the professional relationship and may compromise the quality of intervention. At the same time, Bill understands that this is a difficult time for Mikey's mother and he sees that she is struggling, which makes him uncomfortable with saying no.

Step 2. Bill can think of several possible responses. The obvious one is to simply say no. Another possible solution is to try to advocate for more hours. A third option would be to recommend that the mother apply for respite services. A fourth option would be to find an alternate babysitter.

Step 3. Simply saying no and leaving it at that is the option with which Bill is least comfortable. The mother is clearly struggling and he is concerned that there may be a health or safety risk if she has no support, especially if she is unable to sleep. A recommendation for more hours seems less than ideal from an ethical standpoint, since these hours would not be recommended for clinical reasons. Additionally, they would not be very helpful for the needs of Mikey's brothers or sister. Applying for respite services may be a better solution, but such applications are often complex and time consuming with services taking months to start. The fourth option may be the best bet, and perhaps a babysitter with experience with children with disabilities could be found.

Step 4. Bill believes that an alternate babysitter may be the best option. He believes that a suitable candidate can be found either at the local university's special education department or by finding an RBT who does not work with Mikey.

Step 5. Bill emails Mikey's mother and his supervisor that another babysitter would be best, suggesting that she contact the university or that they "ask around" their pool of RBTs. He gives her contact information for the head of the special education department, along with several professors and suggests that she ask if they know of anyone.

Step 6. After a few phone calls, Mikey's mother is able to find an excellent babysitter who becomes fast friends with all four children. Bill sends an email to Mikey's mom and to his supervisor, saying how glad he is that things have worked out. Bill hears back from his supervisor that she has heard about the struggle to find qualified babysitters before and is concerned that this potential ethics issue may be happening more often. She asks if Bill would like to make this a project. He agrees. They find several names and create a "babysitter referral list" for families.

Bailey and Burch (2016)

Jon Bailey and Mary Burch are often considered the seminal experts in ethics within the field of behavior analysis. As authors of the first textbook in ethics for behavior analysts, they are the "giants" upon whose shoulders the rest of us hope to stand. Jon Bailey also leads the ABA Ethics Hotline, a resource for behavior analysts with ethical questions or problems. Several behavior analysts provide guidance for those who ask questions, and a lawyer also provides legal guidance.

In their third edition, Bailey and Burch proposed a seven-step process for the analysis of ethical cases.

Step 1. Determine if the incident is covered by the Ethics Code.
The first step is to determine if this is actually an ethical violation, rather than something that makes you uncomfortable. What specific Code elements are being violated?

Step 2. Determine the "players."
The "players" in this case refers to those who may have acted and those who are affected by those actions. Who are those who are directly affected by this situation?

Step 3. Develop contingency plans A, B, and C.
It has been said that "If you fail to plan, you plan to fail." It is important not to assume that your first plan will be successful but instead to plan for contingencies in the event that you need to try other tactics.

Step 4. Determine what "skills" and "clout" you possess that are likely to lead to a successful resolution.
What do you bring to the table to resolve this issue? Are you able to negotiate well with others, analyze situations well? Are you skilled at managing difficult people? Being skilled in behavior analysis brings many skills along with it that can be useful in having difficult conversations. "Clout," however, may be more difficult for us to self-assess. This refers to the power and influence that we have in any given situation. It is important to know that power and influence do not need to be ours alone and we can seek out support from supervisors or other trusted colleagues if necessary, including the BACB® if necessary. Knowledge of the law and our ethical obligations may grant us a greater degree of clout.

Step 5. Determine the level of risk to the client, to others, and to yourself.
Just as we would for a treatment plan, we must determine the level of risk for our interventions in ethical situations. Risk may be different to different parties involved, however, the possibility of harm to all parties must be determined before taking any action.

Step 6. Implement your solutions.
Now it is time to put your plans into action. Be sure to be ready with other contingencies in the event that your first plan is unsuccessful.

Step 7. Evaluate the effectiveness of your solution.
Again, evaluating the success of our interventions is necessary. We cannot simply take action and hope for the best, we must also ensure that these actions have had a positive effect on the situation.

The Scenario

Donna is a recent graduate who is thrilled to start her career as a BCBA working with individuals with autism. Shortly after receiving her master's degree, she gets a job at a new company. She interviews with the CEO, a former marketing director who refers to applied behavior analysis as "the hottest field now." She is somewhat concerned that he seems unaware of proper terminology and uses some odd phrases such as "autism kids" and "using all the reinforcements." She decides to take the job anyway, assuming that the CEO will not be involved in any clinical decision-making. She soon realizes it may be worse than feared. In a conversation with an RBT, she learns that RBTs are hired as independent contractors, despite the fact that this is a violation of tax law and prohibited by the BACB®. RBTs are also encouraged to "round up" and bill for longer sessions. When she makes a recommendation for the number of hours that will accommodate a younger child's naps, she is told, "Just request it and we'll have the RBT sit there. We're a startup and this is money in our pocket."

The Process

Step 1. Donna carefully reviews the Ethics Code and determines that there are several legal and ethical violations and that something must be done. First and foremost, she is able to cite Code element 1.02, Conforming with professional and legal requirements.

Step 2. Donna identifies several "players" here. Among these are the CEO and the RBTs. Donna herself is not directly affected, but addressing the issue makes her one of the players as well.

Step 3. Donna develops several contingency plans. For Plan A, she makes a plan to discuss this issue with the CEO. It is possible that he is unaware of the potential legal and ethical ramifications. She does some research as to the possible outcomes and consequences of these actions to make him aware of the seriousness of the situation. For Plan B, she updates her resume and applies to a few other companies. Just because this one doesn't work out doesn't mean that others will not. For Plan C, she researches how to report insurance fraud to her state. If she discovers worse violations, she may need to take such actions.

Step 4. Donna knows that she is very personable and persuasive. Additionally, she has knowledge of the Ethics Code, which her CEO apparently lacks. When it comes to "clout" she finds herself unsure. She contacts her old supervisor, who reassures her that her clout in this situation comes from her value to the company – and to many more companies out there! A few minutes after their conversation, she receives an email from her supervisor with several other recommended places of employment.

Step 5. Donna knows that she risks losing her job and is unsure how to support her family without it. That risk is significant so she wants to be prepared. She prepares her resume and applies to several jobs, reaching out to former professors and colleagues in case things with Plan A do not go well.

Step 6. Donna makes an appointment with the CEO. She explains her concerns and shares with him the research that she has done as to the possible consequences of the current policies. As she suspected, he was unaware of the severity of the consequences and seems genuinely concerned. At the conclusion, he says he will think about what she has said. She asks, "So will you be changing these policies right away?" He sighs and says, "I don't know, I mean, we have a budget we need to keep…"

Step 7. Donna was not reassured that policies would immediately change after her meeting with the CEO, but she was at least comforted that he had not acted out of malice. Since Plan A was a bit less successful than she'd hoped, she considers Plan C (reporting violations). This may not be necessary if policies change, so she decides to move on to Plan B and begins in earnest to apply for other jobs. Donna decides that this time she will hold out for the *right* job, and quickly finds one with a company that serves her area. Several BCBAs hold leadership positions and she is happy to hear that they are familiar with the Ethics Code and insurance law. She submits her notice and makes the transition. Several months later, Donna learns through a colleague that many of her old company's policies had changed, but that the company went bankrupt soon after. They simply had not planned for sustainability to coexist with ethical practice.

Brodhead, Cox, and Quigley (2018)

What if the goal was not response, but prevention? How could we deal with ethics in a more proactive way, rather than forcing ourselves to react to difficult scenarios as they arise? Brodhead, Cox, and Quigley (2018) address precisely this question in their book, *Practical Ethics for Effective Treatment of Autism Spectrum Disorder.* The authors recommend a behavioral systems approach in addressing ethical issues within organizations before problems occur, including the following steps.

Step 1. Analyze
> Take a look at the natural contingencies that encourage (or discourage) ethical behavior. How is ethical behavior reinforced (or punished)?

Step 2. Specify
> The specific behaviors that we would consider "ethical" should be described in behavioral terms: they should be observable and measurable.

Step 3. Design
> At this point the BCBA should describe intervention that would increase ethical behavior. It is important that, whatever behavior is measured, this measure be valid – it should be directly linked to ethical behavior.

Step 4. Implement
> The BCBA would at this point put the plan into place and document its effects.

Step 5. Evaluate
> As always, determining if your solution was effective in resolving the ethical issue or preventing ethical problems.

Step 6. Recycle
> The BCBA ® can repeat any of the steps above if necessary to develop a solution that will build ethical behavior.

The Scenario

Monica is a BCBA who has just started working at a school as a consultant. They are starting a brand new ABA program and she will oversee several ABA classrooms. She is looking forward to supervising and working on staff development and training, but she quickly learns that this may be more complicated. Many of the staff have been there for over ten years and are resistant to any changes in the way they have run their classrooms in the past. When Monica introduces discrete trial teaching as part of the daily schedule, the teachers and paraprofessionals tell it is "too hard" to take data. Monica insists that they try, and they soon begin taking data showing all data at 100%. When Monica observes, she sees that this is not accurate and that data is not being collected during teaching. She confronts them about this and is told, "We told you this was too much for us to do."

The Process

Step 1. Monica sees that the response effort is punishing to the staff that she works with. By requiring that they take data, staff were handing in anything rather than focusing on accuracy. They are being asked to work harder and learn new skills without receiving additional compensation. She decides to do what she can to increase the level of reinforcement.

Step 2. Monica chooses to focus on accurate data collection, since this behavior will allow her to guide the staff to make responsible data-based decisions.

Step 3. Monica decides to implement spot checks to ensure interobserver agreement. In addition she trains staff on how to implement interobserver agreement as well. Every two weeks, she holds two raffles. Anyone who achieved 80% interobserver agreement is eligible for the first raffle. Any pair of staff who observe each other and take interobserver agreement data are eligible for the second raffle.

Step 4. The staff are intrigued about the raffle. Some are enthusiastic, since lottery tickets are being raffled off. A few staff are skeptical and report that they have too much to do. At the next staff meeting, Monica checks in with staff and asks what they learned by observing one another. Several staff report that they realized they had been taking inaccurate data or were running programs incorrectly. One staff member praises her colleague for a creative reinforcer. Most exciting, the winner of the raffle has a lottery ticket worth $50.

Steps 5 and 6. Over the next two months, Monica notices a significant change in staff behavior. Staff begin to take accurate data and more and more spot checks are showing interobserver agreement of 90% or above. Staff are also praising each other's work and are enthusiastic about staff meetings.

Essential Questions

Ethical practice is not always a matter of knowing the right answer. The right answer, after all, may depend far too much on contextual factors to be universal across the board. Rather, ethical practice is often a matter of asking the right questions. In our first edition, we proposed what we called an "essential question" model for making ethical decisions. We recommend that you apply these questions to your everyday practice of behavior analysis. Ask them on a regular basis, not simply when a problem arises, and use them to guide your actions.

Is this for me or is this for them?

In all of our words and actions as we work with clients, this question must be at the forefront. It is imperative that we are able to distinguish those actions from which we benefit and those which benefit our clients. There is nothing inherently unethical in recognizing personal benefit or enjoyment in the work that we do, the people that we become acquainted with, or the relationships that develop as a result. Surely the work that we do will contact reinforcers, as well they should. In the absence of reinforcers of some kind, the behaviors associated with our continued dedication would likely disappear. It is only when the benefit to us begins to eclipse the benefit to the client, or when our own comfort takes precedence over the fulfillment of our professional obligations, that this becomes problematic. Asking the question, "Is this for me or is this for them?" allows us to pause and assess who is really benefiting from our actions and to make decisions accordingly.

Is this socially significant and if so, to whom?

The requirement that treatment be socially significant is one of the cornerstones of applied behavior analysis. The treatment, behavior change program, or dependent variable in question must be considered socially important. This determination of social significance must be at the discretion of those affected by the behavior change. In our clinical practice, this often refers to the clients themselves and their parents or caregivers. The behavior analyst may not have the same views of what is "important," and this difference in priorities may cause conflict. Understanding not only the social significance of any proposed behavior change, but also to whom this change is significant, is essential in ethical practice.

We can teach this skill, but is it the best use of our time and resources to do so?

In applied behavior analysis, we can teach anything. However, the fact that we can teach anything is not to be confused with the assumption that we should teach everything. In some cases, we may discover that a proposed behavior change program does not rise to the level of priority for a particular client. At this point, the necessity of the program should be reevaluated, and perhaps goals and programming could be modified to more closely align with the client and their family. Asking ourselves this question encourages us to be ever mindful of our commitment to the client's goals. This question, however, serves another purpose as well. When working with supervisees, asking this question allows us to take stock of whether the available resources, including our time, effort, and energy, are adequate to the task of teaching this behavior. Ultimately, our resources should be allocated to serve the client, and these resources must be spent wisely.

Is this essential, preferable, or simply preferable to me?

Applied behavior analysis is a science, and as such it is the study of phenomena that already exist. A science is not something that you do. Rather it is something that you can come to understand. The concepts of reinforcement existed for centuries before it was given a name, just as Mount Everest was always there, though undiscovered. Understanding this, we must conclude that there is no "right" way to do applied behavior analysis (ABA). Effective treatment does not depend on specific data-collection systems. Rather, there are often several ways to implement behavioral technologies. There is room for compromise, and for creative problem-solving. In other words, it is characteristic of the responsible and ethical behavior analyst to generalize behavioral analytic skills, rather than remaining rigid in our interpretation of what is necessary. Asking this question allows us to more effectively prioritize and make compromises while still remaining committed to what is actually essential.

Does this behavior interfere with the responsibilities of this professional environment?

Too often the definition of what we consider "professional" is subjective, and far too often, it has little or nothing to do with job performance, but reflects the biases of the observer. Professionalism, however, is associated with the performance of tasks related to their role, and determinations of professionalism must be based on this performance rather than on other factors. Asking the question, "Does this behavior interfere with the responsibilities of this professional environment?" provides the opportunity to assess that the skill set is necessary for "professionalism."

Is this unethical, unprofessional, or does it just make me uncomfortable?

"Unethical" is not a term to be tossed about whenever we encounter a behavior that gives us pause. Nor, however, should it be avoided at all costs. Not everything that we find troublesome is necessarily unethical. Rather, "unethical" refers to those actions which violate the Ethics Code for Behavior Analysts®. While we may find other things troubling, this does not necessarily mean they are unethical. It is essential that the ethical behavior analyst be able to distinguish those situations in which a behavior is unethical and those that may simply make the observer uncomfortable. If an element of the Ethics Code® is in fact being violated, this would certainly require a response. However, if it is simply a matter of discomfort, this presents the behavior analyst with an opportunity for personal and professional growth.

All of these methods of ethical decision-making have in common an emphasis on returning to the Code when in doubt, as well as an awareness that our discomfort, while relevant, is not the only factor to consider. There will, no doubt, be many ethical decisions ahead of you. Some will be minor and some will be more complex. Remember that ethics is not only the big decisions, but the small everyday ones as well. Ask the questions, take the data, and be open to learning.

Works Cited

Bailey, J., & Burch, M. (2016). *Ethics for behavior analysts* (3rd ed.). Routledge.

Behavior Analyst Certification Board. (2020). *Ethics code for behavior analysts*. Littleton, CO: Author.

Brodhead, M. T., Cox, D. J., & Quigley, S. P. (2018). *Practical ethics for effective treatment of autism spectrum disorder*. Academic Press.

Rosenberg, N. E., & Schwartz, I. S. (2018). Guidance or compliance: What makes an ethical behavior analyst? *Behavior Analysis in Practice, 12*(2), 473–482. https://doi.org/10.1007/s40617-018-00287-5

Sellers, T. P., Carr, J. E., & Nosik, M. R. (2020). On the BACB's ethics requirements: A response to Rosenberg and Schwartz (2019). *Behavior Analysis in Practice, 13*(3), 714–717. https://doi.org/10.1007/s40617-020-00463-6

1.4 Ethics Standards Section 1
Responsibility as a Professional

1.01 Being Truthful

Behavior analysts are truthful and arrange the professional environment to promote truthful behavior in others. They do not create professional situations that result in others engaging in behavior that is fraudulent or illegal or that violates the Code. They also provide truthful and accurate information to all required entities (e.g., BACB, licensure boards, funders) and individuals (e.g., clients, stakeholders, supervisees, trainees), and they correct instances of untruthful or inaccurate submissions as soon as they become aware of them.

Explanation

A behavior analyst is obligated to remain truthful to others. This means that our data is accurate, our applications for certification include only truthful information, our academic work is ours and ours alone. We have integrity in our dealings with the Behavior Analyst Certification Board and with other certifying and licensing entities.

Because, as behavior analysts, we know that our behavior affects the behavior of others, we also take responsibility for the truthful behavior of others, including making corrections when necessary. When we are in a position to arrange contingencies, these contingencies increase truthful behavior in those we oversee. It is important to recognize those contingencies which encourage truthful behavior in others, as well as those which encourage deception. As supervisors, are we allowing for the freedom to make mistakes, or are we expecting immediate perfection? Is this an environment where supervisees or trainees feel comfortable asking questions or are they expected to already know the answers? An environment where mistakes are punished is one in which covering them up with deception is a likely outcome.

When we say "behavior analysts are truthful" this means that we also practice humility and encourage humility among others. "I was wrong," "I'm sorry" and "Let me try to say this/teach this/do this better" should be part of the vocabulary of the behavior analyst. We expect perfection neither from ourselves nor from those that we supervise or train and we work to correct mistakes rather than punish them.

Considerations

This would appear to be somewhat obvious: do not lie, cheat, or steal. However, as behavior analysts we should be cautious of any instruction of what *not* to do. As we know, behavior must follow the "dead person's test" (Cooper et al., 2007). This test, in summary, states that if a dead person can do it, it cannot be considered behavior. If the Code element is simply, "Do not be *dis*honest," this would be a problematic definition. It is the second part

DOI: 10.4324/9781003190707-5

of section A, along with section B, that provides some clarification. Not only do behavior analysts avoid acts of dishonesty, they "promote truthful and honest behavior in others."

What would it look like to promote honest and truthful behavior? What contingencies would need to be in place for those in the settings where we work to feel comfortable both being honest and being receptive to honesty in others?

Some aspects of an environment where honesty is actively encouraged might be an environment where growth is encouraged and feedback is given in order to promote that growth. If feedback is only given in a disciplinary manner, or if employees or supervisees believe their jobs are in constant jeopardy, they will be less inclined to accept feedback well and more inclined to cover their tracks when mistakes are made.

Another aspect of such an environment to keep in mind is the creation of a culture where those who would offer an honest assessment of where we can improve are believed and honored. As scientists, we acknowledge that there is always (yes, always) room for improvement and, as ethical professionals, we need to always (yes, always) strive to do better. When we know better, we do better.

Connections

Written by Ann Beirne

Before we begin a discussion of ethical culture, it is important to describe how behavior analysts conceptualize culture. While culture can often be thought of as an ineffable concept, behavior analysts can and have defined this in a way that is far more objective. Sigrid Glenn (1988, 2004) defines culture in terms of interlocking behavioral contingencies. Members of a given culture who respond similarly create the practices which we refer to as "culture" as such behaviors are reinforced by members of the group (Glenn, 1988, 2004). The behaviors become cultural norms as they are maintained by these social contingencies. How can we promote an ethical culture in our workplace? If we are to approach this as an arrangement of the contingencies involved, the task becomes significantly simplified. In this case, the obligation to promote an ethical culture relies heavily on the antecedents and consequences of the behavior we refer to as ethical or unethical. Is the environment one that encourages honesty, communication, and maintaining dignity of clients and others? Are staff encouraged to self-monitor their own ethical behavior? While the idea of promoting a culture may be somewhat elusive to us, the provision of contingencies that encourage and support behavior change is integral to our daily practice. It is essential that we remember that applied behavior analysis is a science. As such, it applies equally to all living things, whether we refer to clients, families, or staff. Contingencies, including the antecedents and consequent conditions in place, should aspire to promote an ethical culture within our workplaces.

Examples from the Field

Written by Jacob Sadavoy

I wish I could say that I have yet to experience dishonesty in my work environments, but that would be dishonest. I have worked with various companies and agencies that did not value honesty and, speaking from experience, those environments are challenging. In one such agency, the first departure from honesty began with a simple request of being asked to tell a small lie. I was asked to inform clients that I had been working with the agency for years despite being on the job for a month. I understand why the business would want clients to think I was a seasoned employee; it builds trust and potentially covers up a turnover issue. I would argue, vehemently, that protecting an agency's image over being truthful is a poor tradeoff. My main objection is not fear of getting caught; rather, it is creating and promoting a workplace culture that is deceitful. You could have very ethical practitioners, but if you put them in an environment in which their ethics are compromised, one of two things will occur: you will lose ethically bound staff or their ethics will regress to the mean.

Another fear of misleading clients with a simple inaccuracy is that if it is reinforcing to the business to do so once, the likelihood is that they will engage in lies in the future. At this aforementioned agency, the first lie I was aware of was about years worked at the agency. I would later learn that there were many more deceptions. Baseline data on assessments would be altered to demonstrate a need for continued services. A therapist who returned from vacation learned that insurance was billed for the duration of the days off, even though the client did not receive any ABA services. This transcends a simple "white lie" dishonesty; it is outright illegal. However, turning a blind eye to the smallest fallacy could leave you vulnerable to ethical violations that are occurring unbeknownst to you. Agencies like this give ABA a bad name and, if not careful, you may be associated with a company with poor ethical conduct or worse, start engaging in behaviors that are aligned with the culture of the organization as opposed to behaviors that are aligned with the Ethics Code(R). We, as practitioners, need to hold ourselves up to a higher caliber of honesty, not only for our clients, but also for the field to combat those agencies who do not value the importance of running an integrous business. The best way to accomplish this is to confront deceit in your workplace and know that any instances of dishonesty, even the smallest white lie, can have damaging repercussions. Taking an ethical stand could be received poorly from the organization but, if that is the case, I would be very wary to continue working in an organization that is not interested in improving their ethical practices.

1.02 Conforming with Legal and Professional Requirements

Behavior analysts follow the law and the requirements of their professional community (e.g., BACB, licensure board).

Explanation

All behavior analysts must follow the requirements of the Behavior Analyst Certification Board®, including those requirements for maintaining professional certification through continuing education, renewing and recertifying one's certification, and, of course, familiarity with the ethical Code.

Beyond that, however, behavior analysts are often beholden to other governing boards as well. Many of us who practice within the U.S. are also licensed by our states and must follow the law and requirements regarding the scope of the practice. We must carry liability insurance. We must maintain licensure according to state's requirements, including the payment of fees, the filing of any necessary paperwork and the submission of any required documentation, including acceptable continuing education, which may have different requirements than those of the BACB®.

As if this were not enough, there are those of us who, like both of the authors of this text, have a background in fields more general than applied behavior analysis such as education, special education, psychology, speech pathology, social work or other fields of study. For these behavior analysts, there are other professional organizations and communities and other licensing boards that must also be maintained.

This Code element, like so many in our Ethics Code, certainly appears simple at first blush. However we quickly find that simple is not the same thing as easy.

Considerations

There are several remarkable aspects to this Code element. One is that this Code addresses the need to familiarize ourselves not only with the BACB's® ethical requirements, but those of other ethical codes as well. Many behavior analysts have backgrounds in social work, education, psychology, or speech pathology. Each of these fields is overseen by governing bodies as well, and each has their own code of ethics, offering guidance as to the principles, values, and ethical practice of each profession. The responsible behavior analyst does not ignore such ethical guidance, but incorporates it into the values espoused by the BACB®. Perhaps the most striking phrase, however, is the phrase, "application to the behavior analyst's work." The emphasis here is not on merely knowing the Code, nor even on understanding it, but in its practical application. The Ethics Code® is not to be placed on a shelf, but incorporated into our practice. The values and principles illustrated in the Code inform all of the work we do. Our ethical practice is not simply an academic exercise, but it is integral to our clinical practice.

Connections

Written by Ann Beirne

As a parent, I often hear this excuse from my own children – "I didn't know I wasn't allowed to do it." Whether the offense is jumping from the top bunk, holding your three-year-old brother upside down, or eating an entire box of cookies half an hour before dinner, ignorance of the rule itself seems, to them at least, a reasonable defense. And there is some logic to this. If they have no way of knowing that such a rule exists, compliance with it would seem to be an unreasonable standard.

In consideration of this Code element, it is paramount that we bear in mind the phrasing here, "Behavior analysts have an obligation to be familiar with this Code." Those who have completed the certification process can reasonably be expected to have familiarity with the professional and ethical Code. Mastery of this material is required as a part of their coursework and continuing education in ethics is required in order to maintain the certification, which would lend evidence to such an assumption. For those pursuing certification through the process of supervision or receiving training through supervision, assuming knowledge of the Code is not necessarily a reasonable assumption. As behavior analysts, educators, or those who work in human services, we acknowledge that skills must be taught before they can be mastered. Within the activities of training and supervision, including supervision of those pursuing certification, learning the Ethics Code® should be a goal of the process. Ethical issues should be discussed openly with the objective of the mastery of the Code, rather than expecting mastery before such training begins. The challenges during fieldwork provide many "teachable moments" in the problem-solving necessary in ethical practice. Allowing a learning curve for those who are beginning their study is not to ignore this Code element, it is simply to be mindful of the purpose of training activities. In supervisory practices, as in all activities, our focus must remain on lasting, meaningful behavior change.

Examples from the Field

Written by Jacob Sadavoy

Like science, the BACB® is always evolving. There exists a responsibility to be aware of the changes. Ways in which I make sure I am aware of changes is: reading I read the BACB®

newsletter, listening to their new podcast *Inside the BACB*, and making sure correspondence from the BACB goes to my inbox. With the change to the Ethics Code for Behavior Analysts, guidelines for practicing the science of applied behavior analysis ethically has changed. With this change I will ensure I have understanding and fluency on new introduced concepts within this Code. For example, I will work towards gaining competence and fluency with the core principles and demonstrate my ability to practice the science of applied behavior analysis through the lens of the core principles for all my professional work. I will understand what personal bias is and how it relates to my ability (or inability) to practice effectively. I will be culturally responsive, compassionate, and strive for self-determination for all my clients. I will read other perspectives on ethics and attend continuing education on topics related to the new Code because it is my responsibility to know the Code thoroughly in order to be able to be an effective supervisor and practitioner for my clients.

1.03 Accountability

Behavior analysts are accountable for their actions and professional services and follow through on work commitments. When errors occur or commitments cannot be met, behavior analysts take all appropriate actions to directly address them, first in the best interest of clients, and then in the best interest of relevant parties.

Explanation

In the immortal words of Spiderman's Uncle Ben, "with great power comes great responsibility"®. Behavior analysts are in the position of caring for individuals who are often in crisis – those who are at their most vulnerable – and with that there comes an immense responsibility to provide high-quality care. That vulnerability may be physical, as in the case of those behavior analysts who provide services for geriatric patients or those in residential facilities, or it may be more emotional as families navigate what the news of a diagnosis may mean for them, their child, and their family. Regardless of the source or type of vulnerability, we must be incredibly careful in our commitments and promise only what we can deliver.

Accountability, however, includes two elements: the prevention of harm and the restoration of well-being when harm occurs. The second half of this Code element is clear. Make no mistake: errors *will* occur. It is not a matter of *if*, but *when*. Behavior analysts are human beings – flawed human beings with complex lives who make mistakes. A mistake becomes unethical only when there is a failure at a good faith attempt to fix it.

We do have great power and we must live up to that great responsibility.

Considerations

This Code seems "commonsensical"; however, the importance of integrity cannot be overstated. As a clinician you have a duty to uphold the science of ABA, but it is equally important to do so in a way that is both truthful and honest. Most professions value honesty; however, we would argue that valuing honesty is not enough in our field. We must be proactive and make sure that we hold ourselves accountable to a higher standard of truthfulness than other professions. We often work with clients who are learning to self-advocate and assist families that are vulnerable, or are considering other pseudoscientific approaches or businesses that are under a great deal of pressure to meet their performance targets. These clients can be crestfallen or desperate at times; they can be rife with risk of exploitation. This is the reality of working with populations that are seeking behavior changes to improve social well-being. It would be naïve to assume that others will approach these same clients with the same concern for honesty and truthfulness. Is there an ethical code to the "doctor" who prescribes hyperbaric oxygen therapy for patients with autism spectrum disorder, a method that has not been demonstrated effective in treating any of the presenting behaviors? Are they obliged to give clients all the information that they have at their disposal? We fully believe that they want to make the lives of their clients better, in some capacity; however, we also believe they really want to sell a $4,000 piece of equipment or, at a minimum, set up recurring appointments. We, as a field, will set ourselves apart by abiding to our ethics and being uncompromisingly truthful.

Examples from the Field

Written by Jacob Sadavoy

I learned early in my career how important accountability was for an organization. I worked in a place that would blame parents for problem behaviors or lack of skill acquisition. By not taking accountability, they were resigned and did not feel a responsibility to make necessary changes to the learners' program because it wouldn't matter since the parents weren't going to follow through anyway. A revelation occurred when I realized that, as a behavior analyst, I can change behavior. That includes increasing parent engagement through reinforcement. If there are legitimate barriers limiting the behavior change program from advancing then discontinuing services must be considered. But the behavior analyst must strive to remove all those barriers and that means looking in the mirror and being accountable for what is working and what is not working. Disempowering your abilities as a behavior analyst to change behaviors and being resigned to barriers when they surface is not serving anyone effectively. Being accountable and owning challenges as they come will promote a dynamic behavior change program which will likely have better outcomes.

1.04 Practicing within a Defined Role

Behavior analysts provide services only after defining and documenting their professional role with relevant parties in writing.

Explanation

Behavior, as behavior analysts understand it, is defined as "anything an organism does." What, then, would be the difference between the scope of practice of a behavior analyst and the scope of practice of a speech pathologist, or occupational therapist, or, for that matter, a pastry chef? If behavior is anything that a dead organism cannot do, then, other than a mortician, would *any* role be out of our jurisdiction?

This is why clarity in our professional role is so essential.

Considerations

Before there was an Ethics Code for Behavior Analysts® – or its previous iteration, the Professional and Ethical Compliance Code – there were the Guidelines for Responsible Conduct®. The Guidelines for Responsible Conduct® was the main document outlining our ethical obligations as behavior analysts. And with repeated use of phrases such as, "to the extent possible," there were many who felt it did not go far enough to keep behavior analysts accountable for maintaining ethical behavior.

And so the Behavior Analyst Certification Board® set to work, creating a document that would be clear and enforceable, and created the Professional and Ethical Compliance Code for Behavior Analysts® and later the Ethics Code. For those of us who have been in the field for a while, the comparison between the two documents has been interesting. And one notable change has been in how our professional relationships are described.

In the Guidelines, our previous resource, professional relationships were described as "remunerative," meaning that such services would be paid. Other definitions include the phrases "financially rewarding" or "earning a salary," but certainly the idea that this should be of benefit to the practitioner – and specifically, of financial benefit – is clear.

This can sometimes be difficult to navigate, especially for those professionals first starting out. Many of us entered the field out of a strong desire to help people, and the desire to profit from what we do can seem antithetical to that idea.

But it is important to remember that, for good or ill, we live in a society that requires that we participate as consumers. We cannot, and should not, provide services without some form of remuneration because we simply cannot do our best work if we are struggling financially.

But perhaps an even better argument is what happens to the professional relationship if we treat our work as a favor rather than a job. When we are not compensated for our work, we are no longer performing a job. Instead, we are doing the client a favor. We have set up an unequal dynamic. Whether we intend to exploit them or not, this client owes us something, and that dynamic can be fraught with problems.

While it may seem unnecessarily cool or distant to formalize our relationships, that commitment allows us to offer clients the clarity that protects them from exploitation. This, again, is the precaution that is ethical, rather than what merely makes us feel good.

Examples from the Field

Written by Jacob Sadavoy

Spending time with my toddler cousin has opened a new social circle for me. I am now surrounded by new anxious parents. It starts with the quiet pleasantries and naturally the conversation always shifts to "What do you do for a living?" Upon explaining the BCBA® acronym or giving them details of what you do for a living, the next thing out of their mouth is a behavioral conundrum; "my daughter refuses to eat vegetables," "why won't my daughter use the potty," "my son goes to bed too late," "what is my daughter's diagnosis?" etc. These are hard questions because you want to be socially appropriate; however, it would be irresponsible to comment because the behavior-analytic services you offer must be in the context of a defined, professional, or scientific relationship or role coupled with the fact that you do not know the whole scenario so offering strategies without data or even an observation is a poor behavior-analytic practice. One simple way to navigate the awkwardness of being seemingly defiantly unhelpful is to provide resources that may prove useful coupled with an explanation as to why it is inappropriate for you to offer recommendations without all the necessary things a behavior analyst needs to be useful (e.g., observations, data, assessments, cultural understanding, an understanding of the environment, etc.).

Upon having a defined behavior-analytic role, one still needs to remain careful that they do not drift to other responsibilities that are not outlined in your roles and responsibilities. What would you do if a parent of the client you are treating enquires about relationship support because their marriage is suffering, or if a business owner likes your work in organizational management so much that they request that you take a quick walk-through of his sister's company? These two examples happen frequently, and it is important to maintain a focus on the behavior-analytic role that is defined and to avoid deviation; otherwise, you may find yourself offering recommendations that are outside your contractual obligations.

1.05 Practicing Within Scope of Competence

Behavior analysts practice only within their identified scope of competence. They engage in professional activities in new areas (e.g., populations, procedures) only after accessing and documenting appropriate study, training, supervised experience, consultation, and/or co-treatment from professionals competent in the new area. Otherwise, they refer or transition services to an appropriate professional.

Explanation

For behavior analysts, a "fake it till you make it" philosophy is ethically unacceptable, and often downright dangerous. As behavior analysts, we know that people will undoubtedly be hurt by attempts to fake what we are not capable of doing well. It is not just doing something *passably*, but doing it *well* that is the standard of ethical practice. Simply put, a behavior analyst will commit to a clinical position only if they are able to perform that job well. When taking on new responsibilities, it is necessary to ask ourselves, "Is this a responsibility that I can fulfill? How can I contribute?" This may lead to some awkward conversations about the details of our experience, when our urge to simply say "yes" may override our ability to make an honest assessment of our own skills as well as the needs of the client. But that honest assessment is essential to ensure that those needs are met.

This does not necessarily mean that we are precluded from ever gaining new experiences, nor that we must immediately drop cases if the client's needs change or as new issues develop. The Ethics Code® clearly allows us to acquire new skills. This Code simply states that we cannot be delivering services responsibly if those skills are not yet acquired from training and supervision under someone who already has them.

Essentially, this Code tells us that we need to seek support when trying new things rather than just learning as we go or doing our best because we want to serve clients even if we don't necessarily know the best way to do that. Having the humility to seek out support is essential in ethical practice. We never need to do it alone.

Considerations

There is a great feeling when you pass your BCBA® exam. You are now an expert in behavior analysis and with that is the feeling that you can change behaviors readily based on the principles you have studied for years. But knowing what you don't know is as crucial as knowing what you do know. You can effectively shape behaviors and develop great task analytic chains, but does that equate to knowing how to create a program to teach a learner to tolerate being in the same vicinity as a hand dryer or redirect masturbatory behavior? If you haven't been exposed to a specific skill or strategy during supervision, you are not an expert in that skill or strategy. Thus, one should consider whether or not to develop an intervention without support from an expert. There is no shortage of continuing education (CEU) or articles to gain exposure to an unfamiliar topic. It is the responsibility of a BCBA® to know what interventions they can competently create, without support, and which interventions are outside their realm of expertise. This allows us to avoid breaking the ethical Code, but also to avoid a scenario in which your client and practitioner are put in harm's way.

This is true for seasoned BCBAs® too. Even though you may have years of experience, it is irresponsible and unethical to develop interventions outside your level of expertise. If you have ten years of experience working in a pediatric center applying the principles of ABA in an early intervention program, would you be a fit for an ABA-based behavioral safety practitioner position in a car manufacturer plant? The answer is clearly no.

However, that can change if that same practitioner completes a few CEUs on behavioral safety and becomes an attentive protégé to an organizational behavior management mentor with expertise in applying behavior-analytic interventions in safety procedures. Another example of this is crisis management. Those who are not certified to train others in crisis management do not; it is both illegal and dangerous. It would be equally harmful to watch a video on crisis management and begin implementing procedures without proper training. That same standard should be applied to unfamiliar behavior-analytic practices regardless of the number of years of experience or how fundamentally rooted in ABA the intervention may be. If in doubt, ask for help. There is no shame in requesting assistance, after all, we are all always adding new experiences into our learning histories.

This can get challenging when working on multidisciplinary teams or on teams where some members are not credentialed. In such a situation, the ABA practitioner must practice within their competency; however, you are also obliged to ensure that the interventions being developed are evidence-based, which is not a hallmark of some related fields. If the learner needs a desensitization protocol for new foods, as a BCBA®, it would be inappropriate to implement that intervention based on anecdotal accounts from a member of a related field or non-credentialed practitioner. If the intervention is unsuccessful, the learner could find eating aversive which has many negative impacts for the learner's health and the future rate of acquisition for the target (e.g. you may need to now target tolerating being in the room with novel foods because of an errant intervention). The best course of action is to take continuing education courses in order to develop expertise in the concept in question so that the learner can rely on a behavioral evidence-based approach as opposed to anecdotal accounts from a practitioner from a related field.

Examples from the Field

Written by Jacob Sadavoy

Early in my career, I was working with a client with severe self-injurious behavior and, if blocked, he would become severely aggressive. Thankfully, I was working at a place that saw the value of contacting outside experts to help analyze the data and come up with an intervention that would reduce the behavior. Had we not consulted an expert and relied on our own experience to reduce the behavior, we could have done tremendous harm both to this young man and to ourselves.

I have had the honor of working abroad and meeting a variety of practitioners from other countries who are just discovering ABA. In these situations, despite being a BCBA®, I am still aware of my limitations as a clinician as I am unaware of the societal norms or what this unfamiliar society deems as socially significant, which is not the case when I oversee ABA programs in North America. My expertise is collaborating with local communities to build an ABA program. I would not go to Lusaka, Zambia, and tell them how they should build an ABA program or provide a one-off training, on a topic that is of interest to me, without subsequent supervisory oversight. That would be wholly irresponsible. I could complete assessments and observations of their students, but without being familiar with Zambian society, how would I be able to address needs that are socially significant? Upon learning about Zambian culture and society, I would be much better at making Zambian-specific recommendations; however, every culture is different and I must realize that my new knowledge of Zambian culture should not be overgeneralized if I have the same position in Tunis, Tunisia (Fallon, O'Keeffe, & Sugai, 2012). The BCBA(R) may be the only individual in the room with a behavior analytic credential or an education in ABA however, unless they ask questions and learn about the environment, the effectiveness of that knowledge in a novel environment is limited. Collaboration is essential when working in a new environment which could be Tunisia but it is also applicable to any new environment (e.g., a new classroom or household).

1.06 Maintaining Competence

Behavior analysts actively engage in professional development activities to maintain and further their professional competence. Professional development activities include reading relevant literature; attending conferences and conventions; participating in workshops and other training opportunities; obtaining additional coursework; receiving coaching, consultation, supervision, or mentorship; and obtaining and maintaining appropriate professional credentials.

Explanation

It may have disappointed you slightly to learn that your academic journey would not end with gaining your Board Certified Behavior Analyst® (BCBA®) certification. After all of this study and work, when can we be considered "experts?" The answer is not that simple, unfortunately. The Behavior Analyst Certification Board (BACB®) has specific requirements that must be met in order to maintain certification and these include continuing your education in order to stay current in the field.

Frankly, we find this Code far from disappointing. In fact, it is one of the more beautiful aspects of scientific inquiry and of our field. Philosophic doubt is one of the assumptions of science and maintains that a scientist must "continually question the truthfulness of what is regarded as fact" (Cooper, Heron, & Heward, 2007). There is always more to be learned. Every behavior analyst is a colleague of every other behavior analyst. There is no one so high above us that they too do not need their continuing education forms signed by the proper authorities.

Rather than being a lifelong title, "expert" is one that needs to be maintained. Think about the medical "experts" of the middle ages, for example. Would their expertise be matched by doctors today?

As a field committed to scientific inquiry and a reliance on scientific knowledge, we must maintain that knowledge. Remaining current within our field is an essential element of delivering high-quality services. The requirements of the BACB® are merely a check on the adherence to this philosophy. It is the ethical obligation of the behavior analyst not only to maintain high standards, but also to maintain the drive and the willingness to learn and grow.

Considerations

In all science-based fields, learning and maintaining your understanding are paramount because science-based fields are dynamic. They change, as new theories are developed and proven to be more effective or parsimonious. As such, as a practitioner, it is an obligation to be aware of the latest research so that you can be the best clinician you can be for your clients. Accessing research can be accomplished in a variety of ways. There are many journals that focus on ABA. Some titles are: *Journal of Applied Behavior Analysis, Behavior Analysis in Practice, Behavioral Interventions, Behavior and Social Issues, Behavior Analyst, Analysis of Verbal Behavior, Behavior Modification*, and *Journal of Experimental Analysis of Behavior*. All of these publications will have articles that will help a practitioner stay informed about the latest research in the field.

In addition to journal publications, podcasts, local ABAI-affiliated chapters, and continued education units are all ways for practitioners to stay informed.

Examples from the Field

Written by Ann Beirne

The Behavior Analyst Certification Board® requires that certain continuing education requirements be met in order for certification to be maintained. There are several options for maintaining certification. Beginning in January of 2020, the BACB® has determined that the continuing education should be acquired in any of the three categories: *learning, teaching,* and *scholarship.*

Gaining continuing education hours through the *learning* category involves any activity on which the BCBA® or BCaBA® is in the role of student. Some of the options are taking college or university coursework in behavior analysis within a verified coursework sequence. This coursework must be at the graduate level for BCBAs®, but can be at the undergraduate level for BCaBAs® and the coursework must be behavior-analytic in nature. One continuing education credit is offered for each 50 minutes of instruction. In North American institutions, this translates into 15 continuing education credits for one semester and ten for each quarter. Documentation must be provided by submitting syllabi and transcripts. The learning category may also include participation in CEU events by BACB®-approved providers as well. In this case, documentation would include the certificate awarded for the CEU event. There are also occasions where the BACB® will offer opportunities to acquire CEUs through events or activities initiated by their organization. These may include participation in surveys or other activities to make improvements to standards and requirements. For these activities, the BACB® adds the documentation directly and there is no additional documentation required.

Within the *teaching* category, teaching behavior analysis can also be used as a continuing education activity. If the applicant is the instructor for CEUs presented by authorized providers, or is the instructor for courses within a verified course sequence, the hours spent in this activity may also be counted toward continuing education. Each event may be counted once, and can be documented with a letter from the approved continuing education (ACE) coordinator or department chair on official letterhead.

Finally, behavior analysts can also acquire continuing education credits through the *scholarship* category. If a behavior analyst publishes an applied behavior analysis article in a peer-reviewed journal, they can receive eight hours of continuing education. Serving as a reviewer or action editor for a journal can also be a continuing education activity and each review is equal to one continuing education credit. These continuing education credits can be acquired through a number of means. Attending live conferences and workshops hosted by ACE providers can be an enjoyable way to gain CEUs, as well as an opportunity to meet and network with other professionals. Many of us missed this terribly when so many conferences were cancelled due to Covid precautions. This may not be practical in all cases, however, and, as we all learned in 2020, gaining CEUs online is a practical solution when traveling or live attendance are not possible.

The requirements may seem daunting at first glance, but the requirements can be easily met with only a minimum of planning. And doing so improves not only our own efforts as professionals, but the profession itself as well.

1.07 Cultural Responsiveness and Diversity

Behavior analysts actively engage in professional development activities to acquire knowledge and skills related to cultural responsiveness and diversity. They evaluate their own biases and ability to address the needs of individuals with diverse needs/backgrounds (e.g., age, disability, ethnicity, gender expression/identity, immigration status, marital/relationship status, national origin, race, religion, sexual orientation, socioeconomic status). Behavior analysts also evaluate biases of their supervisees and trainees, as well as their supervisees' and trainees' ability to address the needs of individuals with diverse needs/backgrounds.

Explanation

For those of us who have done international work, who have worked with vulnerable or marginalized groups, and even for those who watched the events of the summer of 2020 unfold as social justice issues came to the forefront, this was an incredibly exciting addition to our ethical Code. The BACB® has added an explicit requirement addressing the need for us to address diversity within the field. Every BCBA® has the duty and responsibility to examine their biases and expand their skills in cultural responsiveness.

Before we dive into an explanation of this Code element we should pause here for an explanation of "culture" as it is understood by behavior analysts. "Culture", from a behavior-analytic perspective, is a set of meta-contingencies (Glenn, 1988). These social contingencies act as both antecedents and consequences, shaping the behaviors that shape other behaviors, building the series of behavior that we refer to as a "culture." While "culture" may refer to practices, traditions, or societal expectations of different ethnicities or religious practices it may also refer to the habits, idiosyncrasies or inside jokes of families or interest groups.

This is not to diminish the importance of understanding cultures or of approaching those culture with which we lack familiarity with humility and empathy. Nor is it to minimize the impact of dominant culture on that of marginalized groups or the role that privilege may play in our perceptions. Rather, we wish to remind you that an understanding of culture is intended to bring a greater understanding of others, not a greater separation. "Culture" is not to be used as a phrase meaning "*those* people – those *very different* people."

The quality of our work depends on nothing beyond our ability to do it and not on whether or not we accept, understand, or approve of the culture of those with whom we work. Often it is necessary to have a bit of humility about the limitations of our own knowledge. However, it is equally important to be willing to learn more.

We are not required to know everything about a given culture before we begin working with clients. And we do not necessarily need to know everything about it to support our clients' participation in that culture. Part of being a behavior analyst is understanding that learning is a lifelong journey that must be enthusiastically embraced. Rather than shut out new knowledge we need to be open to it.

1.08 Nondiscrimination

Behavior analysts do not discriminate against others. They behave toward others in an equitable and inclusive manner regardless of age, disability, ethnicity, gender expression/identity, immigration status, marital/relationship status, national origin, race, religion, sexual orientation, socioeconomic status, or any other basis proscribed by law.

Explanation

Simply put, behavior analysts do not engage in discrimination in professional environments or in their professional activities. However, a careful examination of this Code element clarifies that it is not merely the absence of discrimination, but the active effort to dismantle it that is required of us.

The second part of this Code element provides a path forward for the behavior analyst who strives to engage in ethical behavior. Rather than simply abstaining from discrimination, an ethical behavior analyst must strive to treat others with equity and to make sure that others are welcomed and included within our circle.

Considerations

It may be necessary here to take a moment to describe the difference between "equality" and "equity." Many of us in dominant groups may have been raised to believe that the most respectful path forward was to acknowledge that the United States is a "melting pot," to have a "colorblind" approach. And many of us may believe that saying "I don't see color" is a way to treat all people equally, and thus, fairly.

A colorblind approach, however, can be extremely problematic. To treat everyone the same is to ignore essential aspects of identity, rather than acknowledging their own unique cultural identity.

Examples from the Field

Written by Jacob Sadavoy

I am disappointed to share that not all my work environments have been positive, and I regret to report that some work environments were discriminatory. I am fortunate that I have not witnessed discrimination across all the categories mentioned within this Code, but I have witnessed discrimination across many. It is hard to witness even when you are the one who is not being discriminated against.

Discrimination can take many other forms as well. In one of my past working environments, I was employed at a private school in which tuition was very expensive. Students were naturally selected into the program based on their socioeconomic status, for those who did not have the funds were unable to attend the program. There was one student in the school who did not have the funds to pay for tuition the following year. Instead of the school doing its ethical due diligence in finding this student an alternate program, she was discharged without a transition plan or a receiving program for her to attend the following school year (which is its own ethical issue). Naturally, the school needed to be compensated, via tuition, for their services; however, it was clear that more effort was made for a student that was being discharged from the program because they were moving to another school compared to the student who was discharged for being unable to afford another year's tuition.

Being male in a mostly female profession has given me an unfair advantage. I have been told how hard it must be working with only women. I have been promoted ahead of candidates who may have been more qualified because I represented "a necessary change in dynamics based on having a Y chromosome," and I have been viewed as a greater authority on ABA topics in meetings with parents because I have "a deeper voice which commands respect." This is wrong, but is aligned with societal norms in other disciplines. As behaviorists that focus on social change, we should be leaders in overcoming gender bias in our workplaces and set an example for other disciplines. At ABAI in Chicago in 2016, one would assume that the percentage of women in attendance would be similar to the percentage of women on stage. This was not the case as the percentage of females in attendance was much greater than the percentage of women who presented. In 2015, 82.2% of Behavior Analyst Certification Board® certificants were female, including 68.3% of those who were certified at the doctoral level (i.e., BCBA-D™), yet female authors accounted for 55.5% of authors who published in the *JABA* in 2014, 27.1% of authors who published in the *Journal of the Experiential Analysis of Behavior*, and 28.6% of the presidents for ABAI

(Nosik & Grow, 2015). Further, there is a gender wage gap in our field too (Li et al., 2018). Why is that? Male privilege. Gender discrimination. Patriarchal favoritism. It is called many different things, but it does exist. And it sadly exists in our field, which is extra concerning as our decisions should be based on behavior and not biased.

Another thing that was apparent at behavior analytic conferences was the percentage of Caucasians in the crowd compared to attendees that were non-white. As a result of this inaccurate distribution of race coupled with the fact that white privilege is societal privilege that benefits Caucasians, the field of ABA is limited from this lack of diversity among practitioners. It is clear that it would be best to have agents for social behavioral change across as many ages, genders, races, cultures, ethnicities, national origins, religions, sexual orientations, disabilities, languages, and socioeconomic status as possible to have more cultural awareness within the field (Fong et al., 2016). Perhaps there is less of a focus on societal structure behavior changes, as the majority of Caucasian practitioners, who reap the benefits of white privilege, are less personally aware and affected by societal discrimination.

We need to do better as a field to accommodate others and overcome our prejudices. ABA should be readily available in all communities. We need to do a better job of dissemination outside the comforts of our own community. This starts with justice in our organizations and promoting those based on merits and ability and not based on a Y chromosome and being white.

1.09 Nonharassment

Behavior analysts do not engage in behavior that is harassing or hostile toward others.

Explanation

Here again, a superficial examination of this Code element would lead us to believe that this would run counter to our attempts to focus on observable measurable behavior. At first blush this would appear to be in violation of the dead person's test. The focus is, after all, on the absence of behavior rather than the behavior itself. In the context of other relevant Code elements, however, we see that the requirement to "do no harm" requires more than simply to avoid engaging in harmful acts. We must also create safe environments for those who are often the victims of harm.

Within behavior-analytic circles, we acknowledge that culture, defined as a set of interlocking social contingencies (Glenn, 1988) has the potential to shape behavior, including behavior that, in the words of this Code element, "is harassing or demeaning toward others." As this behavior was ignored, laughed off, or even encouraged, it was systematically shaped. Those who spoke out against perpetrators of harassment were met with "whataboutism" – what about the alleged harasser's contributions to the field? What about their membership in another marginalized group? What about the accuser's history? Are they simply ignorant, jealous, vengeful, or puritanical? And, perhaps most relevant for this volume, is it ethical to address this with punishment toward an individual rather than shaping behaviors we want to see?

This Code element, however, states clearly that we "do not engage in behavior that is harassing or demeaning to others." And while at first blush this may seem exclusive to the main perpetrator of such actions, we encourage behavior analysts to hold themselves to a higher standard.

Considerations

After the advent of the #metoo movement, there was shock at the breadth of sexual harassment and assault and collective confusion as to what would happen now. As consequences for those who would engage in harassing behavior became more public and widespread, many reacted to this cultural shift, complaining that "the rules have changed."

In reality, however, the rules themselves have not changed. In fact there has been no change to the legal definition of harassment for several decades. As behavior analysts we know that rules without enforcement are often meaningless, and this shift has not been one in which the rules have changed but one in which the *contingencies* have changed.

Examples from the Field

Written by Ann Beirne

True examples of harassment within our field are rare. This is not because they do not happen, but because the victims are often silenced or, after trying to ignore a behavior that has been reinforced for so long it remains entrenched, and they simply give up and leave the field.

Perhaps the best public example of harassment and an appropriate response is from a viral video from a female gamer who was asked by a male player, "What color is your thong today?" Rather than ignoring the question, she responded by calling out his sexism. When he replied, "You can't take a joke," she responded, "What do you think a joke is? ... You haven't gotten to the joke yet. We got to the part where you were being a dick. You haven't told the joke yet."

A joke, by definition, is a statement that is meant to cause laughter, not discomfort. While it is true that many comedians and other artists hold up a mirror to society, they do so *by telling jokes*. If a behavior analyst is incapable of telling jokes which do not victimize others, joke-telling (and perhaps public speaking) would likely be outside of their scope of competence. A class in public speaking such as Toastmasters may be helpful, or perhaps a class in stand-up comedy. But the excuses "it was a joke" or "you can't even joke anymore" are unacceptable. Tell a joke or don't, but do not harass others and call it a joke.

1.10 Awareness of Personal Biases and Challenges

Behavior analysts maintain awareness that their personal biases or challenges (e.g., mental or physical health conditions; legal, financial, marital/relationship challenges) may interfere with the effectiveness of their professional work. Behavior analysts take appropriate steps to resolve interference, ensure that their professional work is not compromised, and document all actions taken in this circumstance and the eventual outcomes.

Explanation

Behavior analysts are human. We are fathers, mothers, daughters, sons, wives, husbands, sisters, brothers, students, citizens, and patients. It is foolish to assume that these other roles would not affect our ability to perform our role as a behavior analyst to the high standards set by the field.

And yet this Code element is consistently compromised. Many employers are of the mindset that your personal life (or lack thereof) is irrelevant, and that mindset often causes behavior analysts to start behaving as if they believe that is the case as well.

Just as in the example of the masks on the airplane, it is essential that we take care of ourselves in order to help others. Application of self-care (including the care of our relationships, our loved ones, or our health) is not selfish, nor is it unprofessional. Allowing ourselves to breathe allows us to give to others.

Considerations

Personal problems and conflicts are unavoidable. What is avoidable is providing subpar behavior-analytic services because of distractions that are happening in one's personal life. The client's therapy should not be negatively affected by intrapersonal conflicts that are unrelated to the client. This is easier said than done and it requires an awareness on behalf of the clinician to know when they need to engage in self-care.

Burnout remains a tremendous issue for our field. This is often described as emotional and physical exhaustion, reduced personal accomplishment, loss of interest, and/or a negative attitude. These are not causes, but rather outcomes of burnout. Under these conditions, one cannot be effective in their work. If you had to pick between getting that assessment completed on time and overcoming burnout, we would argue that the client would be happy waiting a few days for that assessment if it is written thoughtfully and not under exhaustive conditions. After all, a mentally and physically healthy clinician will be able to make a greater impact and make better decisions than one who is despondent.

Being mindful and acting on your self-care needs are different. Do the latter. Set observable and measurable goals, collect data, graph your data, and actively invest in your own self-care. Your client's will benefit from a better you.

Examples from the Field

Written by Ann Beirne

I consider myself to be reasonably socially aware. I am a white woman living in New York City, comfortable with the word "feminist" and happily living in a diverse area where my children attend a New York City public school. As a parent, I make sure that their library at home reflects the diversity we see in the world and, although they range in age from three to eight, they are no strangers to social justice protests, including a march on Washington.

A few years ago, I took the Implicit Attitudes Test on race available from Project Implicit (Xu et al., 2014). This social cognition test is designed to illustrate preferences among races in order to detect implicit biases and data has been contributed by over two million volunteers.

When I had completed the test, I saw the results. There it was in print: "You moderately prefer white people over black people."

It would certainly be easier for me (and far more comfortable) to continue giving myself credit for my inclusivity. Easier, yes, but far less honest.

The fact is that no one is without bias and often it remains invisible until it becomes a problem. In order to engage in ethical practice, we must also engage in some uncomfortable honesty with ourselves. And we must do it repeatedly and often.

Becoming aware of our biases empowers us with knowledge to address them. When we know better, we can do better.

1.11 Multiple Relationships

Because multiple relationships may result in a conflict of interest that might harm one or more parties, behavior analysts avoid entering into or creating multiple relationships, including professional, personal, and familial relationships with clients and colleagues. Behavior analysts communicate the risks of multiple relationships to relevant individuals and continually monitor for the development of multiple relationships. If multiple relationships arise, behavior analysts take appropriate steps to resolve them. When immediately resolving a multiple relationship is not possible, behavior analysts develop appropriate safeguards to identify and avoid conflicts of interest in compliance with the Code and develop a plan to eventually resolve the multiple relationship. Behavior analysts document all actions taken in this circumstance and the eventual outcomes.

Explanation

A multiple relationship is defined by the Behavior Analyst Certification Board as "a comingling of two or more of a behavior analyst's roles (e.g., behavioral and personal) with a client, stakeholder, supervisee, trainee, research participant, or someone closely associated with or related to the client" (BACB, 2021). There are a few essential points to remember here: these relationships co-occur. A relationship that evolves or otherwise changes over time (for example, a colleague who becomes a friend) would not be considered a multiple relationship. However, if one has both a clinical *and* a personal relationship occurring simultaneously, the potential for a multiple relationship could exist and must be analyzed and that outcome of that exploration should be documented. If a multiple relationship exists, a referral can be made or one can opt not to engage in the professional relationship.

Those multiple relationships which are obvious from the outset, such as a clinical relationship with a relative, should be avoided. However, it is often the case that a multiple relationship may develop over time, even if it begins with a strictly professional one. In this case, a relationship that begins with the behavior analyst in a strictly defined professional or scientific role and evolves into one that includes other roles as well. The behavior analyst becomes the friend or the confidant rather than restricting their role to what was their original purpose. Of all of the elements of the Code, this may be the most challenging to explain to new professionals. After all, many of us entered this field out of a strong desire to help people and the emotional gratification of seeing our clients' progress is often our most potent reinforcer. It can be difficult to explain that, although it may seem as if developing these relationships is part of a more compassionate approach, there is the potential for harm. There are certainly situations in which multiple relationships may be difficult, or even impossible, to avoid. Some behavior analysts have brought up that, in rural areas, there are often limited opportunities to avoid these multiple relationships. If there is one car mechanic, or one grocery store owner, or one cardiologist in the area where you live and work, avoiding these relationships may be trickier than it seems (Carr, 2021).

Even when these multiple relationships can be avoided, it is important to consider the level of intimacy that is developed when you enter into a family as a service provider, particularly for those professionals providing home services. We are often working with families in crisis and privy to the most intimate details of their family life at a time when they are incredibly vulnerable. The fact that this relationship is one-sided can be incredibly disconcerting to families. To them, the relationship is not "multiple" or strictly professional, it is just reciprocal, or it is not.

Here is where the provision of safeguards as specified in this Code element becomes important. Clients must understand what multiple relationships are and their dangers. If clients are informed that our distance is to protect and not to offend, the communication can be clearer and we can truly work together to accomplish goals.

Considerations

This is perhaps the most difficult concept for those entering the field to understand. The idea that loving the children we work with is not our job is a pill that is far too bitter for many to swallow. Many teachers will angrily tell the story of the supervisor or professor who told them, "You care too much." "How is that even possible?" they will ask. "There's no such thing as caring too much!"

This is where the breakdown in communication about this Code element begins. And because so many people who work with vulnerable populations are so emotionally tied to their work, it often stays broken down.

One helpful litmus test for whether or not we are forming a potentially harmful multiple relationship is asking ourselves the question, "Is this for them or is this for me?" Often we may begin thinking we are engaged in these multiple relationships for others, but the benefit is for us. So we must ask ourselves: does this allow me to do the job that must be done? Or is it something that makes me feel good?

Our emphasis should not be on feeling good, it must be on *doing* good.

Connections

Written by Ann Beirne

I have learned that one metaphor that seems to work to explain this element of the Code is this: when I bring my children to the doctor for a vaccination, it is not the doctor's job to consider how much the shot will hurt. As the parent, that is *my* job. It is my job to think of what they will need, to plan our trip to the ice cream parlor afterwards, to pack Giddyup and Lulu, their beloved stuffed animals, and to kiss any subsequent boo-boos. If the doctor is preoccupied by all of these things, she would be unable to do her own job efficiently. And that is the job that my children really *need* her to do. While I am certainly happy that my doctor also greets my children excitedly and laughs at their jokes, that is simply not her job. It's a delightful extra, but it is still extra.

Examples from the Field

Written by Ann Beirne

Providing in-home services for children can have a unique set of challenges. When we enter a family's home, we immediately develop a sense of intimacy with them. We see them at their most vulnerable and frequently at their greatest moments of crisis.

You might assume that, in this situation, it would be far more challenging to work with parents with whom you have very little in common. Though working with families where we do not get along comes with its own challenges, I have found that it is harder to maintain ethical practices with people whose company I actually enjoy.

One particular client comes to mind. The client himself was, as most toddlers are, adorable. And the mother was a kind and considerate person, a great listener, and an enthusiastic learner of all things behavior-analytic. She was genuinely interested in me and in my life, was funny and insightful, and simply a joy to be around. She flattered me relentlessly and seemed impressed by everything from my knowledge of the basic principles of behavior analysis to my Play-Doh sculptures and animal noises. As required by my agency's policy, she was present for all sessions and, though it is uncomfortable to admit, I loved chatting with her.

The start of the relationship began innocently enough. As I was leaving a team meeting, I mentioned that I was a singer at an opera company about a block from where the father worked. Since most people are not interested in opera, I expected a polite nod and no future mention of it. But the next time I went to the house for a session, the mother had a copy of my opera company's schedule for the season and asked, "Which operas are you performing in? When can we come and see you?" I was terrified at first, thinking that I had crossed a line by even mentioning it. After discussing it with my supervisor, I realized that I had not created a multiple relationship – not yet, at least. But I knew that I had to start developing some better guidelines to prevent my relationship with the mother from overshadowing my clinical relationship with her son.

Using the question "Is this for me or is this for them?" as a guideline, I set up some "ground rules." Any recreational chit-chat had to be outside of our session time, either before or after. I never volunteered information on any of my performances unless directly asked and then provided only what they asked for. If they attended a performance, I would greet them afterwards, just as I would any other guest, and I would introduce them as friends. During sessions, I would redirect any conversation to a discussion of the programming or other concerns, and I kept a laser focus on his needs. After the client had transitioned and no longer needed my services, I allowed *them* to make a decision about whether or not to begin a friendship. They had my number, and I knew they would call if they wanted to see me socially. They did, and we became friends rather than having a professional relationship. This was possible, in part, because I made every effort to have only one relationship at a time.

I never shared any of these self-imposed rules with the family; I simply enforced them with myself. They did notice, however, and, rather than being offended that I was unnecessarily chilly and distant, they understood that I was focused on the clinical relationship. After the clinical relationship had terminated and a friendlier one began, I shared my personal email address with the mother. In response, she exclaimed, "The boundaries are falling like the walls of Jericho!"

It is natural to want to make friends with friendly people, but we must remember that the *first* relationship is the one that must demand our attention first. We are there as behavior analysts and if we cannot do that, we do not have any business fulfilling any other roles. It is when those other roles begin to take over that the multiple relationship becomes harmful. A bit of self-discipline can go a long way in fulfilling the role we began with.

1.12 Giving and Receiving Gifts

Because the exchange of gifts can invite conflicts of interest and multiple relationships, behavior analysts do not give gifts to or accept gifts from clients, stakeholders, supervisees, or trainees with a monetary value of more than $10 U.S. dollars (or the equivalent purchasing power in another currency). Behavior analysts make clients and stakeholders aware of this requirement at the onset of the professional relationship. A gift is acceptable if it functions as an infrequent expression of gratitude and does not result in financial benefit to the recipient. Instances of giving or accepting ongoing or cumulative gifts may rise to the level of a violation of this standard if the gifts become a regularly expected source of income or value to the recipient.

Explanation

In previous iterations of the behavior analysts' ethical codes, there have been cautions against accepting gifts, followed by a direct restriction on the acceptance of any gift of any value. This was the source of a great deal of debate and even greater confusion. The question, "Is it acceptable to accept a glass of water while working in a client's home?" was the subject of hours of debate, to the great frustration of those of us who felt there were far greater ethical issues worthy of discussion. Worse yet, genuine expressions of gratitude were rejected – often rudely – and trust of stakeholders was broken.

The original intention of those restrictions was to avoid the use of excessive gifts becoming a supplementary income source, which could lead to exploitation. The original intention was that, if we allow a small gift then surely, as incrementalism would indicate, we would allow larger and larger gifts. A plate of homemade cookies would become a five-course meal, which would eventually become a five-day cruise. It is, after all, a slippery slope.

This Code element reminds us however, that slippery slope arguments run the risk of slippery slope *fallacies* – arguments made in the absence of data. To combat this, the BACB® has added the specificity required to make a careful – and ethical – decision. An acceptable gift is one that is of little monetary value and is an occasional expression of gratitude, rather than a supplement to income. In other words, it is the thought that counts.

Considerations

This is often considered to be one of the most controversial elements of the Code, and one that is potentially difficult to navigate in clinical practice when working with children and families. And here again, it is important to remember the essential component of the professional relationship with consumers or their families: *they are not the professionals.* It is our obligation to maintain professional boundaries, not theirs. It is our obligation to uphold the Ethics Code®, not theirs. And this includes this Code element.

So how do we handle the inevitable gift-giving? How do we politely refuse in a way that will maintain the relationship?

First, as is acknowledged by the BACB®, intention matters here. Often the intention of giving a gift is to express gratitude for the impact that treatment has had on a family's life, so a gracious thank you is certainly in order. Following that, sometimes an equally gracious reminder that we are prohibited from accepting expensive gifts is probably in order. I sometimes recommend that behavior analysts (or those in training to become behavior analysts) ask the gift giver for a favorite charity to which the gift can be donated so that the intention is served without any miscommunication regarding a "quid pro quo" relationship.

And, as stated above, what actually constitutes a gift can also be confusing, and a bit of analysis of intention is necessary here too. There may be situations where accepting what would be considered a "gift" might be clinically beneficial. For example, when teaching someone to eat at a restaurant, are we truly preparing them for this activity if no one else at the table is eating? Are we preparing a client to be able to eat at the family dinner table if they never sit next to someone with a plate of food? In these cases, food would not be considered a "gift," it would actually be program materials necessary to teach social skills. In home-based programs, food is often offered during meetings because families are uncomfortable having people in their house who are not eating. In this case, would accepting food establish a "quid pro quo" relationship, would it distract from the work that needs to be done, or would it allow the family the bit of comfort necessary for a working relationship? The answer may not be as clear when offering food as it may be when offering something else.

As for gifts from younger clients, some special consideration would be necessary here as well. I would say that a gift from a child often has the intention of gaining a bit of social reinforcement, something that we should be encouraging if we are to establish ourselves as conditioned reinforcers (or, as they say in other fields, to establish rapport). While it may also be wonderful for us, accepting a handmade card may help the client in this case by encouraging this social interaction. It is more likely to help the professional relationship, and refusing the gift is more likely to harm such a relationship.

As we have all been told about gift-giving, it is the thought that counts. It would be dishonest to pretend that such thoughts are not appreciated – you are permitted, even encouraged, to appreciate the good thoughts of appreciative clients. So appreciate the thought and the intention, but be clear that it's the thought that has your appreciation.

Examples from the Field

Written by Jacob Sadavoy

It was December, and before the holiday break at the end of the month, it was customary for parents to give envelopes (some with gift cards) for staff. Having a niece in preschool, I have learned that this is a common practice across schools (at least in schools in New York City). I was working at a pediatric center at the time and I was one of the four therapists who were given an envelope by one of my client's parents. I was not sure of the contents but I was aware that the others on my team did accept the envelope. I adamantly refused the gift, thinking that this was the right ethical decision and that I would not be swayed by peer pressure. Upon further reflection, it dawned on me that the socially appropriate behavior was accepting the card, and not engaging in that target behavior could have actually produced a greater strain on the relationship between myself and the parent. I was the only one who refused the envelope – what a wonderful way to bring attention to yourself. The reason I did it was to maintain a healthy professional relationship with the parent. I later learned that the parent interpreted the gesture as an expression of displeasure working with her son. The relationship that I sought to protect was damaged because of my socially inappropriate behavior.

When working in a multicultural city like Toronto, one has to be more aware of the cultural differences and expectations. When going to a consult in student's home, there would be times that I was offered to try a homemade dessert, which they had made specifically for the visit. Saying no to food in an Eritrean, Hungarian, or Indian home was not an option. It would have been considered an insult and would have damaged the relationship. The ethical Code, for the most part, is black and white. Avoiding multiple relationships is simple enough. However, when it comes to gifts, one has to consider the cultural relevance in turning down a "gift." It is outright disrespectful for visitors to enter a home and not have something to eat in some cultures. In these cultures, food isn't a "gift," it is a mandatory gesture to welcome someone in your home. It would be an entirely different gesture had I been offered center ice tickets to a Toronto Maple Leafs game, the product of which could be entering a dual relationship or have expectations that exceed professional client-therapist boundaries.

Connections

Written by Ann Beirne

Certainly open communication is helpful, but as we all know, it is the enforcement of rules, rather than simply rules themselves, that have the biggest impact on behavior. In most environments, "no gifts" is a request that is rarely complied with. I know that I personally have written "no gifts necessary" on many a birthday party invitation, only to be greeted by the parents of my children's classmates with, "I know you said no gifts but…" And I have read many party invitations that said, "no gifts" and thought "Well, I can't come empty-handed!" Our history of reinforcement certainly indicates that we should not take this statement too seriously.

1.13 Coercive and Exploitative Relationships

Behavior analysts do not abuse their power or authority by coercing or exploiting persons over whom they have authority (e.g., evaluative, supervisory).

Explanation

Here it is important to explain what is meant by "exploitation." We can all agree that exploitation means, in layman's terms, using someone or taking advantage. As professionals in service fields, we have a tremendous amount of power over vulnerable populations, and it is essential that we refrain from abuse of that power. But are we clear on what constitutes taking advantage?

As in most ethical concerns, the devil here is in the details and it is often the less obvious violation that may be more easily missed. Demanding that a student or a supervisee pick up your laundry in order to get a favorable evaluation would be pretty recognizable to most as exploitation. But other things such as bringing lunch to a meeting, overlooking lateness, or accepting repeated last-minute cancellations may challenge our ability to recognize what goes "above and beyond" expectations.

Also, as in most things in the Code, open communication goes a very long way toward preventing problems. In order to clarify what meets expectations and what exceeds them, we have to make such expectations as clear as possible. We should anticipate at some point running into a supervisee, a student or an employee who may want to treat us with kindness. This is certainly not a license to exploit them, and it is also not their responsibility to avoid our exploitation. It is our responsibility not to exploit them. Just as we clarified in our explanation of the Code involving gifts, setting expectations from the outset may avoid the problems of any feelings of obligation. And, as we also discussed, being gracious is also in order.

In summary, being gracious for generosity is different from expecting excessive generosity. Having the opportunity to exploit is different from exploiting.

Considerations

There may indeed be opportunities for exploitation, as there always are when there is a clear power differential. This does not mean that such power will necessarily be exploited. Just as we are gracious of generosity, we can be equally gracious of vulnerability.

At some point, we must self-manage whether or not we are exploiting others rather than try to rid the world of temptation. We do not have to wear handcuffs to prevent myself from shoplifting – we can choose not to do it because it is wrong. We do not have to live in a convent to avoid cheating on our spouses – we can choose not to because it is wrong.

Just as we have the choice to refrain from shoplifting or adultery, we have the choice to refrain from exploiting those over whom we have some authority, even if, for example, they offer to take us out for dinner to thank us for a recommendation letter. We have the choice to politely decline and to remind them that they got themselves the job, all we did was offer an honest assessment of their abilities. If we choose to go out to dinner with them, I have the choice to order something reasonably priced rather than the lobster and a bottle of the finest wine. And we certainly have the choice to split the check rather than ducking out to the bathroom as the waiter comes to the table.

Exploitation can be a problem, but trying to avoid any opportunity for it means that we are often running in circles.

Examples from the Field

Written by Jacob Sadavoy

Exploitation can be hard to navigate and, in the moment, can be hard to decipher. I unfortunately had one employer who was a master at exploitation. It is how he conducted business. It started off with ridiculously enormous caseloads. The BCBAs® in this agency were expected to see 15–20 cases twice a month. With the vast majority of cases being after-school programs, it does not take a mathematician to see that things did not add up. In sharing my concerns and reminding him of my contract which specified that the work day was from 9:30 to 5:30 and "the odd" later evenings, he was wholly unhelpful and highlighted that the other BCBAs® in the agency did not have a problem with their caseload. The definition of exploitation is the action or fact of treating someone unfairly in order to benefit from their work. We don't associate exploitation with inhumane work hours but that can be an example. I was only able to stay at the job for six months because I was determined to see the students twice a week and provide more if the instructor therapist was new or was struggling with the program. As a result, my days were long… very long. My time was being exploited.

At this same agency, a year later, a former colleague of mine turned down an invitation for the staff holiday party, stating that he would attend his significant other's holiday party, which was scheduled on the same day. The employer threatened to remove his promotion and then proceeded to change the employee handbook mandating all staff attend the holiday party. This colleague was working towards being a state-licensed behavior analyst and was reliant on the agency for necessary paperwork to support that process. It is hard to know if the employer was taking advantage of being in a position in which the employee needed something. Being a Canadian working in the USA, I need working visas, and if I am to leave my job, without another visa for another workplace, I have ten days to leave the country. This puts the employer in a position of power. Unfortunately, power can come to the employer in a variety of different ways and most of the time it will not be abused. But exploitation is in the Code for a reason; it does happen.

If you suspect it is happening to you, ask yourself these three questions:

- Am I being treated differently than my colleagues/classmates?
- Am I having to do more than what is required for the position without acknowledgment or remuneration?
- Am I uncomfortable with this learning/work environment?

If you answered yes to one of the three aforementioned questions, acknowledge that you may be in an exploitative situation. Try to work through the situation with your employer or supervisor as they may be unaware and willing to assist you in making the environment more inclusive. If that is not possible, talk with someone outside your agency. Aside from being unethical, feeling exploited is dreadful. If you find yourself in this situation, it is imperative that you document everything. The impact of the situation on you, all of your correspondence, and every effort to rectify the situation. A good strategy is to write yourself an email. This time stamps an event and supports your documentation efforts for incidents that do not naturally produce a permanent product. I have been fortunate to have the opportunity to reach out to my ethics professor when I have been faced with ethical dilemmas in my past. I encourage you to do the same or reach out to someone who can help you be objective regarding the challenging situation before you.

1.14 Romantic and Sexual Relationships

Behavior analysts do not engage in romantic or sexual relationships with current clients, stakeholders, trainees, or supervisees because such relationships pose a substantial risk of conflicts of interest and impaired judgment. Behavior analysts do not engage in romantic or sexual relationships with former clients or stakeholders for a minimum of two years from the date the professional relationship ended. Behavior analysts do not engage in romantic or sexual relationships with former supervisees or trainees until the parties can document that the professional relationship has ended (i.e., completion of all professional duties). Behavior analysts do not accept as supervisees or trainees individuals with whom they have had a past romantic or sexual relationship until at least six months after the relationship has ended.

Explanation

Unwelcome sexual advances, requests for sexual favors, and other verbal or physical conduct of a sexual nature constitute sexual harassment when this conduct explicitly or implicitly affects an individual's employment, unreasonably interferes with an individual's work performance, or creates an intimidating, hostile, or offensive work environment.

(U.S. Equal Employment Opportunity Commission, 2002)

Behavioral analysts entering a relationship that compromises their work with their client is a destructive voluntary decision. Clinicians break this rule knowing it is wrong, but fully believing that they will be the outlier in which their judgment will remain intact and the relationship remain professional. Perhaps it is naiveté or ignorance, but this train of thought is deeply flawed and can ruin a career, practice, school reputation, marriage, or even a life. It is hard to imagine one's logic when pursuing a sexual relationship knowing that there are a slew of negative life-altering consequences which would immediately put the client, student, and supervisee in an exploitative position.

There could exist a belief that you will not get caught, or that the victim (yes, when one person is in a position of power, the other person is a victim) won't tell anybody. One study of employed women found that 38% had experienced sexual harassment in the workplace (Potter & Banyard, 2011). The reason this is not seen as a problem of epidemic proportion is because it is underreported. With respects to sexual harassment, four out of five women don't report it. For those that do, 80% found no change after reporting, whereas 16% said their situation worsened (TUC, 2016). It is fair to assume that there are probably many examples of sexual relationships that never get reported. Out of sight, out of mind, right? Breaking the Code is never OK and not getting caught could lead to other ethically unsound decisions (assuming the sexual relationship was reinforcing).

Lastly, the ethical Code's intention is not to be the antithesis of Cupid. If there is a chance that this relationship could result in a happily-ever-after scenario, wonderful – all the Code asks is that you wait two years. After all, if you love something, let it go (for two years). If it comes back to you, it's true. If it doesn't, then it was never meant to be.

Considerations

There really are no considerations. This is a bad decision all the time, under every possible circumstance.

In some cases, these relationships are consensual, and both parties agree to take the risk and jeopardize their professional credibility and licensure. In some cases, these relationships are not consensual. These relationships are often entrenched in a history of sexually charged interactions. Let's dissect how one can enter such a relationship and attempt to figure out how it can be plausible given the harsh penalty of being caught.

This is how we interact; we were just having fun. The shift from civilized interaction into threatening behavior is all in the hands of the aggressor. Given the power dynamics, the prey may feel that his or her only option is to comply with a mentor's advances or feel ashamed to address it in public. This could explain why a history of inappropriate interactions is tolerated. If you are unsure whether your behavior is sexually inappropriate, apply the *spouse test*. The spouse test is simply would you engage in the behavior in question in front of your spouse (for those who aren't married a spouse could be substituted for a supervisor, dean, boss, significant other, or parent). If the answer to that question is a hard no, you are doing something wrong. Stop.

I thought she was into it because of the way she dresses. Your supervisee/student dresses provocatively. Whether it is premeditated or accidental, her choice of clothes could bring her unwanted attention and unwanted behavior from men. Isn't it as much her fault as his that an unexpected sexual advance occurred? NO! That assertion is ridiculous. To argue for a scenario in which a woman invites sexual abuse because of her choice of clothing suggests that members of the male gender are incapable of remaining professional when presented with the visual stimulus of a body they find aesthetically attractive. It is wrong and wholly callous to hold the people who are victimized responsible for the crime.

I didn't think she cared. I was just being flirtatious. If your behavior is altered because you are physically attracted to your supervisee, student, or client, you are doing something gravely wrong. It is best not to confuse being personable with being sexually inappropriate. Differentiating how one's interactions can be interpreted can be challenging. A gender-based joke may be delivered with the best of intentions, but it can still be offensive. Putting an errant hand on a shoulder could be seen as comforting or could be viewed as a sexually inappropriate touch. These lines are less blurred when the perpetrator is in a position of power and, in many situations, what someone would call being flirtatious or having fun is in fact sexual harassment and sexual assault, respectively. As a BCBA®, you are to model ethical and professional behavior. If your comment or actions could potentially be misconstrued, it likely was not professional to begin with. A quick test, as stated before, is whether you would engage in the same behavior with your spouse, boss, dean, previous supervisor, or parent.

It was happy hour. I apologized. Believe it or not, being drunk does not excuse one's behavior. No lawyer practices the "blackout drunk defense" because it doesn't exist. If you have a tendency to engage in poor judgment when drinking, do not do so in front of colleagues or clients (that latter should never be a scenario to begin with because a social drink with a client sounds rife for a multiple relationship scenario). Also, an "I am sorry" may not be enough. Sexual abuse/harassment is known to leave emotional scars. Half a minute of poor judgment could trigger symptoms of depression, anxiety, acute stress, or symptoms of posttraumatic stress disorder. As such a simple "I am sorry" likely won't cut it. A good way to avoid sexual relationship with a client, supervisee, and student is to recognize precursor behaviors (e.g., flirting, extra glances, or more salient examples, sweaty palms, increased pulse, etc.) and avoid engaging in any behavior that could be misconstrued as sexual. Pursuing a sexual relationship is under all of our control. It doesn't just happen. If these signs appear, recognize it and alter course immediately.

Examples from the Field

Written by Jacob Sadavoy

Our field is young in terms of years ABA has been around (compared with other scientific disciplines) and young in terms of those practicing. There exists an unofficial direct proportionality between age and maturity. This is not an excuse, but it is the rationale for some of the behaviors I have witnessed at my place of work; perhaps these behaviors exist in other workplaces and have nothing to do with maturity (which is a scary thought). In the first center I was employed in after completing my undergraduate degree, I saw a male staff member slap or kick the bottoms of female staff members. This individual was not in a supervisory role, but he was also not reprimanded for engaging in this behavior. The culture of the organization is now one in which it was acceptable for a man to touch the bottom of a female colleague. Female staff as a result are becoming desensitized to inappropriate physical touch. You may wonder how this relates to sexual intercourse between a supervisor and a supervisee or client. If the culture is created in which staff can be touched inappropriately and the administration is indifferent, is it not possible that a slap on the bottom becomes a caress which could become a grope (simple shaping procedure)? If it escalates and becomes more frequent, and if it is seen as predatory and reported, the organization has a sexual assault issue on its hands when there were numerous opportunities to provide feedback before the escalation. If it goes unreported, the culture in that workplace remains fraught with discord.

1.15 Responding to Requests

Behavior analysts make appropriate efforts to respond to requests for information from and comply with deadlines of relevant individuals (e.g., clients, stakeholders, supervisees, trainees) and entities (e.g., BACB, licensure boards, funders). They also comply with practice requirements (e.g., attestations, criminal background checks) imposed by the BACB, employers, or governmental entities.

Explanation

The mission of the BACB® is focused on maintaining the quality of behavioral interventions. The mission of the BACB® states that its aim is to, "Protect consumers of behavior analysis services worldwide by systematically establishing, promoting, and disseminating professional standards" (BACB, 1998). The vision of how this is accomplished is described by their commitment to "Solve a wider variety of socially significant problems by increasing the availability of qualified behavior analysts around the world." The key phrase is "qualified." The organization itself is devoted to the protection of the maintenance of high standards in order to protect the consumer. The BACB® exists for the protection of consumers, and we are beholden to it; it is not beholden to us. Behavior analysts are subject to the oversight of a governing body. Therefore, it is necessary that we allow that body the opportunity to reasonably govern. The BACB®, in an effort to meet its stated mission and realize its vision, must have the information needed to assess the qualifications of behavior analysts. Professionals will often complain that the BACB® places emphasis on the needs of the consumers rather than the behavior analysts. However, this is precisely the purpose of the organization. To adhere to their guidelines is to maintain the standard of the profession, which benefits not only our own clients, but all clients who receive services.

Considerations

As insurance providers have begun to provide funding or services, there has been a cultural shift in the provision of services, particularly for individuals with autism spectrum disorder. Services are now based on a medical model, and must focus on goals that are "medically necessary," meaning that they address the core deficits as described in the DSM-V's diagnostic criteria for autism spectrum disorder.

In the past, when our advocacy was focused primarily on the educational system, this advocacy was focused on the best services. Services would certainly be provided, but those services may not adequately meet the needs of our clients. Insurance companies, on the other hand, are not coming from a model where something must be provided, making the risks far greater if we do not comply with requirements.

Examples from the Field

Written by Ann Beirne

It is important for behavior analysts to know that, after their certification is complete, there is one additional hurdle – licensure. Licensure requirements, including fees, applications processes, and waiting period, vary state by state. Licensing for the state of residence of the insured is not only an ethical requirement but a legal one.

As the growing practice of telehealth and remote education make our physical borders less relevant, this may seem cumbersome. Several state licenses may be required. In New York, for example, a license for both New York and New Jersey would be convenient. To avoid legal and ethical impropriety, licensing for any and all clients is a necessary addition to our resume.

1.16 Self-Reporting Critical Information

Behavior analysts remain knowledgeable about and comply with all self-reporting requirements of relevant entities (e.g., BACB, licensure boards, funders).

Explanation

The BACB® encourages full disclosure in a timely fashion (i.e., 30 days) as a means to protect clients from changes in one's status based on violations to this Code or public health and safety. A BCBA® must report disciplinary investigations, actions, or sanctions or a public health and safety violation as soon as possible and no later than 30 days. The BACB®, colleagues, and clients do not want a compromised clinician to continue working in the field as that would reflect poorly on the entire profession. A clinician has access to confidential information and if they show themselves to be unlawful and exercise poor judgment, it is best for action to occur to remove them from the case.

Considerations

Among the reporting requirements of the BACB®, one item has caused a great deal of confusion. The public safety requirement in this Code element includes traffic tickets, and much has been debated as to what necessitates reporting to the BACB®. The November 2016 BACB® newsletter offers some clarity on this point. According to this newsletter, the behavior analyst is required to report the incident if the incident indicates a physical or mental health condition, which may interfere with performing the duties of a behavior analyst or indicates a Code violation. In addition, a report is required if the incident involved a client, required reporting to a governmental or regulatory agency, professional liability insurer, or a third-party payer designated by the client. A fine greater than $750 is another indicator of the need to report an incident. Those incidents which do not require reporting include violations where the behavior analyst is not named specifically as the violator, including parking tickets or red light cameras. Additionally, traffic violations that occur at the location of services but do not involve the client or where the client is not present would not need to be reported. Nor would a report be necessary if the incident does not indicate another Code violation or the fine is less than $750. Put simply, there is no need to report every single traffic violation. The Ethics Code, in this as in all things, governs our work as behavior analysts.

Examples from the Field

Written by Ann Beirne

When determining what to self-report, we do not want to leave it to our personal judgment. There are many behavior analysts who will self-report any perceived slight, and many others who will consider even egregious violations unworthy of a report.

Thankfully the BACB® has taken some of the personal judgment from this equation with the Considerations for Self Reporting (BACB, 2019), reprinted here in Appendix C. This document outlines the necessary questions to help make the determination of what rises to the level of requiring a report to the BACB®:

- Have you violated an ethics requirement?
- Have you been the subject of any criminal legal actions, including filing of criminal charges, arrest, plea of guilty or no contest, presentencing agreements, diversion agreements, convictions, and any period of custody in a jail, prison, or community corrections setting such as a "halfway house"?"
- Have you been the subject of any civil legal actions, including filing of lawsuits, or any legal actions in which you have been named or identified (even if not a direct party to the suit)?
- Have you been the subject of any regulatory actions, including investigations, consent agreements, administrative law proceedings, mediation, arbitration, etc.?
- Have you been the subject of any healthcare agency and employer actions, including investigations and sanctions for incompetent or neglectful service delivery?
- Have you been issued a public health- and safety-related ticket or fine related to an incident that may indicate a physical or mental condition that could impact the competent delivery of services?
- Have you been issued a public health- and safety-related ticket or fine related to an incident that is evidence of another Compliance Code violation (e.g., a citation for negligently leaving a client unattended)?
- Have you been issued a public health- and safety-related ticket or fine related to an incident where a client was present (regardless of the amount of the fine)?
- Have you been issued a public health- and safety-related ticket or fine related to an incident that involved the operation of a motor vehicle and the fine was greater than $750?
- Have you been issued a public health- and safety-related ticket or fine related to an incident that you were required to report to your professional liability insurance provider?
- Have you been issued a public health- and safety-related ticket or fine related to an incident that you were required to report to a client's third-party payer?
- Have you been issued a public health- and safety-related ticket or fine related to an incident that you were required to report to a governmental regulatory board?
- Have you been the subject of any investigation, charge, allegation, or sanction that could have placed the client at risk for harm or impacted the competent delivery of services?
- Have you failed to meet the relevant requirements (e.g., number of contacts, % supervision) when providing supervision* to an RBT™ or BCaBA®?

- Have you failed to maintain documentation meeting the relevant requirements when providing supervision* to an RBT™ or BCaBA®?
- Are you an RBT™ or BCaBA® who provided services without a qualified supervisor overseeing your work? Are you an RBT™ or BCaBA® who did not meet the relevant supervision requirements (e.g., number of contacts, % supervision)?
- Are you an RBT™ or BCaBA® who did not maintain documentation meeting the relevant supervision requirements? (BACB, 2019)

With this guidance, we can make objective decisions and uphold our responsibility to the field, to each other and, above all, to our clients.

Works Cited

Behavior Analyst Certification Board. (2020). *Ethics Code for Behavior Analysts.* Littleton, CO: Author.

Behavior Analyst Certification Board. (2019). *Considerations for Self-Reporting.* Littleton, CO: Author.

Carr, R. N. (2021). Rural access to ethical and appropriate behavior analytic treatment in schools. In Sadavoy, J. A. & Zube, M. L. (Eds.), *A scientific framework for compassion and social justice: Lessons in applied behavior analysis* (pp. 247–251). Routledge.

Cooper, J. O., Heron, T. E., & Heward, W. L. (2007). *Applied behavior analysis* (2nd ed.). Pearson.

Fallon, L. M., O'Keeffe, B. V., & Sugai, G. (2012). Consideration of culture and context in schoolwide positive behavior support: a review of current literature. *Journal of Positive Behavior Interventions, 14*(4), 209–219.

Fong, E. H., Catagnus, R. M., Brodhead, M. T., Quigley, S., & Field, S. (2016). Developing the cultural awareness skills of behavior analysts. *Behavior Analysis in Practice, 9*(1), 84–94. https://doi.org/10.1007/s40617-016-0111-6.

Glenn, S. S. (1988). Contingencies and metacontingencies: toward a synthesis of behavior analysis and cultural materialism. *The Behavior Analyst, 11*(2), 161–179. https://doi.org/10.1007/bf03392470.

Glenn, S. S. (2004). Individual behavior, culture, and social change. *The Behavior Analyst, 27*(2), 133–151. https://doi.org/10.1007/bf03393175.

Li, A., Curiel, H., Pritchard, J., & Poling, A. (2018). Participation of women in behavior analysis research: some recent and relevant data. *Behavior Analysis in Practice, 11*(2), 160–164. https://doi.org/10.1007/s40617-018-0211-6.

Nosik, M. R., & Grow, L. L. (2015). Prominent women in behavior analysis: an introduction. *The Behavior Analyst, 38*(2), 225–227. doi:10.1007/s40614-015-0032-7.

Potter, S. J., & Banyard, V. L. (2011). The victimization experiences of women in the workforce: moving beyond single categories of work or violence. *Violence and Victims, 26*, 513–532.

TUC. (2016, August 10). Nearly two in three young women have experienced sexual harassment at work, TUC survey reveals. *TUC.* Retrieved from www.tuc.org.uk/news/nearly-two-threeyoung-women-have-experienced-sexual-harassment-work-tuc-survey-reveals.

U.S. Equal Employment Opportunity Commission. (2002, June 27). Facts about sexual harassment. U.S. Equal Employment Opportunity Commission. www.eeoc.gov/fact-sheet/facts-about-sexual-harassment.

Xu, F. K., Nosek, B. A., Umansky, E., & Greenwald, A. G. (2014). Project implicit creates public archive of 13 years of IAT data from millions of respondents. *PsycEXTRA Dataset.* https://doi.org/10.1037/e512142015-775.

Yahoo! (2021, February 2). "What color is your thong today?" Twitch streamer has the best response to sexist question. *Yahoo!* www.yahoo.com/now/twitch-gamer-shuts-down-sexist-troll-222135344.html.

1.5   Ethics Standards Section 2
Responsibility in Practice

2.01 Providing Effective Treatment

Behavior analysts prioritize clients' rights and needs in service delivery. They provide services that are conceptually consistent with behavioral principles, based on scientific evidence, and designed to maximize desired outcomes for and protect all clients, stakeholders, supervisees, trainees, and research participants from harm. Behavior analysts implement nonbehavioral services with clients only if they have the required education, formal training, and professional credentials to deliver such services.

Explanation

This Code element includes two very important aspects of behavior-analytic service delivery: conceptual consistency and evidence-based practice.

In the very first issue of the *Journal of Applied Behavior Analysis*, the tone was set for what and would not meet the standards of the field. In this article, Baer, Wolf, and Risley (1968) laid out the expectations for publication, and, by extension, for practice. They wrote that, in order to progress, the field should strive to remain conceptually systematic. In other words, any procedures that we use in practice are based on behavior-analytic principles. Any programming that we implement should be based on these behavior-analytic principles without adding "extras" from other fields. Not only would you be very unlikely to see an article that explores the use of past-life regression therapy to teach toilet training, you should not be using it in practice either.

Our programming must adhere to the principles of our field. Just as we practice within the boundaries of our competence, we also practice within the boundaries of the principles of behavior analysis.

In considering this Code element, it is equally important to review what constitutes "scientific evidence." Many professionals working with individuals with autism spectrum disorder describe applied behavior analysis as "the only evidence-based treatment for individuals with autism." This description is troubling for a number of reasons.

The first reason is that the definition of applied behavior analysis has little to do with autism spectrum disorder at all, to say nothing of its treatment. Applied behavior analysis is actually defined by Cooper, Heron, and Heward (2013) as "the science in which procedures derived from the principles of behavior are systematically applied to improve socially significant behavior to a meaningful degree. It is then demonstrated experimentally that these procedures were responsible for the change." By this definition, applied behavior analysis can be used to solve any number of problems from quitting smoking to training guide dogs to encouraging community recycling. There are even behavior analysts working on ending violence within communities and literally working toward world peace

DOI: 10.4324/9781003190707-6

(Mattaini & Thyer, 1996). To describe applied behavior analysis as a treatment for autism spectrum disorder when its potential is so much more far-reaching is unnecessarily limiting to the science itself and to our potential as its practitioners to impact communities.

The second reason this description is troubling is that applied behavior analysis is, at its core, a science. It is not a treatment or a treatment package. It is not a collection of practices, nor a bag of tricks. While there may be many practices that are based on the science that describes how organisms learn socially significant behaviors, describing applied behavior analysis in this way separates it from other sciences and allows for some sloppy interpretations of what it is that we do.

Applied behavior analysis (ABA) is a *science*, not a set of practices. Like any science, it attempts to explain phenomena that already exist. It is not something to *do*, nor is it something to *believe*, since science doesn't care what you believe. Applied behavior analysis is a *science*, and as such it is something to *understand*.

But perhaps the most important reason that this description has never quite sat well is that it is a misplacement of emphasis. It is not that applied behavior analysis is the only treatment that is evidence-based, but that the treatments based on applied behavior analysis rely exclusively on what is evidence-based. Literature reviews of current practices (Wong et al., 2015) reveal that applied behavior analysis is not listed. Practices that are frequently applied are listed, certainly, but not applied behavior analysis itself. And there have been several practices added to this list since we first entered the field 20 years ago, as the evidence grew to support them. As these practices gained evidentiary support, they became part of standard practice within applied behavior analysis. In short, applied behavior analysis does not drive the evidence, it follows it.

So what exactly constitutes this evidence? For those of us working with individuals with disabilities (and specifically autism spectrum disorder), several practices have been identified as "evidence-based." There is some agreement within the scientific community as to how this concept can be defined and it is also described by the National Professional Development Center on Autism Spectrum Disorders (Steinbrenner et al., 2020). Practices gain entry to this list of practices when they have been demonstrated in three randomized or quasi-experimental studies, five single-subject studies, or a combination of evidence – one randomized or quasi-experimental design combined with three single-subject design studies (Odom et al., 2015). The practices with evidentiary support are not limited to those which would be considered "comprehensive treatment packages" for individuals with autism. Evidence is not from conferences, workshops, opinion pieces, anecdotes, or guesswork, but from studies published in peer-reviewed journals.

As discussed previously, the Ethics Code for Behavior Analysts® applies only to professionals within the field of behavior analysis and only behavior analysts are required to adhere to it. The general public does not have knowledge of the science of behavior analysis, of its potential, or of its limitations, and their ability to be effective consumers can be compromised by our inability to adhere to these requirements. Behavior analysts must be mindful of using false or misleading statements. This becomes particularly difficult when other interventions, in particular those which use pseudoscientific or anti-scientific methodologies, continue to make outrageous claims and be well-received by the public. For a behavior analyst, however, honesty is the best policy. Maintaining honesty in both what we say and what we refrain from saying upholds the principles and values of our field. Behavior analysts are mindful not only of making false or misleading information themselves but also aware of how such statements may be received by the general public. In this case it is best to refrain not only from impropriety itself but from the appearance of impropriety as well. If statements about the possible effects of applied behavior analysis are exaggerated, such claims could easily be confused by the general public. What has been stated several times throughout this text bears repeating here, and bears consistent repetition in our clinical practice. Applied behavior analysis is not a set of practices. It is not a set of tools in our toolbox. It is not a bag of tricks. Applied behavior analysis is a science. It is the science of how organisms learn, not a treatment or treatment package for autism spectrum disorder. Though much of our clinical practice is based on this science, our practice is not the science itself. Rather, it is an application of science. A science is not something that you do, it is something that you understand. Here again it is our responsibility to focus our attention on the observable measurable phenomena involved in the methodologies of clinical practice. Whether or not such methodologies effectively treat the behavioral deficits and excesses associated with autism spectrum disorder should not be our primary concern, but simply that these methodologies can affect lasting meaningful behavior change.

Another essential aspect of this Code element is the stipulation regarding nonbehavioral services. Why would the ethical Code for behavior analysts include stipulations for the provision of nonbehavioral services? While there are some behavior analysts whose academic and professional backgrounds are exclusively related to the practice of behavior analysis alone, there are many that began in other fields. Psychology, education, special education, speech pathology, and social work are just some of the fields that may pave a path in a behavior analyst's professional journey. The practices associated with these professions, while not necessarily incompatible with behavior analysis, must be applied responsibly and be competent professionals in that field. Behavior analysts may have a great deal in common with one another, but they are far from a monolith.

Considerations

As behavior analysts who believes deeply in the inherent compassion of effective treatment and the importance of data-based decision-making in the support of meaningful behavior change, we are often dismayed by how applied behavior analysis is described by those who are not practitioners. In describing the day-to-day practice, the words "abuse" and "dehumanizing" often appear, and our hearts break for the family seeking treatment for a child who is struggling. In contrast, many of the alternatives suggested seem to be abuses of inaction, dismissive of the need for a child's health and safety to be protected by interventions aimed at decreasing dangerous behaviors or increasing communication. The Fifth Edition Task List for Behavior Analysts, focuses instead on staff considerations, requires us to, "Use function-based strategies to improve personnel performance" (BACB, 2017). The message is clear: our obligation to analyze behavior. It is necessary to analyze the behavior of those who would choose pseudoscientific methods just as we would analyze the behavior of our clients. The factors affecting choice must be considered when analyzing the reasons for a family to select what we would consider a less desirable option. This then leads us to consider what these options are offering that our own marketing lacks. Much of the "awareness raising" materials that describe autism spectrum disorder paint a dehumanizing and distressing picture of the future for a child with autism. This harrowing picture can provide a powerful motivating operation and set many families on the desperate path for a cure. The power of this distress is a ripe opportunity for an intervention that offers this promise, without necessarily delivering. Many of these interventions describe a sense of community, an opportunity for parents to fight their child, and, above all, hope. While we cannot, should not, and will not promise a cure for any diagnosis, the way that these pseudoscientific "cures" are presented can inform how we describe our interventions. We cannot offer a cure, but we can offer a more accepting and empowering picture of what a diagnosis of autism spectrum disorder can mean for a child and family. We cannot offer false promises, but we can offer community, and we can and should offer hope.

Within this Code element, we arrive at an interesting conundrum. If we are required to restrict our practice to those which are consistent with behavior-analytic principles, how then can we be adequately assured that other practices are inconsistent with scientific evidence? And by extension, how can we be sure that our own principles and the practice that are derived from them are evidence-based? It is often said that the absence of evidence is not evidence for absence. With that in mind, how can evidence be determined? In one study, sensory integration techniques are compared to behavioral techniques in the treatment of challenging behavior (Devlin et al., 2011). It should be no surprise to those of us in the field of behavior analysis that the results concluded that behavioral intervention was far more effective in decreasing challenging behavior. This study would certainly add to the body of research in support of our work, but would it be considered ethical?

In clinical work, this question becomes even more pressing. Can our work incorporate tactics associated with other philosophies and methodologies and remain conceptually systematic? In our explanation of the obligation of behavior analysts to rely on scientific knowledge, we discussed that the efforts to remain consistent in our approach to behavior may be challenged by clients who wish to try methodologies which are not behavior-analytic.

Some of these methodologies, however, can be considered behavior-analytic if framed correctly. While the use of an oral sensory chewable piece of jewelry to decrease self-biting may not be considered behavior-analytic at first, could this be considered a similar procedure to a differential reinforcement of alternative behavior? Perhaps it could if the programming reflected this philosophy. If we were to agree to follow a "sensory diet," could this be planned as a noncontingent reinforcement procedure? Perhaps it could if the activities were preferred and the planning of such activities were done with this philosophy in mind.

Applied behavior analysis is a science, and, as such, explains phenomena that already exist. These phenomena exist in a world that includes sensory activities and these stimuli can be incorporated into a behavior-analytic program.

Connections

Written by Jacob Sadavoy

There exists a larger ethical dilemma when you come across a pseudoscientific approach that defies science and thus ABA. In situations like this, there are many options – from walking away all together at the thought of doing something that is not based in science to biting your tongue and hoping for the best. However, it is important to realize that ABA was not always evidence-based. We deem strong evidence-based scientific evidence as those in which there is a careful assessment of the participants, objective, accurate, and reliable measurements of the intervention, replication (by multiple researchers), and peer reviewed and published in scientific journals. The *Journal of Applied Behavior Analysis* (*JABA*) was founded in 1968. Thus, one could argue that those practitioners, before 1968, were not practicing an evidence-based science based program on the aforementioned criteria. B. F. Skinner was heavily criticized by his contemporaries... and he should be (Chomsky, 1959; Sidman, 1980). His critics were practicing philosophical doubt. Any scientist needs a healthy level of skepticism, as scientific knowledge should always be seen as fleeting. New discoveries can happen at any time. It is crucial for all scientists to come in contact with this research in an effort to be more effective (which is one of the reasons why continued education is mandatory in all science-based fields). The best scientists are those that embrace philosophical doubt and, in doing so, possess a keen intrinsic desire to remain open to other ideas, strategies, and therapies that may counter their own beliefs, which is a healthy, necessary component of scientific reasoning. There are a plethora of interventions for autism spectrum disorder (ASD) with varying levels of popularity and all of which are sworn to work by someone. However, popularity does not have a direct relationship with proof, not all interventions are effective, and even the most well-intentioned will not yield results.

So let us return to the question at hand: what does an ABA practitioner/scientist do when confronted by an intervention that is popular, but not rooted in evidence? There are important considerations that need to be made before the practitioner can feel confident that an ethical decision has been reached. The first and most important question a clinician has to ask themselves is whether or not the intervention is safe. If the intervention in question is not harmful (e.g. extra prayer between lunch and dinner or a change in diet), it may be worthwhile to measure those interventions' effectiveness. The clinical judgment of the Board Certified Behavior Analyst® comes into effect in these situations. With a little education on ABA and demonstrating no link between acquisition of skills/maladaptive behavioral reduction for learners on a gluten-free/casein-free diet, the guardians may opt to avoid dietary intervention. If they are insistent on pursuing a dietary approach, does it impede ABA principles? Is there a safety concern? The likelihood is that the answer to both questions is no. In ethics, the phrase "Is this the hill to die on?" can be used a lot. I would argue that, in most cases, a gluten-free/casein-free diet and ABA can coexist if that the dietary intervention does not make food-aversive or promote food deprivation effects within therapy. Now, if you ask yourself whether the intervention being proposed is safe and the answer is "no," like the industrial bleach sold as the supplement "Miracle Mineral Solution" or putting your child downstream in a basket as a means to ward off the evil spirits, you are obligated to share your concerns and provide supportive scientific-based evidence to protect the client. ABA and harmful therapies cannot coexist.

Maintaining a client, if they are involved in a pseudoscientific therapy, is certainly not ideal. However, it can be worthwhile if the guardians desire to pursue the unsafe intervention can be shaped and eventually extinguished. It is also important to realize that our clients are allowed to have philosophical doubt too. I have seen many cases in which parents are vilified for trying something we know is harmful yet they feel could be a miracle "cure" from a blog or a testimonial. It is our responsibility to educate and ensure the health and safety of those we serve. When presented with a new treatment strategy, a scientist would not say, "this is flawed because I practice something else," rather they would say, "I practice ABA, which is evidence-based and shown to be effective and backed by decades of research. Could you please share some research for your intervention? I want to do what is best for the client and it will be helpful for me to understand the effectiveness of your strategy coupled with the risks involved."

As mentioned earlier, ethical decision-making can be complex and sometimes decisions can be ethically sound yet off-the-mark at the same time. Imagine a scenario in which a clinician has agreed to suspend services because the guardians of a client they are treating are looking at alternative therapies. Suspending services for this reason would be acceptable (i.e., ABA hours are being decreased in favor of a pseudoscientific therapy). Instead, a worthier response would be to examine why this behavior is happening. The likelihood is that the client is dissatisfied with the learner's progress or does not fully understand the principles of ABA. Conveniently, both deficits are within the BCBA's® repertoire of mastered skills to educate the client. After providing more information, if the guardians wish to pursue other interventions, they are exercising their philosophical doubt which should not be the sole reason for suspending services for a client. Clinician that sever services due to pseudoscience interventions are not taking into account the safety of the client (by not having ABA) or their role to promote ABA.

Examples from the Field

Written by Jacob Sadavoy

Imagine you are working with a client who is making slow progress across his skill acquisition plan and this same client also participates in a Facilitated Communication (FC) program where he is making rapid progress on his FC targets. You recently learned that his parents are considering cutting his ABA hours in favor of giving him more time to finish a book on poetry he is writing with his facilitator. As a BCBA®, what is the right thing to do? I can tell you that being in this situation was not fun. It is especially challenging to promote the benefits of ABA when the parents are clearly more reinforced by the "results" and promises that come from FC. However, who can blame them? It is not the fault of the parents but rather the responsibility of the BCBA® to promote and teach the parents why evidence-based practices are so important and why investing time and resources in FC is fruitless. An inappropriate reaction would be termination of services. The BCBA® is incorrect to assume that the parents should intrinsically favor ABA: further the BCBA® is obliged to help the client access the best services available (ideally one without FC). Some potential ways a BCBA® can accomplish this is by pointing out some of the shortcomings of FC (e.g., "why isn't he able to mand or answer questions across novel keyboards with novel people?," "why is his language and grammar so sophisticated despite not having formal language art lessons?" "when did the client gain his knowledge on Norse Mythology to write a sonnet about Vikings and Valhalla?" etc.) or highlighting the research that demonstrates the effectiveness of ABA coupled with the research that demonstrates FC's ineffectiveness.

A consulting firm hires a BCBA® to develop organizational behavior management strategies to help a construction company meet targets on time while promoting a safe work environment for their employees. Despite a concerted effort by the BCBA® to offer simple reinforcement strategies and incentives based on staff performance, upper management continues to reprimand and berate subordinates when targets are not met. One course of action is to refuse providing recommendations for a management staff who is content employing a positive punishment approach to supervision. However, just as in the previous example, it is the BCBA's® responsibility to teach this management group the benefits of the science so that they can learn that positive punishment will not be successful in the long term and how the recommendations made by the BCBA® will yield optimal results (if attempted). The company will not intrinsically know the pitfalls of employing a positive punishment approach (it is likely entrenched in their learning history hence resistant to behavior modification). The BCBA® once again not only has to come up with an intervention plan, but relate it back to the science to give the clients the "why" they need in order to follow through on the recommendations.

The common thread in both examples is return to the science. There is no sense in vilifying those who do not readily access proofs or seek evidence-based interventions. It is the responsibility of the behavior analyst to support their client's ability to engage in philosophical doubt. Hopefully it overgeneralizes, as there is no such thing as too many scientists.

You are a client and you are offered a choice of service: a miracle that will change your child's behavior within two months or a time-consuming, expensive, approach that will be gradual, systematic, and data driven. It is not hard to see the temptation of the claims of the former service. It is hard, for me, to see behavior technicians refusing to work with clients who entertain a pseudoscientific approach. It is best not to take it personally, understand that the client wants the same socially significant gains that you do, and understand that this is the reality. We are not going to make false claims, other therapies will, and that will attract prospective clients. We will continue to provide evidence-based strategies, we will continue to improve based on research literature, and we will continue to be an alternative for clients when they are ready for something that is time-consuming, expensive, gradual, systematic, but effective.

2.02 Timeliness

Behavior analysts deliver services and carry out necessary service-related administrative responsibilities in a timely manner.

Explanation

In the words of Shakespeare, "Brevity is the soul of wit." In this brief Code element, we have a clear requirement to work efficiently to ensure that our clients have access to necessary services. Behavior analysts must be responsible for adherence to deadlines as stipulated by funders, academic institutions, or legal entities.

Considerations

This is in line with core principle about being integrous. If one carries out necessary service-related duties in a timely manner you are doing more than following through on your commitments. You are being reliable in the eyes of your client and your supervisee/supervisor. Establishing yourself as honest and trustworthy will facilitate richer more open relationships and a greater access to compassion. If one is unreliable, the client will be less inclined to share because you have a history of not doing what you say you do.

Examples from the Field

Written by Jacob Sadavoy

Audit! I never understood why there would be a frenzy during the time of an audit unless there was something amiss with respect to the documentation of the client's file. This should never be the case. The file should be updated regularly and, if it isn't, which I have known to be the case in several of my work environments, interventions need to be implemented to support staff in being able to accomplish this basic requirement. I was recently asked for my clinical notes after performing a classroom consultation. I always surrender my notes with an apology for the handwriting. Transparency is important as is keeping good notes in the moment and penmanship, a skill that I have yet to master. Other times, the teacher is adamant that I do not take notes. In these situations, I waver and assess the situation as to whether to take consultation notes in the moment.

It is definitely my preference to do so; however, I have been given feedback that it can be unnerving to the teacher. It was shared that most professions do not have an analyst taking notes on their performance. I assured the teacher that it was about the student, and the notes would be helpful for both of us later. I also realize the teacher's lack of comfort is an unfortunate reality that they are not familiar with someone providing feedback for their performance which is a problem in itself. In the end, I will pair with the teacher, but, under some circumstances, I will collect notes after the session to respect the preferences of the teacher and to limit reactivity in the teacher's behavior. This is not possible when collecting data for the student, but, in those situations, I make it clear what I am writing and, most of the time, the teacher is pacified as long as it is not about their performance.

2.03 Protecting Confidential Information

Behavior analysts take appropriate steps to protect the confidentiality of clients, stakeholders, supervisees, trainees, and research participants; prevent the accidental or inadvertent sharing of confidential information; and comply with applicable confidentiality requirements (e.g., laws, regulations, organization policies). The scope of confidentiality includes service delivery (e.g., live, teleservices, recorded sessions); documentation and data; and verbal, written, or electronic communication.

Explanation

Consent is an essential concept and, according to the Professional and Ethical Compliance Code®, one that is an essential component in many aspects of our work. Clients and client surrogates, such as parents or guardians, have a right to both privacy and confidentiality. Privacy refers to the client's right to decide what is disclosed, whereas confidentiality refers to the right to decide to whom such information is given. To review information without such consent may not violate a client's right to privacy, since this has already been revealed, but does violate confidentiality.

Considerations

Many inexperienced clinicians will believe that revealing confidential information might be possible, or even ethically excusable, in certain spaces. Spaces where the individual being discussed is unlikely to be present might be considered sufficiently secured, so that information might be shared. The odds of encountering the client themselves, or anyone who may know the client, may be reduced. Revealing information in this context may seem like a victimless crime. After all, who would know? The Birthday Paradox (Flajolet, Gardy, & Thimonier, 1992), however, would be an example of the caution that must be taken when asking the question, "What are the odds?" This paradox states that among 24 people, it is likely that two will share the same birthday. While one might logically assume that the odds of two random people sharing the same birthday might be 1 in 365, this probability is affected by the number of people.

However, there is a more important reason to refrain from violating confidentiality than the possibility of repercussions. To do so is disrespectful of families, regardless of who may be aware of this violation. It is our responsibility to maintain confidentiality, not simply to avoid getting caught.

Maintaining confidentiality can be a simple matter of redacting any unnecessary information when communication is necessary. For example, using a numerical or alphabetic code rather than a client's name in the listed contacts on your phone may be a simple way to avoid this information being shared unnecessarily.

Examples from the Field

Written by Ann Beirne

As a clinician in home-based programs, I would frequently have cases referred to me by word of mouth. My work was of sufficient quality, so that I began to develop a reputation among other service providers. One such case was referred to me by the director of a school where another client was seen by a psychologist and special education team.

On the day before I began this case, I spoke to my current client about the scheduling, explaining that there was a possibility I may be a few minutes late as I traveled from a new location. The mother asked, "Oh, is his name Billy [a pseudonym]?" I smiled and said, "I can neither confirm nor deny!" The mother, understanding that I was ethically obligated to maintain confidentiality, laughed and dropped the subject. The next day, I was, as predicted, a few minutes late. As I arrived, I explained, without revealing any information, that I had traveled from another case. The mother, becoming visibly uncomfortable, said, "I want to stop you right there. I know that your new case is Billy. In fact, I know much more about it than I should." The mother then explained that the director of the school had asked her for my contact information, saying that there was a case where I might be able to help. The mother offered the information requested, and the director thanked her, explaining many of the details of the case, in addition to using the child's first and last name. "I know that little boy," the mother said, "and his mother. They attend my church." "Oh my goodness," said the director, "I shouldn't tell you this," but proceeded to give more information. Even in a large metropolitan area like New York City, there can be unexpected connections (Hope & Kelly, 1983). It is best not to reveal any identifying information.

2.04 Disclosing Confidential Information

Behavior analysts only share confidential information about clients, stakeholders, supervisees, trainees, or research participants: (1) when informed consent is obtained; (2) when attempting to protect the client or others from harm; (3) when attempting to resolve contractual issues; (4) when attempting to prevent a crime that is reasonably likely to cause physical, mental, or financial harm to another; or (5) when compelled to do so by law or court order. When behavior analysts are authorized to discuss confidential information with a third party, they only share information critical to the purpose of the communication.

Explanation

This Code element refers to the situations in which the behavior analyst can disclose information. Essentially, information cannot be disclosed simply for the sake of disclosing it, there must be some other purpose for the disclosure and that should be directly related either to the specifics of the contract (in the case of obtaining payment) or to the best interests of the client.

For those of us working in areas where there are laws that mandate reporting the reasonable suspicion of child abuse or neglect, this legal requirement supersedes any confidentiality requirement. The protection of our client, as well as the protection of the general public, is our primary concern.

Considerations

Some behavior analysts will go through their entire career and never have to disclose confidential information without consent while others will do this on a daily basis (e.g., behavior analysts working in high-risk residential facilities). It should be clear either in an employee manual or in the organization's policies and procedures as to the circumstances in which disclosure of confidential information can be shared without consent and what information can be shared. The client and the client's legal guardian must also be aware when you are obliged to share confidential information without their signed consent. This is not negotiable. This is to provide information to the client and employees in advance to limit errors and misunderstandings if a situation arises.

When working abroad, things get murky. In North America, if you are not paid for services rendered, the natural progression of this infraction would lead you to small claims court. Many countries do not have a small claims court. In those countries, collecting outstanding payment could prove to be challenging or perhaps impossible.

Internationally and domestically, laws protecting minors vary. Does the behavior analyst change the way he or she handles a situation if a minor is being threatened in one of the other countries or states in which minors' rights are limited? It is a very challenging situation because no crime has been committed and that society accepts the behavior as appropriate. There is nothing to report. There is, however, an obligation to train. An obligation to disseminate. An obligation to provide needed professional services to the client.

Therefore, it is important to know the local laws and be aware of your environment. You can find yourself in trouble if you disclose confidential information without consent for an infraction in your home state or country, but not in the state or country you are serving.

Examples from the Field

Written by Jacob Sadavoy

I remember the first time I had to disclose confidential information without consent. I had to report a paraprofessional for upbraiding a student. It was an awful feeling, because the student's information was being shared widely as the complaint escalated past the school and into the school board and legal team. It was difficult to discuss the student with professionals that were not involved in the behavior change program and who were not stakeholders. They were focused on the incident I observed. I do not wish a similar situation to happen to anyone reading this; however, if it does, I hope sharing the client's information so broadly will be as uncomfortable to you as it was for me because that suggests that you uphold confidentiality and take great care in protecting your clients.

I was working in a home program in which I was told that the learner's mother mentioned killing her daughter "to make her life easier" by one of the learner's therapists. I was confident that the mother would not do such a thing because it was mentioned more as an exasperated expression; however, I immediately became concerned for the daughter, who had very low self-esteem, was incessantly seeking positive feedback from her mother, and took things very literally. I did not feel this was a safe environment and upon reporting it to the BCBA-D™ and owner of the agency, I was told not to disclose. It is a hard situation to be in. Had something happened, both of us would be liable for having clinical notes in which the incident was reported and discussed, and no action was taken. Fortunately, nothing did happen, but I regret not reporting as the environment was clearly volatile.

2.05 Documentation Protection and Retention

Behavior analysts are knowledgeable about and comply with all applicable requirements (e.g., BACB rules, laws, regulations, contracts, funder and organization requirements) for storing, transporting, retaining, and destroying physical and electronic documentation related to their professional activities. They destroy physical documentation after making electronic copies or summaries of data (e.g., reports and graphs) only when allowed by applicable requirements. When a behavior analyst leaves an organization these responsibilities remain with the organization.

Explanation

Our primary obligation in terms of maintaining records is to be accountable for them, rather than to simply complete them. Behavior analysts must be held accountable for these records, not only in terms of their content, but also in terms of who can access them and how.

In order to preserve the confidentiality of the information, the phrase that is perhaps most relevant here is "under their control." In order to maintain the confidentiality of these records, it is essential that you yourself maintain them. It is ultimately the behavior analyst's responsibility to make sure that these records *remain* under their control.

In the fields of human services, behavior analysts are set apart by our emphasis on data collection and documentation. The necessity of this consistent documentation is foundational in our approach to practice. What cannot be documented cannot be proven, and as a scientific field, we rely upon evidence rather than guesswork. This acknowledgment of the importance of documentation brings with it a greater responsibility that such documentation be maintained responsibly, and greater difficulty in doing so. Within the USA, there are two statutes which govern how this information is managed, and the decision of which statute's regulations to follow is dependent on the role of the behavior analyst, including the clinical setting and the funding source. These are the Health Insurance Portability and Accountability Act (HIPAA) and the Family Education Rights to Privacy Act (FERPA) (in Canada they use Personal Information Protection and Electronic Documents Act (PI-PEDA), in Europe they use General Data Protection Regulation (GDPR), and Australia uses the Australian Data Privacy Regulations). HIPAA regulates the use, disclosure, and protection of health information and is applicable to therapists as well as those in the medical profession. Given that HIPAA addresses issues of electronic record keeping, it is often considered an appropriate standard. Any communication that includes individually identifying health information must be protected according to this standard. Email communication should include a HIPAA disclaimer and the use of identifying information (including names and images) should be avoided in texts or other communication. If records are kept on paper, these must be kept secure from the view of anyone else. FERPA not only ensures that educational records be kept private, but also maintains that families must have access to them if requested. Any educational records, defined here as information allowing for programmatic decisions, are subject to the protections ensured by FERPA. This statute applies to any and all educational records maintained by professionals in educational settings. A full analysis of the legal requirements of HIPAA and FERPA are beyond the scope of this volume. However, there are several options for adhering to these requirements, and there is often little need for behavior analysts to reinvent the wheel. It is important to note that agencies and schools will likely have their own policies in place to address compliance with either HIPAA or FERPA. Additionally, many of the technologies used to share information such as program data will have addressed compliance with HIPAA and FERPA. An excellent guideline is to restrict communication to those technologies which have established such security and refrain from using identifying information outside of these platforms.

Connections

Written by Jacob Sadavoy

Article 17 of the General Data Protection Regulation (the European equivalent to HIPAA) states, "The data subject shall have the right to obtain from the controller the erasure of personal data concerning him or her without undue delay and the controller shall have the obligation to erase personal data without undue delay where one of the following grounds applies" (General Data Protection Regulation, 2018). This directly conflicts with the behavior analysts' requirement to keep records for seven years. The way around this is to have the clients request, in writing, that they wish their files and data to be terminated. I also highly recommend stipulating concerns regarding their decision for erasure of the file and have the client initial acceptance of each of the stipulated concerns.

Considerations

There is often only one alternative presented to a behavior analyst, teacher, or other human services professional who is unable to complete their paperwork during office hours – take it home and do it there.

This of course, significantly increases the difficulty of maintaining confidentiality. The apparent inconsistency can be confusing, and the devil is certainly present in these details. Many teachers bring work home, and many spend evenings or weekends grading papers, planning lessons, or creating materials. While this may be a common practice in grading, it can easily compromise confidentiality. In many cases, the information we have at our disposal is far more sensitive than the results of a quiz or the grade on an essay. It is essential to make sure that such information is protected.

Still, this may be an alternative if the behavior analyst lives alone, and can be assured that no one – no spouses, roommates, guests, or children – will be able to view confidential information… or is it? Can records also be transported in a way that allows for confidentiality to be maintained? Or would something as simple as a flat tire compromise this effort?

A home office may not be the best option, and options for taking paperwork home must be considered carefully before agreeing to do so. It is important to consider all possible violations of confidentiality when assessing the best way to store, maintain, and transport records.

For those behavior analysts in private practice, the greatest challenge in complying with this Code is not simply whether or not to do so, but how to do so. Many professionals do not have a dedicated office space, particularly as their practice begins. The need to maintain affordable options for compliance with HIPAA or FERPA is an important element to consider when establishing a private practice.

One possible solution is to simply have a locking cabinet or file box where paperwork is stored and to keep this in the behavior analyst's home, or even their car. This, however, does not meet the requirements of maintaining, storing, or disposing of records in a manner consistent with the requirements of this Code element. A residence is not a sufficiently secure environment. A car is even less secure, and does not adhere to the standard of the safe transportation of these materials.

Another solution that cuts down on cost is to use open-source documentation and simply redact any identifying information. Without such information, the use of such measures would comply with the letter of FERPA and HIPAA, though not their spirit.

The use of documentation is integral to the effective application of behavior analysis. Redacting identifying information does not allow for the use of these records in advocacy for services or the provision of records to necessary entities, including insurance providers. Though this may be an appropriate stopgap measure, it may also prevent us from fulfilling other responsibilities.

Though the cost is certainly a consideration, the simplest and most ethical solution is the use of management software designed for this purpose. The increase in effort and cost is more than made up for by the security of ethical practice.

Examples from the Field

Written by Jacob Sadavoy

I have never been required to produce clinical notes or data from years ago, but it is absolutely essential to be prepared if that time comes. It is not easy to maintain records securely. Physically, I moved homes frequently in the last decade and because I have only recently learned the value of investing in a quality computer, I have gone through an absurd number of hard drives. Client safety is my responsibility as is maintaining their clinical records for years after I leave the case. Had I had my client files on my computer during one of my hard drive meltdowns, I would have lost all the files. I would then have had to call the client, who I had not spoken with in several years, and explain what had happened. For this reason, and the challenge of physically moving, having a good quality locked filing cabinet has been (and continues to be) very beneficial. I use a secure password-protected encrypted hard drive that I keep with me or have locked in a desk drawer when I am not working. This gives me peace of mind that my clients' records are safe and are all in one place able to be accessed by only me.

Connections

Written by Ann Beirne

How much documentation would be considered "enough"? This particular Code element does allow for some interpretation on this point. Though the requirement to provide documentation as required by law may provide some guidance, it is certainly not expansive enough to fulfill the other requirements of this Code element.

When considering the appropriate amount of documentation, I find it helpful to describe the concept of "enough" as behavior analysts describe many other concepts – by function, rather than the topography of what a correct volume of document might look like. Rather than taking data out of habit, it is perhaps best to occasionally revisit the role that data serves in our clinical work. I will often explain to trainees or supervisees that there are only three critical requirements of data:

Data must be taken. Though this may seem simple, simple is very rarely the same as easy. Is data being collected on a regular basis as recommended? Is the system clear and simple enough for others to collect data in our absence? Is the complexity of the system such that accuracy is being sacrificed? In order for data collection systems to give us the necessary information to move forward, these systems must work effectively to collect such information.

Data must be looked at and analyzed. Who is examining the data and how often? Are those direct service providers also advised to look for patterns in the trends of data? If patterns indicating progress are not evident, are they knowledgeable in what to look for that they can ask for help? Data must never be taken only to be sent into a black hole. It must be monitored, so that trends in progress – or lack thereof – can be detected.

Data must be used to modify behavior-change programs. This is the final, and perhaps most important, requirement of any data collection system. The information that is gained and shared through our data collection systems must inform our programming. All programmatic changes must be based on this data collection system and our review of the trends of the data. Ours is the science of behavior change, and our programming must always move forward.

Data must accomplish these three goals. However, anything beyond this is subject to other factors, including agency required practices, financial and human resources, and the preferences of the behavior analyst. Whether data is collected daily, weekly, or even less frequently, these requirements must be adhered to. There is considerable freedom in the way in which we collect and analyze, as long as we retain the ability to make data-based decisions.

It is perhaps best to approach our documentation systems with a healthy level of pessimism – hoping for the best, but preparing ourselves for the worst.

2.06 Accuracy in Service Billing and Reporting

Behavior analysts identify their services accurately and include all required information on reports, bills, invoices, requests for reimbursement, and receipts. They do not implement or bill nonbehavioral services under an authorization or contract for behavioral services. If inaccuracies in reporting or billing are discovered, they inform all relevant parties (e.g., organizations, licensure boards, funders), correct the inaccuracy in a timely manner, and document all actions taken in this circumstance and the eventual outcomes.

Explanation

Here again we have a requirement that we do the bare minimum: that we are honest in our billing, as is frequently required by law or agency policy. However, as is often the case, there is a bit more to it.

Billing requirements may be complex, especially as insurance companies and government agencies become involved in the oversight of applied behavior analysis programs, and errors can be very costly. At best, such errors could delay your income and at worst, could be interpreted as fraud. Many of the errors could be based on assumptions from previous practices. For example, many behavior analysts bill in 10- or 15-minute increments, but such practices may not be acceptable when billing agencies.

It is best to have a clear idea of what such billing requires. Read all regulations carefully and be sure to know who to ask if you have any questions. Assume nothing.

Considerations

Behavior analysts are ultimately responsible for billing that is done in their name, even if this billing is done by someone else. Even if an agency or other organization submits billing to a funding source on your behalf, errors can have detrimental effects.

Despite the common discomfort discussing fees and billing arrangement, it is vital to ask question regarding billing procedures, including the person responsible for submission. The opportunity to review billing can prevent a simple billing error from becoming a much greater problem.

Examples from the Field

Written by Jacob Sadavoy

I often wonder, as a BCBA®, am I doing enough to oversee the billing of my clients? This is not a problem when in my private practice as I am solely responsible for billing and can ensure that invoices that I generate are accurate and descriptive.

My concern lies when working at a school or agency. In most cases, I never see the bills. I register hours or it is done centrally, and an invoice is generated by the finance department and sent to the client. An additional concern occurs when invoicing a client through insurance as each individual insurance company has its own specific standards as to what they want on the invoice. Some are elaborate, and others require just the hours and whether the service hours were direct or indirect. In the latter case, relevant outcomes and other descriptive data are absent from the invoice. More concerning is there have been times when an invoice has been returned and I have to cross-reference my hours. This gives me immediate fears that the finance department could be making more errors and potentially overcharging clients inadvertently (or not!). A BCBA® cannot plead ignorant. They are responsible for all aspects of their services and even if another individual generates invoices, the ethical violation would be the BCBA's® (the illegal billing fraud, on the other hand, would be attributed to everyone).

As BCBAs®, we need to be more involved in all aspects of our work especially if we are not in a private practice (and reliant on others to produce on our behalf). We need to make sure that our ethical Code is being upheld by those in our organization who we are ultimately relying on to maintain our ethical standard.

2.07 Fees

Behavior analysts implement fee practices and share fee information in compliance with applicable laws and regulations. They do not misrepresent their fees. In situations where behavior analysts are not directly responsible for fees, they must communicate these requirements to the responsible party and take steps to resolve any inaccuracy or conflict. They document all actions taken in this circumstance and the eventual outcomes.

Explanation

This Code element addresses an area of great discomfort for many of us in the human services professions: compensation. This Code element does not demand that we set rates at a certain point, but simply that we communicate our fees and determine the rate to be charged. Behavior analysts should provide a written invoice at the time of service or shortly thereafter. These invoices should be sufficiently detailed, so that the cost of services and the specific services provided are clear, and the required information must be accurate.

This is one case in which honesty is indeed the best policy. Open communication regarding the financial compensation for providing services is essential in ethical practice.

Considerations

We should all be cautioned against undercharging for services. The urge to do so may come from a good place – they do not want to unnecessarily burden families. In some cases, it may come from a less admirable position – undervaluing our own worth.

This is a particular challenge because our clients and their families are in a uniquely vulnerable position. What would you pay to hear your child's voice for the first time, to be able to have dinner as a family, or to overcome your own fear of flying? For many of us, the value services that behavior analysts provide would be priceless. As one parent of a client once told me, "We will never be even." Those of us who work in human services often have an uncomfortable relationship with money. Many of us will say that we are not "just in it for the money." However, it is important to remember that applied behavior analysis is not a hobby, it is our livelihood.

Behavior analysts do need to be mindful of charging prohibitive rates, but they must also be mindful of meeting their own needs. Many behavior analysts have families to support, student loans to repay, and many other expenses. Ignoring our own need for financial security does not do a service to our clients, and often forces us to provide inconsistent services or take on a caseload that compromises our effectiveness.

Discomfort with conversations about financial arrangement is not an excuse to compromise the quality of our work. Though it may be uncomfortable, it is a necessary part of our work.

Examples from the Field

Written by Jacob Sadavoy

I am going to repeat it again because it cannot be overstated. Though conversations about financial arrangements may be uncomfortable, it is a necessary part of our work. For some behavior analysts, it is not uncomfortable; it is part of the job and an important part of the contractual obligations of the behavior analysts. Personally, it can be uncomfortable, as you will see in the following example.

In this anecdote, an agency in which I was not employed requested that I observe a client and provide professional crisis management for the family and therapists in the home program (as I was a trainer at the time). We had discussed that compensation would have to come from the parents as I was not employed by this agency, but first, I was going to get a sense of what the needs were and if it made sense for me to join the home program. This was a mistake. A contract should have been discussed at this point with a rate known and agreed upon by the client and me, the behavior analyst.

I went for an observation. I went for a second observation, to observe the other therapist working with the client. I inquired about visiting the school, in which it was reported he had no problem behaviors and nobody had thought to see him in that setting. I didn't see the aggressive outbursts that were reported (granted it was only three observations, I went again to see the morning routine). I was called in to provide professional crisis management for therapists and caregivers; however, in the end it was decided that only the mother would receive the training (which is hugely problematic because of behavior contrast not to mention likelihood of damaging the relationship between the son and the mother if she is the only person who is performing the crisis management protocols).

At this point, still no contract. There was a discussion about my rate, but my involvement was clouded by the fact that crisis management was no longer being sought by the therapists and the entire family. In the end, I wrote a report, to provide strategies that could be effective for the client and we went our separate ways as the agency retained the responsibility of the client's clinical needs. I was not compensated for several hours of work. I was more disappointed that I devalued the science by providing my services for free than not getting a paycheck. Moral of the story, even if you are unsure of your role upon starting a relationship with a client, get a signed contract with remuneration stipulated before you invest any time.

2.08 Communicating About Services

Behavior analysts use understandable language in, and ensure comprehension of, all communications with clients, stakeholders, supervisees, trainees, and research participants. Before providing services, they clearly describe the scope of services and specify the conditions under which services will end. They explain all assessment and behavior-change intervention procedures before implementing them and explain assessment and intervention results when they are available. They provide an accurate and current set of their credentials and a description of their area of competence upon request.

Explanation

There are few things more alienating than the feeling that you are in a conversation with someone who is not talking to you. In an effort to assert our own authority, or even simply out of habit, it may be tempting to discuss principles of behavior analysis as if the listener already knows all of the same terminology. However, it is important to realize that many do not, and even some of the words that sound familiar to the general public can have very different meanings in our field. Using a common language is not "dumbing down" the information and is no more unethical or unprofessional than the use of translators at the United Nations.

The onus is not on our potential clients to be able to understand the services that we provide or the science behind how we provide them. Instead, the onus is on *us* to help support them and promote greater understanding. Simply put, behavior analysts do not discriminate. The quality of our work depends on nothing beyond our ability to do it and not on whether or not we accept, understand, or approve of the culture of those with whom we work.

Often it is necessary to have a bit of humility about the limitations of our own knowledge. However, it is equally important to be willing to learn more.

We are not required to know everything about a given culture before we begin working with clients. And we do not necessarily need to know everything about it to support our clients' participation in that culture. Part of being a behavior analyst is understanding that learning is a lifelong journey that must be enthusiastically embraced. Rather than shut out new knowledge we need to be open to it.

Considerations

Imagine that two parents arrive at a meeting with the Board of Education and try to advocate for services. Parent #1 says, "My son is doing so much better than last year. He is learning so fast! When we walk down the street, he is pointing things out and saying their names. He's also asking for things all the time, even if I don't ask him what he wants." The second parent walks into the meeting and says, "My daughter's communication across all verbal operants has improved. She has mastered over 50 targets in the past six months! Her tact repertoire is much greater and she is engaging in pure tacts under naturalistic conditions. Her spontaneous and independent mands have also increased and they are controlled by the motivating operation without the need for a verbal stimulus at all." It is easy to see who is more likely to get the services they ask for, even though they are essentially saying exactly the same thing.

While we certainly want to make our language understandable to the recipients of our services as well as stakeholders, we also want to empower them to be able to effectively advocate for themselves or for their children. This cannot be accomplished by remaining entrenched in our ivory tower.

Examples from the Field

Written by Jacob Sadavoy

I used to be that guy. That guy that would go to a meeting, armed with my knowledge of the ABA glossary in the back of Cooper, Heron, and Heward, and proceed to flaunt. I would explain at length about how behavior contrast is the root of the problem or how ratio strain was the cause of poor rate of skill acquisition. I soon learned that this strategy was a brilliant way of being ignored by the teaching staff. My goal going into this meeting was not that the staff at the school were impressed with my vocabulary; my goal was to fuse behavior-analytic strategies in an educational environment for our mutual student. The staff had not studied ABA in teacher's college. They did not care that I had several years of experience in behavior-analytic programming. They wanted solutions to help their students, not hear some gibberish from a supposed expert. So, my behavior was shaped pretty quickly upon learning that my recommendations were not applied because the school team were unable to understand me. Conversely, I was more successful when I started to provide strategies using colloquial terms that were familiar to the classroom staff and not rhyming off ABA concepts from the back of the *White Book*.

Providing telehealth supervision has also been instrumental in helping me deliver recommendations that are clear and concise. In these situations, communication is of the utmost importance and can be extremely challenging at times as a supervisor cannot be onsite observing the program and video samples of a program can only go so far. It is the supervisor's responsibility to establish a sound behavior-analytic program for their client, part of that would be to make sure that the recommendations are understood and practiced so that the data reflects the interventions put in place. There is no benefit from the supervisor "talking over" their target audience. They will not get accurate information and since they are unable to provide in-person observations, they will have to wait until the next supervisory call in order to learn that there was a miscommunication which is inefficient and unnecessary.

This challenge is compounded when you require the need of a translator to help with your supervisory discussion. When using interpreters, it is important to be aware of best practices for disseminating information. I have provided weekly clinical recommendations for a school in Nanchang, China. None of the clinicians at this school speak English, so my discussions with them require an interpreter. I cannot be sure what I am saying is understood. What I can do is:

- Speak clearly and concisely
- Ask questions about the concepts being discussed to learn if the clinicians are able to repeat the recommendation accurately
- Ask for videos of the content you are discussing to see if it is understood (if a picture says 1,000 words, surely a video will be informative)
- Provide an agenda and common terms that will likely be discussed to help prime the interpreters for greater chance of understanding
- Presume competence; always presume competence

Understanding recommendations and ensuring that they are understood is my responsibility as the BCBA®. Failing to do so is failing the clinical integrity of the program and I firmly believe that not all programs can move forward with an interpreter. Fortunately, for me, I have video and data that demonstrate the effectiveness of my supervisory call; however, I am not going to fool myself into thinking that this supervision is ideal. This school would benefit from a Mandarin-speaking BCBA® and, with one, I would anticipate an improved rate of acquisition of the concepts being discussed.

2.09 Involving Clients and Stakeholders

Behavior analysts make appropriate efforts to involve clients and relevant stakeholders throughout the service relationship, including selecting goals, selecting and designing assessments and behavior-change interventions, and conducting continual progress monitoring.

Explanation

Clients must be involved in their own programming. There it is, explicitly stated in the Code. In order for our programming to be successful, it helps if clients can approach it with enthusiasm. It would stand to reason that the things that are the easiest to learn are those things you really want to learn. After all, the learning itself could then serve as a reinforcer. As the behavior change begins to take hold, that change would be supported.

Which means that we do our work with them, rather than for them. Rather than make assumptions about the appropriateness of proposed interventions in a country we have never visited, with our feedback translated into a language we do not speak, we have to begin by listening. What do these individuals in this situation need? What do they want? What are the unique challenges and hopes of this particular center, here and now? If we begin by involving our clients in the programming, the results can surpass our greatest expectations.

Considerations

Many of the practitioners of applied behavior analysis are neurotypical individuals working with individuals on the autism spectrum. And many of us may have entered the field having heard that applied behavior analysis was "the most effective treatment for autism spectrum disorder." And some may have tossed about the words "recovery," or even "cure."

As the voices of individuals with autism begin to be heard, there is a bitter truth that rises to the surface: many autistics (as self-advocates often refer to themselves) are not interested in a cure. In some cases, the term used for recovery from autism spectrum disorder is "best outcomes." Surely, many behavior analysts say, through a neurotypical lens, recovery from autism is the best outcome. What other outcome could we want? But to many autistics, this erases an integral part of their identity. The best outcome is not necessarily being "indistinguishable from peers," as many describe recovery, but being able to live full and rich lives. Having a life that includes health, safety, relationships, gainful employment, pursuing one's own interests, happiness in all of its forms – this is a life that many would consider the best outcome. Who among us really wants to be indistinguishable from peers?

Applied behavior analysis, referred to as ABA, places great emphasis on social significance. In fact, the first "A" in "ABA" stands for "applied." The question then becomes "socially significant to whom?" Is the goal here to promote meaningful behavior change or to make everyone else more comfortable? What is the benefit of this program to this client? Applied behavior analysis does not need to be a curative intervention. It can instead be a supportive one. We do not need to "cure" autism, or even imply that such a cure is necessary or beneficial. Instead, we can focus on meaningful behavior change – reducing self-injury, promoting communication, and establishing autonomy. It has been said that we have two ears and one mouth, so that we can listen twice as much as we speak. It is the responsibility of every behavior analyst to listen to their clients, even when what they say is a bit difficult for us to hear. This is the best way to promote lasting and meaningful behavior change.

Examples from the Field

Written by Jacob Sadavoy

This Code element is aligned with self-determination from the core principles. I can safely say this is something I reflect on regularly now. However, earlier in my career,

I would work on completing programs as designed and there was very little client involvement in the treatment planning. In my interactions with the autistic community (please read Joy Johnson's fantastic essay contribution later in this text, Chapter 3.5) I learned how harmful it is creating a behavior change program for an individual without getting their input. In some cases, self-determination is more challenging than for other clients. Regardless, it will be attempted otherwise the program is going to reflect my biases and experiences and imposed on another who will have different values, desires, and concepts of social significance. Our Ethics Code recognizes the importance of the client to have an active role in their own program; choice is critical (Parsons et al., 2012). Who is better to tell us how to proceed with a behavior-analytic program than our clients?

2.10 Collaborating with Colleagues

Behavior analysts collaborate with colleagues from their own and other professions in the best interest of clients and stakeholders. Behavior analysts address conflicts by compromising when possible, but always prioritizing the best interest of the client. Behavior analysts document all actions taken in these circumstances and their eventual outcome.

Explanation

Within each of the sections of this Code element, there are two things to consider: when to seek out and cooperate with consultants and when not to. Behavior analysts, while they are expected to have some level of competence, are not expected to be omniscient. Challenges may arise in the course of our work that necessitate an outside observer, and it is our obligation to seek this out when necessary. When such referrals are made, it is our obligation to work collaboratively for the client's benefit.

There should be some limits, however, to our willingness to make such referrals as well as our willingness to collaborate. These referrals must be made in the best interests of the client and must be done openly, honestly, and within the boundaries of our other responsibilities. In addition, our cooperation must be within certain limits. When seeking consultation or collaborating with those who provide such consultation, we are behavior analysts first and foremost and must adhere to our other professional and ethical obligations. These include our responsibility to rely on scientific knowledge in making recommendations (2.01). Although other fields may not have similar ethical requirements, we must consider these obligations when working with others.

There are two relationships to be considered when discussing the Code element: the relationship with the client and the relationship with another entity.

It may be helpful to clarify, in writing, the roles of each entity at the start of service. This can be easily incorporated into a contract. A simple "phone tree" listing the people responsible for various areas that clarifies which types of questions they are most able to answer can work wonders for providing this clarity for consumers.

When considering the relationship with another party, clarity also goes a long way. A contract here is required which includes the responsibilities of all parties involved. The negotiation of this contract is a good opportunity to clarify your commitment to the Ethics Code.

Honesty with all parties is the best policy in this case, and can often prevent later problems.

Considerations

Collaborating with professionals from other fields can frequently be challenging for behavior analysts, since behavior analysts view behaviorism not simply as a job, but as an overriding philosophy. Behavior analysis after all is a science, and as such it is not something to *do*, but something to *understand*.

While it may be tempting to examine all decisions through the narrow lens of what is right or wrong, it is important to acknowledge that each professional from each field brings expertise. It would further behoove us to remember that each profession has its own ethical standards and that "different" is not necessarily synonymous with "wrong."

It is always important to remember that, whether we are discussing individual clients, service agencies, or corporate entities, everyone comes to a situation with their own distinct responsibilities. The client's family is responsible primarily for the safety and care of the client and any other concern is secondary (often by a wide margin). Our obligation is to our ethical practice and we are required to follow this Code. An agency or corporate entity is accountable to state agencies in the case of a nonprofit organization and may be accountable to investors if such an organization is for-profit. While these may be different responsibilities, it is important that each be acknowledged.

In the case of conflict, it is essential that the behavior analyst prioritize the needs of the client while also acknowledging the responsibilities of other parties. Without understanding the perspectives of each side, any negotiation becomes impossible.

Examples from the Field

Written by Jacob Sadavoy

One of the best teams I had the pleasure of working on was a multidisciplinary team comprised of a psychologist, speech and language pathologist, occupational therapist, physiotherapist, social worker, special educator, and paraprofessional. We would go out in teams of two, and we would bring our collective learning histories to classrooms. It was enriching and insightful and even though we did not always speak the same language, having shared observations with a common goal made collaborative efforts within this consultative model very positive.

I would be lying if I said all my collaborative efforts with other service providers were fruitful. I would also be lying if I said all my collaborative efforts with other BCBAs® yielded favorable results too. It can be incredibly challenging when you are working through an extinction procedure for a behavior in which you know the function is to gain attention and another service provider runs to the learner to commence a sensory diet. Similarly, decisions that are suggested without data can be very challenging to take seriously. However, it is in the best interest of your client (whether it is the school, center, learner, parents, organization, employee, etc.) to be an active participant in consultative meetings. Part of being an active participant is being an active listener, being respectful, and speaking colloquially. You are not helping your client by limiting the collaborative efforts of a multidisciplinary team. I personally have benefited greatly by using some of the strategies that were published by speech and language pathologists, occupational therapists, psychologists, and social workers.

In the previous chapter we discussed the importance of dissemination. When in a multidisciplinary meeting I always view it as an opportunity to disseminate the science. I am excited when I am met with related-service professionals who do not agree with ABA or disagree with a behavioristic approach. Sometimes, their concerns are sound and based on their learning history working with an ABA team who were not collaborative or successful applying the principles of ABA. Other times, they are unfamiliar with ABA or focused on promoting their discipline. Regardless of the considerations, when in meetings with related-service professionals who would rather I not be at the table, I focus on the mutual client and our shared common goal. I provide a thick schedule of reinforcement and begin to disseminate what I know will work for the client referencing the work of the related-service professionals throughout. This may be a lengthy process (largely based on a history of aversive pairing) but behavior analysts are obligated to disseminate and who better to disseminate the science to than a related-service professional who may work with similar clientele and whose collaborative support is instrumental to the success of your shared client.

2.11 Obtaining Informed Consent

Behavior analysts are responsible for knowing about and complying with all conditions under which they are required to obtain informed consent from clients, stakeholders, and research participants (e.g., before initial implementation of assessments or behavior-change interventions, when making substantial changes to interventions, when exchanging or releasing confidential information or records). They are responsible for explaining, obtaining, reobtaining, and documenting required informed consent. They are responsible for obtaining assent from clients when applicable.

Explanation

Clients must approve the behavior-change program before its implementation and when any significant changes are made. Simply put, programs cannot be implemented without such consent.

As Wolf (1978) states in his description of social validity, this concept includes the social appropriateness of the procedures. If we do not have the consent required, such social appropriateness cannot be established and thus our programming would no longer be considered "applied."

The social significance of our programming is not secondary to our work. It is the cornerstone of it. Before beginning an assessment or behavior change program, client consent must be obtained, and such consent must be documented. While the latter may seem an unnecessary component, the documentation of the procedure itself, along with all of the information that must accompany the description of this procedure, performs an essential component in the consent process. This documentation allows the client or client's surrogate the time necessary to review information, and the ability to continue to review it periodically.

Connections

Written by Jacob Sadavoy

I am a huge proponent of meetings related to gaining consent. I make it a point to discuss the desired assessment outcomes with parents and my goal is not necessarily to get signed consent, even though that is a common outcome, but rather to create a positive dialogue on how to effectively manipulate the independent variable across all learning environments. In many cases, this is a phenomenal opportunity to brainstorm how to problem solve the challenging behavior if it presents itself at home or in the community with the consenting adult and know how much to reduce the behavior in the clinical environment before an opportunity for generalization could present itself based on their level of comfort. I have heard many clinicians complain about the lack of parental involvement in their client's program. In those situations, I question whether or not we are truly supporting the parents' involvement in the assessment process, for if we are taking the time to explain the procedures of all assessments to the parents, it would be exceedingly difficult for them not to be involved. I would argue that the goal is not for involvement, but for engagement or active participation. Fortunately, behavior analysts know a few things about promoting and reinforcing engagement.

Considerations

It has often been said that patience is a virtue. In behavior analysis, particularly for those of us who work with vulnerable populations, the opposite may in fact be true. It is our impatience, rather than our patience, that provides the motivating operations necessary for us to engage in the difficult work of human services and to maintain our "teaching behavior." Our impatience is what motivates us to promote meaningful behavior change rather than waiting and seeing what will happen without our intervention. It is central to the right to effective treatment that we intervene in the establishment of behavior change. Impatience, in behavior analysis, is a virtue. And it is a virtue that many of us have in great supply.

It is in our adherence to the Code element that we return to the idea of patience being a virtue. Our drive to resolve the issues and the motivation of own desire or the desire of others to change a problematic behavior can often cloud our judgment. We may be pressured to complete evaluations before consent is given by school administrators or other stakeholders who fail to understand why we "can't just take a look." We must guard against either the internal or external pressures to move forward with an assessment, and certainly a behavior plan, until consent is acquired. Additionally, we must understand that their impatience is also often a virtue, and guard against our impatience acting as a vice in this case.

When working with families and children, it is often tempting to simply get to work, rather than take the time to stop and review the procedures and goals. However, the importance of the words "in writing" cannot be overstressed in this case.

It is important to remember that, like any human service profession, behavior analysts are often working with clients or families in crisis. Many families come to us in desperation, ready to do virtually anything to ensure their child's health and safety. The professionals who work with these families may not take into account how distracting this desperation can be without every opportunity to understand the procedures used in behavior-change programs. Even with the best of intentions, families may unwittingly commit to more than they can reasonably do, or more than they can completely understand. We have encountered many families who have not understood the details of a behavior-change program, or even the fact that such a program had been put in place, simply because they had only given verbal consent. Having the procedures clarified in writing allows the client or client surrogate the time necessary to review the components of the behavior-change plan, to ask any necessary questions, and to gain a full understanding of the procedures and their rationale.

Equally important is the stipulation that is highlighted in section (b): written approval must be obtained. While this certainly allows us to ensure that we have some basis to our claims should a disagreement arise, there is a more compelling reason to provide this documentation. Having written consent allows the time to sit down and review the procedures, to answer questions and to check for clarification. The act of reviewing such a document allows the client and client surrogates to give informed consent to any assessment or programs.

When working with families, we may encounter some resistance to assessments. There are several reasons why this may occur, and among them are the possible misuse of such information and the misunderstanding of why (or if) such information is necessary.

The idea of "testing" children may indeed be a foreign one to many of the families that we work with, and the particular way in which educational testing is performed may be particularly unnerving. Many families will be offended if we cannot simply take their word that "he can do that, he does it at home." The methods of assessment and the information that will be used must be made as clear as possible.

Connections

Written by Ann Beirne

When my daughter was very little she had a terrible habit of chewing on her hair. One day, after being told for the hundredth time to stop, she said, "I just want to chew something!" and I realized that a DRA was probably the best bet. I started allowing her to chew gum and it quickly solved the problem. A few days later, the babysitter – who did not realize what had gone on behind the scenes – told me she didn't think such young children should chew gum. Good point, I agreed. No more gum.

It wasn't until hours later that I realized that, without any intention or malice, I had completely forgotten my own rationale, just from the suggestion that it was a bad idea. It made me wonder how often I had done this inadvertently, in an effort to advocate. Had I gained consent, or had I inadvertently coerced it?

In the cases where consent is not given, we often have little choice but to accept that the individual or the individual's family is simply not ready to begin this process. It may not, at this point, represent a persistent or severe enough referral problem to necessitate assessment or intervention. And, in those cases, we must accept that an assessment should not be performed.

The science of behavior analysis is one of tremendous power and that power must be used responsibly. Using the science of behavior analysis, we can teach anything. However, this is not an indication that we should treat everything. Nor is it an indication that every behavior should be assessed, regardless of our opinion on its importance.

Only those behaviors which have relevance that is indicated by consent to assess should become a priority for teaching. Priorities are not decided by the behavior analysts, but by the clients.

Examples from the Field

Written by Jacob Sadavoy

Whoever coined, "It is better to beg for forgiveness than ask for permission," was not a behavior analyst. Under no circumstances should a behavior-change program be implemented or altered without signed consent. I recall a horrific situation in which a client was on a behavior plan for screaming. His strongest reinforcer was watching YouTube videos on his computer. The protocol is that the computer would be removed from his visual field if he screamed. I would be lying if I said this was a successful protocol and the classroom lead's frustration was mounting as the behavior was not lessening. In an instant, this therapist broke protocol and, in that moment, which he later called "probing," removed the student and put him in a closet as opposed to his computer. There are no words to describe how awful this is for a behavior-analytic perspective or through the lens of client dignity.

Any behavior analyst would agree that the above example does not constitute a probe. Further, one is not allowed to try something new in the middle of a behavior-change program. Sudden changes in protocol need to be discussed and signed consent secured before moving forward. It is a method to ensure that everyone is in agreement and prevent rogue and ill-conceived decision-making "probes."

2.12 Considering Medical Needs

Behavior analysts ensure, to the best of their ability, that medical needs are assessed and addressed if there is any reasonable likelihood that a referred behavior is influenced by medical or biological variables. They document referrals made to a medical professional and follow up with the client after making the referral.

Explanation

There is a common cognitive bias that plagues all of us, but it is of particular interest to those of us in human services professions. Known as the law of the instrument, it is best explained as Abraham Maslow did in 1966, stating, "I suppose it is tempting, if the only tool you have is a hammer, to treat everything as if it were a nail" (Maslow, 1966). Behavior analysts are not immune to such cognitive biases and it is our responsibility to ensure that we actively prevent their interference with our effective work with clients.

It is important that we are observant not only of the circumstances in which the learner exists, but also of the indicators that there may be other factors that affect behavior. There may be precursor behavior to the target behavior that offers some indication of a medical or biological cause, and those need to be noted.

Considerations

While it is true that behavior can be analyzed according to antecedents and consequences and that these are often observable, it is equally true that many of the things that affect behavior are internal. Even the most radical of radical behaviorists acknowledges that pain and fatigue exist. It is not that we do not acknowledge the existence of these phenomena. B. F Skinner himself did so, stating "a private event may be distinguished by its limited accessibility but not, so far as we know, by any special structure or nature" (Skinner, 1965). There certainly exist those factors which cannot be directly observed. Our inability to see them does not mean that they do not exist.

And yet, many of us would take issue with the clinician who consistently claims that self-biting is "because he's hungry" or that inconsistency in responding is not a reflection of whether or not the client knows the skill, but a symptom of illness. Acknowledgment that such factors exist does not mean that we are assuming that they are always responsible for behavior – we are merely acknowledging that behavior can be influenced by such factors.

Examples from the Field

Written by Jacob Sadavoy

I can think of numerous examples in my career in which both behavior analysts and related service providers are quick to chalk up a medical or biological cause for an inappropriate behavior. As behavior analysts, we are required to seek medical consultation if there is a reasonable possibility that a referred behavior is influenced by medical or biological variables. Reasonable possibility is quite vague and, oftentimes, there are benefits to playing it safe. However, if a behavior plan is not working, it is more likely a result of the plan itself or the execution of that plan as opposed to a medical or biological challenge (Carr, 1994). I have found this to be true.

The neighboring classroom had a student who was vomiting his meals. As per the sick policy, the student was promptly sent home. Many professionals were worried about the possible development of gastroesophageal reflux disease or the potential for malnutrition by not absorbing nutrients from lunch. As a behavior analyst, I was curious about context.

Was this happening at breakfast and dinner? Is there something different about his lunch food items? Upon learning that this was something that was only happening at lunch, we changed some of the variables and learned that, if the food was heated, he would eat his meal thoroughly without any instances of regurgitation. In this instance, adopting a behavior-analytic approach yielded a positive outcome whereas waiting for an appointment to see a gastroenterologist while the learner practices the behavior would not have been the best course of action.

2.13 Selecting, Designing, and Implementing Assessments

Before selecting or designing behavior-change interventions behavior analysts select and design assessments that are conceptually consistent with behavioral principles; that are based on scientific evidence; and that best meet the diverse needs, context, and resources of the client and stakeholders. They select, design, and implement assessments with a focus on maximizing benefits and minimizing risk of harm to the client and stakeholders. They summarize the procedures and results in writing.

Explanation

This section of the Code begins with a warning: we are only to use assessments for "appropriate" purposes. In order to determine the appropriateness of our intended use, it may be helpful to review the purpose of assessments in general. A behavioral assessment is essentially a compilation of data that reflects a client's skills and needs. In order to do this, we need to use assessments in ways that reflect these needs honestly and conservatively, so that we detect those areas which need to be addressed.

Such assessments must honestly reflect the current skill level of the client where they are. In the case of assessments to determine the function of a given behavior, these assessments must accurately reflect the antecedent and consequent conditions that are likely to control behavior.

A skills assessment is an evaluation of the client's current needs and level of progress. In order to address behavioral deficits, these deficits must be made clear. I will often explain to supervisees that data must meet three requirements: (1) data must be taken, (2) data must be looked at and analyzed, and (3) data must be used to modify behavior-change programs. Anything beyond these requirements is at the discretion of the behavior analyst, who can decide on other factors based on any criteria – personal preference, convenience, or aesthetics.

Considerations

Where the assessment is a skills assessment, as might be required periodically for a program update or at the start of services, this would mean determining the clients' needs in the most conservative manner. This conservatism is not necessarily common to practitioners at other levels, or to families, and we will often need to train others in the responsible implementation of assessments. It is a natural instinct to want the client to do their best, which may lead us to gloss over areas where responding is inconsistent in an effort to "give them credit." However, this may lead to an assessment of the skills we anticipate that the individual will have rather than those they actually do have. We might explain the importance of "meeting our clients where they are," so that we can carefully shape those behaviors which are going to be most meaningful, as assessment is often referred to as a "snapshot" – an honest and objective picture of the client in this moment. It is not a vision for where they could be, but an evaluation of where they are now. Without the assessment of where we begin, we cannot possibly track progress accurately.

Examples from the Field

Written by Jacob Sadavoy

In my career, I have been asked to do a variety of assessments to assess current level of performance of my clients. The assessments I have used most often are The Assessment of Basic Language and Learning Skills—Revised (ABLLS-R; Partington, 2006), The Verbal Behavior Milestones Assessment and Placement Program (VB-MAPP; Sundberg, 2008), The Assessment of Functional Living Skills (AFLS; Partington & Mueller, 2012), and Promoting Emergence of Advanced Knowledge (PEAK; Dixon, 2016). All of the afore-mentioned assessments are criterion-referenced, in which the assessor will collect data via timed observations, interviews, probes, and direct measurement to evaluate a client's language and cognition skills and academic repertoires across several domains (LaFrance & Miguel, 2014). It should be noted that no data on these assessments' psychometric prop-erties have been published and yet many practitioners continue to implement and create programs based on the results of one or more assessments (Carr and Miguel, 2013; Dixon et al., 2017; Love et al., 2009; Odom et al., 2010). These assessments provide invaluable in-formation regarding current level of performance across a variety of domains but they are not a curriculum and they should not be the sole resource for any behavior change program.

Earlier in my career, I made two substantial errors when it comes to assessments – I com-pleted assessments alone, too soon, without direct supervision, and I developed programs as stipulated by the assessment. Both these errors have a tremendous impact for the client and the effectiveness of the program. Before detailing both ethical gaffes it should be noted that assessment choice is important. There are fundamental differences between each and, in my experience, the assessment I had opted for was stipulated by the agency and not cli-ent-directed. In hindsight, I would have liked to discuss the merits (and limitations) of each assessment, with the client, and collaborate on an assessment based on the client's profile and preference and not on convenience or the preference of the agency or center.

I remember being new to the field and it was assessment time. I was required to do the ABLLS-R and was told by my supervisor that I was able to do it alone. I was ecstatic. I thought this was a positive reflection of my skills and willfully took the assignment as a complement and a reflection of my competency. Unfortunately, it was a competency I had not yet earned. I was ill-prepared to do the assessment without direct supervision and I should have voiced those concerns to my supervisor. The results of an assessment are a snapshot into the client's current performance but errors in the assessment have a tremen-dous negative impact on program development and integrity of both the program for the client but the agency or center too.

I remember, also early in my career, using the assessment to derive program recommen-dations. I would look at the empty boxes and develop targets based on the gaps on the visual grid of the assessment. This should never happen. This is ineffective programming as it is not taking the client's needs into consideration if programming decisions are based solely upon assessment data. The value of these assessments is a practitioner's ability to identify targets especially in the realm of language development (LaFrance & Miguel, 2014). These assessments must be used in conjunction with client conversations related to areas of need, culture, and values and an environmental analysis to ensure that the behav-ior change program is individualized and not an attempt at teaching to an assessment with the hopes of coloring more boxes for the next assessment.

2.14 Selecting, Designing, and Implementing Behavior-Change Interventions

Behavior analysts select, design, and implement behavior-change interventions that: (1) are conceptually consistent with behavioral principles; (2) are based on scientific evidence; (3) are based on assessment results; (4) prioritize positive reinforcement procedures; and (5) best meet the diverse needs, context, and resources of the client and stakeholders. Behavior analysts also consider relevant factors (e.g., risks, benefits, and side effects; client and stakeholder preference; implementation efficiency; cost effectiveness) and design and implement behavior-change interventions to produce outcomes likely to maintain under naturalistic conditions. They summarize the behavior-change intervention procedures in writing (e.g., a behavior plan).

Explanation

One of the unfair criticisms of applied behavior analysis programming as it is generally done is that it does not design programming to address a client's individual needs. According to Baer, Wolf, and Risley (1968), the dimension indicating that programs must be conceptually systematic would indicate that there is some basis to this. We are restricted to those procedures which are based on behavior-analytic principles, which frequently means that we may recommend certain practices repeatedly for several different clients. To the outside eye, it may appear that we have blanket recommendations that are made for many rather than individualized programming designed for each client. However, this Code element requires that we address the many other factors that may interfere with or enhance the effectiveness of behavioral programming. As behavior analysts, we acknowledge that behavior does not occur in a vacuum and we must also acknowledge that promoting meaning and lasting behavior change also cannot occur in a vacuum. The cost-effectiveness of interventions, in terms of both financial cost and the cost of time and resources, must also be considered if our programming is to be effective. The risks of the interventions themselves must be assessed, along with the likelihood of proper training mitigating these risks and a description of what this training would entail. And perhaps most importantly, does this meet with the client's preferences as well?

Connections

Written by Ann Beirne

Many of us in behavior analysis came to this field with a deep desire to promote lasting behavior change and make a difference in the lives of our clients. To some extent, every case begins with a wish list of what we hope to accomplish – the difference that we hope to see and the support and enthusiasm of those who are responsible for implementing the plans we develop. This is an admirable trait and one that should be cultivated in supervisees and newly minted BCBAs®. However, it is equally important to be realistic about the resources in terms of manpower and time.

A behavior-change program must promote change. If such a plan fails to do so, then it must be modified until a meaningful change in behavior is achieved. When we say that behavior-change programs must be effective, what that means is that if such programs do not produce meaningful behavior change, they are modified again and again, and the environmental conditions are also continuously and repeatedly modified.

Over-ambition is the downfall of many behavior-change programs. It is essential to be realistic enough to base behavior-change programs on what is currently available while also being flexible enough to modify plans based on what can be done given the resources available.

Considerations

This Code element clearly states that clients have the right to effective treatment and that this is defined as "scientifically supported." However, have we ensured that clients actually want it?

Why would a parent reject a treatment based on the best available scientific evidence? Particularly now, when we are inundated with more information at our fingertips than many of our grandparents could have imagined having access to over a lifetime, such willingness would seem implausible. Why would a family opt instead for fad treatments or those which have been tested through research?

For those of us in behavior analysis, the question "why would they do that?" is not a rhetorical one. Despite the fact that our work is dedicated to the science of how organisms learn and behave, we tend to overlook the contingencies in place for those who select pseudoscientific methods. It is essential that we understand that there are often powerful reinforcers for selecting pseudoscientific practices. They might include a sense of community, a listening ear, reassurances that everything will be okay in the face of uncertainty.

It is beneficial to take a look at these reinforcers, just as we would when analyzing the behavior of a client. Is the behavior of following through on behavioral programming sufficiently reinforced? If not, we run the risk that other behaviors may take its place.

Examples from the Field

Written by Jacob Sadavoy

There are many protocols for toilet training. I have used a variety; some I like more than others, but the reality is most ABA toilet training strategies get the job done (Leader et al., 2018). I was working at a center and the BCBA® was adamant on using a standard toilet training strategy. We had used it with many learners in the school and it was effective. However, the strategy, as written, word-for-word, was applied to a learner with greater cognitive understanding around bathroom expectations. This strategy is effective; however, the BCBA® in this situation was guilty of overgeneralization and neglected to consider the individual learning profile of the new client. The previous learners, for whom the toilet training protocol was used, had limited verbal vocabulary. In comparison, this new student demonstrated greater command of all verbal operants. It made little sense not to have him involved in the toilet training procedure and having an overcorrection procedure for the first error seemed wholly inappropriate when the desired behavior could have been explained to the client.

2.15 Minimizing Risk of Behavior-Change Interventions

Behavior analysts select, design, and implement behavior-change interventions (including the selection and use of consequences) with a focus on minimizing risk of harm to the client

*and stakeholders. They recommend and implement restrictive or punishment-based proce-
dures only after demonstrating that desired results have not been obtained using less intrusive
means, or when it is determined by an existing intervention team that the risk of harm to
the client outweighs the risk associated with the behavior-change intervention. When recommending and implementing restrictive or punishment-based procedures, behavior analysts
comply with any required review processes (e.g., a human rights review committee). Behavior analysts must continually evaluate and document the effectiveness of restrictive or punishment-based procedures and modify or discontinue the behavior-change intervention in a
timely manner if it is ineffective.*

Explanation

The phrasing of this Code element is abundantly clear. Reinforcement strategies are the intervention of choice if any choice is available. Many beginning behavior analysts interpret
this to mean that punishment is never recommended, or that punishment is ineffective.
I have heard many students of behavior analysis claim that punishment "doesn't work."

The belief that punishment does not work is, unfortunately, easily refuted. Punishment,
by definition, is a procedure that results in a decrease in behavior. Given that it is defined by its effect, punishment must be effective. Punishment, by definition, does decrease
behavior and to perpetuate the idea that it does not is both naive and unscientific.

Where then does punishment fit into our understanding and why is reinforcement preferred? Is our preference for reinforcement yet another example of action that feels good
rather than one that is good? Does this stance allow us to maintain a high standard of ethics, or are we allowing our ego to interfere with our ability to support meaningful behavior
change that would make a difference in the lives of our clients?

In order to determine what constitutes meaningful behavior change, it may be helpful to
review what is meant by the term "behavior" – anything that an organism does. Behavior
must be actively performed and must pass the "dead person's test," which states that if a
dead person can do it, it does not meet the criteria to be considered "behavior." By this
standard, the behavior change caused by the use of punishment alone would be substand-
ard. The focus of such a procedure would in fact be in the absence of behavior rather than
behavior itself. While such a procedure may be effective, an emphasis on non-behavior
is not the same as an emphasis on behavior itself. An emphasis on termination of behavior would violate the "dead person's test." In other words, punishment does not promote
learning, but rather stops it. By emphasizing behavior increase, however, behavior analysts
are engaged in the work of learning – the establishment of meaningful behavior change.

Considerations

The considerations within this Code element are embedded in the phrase, "whenever possible." Here we are challenged to question what would be within the realm of "possible."
What are the limits of this possibility? There is considerable room for judgment in this
case and there are certainly behavior analysts whose views fall on either extreme. There
may be some who claim that to stand idly during the painstaking process of more gen-
tle teaching approaches would be a less ethical choice than an intervention that would
take hold more immediately. If safety or health is a concern, there are those who may
argue that a more time-consuming but less restrictive approach represents a failure to act
in the best interests of the client. However, there are many other behavior analysts who
would argue that punishment procedures are rarely, if ever, necessary. These professionals

maintain that any behavior problem can – and moreover, should – be treated through the use of reinforcement for alternative behaviors.

The phrase, "whenever possible" brings with it, to some extent, a burden of proof. We must be able to demonstrate – through the analysis of baseline data, through the analysis of the effects of various treatments, and through a thorough risk-benefit analysis – that such a procedure is necessary. This burden is on us to demonstrate that punishment procedures are a necessity.

Though the Behavior Analyst Certification Board® does not directly prohibit the use of punishment, it does not allow punishment procedures to be implemented as a first course of treatment without further consideration.

Examples from the Field

Written by Jacob Sadavoy

I firmly believe that reinforcement should be exhausted before punishment is considered (unless certain circumstances require a punishment approach immediately because the target behavior puts the client or others in the client's environment in danger). This needs to be stated in the ethical Code because punishment can be as effective as, and oftentimes more effective than, reinforcement.

I was working with a client and was shown an approach, by a related service provider, that was used whenever the client screamed. The client would be propped up against the wall, unable to move and his lips were kept shut by the practitioner's dominant hand. The parents were on board because it was effective; the behavior was decreasing. Our ethical Code did not allow me to perform such a protocol. Previously, I promoted a reinforcement system for positive behaviors, which was also effective. The challenge was that the latter approach was not used consistently, whereas the punishment approach provided immediate positive reinforcement for the practitioner.

Another common example of punishment I see in practice is token removal. Some ABA practitioners may think that removing tokens is not thought of as a punishment procedure but it is; you are decreasing the likelihood of the behavior from reoccurring by removing something desired (in this case, a token). Similar to the previous example, this strategy (also called a response cost procedure) can yield desired results but employing a response cost needs to be carefully thought out. A target behavior must be known to the learner and the instructor before a response cost is implemented, but, more importantly, it needs to be decided as to whether a response cost is needed at all. A clinical decision based on data as to whether to remove tokens is very different than an emotional decision based on a practitioner's "feeling" that the student does not deserve the token or reinforcement. The latter scenario would benefit the practitioner, whereas the former scenario would support the client.

2.16 Describing Behavior-Change Interventions Before Implementation

Before implementation, behavior analysts describe in writing the objectives and procedures of the behavior-change intervention, any projected timelines, and the schedule of ongoing review. They provide this information and explain the environmental conditions necessary for effective implementation of the behavior-change intervention to the stakeholders and client (when appropriate). They also provide explanations when modifying existing or introducing new behavior-change interventions and obtain informed consent when appropriate.

Explanation

This Code element requires that we describe the goals of the intervention. What do we hope to gain from this behavior-change program? How will we know when this goal is met? What procedures are in place to meet this goal? And finally, is the recommended procedure the most effective and least hazardous way to accomplish these goals? In order to meet the requirements of this Code, any program description must include these elements: a description of the goal, a description of the procedure, a rationale for the proposed procedure, and a rationale for the consideration and rejection of other interventions. In addition to a description of the goal and a criterion to determine the mastery of this goal, an analysis of the risks and benefits of the proposed intervention and those of different interventions must be included as well. It has been said that if you fail to plan, you plan to fail. In order to ensure the success of behavior-change programs, planning for success is necessary.

What provisions are necessary for a behavior-change program to, in Baer et al.'s words, "produce practical results for the client" (Baer et al., 1968)? The answer to this question differs depending on several factors, including the complexity of the task being taught, the prerequisite skills involved, the communication needs of the client, and the resources available.

It is essential that the necessary provisions for the success of the program be explained as part of the behavior-change program. An honest assessment of what is needed is necessary to move forward with any behavior-change program.

Considerations

What should a goal in a behavior analysis program look like? Certainly as more and more behavior analysts are advocating for the provision of services through health insurance companies, it becomes a pressing issue. How can we adequately state the goals of our intervention in order to ensure that such interventions are adequately funded? And how do we ensure that these goals are relevant for a given purpose?

It would seem that an appropriate area of focus in this case would be the application of these goals to two of the current dimensions of behavior analysis. Goals must be behavioral – behavior that is observable and measurable must be the focus of programming. The outcomes of behavior-change programs must also be effective – the success of such a program must achieve practical results for the client (Baer et al., 1968). Additionally, goals must be applied – they must be socially significant.

Here we may look at the recommendations that are often made in educational settings. Teachers are often encouraged to "S.M.A.R.T. goals" in the development of educational objectives for their students (O'Neil & Conzemius, 2006). The acronym "S.M.A.R.T. goal" refers to goals which are strategic and specific, measurable, attainable, results-based, and time-bound. Beginning with the first element, a strategic and specific goal would relate to a particular response or a particular response class. A goal which states, "Jimmy will ask for up to 15 items when these items are present in the room" would be an example of such a goal, whereas "Jimmy will increase his language" would not. The second element states that such goals must be measurable, which certainly aligns with the behavior analysts' obligation to focus on objective observation in the development of programming. It could be argued that the behavior analyst is separated from other human service fields by exactly this distinction – behavior analysts do not guess what individuals think or feel. Rather, they observe what they do. A S.M.A.R.T. goal must also be achievable. Every effort must be made to ensure the success of the behavior-change program and to eliminate or compensate with factors that may affect the success of a program. Goals that would be considered S.M.A.R.T. goals must also be results-based.

The requirement to create goals that are results-based and time-bound is directly related to the effectiveness of proposed interventions. Baer et al. (1968) describe the effectiveness of interventions in applied behavior analysis by stating that such behavior-change programs "produce practical results for the client." Goals focus on these practical results and place a time limit on meeting them.

Examples from the Field

Written by Jacob Sadavoy

I had practiced ABA for several years, as a behavior therapist, before coming across a risk-benefit analysis in a behavior-change program (hopefully all the Board Certified Behavior Analysis® I had worked under previously now include them in their behavior-change plans). I find them extremely helpful. Conducting a consent meeting for a behavior-change program, I make it a focus to discuss the risk-benefit analysis. Most of the time, the client and I agree; other times, I learn that the behavior is not a concern. One instance in which the latter prevailed was around a food desensitization program; the client's food repertoire was either a specific brand of chicken nuggets or frozen pizza. I was concerned about the client's nutritional needs. Upon discussing the risk-benefit analysis, we agreed to target the behavior. The purpose of the risk-benefit analysis was not to convince the client to sign off on a behavior-change program but rather to discuss the scenarios in which the problem behavior may as to progress or maintain without an intervention and from this discussion decide accordingly in whether or not to proceed with the behavior-change program.

I was consulting a home program and the protocol for aggressive behavior was to put the learner in the closet and wait for him to de-escalate. The closet was located at the other end of the main hall, in the parent's bedroom. Nowhere in the behavior-change program was it stipulated on how a clinician or a parent would physically transport him from the location of the incident to the closet (none of the team members or parents had crisis management training) or whether the closet would be available during every session. By not clearly describing the environment, I anticipate the consequence for this behavior-change program would be highly variable; many of which are outside the control of the therapists. One can reduce confounding variables and inaccuracies in execution by providing clear and concise expectations regarding the environment in behavior-change programs; otherwise, there will be various contingencies for the same target behavior which will greatly limit progress (Alwell et al., 1989).

2.17 Collecting and Using Data

Behavior analysts actively ensure the appropriate selection and correct implementation of data collection procedures. They graphically display, summarize, and use the data to make decisions about continuing, modifying, or terminating services.

Explanation

Before discussing assessment through data collection, it is necessary to, as behavior analysts frequently do, begin by defining the concept we are discussing. Cooper, Heron, and

Heward (2007) describe assessment as a "full range of inquiry methods" that allow us to determine the scope of an individual's strengths and needs.

To speak in more simplistic terms, assessment refers to the array of information-gathering activities that allow us to arrive at a hypothesis. These hypotheses may address the topography of a given behavior, the reinforcer that maintains behavior, or the behavioral deficits that must be addressed in a skill acquisition program. The clinical practice of applied behavior analysis can accurately be described as the application of behavioral principles to promoting lasting meaningful behavior change. Assessment, in a sense, is the overall picture from which we draw conclusions. These conclusions allow us to engage in the work of promoting lasting meaningful behavior change.

This section of the Code begins with a warning: we are only to use assessments for "appropriate" purposes. In order to determine the appropriateness of our intended use, it may be helpful to review the purpose of assessments in general. A behavioral assessment is essentially a compilation of data that reflects a client's skills and needs. In order to do this, we need to use assessments in ways that reflect these needs honestly and conservatively, so that we detect those areas which need to be addressed. Such assessments must honestly reflect the current skill level of the client where they are. In the case of assessments to determine the function of a given behavior, these assessments must accurately reflect the antecedent and consequent conditions that are likely to control behavior.

A skills assessment is an evaluation of the client's current needs and level of progress. In order to address behavioral deficits, these deficits must be made clear.

Considerations

Where the assessment is a skills assessment, as might be required periodically for a program update or at the start of services, this would mean determining the clients' needs in the most conservative manner. This conservatism is not necessarily common to practitioners at other levels, or to families, and we will often need to train others in the responsible implementation of assessments. It is a natural instinct to want the client to do their best, which may lead us to gloss over areas where responding is inconsistent in an effort to "give them credit." However, this may lead to an assessment of the skills we anticipate that the individual will have rather than those they actually do have. We might explain the importance of "meeting our clients where they are," so that we can carefully shape those behaviors which are going to be most meaningful, as assessment is often referred to as a "snapshot" – an honest and objective picture of the client in this moment. It is not a vision for where they could be, but an evaluation of where they are now. Without the assessment of where we begin, we cannot possibly track progress accurately.

Examples from the Field

Written by Jacob Sadavoy

I was working on a public washroom desensitization program with a girl in a school. We moved her closer and closer to the washroom. The consulting BCBA® checked data biweekly and we were moving a few centimeters each interval. In a different program, we were collecting three term contingency data for months and months and when shared with the consulting BCBA® the team was instructed to collect more. This went on for months and months too. Data is collected to be analyzed and to inform treatment. I remember in sharing my frustrations with a mentor, they shared, "data should not be taken for taking data's sake." Essentially what she was saying was that we are obligated to take data but if we are not going to use the data, do not waste time collecting it.

When I became a BCBA®, my supervisees would joke that they knew not to bother asking me question without being armed with data and graphs. I wanted to be the other extreme. I continue to feel it is necessary to demonstrate the need and usefulness of the data that is being collected. This is especially critical when asking stakeholders that are not familiar with taking data (e.g., parents, teachers, paraprofessionals, etc.). It is necessary to have a thick schedule of reinforcement for data-collecting behavior especially if it is a new skill. Taking data is added task demand. It is necessary to bring weight and value to the data being collected otherwise you risk drift and resignation.

Finally, during meetings, one of my primary goals is to demonstrate my problem solving and treatment decision-making outloud which will be rooted in the data that was collected by the team. One of my favorite things to do, is to encourage critical thinking skills in my team members and by bringing the graphs and asking the question, "what do you think?," team members are now practicing data analysis and thinking of next steps.

2.18 Continual Evaluation of the Behavior-Change Intervention

Behavior analysts engage in continual monitoring and evaluation of behavior-change interventions. If data indicate that desired outcomes are not being realized, they actively assess the situation and take appropriate corrective action. When a behavior analyst is concerned that services concurrently delivered by another professional are negatively impacting the behavior-change intervention, the behavior analyst takes appropriate steps to review and address the issue with the other professional.

Explanation

In order to make sure that our programming is making a difference for our clients, we must continually evaluate the program's effectiveness. there will certainly be opportunities to correct course, or determine a different destination altogether. But wandering aimlessly is unacceptable. We must know where we are going and have a clear idea of our progress getting there.

Considerations

As many of us know, the path of progress is very rarely straightforward. In fact, those of us who work with children are particularly aware that with each step forward there is a new set of challenges, and as children grow, there may be occasional stumbles in progress. So how do we determine if sufficient progress is being made when that progress may be slower than we expect? First, we need to carefully consider if our data collection is capturing the relevant factors. Do we have enough information about the nuances of the progress being made? Would a different system, such as trials to criterion (how many prompts are necessary before a single independent response) vs percentage correct (how many independent responses?) be appropriate? Have we accounted for other variables? Would a food diary, sleep diary, or activity diary give us relevant information? While the Code element requires us to evaluate the efficacy of our programming, it also allows us to analyze those factors that affect it.

Examples from the Field

Written by Jacob Sadavoy

Practicing in New York City, it was commonplace for clients to dabble in other therapies. In addition to behavior-analytic services, I have worked with clients who were also implementing biofeedback therapy, therapeutic listening, Son-Rise, camel's milk consumption protocol, facilitated communication, primitive reflex therapy, and so on. These strategies could overlap with behavior-analytic clinical hours and could erroneously be credited for gains made due to their behavior-analytic program or maturation. It was important to consider these treatments in the data and graphical analysis to appraise their effects and support the client in being able to ascertain which therapy was yielding positive results. Under these circumstances, the behavior analyst can demonstrate that applied behavior analysis is the most effective of the therapies. A concern and risk exists that the client may favor one of the pseudoscientific approaches largely due to false claims or, in my experience, to justify the financial and temporal investment. It is also important to note that "data" from those intervention strategies are subjective and not replicable. Thankfully, the behavior change program is replicable and when I am in this situation, I look to ramp up parent training initiatives. Doing this will allow the parents to contact ABA strategies which, if delivered effectively, can result in acquisition of socially significant skills an outcome that can't happen with facilitated communication or therapeutic listening.

2.19 Addressing Conditions Interfering with Service Delivery

Behavior analysts actively identify and address environmental conditions (e.g., the behavior of others, hazards to the client or staff, disruptions) that may interfere with or prevent service delivery. In such situations, behavior analysts remove or minimize the conditions, identify effective modifications to the intervention, and/or consider obtaining or recommending assistance from other professionals. Behavior analysts document the conditions, all actions taken, and the eventual outcomes.

Explanation

At first glance, it might appear that (a) and (b) are talking about the same thing – an environmental constraint that is an obstacle to program implementation. But there is a subtle distinction that deserves some closer attention here. The first part of this Code element deals with conditions that prevent implementation of programming. This means that programming is not possible. Being in a full-leg cast prevents a client from learning to ride a bike. It is time to bring in another professional. There may other medical conditions, along with other considerations that would prevent implementation, certainly. But I would hesitate to call many environmental conditions those which would preclude implementation. The second part of the Code refers to environmental conditions which hinder implementation. This means that programming is more difficult, but not necessarily impossible. Those environmental conditions which hinder implementation can be worked around, or possibly eliminated through careful consideration and adjustment to the training procedures, data collection systems, or adjustment of other aspects of the environment. Understanding and carefully identifying those conditions that either prevent or hinder implementation is a necessary skill for a behavior analyst. However, even more essential is understanding the distinction between them.

Considerations

Ethical practice is often a question of self-management. I have found that one of the keys to effective self-management is the mediated response of asking oneself questions in order to self-monitor ethical (or unethical) behavior.

In our discussion of multiple relationships, we explained the importance of asking the question, "Is this for me or is this for them?" Here there is an equally important question to be asked, "Is this essential, preferable, or preferable to me?"

Those environmental considerations which are essential would be those conditions on which the success of a behavior program depends. There must be adequate staffing to implement the plan in the first place, there must be reinforcers available, and there must be data collected. For those aspects that would be considered preferable, there may be greater flexibility. Is it necessary for staffing to be limited to a few trained individuals, for the reinforcers to be edible, or for data to be collected daily? Those elements which are described as "preferable to me" would be those aspects which are a factor of habit more than that of the impact on effectiveness. Is it necessary for those implementing programs to be BCBAs®, for data to be collected during certain times, or for chocolate chip cookies to be used as reinforcers? Asking yourself the question, "Is this essential, preferable or preferable to me?" is one way to acknowledge the differences between those environmental conditions that prevent implementation and those that merely hinder it.

Examples from the Field

Written by Jacob Sadavoy

Upon being certified as a trainer in professional crisis management, one of the focal points when a crisis happens is being aware of the environment. All scenarios need to be carefully thought out, discussed, and consent signed before an intervention is implemented. In some cases, it is necessary to have two staff for transport or immobilization. If there is only one staff member available, the crisis management plan changes accordingly. A colleague once shared his frustration regarding a physical behavior-change program for a larger client. He was successfully able to follow the protocol as written, but nobody else on the team could assist, and the client's mother certainly could not. In this scenario, environmental conditions hindered implementation of the behavior-change program, thus my colleague should have sought to eliminate the environmental constraints, which in this case was implementing the protocol as written, because of the lack of support. If this cannot be rectified, my colleague should acknowledge the obstacle in writing and seek an amendment in the behavior-change program, so that it can be carried out as written by all members of the team.

Works Cited

Alwell, M., Hunt, P., Goetz, L., & Sailor, W. (1989). Teaching generalized communicative behaviors within interrupted behavior chain contexts. *Journal of the Association for Persons with Severe Handicaps*, *14*(2), 91–100. <ds>https://doi.org/10.1177/154079698901400201.</ds>

Baer, D. M., Wolf, M. M., & Risley, T. R. (1968). Some current dimensions of applied behavior analysis 1. *Journal of Applied Behavior Analysis*, *1*(1), 91–97. <ds>https://doi.org/10.1901/jaba.1968.1-91.</ds>

Carr, E. G. (1994). Emerging themes in the functional analysis of problem behavior. *Journal of Applied Behavior Analysis*, *27*(2), 393–399. <ds>https://doi.org/10.1901/jaba.1994.27-393.</ds>

Carr, J. E., & Miguel, C. F. (2013). The analysis of verbal behavior and its therapeutic applications. In G. J. Madden (Ed.), *APA handbook of behavior analysis. Volume 2.* American Psychological Association.

Chomsky, N. (1959). Review of B. F. Skinner, *Verbal behavior. Language, 35,* 26–58.

Cooper, J. O., Heron, T. E., & Heward, W. L. (2013). *Applied behavior analysis.* Prentice Hall.

Devlin, S., Healy, O., Leader, G., & Hughes, B. M. (2010). Comparison of behavioral intervention and sensory-integration therapy in the treatment of challenging behavior. *Journal of Autism and Developmental Disorders, 41*(10), 1303–1320. <ds>https://doi.org/10.1007/s10803-010-1149-x.</ds>

Dixon M. R. (2016). *The PEAK relational training system.* Carbondale, IL: Shawnee Scientific Press.

Dixon, M. R., Belisle, J., McKeel, A., Whiting, S., Speelman, R., Daar, J. H., & Rowsey, K. (2017). An internal and critical review of the PEAK relational training system for children with autism and related intellectual disabilities: 2014–2017. *The Behavior Analyst, 40*(2), 493–521. <ds>https://doi.org/10.1007/s40614-017-0119-4.</ds>

Eikeseth, S., Smith, T., Jahr, E., & Eldevik, S. (2007). Outcome for children with autism who began intensive behavioral treatment between ages 4 and 7: a comparison controlled study. *Behavior modification, 31*(3), 264–278. <ds>https://doi.org/10.1177/0145445506291396.</ds>

Epstein, R. (1984). The principle of parsimony and some applications in psychology. *Journal of Mind Behavior, 5,* 119–130.

Flajolet, P., Gardy, D., & Thimonier, L. (1992). Birthday paradox, coupon collectors, caching algorithms and self-organizing search. *Discrete Applied Mathematics, 39*(3), 207–229.

Hope, J. A., & Kelly, I. W. (1983). Common difficulties with probabilistic reasoning. *Mathematics Teacher, 76*(8), 565–570.

LaFrance, D. L., & Miguel, C. F. (2014). Teaching verbal behavior to children with autism spectrum disorders. In J. Tarbox, D. R. Dixon, P. Sturmey, & J. L. Matson (Eds.), *Handbook of early intervention for autism spectrum disorders: Research, policy, and practice* (pp. 403–436). New York, NY: Springer.

Leader, G., Francis, K., Mannion, A., & Chen, J. (2018). Toileting problems in children and adolescents with parent-reported diagnoses of autism spectrum disorder. *Journal of Developmental and Physical Disabilities, 30*(3), 307–327. <ds>https://doi.org/10.1007/s10882-018-9587-z.</ds>

Lovaas, O. I. (1987). Behavioral treatment and normal educational and intellectual functioning in young autistic children. *Journal of Consulting and Clinical Psychology, 55*(1), 3–9. <ds>https://doi.org/10.1037/0022-006X.55.1.3.</ds>

Love, J. R., Carr, J. E., Almason, S. M., & Petursdottir, A. I. (2009). Early and intensive behavioral intervention for autism: a survey of clinical practices. *Research in Autism Spectrum Disorders, 3*(2), 421–428. <ds>https://doi.org/10.1016/j.rasd.2008.08.008.</ds>

Maslow, A. H. (1966). *The psychology of science: A reconnaissance* (p. 15). Washington, DC: Gateway Editions.

Mattaini, M. A., & Thyer, B. A. (Eds.) (1996). *Finding solutions to social problems: Behavioral strategies for change.* American Psychological Association. <ds>https://doi.org/10.1037/10217-000.</ds>

Newman, B. (2002). *Graduated applied behavior analysis.* Dove and Orca.

O'Neill, J., & Conzemius, A. (2006). *The power of SMART goals: Using goals to improve student learning.* Bloomington, IN: Solution Tree.

Odom, S. L., Boyd, B. A., Hall, L. J., & Hume, K. (2009). Evaluation of comprehensive treatment models for individuals with autism spectrum disorders. *Journal of Autism and Developmental Disorders, 40*(4), 425–436. <ds>https://doi.org/10.1007/s10803-009-0825-1.</ds>

Parsons, M. B., Rollyson, J. H., & Reid, D. H. (2012). Evidence-based staff training: a guide for practitioners. *Behavior Analysis in Practice, 5*(2), 2–11.

Partington, J. W. (2006). *The assessment of basic language and learning skills: Revised.* Behavior Analysts, Inc.

Partington, J. W., & Mueller, M. M. (2012). *The assessment of functional living skills.* Partington Behavior Analysts.

Reynolds, G. S. (1961). Behavioral contrast. *Journal of the Experimental Analysis of Behavior, 4*(1), 57–71. <ds>https://doi.org/10.1901/jeab.1961.4-57.</ds>

Sidman, M. (1980). A note on the measurement of conditional discrimination. *Journal of the Experimental Analysis of Behavior, 33*(2), 285–289. https://doi.org/10.1901/jeab.1980.33-285

Skinner, B. F. (1965). *Science and human behavior.* New York, NY: Simon & Schuster.

Steinbrenner, J. R., Hume, K., Odom, S. L., Morin, K. L., Nowell, S. W., Tomaszewski, B., Szendrey, S., McIntyre, N. S., Yücesoy-Özkan, S., & Savage, M. N. (2020). *Evidence-based practices for children, youth, and young adults with autism.* The University of North Carolina at Chapel Hill, Frank Porter Graham Child Development Institute, National Clearinghouse on Autism Evidence and Practice Review Team.

Sundberg, M. L. (2008). *Verbal behavior milestones assessment and placement program.* Concord, CA: AVB Press.

Van Houten, R., Axelrod, S., Bailey, J. S., Favell, J. E., Foxx, R. M., Iwata, B. A., & Lovaas, O. I. (1988). The right to effective behavioral treatment. *Journal of Applied Behavior Analysis, 21*(4), 381–384. <ds>https://doi.org/10.1901/jaba.1988.21-381.</ds>

Wolf, M. M. (1978). Social validity: the case for subjective measurement or how applied behavior analysis is finding its heart. *Journal of Applied Behavior Analysis, 11*(2), 203–214.

Wong, C., Odom, S. L., Hume, K. A., Cox, A. W., Fettig, A., Kucharczyk, S., Brock, M. E., Plavnick, J. B., Fleury, V. P., & Schultz, T. R. (2015). Evidence-based practices for children, youth, and young adults with autism spectrum disorder: A comprehensive review. *Journal of Autism and Developmental Disorders, 45*(7), 1951–1966. <ds>https://doi.org/10.1007/s10803-014-2351-z.</ds>

1.6   Ethics Standards Section 3
Responsibility to Clients and Stakeholders

The term *client* as used here is broadly applicable to whomever behavior analysts provide services, whether an individual person (service recipient), a parent or guardian of a service recipient, an organizational representative, a public or private organization, a firm, or a corporation.

In this chapter, we will discuss the section of the Professional and Ethical Compliance Code® related to our responsibilities to clients. How do we operate in their best interests? Are the ways in which we assume accomplishing this goal actually standing in the way?

These are not insignificant questions for those of us who provide direct clinical services. And they are questions that have always challenged behavior analysts. In his 1978 article, *Social Validity: The Case for Subjective Measurement or How Applied Behavior Analysis Is Finding Its Heart*, Montrose Wolf writes:

> Colleagues, editors, and community members were asking us about the behavioral goals that we had chosen for training the teaching-parents and the youths participating in the community-based, family-style, behavioral treatment program at Achievement Place. They would ask us: "How do you know what skills to teach? You talk about appropriate skills this and appropriate skills that. How do you know that these are really appropriate?" We, of course, tried to explain that we were psychologists and thus the most qualified judges of what was best for people. Somehow, they didn't seem convinced by that logic.
>
> (Wolf, 1978, p. 206)

In this chapter, we will be exploring the very messy process of addressing the needs of our clients rather than assuming that we know best.

3.01 Responsibility to Clients

Behavior analysts act in the best interest of clients, taking appropriate steps to support clients' rights, maximize benefits, and do no harm. They are also knowledgeable about and comply with applicable laws and regulations related to mandated reporting requirements.

Explanation

As explained in our introduction, the lowest rung on the ladder of being a "good person" or a "good behavior analyst" is following the law. Client rights under the law must be maintained. A few distinct client rights are highlighted here.

DOI: 10.4324/9781003190707-7

The right to safety. This involves not only being safe but also *feeling* safe. Clients must have access to a clinician's relevant information, including credentials and any criminal background.

The right to consent. Clients must consent both to recording and to any future uses of recording.

The right to a redress of grievances. Clients must be informed as to how to make complaints.

For each of these rights, we must not only uphold clients' rights but also explain to clients what their rights are and empower them to do the same for themselves. We cannot expect or require that clients be their own advocates without the knowledge to do so.

Considerations

There are several considerations here that are spelled out for us, making the behavioral expectations for recording sessions, sharing qualifications, and compliance with background checks clear. However, there are two aspects of how to follow that can be a bit unclear without further research.

Many practitioners may not necessarily understand their clients' rights under the law. Having provided consultation in countries where there are no laws currently in place protecting children, the standard of rights under the law becomes irrelevant. It may instead be more relevant to rely equally on two other sources: the United Nations Declaration of Human Rights and the seminal article, "The right to effective behavioral treatment" (Van Houten et al., 1988).

Within these documents, several key points are made clear. According to the United Nations, every person, regardless of their nationality, gender, sexual orientation, or any other factor, has the right to personal safety and autonomy, the right to express themselves, and the right to have fulfilling work, relationships, and leisure activities. According to Van Houten and colleagues, the responsible behavior analyst must be prepared to assist clients to access them in the most effective ways possible.

If we are to summarize the rights spelled out within these two documents, several common themes emerge. Individuals have a right to safety, to education, to autonomy, and to free expression. To uphold these rights and enable clients to execute them should be our primary goal.

Examples from the Field

Written by Ann Beirne

One example that comes up frequently in addressing the needs of young children is the use of straps on high chairs or other seating. For those of us who work in early intervention (or who have children of our own), we know the importance that these have for the safety of children while in the seats. It is important to make a distinction, however, between the use of a strap for *safety* and the use of a strap for *restraint*. If sitting is a behavioral problem, it requires a behavioral solution – first and foremost among these being the provision of adequate reinforcers when seated. Restraint neither addresses the reinforcers that maintain behavior, nor does it teach them to attend to tasks.

We are not permitted to use straps for restraint, even if the client "won't sit" and even if the parent requests it. We must remember that we are there precisely to offer these behavioral solutions.

Connections

Written by Ann Beirne

The use of unnecessary restraint by professionals is clearly unethical. But what about parents? What about the use of these safety straps or of safety harnesses and leash backpacks for parents who are concerned about elopement?

The first thing to remember in this case is that *parents are not professionals* and as such they have no obligation to adhere to our Ethics Code®. These are our requirements, not theirs. Prioritizing the ease of the session of the necessity of teaching is not the same as prioritizing safety over the time to teach. The expectations simply cannot be the same because the roles are not the same.

To the parents who find themselves relying upon safety harnesses or other specialized equipment for safety, I will often explain why I take issue with such equipment in general: it does not teach the child safety. The child does not learn how to walk safely in the street, how to stay in proximity of an adult, how to return to an adult when their name is called, or any other necessary safety skills. And then I say, "That said, I get it." Rather than an "all or nothing" approach, I encourage families to practice under safe conditions and use this equipment when necessary. We do not need to choose between safety and teaching, each can be done in their own time.

3.02 Identifying Stakeholders

Behavior analysts identify stakeholders when providing services. When multiple stakeholders (e.g., parent or legally authorized representative, teacher, principal) are involved, the behavior analyst identifies their relative obligations to each stakeholder. They document and communicate those obligations to stakeholders at the outset of the professional relationship.

Explanation

There can be many parties who might be considered to have a "stake" in the outcomes for our clients – among them may be the parents, teachers, other services providers, employers, siblings, and even peers. Our concern in this case is not only the effect that our services will have on the client, but the effect those services will have on others.

This Code element may be particularly relevant to those situations in which a behavior analyst is working for a corporate entity. A behavior analyst working for a large corporation and providing organizational behavior management services, for example, must have a clear idea of the primary beneficiary of services. In such a situation, the behavior analyst might ask themselves, "Should my suggestions benefit labor or management? Should my primary concern be employees' safety or the company's profitability?"

However, even for those of us who provide behavior-analytic services for individuals with developmental disabilities, as many of us do, the question could have multiple answers. A child, a parent, or a school could be considered clients. In this case, a determination must be made regarding who is considered the primary client, and it is this individual's benefit that must be our primary concern.

Considerations

So who exactly are we working for? That question may have a less obvious answer than we think. In some cases, the interests of one party considered to be a client may conflict with another. While teaching the skill of verbal refusal may be in the best interests of an individual client, for example, it can be complicated in a school setting.

It is in this situation that the stipulation "a hierarchy of parties must be established and communicated from the outset of the defined relationship" becomes relevant. We might also add to this stipulation that such a hierarchy must also be communicated *throughout* the defined relationship.

In addition, some situations may more clearly indicate a hierarchy than others. When we are, for example, presenting workshops or training, what is our role with respect to participants, which may include family members, students, or other professionals?

This might be considered a variant of the issues involving multiple relationships discussed in Section 1. Although we are providing a service that ultimately improves the quality of life for others, *our primary relationship is our first concern*. It is from this relationship that the hierarchy develops.

Examples from the Field

Written by Jacob Sadavoy

Who is your client? This can be confusing. Is it the learner? Center/educational institution? Insurance provider? Parents? Employee? Organization? The science? The quick answer is the learner, but that is not always the case. When you sign a contract and work for your employer, you are obligated to follow their organizational policies (within reason). This is ultimately best for the learners as they will be working in a program in which all team members are working in unison following the same rules and procedures. This can become difficult when you are faced with a center-wide intervention that counters your beliefs based on your learning history. For example, I was faced with an intervention where I was required to swab the lips of a client with hot sauce every time he aggressed. I was new to the field of ABA. I was unaware of the factors that lead to that decision. I did, however, know that I absolutely did not want to perform this intervention, and I was also aware of the challenges for the learner, to have individual consequence procedures by individual staff members. Here, my responsibility was to voice my concerns with the center, but follow through on the consented treatment procedure for aggression.

As a clinician, you are responsible for improving socially significant behaviors. But who is it that prioritizes socially significant behaviors? I worked with a student who would track his index finger as he moved it across his face from his right temple to his left temple. This learner's parents wanted this behavior reduced as did the center in which I was employed. We took partial interval data and would interrupt the behavior by providing a verbal "hands down" and a physical redirection. Some autistic self-advocates would argue that this behavior could be a means of expressing himself or a coping mechanism. Would it be socially significant for the learner? How far does a behavior analyst go in reducing behaviors that are not harmful, while taking into account that social significance is a factor of a society that stigmatizes behaviors that are not perceived as normal? It is important to review and be aware of all the various stances that inform your clinical decision-making, especially your data and research. In this example, research would support intervening, as stereotypical behaviors can increase in duration and intensity if left untreated and social validity from research targeting stereotype has shown favorable results by autistic participants (Cunningham & Schreibman, 2008; Hanley, 2010; Militerni et al., 2002; Potter et al.,

2013); It should be noted that not all stereotypical behaviors increase in duration and intensity. At this early stage in my career, and upon reflection, I realize that the intervention was misguided in that non-harmful stereotypy was a programming focus, when it should have been communication and supporting autonomy.

3.03 Accepting Clients

Behavior analysts only accept clients whose requested services are within their identified scope of competence and available resources (e.g., time and capacity for case supervision, staffing). When behavior analysts are directed to accept clients outside of their identified scope of competence and available resources, they take appropriate steps to discuss and resolve the concern with relevant parties. Behavior analysts document all actions taken in this circumstance and the eventual outcomes.

Explanation

This is very similar to our obligation to maintain professional competence, which reminds us that we must do the tasks that we can perform well, and seek out additional support if and where we feel we cannot provide services, teach, or train others. Our obligation here is very similar. There is simply no, "fake it till you make it" when the real lives of clients are at stake. Such risks *cannot* be taken.

However, in both of these Code elements, we also have some exceptions. When accepting clients, it is permissible to expand our skill set by taking on new challenges. New experiences can be undertaken, but only if the conditions for success are ensured. Simply put, we are prohibited from taking on these challenges alone. The only ethical way forward is to do so with the support and oversight of those qualified to provide training.

Considerations

The Dunning-Kruger effect is simply that those with a skill deficit are often unaware (Dunning, 2011). This deficit is often exacerbated by continuous mistakes and erroneous assertions due to ongoing ignorance as a result of not knowing what you don't know. This concept makes sense. In the field of applied behavior analysis, this could not be truer. As mentioned earlier, we discussed working within your expertise in our core principles. Knowing what client to take and what client you cannot take is based on your level of expertise. The Dunning-Kruger effect is a cautionary social psychological effect that suggests that we know less than we presume; essentially, we overestimate our competence (Dunning, 2011). So, extrapolating the Dunning-Kruger effect into practice, when assessing a new client, one should thoroughly look objectively at the projected program and ensure that you, as a clinician, can provide thoughtful, informed, and sound treatment for this prospective client. When doing this, anticipate the needs of the client and the environments in which the client will require services. Have you performed similar interventions effectively? Have you had success across similar learning environments? If you are about to take on a client who seems to differ from your typical case, it is worthwhile to explore what the difference is and whether or not the difference is within your competency to treat. As stated earlier, competency is not stagnant; it is not a quantifiable number you get upon becoming a licensed Board Certified Behavior Analyst (BCBA®) and goes unchanged throughout your career. We are obligated to enrich our experiences and improve upon our level of expertise through continuing education (CEUs) and by being aware of the latest literature in our field. Remember to follow our last core principle; *ensure competence.*

Being aware of your deficits is challenging. As a BCBA®, we often work in isolation where the only feedback we receive is from the client themselves or behavior technicians, neither of which will likely be able to offer you critical analysis of your treatment plans. A saying you have probably heard is that "that data never lies." If your client is not making gains, it could be due to a variety of reasons. One of the reasons that needs to be ruled out is that the treatment plan is the root of the ineffectiveness and perhaps the required treatment plan is outside your realm of expertise. It is best to anticipate before accepting a client whether or not it will be a fit. If, after some time, the client is not making gains, take into consideration whether another BCBA®, with different expertise would have better results.

Connections

Written by Ann Beirne

Like many people I know, I often suffer from imposter syndrome. I will often torture myself about knowing or doing enough, especially for those tasks that I really care about. Determining if a particular task is within our scope of practice can be more complicated than it seems. We must contend not only with the Dunning-Kruger effect, but also with its equally dangerous opposite.

Fortunately, our colleagues Matthew Brodhead, Shawn Quigley, and Susan Wilczynski (2018) have offered some guidance on a more objective way to determine our scope of practice. In their article, they advocate the use of fours simple questions:

- Given this behavior problem, what is my level of confidence in procedures and strategies, populations, and settings?
- What is my level of confidence in treatment success, based on my past experiences, familiarity with the literature, and available resources?
- How similar is this situation to my past experiences and available resources and the conditions and characteristics of participants described in the literature?
- Considering the answers to these questions, what is my level of competence (Brodhead, Quigley & Wilczynski, 2018)?

Addressing each of these questions can lead us to an answer that relies on objective information rather than our own faulty judgment.

Examples from the Field

Written by Jacob Sadavoy

All behavior therapists need to analyze their own competence and assess whether they can effectively provide a behavior-analytic program when presented with a new client. There are not many clinicians who have had the opportunity to provide sustainable international telehealth behavior-analytic services. As such, a BCBA-D™ or a well-published clinician, who may have vast experiences providing behavior-analytic services in North America, could find themselves not possessing the expertise required to create a behavior-analytic program for a client in an under-resourced area outside their continent. Just a few things to consider would be ways to build capacity and engage stakeholders, learning what is considered socially significant in an unfamiliar culture, and knowing where to start in order for the staff to build behavior-analytic skills to promote sustainability. These considerations would not be common in the typical North American work environment. Had that client been in North America, a BCBA-D™ or a well-published clinician would have been within their level of competence to provide ABA strategies. Extrapolating those experiences and presuming competence internationally would be erroneous.

Once upon a time, I flirted with the idea of a career change into the field of organizational behavior management (OBM). I was attracted to the challenge of taking the concepts that I have used with students and applying them to organizational systems. I took a six-month course which supported my fascination. I was ready. I changed my resume to reflect competency as an OBM practitioner and was ready to pound the online pavement. I started getting interviews. That is when it dawned on me that even though I had taken a six-month course and was competent applying the principles of ABA in an educational, home, community, or clinical setting, I did not have the expertise assessing performance metrics to a company's mission or shifting communication processes and feedback to ensure staff meets performance goals. It became clear that I would need a mentor and that I would need to volunteer in order to gain the experience that I needed in order to competently work as a responsible OBMer. Personally, the volunteer experience and mentoring were invaluable and now, I am able to practice OBM responsibly thanks to the six-month course, volunteer experience, mentoring, and staying informed by reading the latest OBM publications.

3.04 Service Agreement

Before implementing services, behavior analysts ensure that there is a signed service agreement with the client and/ or relevant stakeholders outlining the responsibilities of all parties, the scope of behavioral services to be provided, the behavior analyst's obligations under the Code, and procedures for submitting complaints about a behavior analyst's professional practices to relevant entities (e.g., BACB, service organization, licensure board, funder). They update service agreements as needed or as required by relevant parties (e.g., service organizations, licensure boards, funders). Updated service agreements must be reviewed with and signed by the client and/or relevant stakeholders.

Explanation

It has been said that honesty is the best policy. In this case it is not only honesty but the clarity that comes with honesty that we must also prize in order to be considered ethical professionals. Service agreements, regularly updated, signed by all parties, and reviewed periodically can prevent disagreements and conflicts, as well as uncomfortable situations.

Considerations

In contracts with clients, it is wise to include a paragraph outlining what to do if they have a complaint with a BCBA's® service. It is important to share this information, in the beginning of a professional relationship, so the client is aware that there are consequences for the supervising BCBA®, for being negligent in their duties. It also provides an opportunity to discuss the BACB® and the behavior analyst's ethical Code; two things that should be known to clients. Prospective clients are bombarded with options and therapies for services. It is important that we as a science ensure that we are informing clients of their rights regarding procedures and inform them how to lodge complaints about professional practices. This will provide a stark contrast from the competition by demonstrating credibility and assurance of services for the client.

Examples from the Field

Written by Ann Beirne

There have been many times over the years that I have been asked to do things I was not comfortable with. And, without a written justification to point to, I was often considered "rigid" and asked to "be flexible" during times that I felt there had to be limits.

A written agreement would have clarified and prevented this from happening. Potentially contentious conversations regarding the appropriateness of a behavior analyst being alone in the home with the client and no caregiver, administering medicine, or when to begin a behavior plan could have been avoided. Even a dispute as simple as whether or not I would be expected to work on the weekends or holidays could have been resolved easily.

Written agreements can resolve these issues before they start – when they are resolved most easily.

3.05 Financial Agreements

Before beginning services, behavior analysts document agreed-upon compensation and billing practices with their clients, relevant stakeholders, and/or funders. When funding circumstances change, they must be revisited with these parties. Pro bono and bartered services are only provided under a specific service agreement and in compliance with the Code.

Explanation

Document, document, document. With respect to financial agreements, remuneration must be stipulated, and that includes timeliness, rate, and re-evaluation after which the contract is set to expire contingent on achieving goals or termination of services. Having this information available in the beginning of the relationship allows the client or supervisee to know what the expectations are and, if there are disagreements related to pay, the contract or service agreement can be referenced for clarification and resolution.

If funding circumstances change, it is critical that a conversation happens immediately and a new service agreement is agreed upon before any changes can be made to the financial arrangement. Under no circumstances can a rate change without a signed agreement.

Considerations

Many behavior analysts been asked how much is the going rate for services, for a one-off FBA, for supervision, etc. There does not exist a centralized place for one to get this information and for good reason. There are many factors that go into a rate-for-service, such as: years of experience, state or provincial norms, nature of relationship, resources, direct-care versus service oversight, environment, and responsibilities. As a result of all of these factors, a behavior analyst must make a decision not to undersell or oversell their services.

Three considerations follow. First, an agreement could stipulate that fees can change based on changes in the scope of competence or practice. Second, despite one's years of service in the field of applied behavior analysis, if a practitioner is new to applying behavior-analytic principles with a new clientele or industry, the rate they are accustomed to would likely be different. Third, it is encouraged that schedules and late penalties are also drafted in the contract. It is important to promote timeliness in the relationship for all parties involved.

Examples from the Field

Written by Jacob Sadavoy

I entered a situation in which I agreed to work with a supervisee, on a temporary basis, until he secured another supervisor (I was the supervisor who oversaw his Registered Behavior Technician® competency assessment). My rationale for doing so was due to his financial situation, a national BCBA was available to supervise him in a couple of months, and the challenges of working internationally (with limited access to supervisors) of which alternatives were overpriced and would likely not be culturally responsive as most North American supervisors had not worked in his part of the world. The BCBA who was set to work with him was delayed and I was obligated, based on my supervisory contract, to continue supervision without a stipulated financial arrangement. This is not workable and sets a poor precedent for someone who is just starting in the field. Eventually, the supervisor that was scheduled to work with him did so, but that relationship lasted three months and then left the agency; a reality of international dissemination with current supervisory structures. The situation could have been averted if there had been a clearly defined contract in place with a completed, agreed upon section for remuneration.

Under similar circumstances, someone may find themselves doing a favor for a client as opposed to a supervisee. This cannot be done, and should it be a stopgap, make sure the duration of the relationship is stipulated in the contract along with responsibilities, with a clear understanding that the rate of behavior-analytic services should not be charitable, as this creates a power imbalance that can have deleterious effects on the relationship. For example, a supervisee or a client who is receiving services for a lesser fee may be less inclined to voice dissatisfaction in an effort to maintain a lower cost of service. This would not allow for an informed, collaborative program.

3.06 Consulting with Other Providers

Behavior analysts arrange for appropriate consultation with and referrals to other providers in the best interests of their clients, with appropriate informed consent, and in compliance with applicable requirements (e.g., laws, regulations, contracts, organization and funder policies).

Explanation

Within each of the sections of this Code element, there are two things to consider: when to seek out and cooperate with consultants and when not to.

Behavior analysts, while they are expected to have some level of competence, are not expected to be omniscient. Challenges may arise in the course of our work that necessitate an outside observer, and it is our obligation to seek this out when necessary. When such referrals are made, it is our obligation to work collaboratively for the client's benefit.

There should be some limits, however, to our willingness to make such referrals as well as our willingness to collaborate. These referrals must be made in the best interests of the client and must be done openly, honestly, and within the boundaries of our other responsibilities. In addition, our cooperation must be within certain limits. When seeking consultation or collaborating with those who provide such consultation, we are behavior analysts first and foremost and must adhere to our other professional and ethical obligations. These include our responsibility to rely on scientific knowledge in making recommendations. Although other fields may not have similar ethical requirements, we must consider these obligations when working with others.

Considerations

Collaborating with professionals from other fields can frequently be challenging for behavior analysts, since behavior analysts view behaviorism not simply as a job, but as an overriding philosophy. Behavior analysis after all is a science, and as such it is not something to *do*, but something to *understand*.

While it may be tempting to examine all decisions through the narrow lens of what is right or wrong, it is important to acknowledge that each professional from each field brings expertise. It would further behoove us to remember that each profession has its own ethical standards and that "different" is not necessarily synonymous with "wrong."

This will be further explored in an upcoming chapter, *The Behavior Analyst and the Team*.

Examples from the Field

Written by Jacob Sadavoy

Oftentimes, my client will request that I collaborate with other professionals on the team whose goals overlap (e.g., communication with a speech and language pathologist, bike riding with an occupational therapist, behavior change with a prescribing physician, etc.). In all these situations I must do a few things. First, written informed consent for sharing information must be documented. A BCBA® cannot honor requests to share information if the request is informal. For example, if the parent starts a group text or provides an ABA practitioner with an email introduction connecting you with a related service professional. In that consent, I would like to stipulate the basis of the communication. I have been in situations in which a school team member was sharing concerns about the client's parents decisions. I was able to reference the contract and ensure that all communication was centered around our mutual client. Secondly, it is in the clients best interest for the collaboration to be fruitful so, I make sure I provide a lot of reinforcement, I speak colloquially, and I listen (and by listen, I am listening to learn not to simply wait for my turn to speak). Thirdly, I ask the client if they want to be invited and involved in the conversations. There is great value in transparency.

3.07 Third-Party Contracts for Services

When behavior analysts enter into a signed contract to provide services to a client at the request of a third party (e.g., school district, governmental entity), they clarify the nature of the relationship with each party and assess any potential conflicts before services begin. They ensure that the contract outlines (1) the responsibilities of all parties, (2) the scope of behavioral services to be provided, (3) the likely use of the information obtained, (4) the behavior analysts' obligations under the Code, and (5) any limits about maintaining confidentiality. Behavior analysts are responsible for amending contracts as needed and reviewing them with the relevant parties at that time.

Explanation

Here, again, we have a situation in which honesty *and clarity* become the best policies. And again, dealing with these potential conflicts before they happen is the best way to address them.

Clients and client surrogates must always be aware of what to expect from behavioral services: of their rights and the responsibilities of behavior analysts and other parties. As these circumstances change, written agreements must be changed to reflect that.

Considerations

One of the more complex aspects of the "new normal" in which we find ourselves in the aftermath of 2020 is the growth of telehealth and its impact on the field. As the distinction between "work" and "home" have become blurred by the increased frequency of working from home, we may find ourselves with newfound limits to confidentiality.

The potential risks of telehealth must always be explained and clients and clients' surrogates must give written consent to engage in telehealth. Precautions in the use of platforms must be adhered to. Be sure to use only HIPAA compliant platforms for communication and for service provision.

Examples from the Field

Written by Ann Beirne

I have been fortunate enough to work for some wonderful organizations over the years (and, certainly, some that were less so). Though, even in situations where I felt a profound sense of loyalty to my employer, my loyalty was always split, and it was always the client who was favored.

I remember I was once at a meeting at one of those wonderful organizations and we were discussing pendency, an aspect of education law that could be used to advocate for services to continue after a student had aged out. "Don't tell parents about this," we were urged.

Despite my loyalty to this agency, I immediately planned my rebellion. I would tell *every* parent about this. Maybe I would get T-shirts made…

It turned out that there was good reason to be cautious. Pendency was a good option for some clients, but not all clients. When used as designed – to avoid disruption until a decision can be made and appropriate placement can be found – it can keep progress going and prevent regression. But my rebellion became tempered with caution, and as new high-quality programs began to grow in number, I encouraged parents to consider all options.

Our first obligation is to the client. Wherever that obligation may lead us.

3.08 Responsibility to the Client with Third-Party Contracts for Services

Behavior analysts place the client's care and welfare above all others. If the third party requests services from the behavior analyst that are incompatible with the behavior analyst's recommendations, that are outside of the behavior analyst's scope of competence, or that could result in a multiple relationship, behavior analysts resolve such conflicts in the best interest of the client. If a conflict cannot be resolved, the behavior analyst may obtain additional training or consultation, discontinue services following appropriate transition measures, or refer the client to another behavior analyst. Behavior analysts document all actions taken in this circumstance and the eventual outcomes.

Explanation

In addition to the organizational flow chart of various responsibilities mentioned earlier, it is imperative that behavior analysts clarify a distinct hierarchy: the client's needs supersede any others. We cannot allow our egos, professional relationships, or eagerness to please allow us to make decisions that would – even inadvertently – place them in harm's way.

This element does, however, allow us to collaborate ethically by obtaining necessary training or by transitioning to the services of another professional if necessary. And, as always, we must document our efforts at working through these conflicts.

Considerations

It is always important to remember that, whether we are discussing individual clients, service agencies, or corporate entities, everyone comes to a situation with their own distinct responsibilities. The client's family is responsible primarily for the safety and care of the client and any other concern is secondary (often by a wide margin). Our obligation is to our ethical practice and we are required to follow this Code. An agency or corporate entity is accountable to state agencies in the case of a nonprofit organization and may be accountable to investors if such an organization is for-profit. While these may be different responsibilities, it is important that each be acknowledged.

In the case of conflict, it is essential that the behavior analyst prioritize the needs of the client while also acknowledging the responsibilities of other parties. Without understanding the perspectives of each side, any negotiation becomes impossible.

Examples from the Field

Written by Jacob Sadavoy

I had submitted a reauthorization assessment for a client who had made wonderful gains. Based on the data which showed zero occurrences of the targeted challenging behaviors over several months coupled with an ongoing successful school integration transition plan (in which the therapist was only present twice a month), I recommended discharge. My employer had shared that they would like me to change that recommendation to get a mandate for another six months of services. The rationale was that he may need assistance when his teacher changes in the following school year and a "reauthorization is easier to get than putting in a new claim in September." Am I responsible for the client (where assigning a shadow could adversely affect his dignity, socialization skills, and independence) or the employer? Is the employer acting in the best interest of the client or the insurance provider? It was commonplace for reports to be returned or altered based on the needs of the individual's insurance provider. Is this to maximize hours? Is that in the learner's best interest? Insurance has given access to ABA services to learners that would not have had it otherwise. However, we must be mindful and ensure that our reports and practice are not shaped by the whims of the insurance provider who are a third party and whose interests may not be aligned with your clinical recommendations.

In many cases, the third party's preference is for the clinician to do a job as quickly as possible. While working in Nigeria, I was working with a clinician who did a masterful job supporting a student's transition to school. His behaviors, that were impeding his ability to be successful in the classroom, had reduced greatly and we were discussing a gradual and systematic fade-out procedure. Unfortunately, that was compromised in support of an immediate fade out. The clinician is responsible for the client's successful inclusion. She did the correct thing by voicing her concerns, providing an alternative, and sharing that she would try to be available if the challenging behaviors reoccurred. Unfortunately, they did.

Stipulating your clinical and ethical needs in a contract with a third party is essential. Anticipate what resources and time you will need and have that agreed upon before investing in the case.

3.09 Communicating with Stakeholders About Third-Party Contracted Services

When providing services at the request of a third party to a minor or individual who does not have the legal right to make personal decisions, behavior analysts ensure that the parent or legally authorized representative is informed of the rationale for and scope of services to be provided, as well as their right to receive copies of all service documentation and data. Behavior analysts are knowledgeable about and comply with all requirements related to informed consent, regardless of who requested the services.

Explanation

There are two relationships to be considered when discussing the Code element: the relationship with the client and the relationship with another entity.

It has been said that "too many cooks spoil the broth." If there are several parties involved in the provision of services, it can be confusing to consumers who exactly is in charge and what recommendations to follow. It is essential therefore to bring as much clarity to these roles as possible. It may be helpful to clarify, in writing, the roles of each entity at the start of service. This can be easily incorporated into a contract. A simple "phone tree" listing the people responsible for various areas that clarifies which types of questions they are most able to answer can work wonders for providing this clarity for consumers.

When considering the relationship with another party, clarity also goes a long way. A contract here is required which includes the responsibilities of all parties involved. The negotiation of this contract is a good opportunity to clarify your commitment to the Ethics Code®.

Honesty with all parties is the best policy in this case, and can often prevent later problems.

Considerations

It is clear from the research on intensive behavioral programs for individuals with autism spectrum disorder that parent training is a component in the most successful programs. It is little wonder, therefore, that insurance companies often require that parents training be a part of a treatment plan.

Because of the parent training component, we are often the professionals with the most "face time" with the clients. Though they may receive other therapies or services from other professionals, these professionals do not necessarily have the time to discuss recommendations or goals, and may not have the same relationship with parents that we do.

Therefore, it may take considerable effort for us to remain within our scope of competence. We may have to be persistent in our communication with other professionals, and clear with parents as to what questions we can and cannot answer.

Examples from the Field

Written by Ann Beirne

I started working for a large company where I knew several people, all of whom were extremely competent and each of whom worked in different departments. I had friendly relationships with each and I knew that, as I adjusted, any would be happy to answer my questions.

Still, it was one friend at that company whose advice was the most helpful. She said simply, "Let me tell you who to talk to about what."

We cannot assume that clients or families will know who is capable of answering what kind of question. Simply telling them, "Let me tell you who to talk to about what" can avoid frustration and allow us to remain within our scope of competence and our job responsibilities.

3.10 Limitations of Confidentiality

Behavior analysts inform clients and stakeholders of the limitations of confidentiality at the outset of the professional relationship and when information disclosures are required.

Explanation

Behavior analysts are expected to maintain the confidentiality of their clients, but as was explained in previous chapters, this commitment to protecting confidentiality cannot come at the expense of client safety or the safety of the public.

Clients must be made aware of our commitment to client safety above all else.

Considerations

Communication is an essential aspect of our role as behavior analysts. Not only must we be equipped with adequate communication skills, we must also have the technology to use them.

Email should be encrypted to avoid client information falling into the wrong hands. Texting and phone calls would not be considered secure and should be avoided if possible. Certainly voicemails and messages should not include any identifying information.

In the "information age" everything has changed about the way we communicate and, like any responsible professional, behavior analysts must change with the times. We must be aware of the limitations of the platforms we use and the potential for client information to be compromised.

Examples From the Field

Written by Ann Beirne

I am a fan of texting. I enjoy a good emoji (or better still an amusing gif or meme) showing up on my phone and it is certainly a fun and easy way to communicate with family and friends.

With clients, however, texting has simply too many pitfalls. The potential of misuse of information is too great. If possible, I prefer to avoid it. But there are times when this is a family's preferred mode of communication. What to do then?

Fortunately, the medical field has also dealt with this phenomenon and several apps are available that allow for texting that remains compliant with medical privacy laws. This simple adjustment allows a compromise between ease of communication and our ethical obligations.

3.11 Documenting Professional Activity

Throughout the service relationship, behavior analysts create and maintain detailed and high-quality documentation of their professional activities to facilitate provision of services by them or by other professionals, to ensure accountability, and to meet applicable requirements (e.g., laws, regulations, funder and organization policies). Documentation must be created and maintained in a manner that allows for timely communication and transition of services, should the need arise.

Explanation

There are several aspects of these Code elements that behavior analysts must be aware of. This Code element, rather than simply stating a behavioral expectation of, explains the rationale behind it. Documentation is not simply for its own sake, but plays a pivotal role in the work that we do.

To facilitate the continued provision of services. In order to ensure that services are continued in our absence, it is important to have contingency plans in place. If the behavior analyst is unable to continue on the case for whatever reason, the client's right to effective treatment remains intact. Behavior analysts must ensure that services can be continued with some degree of fidelity in their absence.

To ensure accountability. Throughout the Ethics Code®, the responsibility of behavior analysts is to provide services of the highest quality possible. It is only through consistent and well-maintained documentation that we can ensure such responsibilities are upheld.

To meet other requirements of organization or the law. Many organizations, including educational or health care agencies, will have specific requirements that must be adhered to. These regulations may deal with legal issues, such as insurance or Medicaid regulations, and the repercussions of their violation could be serious. It is the obligation of the behavior analyst to understand such regulations and to follow them to the greatest extent possible. As always, it is best to research the information needed rather than guess. Be sure to ask compliance officers, immediate supervisors, or colleagues with more experience about the specific legal requirements at your fieldwork site.

Considerations

How much documentation would be considered "enough"? This particular Code element does allow for some interpretation on this point. Though the requirement to provide documentation as required by law may provide some guidance, it is certainly not expansive enough to fulfill the other requirements of this Code element.

When considering the appropriate amount of documentation, it is helpful to describe the concept of "enough" as behavior analysts describe many other concepts – by function, rather than the topography of what a correct volume of document might look like. Rather than taking data out of habit, it is perhaps best to occasionally revisit the role that data serves in our clinical work. To review what has been detailed in a previous chapter, data collection has a few essential elements:

Data must be taken. Though this may seem simple, simple is very rarely the same as easy. Is data being collected on a regular basis as recommended? Is the system clear and simple enough for others to collect data in our absence? Is the complexity of the system such that accuracy is being sacrificed? In order for data collection systems to give us the necessary information to move forward, these systems must work effectively to collect such information.

Data must be looked at and analyzed. Who is examining the data and how often? Are those direct service providers also advised to look for patterns in the trends of data? If patterns indicating progress are not evident, are they knowledgeable in what to look for so that they can ask for help? Data must never be taken only to be sent into a black hole. It must be monitored, so that trends in progress – or lack thereof – can be detected.

Data must be used to modify behavior-change programs. This is the final, and perhaps most important requirement of any data collection system. The information that is gained and shared through our data collection systems must inform our programming. All programmatic changes must be based on this data collection system and our review of the trends of the data. Ours is the science of behavior change, and our programming must always move forward.

Data must accomplish these three goals. However, anything beyond this is subject to other factors, including agency required practices, financial and human resources, and the preferences of the behavior analyst. Whether data is collected daily, weekly, or even less frequently, these requirements must be adhered to. There is considerable freedom in the way in which we collect and analyze, as long as we retain the ability to make data-based decisions.

Examples from the Field

Written by Jacob Sadavoy

I have been in situations in which outstanding documentation needed to be recreated because of disorganization (e.g., I had to wait months to collect my supervisee experience forms from a supervisor from a previous agency). As a result of this experience, and anecdotes from others of similar challenges, I am extremely timely when it comes to documentation and feedback. For me, not naturally an organized person, it helps ensure that documentation does not fall through the cracks. The last thing I want to do is rely on my memory for notes. Another beneficial byproduct of being diligent around documentation is to effectively model the importance of the relationship between a BCBA® and paperwork. By positively pairing case notes, reports, and data with positive outcomes, your client may have a greater likelihood of contacting all three more intimately, or even collect their own generalization data outside of sessions.

For clients, documentation is critical. It is your way of making claims to advance the program forward. Without supporting documentation or data, recommendations are subjective and in the world of behavior analysis, worthless. I reference the assessment, data, clinical notes, and sometimes even the service agreement, periodically, as a reminder for clients to appreciate and access the foundation in which I deliver service. If anything is challenged, it is now normalized to refer back to the assessment, data, clinical notes, or the service agreement.

3.12 Advocating for Appropriate Services

Behavior analysts advocate for and educate clients and stakeholders about evidence-based assessment and behavior change intervention procedures. They also advocate for the appropriate amount and level of behavioral service provision and oversight required to meet defined client goals.

Explanation

As behavior analysts, it is our responsibility to ensure that the behavior-change programs that we design are set up for success. Part of acknowledging the importance of our work is making sure that we allow for the proper time and resources needed to accomplish the goals of our program. In order to do this, we must have both clearly defined goals and clearly explained conditions that are necessary to meet them.

Make sure that the oversight you propose will be ongoing. Leave nothing to chance in the implementation of behavior-change programs and allow more time than you think will be necessary for training and supervision of those responsible for carrying out programs. You may be surprised by what people have difficulty getting used to when it comes to implementation. A bit of planning can go a long way in the successful implementation of behavior-change programs.

Considerations

How much applied behavior analysis would be considered "enough?" In his 1987 study, Lovaas described what is often considered the standard for "intensive" programming by stating,

> Each subject in the experimental group was assigned several well trained student therapists who worked (part-time) with the subject in the subject's home, school, and community for an average of 40 hr per week for 2 or more years. The parents worked as part of the treatment team throughout the intervention; they were extensively trained in the treatment procedures so that treatment could take place for almost all of the subjects' waking hours, 365 days a year.

(Lovaas, 1987)

In this study, there were two experimental groups: one which received more eclectic special education services and one that, because they lived too far from the center for a home program to be adequately staffed, received ten hours a week of services (Lovaas, 1987). This study was historic in its impact on the field, since it offered (or perhaps more accurately, popularized) a treatment option to families that had not been readily available. Eikeseth, Smith Jahr, and Eldevik (2007) also explored the effects of intensive programming and found similar effects, even for children who were elementary school age. But perhaps a better explanation of what would constitute "enough" behavior analysis is explained by Dr. Bobby Newman (2002) who, when asked how many hours are needed, replies, "all of them." As addressed in a previous chapter, applied behavior is not a treatment, and is not a set of practices. It is instead a science, and as such it is not something that one can do or not do. It is instead something that we come to *understand*. When this science becomes a guiding principle of our programming, the approach informs all programmatic decisions.

Examples from the Field

Written by Jacob Sadavoy

A client will be prescribed an appropriate amount and level of service based on the results of the client's assessment and behavior-change program needs. Personally, when making a decision of this nature, I will often refer back to the literature. Prescribing too few service delivery hours may compromise the client's gains by not providing enough opportunities for the student to learn. Prescribing too many service delivery errors would be an inefficient use of resources and time. Thus, it is important to take into account a multitude of variables in the hopes of procuring an appropriate number of hours of behavior-analytic services per week.

I once consulted at a small center-based program, which would recommend the number of service hours they could provide based on their schedule. This is problematic for several reasons. First, the number of service hours must be based on the clients' needs and not the needs of the program. Second, if the client needs 30 hours per week of ABA but is being prescribed 10 based on availability and center capacity, the likelihood is that the gains made by the client will be limited by not having an appropriate number of clinical hours. Now, if the assessment called for 30 hours, but the client was only receiving 10, then one could come to the conclusion that the client needed more applied behavior analysis. However, since the report suggests 10 hours, which is what he is receiving, the minimal gains made will be a reflection of the program or the center which would be a false assertion if one had all the facts. Lastly, the perception of a client who needs 30 hours of services per week vs. 10 hours per week would be vastly different. The parents and receiving school will get an inaccurate profile and minimize the clinical support required.

It should also be acknowledged that the opposite scenario is also problematic. Some programs may feel it is best to maximize the number of service delivery hours (i.e., have the client receive clinical services for as many hours as can be authorized). This is inaccurate reporting and demonstrates a greater need for services than necessary which would be dishonest.

3.13 Referrals

Behavior analysts make referrals based on the needs of the client and/or relevant stakeholders and include multiple providers when available. Behavior analysts disclose to the client and relevant stakeholders any relationships they have with potential providers, and fees or incentives they may receive for the referrals. They document any referrals made, including relevant relationships and fees or incentives received, and make appropriate efforts to follow up with the client and/or relevant stakeholders.

Explanation

Here again we are reminded that the client's individual needs must be our primary concern. As with many of the Code elements, this is cautionary. We are not instructed not to make referrals, only to make sure that such referrals are made in the best interests of the client, rather than our own. And here again, honest and open communication is the prevention that is worth a pound of cure.

Considerations

The need for qualified providers, it seems, is always greater than the number of qualified staff available. Many human resources departments have responded to this by incentivizing referrals from current employees. What they offered was an incentive for clinicians to recruit friends and colleagues. An employee who made a referral would receive a stipend once the clinician they referred had been employed for six months. Would this be considered an ethical violation?

It is important here to consider the "why" of the rule in order to determine if an ethical violation has been made. Who is this element designed to protect and how does it ensure that they are protected?

It might be helpful here to use an illustrative example. If a behavior analyst were to receive a referral fee each time a referral was made to an occupational therapist, for example, this behavior analyst may refer all of their cases to this occupational therapist, regardless of the clients' needs. If the behavior analyst maintained another relationship with this occupational therapist without disclosing this relationship to the clients, referrals may be made that would lead to personal gain. Even if such referrals were made in the best interests of the clients, it would be difficult to avoid the appearance of impropriety.

The needs of our clients must always be our primary concern – this is the cornerstone of the Ethics Code®. Certainly a person-to-person agreement between independent providers, which compromises this ideal, would be in violation of it. If an agreement with another provider leads to decisions that may not be in their best interests, this should be avoided.

However, referring a colleague (or even a friend or relative) for employment at an agency where you work has several important distinctions from such an example. The referral in this case would be to the agency rather than a specific client. The agency could then assign cases based on the specific clients' needs. Rather than a referral that has no basis in the needs of the client or the skills of the therapist, we adhere to the requirement that referrals be based on the alignment of both factors. In addition, agencies offering this incentive would likely receive more than one referral, which would additionally meet the requirement that multiple options be presented. The specific assignments of clinicians to clients can reflect both of these factors.

While such business practices may raise important questions to be asked, the questions themselves are not necessarily indicators of wrongdoing. Remembering both the details of the Code element and the rationale behind it can allow us to see more clearly.

Examples from the Field

Written by Jacob Sadavoy

I imagine many clinicians have been in the situation in which you have to refer a client to another BCBA® or a related-service professional. Personally, I have not come across a situation in which money, gifts, or other inappropriate forms of gratitude were exchanged between clinicians for a referral. However, I have worked in an environment in which parents could get a psychological, speech, behavioral, and occupational therapeutic assessment all under one roof. That roof also contained an intensive behavior intervention program as well as a private school that focused on speech-related clinical needs and small class sizes. Naturally, recommendations from that report would often lead parents to one of the two programs. This can be seen as unethical. A way to be able to offer assessments and clinical programs in the same location is to ensure that there are multiple referral options made based on objective determination of the client's needs based on the assessment. This can prove to be challenging for facilities in smaller populated communities that do not have multiple options for programming in the area. If that is the case, I would inform the client of this limitation.

If you are a behavior analyst, your decisions should be based on the individual needs of your client. Clinicians are obligated to provide their rationale for referrals, which should be based on the individual needs of your client coupled with why you anticipate a match with the referred clinician. In all cases, try to make an effort to provide multiple options. This can be difficult especially if you are taking into consideration the individual needs of your client and foresee a fit with a specific clinician. Even if you foresee an optimal match, it is best to provide multiple referrals whenever possible to ensure that your client has choices.

3.14 Facilitating Continuity of Services

Behavior analysts act in the best interests of the client to avoid interruption or disruption of services. They make appropriate and timely efforts to facilitate the continuation of behavioral services in the event of planned interruptions (e.g., relocation, temporary leave of absence) and unplanned interruptions (e.g., illness, funding disruption, parent request, emergencies). They ensure that service agreements or contracts include a general plan of action for service interruptions. When a service interruption occurs, they communicate to all relevant parties the steps being taken to facilitate continuity of services. Behavior analysts document all actions taken in this circumstance and the eventual outcomes.

Explanation

In previous iterations of our ethical Code, our obligation was simply stated, "Behavior analysts do not abandon clients." Whether that abandonment be short or long term, it should be avoided at all costs.

Behavior analysts must expect that they will take vacations, sick days, and personal time and prepare for such eventualities. With enough preparation, behavior analysts can continue services smoothly and return to a well-run program even in their absence.

Considerations

It is important that behavior analysts prepare not only for expected breaks, but for the unexpected as well. Be mindful that disruptions in service can happen for any number of reasons, and only some of these are within our control.

Here we have a strong argument for family involvement. If family members are able to continue with behavioral programming during a disruption of services, then services will not be disrupted after all. Empowerment of the families to continue on their own creates the environmental support that allows our clients to thrive.

Examples from the Field

Written by Ann Beirne

For many service providers, the Covid-19 pandemic and the lockdowns that resulted from it were a rude awakening. We were ready to prepare for a long weekend, for vacations, or for a maternity leave. But when a sudden two-week disruption came with no notice, and when that two weeks turned into months, we were forced to examine what "prepared" really looked like.

For myself, I realized that I needed to put greater emphasis on three things: generalization, parent empowerment, and social validity.

If the skills I had taught had not generalized so that the client had learned to perform these skills without my presence, then how had my presence benefited them at all? If the parents were not able to continue to provide teaching in my absence, then how have I helped them? And finally, if I had not been teaching goals that the client would deem "important" – skills they would be practicing and using everyday – then how were my priorities in sync with their needs?

Preparation involves more than a list of responsibilities. It involves a philosophical approach toward empowering clients to move on.

3.15 Appropriately Discontinuing Services

Behavior analysts include the circumstances for discontinuing services in their service agreement. They consider discontinuing services when: (1) the client has met all behavior-change goals, (2) the client is not benefiting from the service, (3) the behavior analyst and/or their supervisees or trainees are exposed to potentially harmful conditions that cannot be reasonably resolved, (4) the client and/or relevant stakeholder requests discontinuation, (5) the relevant stakeholders are not complying with the behavior-change intervention despite appropriate efforts to address barriers, or (6) services are no longer funded. Behavior analysts provide the client and/or relevant stakeholders with a written plan for discontinuing services, document acknowledgment of the plan, review the plan throughout the discharge process, and document all steps taken.

Explanation

Target behaviors must be clarified at the outset of treatment and the criteria set for the mastery of these goals. Criteria for the reduction of services or the transfer of oversight to others must also be included. We must begin every case with a plan to let go.

Our goal as behavior analysts is to "work ourselves out of a job." There will certainly always be new goals to be taught and new challenges for the client to meet, but rather than expecting that we will be their constant support, we must empower the client to meet those challenges on their own.

Connections

Written by Ann Beirne

For those of us in the field of autism treatment, this particular Code element seems counterintuitive. The notion of "success" in the education of individuals with autism is often considered a moving target. Each step forward brings with it a new set of goals to be worked on and lessons to be learned. If we understand "autism spectrum disorder" as the referral problem, it may stand to reason that the only possible measurable criteria for discontinuation would be if an individual no longer meets the description of the diagnosis.

Although the diagnostic label of autism includes the word "disorder," Baron-Cohen (2017) argues that this distinction may not be warranted. Autism is often referred to as a "disability"; however, this label can also be considered functional (Baron-Cohen, 2017). "Disability" suggests that an individual requires support in order to function in a given environment (Baron-Cohen, 2017). Baron-Cohen (2017) writes, "If someone is tone-deaf, that is only a disability in a situation where the person is expected to sing." Expanding on the quote attributed to Einstein, a fish will appear as having a disability if required to climb a tree. And to expand on the quote attributed to a person with autism, "We are fresh water fish in salt water. Put us in fresh water and we are fine. Put us in salt water and we struggle to survive." "Difference," on the other hand, implies that an individual may be different in some way than is typical, but that this difference does not impede their ability to function (Baron-Cohen, 2017).

Our responsibility, therefore, is not necessarily to ensure that an individual with autism can be "indistinguishable from peers" (Lovaas, 1987). Rather, our responsibility is to support behavior change that will allow them to function in environments in which they are accepted and have as much choice and self-determination as possible. Autism spectrum disorder is not necessarily a referral problem, or indeed a problem at all. Rather, it is the behavioral deficits and excesses which impede an individual's full inclusion in their community that must be addressed. Our goals must reflect the goals of the individual. To expand on the metaphor attributed to Einstein, our goal should not necessarily be to teach a fish to climb a tree, but to help them to be the best swimmers they can be and increase their access to more welcoming water.

It is necessary for behavior analysts to develop clear and measurable goals, aligned with the goals of the client and/or client surrogate and for our programming to reflect the target behaviors that will indicate the accomplishment of these goals. I often say to students of behavior analysis, "In applied behavior analysis, we *can* teach *anything*, but that doesn't mean that we *should* teach *everything*."

Considerations

There is a delicate balance to be struck between adherence to our obligation to discontinue services that are no longer needed and our obligation to make these transitions as smooth as possible. Discontinuation of services should not be avoided for the sake of teaching what does not need to be taught. However, it should also not be entered lightly.

Determining if the goal of treatment has been met may mean looking beyond the data-based criterion and addressing the practical results for which we had hoped. Cooper, Heron, and Heward's definition of validity as it relates to data refers to the relevance of a given measure to the behavior of interest (Cooper et al., 2007). Wolf's definition of social validity addresses the importance of the given goal within an individual's community and the acceptability of all results (Wolf, 1978).

One tactic useful here would be to combine these two definitions and determine if the stated goal of the intervention is one that has addressed the presented need. A "valid" result would be one that is not only reflected by data which is relevant to the target, but also reflects social importance. However, it is equally important that the results of intervention themselves address the referral problem. If improvement is noted, this must make an impact on the problems identified in the assessment process. These "practical results" that serve as a definition of a program's effectiveness (Baer et al., 1968) must be reflected in the story that the data tells. Programming must address not only the targeted behavior, but also the socially significant impact of the target behavior.

Examples from the Field

Written by Jacob Sadavoy

I was working in a school and, to this day, question the discharge plan for three clients in the same school year.

Student A engaged in no challenging behaviors that impeded his learning. He was sometimes rude to his teachers, but that was largely due to his thirst for knowledge and being frustrated that he was in a classroom with students who had challenges accessing the curriculum for a variety of reasons related to the learning environment. This student demonstrated the prerequisite skills needed to be successful in a regular education placement; socially he may struggle, but he certainly wasn't getting the social exposure he needed from his current classmates. The parents were concerned about bullying in a regular education placement and preferred that he stayed in a sheltered, center-based program. The client's data demonstrated that he is neither needing the service nor benefiting from the service. You could make an argument that impeding his socialization skills is causing unjustified harm by continued services. It is difficult to discharge a client if the parents are adamantly against the decision but I would argue it is more difficult denying a student access to their least restrictive environment in favor of parents' non-clinical determination.

Student B formally requested to be discharged from the program. The program felt he would benefit from an extra year. The reality was that he was leaving. No transition support plan was provided because they felt he was being discharged too early. This is inexcusable. You may not agree with the decision but providing a transition plan, a tour of the receiving school, or teaching some of the new expectations to prime Student B would have gone a long way.

Student C was discharged from the program because she could no longer afford services. She was given a lengthy discharge. However, toward the end of the discharge date, a receiving school was still not known. The student was without a learning environment. I was told that effort was made to assist the parent in finding a new school placement and there were accusations that the parent was not actively seeking a new learning environment hoping to stay in the program. This is a challenging situation. The fact that the student went from being under the care of a BCBA® to not being in any learning environment is an ethical violation.

As a BCBA®, document everything, including your rationale as to why a discharge is appropriate and why it may not be. This rationale should be connected to the discharge criteria that should be featured on the initial service agreement or contract for services. The BCBA® is obligated and responsible to make sure every effort is made to support a clinically-sound transition for a discharged client.

3.16 Appropriately Transitioning Services

Behavior analysts include in their service agreement the circumstances for transitioning the client to another behavior analyst within or outside of their organization. They make appropriate efforts to effectively manage transitions; provide a written plan that includes target dates, transition activities, and responsible parties; and review the plan throughout the transition. When relevant, they take appropriate steps to minimize disruptions to services during the transition by collaborating with relevant service providers.

Explanation

Behavior analysts must prepare for and facilitate the transition of services to other parties when necessary. There should be no questions left unanswered for the client or client surrogates during this process. Again, clarity is essential.

Considerations

There is considerable debate within the field of behavior analysis as to what constitutes an ethical refusal to treat behavior or take on a client, and much of it centers around the phrase, "when the client ... is not benefiting from the service." This determination can be somewhat subjective. There are some behavior analysts who might say that if a client's family is also pursuing pseudoscientific methods to treat behaviors or developmental disorders that this would run counter to our efforts and compromise benefits.

There are others who might argue that an approach focused on reinforcing the behaviors we hope to see – specifically following through on recommendations that are based on behavior-analytic principles – might be more consistent with our science.

At another extreme, there might be resistance to leaving a case, even when a situation becomes untenable, for fear of abandoning a client. We might propose a radical idea here: if the safety or well-being of the clinician is compromised, this would compromise benefit to the client. If you are not being treated well as an employee, either by supervisors or by clients, the quality of your work will undoubtedly be compromised. The effects of harassment, for example, can have serious impacts upon physical and emotional health, causing excessive absenteeism and a loss of productivity. Certainly, this does not benefit clients.

Your first job does not have to be your last job. If you are unhappy, this Code element does not obligate you to stay.

Examples from the Field

Written by Jacob Sadavoy

I was taught, early in my career, that the ultimate goal is to work yourself out of a job. I had taken over a home program from another clinician and was told the goal for the client was to reduce several socially inappropriate behaviors that were impeding the client's ability to be successful in the community (e.g., the local grocery store and synagogue) and at home. With an individualized behavior-change program, the client was successful both in the community and at home. I could have stayed involved and targeted other pertinent skills (e.g., self-advocacy, prosody, or conversation skills); however, the established criteria for discontinuation were attained and the series of agreed upon goals were achieved. I did not want to change the nature of my involvement for that would be unethical even though there were other skills, in my estimation, needed to be taught. Instead, I referred the client to a speech and language pathologist (SLP) with the hopes that the client and the SLP would develop new criterion for discontinuation, upon mastery of a series of predetermined goals.

Works Cited

Baer, D. M., Wolf, M. M., & Risley, T. R. (1968). Some current dimensions of applied behavior analysis. *Journal of Applied Behavior Analysis*, *1*(1), 91–97.

Baron-Cohen, S. (2017). Editorial perspective: Neurodiversity: a revolutionary concept for autism and psychiatry. *Journal of Child Psychology and Psychiatry*, *58*(6), 744–747. https://doi.org/10.1111/jcpp.12703.

Behavior Analyst Certification Board. (2020). *Ethics Code for Behavior Analysts*. Littleton, CO: Author.

Brodhead, M. T., Quigley, S. P., & Wilczynski, S. M. (2018). A call for discussion about scope of competence in behavior analysis. *Behavior Analysis in Practice*, *11*(4), 424–435. https://doi.org/10.1007/s40617-018-00303-8.

Cooper, J. O., Heron, T. E., & Heward, W. L. (2007). *Applied behavior analysis*. Upper Saddle River, NJ: Pearson.

Cunningham, A. B., & Schreibman, L. (2008). Stereotypy in Autism: The Importance of Function. *Research in autism spectrum disorders, 2*(3), 469–479. https://doi.org/10.1016/j.rasd.2007.09.006

Dunning, D. (2011). The Dunning-Kruger effect. *Advances in Experimental Social Psychology*, 247–296. https://doi.org/10.1016/b978-0-12-385522-0.00005-6.

Eikeseth, S., Smith, T., Jahr, E., & Eldevik, S. (2007). Outcome for children with autism who began intensive behavioral treatment between ages 4 and 7: a comparison controlled study. *Behavior Modification*, *31*(3), 264–278.

Hanley G. P. (2010). Toward effective and preferred programming: a case for the objective measurement of social validity with recipients of behavior-change programs. *Behavior analysis in practice, 3*(1), 13–21. https://doi.org/10.1007/BF03391754

Lovaas, O. I. (1987). Behavioral treatment and normal educational and intellectual functioning in young autistic children. *Journal of Consulting and Clinical Psychology*, *55*(1), 3–9. https://doi.org/10.1037/0022-006x.55.1.3.

Militerni, R., Bravaccio, C., Falco, C., Fico, C., & Palermo, M. T. (2002). Repetitive behaviors in autistic disorder. *European Child & Adolescent Psychiatry, 11*(5), 210–218. https://doi.org/10.1007/s00787-002-0279-x.

Potter, J., Hanley, G.P., Augustine, M.T., Clay, C.J., & Phelps, M.C. (2013). Treating stereotypy in adolescents diagnosed with autism by refining the tactic of "using stereotypy as reinforcement". *Journal of applied behavior analysis, 46*(2), 407-23 .

Van Houten, R., Axelrod, S., Bailey, J. S., Favell, J. E., Foxx, R. M., Iwata, B. A., & Lovaas, O. I. (1988). The right to effective behavioral treatment. *The Behavior Analyst, 11*(2), 111–114. https://doi.org/10.1007/bf03392464.

Wolf, M. M. (1978). Social validity: the case for subjective measurement or how applied behavior analysis is finding its heart. *Journal of Applied Behavior Analysis, 11*(2), 203–214. https://doi.org/10.1901/jaba.1978.11-203.

1.7   Ethics Standards Section 4

Responsibility to Supervisees and Trainees

4.01 Compliance with Supervision Requirements

Behavior analysts are knowledgeable about and comply with all applicable supervisory requirements (e.g., BACB rules, licensure requirements, funder and organization policies), including those related to supervision modalities and structure (e.g., in person, video conference, individual, group).

Explanation

A behavior analyst must maintain a high standard of integrity. Honesty is a value that must be upheld by the responsible behavior analyst. This value permeates the work of the behavior analyst and is the core component of communication in ethical practice. One of the most important demonstrations of this commitment to honesty is in our association with the BACB® itself, including the necessity of upholding the requirements of supervision. Although the BACB® has some capacity to oversee the provision of coursework, continuing education, and supervision, the mission of the organization itself would preclude intensive oversight over every program, every continuing education offering, or every supervisor. The system as it currently stands allows for audits of documentation and requires that syllabi be submitted to the Association for Behavior Analysis International in order for coursework to be approved. However, the goal of disseminating behavior analysis and increasing the number of qualified behavior analysts worldwide necessitates that oversight be limited if it is to be sustainable. Although there could certainly be consequences of failing to meet such standards, and these consequences could be quite harsh, it is not the responsibility of the BACB® to directly oversee each aspect of the programs which we develop. Behavior analysts who oversee such endeavors are required to self-manage their adherence to this Code.

Considerations

Once one begins their coursework toward their pursuit of certification with the BACB®, there are several steps that need to be taken as supervised fieldwork. The first of these is to establish an account at the BACB® Gateway. Once the account is established, you will be able to receive emails from the BACB®. These may be job offers, requests to participate in surveys or academic research, announcements of publications, or other information from organizations that either seek services from or provide services to behavior analysts. As required by law, each email will include a link to unsubscribe. However, the BACB® urges certificants and those pursuing certification to consider adjusting their email preferences instead. By logging into their portal, those with a Gateway account can manage their

DOI: 10.4324/9781003190707-8

subscriptions to receive only the information that they find relevant and avoid the "noise" of emails that they are not interested in receiving. Though it may seem simpler to simply unsubscribe, doing so would come at a great cost. Among the emails that offer or request services, those with a Gateway account can also receive the BACB® newsletter. These newsletters often contain crucial information, including changes to standards and regulations, insights as to the challenges of adhering to the Ethics Code for Behavior Analysts®, and updates from the BACB®'s legal department. The simplest route to maintaining one's knowledge of upcoming changes, perspectives from the BACB® on current requirements, or practical solutions to common issues faced by BCBAs® is to keep the lines of communication open.

Examples from the Field

Written by Jacob Sadavoy

I have had the pleasure of being an ACE Provider coordinator, VCS coordinator, co-created an RBT® course sequence, and BCBA® supervisor. All require considerations to ensure that the BACB® standards are upheld. For example, the RBT® course sequence and continued education units have a temporal component. In order to ensure that we are honoring the stipulated amount of time as per the BACB®, we developed the content on a program that does not allow videos to be fast forwarded. This ensures that the audience (either a BCBA® seeking a CEU or a clinician completing the RBT® course sequence) is engaged in the material for the allotted time. The reason that this is so important is that ABA practitioners cannot cut corners. We are bound by our ethical Code to be professional, truthful, and adhere to the stipulated requirements regarding supervision. If a BCBA® takes on a supervisee, they agree to take on all the responsibilities that come from that. The reminder of this chapter outlines what that looks like.

4.02 Supervisory Competence

Behavior analysts supervise and train others only within their identified scope of competence. They provide supervision only after obtaining knowledge and skills in effective supervisory practices, and they continually evaluate and improve their supervisory repertoires through professional development.

Explanation

Again we hear a variation on a familiar theme: behavior analysts do the work that they can do well. A responsible behavior analyst neither experiments with what they cannot do nor uses the client as a learning opportunity. The time spent on the "learning curve" must not be at the expense of the client. Mastery of skills is required before a behavior analyst can responsibly train others in the acquisition of those skills. When it comes to Supervision toward the Board Certified Behavior Analyst®, or BCBA®, this may become problematic. How can one adequately gain the skills required if the supervisor lacks the necessary experience? The Behavior Analyst Certification Board®, or BACB®, does, however, encourage those pursuing certification to "have multiple experiences" (BACB, 2012). Supervisees should work in multiple settings, with different populations and highlighting different activities. While this may not always be practical, since many students of behavior analysis pursue certification at their places of employment, it is still a worthy goal to be strived for. Even within the same organization, different supervisors may have different skill sets and different areas of interest. Earlier in the Ethics Code®, we reviewed the behavior analyst's obligation to remain within the boundaries of his or her areas of competence. However, there remained the caveat that new experiences and the acquisition of new skills were encouraged, so long as the development of these skills was not at the expense of the learner's time and resources. When in the position of a supervisor, we must address the client's need for high-quality services and the supervisee's need for the skills necessary to help them. We begin with a degree of humility. Are we, as supervisors, able to assess what the needs of the client are and what behavior change programs might be necessary to address them? Are we, as supervisors, able to select an intervention that would adequately address these needs? And are we, as supervisor, capable not only of implementing this intervention, but also of training others to implement it as well? Many of us understand the concept of generation loss – the fact that a copy of a copy loses the quality of representation of the original. In terms of training, generation loss can also occur. If we as supervisors lack true fluency in the techniques that we are teaching, there are likely to be several elements missing, several aspects of the procedure that we have overlooked. Perhaps one of the most valuable lessons that we can teach, particularly to those who are receiving supervision, is the task analysis of practicing this humility. Begin by seeking out experts in the area of need. Begin by reaching out to your immediate circle. How many colleagues may have some expertise in this area? Then widen your circle of community – who has published in this area? Are these publications sufficiently technological? Where do these experts currently practice? Would they be open to questions, or do they have students or protégés who might be willing to discuss the procedures? Would they be able or willing to make referrals? Just as we are not responsible to know all of the answers as clinicians, we are also not expected to know all of the answers as supervisors. Perhaps the best we can do is to model how to ask the right questions and how to find the person to ask.

Considerations

A good behavior analyst is not necessarily a good supervisor. In some cases, supervision may be an afterthought; a conversation about one's current caseload and, if they are lucky, a discussion on a related research article. Quality supervision is essential; it is what helps our science evolve. If we are not effectively passing down the skills necessary to be an effective behavior analyst, we are inadvertently promoting a generation of behavior analysts that will practice the science incorrectly. The BACB® mandates 1,500 supervision hours (for independent fieldwork) and on January 1, 2015, supervising BCBAs® were required to complete an eight-hour Supervision Training with the purpose of facilitating the delivery of behavior-analytic procedures while reading supervisees to be able to apply the science professionally, analytically, and ethically (BACB, 2012). Supervisors have an obligation to the supervisee. I would argue that a supervisor that does not take this responsibility with the utmost sincerity is incompetent. They may have the clinical skills to supervise, but they should not for the betterment of the supervisee and the science

Examples from the Field

Written by Ann Beirne

During my own supervisor experience with Dr. Bobby Newman, he would routinely use stories from his own experience to illustrate his points. While giving an example of a descriptive analysis to determine the function of behavior, he recalled an example of a child in a school who had refused to leave the lunchroom. The student had been slightly aggressive with his paraprofessional and that paraprofessional had left, citing union requirements for immediate trauma counseling. Dr. Newman explained how the school principal had dressed in a costume and led him from the lunchroom, offering the student ice cream. My colleagues and I were shocked, which was the intention, of course. My response was, "Bobby, how did you keep yourself from saying, 'What are you people using for brains?'" Bobby, wisely, replied, "If someone is hiring me, they are hiring someone to say, 'What are you guys using for brains?' If they hire you or some other of my colleagues, they are hiring someone to finesse it a bit more." Years later, I retold this conversation, which Dr. Newman had not remembered, as an example of some of the best advice I had ever received. Though Dr. Newman jokingly accused me of implying a lack of social skills on his part, nothing could be further from the truth. In fact, I realize that if the role I was to play was one of a sterner consultant, it is unlikely I would do so successfully. I believe that this story was an excellent example of knowing one's strengths and embracing them. I will often explain to supervisees that there are many different kinds of behavior analysts. Whatever kind of behavior analyst you are, there is a client that needs precisely that kind of behavior analyst. When overseeing the supervision of future behavior analysts, it is perhaps best to make sure we are addressing the strengths and needs of this particular future behavior analyst. Does this supervisee have a model for the type of behavior analyst they will be, or hope to be? And do they have the skills to do so in a way that enhances their ethical practice? It is not a requirement of the supervised experience to emulate the supervisor, but to enhance their own skills. Encouragement of personal growth is an essential piece of this puzzle.

4.03 Supervisory Volume

Behavior analysts take on only the number of supervisees or trainees that allows them to provide effective supervision and training. They are knowledgeable about and comply with any relevant requirements (e.g., BACB rules, licensure requirements, funder and organization policies). They consider relevant factors (e.g., their current client demands, their current supervisee or trainee caseload, time and logistical resources) on an ongoing basis and when deciding to add a supervisee or trainee. When behavior analysts determine that they have met their threshold volume for providing effective supervision, they document this self-assessment and communicate the results to their employer or other relevant parties.

Explanation

Here we also see similarities to other Code elements for behavior analysts. A behavior analyst refrains from making commitments that they cannot keep. This is true not only of our clinical practice, but our supervisory practice as well. The requirements for BCBA® supervision are sufficiently involved so that supervisory volume must be managed. The hours of group supervision cannot exceed the number of hours of individual supervision in any supervisory period; a supervisor contact must be a minimum of two observations or two contacts per month. In addition, meetings must represent 5% of the hours accrued toward the certification. Meeting these requirements alone would make it challenging to create an unmanageable volume of supervisees. Challenging, however, is not the same as impossible, and it is necessary to evaluate whether we are in fact offering the best experience to our supervisees in the activities of supervision. And, just as is our responsibility when assessing our effectiveness in our clinical work with clients, it is necessary to continually assess if the needs of each supervisee is being met. The requirements of the

Behavior Analyst Certification Board® provide a minimum standard for adequate supervision, which includes a minimum number of contact hours between the supervisor and the supervisee. Meeting this minimum requirement does not adequately meet the needs of the clients this supervisee will serve. It is necessary to continuously ask ourselves not only, "Is there adequate time to meet with supervisees?" but "Is there adequate time to support supervisees?" If this is our guideline for the provision of supervision, we can build a schedule that considers the needs of everyone involved, as well as everyone ultimately affected.

Considerations

This question is somewhat easier to consider given the requirements of supervision toward board certification in behavior analysis than it is when engaged in the activities of supervision, or the oversight of direct service providers. Often such providers are poorly paid and give little training and support. Even in the best-case scenario, in which direct service providers would qualify as Registered Behavior Technicians®, this would involve only one week of didactic training in behavior analysis and the successful completion of the competency assessment. Though annual renewals are required, there is room here for considerable error. Our first author has often said when discussing training of professionals in school that there are two kinds of supervisees. One will immediately launch into a litany of complaints, presenting a list of those behaviors which must be treated. While this may be problematic, there is a strange comfort in knowing precisely where to start in planning interventions. The other type of supervisee is certainly pleasant but presents a greater challenge for the supervisor. This supervisee replies that everything is "fine" when asked about ongoing programs and replies "no" when asked if they have any questions or concerns. However, problems become more evident as more observation continues and reveals the gap in understanding. The Dunning-Kruger effect (Dunning, 2011) is a phenomenon which might also be described as "meta-ignorance." In short, this phenomenon is best described by the phrase "you don't know what you don't know." It is difficult for one to be knowledgeable of the gaps in one's own knowledge, and this becomes particularly challenging when learning new skills. We cannot rely on our supervisees to ask us to fill in the gaps in their knowledge, since this assumes they will be knowledgeable in the boundaries of their knowledge. When providing training and oversight in the activities of supervision, it is necessary to provide additional guidance to ensure that the inevitable gaps in a trainee's knowledge do not impair the client's programming in any way. It is not their responsibility to understand the breadth of what must be learned, it is ours. And this responsibility, both to the supervisee and to the clients, must be fulfilled.

Examples from the Field

Written by Jacob Sadavoy

Supervision should be time consuming. If done correctly and thoroughly, the supervisor may invest more time on a supervisee than some of his or her clients on any given week. A behavior analyst is expected to manage time accordingly to ensure that all roles and responsibilities are done meticulously and accurately (similar to Code element 2.02). Therefore, when I agree to supervise, I ensure that I can afford the time to plan each supervisory meeting in advance, meet for the prescribed length of time stipulated by the number of hours they have worked, have comments prepared based on observations of their performance, and have sent resources and latest research on the topic of discussion a week in advance. I am not doing my due diligence as a supervisor if I cannot deliver on all these requirements. A supervisor must put quality over quantity. Overseeing too many clients will adversely affect one's ability to provide behavior-analytic services, similarly too many supervisees will impede supervisory effectiveness and quality.

4.04 Accountability in Supervision

Behavior analysts are accountable for their supervisory practices. They are also accountable for the professional activities (e.g., client services, supervision, training, research activity, public statements) of their supervisees or trainees that occur as part of the supervisory relationship.

Explanation

When behavior analysts are functioning as supervisors, they must take full responsibility for all facets of this undertaking. Before we begin to discuss supervision, it is helpful to begin with a few definitions. As you begin (or perhaps continue) the process of gaining the required hours for your supervised fieldwork, you may have already begun the process of what you and your supervisor refer to as supervision. For the purposes of attaining your certification in behavior analysis, supervision has a specific definition and purpose. The pursuit of your certification requires specific documentation and practices. Supervision in this case is so specific that there is little room for compromise, and the rigidity of those requirements allows for the quality of such supervision to be maintained. Within the confines of the requirements of this type of supervision, which will be referred to here as Supervision, the practices are clear. Outside the confines of Supervision, however, we have supervision which involves the oversight of employees or other professionals. In this role, the supervisor has fewer requirements, but also less structure. How then can the same high standards and focus on the quality of supervision be achieved? This section of the Ethics Code for Behavior Analysts® provides some insight as to how such a goal can be accomplished. In this chapter, we will address not only the requirements of Supervision, but also the ethical requirements of the behavior analyst in the roles required during supervision.

Considerations

Gerald Shook (2005) labeled a challenge that we see in today's behavior-analytic processes; "BACB certificants are certified as meeting the minimum standard in behavior analysis" (p. 571). Fifteen years later, the field has grown and evolved as have the requirements to be a credentialled behavior analyst by the BACB. In response to the exponential growth in the field, the BACB initiated a Supervision Task Force "perhaps in response to the lack of explicit instruction and non-optimal supervisory practices" (Sellers et al., 2016, p. 274). Sellers and colleagues (2016) went on to highlight five overarching recommended practice guidelines for individual supervision in the field of ABA: establish an effective supervisor-supervisee relationship, establish a plan for structured supervision content and competence evaluation, evaluate the effectiveness of supervision, incorporate ethics and professional development into supervision, and continue the professional relationship post-certification. The Ethics Code for Behavior Analysts (2020) mandates that BCBAs are obligated to be responsible for the clinical needs of clients but also do their due diligence with respect to their supervisees. At times, managing both responsibilities can be challenging. The outcome of supervision is not to promote certification or have supervisees possess minimal viable competency in the field of behavior analysis (Eikeseth, 2010). Rather, each supervisor should seek to promote the sustainability and evolution of the science. In order to promote thoughtful and effective supervision, supervisors must go beyond the Task List and exam preparedness and instill clinical competency, cultural responsiveness, critical thinking skills, willingness to collaborate, commitment to ethical and professional behavior, ability to speak about behavioral concepts professionally and colloquially, and owning one's competence.

Examples from the Field

By Jacob Sadavoy

The supervisee is an extension of the supervisor. Any errors made by the supervisee are a reflection of the supervisor. If something arises, it is a learning opportunity, which is great (better errors happen during supervision than when they become a supervisor). I was sent an official letter of complaint from a BCBA regarding public statements made by my supervisee. It was a fantastic learning opportunity to talk about posting behavior-analytic information and ensuring that posts are truthful, coming from a place of compassion, and never anything specific about a client.

It is imperative that supervisors take this responsibility seriously. If a supervisee is struggling or if you are dissatisfied with the thought that their performance is a representation of you, then, similar to a client who is not making gains, change the program. Analyze what isn't working. For me, I was spread thin working at one of my agencies. I could not give my supervisees the attention they needed which was my responsibility. Not surprisingly, feelings of burnout followed a lack of personal accomplishment, feelings of inadequacy, or emotional exhaustion (Hayes, 2020; Plantiveau et al., 2017). I asked to have fewer cases or cases closer together but both requests were rejected. I could have simplified the targets but that would be creating an inferior behavior change program so I ended up leaving that position because I was disheartened by the quality of work by my supervisees which was my responsibility.

4.05 Maintaining Supervision Documentation

Behavior analysts create, update, store, and dispose of documentation related to their supervisees or trainees by following all applicable requirements (e.g., BACB rules, licensure requirements, funder and organization policies), including those relating to confidentiality. They ensure that their documentation, and the documentation of their supervisees or trainees, is accurate and complete. They maintain documentation in a manner that allows for the effective transition of supervisory oversight if necessary. They retain their supervision documentation for at least 7 years and as otherwise required by law and other relevant parties and instruct their supervisees or trainees to do the same.

Explanation

All documentation is important, so it is not surprising that documentation related to supervision needs to be taken seriously. This includes having safeguards in place to ensure that it is accurate but also updated regularly (ideally once a week but daily is preferable), stored safely so that everyone on the supervision team can access, and if a transition occurs, the documentation is so concise, that a new supervisor is able to continue seamlessly. Paperwork goes both ways. The supervisee is responsible for understanding and knowing what the expectations are for the supervisor to complete and should make a concerted effort to contact the paperwork often to ensure that there are no irregularities.

Considerations

Being familiar with supervising documentation requires understanding of the entire process from inputting your first hours on the monthly tracker to what the BACB® is to receive upon the completion of your supervised hours. The monthly tracker ensures that errors are not tabulated into the calculated fields; however, the supervisee (and the supervisor) should be fully aware as to what they need to get credit for up to 30 hours (i.e., two contacts and one live or video observation) and what constitutes direct and indirect service hours. There are many nuances so it is encouraged that all of this should be explained in detail in the first or second supervision meeting following going over the supervision contract. We recommend going over the BACB® *BCBA/ BCaBA EXPERIENCE STANDARDS: Monthly System* (BACB, 3/2020). Lastly, it is paramount that all this is saved. I have heard too many anecdotes in which the BACB® requests proof of hours and forms are missing. Forms need to be kept and protected for seven years. An additional recommendation is to promote organization of supervisory work by keeping notes, assessments, feedback (for both the supervisor and supervisee), contract, videos, and action steps in a HIPAA, PIPEDA, or GDPR compliant format that can be accessed by the supervisory team. This way information is always available promoting transparency and efficiency as it is helpful for supervision sessions to build on one another. It is a serious offense to err in the realm of supervisory documentation. It is so critical to be prepared and organized in order to have a smooth supervisory documentation process.

Examples from the Field

By Jacob Sadavoy

If you have been a supervisor or a supervisee, you hear the words experience tracker or supervision paperwork and you may flinch. There is a lot but if organized it is all manageable. I had the greatest success when I was either the lone supervisor or I shared supervision duties but someone was appointed responsible for the paperwork. Without clear expectations, it is easy to have things get muddled which could negatively affect your supervisees hours.

   Oftentimes, I will purposely make errors on supervision forms. My reasoning for causing added stress is for the supervisee to access these forms ongoingly and examine them for any inaccuracies. When my supervisees become supervisors, they are responsible for the supervision forms (as are the supervisee). I want them to practice interacting with the forms thoroughly from Day 1.

4.06 Providing Supervision and Training

Behavior analysts deliver supervision and training in compliance with applicable requirements (e.g., BACB rules, licensure requirements, funder and organization policies). They design and implement supervision and training procedures that are evidence based, focus on positive reinforcement, and are individualized for each supervisee or trainee and their circumstances.

Explanation

It is important to separate an explanation of this Code element into the two contexts in which supervision is provided: that of supervision and Supervision. In the context of the oversight that we refer to as supervision, we are often tasked with designing training for those who are entirely new to the field, many of whom have not had any training or experience in working with the population that we serve. It is essential that these trainings be adequate to ensure that they are able to perform all of the tasks required. In their book, *The Supervisor's Guidebook: Evidence-Based Strategies for Promoting Work Quality and Enjoyment Among Human Services Staff*, Reid and colleagues (2012) provide several strategies for assuring quality in staff training.

As a first step, it is extremely important that supervisors have a clear idea of the responsibilities of staff and that these duties be task-analyzed. Written descriptions must be provided and staff must have an opportunity to practice and receive objective feedback on their performance (Reid, 2012). These steps should be repeated until staff demonstrate competency in the target skills. This requires a considerable amount of time, but the return on this investment ultimately benefits the client to a much greater extent than what is saved by forgoing effective training. In the context of supervision toward BCBA certifcation, we are provided some guidelines in the provision of effective training and the requirements both for us and our supervisees. Supervision must address the core areas of the current Task List published by the BACB®, and this does allow a framework from which to develop our supervised experience. Although many of the items on this list may come up organically as part of the conversation during the required meetings, there will undoubtedly be those that will be missed. It is certainly a challenge to address the needs of each supervisee in this context, since not every work environment will have ample opportunities for each item. However, opportunities to address these basic skills should be provided.

Considerations

Is it true that those who can do and those who can't teach? Reid and colleagues (2012) would disagree with this statement and attest that supervisors must have intimate knowledge of the procedures they are training. As a consultant in a new applied behavior analysis (ABA) program in a preschool, our first author had banned the use of one word: just. The intention was to raise the awareness of how we might diminish a student's skills or the goals of our teaching, since the phrase "He's just playing" is remarkably different from the phrase, "He's playing." However, it may offer an insight into the assumptions of a supervisor as well. How many times have we heard or even used the phrase, "Just do this," as if the completion of the task was utterly simple? In some cases, staff members may not have the fluency with the skills needed to "just" do what is required. And in some cases what seems simple to us may in fact be more complicated. What appears to be a simple task is often simple because we have gained fluency on the task, not because the task was simple to begin with. In this case more training would be necessary, so that the supervisee could gain fluency as well. And, in other cases, the task itself may be more difficult than we can anticipate. There may be other factors that affect the ability of our supervisees to implement the strategies that we suggest or the plans that we develop. When making recommendations, it is best to model the procedures ourselves. We must have a complete sense of what the obstacles may be to successful implementation in order to address these obstacles. Determinism, the belief that all phenomena occur as the result of other events (Cooper, Heron, & Heward, 2013), is among the cornerstones of scientific inquiry. In layman's terms, this means that everything happens for a reason. Rather than simply say, "Just do this," we need to reframe this statement into the question, "Why isn't this being done?" Whether the answer is that the supervisee has not yet gained sufficient fluency in the skills or perhaps that the tasks were more complicated than originally supposed, it is a question that deserves an answer.

Examples from the Field

Written by Jacob Sadavoy

When I was a supervisee, the content of my supervision meetings were almost exclusively focused on my clients and all references to Task List items would be discussed in relation to the week's events. I thought nothing of it. From my supervisor's standpoint, they were reviewing their caseload while providing BCBA® supervision at the same time. I copied this model when I started supervising. In discussing the poor pass rate with one of my supervisees, I began to wonder if this was a symptom of the educational institutions or if it was supervision (Shepley et al., 2017). Because I had no control over the former scenario at that time, I began to look at the model of supervision that was used for my independent fieldwork hours which I passed on to my supervisees. As a supervisor, it is my duty to ensure my supervisees are clinically competent, critical thinkers, committed to ethical behavior, culturally competent, possess the ability (and willingness) to collaborate, and able to talk about behavior-analytic principles fluently both professionally and colloquially. Reciting the Task List or even passing the exam are secondary responsibilities for the supervisor. In order for the science to advance, more focus needs to be invested in providing quality supervision. The future of the science is at stake if the focus of future BCBAs is on memorizing the Task List or exam preparation courses.

4.07 Incorporating and Addressing Diversity

During supervision and training, behavior analysts actively incorporate and address topics related to diversity (e.g., age, disability, ethnicity, gender expression/identity, immigration status, marital/relationship status, national origin, race, religion, sexual orientation, socioeconomic status).

Explanation

Beaulieu and colleagues (2018) demonstrated, via a survey, that the vast majority of behavior analysts that were surveyed believe that they are either extremely skilled or moderately skilled in developing culturally competent care programs. A similar majority also reported having no or a little in the way of diversity training. Cross and colleagues (1989) show a spectrum of cultural understanding where cultural destructiveness is at the bottom and gradually moves to cultural proficiency with cultural incapacity, cultural blindness, cultural pre-competence, and cultural competence in the middle. Based on the survey, it would seem that those polled in Beaulieu's study fell into cultural blindness in which they think they are unbiased despite not having any formal training in understanding, responding, or enacting diversity-informed practices. It should be noted that the authors of this paper do not believe there exists a state of cultural proficiency as cultural humility is a behavioral cusp and requires lifelong learning and understanding as cultures adapt within different and often challenging social contexts especially when working with a vulnerable population.

Thus, it is critical to ask questions and learn about your client in order to build a culturally responsive program that will drive socially significant behavior change deemed necessary by the client and not be informed by the practitioner's learning history. Henrich and colleagues (2010), coined the acronym WEIRD for the following: western, educated, industrialized, rich, and democratic. The science of ABA is a growing field based on increases in both the volume of research and credentialled practitioners; however, an important distinction needs to be made in that the foundation and seminal work in ABA is largely WEIRD and male. This fact coupled with the aforementioned survey in which the majority of behavior analysts think they are culturally competent, have minimal to no diversity training, and are taught to create a behavior change program based on assessment, past literature, and their learning history promotes client targets that are not individualized and informed by WEIRD. Without diversity training, cultural responsiveness cannot exist and if culturally informed program decisions are not being made, the behavior change program is not meeting the requirement for individualization of client programming.

For supervisors, bringing this to the attention of supervisees is essential. Helping them understand their biases and allow them to enter new situations willing to learn and interact with new clients from a place of listening as opposed to a place rooted in their past experiences is invaluable in connecting with clients and establishing an individualized program that accommodates their individuality.

Considerations

Our second author has learned many things traveling the world (15 different countries) implementing behavior change programs but the need to be humble and how culture influences the environment are two lessons we continue to access regardless of where we are. A first step in incorporating and addressing diversity is to recognize your own culture and lens. We may be familiar with centers and schools in Manhattan and Toronto. We might use those experiences to help inform the way we approach schools and centers in other parts of the world; however, we would be foolish to impose or attempt to recreate these learning environments that we are familiar with in another part of the world. In order to feel comfortable providing recommendations we would need to learn the following: culture, staff experiences and learning histories, social significance, values, and the clients. That can't happen in a one-and-done training or a week- or month-long trip. In order to be successful, one has to understand their bias, and listen. Listen for what can be created by the sharing of local practitioners who are trying to make a difference in their community. We may have letters after our name and may think we can change behaviors but, by being humble, we realize we have a lot to learn in a new environment.

We would get the same feeling when going to a new school or a new home. Different learning histories, different cultures, different needs and values, and if we hope to have any success we need to individualize our behavior-analytic relationship contingent on my audience.

Examples from the Field

By Jacob Sadavoy

I am constantly working on ways I can be more culturally responsive. It starts with knowing who I am, the biases I have because of who I am, and listening to stories from those that have different identities than my own. When in Asia, it was important for me to realize the different social and cultural contingencies that make a country like China, India, or Vietnam different than North America. I could go into those environments and insist that they do 1:1 therapy for their autistic population; however, that is unrealistic based on need, population, and resources. In doing distance supervision it is critical that there is an understanding of these limitations and barriers to implementing ABA services familiar to the supervisor. If a supervisor ignores the resource barriers, the learning histories of their supervisees, or the environmental landscape of the region, they don't have a hope of providing individualized, informed supervision.

4.08 Performance Monitoring and Feedback

Behavior analysts engage in and document ongoing, evidence-based data collection and performance monitoring (e.g., observations, structured evaluations) of supervisees or trainees. They provide timely informal and formal praise and feedback designed to improve performance and document formal feedback delivered. When performance problems arise, behavior analysts develop, communicate, implement, and evaluate an improvement plan with clearly identified procedures for addressing the problem.

Explanation

It is ingrained in the culture of behavior analysis that reinforcement is the way that we change behavior. As addressed in our review of the Code elements regarding punishment, behavior analysts are cautioned against using punishment and are required to following the procedures outlined in the Ethics Code®. Punishments are not to be recommended or implemented without careful consideration. In fact, in clinical practice, many behavior analysts refrain from punishment altogether. However, as is reviewed in our analysis of the Ethics Code's® restrictions on the use of punishment, this is not merely because it meets the criteria for what we would consider ethical, it is because reinforcement is more effective in the formation of new behavior. Punishment does not encourage or sustain learning. Punishment can only stop or prevent it. In order to teach the skills necessary for the practice of behavior analysis, behavior analysts must remember that this applies to any learning activity. Whether we are teaching the skills necessary to become a behavior analyst in the activities of Supervision or training direct service providers as we engage in the activities of supervision, skills are taught through reinforcement and this reinforcement must be consistent enough to ensure that the skills will be supported and maintained.

Considerations

It is inspiring to see so many new professionals, to be swept up in their excitement and enthusiasm at the potential of applied behavior analysis to change lives. Our first author has been fortunate enough to work with some incredibly dedicated professionals. However, the transition from direct service to a more administrative and supervisory role can come with many challenges, the greatest of which was the adjustment of the concept of what could be taught. As a clinician, the underlying assumption of every program was confidence in the client's capabilities. Though the road ahead may be long and the journey tiring, we began with the assumption that the client was limited in their ability to learn only by my ability to teach. If they struggled to learn a skill, the struggle is to find a way to teach them. "There is no such thing as an unsolvable problem. There are only solutions that we have not yet found." When making the transition to a supervisory role, that idea needed to be adjusted. The science was still the same; the capacity of every organism to learn what was effectively taught still remained the same. But the time and energy required for teaching now came at a greater cost – the time and resources of the client. While it may still be true that anyone can learn anything, here again we have the questions, "If we can teach anyone anything, does this necessarily mean that we should teach everyone everything?" When working with a client, one may have less inclination to assume that a particular skill was not worth the effort involved in teaching it, as the socially significant behaviors we are teaching have already been identified as important. However, when working with staff or supervisees, the learning curve comes at a cost to the client in time and resources. We are forced to ask ourselves, "While it may be true that this staff member is capable of learning the skill I am trying to teach, is teaching them the best use of my time and resources?" The time spent in staff training could be spent on treatment plan development, data review, or other tasks that could be of direct benefit. If the supervisee does not correct their performance, we may have to make the difficult decision that the training they are receiving is not working out, and may even have to terminate their employment.

Examples from the Field

Written by Jacob Sadavoy

I find it helpful to look at my supervisees as clients. Similar to my clients, I am invested in seeing skill acquisition in their behavior-analytic skills and, in order to do so, I must assess their current level of achievement and collect data to monitor their progress. I strive to personalize supervision like I personalize a behavior change program for a client. For example, if the supervisee shows low scores on their assessment for ethics and high scores on data analysis, I would focus my supervision time with my supervisee on ethics and not on data analysis. I would also strive to have them practice explaining concepts colloquially and technically as these are both critical skills for supervisors to possess when talking to clients and colleagues, respectively. Lastly, with the Ethics Code for Behavior Analysts® (2020), I will now collect data on the supervisee's fluency when it comes to the new critical features (e.g., personal bias, cultural responsiveness, compassion, dignity, self-determination, and respect).

The responsibility of the supervisor is daunting and oftentimes they are not afforded the indirect hours necessary to supervise at a level to mold a supervisee into a supervisor themselves. There are many resources that are tremendously helpful so one does not have to recreate the wheel. Some of my favorites include: *Building and Sustaining Meaningful and Effective Relationships as a Supervisor and Mentor* by Linda A. LeBlanc, Tyra P. Sellers, and Shahla Ala'i, *The Supervisor's Guidebook: Evidence-Based Strategies for Promoting Work Quality and Enjoyment among Human Service Staff* by Dennis H. Reid, Marsha B. Parsons, and Carolyn W. Green, *Remote Fieldwork Supervision for BCBA® Trainees* by Lisa N. Britton and Matthew J. Cicoria, and *Fieldwork and Supervision for Behavior Analysts: A Handbook* by Brian Rice, Ellie Kazemi, and Peter Adzhyan.

4.09 Delegation of Tasks

Behavior analysts delegate tasks to their supervisees or trainees only after confirming that they can competently perform the tasks and that the delegation complies with applicable requirements (e.g., BACB rules, licensure requirements, funder and organization policies).

Explanation

There is a term from the information technology and design fields that is useful to remember here: "end-user." In the technology or design this refers to the individual who will ultimately use the product or service designed. While a company may hope to provide a product that will be easy and inexpensive to manufacture and sell, what purpose will this product serve for the "end-user?" What need will be addressed by this product or service and how well will this product meet it? In their capacity as supervisors, it is necessary that we take a long view and remember that we too must consider the needs of our "end-user" – the client. Even when we are working directly with staff members or those pursuing certification, our ultimate responsibility is to the clients that they serve. It is essential that we as behavior analysts remember the great responsibility of our role. Whether we work in direct services or provide supervision oversight or training to those that do, our ultimate responsibility is to the "end-user" of our services. How will our services, even when these are indirect, positively impact the lives of clients? One way is to ensure that our supervision has a positive impact on the clients who will ultimately be served. For those who are pursuing BCBA® certification in the process we refer to as Supervision, the skills we teach must be taught in a way that allows the supervisee to perform them independently, at a minimum, at the conclusion of their supervision. Until mastery of these skills has been achieved, continued supervision and training must be provided, and the mastery of these skills must be supported.

Connections

Written by Ann Beirne

As many working mothers do, I often fall prey to "it's easier if I just do it" syndrome. Rather than invest the time and energy teaching my young children how to clean their room, I will often do it myself, even though I do acknowledge that, in the long run, this is certainly not easier. And it is not necessarily the best thing for my children if they cannot engage in this task or other household tasks independently. It is also a necessary stage of the supervision process to transition to providing less guidance and more opportunities. I will often say to supervisees at this stage that I am now offering them "tricks" rather than necessary skills from the current Task List. It can be difficult to have the self-discipline to allow supervisees to come to their own answers rather than providing them. This, however, is a necessary part of the process of supervision. Supervisees must be allowed the space to thrive and they cannot do so under the weight of our agendas or our need to control the experience. Just as we must "work ourselves out of a job" when working directly with clients, so too must be our aim when working with supervisees. In the case of those, whose work we oversee, as they fulfill more subordinate roles, we must ensure that they are able to complete the responsibilities of these roles independently.

Considerations

The BACB®, in their experience standards, have outlined the acquisition of indirect hours as a necessary requirement for the BCBA® credential. Any BCBA® candidate, no matter their fieldwork experience setting, must acquire experience hours in tasks other than direct service provision.

Why this requirement? Because the tasks of the BCBA® go far beyond direct service and candidates must have supervised experience in all of these tasks. Program design, data collection and observation, training – each task requires a different set of skills.

The requirement to delegate responsibly and the requirement that we provide opportunities to learn all necessary skills are intimately linked, and both must be considered in the design of supervision.

Examples from the Field

Written by Jacob Sadavoy

As a supervisee, I was writing behavior plans and skill acquisition programs with minimal oversight. In some cases, the supervisor would be absent for weeks and the Educational

Director, who was not a behavior analyst, would make the decision to implement the plan as written. In conversations with other BCBAs®, I learned that others were unfortunate to be put in a similar position. As a supervisee, I admit, it felt liberating and exciting to see my plan implemented as designed. However, as a supervisee, I am entitled for feedback and support on all proposed plans. This way, I can improve my ability as a behavior analysis as opposed to learning through trial and error. The roles and responsibilities of the supervisee should be stipulated in the contract. If you are a supervisor, make sure you demonstrate professionalism and model appropriate clinical judgment by ensuring the supervisee is performing the duties in which they are responsible or provide direct oversight for duties that go beyond their responsibilities. If you are a supervisee, ask questions. Demand that your supervisor supervises. Your clinical hours are precious; avoid accruing them in silence.

4.10 Evaluating Effects of Supervision and Training

Behavior analysts actively engage in continual evaluation of their own supervisory practices using feedback from others and client and supervisee or trainee outcomes. Behavior analysts document those self-evaluations and make timely adjustments to their supervisory and training practices as indicated.

Explanation

This should be a familiar refrain. In our interactions with clients, behavior analysts acknowledge the need for continued evaluation in order to assess progress and current needs. The ongoing documentation of behavior change is acknowledged as necessary in order to make data-based decisions. When providing supervision, however, this is often overlooked. Despite our knowledge of the science of behavior and the importance of reinforcement, we often overlook it when supervising staff. Consistent evaluation of the effects of our intervention is acknowledged as important in our direct work with clients, though not necessarily in our work as supervisors. In the case of the oversight referred to as supervision, it is necessary to have a clear understanding of the responsibilities of those requiring our oversight. What are the tasks that they are required to perform? Are there clear task analyses for these responsibilities? Are the behaviors we hope to see operationally defined? Just as in our clinical work, our measure of the success of our intervention must be in the behavior change that we see. Just as assessments, well-defined goals and clear roadmaps must be present in our clinical work, so it must be in the supervision of others.

Considerations

In order to evaluate the effectiveness of supervision, it is necessary to define the goals of the supervision process. In the case of the process toward gaining board certification in behavior analysis, this may be considered a goal. However, if our goal is simply to gain a certification, more letters to be placed after our name on a resume or business card, then this goal would not uphold the values which bring us to this field. How many of us entered this field to change lives, to improve the quality of life for children and families, or to increase independence and agency for some of society's most vulnerable citizens? Certainly, the accolades and acknowledgment are wonderful, but many of us are more motivated by the possibility of promoting lasting meaningful behavior change. The goal of the supervision process is not simply to become certified, but for that certification to be meaningful. The goal is not to be a behavior analyst, but to be a good one. One possible solution to this issue is to develop a clear curriculum for supervision. What are the necessary skills to be learned and what is a reasonable timeline to meet to develop these skills within the supervised experience? Having clear benchmarks for a successful supervised experience will allow us to measure whether or not those benchmarks are being met. Supervision must be based on the current Task List and address the supervisee's needs and goals. It so a delicate balance to provide for the individual needs of supervisees, but to do so is an effort worth making. This individualization of goals and activities is a vital aspect of behavior-analytic practice, and a valuable skill to model for supervisees.

Examples from the Field

Written by Jacob Sadavoy

In Montrose Wolf's seminal article (1978), he makes the distinction that analysts cannot report their own performance accurately. Thus, program modifications that are derived by self-evaluation will be wholly insufficient. Wolf insisted that behavior analysts make data-based decisions based on the delivery of the behavior change program which must be informed by the client via social validity to measure effectiveness, maintenance, and ease of use. These principles were adopted by BACB when they mandated that supervisors must adopt a supervision contract with supervisees, engage in behavior skills training (BST), and receive performance feedback based on their performance (Turner et al., 2016). Until course sequence programs place an onus on soft skills, training supervisees how to engage in cultural competemility and compassionate care is the supervisors' responsibility (Fong et al., 2017; Taylor et al., 2019). In order to engage in ethical and responsible supervision, data must be collected on both the supervisors and supervisee and the data collected must inform supervisory objectives. This is paramount in their ability to be an effective supervisor.

Turner and colleagues' (2016) *Supervision Monitoring and Evaluation Form* is a quick questionnaire for supervisees to share information about the performance of the supervisor. Supervisors must collect data on their performance and develop interventions to improve their performance. As a behavior analyst knows, data is required in order to measure and monitor behaviors and that includes our own in an effort to demonstrate and ensure that we are effective, responsive supervisors.

4.11 Facilitating Continuity of Supervision

Behavior analysts minimize interruption or disruption of supervision and make appropriate and timely efforts to facilitate the continuation of supervision in the event of planned interruptions (e.g., temporary leave) or unplanned interruptions (e.g., illness, emergencies). When an interruption or disruption occurs, they communicate to all relevant parties the steps being taken to facilitate continuity of supervision.

Explanation

Just as we must plan for our clients, we must plan for our supervisees. A great deal depends on the continuity of our ability to provide oversight, in both cases. Without our supervision, supervisees may be restricted from providing direct services, which would have a direct impact on clients. And moreover, models poor supervision practices.

Everything that we do, including supervision, has an effect on vulnerable populations.

Considerations

Some of us are fortunate enough to work for large companies with adequate resources to provide supervision for candidates when absences or interruptions inevitably happen. For others, a bit more direct action is necessary.

If you are embarking on independent work, make sure that you create a network of trusted colleagues you can recommend to cover absences, address areas where you have less expertise, or simply enrich the experience for your supervisees. As discussed on Shane Spiker's interview in Part 3, we do not make referrals in this field often enough. If you and your colleagues can make arrangements to facilitate that continuation of services, you will have done a great service to your colleagues, your supervisees, and the field as a whole.

Connections

Written by Ann Beirne

I have often been dismayed at how many new BCBAs® seek out guidance for programming on social media. This is, for a variety of ethical reasons addressed in the new Ethics Code®, questionable, but it also points to a serious issue. After supervision, new professionals do not know where to turn, and instead of turning to a trusted resource, they turn to any and every resource available.

For this reason I often offer supervisees "lifelong membership to the Ann Beirne pick-a-brain society." They very rarely need it, but we all feel better knowing that safety net is there.

Examples from the Field

Written by Ann Beirne

When I was pregnant with my third child, I was providing supervision to several candidates and decided that, since I could work from home and nurse, a maternity leave would be unnecessary. When I went into labor, I sent out assignments, and I returned a week later.

Of course, this didn't go well. Two weeks later I had pneumonia. My doctor was shocked. Not that I was sick, but that I had been so foolish in not expecting this to happen.

I had originally thought that my supervisees needed me and I didn't want to let them down. But that was not heroism or dedication, that was hubris. I took the opportunity to discuss my foolishness with my supervisees, cautioning them about the importance of self-care, but a better model would have been demonstrating self-care before becoming sick, and making the appropriate referral.

Absences happen, and avoiding them is an exercise in futility. But planning for them can be a valuable lesson for supervisees.

4.12 Appropriately Terminating Supervision

When behavior analysts determine, for any reason, to terminate supervision or other services that include supervision, they work with all relevant parties to develop a plan for terminating supervision that minimizes negative impacts to the supervisee or trainee. They document all actions taken in this circumstance and the eventual outcomes.

Explanation

Appropriate closure for either our clients or our supervisees is essential. No matter the reasons for the termination of supervision, they should be able to pick back up with another supervisor when they are ready, just as we would expect a client to be able to move on. It is vitally important that any supervision paperwork be stored and also provided to the supervisee and that any logging of hours be transferred to the appropriate person, whether that be the supervisee themselves or a new supervisor.

As always, communication is essential.

Considerations

Many of us who work with vulnerable populations come from a viewpoint that assumes competence. We face each case saying, "You are limited only by my ability to teach." There is no unsolvable problem. With enough time and enough patience and enough compassion, anyone can learn anything.

That may not always translate to the world of supervision, however, when that time, patience, and compassion must also be spent on the vulnerable populations we serve. Sometimes in this case we must ask ourselves, "While it is true that you can learn anything, is it worth the expenditure of my time and energy to teach you, knowing that both of these are in limited supply?"

While some patience with learning new skills and information should be expected, clear expectations should be made clear from the outset of the supervision experience. Clear behavioral expectations and their consequences should be outlined in the supervision contract, along with what conditions would necessitate termination and where the supervisor and supervisee would go from there.

Examples from the Field

Written by Ann Beirne

I once worked as a consultant at a school where I also provided BCBA® supervision to a few candidates who were employed there. Unfortunately, as often happens, funding became an issue and I was no longer able to continue with my employment there.

I was, thankfully, allowed the time to inform them, provide the necessary paperwork, and introduce them to the staff member who would be taking over. That time allowed me the opportunity to make the transition.

A smooth transition requires care, thought, and time. Take the time to make it as smooth as possible.

Works Cited

Beaulieu, L., Addington, J., & Almeida, D. (2018). Behavior analysts' training and practices regarding cultural diversity: the case for culturally competent care. *Behavior Analysis in Practice, 12*(3), 557–575. https://doi.org/10.1007/s40617-018-00313-6.

Behavior Analysis Certification Board. (2020, March 20). BACB – Behavior Analyst Certification Board. www.bacb.com/wp-content/uploads/BACB_Experience-Standards_200501.pdf.

Behavior Analyst Certification Board. (2020). *Ethics Code for Behavior Analysts*. Littleton, CO: Author.

Britton, L. N., & Cicoria, M. J. (2019). *Remote fieldwork supervision for BCBA® trainees*. Academic Press.

Cooper, J. O., Heron, T. E., & Heward, W. L. (2013). *Applied behavior analysis*. Upper Saddle River, NJ: Pearson.

Cross, T. L. (1989). Towards a culturally competent system of care: a monograph on effective services for minority children who are severely emotionally disturbed.

Dunning, D. (2011). The Dunning-Kruger effect. *Advances in Experimental Social Psychology*, 247–296. https://doi.org/10.1016/b978-0-12-385522-0.00005-6.

Eikeseth, S. (2010). Examination of qualifications required of an EIBI professional. *European Journal of Behavior Analysis*, *11*(2), 239–246. https://doi.org/10.1080/15021149.2010.11434348.

Hayes, S. C. (2020). *A liberated mind: How to pivot toward what matters*. New York, NY: Avery.

Henrich, J., Heine, S. J., & Norenzayan, A. (2010). The weirdest people in the world? *SSRN Electronic Journal*. https://doi.org/10.2139/ssrn.1601785.

Fong, E. H., Ficklin, S., & Lee, H. Y. (2017). Increasing cultural understanding and diversity in applied behavior analysis. *Behavior Analysis: Research and Practice*, *17*(2), 103–113. http://dx.doi.org/10.1037/bar0000076.

Kazemi, E., Rice, B., & Adzhyan, P. (2018). *Fieldwork and supervision for behavior analysts: A handbook*. New York, NY: Springer.

LeBlanc, L. A., Sellers, T. P., & Ala'i, S. (2020). *Building and sustaining meaningful and effective relationships as a supervisor and mentor*. Cornwall on Hudson, NY: Sloan Publishing.

Neuringer A. (1991). Humble behaviorism. *The Behavior Analyst*, *14*(1), 1–13. https://doi.org/10.1007/BF03392543.

Plantiveau, C., Dounavi, K., & Virués-Ortega, J. (2018). High levels of burnout among early-career board-certified behavior analysts with low collegial support in the work environment. *European Journal of Behavior Analysis*, *19*(2), 195–207. https://doi.org/10.1080/15021149.2018.1438339

Reid, D. H., Parsons, M. B., & Green, C. W. (2012). *The supervisor's guidebook: Evidence-based strategies for promoting work quality and enjoyment among human service staff*. Springfield, IL: Charles C. Thomas.

Sellers, T. P., Valentino, A. L., & LeBlanc, L. A. (2016). Recommended practices for individual supervision of aspiring behavior analysts. *Behavior Analysis in Practice*, *9*(4), 274–286. https://doi.org/10.1007/s40617-016-0110-7.

Shepley, C., Allan Allday, R., & Shepley, S. B. (2017). Towards a meaningful analysis of behavior analyst preparation programs. *Behavior Analysis in Practice*, *11*(1), 39–45. https://doi.org/10.1007/s40617-017-0193-9.

Shook, G. L. (2005). An examination of the integrity and future of the behavior analyst certification Board®Credentials. *Behavior Modification*, *29*(3), 562–574. https://doi.org/10.1177/0145445504274203.

Taylor, B. A., LeBlanc, L. A., & Nosik, M. R. (2018). Compassionate care in behavior analytic treatment: can outcomes be enhanced by attending to relationships with caregivers? *Behavior Analysis in Practice*, *12*(3), 654–666. https://doi.org/10.1007/s40617-018-00289-3.

Turner, L. B., Fischer, A. J., & Luiselli, J. K. (2016). Towards a competency-based, ethical, and socially valid approach to the supervision of applied behavior analytic trainees. *Behavior Analysis in Practice*, *9*(4), 287–298. https://doi.org/10.1007/s40617-016-0121-4.

Wolf M. M. (1978). Social validity: the case for subjective measurement or how applied behavior analysis is finding its heart. *Journal of Applied Behavior Analysis*, *11*(2), 203–214. https://doi.org/10.1901/jaba.1978.11-203.

1.8   Ethics Standards Section 5
Responsibility in Public Statements

Responsibility in Public Statements

Behavior analysts maintain high standards of ethics when representing the field on public statements. In this chapter, we will review the requirements for ethical practice in public statements according to the Ethics Code for Behavior Analysts®, including responsibilities of maintaining ethical marketing practices, social media postings, and use of intellectual property. We include a discussion of each Code element, including an explanation, examinations of the considerations of complying with the Code element, and examples from the field.

Section 5 of the Ethical Code for Behavior Analysts addresses the behavior of professionals in the use of public statements. Before we dive too deep into the ethical issues that may arise from their use, let us take a moment here and address the purpose of public statements and their benefit to the field of behavior analysis.

There are specific common pitfalls in our representation, which can be problematic. These arise a repeatedly throughout this section of the Ethics Code®:

Confidentiality and consent. Data should not be presented publicly without consent. Even with consent to share data, information about specific clients should never be revealed, nor should any information that could lead to their identification be revealed. Pseudonyms should be used in any presentations.

Boundaries of competence. Marketing materials should send a clear picture as to what a practitioner does, without including areas outside of this demonstrated competence.

Misrepresentation. Marketing materials, presentations, lectures, and publications must clearly identify the behavior analyst's true credentials and to the best available scientific evidence.

Given these pitfalls, what is the benefit of making public statements? Public statements by behavior analysts often serve one of two purposes, both of which are important for the growth and development of the field:

Internal dissemination

Dissemination refers to the sharing of information with the public. Internal dissemination is the translation of scientific information and sharing of technologies to those within our own ranks: professionals within the field of behavior analysis.

This could be perceived as "preaching to the choir," and some may wonder what is the point of sharing within the ranks of those who have already had favorable responses. There is some value, however, to "preaching to the choir." That is, after all, how they are inspired to sing. Sharing resources, technologies, and information within our field is a valuable practice. We may be somewhat uncomfortable with highlighting our own materials or benefiting financially from materials or resources that they have developed.

DOI: 10.4324/9781003190707-9

External dissemination

Like many behavior analysts, we believe that there is life-saving potential within the technologies developed from this science. Which compels us to ask, "If we knew something that could save someone's life, would we hesitate to share it?" Would we hesitate to offer an antidote to a snakebite, or to help a choking victim? If not, why would we hesitate to share technologies which could allow vulnerable people to be healthy and safe? Dissemination is our ultimate goal, and the same types of activities that make our marketing successful are the tools that we use to accomplish it.

5.01 Protecting the Rights of Clients, Stakeholders, Supervisees, and Trainees

Behavior analysts take appropriate steps to protect the rights of their clients, stakeholders, supervisees, and trainees in all public statements. Behavior analysts prioritize the rights of their clients in all public statements.

5.02 Confidentiality in Public Statements

In all public statements, behavior analysts protect the confidentiality of their clients, supervisees, and trainees, except when allowed. They make appropriate efforts to prevent accidental or inadvertent sharing of confidential or identifying information.

Explanation

Because of the similarity between these two Code elements with regard to public statements, we can address their requirements together.

It is necessary here to define what is meant by confidentiality and privacy. According to the Office for Protection from Research Risks (1993),

> Confidentiality pertains to the treatment of information that an individual has disclosed in a relationship of trust and with the expectation that it will not be divulged to others, in ways that are inconsistent with the understanding of the original disclosure without permission.

Privacy is defined as, "having control over the extent, timing, and circumstances of sharing oneself (physically, behaviorally, or intellectually) with others." Clients should expect that they need only share what is relevant to the behavior-analytic program. Clients also have a right to expect that the information that they choose to share with us will be used only for the purpose for which it was originally shared. Without our respect for confidentiality, we afford our clients neither confidentiality nor privacy.

Considerations

This is an easy Code element to follow. By not providing public statements in the first place, you are golden; after all, sharing confidential information over public statements is incompatible if one does not make public statements at all. With that being said, upholding the science of applied behavior analysis through dissemination may be appropriate and, in some cases, necessary depending upon where you live (e.g., if there are limited resources available, to combat pseudoscientific campaigns, defend the science, etc.). In these cases, considerations must be made to ensure that the information that is being shared is truthful and identifying attributes related to the client are never shared. Using a pseudonym may not be sufficient, should there be other variables that the reader can use to decipher the identity of the individual mentioned in the public statement. This protection extends to stakeholders and colleagues. Even if the public statement is glowing, obtain signed permission ahead of time to ensure a public statement is both known beforehand and approved. Further, this necessity extends beyond vulnerable populations. For example, if you work as an Organization Behavior Management practitioner, you must get consent to share work related to organizations in which you have worked. A conversation around testimonials is upgoing within this chapter for greater clarification on public statements related to advertising and nonadvertising purposes.

Examples from the Field

Written by Jacob Sadavoy

One of the hats I wear is a vocational counselor in the food industry. In an effort to protect the information of individuals with whom I work, I need to be aware of what I share in an effort to maintain confidentiality of my colleagues. Upon sharing information related to the location of the kitchen and what we produce, additional demographic information of colleagues would make it fairly easy for the audience of a presentation to decipher the individual within my statement even if I use a pseudonym. This is less of a concern for larger organizations or organizations in saturated marketplaces. With that being said, those in larger organizations or within saturated markets still need to be careful and mindful of not providing too many details.

I had the unpleasant experience of working for an organization that used an image of a client without consent. The parent of the client was rightfully livid. A more thorough means of gaining informed consent was devised to avoid future transgressions; however, it made me think about other images of clients that this organization wrongly used to promote their work in situations such as; the parents were unaware, language barriers existed, social media was inaccessible, or there was a perceived power imbalance, where their concerns were not voiced for fear of negative repercussions. In all cases, these and other concerns *must* be addressed prior to sharing a personal statement. Consent must be informed and ideally, the client would agree on all images or statements, even with consent, to ensure the public statement is both accurate, transparent, and the client's identity is deemed protected.

5.03 Public Statements by Behavior Analysts

When providing public statements about their professional activities, or those of others with whom they are affiliated, behavior analysts take reasonable precautions to ensure that the statements are truthful and do not mislead or exaggerate either because of what they state, convey, suggest, or omit; and are based on existing research and a behavioral conceptualization. Behavior analysts do not provide specific advice related to a client's needs in public forums.

Explanation

Behavior analysts often have some resistance to marketing their services. It is often said that behavior analysts do not need to market or advertise their services or that they should refrain from doing so. The rationale is often that "most behavior analysts have more work than we know what to do with" and that such efforts are unnecessary. Another concern raised in such discussion is that we should be cautious in presenting ourselves as excessively polished. Given that so many pseudoscientific methodologies engage in slick and artful marketing with no evidence to back up their claims, we would be engaging in similar unethical behavior if we were to market our services.

However, it is not the marketing of such interventions that causes us to question the ethics of those involved. The questionable ethics are demonstrated by the *methods these individuals use*. It is not the description of the behavior that is unethical, it is the behavior itself. I would also caution against the idea that we do not need to market our services because "we have more work than we know what to do with." It is reasonable to assume that marketing efforts can and should lead to more clients and allow us to make our businesses sustainable, and that is the primary purpose of most marketing activities. However, marketing is often described as saying what you do repeatedly and often. Explaining applied behavior analysis repeatedly often allows us to disseminate the science and its power to support lasting meaningful behavior change. Our efforts at marketing have the potential to reach anyone who is interested in behavior analysis as a potential client, an advocate, or a future clinician. Therefore, it is not a question of whether or not every behavior analyst has enough work, but a question of whether or not every client has access to effective treatment. If we truly believe in the right to effective treatment, the onus is on us to ensure that applied behavior analysis is the first and most appealing treatment option that families hear about. In order to do this, we do not have the luxury of viewing marketing as an unsavory concept. Marketing our services does not imply that deception is taking place. Deception is deception and marketing is marketing, and they are not interchangeable just because they are not mutually exclusive.

Considerations

It is necessary when reviewing this Code element to address the various audiences to whom we would be communicating and the types of ethical pitfalls that we must avoid.

Potential audiences would be:

Potential employers. These individuals would view resumes and curriculum vitae. This would be a somewhat narrow audience and we could reasonably expect more knowledge of the science of behavior analysis and the ethical obligations of behavior analysis, though this expectation may not always meet the reality of every work environment.

Potential clients. This category refers to those who would be viewing advertisements, finding our names in directories, or reading brochures. If asked, we must provide other credentials as well. However, they are the target audience for our marketing.

Community members. This category applies to the audience of our most public of public statements. It refers to those who view public presentation, including those in social media, blog posts, or other media or publications. This would be our widest audience and we might reasonably expect little knowledge of the science, of applied behavior analysis methodologies, or of our ethical obligations as behavior analysts. Because some of these audiences would not have a level of expertise in the ethical obligations of our field, it becomes all the more important to be conscientious of these obligations.

Examples from the Field

Written by Jacob Sadavoy

This textbook has many contributors, many citations, and many referrals to trademarked and copyrighted material (e.g., the Ethics Code). Before we started this process of writing this textbook, we contacted the BACB® Compliance Coordinator asking for permission to reprint and/or display the BACB document entitled "Ethics Code for Behavior Analysts." Permission was granted upon sharing legal name/title, the exact materials we were requesting to cite or use, the exact nature of intended use, the period of time during which we will be offering the cited materials (i.e., period of publication), and to identify the publisher. The BACB® has a Compliance Coordinator in order to ensure that the material they produce is protected and will not be misrepresented in any form or medium. We have contributors to enrich the ethical dialogue for our readers. I do not take credit for their words as they would not take credit for mine. In some cases, I may disagree with a view they have written in their reflection or they may find issue with one or more of my examples. The ideas in this textbook are the intellectual property of the authors. It is to invigorate conversations about ethics and hopefully generate future publications from other voices in the field.

Perhaps more important is the addition, "behavior analysts do not provide specific advice related to a client's needs in public forums." This seems obvious as a behavior analyst would be unable to provide a sound clinical recommendation without data, context, past reports outlining objectives and goals, and consent (direct observation and conversations with other members of the collaborative team would also be of value). However, specific clinical advice has been shared on public forums, hence this addition to the Code. For those in parts of the world or in rural communities in which a behavior-analytic community is sparse, public forums can be integral to gain access or ideas on available resources and for connection with other behavior analysts in an effort to build a behavior-analytic community. Both of those activities do not involve sharing specific client-specific recommendations. A public forum should not be a substitute for supervision; however, in looking at the consequences of behavior for an inquirer, public forums are likely more responsive with greater access to reinforcement (via hearts and thumbs up) than what might be present in one's supervision. If this is the case, let your supervisor know you would like more timely feedback.

5.04 Public Statements by Others

Behavior analysts are responsible for public statements that promote their professional activities or products, regardless of who creates or publishes the statements. Behavior analysts make reasonable efforts to prevent others (e.g., employers, marketers, clients, stakeholders) from making deceptive statements concerning their professional activities or products. If behavior analysts learn of such statements, they make reasonable efforts to correct them. Behavior analysts document all actions taken in this circumstance and the eventual outcomes.

Explanation

As behavior analysts we are responsible for the image that we present to the world, but this Code element makes another point abundantly clear: we are also responsible for our image *as presented to the world*, regardless of whether or not the words or images are ours. It is important to monitor these public statements and correct any errors as soon as we become aware of them.

Considerations

Many of us in the field of behavior analysis began in a position that would evolve into what is now known as a Registered Behavior Technician®. Before there was such a certification, the role was still fulfilled and was called many other things, including "line therapist" or "direct service provider," but the responsibilities were similar. Less training and structure was available to the "line therapist," but there were many who, like myself, pursued this training over several years or decades and eventually became behavior analysts. After many years of receiving such training and decades spent in the field, our fluency increases and we are faced with an interesting dilemma – how to determine what constitutes "common knowledge." Common knowledge within our field is not necessarily common knowledge to the rest of the world, but, when the skills begin to come naturally to us, it is easy to conflate knowledge of the science with common sense. The "common sense" guideline refers to common sense among the general public, not merely common sense among those who have already learned the scientific support for various methodologies. When communicating clients or clients' families, citing this scientific support for our suggested interventions is a necessary step.

Examples from the Field

Written by Jacob Sadavoy

In my experience, negative statements about ABA are not generated in a vacuum and a great way to get to the root of the problem is to ask questions and not take their experiences personally. I was speaking to a headteacher in the United Kingdom who was against the use of ABA in the school setting. Instead of correcting her and delivering a speech regarding the necessity for evidence-based practices, I asked her to share her experiences. She provided an example in which a BCBA® came into her school and openly criticized the teacher for allowing a student to engage in physical stereotypy by saying, "you just let him do that" in front of the student and his classmates. The comment is insensitive and undermines the student's dignity. I cannot align myself with the fellow BCBA® from this story. She is correct. That should never have happened but that is not a flaw of ABA but a glaring lapse of judgment by an individual.

I remember when I first came into the field it was drilled into me that when referring to autistics, I had to use person-first language. I was given the rationale that you don't say "cancerous woman" but "women with cancer," and you should show the same respect for individuals with autism because the person comes before the disability. I no longer use person-first language to describe autistics because I make it a point to listen to the autistic community in an effort to be a more mindful and thoughtful behavior analyst. Self-advocates are on a crusade to own and celebrate their autism, as they should. Many self-advocates have also painted a negative picture of ABA. In a speech delivered on February 1, 2017, Ari Ne'eman, leading autism rights advocate and founder of Autistic Self Advocacy Network, said of Lovaas that he set out to "recover" autistic children and make them "indistinguishable from their peers." One could easily provide the argument that ABA in 1973 looks differently than it does in 2019, but I would argue that the concern here has less to do about Lovaas and has more to do with what is defined as socially significant. An autistic does not have to be indistinguishable from their allistic peers or recovered from their autism (essentially making them an entirely different person, which I would argue nobody would want) to be successful members of society. Self-advocates are demonstrating success across all facets of society. ABA practitioners need to be aware of these successes while focusing on the behaviors that are truly socially significant in order to be autistic and an independent contributing member of society. It is critical for the ABA community to listen and learn from self-advocates who can share their learning history and perspectives which are invaluable for practitioners working with the autistic population.

Please reference BCBA Joy Johnson's chapter (Chapter 3.5) within this textbook to gain a deeper understanding on how the science of applied behavior analysis can be enriched via inclusion and compassion.

It is also important to acknowledge that the non-autistic population would also benefit from ABA to help improve socially limiting behaviors. Personally, I have a hard time saying, "no" and being vulnerable; both socially significant behaviors for choice-making and social-emotional health and relationship building. I would likely benefit from behavior-analytic services to help me with those two deficits with the goal of reaching my full potential and not "being indistinguishable from my peers" or "to be recovered."

5.05 Use of Intellectual Property

Behavior analysts are knowledgeable about and comply with intellectual property laws, including obtaining permission to use materials that have been trademarked or copyrighted or can otherwise be claimed as another's intellectual property as defined by law. Appropriate use of such materials includes providing citations, attributions, and/or trademark or copyright symbols. Behavior analysts do not unlawfully obtain or disclose proprietary information, regardless of how it became known to them.

Explanation

Credit of authorship is essential. Any student knows that they claim as their own ideas at their own peril. Plagiarism is often severely punished in academic circles and a student who engages in academic dishonesty can risk failure in an assignment or class or even expulsion from an academic program. In a description published by the Writing Program Administration, plagiarism is defined as, "when a writer deliberately uses someone else's language, ideas, or other original (not common-language) material without acknowledging its source" (Council of Writing Program Administrators, 2003). Essentially any statement that goes beyond that is considered "common knowledge" must include a citation. The general recommendation is that if you are in doubt, a citation is the best option. Beyond our academic life, use of intellectual property without the proper trademark and copyright symbols can also come with steep consequences. It is essential to use the correct symbol when referring to trademarked materials. Inclusion of such a symbol indicates a trademark (^{TM}) or a registered trademark ($^{\circledR}$). Be sure to check the accuracy of such symbols if there is any room for doubt. An additional point to discuss is that such a symbol does not indicate affiliation with an organization or company, and such an affiliation should not be indicated. As our repeated theme in the Professional and Ethical Compliance Code$^{\circledR}$ suggests, honesty is the best policy.

This may seem to be one of the more fastidious Code elements. The rationale may be difficult to discern, as discussion of intellectual property is where we begin to depart from the comfortable realm of human services and enter a business mindset. The practice of creating a name and visual representation which differentiates a business or product is referred to as branding. Branding of materials is an essential element of establishing the identity of one's business, including non-profit entities such as the BACB$^{\circledR}$. The necessity of establishing this identity has a distinct purpose – to grant assurance to clients and their families seeking out highly qualified professionals. If this branding is not protected by intellectual property, the risk is that it will lead to confusion among consumers. It would be difficult to distinguish a board-certified behavior analyst$^{\circledR}$ from a practitioner who calls themselves "trained in behavior analysis" if the use of the logo and trademarks of the BACB$^{\circledR}$ are not carefully controlled. A university which offers coursework using the logo and mentions the credentials could reasonably be assumed to meet the coursework requirements for certification. In order to achieve the stated goal of meeting the needs of certificants as well as clients, this branding allows the BACB® to preserve the sanctity of this certification.

Considerations

It is not particularly natural to add a registered trademark symbol to a description of our credentials, since this is not required when indicating a degree. As a result, it may look a bit unusual and we may begin to question the necessity of this level of caution. When discussing how to avoid plagiarism, professors often advise their students, "when in doubt, provide a citation." Just as in our obligation to maintain academic integrity, it is best to be conservative in our compliance with this Code element if in doubt. Some of this doubt can be removed, however, by carefully examining which descriptors require a registered trademark symbol or require permission and which do not. The terms Behavior Analyst Certification Board®, board-certified behavior analyst®, board-certified assistant behavior analyst®, registered behavior technician®, and their abbreviations, BACB®, BCBA®, BCaBA®, and RBT®, respectively, are all protected trademarks. Descriptions of our job responsibilities or the philosophy behind them, such as natural environment teaching, discrete trial teaching, functional analysis, or functional communication training would not require registered trademark symbols. To speak somewhat loosely, the essential difference here is that the registered trademark is required for the description of who we are – the brand with which we align ourselves. Description of what we do would not be subject to this requirement.

Connections

Written by Ann Beirne

When the majority of my work was with young children, parents would often say to me, "We don't like ABA, but we like you. You don't really do ABA, it's more like modified ABA." I would often cringe when I heard it, thinking of Bobby Newman's words, "You can't do modified ABA any more than you can have a modified pregnancy." Using the science of behavior analysis is binary state – either the science guides practice or it does not. One day my husband pointed out the obvious by asking, "Why do they call it modified? Is it because you're nice?" The term "modified ABA" has been a popular one in educational circles. However, it is often unclear what exactly is modified about it if the intervention is focused on specific goals and emphasizes data-based decision-making. Applied behavior analysis, after all, is the science of how organisms learn, not treatment or treatment package. The analysis of antecedents and consequences and the use of data to make decisions as to the success of interventions to treat socially significant behavior are not modified in many cases. There is nothing within the science that mandates, or even suggests, that interventions cannot be compassionate or playful. There is nothing that mandates compliance above all else, regardless of the public perception of applied behavior analysis programs. The only thing that is modified in this case is the perception of applied behavior analysis as an intervention that promotes blind obedience. If practitioners use this terminology, however, it is understandable that consumers would view applied behavior analysis programs as being stodgy and robotic at best and cruel and abusive at worst. To refer to intervention as "modified ABA" implies that applied behavior analysis requires modifications in order to be attentive to the social significance of our interventions. Rather, it is the "applied" that comes before the "analysis." Our interventions must reflect a commitment to social significance and our messaging must clearly communicate that doing so is not a modification. It must communicate that playful behavioral interventions are still behavioral interventions, and that joy can be part of a responsible program. Kindness and compassion are not modifications, but they should be integral to programming.

Examples from the Field

Written by Jacob Sadavoy

Branding is important. Companies use branding so that stakeholders, at a glance, are aware of the product and quality. The symbols and names within the field of ABA established by the BACB® serve a similar purpose. If anyone could post the BACB® logo or call themselves an RBT, how would prospective clients discern which are true BACB®-associated clinicians. For the same reason, if you are wanting to purchase a Coke, you would know something is wrong if there is blue on the can. In working with a team in China, they were unaware of the importance of this Code element and had the BACB® logo on their site and were going to call participants of a two-day training an RBT®. Both are egregious errors that would confuse their clients. The prior error suggests that the program is affiliated with BACB® which is inaccurate and the latter error is falsifying a credential. Both of these mistakes where misleading and in violation of this ethical code element.

5.06 Advertising Nonbehavioral Services

Behavior analysts do not advertise nonbehavioral services as behavioral services. If behavior analysts provide nonbehavioral services, those services must be clearly distinguished from their behavioral services and BACB certification with the following disclaimer: "These interventions are not behavioral in nature and are not covered by my BACB certification." This disclaimer is placed alongside the names and descriptions of all nonbehavioral interventions. If a behavior analyst is employed by an organization that violates this Code standard, the behavior analyst makes reasonable efforts to remediate the situation, documenting all actions taken and the eventual outcomes.

Explanation

This might be a bit confusing at first glance, since this Code element would appear to be contradictory. Behavior analysts do not implement non-behavior-analytic intervention, and yet when they do there are certain restrictions on how to do what they are not permitted to do. Some clarification is certainly in order. In the early years of certification in behavior analysis, there was no restriction on the area of concentration for the master's degree. If an applicant for certification had a degree in Russian literature or French pastry, the answer was an enthusiastic "yes." This has been changed in response to the needs of consumers to assure the quality of intervention, but the intention was a broader interpretation of the science. Given that this is the science explaining the processes of learning for all organisms, a focus on the effective teaching and learning strategies could benefit anyone in any field, including Russian literature and French pastry. There are behavior analysts who are also speech therapists, personal trainers, or even novelists. Just as the original intention of the BACB® suggested, their knowledge of the science of behavior informs their practice in these areas. However, the intention of this Code is to clarify to the general public what is applied behavior analysis and what is not. Once a practice deviates from the scientific validity and data-based decision-making, that differentiates behavior-analytic practice. Behavior analysts are not restricted from following other interests and in fact many do. This Code element does not require restriction of our activities, whether they be personal or professional pursuits. This Code element requires that the behavior analyst be clear about what activities are behavior-analytic and what are not, and to maintain that clarity for the consumer.

Considerations

One of the trickier aspects of the transition from student to behavior analyst is how to explain that transition to potential employers or clients. Finding a way to explain the state of being "not quite a behavior analyst yet" can be complex. The reality is that being a certified behavior analyst is a binary state: you either are a certified behavior analyst or you are not. Presenting oneself as "almost a behavior analyst" or "Board Certified Behavior Analyst® (BCBA®) eligible" is not only confusing to potential clients, but it also misrepresents the field as a whole. It is worthy of note here that using the phrase "pending" is not authorized and would be considered misrepresentation. This is a situation in which an absolutist approach to ethics would be necessary. Misrepresenting one's credential is a violation of the Code which could interfere with an applicant's eligibility for the exam, and the importance of adherence to this requirement cannot be overstated. The status of pursuing certification is not an irrelevant detail in pursuing employment, however. The question then becomes how advanced coursework, an interest in opportunities for advancement, or the need for supervision, observation, or even simply flexibility can ethically be conveyed. Rather than placing emphasis on a credential that has not yet been acquired, it would be best in this case to do what behavior analysts do best: focus on observable and measurable phenomena, and this is essentially the guidance provided by the BACB® on this matter. According to the BACB®'s September 2008 newsletter (BACB, 2012), the best alternative is to simply list the coursework and experience as part of the resume. Include your status as a student under your education and your responsibilities under your work experience without mention of eligibility for the credential itself. Those familiar with the BCBA® credential will recognize your pursuit, and those who are not need only know that it is an international credential in behavior analysis.

Examples from the Field

Written by Jacob Sadavoy

I started out in the field as a home programmer. I was supervised by a BCBA® and I invoiced the family as a therapist doing ABA services. However, not all of my duties were as an ABA therapist (your multiple relationship radar should be gong off). There were times I was asked to spend an evening with the learner and provide respite for the parents. I am not technically doing the home program; however, I am doing ABA (I don't think I could stop seeing the principles of ABA in my everyday life if I tried). When in doubt, it is best to stipulate that the services rendered are different and to denote that on the invoice. Sometimes costs of services can vary and a remuneration breakdown would be beneficial. I have done so in the past in which school training, parent training, and professional crisis management course training were all at different rates. An old client of mine, from four years ago, still sends me inquiries about whether I can come visit her son. Her son has never really had a home program, as she does not wish for the principles of applied behavior analysis to be used at home because it "impedes her son's happiness" and she is happy having her son do whatever he likes because his happiness is paramount. It is a longer story. In any case, if I decided to go and work with this client again, I would have to stipulate that my time, which I am billing the client for, is "not behavior-analytic in nature and are not covered by my BACB® credential." I have zero interest to do so and create an invoice identifying non-behavior-analytic services and developing a rate for those services.

This gets confusing for those that have certification expanding their scope of practice. For some, having a behavior-analytic worldview is mutually exclusive to another worldview. However, I would argue there is value having multiple credentials in which one can inform the other. Take, for example, being an American Association of Sexuality Educators, Counselors and Therapists (AASECT) professional or a Speech and Language Pathologist who are dual certified as an ABA practitioner; for these individuals they will utilize the principles of ABA but also enrich client outcomes related to sexual health or speech and language based on the additional coursework and supervised hours in increasing their scope of competence outside the scope of behavior-analytic practice. As such, when they are making recommendations related outside a behavior-analytic scope of practice, it is best to label that as such. Further, it is also recommended that all of this is shared at intake and during the contractual agreement conversation so the client is aware of the different worldviews and knows when they are receiving behavior-analytic intervention and when they are receiving intervention from an auxiliary credential or licensure.

5.07 Soliciting Testimonials from Current Clients for Advertising

Because of the possibility of undue influence and implicit coercion, behavior analysts do not solicit testimonials from current clients or stakeholders for use in advertisements designed to obtain new clients. This does not include unsolicited reviews on websites where behavior analysts cannot control content, but such content should not be used or shared by the behavior analyst. If a behavior analyst is employed by an organization that violates this Code standard, the behavior analyst makes reasonable efforts to remediate the situation, documenting all actions taken and the eventual outcomes.

Explanation

This Code element encourages us to consider the effects of our actions on two distinctly different but equally vulnerable groups: those who give the testimonials and those who read them. The rationale behind this particular element deserves some explanation. Current clients can be influenced and even exploited, particularly by those who provide direct services. Particularly for those behavior analysts who work with families directly in home-based services, there is a great deal of intimacy in the professional relationship, even if behavior analysts are committed to maintain professional boundaries. If we enter these families' lives in the early days or weeks following a diagnosis of autism spectrum diagnosis, we may offer hope in a time of great uncertainty. For clients with other needs, we are still often coming into their lives in times of crisis, and this dynamic often permeates the relationship for as long as the relationship itself continues. Despite our efforts to the contrary, it is an inequality that often causes clients to feel indebted to us – a debt that can never be fully repaid. In this context, asking a simple favor such as a small testimonial becomes far from simple. The likelihood of exploitation is simply too great, even if there is no intention of exploitation on behalf of the clinician. Those seeking services are an equally vulnerable population. They also seek out services during a time that is likely marked by desperation and confusion. Interventions offered at this time can offer hope in the face of this bewilderment, but the responsibility of offering such hope cannot be overstated. It is a terrible disservice to offer hope if such hope is false. The rationale behind this Code element is to avoid exploitation through the promise of unrealistic expectations of treatment outcomes. While elements of the Ethics Code® often allow behavior analysts to develop their own alternatives to potentially unethical behavior, this particular element offers several. Rather than promise what cannot be honestly offered, a behavior analyst restricts their materials to what can be honestly offered. A behavior analyst offers information of what benefit their services actually offer rather than the promises that such services could offer.

Considerations

Marketing is marketing and deception is deception. Just because they are not mutually exclusive does not mean that they are the same thing. A behavioral definition of deception must include some act or statement which is not true, and the lack of accuracy is a defining feature of deception. A behavioral definition of marketing, on the other hand, is simply talking about one's work to as many people as possible as often as possible. There are many behavior analysts who believe that to offer marketing materials with mass appeal is by its nature unethical. After all, they often point out, this is what pseudoscientific methods do. Cloaked in the veneer of beautiful pictures and moving stories, they offer hope without evidence, and many behavior analysts recoil at sophistication of their messaging, assuming that it implies there is little underneath their lofty promises. Many hope to avoid the appearance of impropriety by avoiding the appearance of this sophisticated messaging entirely, which I believe misses the point. As behavior analysts, it is important to exercise the skills we so often use with our clients and determine the function behind the actions of potential clients and their caregivers. Behavior occurs in the context of the environment, and behavior that persists is maintained by reinforcement. To ignore the potential reinforcers of these methods or the persistence of the behavior associated with their access and insist that caregivers should seek out scientifically validated methods is to ignore data, and there is no greater sin in any of the sciences. If we fail to deliver a message that is likely to be well-received in a way in which it will be well-received, we need not congratulate ourselves for our ethical stance. Rather, such a refusal restricts access to services for those who most desperately need it. Every client has a right to effective treatment, including those who happen to enjoy a beautiful brochure.

Examples from the Field

Written by Jacob Sadavoy

When working with clients, I am aware that they are bombarded with recommendations from everywhere from an often-well-intentioned safety net. Once they are clients, it is my ethical responsibility to showcase the profession as the gold standard. If they are drawn to a new therapy, I take that as feedback of my performance in presenting the field of ABA and will make a concerted effort to refocus the client on using ABA principles. I can accomplish this goal without employing testimonials due to the plethora of resources and research that other pseudoscientific therapies simply do not have. It has been mentioned throughout this textbook that there is a plethora of other therapies for clients to explore. When I am deciding on a restaurant, I go to an app on my phone, Yelp, to help me decide based on the testimonials of other diners. For hotels, I read reviews and look at the number of stars. I do this 100% of the time. There are sites where teachers and physicians are given a grade based on past students and patients, respectively. If you are a parent of a recently diagnosed child and you are looking at therapeutic options, I anticipate that they will also read testimonials and may opt to try a program centered around Sensory Integration or, worse, the Miracle Mineral Solution. Similarly, the business owner looking for a consultant to provide an analysis on existing operations is likely to Google for testimonials and may make a decision based on reviews. As a parent, it is challenging to discern what therapies are right and which are harmful as there are resources that show that each therapy is the right one and likewise there are materials that demonstrate that each therapy is harmful, including ABA. Not every parent will know to intrinsically type "evidence-based practices" in a search engine. Is our advertising silence inadvertently supporting those therapies that do advertise?

5.08 Using Testimonials from Former Clients for Advertising

When soliciting testimonials from former clients or stakeholders for use in advertisements designed to obtain new clients, behavior analysts consider the possibility that former clients may re-enter services. These testimonials must be identified as solicited or unsolicited, include an accurate statement of the relationship between the behavior analyst and the testimonial author, and comply with all applicable privacy and confidentiality laws. When soliciting testimonials from former clients or stakeholders, behavior analysts provide them with clear and thorough descriptions about where and how the testimonial will appear, make them aware of any risks associated with the disclosure of their private information, and inform them that they can rescind the testimonial at any time. If a behavior analyst is employed by an organization that violates this Code standard, the behavior analyst makes reasonable efforts to remediate the situation, documenting all actions taken and the eventual outcomes.

Explanation

In this case, concerns about the exploitation of current clients is eliminated, but we must still be aware that testimonials should be used responsibility. There are several aspects of this element that deserve careful review.

Confidentiality. Client information should not be shared as part of a testimonial, even if that client is no longer receiving services. Our responsibility to protect the rights of clients does not disappear when services stop, it continues long after.

Consent. Consent must be *informed* and *voluntary.* Even clients who no longer receive services must have full and complete information about how these testimonials will be used.

Responsibility. The full responsibility for how these testimonials will be used and the adherence to the Ethics Code is ours and our alone. We cannot expect those with expertise in marketing to also have expertise in our Ethics Code. Clear communication about appropriate use and the correction of any misuse is essential.

Considerations

Many professionals use the word "consent" as synonymous with "form that is signed indicating consent." In reality a consent form is to consent as a photograph is to a person. A photograph is not synonymous with that person. Rather it is documentation of that person at a particular moment in time. Similarly, a signed form indicating consent is merely documentation that, at a particular moment in time, consent was given. It is not a commitment to consent.

A necessary element of consent is that it is voluntary and can be withdrawn at any time. Make sure that clients and families know that this is not a contract, it is the documentation of your conversations. Their consent today can be withdrawn tomorrow.

Examples from the Field

Written by Ann Beirne

Many years ago I received a "cold call" – a phone call from someone I did not know asking for my services. It was so long ago, in fact, that it was on a landline. This woman, a parent of a child with autism, had gotten my number from someone else – another person that I did not know, and had heard wonderful things about me. Unfortunately, I did not have any room in my caseload, I explained, but if she was unable to find anyone in a week she should call me back. "This is what I tell people every time I can't do it," I said, "and no one has ever called me back, so I'm confident you will be able to find someone." The mother laughed and said, "That's exactly what she said you would say!"

Testimonials are powerful instruments and often, as in this example, their reach can surpass our expectations, or even our intentions. Their power to generate enthusiasm and hope cannot be matched, even by the power of the evidence that supports our methods. and must be used responsibly.

5.09 Using Testimonials for Nonadvertising Purposes

Behavior analysts may use testimonials from former or current clients and stakeholders for nonadvertising purposes (e.g., fundraising, grant applications, dissemination of information about ABA) in accordance with applicable laws. If a behavior analyst is employed by an organization that violates this Code standard, the behavior analyst makes reasonable efforts to remediate the situation, documenting all actions taken and the eventual outcomes.

Explanation

Our responsibility as outlined in this Code element is to be aware of applicable laws. Has written consent been obtained? Has this written consent specified how testimonials will be used? And, above all, have the privacy and confidentiality of the client or family member been protected?

As is true for other Code elements involving our legal obligations, it is our responsibility to be aware of the laws that apply and to take the initiative to correct any violations.

Considerations

How do you ask for someone to endorse your services, skills, or experience? First, be willing to accept "no" as a full sentence. The goal is to ask your most enthusiastic cheerleaders, and anyone who is resistant is not a good candidate. Second, tell them a bit about the position or the key elements of what the deciding parties are looking for so that they can tailor the letter accordingly. Even if they ask, do *not* write a letter yourself for them to sign. Finally, encourage them to "write what they know." A testimonial from a parent that describes your compassion, enthusiasm, and creativity is appropriate. A letter of recommendation from a professor describing your work ethic and research skills is equally appropriate.

Connections

Written by Ann Beirne

Perhaps the most powerful example of a testimonial written for nonadvertising purposes is the book *Let Me Hear Your Voice* by Catherine Maurice. Maurice, writing under a pseudonym to protect the privacy of her children, writes about the diagnosis of her two children and the use of applied behavior analysis. Both of her children were considered "recovered" – meaning that they no longer meet the diagnostic criteria of autism. The power of her story was not just in the results, but in the beauty of her writing and the emotion of her journey – her search for appropriate services, her heartbreak at the persistence of theories that attribute autism's cause to bonding or to inadequate parenting. And, most important, she described the experience – the joys and triumphs – of an ABA program.

It was this testimonial that brought many parents their first stories of how applied behavior analysis could be used in loving supportive ways and how it could offer evidence-based alternatives based on positive reinforcement. It was this testimonial that created the demand for services – that literally created the field as it is today.

Examples from the Field

Written by Ann Beirne

I once applied for a scholarship that presented a unique opportunity to mentor with one of the most well-known behavior analysts in my state. The committee that would decide on the recipients of this scholarship, sponsored by an organization that was founded by parents, required several elements to the application, including letters of recommendations specifically from parents. As parents themselves, those on the committee knew what they were looking for, and had confidence that the parents of my clients had the viewpoint they needed.

I explained the scholarship, what I hoped to gain, and asked for the letter. When I received it, I took it, without looking, and gave them my sincere thanks. Each was unique, as was my relationship with each client and each family.

5.10 Social Media Channels and Websites

Behavior analysts are knowledgeable about the risks to privacy and confidentiality associated with the use of social media channels and websites and they use their respective professional and personal accounts accordingly. They do not publish information and/or digital content of clients on their personal social media accounts and websites. When publishing information and/or digital content of clients on their professional social media accounts and websites, behavior analysts ensure that for each publication they (1) obtain informed consent before publishing, (2) include a disclaimer that informed consent was obtained and that the information should not be captured and reused without express permission, (3) publish on social media channels in a manner that reduces the potential for sharing, and (4) make appropriate efforts to prevent and correct misuse of the shared information, documenting all actions taken and the eventual outcomes. Behavior analysts frequently monitor their social media accounts and websites to ensure the accuracy and appropriateness of shared information.

Explanation

It is safe to say that social media is everywhere. The ubiquity of social media, and the expectation that we will use this method to communicate, make it difficult to opt out of the social media age.

This Code element does not require that you refrain from social media, merely that you use this powerful tool responsibly. Personal and professional social media accounts should be kept separate and, as with all of our professional activities, all of our communication must adhere to the requirements of the Ethics Code®.

Considerations

One important element here deserves attention: *the potential for sharing*. In contrast with other Code elements that address our clients' right to confidentiality, we must be keenly aware that once information is posted, we no longer control it. At a minimum we must regularly check our privacy settings and any new posts to or professional pages, ensuring that any and all statements meet with the requirements of the Ethics Code®. Any information at all should bear in mind this potential for widespread use, and the behavior analyst who posts it must share responsibly.

Examples from the Field

Written by Ann Beirne

I once had a confrontation online that took an unexpected turn. When I saw what I felt was a sexist post, I commented on that opinion, saying that it should be taken down. Several of my colleagues, as it turned out, had agreed, and quite a controversy had stirred up.

A few days later, with that controversy still brewing, I received a message, sent by someone I did not know. She accused me of hypocrisy and said I should not be making such accusations. Her evidence was a post of mine from three years earlier. It was a clip from the movie Miss Congeniality that she claimed could be interpreted as offensive to blondes, posted on April 25, described in the video as "the perfect date" with the comment "I hope you all have the perfect date today!"

I read the message with a mix of horror that someone had combed through my posts so thoroughly and pride that she had found so little offensive material. As a mother of three who enjoys baking and trips to the zoo, I can only imagine how much cake decorating and baby pictures she must have searched in those three years of posts before arriving at what she chose.

5.11 Using Digital Content in Public Statements

Before publicly sharing information about clients using digital content, behavior analysts ensure confidentiality, obtain informed consent before sharing, and only use the content for the intended purpose and audience. They ensure that all shared media is accompanied by a disclaimer indicating that informed consent was obtained. If a behavior analyst is employed by an organization that violates this Code standard, the behavior analyst makes reasonable efforts to remediate the situation, documenting all actions taken and the eventual outcomes.

Explanation

In the use of digital content the same rules apply – perhaps even more rigidly, as this content is often visual, leaving greater opportunity for "identifying information" to be gleaned. Digital media, including recordings and photos, must be obtained with consent that is both *informed* and *voluntary*. Clients and their caregivers must be informed how and when such content will be used – every time that it is used. And they must be informed that such consent can be withdrawn at any time.

Considerations

Again, it is the behavior analyst's responsibility to adhere to the Ethics Code® and not others who may be affected by our decisions, including those who market our services. Though obtaining consent to share media each time it is shared and for each purpose may seem cumbersome, we may find ourselves explaining that it is a necessary component of ethical practice. Communication, whether it be with clients, families, or those in management positions, must be done with honesty. That communication should be the preventive response, not the reactive one.

Connections

Written by Ann Beirne

I occasionally use video models in my training of staff or parents, and occasionally use pictures of children in social narratives as the instruction phase of behavioral skills training. When using other children as models I usually rely on the consent of a parent I know quite well – myself. My own children have served as models for attentive listening, manding items by pointing, use of sign language, and prompting strategies. I generally explain this to clients or to participants if these are presented so that there is no misunderstanding and so that consent is clear.

A bit of creativity in the use and development of materials can avoid many ethical pitfalls in the use of digital materials.

Examples from the Field

Written by Ann Beirne

A colleague of mine did a presentation on the use of pairing techniques and appropriate goals and data collection systems to monitor their progress. Pairing is the process by which behavior analysts and other clinicians establish rapport. This is repeated as the therapeutic relationship continues but is most important at the start of service. As one might well imagine, it would be very difficult indeed to gain consent for filming this process with a new client, and the discomfort for all involved as clinicians and client get to know one another would make it questionable.

Instead, this colleague used a different video model – one of E.T. As E.T. gradually approaches Elliott, she explained the process of and approaching the client gradually by being mindful of behavior. As E.T. drops Reese's Pieces into Elliott's hand, she explained noncontingent reinforcement. The humor made it memorable; the creativity made it ethical.

Works Cited

Autistic Self Advocacy Network. (2017, February 1). Autism and the disability community: the politics of Neurodiversity, causation and cure. https://autisticadvocacy.org/2017/02/autism-and-the-disability-community-the-politics-of-neurodiversity-causation-and-cure.

Behavior Analyst Certification Board. (2008, September). BACB – Behavior Analyst Certification Board. www.bacb.com/wp-content/uploads/2020/05/BACB_Newsletter_9_08.pdf.

Behavior Analyst Certification Board. (2020). *Ethics Code for Behavior Analysts*. Littleton, CO: Author.

Council of Writing Program Administrators. (2003, January). *Defining and avoiding plagiarism: The WPA statement on best practices.* CWPA. https://wpacouncil.org/aws/CWPA/pt/sd/news_article/272555/_PARENT/layout_details/false.

Maurice, C. (1994). *Let me hear your voice: A family's triumph over autism.* New York, NY: Ballantine Books.

The Office for Protection from Research Risks. (1993, August 13). *NIH guide: Protecting human research subjects: Institutional review BOARDGUIDEBOOK.* NIH Grants Site. https://grants.nih.gov/grants/guide/notice-files/not93-209.html.

U.S. National Institutes of Health, Office for Protection from Research Risks, Protecting Human Research Subjects: Institutional Review Board Guidebook, 3–27 (U.S. National Institutes of Health, Bethesda, Maryland, 1993, with later addenda).

1.9 Ethics Standards Section 6
Responsibility in Research

6.01 Conforming with Laws and Regulations in Research

Behavior analysts plan and conduct research in a manner consistent with all applicable laws and regulations, as well as requirements by organizations and institutions governing research activity.

Explanation

It is necessary to have a deep understanding of the laws involving research subjects. While many of these may seem obvious, there may be some that escape our attention. For younger subjects, laws and regulations may govern how frequently they are offered snacks or an opportunity to rest. Protocols which involve extended direct teaching may not be aligned with children's needs, including snacks and naps, and this should be taken into account when designing intervention. Laws involving the treatment of animals should be considered as well. As discussed in our introductory chapter, legality is the minimum standard for the behavior we consider consistent with being a "good person." However, when conducting research, the considerations of relevant legal requirements may take a bit of research. Ignorance of such laws is an inadequate defense, for both legal and ethical violations.

Considerations

In any mention of mandated reporter requirements, a certain amount of discomfort should be expected. Many of us in human services believe passionately in the rights of clients, particularly children, to safety, and many of us are staunch advocates for children and are, at least in theory, prepared to make reports of abuse or neglect if necessary. To be prepared in theory, however, is very different from being prepared in practice. The reality is that making such reports is often difficult. It is not a decision to be made lightly, and I know very few clinicians who have done so easily or without regard for the consequences for the family. In the case of research, other, less noble but no less valid concerns may also interfere with our judgments. If grant funding or the completion of a degree is in question, this may color our clinical judgment. It is always important to remember that our first and most important obligation is to the client – for the benefit of their personal safety and welfare. Though the process is difficult and often traumatic, families often cannot be helped without the services provided. To hesitate on reporting abuse or neglect is often to deny families the support that is needed to maintain health and safety for everyone.

DOI: 10.4324/9781003190707-10

Examples from the Field

Written by Jacob Sadavoy

Completing research is an essential part of any scientific discipline. It is the evidence in "evidence-based" practice. If you look at the history of applied behavior analysis (ABA), there were 36 articles published between 1959 and 1967 (Morris et al., 2013). In the same eight-year time period between 2009 and 2017, a search for all ABA-related research in just the *Journal of Applied Behavior Analysis* alone produced 79,936 results. Similarly, if one were to do an analysis on the prevalence of articles on alchemy, geocentric model of the universe, or facilitated communication, you would see a reverse trend in research production over time. A scientific theory will either gain more prominence as it is shown to be replicable, true, and of importance, otherwise the theory will fade into obscurity. It is the science community's way of using natural selection to ensure that true science propagates at the expense of pseudoscience which does not survive. However, generating articles is only a measure of success in the scientific world if there are regulations, rules, and laws to ensure that there are professional standards governing the conduct of that research. Internationally, in developing countries, there would be fewer provisions on researchers and consent procedures; as a result, the behavior Analyst Certification Board® is making a clear delineation that, even in under-resourced areas, a Board Certified Behavior Analysis® must conduct research ethically and uphold the standards required to conduct research as a BCBA® researcher. The Nuremberg code of 1947 was generally regarded as the first document to set out ethical regulations in human experimentation based on informed consent as a result of the Nazi experiments on concentration camp detainees. However, the Prussian guidelines of 1900 predate the Nuremberg code and should have been implemented to prevent the atrocities that befell victims of the Holocaust (Vollman & Winau, 1996). Thus, applicable laws and regulations cannot be solely relied upon. Similarly, an independent, formal research review board cannot be the sole guarantor that research practices are ethical. The researcher has an obligation to go through our Code and uphold its requirements regardless of where they are conducting the research and the laws that may be too lenient.

6.02 Research Review

Behavior analysts conduct research, whether independent of or in the context of service delivery, only after approval by a formal research review committee.

Explanation

As an attendee at conferences and workshops, it may appear that research is simply the public posting of data that we already have. As a data-based intervention, it may seem that we can simply present data from a successful program as part of a research study, collect our accolades, and call it a day. There are, however, several steps to be taken before research can be conducted ethically. As a preliminary step, many institutions require a course in the ethics of research with human subjects, along with certification of the course' completion, which expires in three years. Such research also requires the oversight and approval of an Institutional Review Board. The members of this advisory group, which includes both scientists and nonscientists, must approve the methods proposed by the researchers, including the use of potentially sensitive information, the protection of confidentiality, and the potential harm and/or benefit of the procedures. The oversight of an Institutional Review Board and the requirement of its approval certainly add a safety net, so to speak, for the protection of research participants. However, individual behavior analysts must also take responsibility for the welfare of those who participate in research. Contributing to the overall knowledge in the field is a tremendous undertaking and should not be taken lightly. Those who assist us in this endeavor must be protected and it is the responsibility of all of those who oversee or design research to do so.

Considerations

Perhaps the most infamous of psychological experiments is the Stanford Prison Experiment (Drury et al., 2012). In this experiment of the situational effects of a prison environment, college-aged young men were randomly assigned the roles "prisoner" or "guard" and agreed to play these roles in a mock prison on the Stanford campus. The lead researcher, Philip Zimbardo, played the role of "prison superintendent." The experiment, originally planned to last two weeks, was cut short after six days. In that time, the "prison guards" repeatedly isolated, abused, and humiliated the "prisoners." Despite the fact that each of the participants expressed a preference for being a prisoner rather than a guard, the prison guards became absorbed in their roles, and grew to accept as normal the dehumanization of the "prisoners." Even Dr. Zimbardo himself became a participant in the environment, and was absorbed in the role of the "prison superintendent" as well, until he was finally urged to put a stop to the abuse and the experiment itself. In Philip Zimbardo's later work, he has been forthcoming about the ethical violations of this experiment and describes the experiment as "both ethical and unethical." Following the termination of the Stanford Prison Experiment, Zimbardo himself called for an ethics review by the American Psychological Association. Given that the subjects had freely consented to participate, it was determined that there had not been ethical violations as they currently stood, and the experiment could therefore be fairly described as "ethical." However, many of the most egregious abuses of the "guards" were not anticipated, leading Zimbardo to describe it as "unethical." It is important to acknowledge, however, the value of this experiment in terms of its impact on our knowledge of the abuses of power. Disturbing though the Stanford Prison Experiment may be – and it certainly is – the knowledge gained from its efforts has given us greater understanding of the nature of similar oppression of abuse of power. Dr. Zimbardo has offered his expertise in this area to consult in other situations outside the laboratory, including an understanding of the psychology behind genocide and torture. Research could accurately be described as a search for the truth. Bearing this in mind, it is difficult to deny the "bright side" of this particularly dark tale. Our understanding of the nature of what could be described as "evil" was undeniably changed by the knowledge gained by the Stanford Prison Experiment, and certainly one of our obligations as researchers is to the truth. Our first and most critical obligation, however, is to the welfare and dignity of those who join us in this search for the truth. Whatever can be gained does not compare to this. Because of this experiment and others, we are able to know better, and when we know better, we are able to do better.

Examples from the Field

Written by Jacob Sadavoy

When research and clinical needs conflict, behavior analysts prioritize the welfare of the client. This seems simple, but this cannot be overstated as it has been challenged for decades, around the world. We had mentioned the horrific experiments executed by the Nazis under the guise of scientific advancements. Here in the USA, the Tuskegee syphilis experiment's goal was to observe the natural progression of untreated syphilis in rural black men in Alabama (Emanuel et al., 2011). In both cases, highly vulnerable populations were exploited: German medical doctors undertook their experiments on concentration camp detainees while US medical doctors exploited black US citizens by studying the natural progression of syphilis without providing available cures, for four decades. In both cases, informed consent was foregone. There was no mechanism to ensure compliance of ethical practices despite the existence of ethical guidelines for conducting research at the time. Experiments like this gave birth to the IRB process to ensure that research went through strict measures to ensure that participants were protected and designs were ethical.

The previous examples, though not in ABA, are critical to understand that humans have sought answers, through scientific reasoning, at the expense of human lives. The field of ABA has no shortage of controversy as well. The role of societal intolerance in choosing target behaviors was mentioned in one of the Rekers/Lovaas studies where the authors concluded that it is more realistic to change those affected by intolerance than to change the intolerant behaviors of society. As a result, the Feminine Boy Project was created as a means to replace feminine behaviors (e.g., "maternal nurturance" and playing with girls) with masculine behaviors (e.g., playing with a toy submachine gun and roughhousing with boys) in gender-role-deviant young boys (Rekers & Lovaas, 1974). This is hugely problematic for several reasons despite the fact that homosexuality, at the time, was illegal and the parents provided informed consent for their child to partake in the study. For starters, there is no research/truth that suggests the life of a heterosexual male is superior to that of a homosexual male or that a boy having "feminine behaviors" results in adverse development. Thus, the Feminine Boy Project did not have a socially significant dependent variable and further, how can the dependent variable in this study be accurately measured when defining behaviors as being gender specific is absurd (with few exceptions, e.g., menstruating, lactating, penile erections, etc.). Today, an IRB would not accept this experiment as it is unethical and dehumanizing.

6.03 Research in Service Delivery

Behavior analysts conducting research in the context of service delivery must arrange research activities such that client services and client welfare are prioritized. In these situations, behavior analysts must comply with all ethics requirements for both service delivery and research within the Code. When professional services are offered as an incentive for research participation, behavior analysts clarify the nature of the services, and any potential risks, obligations, and limitations for all parties.

Explanation

In casual assessments of risk, it is often stated that crossing the street also comes with risk. Certainly, this statement is true, but it can easily be argued that such a statement is also incomplete. Crossing the street comes with risk, but such risk is known to the pedestrian.

It is essential that we have an understanding of any and all anticipated risks of participation in a given study. It is equally important that such an understanding is conveyed to potential participants. We must make every effort to be honest and forthright in our descriptions of the risks involved to safety, dignity, and privacy.

Considerations

This Code element urges us to consider our obligations *to the participant* in research. In addition to the consideration of risks of participation, we must also be mindful of the *benefits* of research.

In Baer and colleagues' article (1968), the requirements for what is considered acceptable research in applied behavior analysis were made clear. These dimensions of behavior analysis, but primarily they are intended to be criteria for behavior analytic research. A behavior change program must be *effective*. This is described by Baer, Wolf and Risley as producing "large enough effects for practical value" (Baer, et al., 1968). There is considerable overlap with the requirement that such research also be *applied,* defined by Baer, Wolf and Risley (1968) as being a reflection of the social significance of the behavior. As the authors state it, "a primary question in the evaluation of applied research is: how immediately important is this behavior or these stimuli to this subject?" (Baer et al., 1968).

It becomes necessary for those of us engaging in research activities to ask ourselves, "Do the potential benefits of participation in this study have practical value? Will the behavior change that results be relevant to the participant?"

A focus on practical benefits to clients runs deep within our science, and research activities are not an exception to this focus.

Examples from the Field

Written by Jacob Sadavoy

It is important to acknowledge that there are always risks associated with research. Sometimes those risks are minimal but other times those risks outweigh the value of the benefit of seeking scientific validation. This Code element is a reminder to reflect on the value of conducting research both on the research participant but also everyone else affiliated with the project. In Watson's Little Albert experiment, contriving the environment to evoke reactions of fear in humans under laboratory circumstances would be considered unethical by our present-day standards.

I often think about ways I can support those I work with internationally to produce research to showcase their wonderful work coupled with promoting dissemination in their local communities. Currently the majority of international partners are working on maintaining the treatment integrity of their program and engaging stakeholders in their community. Research is rightfully a lower priority for them. Further, in order for them to do a research assignment, they would have to invest resources in getting the necessary data and IOA which would mean withdrawing resources from other aspects of their work. In time, once they have built capacity and have a stronger foundation, they will have the resources to maintain their clinical integrity and conduct research concurrently. Applied research is challenging and research initiatives should not undermine or negatively alter progress of the behavior change program.

6.04 Informed Consent in Research

Behavior analysts are responsible for obtaining informed consent (and assent when relevant) from potential research participants under the conditions required by the research review committee. When behavior analysts become aware that data obtained from past or current clients, stakeholders, supervisees, and/or trainees during typical service delivery might be disseminated to the scientific community, they obtain informed consent for use of the data before dissemination, specify that services will not be impacted by providing or withholding consent, and make available the right to withdraw consent at any time without penalty.

Explanation

In this Code element we see the overlap of our obligations to participants and our obligation to the truth.

"Consent" is often ill-defined as synonymous with "permission slip." There is, however, a meaningful distinction to be made between consent and the documentation of this consent. Though the documentation of consent is a necessary element, this is merely an indication of consent, and not consent itself.

In order for such consent to be truly "informed" as required, all participants must have a clear understanding of the fact that they will be participating in a research study, the procedures to be used and the study's purpose, as well as any risks and benefits of participation. Alternative treatment plans must also be addressed and fully understood. Participants must also be informed that their consent is voluntary and told who will be available to answer any further questions.

As with any communication, however, what we say is only half of what must be considered. Even with a signed consent form, if a true understanding of the procedures, purpose, benefits, and risks of the study is to be achieved, what is heard is equally important.

Considerations

When doing research, particularly with vulnerable populations, it is important to be aware of our influence and the power that we hold. Coercion can happen even if it is unintentional and even if it is subtle.

The essential components of informed consent are the understanding of both the freedom to participate and the freedom to decline to participate. Consent must be given freely and without coercion. If the study was being conducted by service providers, it may imply that participation is a required aspect of service. The appearance of supervisor may add to the pressure to participate, even if the intention is only to ensure fidelity.

Once a potential participant has declined to participate, the conversation must end. Whether or not any coercion is intended, even the appearance of it must be avoided.

Connections

Written by Ann Beirne

My father once worked as a risk management consultant for a medical malpractice insurance company. When giving lectures to doctors on ways to minimize their risk of lawsuit, he would stand at a dais and ask the question, "What is the most important piece of equipment you can have when getting consent for a medical procedure?" There were several guesses: a pen, a clipboard, a written description of the procedure. After the doctors had run out of ideas, he would explain that many patients who sued their doctors knew they would sue even before the incident occurred. He said that they reported that they consistently felt rushed, that their doctor was too busy to talk to them, that they were not paying attention. Even if the doctors said that they gave them ample opportunity to ask questions, that was not the patient's experience. Then he would give them the answer to the question, "What is the most important piece of equipment when getting consent?" He would take a chair and place it on the table, saying, "This is it. A chair. When you are getting consent, sit down. It tells the patient that you are making time for them."

Informed consent should not only follow the letter of this Code but also its spirit. In order for consent to be truly informed it should also feel that way to the participant. It is worth the extra effort and time to address all of the client's concerns and let them know we will make that time for them.

Examples from the Field

Written by Ann Beirne

When my son, at age ten, participated in a research study, we were both asked to sit and give consent to the study. During the discussion with me, all of my questions were answered and I was told of the ability to withdraw consent. I signed my assent. Then they turned to him. They explained the procedures. And answered all of his questions. As part of the consent, they clarified, "No one will be mad at you if you say you don't want to do the study."

This beautifully clarified his right to refuse and his right to withdraw consent. Consent, as we will repeat again and again, must be *voluntary*.

6.05 Confidentiality in Research

Behavior analysts prioritize the confidentiality of their research participants except under conditions where it may not possible. They make appropriate efforts to prevent accidental or inadvertent sharing of confidential or identifying information while conducting research and in any dissemination activity related to the research (e.g., disguising or removing confidential or identifying information).

Explanation

The researchers' obligation to the participants includes not only the respect for the safety and comfort of participants but also respect for their personal information. Participants must be assured that their efforts to add to the field of knowledge will not be rewarded with a violation of their privacy.

Just as we must protect the privacy of our clients, we must also protect the privacy of research participants.

Considerations

One aspect to be considered here is that any research should have some level of external validity. This refers to the extent that the results of a particular study will be applicable to the general public. Seeing impressive results decreasing gum-chewing in a population of eight-year-old boys is unlikely to generalize to decreasing smoking in college-aged women. However, the issue of the relevance of some information. In this example, the age and general health of the participants in a smoking cessation study may be relevant, but religious affiliation, parents' income, or sexual history would not be.

As the old adage says, "tell the truth but don't always be telling it." Information that is obtained in the context of a research study, and certainly the information that is communicated as a part of the study's description and results, should be relevant to the study itself. What we do not have access to, we do not fear revealing.

Examples from the Field

Written by Ann Beirne

In perhaps the best example of maintaining confidentiality, I once had the pleasure of watching Dr. Dana Reinecke present her finding on her study increasing reinforcer repertoire. As the mother of a young child and a fan of the Muppets, she had selected unique pseudonyms for her participants – Bob, Luis, and Maria, the adults who lived on Sesame Street. As a practitioner working with young children I recognized the names immediately, but for those who did not she also made reference to this as a discussant.

The cleverness of this tactic was not only that she *used* pseudonyms, but that she used ones that were *easily identifiable as pseudonyms*. This avoided not only breaches of confidentiality but also the appearance of those breaches. It is essential to maintain the confidentiality of participants and, by using the names of the adults rather than other characters, she treated participants with dignity while demonstrating creativity, humor, and respect.

6.06 Competence in Conducting Research

Behavior analysts only conduct research independently after they have successfully conducted research under a supervisor in a defined relationship (e.g., thesis, dissertation, mentored research project). Behavior analysts and their assistants are permitted to perform only those research activities for which they are appropriately trained and prepared. Before engaging in research activities for which a behavior analyst has not received training, they seek the appropriate training and become demonstrably competent or they collaborate with other professionals who have the required competence. Behavior analysts are responsible for the ethical conduct of all personnel assigned to the research project.

Explanation

As clarified in many Code elements, behavior analysts do not dabble in those activities in which they do not have expertise. "Fake it till you make it" is not an ethical stance, and to do so would be grossly irresponsible. Behavior analysts must gain the skills and experience necessary to engage in professional activities competently before allowing clients to be put at risk.

This is equally true when engaged in research activities. We must first acquire the skills necessary to responsibly engage in research before taking on this role. Research is central to our field, and its implementation must be taken seriously.

Considerations

I remember being asked to guess the most common participant in a psychological experiment. I often repeat this activity when teaching exam prep or in discussions with supervisees, and many are surprised by the answer – college sophomores.

There are many opportunities to engage in research, both as a participant and as a researcher. If opportunities to learn from researchers present themselves, it would be beneficial to take them. This may mean being the participant in a study and gaining some insight into the study's design and demonstration of a functional relationship. It may mean participating as a confederate and implementing the procedures studied. Whatever your involvement, much can be gained from the experience of engaging in research activities.

Understanding how such knowledge is gained at each level of involvement can inform and enhance the skills of any clinician.

Examples from the Field

Written by Jacob Sadavoy

Conducting research requires a specific skill set. Reading countless articles does not equip one to attempt to do a research project independently. There are many "behind-the-scenes" variables that an inspiring researcher should be comfortable performing independently and the only way in which to ensure that is the case is to have successfully conducted research under a supervisor in a defined relationship (e.g., thesis, dissertation, specific research project). This Code element acknowledges that research has its own specific skill set and expertise in conducting research can only be obtained with supervision from a seasoned researcher. It is the responsible way to support continued ethical contributions in ABA literature.

There are many barriers that limit practitioners from authoring their own research studies. One barrier, having access to an IRB (which is often available for larger organizations committed to research or educational institutions) can be mitigated via the creation of a research review committee (see LeBlanc et al., 2018). In wanting to do research, I sought to create an RRC. However, there are stringent measures in place to ensure that the articles published in our respected journals are quality (via the peer review process) and, from a responsibility perspective, it is vital to have mentorship when starting research.

6.07 Conflict of Interest in Research and Publication

When conducting research, behavior analysts identify, disclose, and address conflicts of interest (e.g., personal, financial, organization related, service related). They also identify, disclose, and address conflicts of interest in their publication and editorial activities.

Explanation

A conflict of interest can occur when there are two or more contrasting interests related to the same event either by the researcher or the researcher's organization. Conflicts of interests must be disclosed. This is critical information to the reader of a study as that conflict of interest could impact the findings and disclosure is critical so the reader is aware. When a conflict of interest presents itself it must be acknowledged, shared in the study, and addressed as to how it did not impact the findings. A conflict of interest is not necessarily wrong, it could be circumstantial as it does not involve the participants or researcher directly but rather environmental variables that could pose a biased lens. In disclosing, a researcher has an opportunity to clarify and explain those variables.

Considerations

You may notice at the end of some recent journal articles you will see a conflict of interest statement. In many cases a typical conflict of interest statement would read something along the lines of, "the authors declare no conflicts of interest regarding this article" or "the author has no conflict of interest to declare." Ways in which a conflict of interest could present itself in a research paper is if there is an opportunity for financial gain contingent on the findings or a multiple relationship is created by being both a research investigator and a behavior analyst as well as a research participant and a client. There could also be added financial incentives to the organization which must be disclosed if that possibility exists.

Examples from the Field

Written by Jacob Sadavoy

I am currently doing a research project in my place of employment. A potential conflict of interest is my desire to demonstrate that I am excelling and the data generated from the research study, if positive, would be an indication of good workplace performance. This is a common trap that can befall any behavior analyst; as positive trends in data are reinforcing and, at times, we want clients or participants, to succeed to demonstrate effectiveness of behavior change program or research design. A conflict of interest would be created if I received a financial bonus for research results. Data should objectively be based on participants' behaviors without any additional incentives. For my research study, I want it to be successful but there is no added incentive aside from personal accomplishment which is less reinforcing than contributing something of substance to the field of behavior analysis.

6.08 Appropriate Credit

Behavior analysts give appropriate credit (e.g., authorship, author-note acknowledgment) to research contributors in all dissemination activities. Authorship and other publication acknowledgments accurately reflect the relative scientific or professional contributions of the individuals involved, regardless of their professional status (e.g., professor, student).

Explanation

Our obligation to our colleagues, as indicated in this Code element, is to give credit for work when credit is due. The criteria for credit of authorship are dependent on the amount of work and not on any other factor.

This requirement fits neatly within our general practice, as it is particularly objective and behavioral. The more subjective aspects of one's qualifications are irrelevant for the consideration of crediting authors. The behaviors included in the research activity are reinforced with acknowledgment of authorship and such reinforcers are only delivered contingent on those behaviors.

Considerations

If it is true that many hands make light work, it is equally, or perhaps more true that many hands are necessary to make published research. Research studies are frequently implemented with a team of those who contribute.

When discussing the need to acknowledge contributions of primary and secondary authors as such, it is also important to consider how to acknowledge the more minor contributions of those who assist in the implementation of a research study. Not every contribution warrants acknowledgment as author, but each contribution should be acknowledged.

Here we see the significance of the phrase, "The authors wish to express their gratitude to…" This phrase allows acknowledgment to be offered to every person who contributed to the success of a study. The success of a study, after all, depends on each of these actors, and this simple sign of respect costs us nothing.

Examples from the Field

Written by Jacob Sadavoy

Another way in which researchers may mislead their audience is by omitting credit when due or taking credit for someone else's work. A colleague of mine saw her work posted, verbatim, in another language, on a co-presenter's website. This colleague's ideas and work were used without adequate acknowledgment or any credit. This is academic exploitation, which is a type of plagiarism. A website is not considered a reliable source for research literature; however, plagiarism is plagiarism regardless of the medium and a BCBA should never plagiarize, ever. By not citing or acknowledging the work of the co-presenter, the owner of the website is guilty of stealing her contributions which is unethical.

Another example of this, is a professor or research head adding their name, or the names of others, to a research project with whom they have no affiliation. This is commonplace in some academic programs despite being unethical and a misrepresentation of authorship. The benefit of having one's name on a research paper is to access the prestige and honor associated with advancing a scientific field. However, it is unethical for credit to be taken for someone else's work. There would likely be fewer instances of academic exploitation with harsher penalties. Thankfully, our ethics Code considers this a serious offense.

6.09 Plagiarism

Behavior analysts do not present portions or elements of another's work or data as their own. Behavior analysts only republish their previously published data or text when accompanied by proper disclosure.

Explanation

In this Code element there is considerable overlap between two of the obligations mentioned here: our obligation to colleagues and our obligation to the truth.

In academic institutions, our obligation to academic honesty is clear, and clear contingencies are in place to prevent, detect, and, if necessary, punish violations to policies aimed at maintaining high standards of integrity. Once such contingencies are no longer in place, however, the behavior change may lack the support necessary to continue.

Avoiding plagiarism is not merely an exercise intended to ensure the quality of work for individual students, and it is not intended exclusively for assessing students in academic settings. Rather, the behaviors that result in the avoidance of plagiarism must be learned and practiced in academic environments and then maintained throughout the behavior analyst's practice.

Considerations

Many academics and researchers rely on the "common sense" rule of citation. In other words, if a statement is neither an original thought nor something that would be considered "common sense" by the general public, a citation must be given.

However, it has often been said that there is nothing more *uncommon* than "common sense." The longer we spend in highly specialized fields such as behavior analysis, the more what we define as "common sense" may be determined more by our own level of fluency than by what is known by the general public.

As a field dedicated to the practice of evidence-based strategies it is essential that such evidence be cited. What may be common knowledge within our own circle may be quite uncommon outside of it.

Examples from the Field

Written by Jacob Sadavoy

You were likely first introduced to plagiarism in middle school as a grave form of academic dishonesty and likely discussed, in syllabi, for the remainder of your academic life. Committing plagiarism is a serious offense where penalties range from being given a zero on an assignment to expulsion and/or fine. Under no circumstances is it acceptable to steal someone else's work as your own. Conversely, it is encouraged that new academic and research works make use of the available literature as a means of communicating truths. Publishing research is the most effective way for the scientist to take a position and operate in the free exchange of ideas and findings. The sharing of published works as an ideal forum for this exchange as long as those contributing are abiding by their ethical obligation as researchers and colleagues in the pursuit of new discoveries.

6.10 Documentation and Data Retention in Research

Behavior analysts must be knowledgeable about and comply with all applicable standards (e.g., BACB rules, laws, research review committee requirements) for storing, transporting, retaining, and destroying physical and electronic documentation related to research. They retain identifying documentation and data for the longest required duration. Behavior analysts destroy physical documentation after making deidentified digital copies or summaries of data (e.g., reports and graphs) when permitted by relevant entities.

Explanation

Participant data must be kept confidential and to maintain confidentiality safeguards must be in place. All of these safeguards must be shared with the IRB and the participants. Under no circumstances should your data be allowed to be accessed by an individual or party that is not authorized. This means data storage, transporting data, encryption, and password protection for data sets on research computer as well as desks, offices, and filing cabinets need to be considered and planned fully in advance.

When the research project comes to an end, the duration of time before data can be erased varies. In some cases, the time period is at the discretion of the principal investigators; however, many IRBs require that data be retained for a minimum number of years upon completion. Three years are common but some research institutions insist on longer durations of time (National Institutes of Health, 2020).

Considerations

Once the minimum storage period has been met, the principal investigator has a decision to make – delete and store. Technically one could keep data indefinitely, however the principal investigator must assess the merits and risks of storing data for a longer period of time as opposed to destroying that data. A reason to store the data for longer is because readers may request to see the raw data or the findings may be questioned. In both those cases, it would be helpful to have the data to share and confirm, respectively. The longer data is stored and exists the longer you run the risk of a potential breach of confidentiality. Further, there are financial costs related to data storage and security. Upon weighing out the pros and cons and deleting the data is the outcome, the principal investigator must ensure that the data is completely destroyed which includes temporary files, emails, and other correspondence notes related to the research.

Examples from the Field

Written by Jacob Sadavoy

It is my responsibility to produce data when requested, within the stipulated timeframe. Maintaining and keeping data is a wonderful way to practice one's organizational skills. It is essential that things are kept securely and organized for losing files with terminating them fully puts you and the participant at risk of someone accessing data that they shouldn't. Your participants sign consent to participate. They trust the principal investigator to keep their end of the bargain with respect to maintaining, storing, and, eventually, terminating their data. Failing to do so would require the principal investigator to inform all the participants which is a conversation that should be aversive.

6.11 Accuracy and Use of Data

Behavior analysts do not fabricate data or falsify results in their research, publications, and presentations. They plan and carry out their research and describe their procedures and findings to minimize the possibility that their research and results will be misleading or misinterpreted. If they discover errors in their published data they take steps to correct them by following publisher policy. Data from research projects are presented to the public and scientific community in their entirety whenever possible. When that is not possible, behavior analysts take caution and explain the exclusion of data (whether single data points, or partial or whole data sets) from presentations or manuscripts submitted for publication by providing a rationale and description of what was excluded.

Explanation

There are ethical requirements within this Code element which can affect the integrity of a research study. In this Code element, the emphasis is placed upon the behavior analyst's responsibility to the truth. Anything that threatens either the interpretation or the execution of a research study should be attended to.

The Stanford Prison Experiment again clearly demonstrates how insidious this influence can be. In the span of only six days, the researchers became as immersed in their roles as the participants. In his book, *The Lucifer Effect* (Zimbardo, 2007), Dr. Zimbardo recounts the impulse to protect "his prison" from insurgency when "prisoners" appeared ready to revolt. Though this immersion in his role as superintendent, and moreover his protection of the Stanford mock prison, appears, with the benefit of 20/20 hindsight, to be a clear example of interference.

We must not allow our own influence to impact results or interpretation. This remains true, whether such influence be in the subtle form of our own financial or personal entanglements, or in the more direct form of our actions within the study.

This Code element clearly states our obligation to the truth. On our efforts to communicate our findings, we must be mindful of the honesty of such communication will be received. The necessity of honesty and forthrightness in scientific writing cannot be overstated.

I have often advised supervisees that, "Data is a fancy word for information. There is no such thing as bad data, though there may be information that you didn't want to hear." Data that is part of a research study must be presented and must be presented on its entirety, even if it includes results that may not be expected – or hoped for – by the researchers.

Considerations

British Prime Minister Benjamin Disraeli famously said, "There are three kinds of lies: lies, damned lies, and statistics." Although the science of behavior generally uses visual analysis rather than statistical analysis and focuses on clinical significance rather than statistical significance, the skepticism of this statement can still apply to our own research.

Often research is assumed to be biased by those most skeptical about the results. Studies showing the benefit of vaccines are dismissed or not accessed as a result of click optimization by populating feeds and searches with similarly read articles. Discerning scientific research from opinion will continue to be an ongoing challenge.

Biases can inevitably impact research. Personal biases can impair judgment, which can affect results or how those results are expressed.

Examples from the Field

Written by Jacob Sadavoy

It is of the utmost importance for research to be objective and not influenced by superfluous factors that could detract from the content of the research whether purposefully or inadvertently. Research should be conducted in environments that are as close to *in situ* as possible and free of extraneous factors that could influence the outcome or pose a conflict of interest.

When I was new to the field, I remember voicing displeasure when my supervisor had a colleague perform the ABLLS-R assessment on my assigned primary student (whom I was responsible for the graphs and maintaining the program). She correctly assessed that I was personally invested in the results and she was concerned that I would inadvertently give my client the benefit of the doubt as opposed to being more objective. This can be a challenge for researchers. Sometimes you want to manifest your hypothesis so much that you lose that objectivity needed in order for the research to be sound. Having an accurate ABLLS-R is of greater benefit for me even if it does not depict the growth between assessments that I was seeking. Similarly, thorough and valid research is of more value than a correct hypothesis.

Data is necessary to measure the effectiveness of an intervention. There are many ways a behavior analyst can measure behavior and as such there are many ways data can be collected. This Code element acknowledges that data can be manipulated and stress the importance of data being reported accurately and honestly and be available for professionals who inquire to see data from a study. Any inaccuracies are often uncovered during the peer review process whose primary focus is to vet studies and ensure the data that is being reported appropriately.

For a poster presentation at ABAI, data was collected for two dozen students' performance on a series of task analyses with the goal to produce holi powder from scratch to a sellable bagged product in India. There were many ways the data could be shared: a few cases could be used, an average of all of the students, completed steps as opposed to percentage of steps completed accurately, etc. Had we removed the clients who did a poor job on their task analyses and present the average of the participants, we would have been omitting data, fabricating the results, and submitting unethical research. Cause of error is moot, the behavior analyst is responsible for submitting quality data that reflects their findings explicitly.

Works Cited

Baer, D. M., Wolf, M. M., & Risley, T. R. (1968). Some current dimensions of applied behavior analysis. *Journal of Applied Behavior Analysis, 1*(1), 91–97. https://doi.org/10.1901/jaba.1968.1-91.

Drury, S., Hutchens, S. A., Shuttlesworth, D. E., & White, C. L. (2012). Philip G. Zimbardo on his career and the Stanford Prison Experiment's 40th anniversary. *History of Psychology, 15*(2), 161–170. https://doi.org/10.1037/a0025884.

Emanuel, E. J., Grady, C. C., Crouch, R. A., Lie, R. K., Miller, F. G., & Wendler, D. D. (2011). *The Oxford textbook of clinical research ethics.* New York, NY: Oxford University Press.

LeBlanc, L. A., Nosik, M. R., & Petursdottir, A. (2018). Establishing consumer protections for research in human service agencies. *Behavior Analysis in Practice, 11*(4), 445–455. https://doi.org/10.1007/s40617-018-0206-3.

Morris, E. K., Altus, D. E., & Smith, N. G. (2013). A study in the founding of applied behavior analysis through its publications. *The Behavior Analyst, 36*(1), 73–107. https://doi.org/10.1007/bf03392293.

National Institutes of Health. (2020, November 3). *NIH data sharing policy and implementation guidance.* NIH Grants Site. https://grants.nih.gov/grants/policy/data_sharing/data_sharing_guidance.htm.

Rekers, G. A., & Lovaas, O. I. (1974). Behavioral treatment of deviant sex-role behaviors in a male child. *Journal of Applied Behavior Analysis, 7*(2), 173–190. https://doi.org/10.1901/jaba.1974.7-173.

Vollmann, J., Winau, R., & Baron, J. (1996). History of informed medical consent. *The Lancet, 347*(8998), 410. https://doi.org/10.1016/s0140-6736(96)90597-8.

Zimbardo, P. G. (2007). *The Lucifer effect: Understanding how good people turn evil.* New York, NY: Random House.

1.10   Study Guide

Facts About the BCBA® Exam

At one point on my career, I took an unexpected but nonetheless fascinating turn when I was the creator and instructor of the Prepare to Pass® exam preparation program. I must admit that, when I first started on this endeavor, my assumption was that those who struggled to pass the exam simply had not studied hard enough. If only they had fluency with the material, they would obviously pass the exam. Just memorize the terms and there you go – easy!

However, as we have said over and over again in this volume, simple is very rarely the same thing as easy. Behavior change is complicated, whether the change in question is the behavior of our client or our own. And, as bears repeating, applied behavior analysis is the science of how organisms – *all organisms* – learn. Fluency is defined as "flowing, effortless, well-practiced, and accurate performance" (Johnson & Layng, 1996). This is achieved not only by churning out the same memorized definition without attention to their meaning but reflects several other elements of understanding. The best way to understand fluency is to think of it as the way we "know" the knowledge with which we are most intimately connected, the knowledge where it would be more difficult to respond incorrectly than correctly: our own birthdays, or our middle names. Placing our emphasis on fluency will allow us to become not only proficient test-takers, but proficient behavior analysts.

Fluency and Your Study Plan

As explained by Johnson and Layng (1996), fluency is characterized by several learning processes: retention, endurance, stability, application, and adduction, which are summarized by the mnemonic *RESAA*.

Retention refers to the maintenance of behavior change over time. A behavior that is that is truly learned must cause a durable change rather than a fleeting one. Behavior that is truly fluent will not be abandoned the day after the final exam. Much of the coursework necessary for behavior analysis is scaffolded – each course builds on the one before it and fluency will therefore be more easily accomplished. However, there is always the temptation to abandon what has been learned and focus only on new content. When addressing retention in our clinical work, there are a number of strategies we can use to encourage it, many of which were specified in the seminal article on the topic, Stokes and Baer's 1977 "An implicit technology of generalization".

Among these strategies might be the incorporation of *"natural maintaining contingencies"* (Stokes & Baer, 1977). By teaching behaviors that will be reinforced by the natural environment, and by allowing access to an environment that supports them we can be more confident that behavior change will persist long after the teaching phase is complete.

DOI: 10.4324/9781003190707-11

The use of *indiscriminable contingencies,* or the provision of reinforcers on an intermittent schedule, can also maintain behavior change over the long term. Another possibility – a powerful tool in our proverbial toolbox – is to *mediate generalization.* Using this tactic, a learner would be taught an additional behavior that would promote generalization. This method of generalization, Stokes and Baer (1977) point out, is used throughout the literature on self-management. The behaviors of self-monitoring, self-recording, and self-reinforcement allow a client to maintain behaviors for the long term on their own. Such methodologies work equally well whether the behavior change we hope for is our clients' or our own. Begin by creating a study group in order to contact reinforcement for the frequent and correct use of terminology. Create a pact (and perhaps a schedule) to provide intermittent reinforcement for one another for the behaviors that will increase your fluency, including using terminology in examples and study activities. Access these reinforcers by showing off occasionally. Brag about it when a concept you have difficulty with finally clicks.

Endurance refers to a behavior's resistance to extinction. This is certainly a very important factor in our clinical programming for our clients, and the use of *indiscriminable contingencies* (Stokes & Baer, 1977) may also influence this aspect of fluency. Patterns of responding to intermittent schedules of reinforcement tend to indicate that behaviors that are reinforced on more variable schedules of reinforcement can persist far longer in the absence of reinforcer delivery. For many behaviors that we teach, we want to be mindful that we are moving from very contrived, thick schedules of reinforcement to the far thinner reinforcement schedules provided naturally. Given that we should always be focused on the use of positive reinforcement, this emphasis on adjusting toward thinner schedules of reinforcement is a sensible and ethical consideration. However, for the self-managed study program, the issue of endurance may in fact be irrelevant. Many aspiring behavior analysts begin their study process (one would hope as early as possible on their coursework) with a fair amount of anxiety about their knowledge and proficiency in the material. It is often that anxiety that drives them to create a plan to study in the first place. Anxiety becomes the antecedent and studying becomes the behavior, leading to some relief when mastery of concepts is achieved. Studying – in the beginning at least – is often maintained by negative reinforcement. As the behavior continues however, a shift takes place. More comfort with the terminology and the concepts means that more reinforcers are accessed than aversives avoided. In other words, the satisfaction that comes with increasing success *thickens* the schedule of reinforcement rather than having it thinned. As the natural contingency of increased knowledge begins to take over, the importance of maintaining performance under thinning schedules of reinforcement becomes far less important.

In order to increase your contact with these reinforcers, taking data should be integrated into your study plan. Using data collection to monitor your progress can not only allow you to be more precise on your approach to the material but also can increase your access to reinforcers. Seeing your performance improve is perhaps the most effective reinforcer for all of your hard work.

When it comes to data collection, one very helpful strategy is to use *SAFMEDS* (Stockwell & Eshelman, 2010). This acronym, first coined by Ogden Lindsley, stands for "*Say All Fast* [for a] *Minute Each Day, Shuffled*". Begin by creating flashcards. Write a term on one side of an index card and three to five words describing its essential elements on the other. Not a full sentence, not a full description – simply three to five words. Once you have an impressive pile of index cards (30–50 will do nicely), you can begin your timings. Set a timer for one minute. Test yourself, either by looking at the term and proving the description or by looking at the description and providing the term. As you go through the terms, make a pile of those that were correct and those that were incorrect. Chart your day-to-day performance. As you continue to learn new terms, add these to your pile and continue to test yourself and chart daily. Watching documentation of your improvement over time will soon increase your confidence and act as a powerful reinforcer.

Stability. Stability refers to the consistency of behavior change. Rather than focusing exclusively on generalization, this aspect of fluency requires that the skill reach a performance criterion. Does the client demonstrate sufficient independence with this skill? Are their responses consistently accurate?

Many programs that focus on fluency examine the rate of response as a primary measure. For that reason it is often assumed that increasing speed should be the emphasis of programming. To some extent, this would seem to make sense. If we think logically about those pieces of information with which we have fluency, they are often those things that we list off quickly, the responses we can provide without a moment's hesitation.

If our responses are not accurate, however, then all we have is faster errors. And practicing errors may make them far more entrenched. If we cannot achieve a level of proficiency, we cannot hope to gain fluency. Fast mistakes are still mistakes, and fluency with mistakes takes us further from the goal.

In order to prevent this when studying, refer back to that pile of incorrect responses. Once the data is collected, take a moment to review them. Not to simply read through them, but to take a more systematic approach. A multistep process is often what I recommend to test-takers: *First, start with plain English.* It is often surprising how many of the terms we use within behavior analysis have very similar meanings when used in more colloquial settings. Prediction, for example, may be used in casual conversation to mean "saying something will happen before it does." What would be the difference then when defining the aspect of baseline logic "statement of an anticipated outcome?" We can all agree, even without seeing the movie, that *Escape from Alcatraz* likely takes place in Alcatraz. Why then would so many test-takers struggle to remember that "escape" involves an ongoing stimulus? See what you can guess without allowing anxiety or intimidation with scientific terminology get in the way. *Refer back to the source.* Reread the full definition from your source material, whether it be an assigned article or your text. Reread it several times to make sure you understand the phrasing. *Rephrase the definition in your own words.* Strip away the academic vocabulary and think of the desperate parent who needs an explanation. How would you describe this term to them? Then, and only then, *think of an example.* The timing of this step is crucial. It is important to understand the distinction between a definition and an example. Too often, this leads to a lack of generalization. A clinician who has learned that a discriminative stimulus is the instruction in discrete trial teaching may struggle to think of other examples. Learning that a discriminative stimulus is the signal that a reinforcer is available clarifies not only our DTT example but further examples as well. Once you have your example in hand, *develop a mnemonic.* This step is not 100% essential, though many students find it helpful. The mnemonic should be something that makes sense to you. Finally, *make a commitment* to our final two aspects of fluency: *Application* and Contingency *Adduction*.

Application and *Adduction.* Although these represent two different aspects of fluency, for the purposes of your study for the exam they can be accomplished with similar tactics. *Application* refers to the "real life" performance of a given skill. Reciting definitions accurately while reviewing SAFMEDS is incredibly helpful, but mastery can only be accomplished if you can also use these terms clinically. Can you define them in discussions with clients, or with your supervisors or colleagues? Contingency *Adduction* refers to the response generalization that occurs when behavior change that has been reinforced under teaching conditions expands to different behaviors. The recognition of behavioral terminology has been reinforced in classes, and now in your independent study. What, then, would be the natural extension of this behavior?

Remember that applied behavior is a science and, as such, is an explanation of phenomena that already exist. Long before this science was applied to organizational behavior management, the learning processes described in this way existed in the same way. Seeing something makes it more clear, but it existed just the same. All around us, the behavioral phenomena described by this terminology have been shaping behavior. As the final aspect of your study plan, *make a commitment* to identifying those phenomena in your everyday surroundings. You may also choose to keep track of the number of examples you find and add it to your data collection.

Emphasizing fluency in your study will allow you to approach your exam with confidence. It will increase both your efficiency in studying and your chances of success.

Purpose

Any high-pressure exam can bring about a great deal of anxiety. I would often counsel anxious test-takers by telling them, "This test does not mark the end of your career, and it doesn't mark the beginning. It's simply one point in the middle."

I have discussed the exam with behavior analysts who struggled to pass and who called into question their competence. They wondered if their excellent grades, wonderful feedback from supervisors and clients, and the success of their clients had been, somehow, an illusion? Had they really been unqualified all along?

The purpose of the BACB® exam is not to create an obstacle for qualified professionals but to maintain a *minimum standard* of knowledge and academic performance. In order to allow as many universities as possible in as many locations as possible to create programs with different areas of emphasis, different teaching styles, and different student populations, it is necessary to have a system by which we can determine some "apples to apples" comparison among our field.

The exam cannot measure all of the responsibilities of the competent behavior analyst. It is not intended to. It cannot measure how you would respond in a professional situation, how much you care about your clients, or how devoted you are to the study of behavior and the potential of the science of applied behavior analysis. It is not intended to do that either. Expecting the exam to be a measure of your worthiness to practice rather than *an objective measure of your academic understanding of the science* is a surefire way to bring yourself anxiety, frustration, and bitterness. And it will do little to help you pass the exam.

It is not a perfect system, but it is best to remember how I counseled those frustrated test-takers: it is not the beginning of your career, nor the end, but a point in the middle. It is the best estimate of an objective measure that can be offered.

Structure

Tests are administered at Pearson Vue testing sites at various locations and test-takers, once approved to sit for the exam, are able to select an appointment time and location that works for them. The computer-based testing site will be offering a variety of tests for a variety of professions. Some may be testing to become registered nurses, lawyers, or certified public accountants. These testing sites have strict security measures that must be adhered to. There is no food or drink allowed in the testing area, no access to phones or electronic devices, and no use of scrap paper. You will be given a laminated paper and a pen to make notes and a calculator is available on the computer as well.

There is a tutorial available through Pearson Vue and it is highly recommended that you familiarize yourself with the way that the test is organized and administered. Understand how to answer questions, how to monitor time, and how to access any needed information before walking into the exam.

The BACB® exams are made up of 160 multiple choice questions. Ten of these questions will be unscored – they are being assessed for future test administrations, leaving 150 questions from which the scores will be derived. Your testing appointment is four hours, and after logging in you will have approximately three hours and 55 minutes to complete the exam. Once the exam is complete, you will receive information as to whether you have passed or failed. If you have passed, you will receive an email confirming this and your information will be updated with the BACB within a week. If you have failed you will receive your score, along with a report that will allow you to focus your study in the areas where you had more difficulty.

Test questions are selected from a large pool which have been tested as part of those pilot questions which are unscored. Scoring is based on a statistical analysis of the questions and answers based on the answering patterns of subject matter experts. This method, known as the modified Angoff method, is one in which subject matter experts review the questions and answer selections and determine what percentage of "minimally acceptable" test-takers would be able to respond correctly. Based on this information, a value is determined for each test item and that is used to determine the score. A scaled score is then determined out of a possible 500, with 400 as a passing score. Test-takers are not competing with one another and, depending on the test items selected, the number of correct answers may vary from one test to another

Although there is a space to offer comments it is critical to remember that the answer that will be scored is *only* the multiple choice answer. Your comment, no matter how well-argued, will not be considered as part of your answer. Your answer will be considered correct or incorrect, and no amount of advocacy will change how it is scored.

In short, though the system of scoring may be new to you, the test is based on information that is familiar. By the time you have been approved to sit for the exam, you would have already met a criterion for mastery of the materials and should have also met criterion for experience which would have allowed you to apply this knowledge. Though the test itself may be intimidating, it is merely a step in your journey – and moreover, it is one along a familiar path.

Pass Rates

All of the test items are determined by the BACB and derived directly from the task list. All verified coursework sequences also were also determined from the task list, so there should be considerable alignment. Each course in your coursework should lead organically to the next and all of it should be directly relevant to the exam.

All of this begs the question: shouldn't the pass rates be far closer to 100%? After all, coursework is standardized by the verified coursework approval system. Many courses use the same textbooks and even those that do not often have textbooks derived from the same or similar source material. And yet, pass rates have historically hovered at 60–70% overall. Though there is considerable variability by university programs, and many boast 100% pass rates, the lack of consistency is, at a minimum, an interesting phenomenon. Even more concerning is the significantly lower pass rate for those who are retaking the exam. According to the 2020 annual data report, those who retake the exam had only a 31% pass rate for the BCBA® exam and 41% for the BCaBA® exam. Exposure to the questions does not seem to improve performance.

Rumors swirl about the exam itself: do those who have failed the test in the past get a harder version of the exam? Is the exam even a fair way to test? Should "none of the above" be an answer choice for all questions? After all, sometimes in life nothing we try works, sometimes in life the answers are not clear cut.

The exam, of course, is not life. It is not even the small slice of life that makes up our cynical practice. It is merely the objective assessment of academic understanding that provides a minimum standard for a knowledgeable and competent behavior analyst. It does not speak to your experience or your client care, only to your mastery of those academic concepts.

Difficulty with the Exam

The areas covered in the BACB exam include the areas of the task list, which in turn include behaving in accordance with the Ethics Code for behavior analysts. Fluency with the terminology is the first step toward success on the exam, and perhaps the easiest to immediately implement. Begin by examining the glossary accompanying the Ethics Code.

It is true that this is merely a cursory examination of the Code. However, this supplement to your more in-depth study of the Code can clarify some of the critical misunderstandings that can lead to unethical practices. For example, there is often a great deal of confusion as to what constitutes a multiple relationship. If a behavior analyst were to attend a fundraiser for the school which employed them, would that constitute a multiple relationship? If a behavior analyst were to lend a sympathetic ear as a parent began to weep during a moment of vulnerability, would this constitute a multiple relationship? The definition of a multiple relationship as specified by the BACB offers some clarity on this point. A multiple relationship is defined as, "a *comingling* of two or more of a behavior analyst's roles" (BACB, 2020). In the case of our two examples, though they may be a bit uncomfortable for different reasons, these do not constitute a multiple relationship. A behavior analyst attending a fundraiser for their employer is still a behavior analyst. A sympathetic and compassionate behavior analyst is still a behavior analyst. Our humanity does not constitute a different role and its appearance would not be considered "comingling."

Just as the vocabulary for behavior analysis enables us to use these building blocks to build the foundation of our understanding of the science, so too can the vocabulary clarify and build our understanding of ethical concepts.

Understanding and avoiding the pitfalls of the exam itself, and specifically what makes it so difficult for many test-takers, is the next most important strategy. Once mastery of the material has been accounted for, what remains is the ability to answer the questions themselves. There are a few obstacles to success in this area beyond understanding the concepts.

Clinical vs. Multiple Choice Thinking

Perhaps the biggest challenge to those taking the exam is the wide difference in behavioral expectations between clinical work and success on a multiple choice exam.

Good clinicians approach a new case with an open mind. They take in all the information available, and they are ready to approach problems from several angles. The best clinicians understand that the behavior of the client will ultimately guide their decision making, both in the assessment process and the evaluation process. It is the client's behavior that determines whether a program is necessary and whether or not a program is working as it should. A clinician should be aware that the best solutions may not be the obvious ones, or perhaps they are sometimes so obvious that they manage to elude us. Is bedtime reading a struggle? Try reading in the afternoon instead. Client refuses to shower in the morning? Try a bath in the evening. Thinking outside of the arbitrary boxes of our own making is a mark of excellence in a clinician.

The skills involved in multiple choice test-taking are markedly different, however. These involve the understanding that all of the information available is already apparent. One of the most important skills in multiple choice test-taking is to limit the possible responses to those already available and to assume that the information provided is all that is needed to answer the question. While an excellent clinician must challenge themselves to think "outside the box," excellence in multiple choice test-taking often depends on remaining firmly inside the box.

This becomes particularly challenging when faced with scenario questions. For example, if a question states, "You decide to use prompt fading. What would you do?" many test-takers become distracted by the question, "What would you do?" and answer the question as if they were asked what they personally would do in that scenario. In this case, however, you were not asked what you would do. You were asked what you would do *once you had decided to use prompt fading*. This is not a question about your recommendations, it is a question that asks which of the following examples meets the definition of prompt fading.

Overthinking and Over-answering

Let us take a slight detour to describe two schools of thought within behavior analysis. The *radical behaviorist* takes the view that all events can be explained by one's biology and learning history. In other words, all behavior, observable to the outsider or not, is both relevant and open to analysis, and the science of behavior has the key to unlocking these mysteries. Anything that an organism does is considered behavior, including those behaviors that are covert, or take place "under the skin." These behaviors, like any others, are shaped by their antecedents and consequences. They can, therefore, be analyzed and changed.

The *methodological behaviorist* does not necessarily disagree from a philosophical standpoint, but takes a more practical view. While all behavior may be subject to the influences of antecedents and consequences, that does not mean that all behavior can be responsibly studied by an outsider. A methodological behaviorist acknowledges that behavior under the skin is still behavior and, as such, is subject to the same processes that govern learning of covert behavior. A methodological behaviorist, however, maintains that, because these behaviors cannot be directly observed by outsiders, they are not appropriate for study.

Thinking, therefore, would be considered a behavior. Though it occurs "under the skin" it is nonetheless shaped by antecedents and consequences. Both radical and methodological behaviorists would agree that it is a behavior that can be shaped.

The conflict between these two philosophies, however, raises a question relevant to study: given that we cannot observe another person's "overthinking," how can we define it? Are we actually overthinking or is someone else underthinking? How can "overthinking" be distinguished from thinking the optimal amount?

Overthinking, like our example of "outside the box" clinical problem solving, is not necessarily a problem in different contexts. Overthinking can be an advantage if the context is planning a trip to the airport, for example, since it is far better to be two hours early with everything prepared than five minutes late without identification. In this case, overthinking would allow us to anticipate problems and plan for them. What if we can't get a taxi? No problem, we'll call ahead. What if the alarm doesn't go off and we oversleep? No problem, an extra alarm will give us a safety net. This type of contingency planning involves creative thinking of potential problems and their solutions.

Multiple choice questions, on the other hand, do not involve a search for extra information. In fact a search for extra information will almost certainly lead to *adding information that is not in the question*. Which will almost certainly lead you in the wrong direction.

Many test-takers who have mastery of the material itself struggle with deciphering what the question is really asking and answering only that. Rather than offering a simple answer to a simple question, they take a more holistic approach. They ask the question "what if" just as they would when assessing risks and benefits, thinking through every possible scenario, both in the best and worst cases.

Overthinking can only be identified by the individual doing it, and is often marked by both its context and its precursors. *One clearly identifiable precursor in these examples is the word "if".* "If" introduces a new condition – one that is not there in the first place. *If* we hit a traffic jam on the way to the airport... *If* we oversleep... *If* the client engages in more severe aggression. In each case, these have not yet occurred but may occur in the future.

In the case of a multiple choice test, however, when all of the information is needed to answer the question, adding additional information can be hazardous. When we begin to add what isn't there, we are not just strategizing or planning, we are *overthinking.*

So here we have a clue which, while it may not be 100% consistent, may be generalizable enough to help you discover the precursor behaviors to your own overthinking. Thinking the word "if." Addition of "if" indicates that we are no longer restricting ourselves to the words on the page, but we are adding more information.

One helpful metaphor is to think of the process of retrieving information on the exam as if you are asked to get something from the closet. You've been asked to get an umbrella, that's all. Do not stand in the closet, grabbing all of the items that might be useful in the rain or cold. If you are asked for an umbrella, grab the umbrella and get out.

Practice Questions and Analysis

In this section we will review some sample questions and analyze what may make a similar exam question difficult, and how to approach it. These questions are not taken from the exam itself (to do so would be a violation of our Code), they are simply meant to point out some common challenges on the exam. In this case we will take a three-part question based on one scenario.

> You have been asked to consult on a case in a school for children with developmental disabilities. The student is engaging in frequent out of seat behavior that is interfering with the classroom. Teachers have expressed difficulty with managing the classroom and attempts to redirect him back to his seat. Many of these attempts are time consuming and often unsuccessful. How would you begin?
>
> a.   implement a treatment plan to be carried out by you
> b.   train teachers in more successful techniques
> c.   *schedule an observation to determine function*
> d.   graph data that they have reported

For this question we are given several possibilities. In fact, we are given several necessary steps on the development of a sound behavior plan. Given the difficulty the teachers are having managing the classroom when this behavior occurs, a behavior analyst should certainly implement a behavior plan. And training teachers and collecting data would also be necessary steps. But which answer reflects how we would begin? Though these steps are necessary, are they a beginning or are they the later steps? Remember that this question asks for how you would begin, not all of what you would do. The answer must be *schedule an observation to determine function.*

What would the best data collection system to use in this case?

a. frequency
b. latency
c. *duration*
d. permanent product

In order to select the best data collection system, we need to have a sense of what question we are trying to answer. Given that the behavior continues for long periods of time, taking frequency data may not readily reflect how much behavior we are actually seeing, since an incident lasting ten seconds would be counted the same as one lasting three hours. Without a clear onset stimulus, latency would also be an inappropriate measure, and there is no permanent product. Which leaves us with the best answer: duration. Are there other data collection systems that would be a better choice? Maybe, but that should not be our focus here. *The right answer can only be among these selections.* If it isn't here, don't allow it to distract you.

You determine that the behavior is maintained by escape from demands and decide to use a DRA procedure to address this behavior. Which of the following would be an example of this procedure?

a. three-minute breaks are provided contingent on remaining in seat behavior for a given interval
b. *three-minute breaks are provided contingent on raising hand and requesting a break*
c. three-minute breaks are given contingent on out of seat behavior below a certain frequency
d. out of seat behavior is ignored

This question is asking for which of these examples describes a DRA (a differential reinforcement of an alternate behavior). However, the most confusing aspect of this question is not a lack of understanding of what constitutes a DRA, but what the question is actually asking. There may be situation where the best course of action is to use extinction (ignore the behavior) or a DRI (remaining in seat is met with reinforcement). To promote progress in this goal, a DRL may also be used (providing a reinforcer for behavior below a given criterion). However, we are not asked what is the most appropriate intervention. We are being asked which one describes a DRA. What you would do personally is not the question, you have already been told what you will do, and now you just have to identify it.

Understanding what makes these examples tricky will help you avoid such pitfalls on the exam itself. To summarize, the best way to approach the exam is by taking each question assuming that the answer is there. After all, it is: printed right in front of you. You do not have to search for it or add extra information, you simply have to select from what is already there. Use your knowledge. Have faith in your education. Work toward fluency. And embrace the beautiful elegance and simplicity of the science of behavior analysis.

Works Cited

Johnson, K. R., & Layng, T. V. J. (1996). On terms and procedures: fluency. *The Behavior Analyst*, *19*(2), 281–288. https://doi.org/10.1007/BF03393170.

Stockwell, F., & Eshleman, J. (2010). A case study using SAFMEDS to promote fluency with Skinner's verbal behavior terms. *Journal of Precision Teaching and Celeration, 26*, 33–40.

Stokes, T. F., & Baer, D. M. (1977). An implicit technology of generalization. *Journal of Applied Behavior Analysis*, *10*(2), 349–367.

Part 2

Professional Behavior and the Behavior Analyst

Beyond the Code

2.1   Professionalism

Professional, Unethical, Uncomfortable: Introduction to Part 2

In Part 1, we discussed the nature of "goodness" and the many facets which make up what we consider to be "being a good person." We proposed examining the different facets of "goodness" by envisioning this concept as being multitiered. There is legality, which involves being a law-abiding citizen and doing the bare minimum required as a member of society to allow for, though not necessarily work to preserve, the rights of others. Legality is the lowest standard of what we refer to here as "goodness." It would be naive to suggest that legality is not a concern in our professional lives, or that there are not board-certified behavior analysts who engage in illegal activities. On the contrary, violations of the law, which may include fraudulent billing or even abuse, occur far too frequently. We must be ever vigilant to maintain this standard and ensure that others maintain these standards as well.

Then there is *ethical behavior*, which refers to adherence to the Ethics Code®. Ethical behavior is not a matter of following one's conscience, but of following the guidance of a governing body. Though this may appear impersonal at first, it maintains our professional relationships. And finally we have the aspect of *morality*. To the inexperienced behavior analyst, it may seem that ethical and moral "goodness" would be interchangeable. And certainly, it would seem that if one meets the standard of moral goodness, the ethical standard would take care of itself. However, as discussed in Part 1, ethical and moral standards are not necessarily hierarchical. In our professional practice, our first obligation is to maintain ethically responsible professional relationships. If we fail to maintain adherence to the Ethics Code®, we have failed at both the ethical and moral standards of "goodness."

As suggested in Part 1, one helpful self-management tactic is to ask ourselves, "Is this for me, or is this for the client?" A focus on the moral standard of goodness at the expense of the ethical standard may in fact stoke the behavior analyst's ego and self-esteem more than it addresses the clients' needs. Our first obligation is to the client, and their needs must be our top priority. The occasional conflict between the moral level of goodness and the ethical level can be a bitter pill to swallow for many behavior analysts. This is particularly true for those of us who enter the field through direct service. In this case, the relationships we develop with our clients are our most potent reinforcer. Complicating this further, our ethical obligation to maintain professional relationships is often poorly explained. Many service providers have a story of the supervisor who told them, "You care too much." Such admonishments often either become a rallying cry against any similar advice or they fall on deaf ears.

In this volume, I encourage behavior analysts to care. Caring is good. Caring is helpful. The problem is not caring too much. The problem is that "caring" often becomes more

DOI: 10.4324/9781003190707-13

about the relationship and its inherent reinforcement than it is about the client's long-term benefit. It is helpful and appropriate for our emotional investment to inform our work. However, we cannot allow our emotional investment to overwhelm the work that we do.

Among the descriptions of behavior as "ethical" and "moral," behavior analysts are also required to engage in *professional behavior.* Though definitions of ethical and moral behavior come with their own set of challenges, defining professional behavior is often the most similar to nailing jelly to the wall. Often, we are forced to rely on personal judgments without having a clear idea as to what "professional" means. It is often defined as Supreme Court Justice Potter Stewart once described pornography, "I shall not today attempt further to define the kinds of material I understand to be embraced within that shorthand description, and perhaps I could never succeed in intelligibly doing so. But I know it when I see it" (Stewart, 1964). In this introductory chapter, we will attempt to gain more specificity toward a definition of "professional" behavior by examining the responsibilities of the behavior analyst in each of the most common roles we may fulfill. We will also address some of the challenges inherent with developing this specificity.

Corporate Culture and the Behavior Analyst

As behavior analysts, particularly those who ascribe to a radical behaviorist approach, we believe that all behavior can be analyzed in terms of controlling variables in history and biology. Such a philosophical stance is not restricted to the behavior of our clients, but it permeates all of our interactions. Behavior analysts also understand culture in terms of these controlling variables. Sigrid Glenn in 1988 described culture using the term, "interlocking behavioral contingency" (Glenn, 1988). The behavior of new members of a group is shaped by current members of a given culture. Individual behavior, in other words, is affected by the behavior of others in any environment. When we adopt this definition of culture, it liberates our thinking by allowing us to shake off the restrictions of discussion of culture in a strictly nationalistic or ethnic framework. Culture can be adopted by any group. When we refer to "corporate culture," this definition of culture is an essential one to bear in mind. No culture exists in a vacuum and each member of a culture is shaped by the behavior of others. Every corporate culture is created by the people within that corporate entity. Their behavior shapes the behavior of others.

Our ideas of "right" and "wrong" are often informed, or perhaps even determined, by our own biases. The same is true of our concepts of "professional" and "unprofessional." There is actually considerable room for interpretation in these labels, and whether or not a given behavior meets the criterion for what we would consider "professional" is, to some extent, determined by the professional environment as much as by the Ethical Code® or by the behavior itself.

Professionalism as Competence

The importance of competency-based training for supervisees, trainees, and employees cannot be overemphasized. One of the repeated themes in the Ethics Code® is the necessity of ensuring that the behavior analyst establishes competence before allowing ourselves or those under our supervision to perform tasks or implement procedures which require oversight. Several Code elements address this concern directly, but the importance of maintaining competence is repeated throughout the Code. Within the Fifth Edition Task List we are also required to utilize competency-based assessment in the evaluation of staff performance. Competency in behavioral circles is not the vague, ambiguous descriptor within our practice that it often is when used colloquially. Rather, it refers to specific behavior and performance on specific tasks. Professionalism, therefore, should be objectively defined based on the behaviors expected in a particular environment. These behaviors should be directly related to task performance and the efficient completion of responsibilities.

Ethical, Professional, and Uncomfortable

There are behaviors that would be considered unethical – those which violate some aspect of the Ethics Code®, and there are those which would be considered unprofessional. Ideally, these behaviors would be addressed in company policies and documented in employee handbooks or other literature for starting employees. However, some of these may go unspoken, unwritten, and assumed by members of a given corporate culture. And these may not be reflections of unprofessional behavior at all, but rather behavior or aspects of the culture that simply rub an individual the wrong way. The behavior of the individual is not necessarily in question, but rather the reaction of the community. In order to create a more objective definition of professionalism, it is necessary to look at this class of behaviors in the same way that we look at any behavior – through the lens of what is applied. "Applied" in terms of the dimensions of behavior analysis refers to the social significance (Baer, Wolf, & Risley, 1968). Such determination is dependent on context. What is socially significant in one environment may not be socially significant in another. The essential question to ask in this case is, "Does this interfere with the performance of professional tasks?" In some cases, what makes us slightly (or perhaps more than slightly) uncomfortable may not be a reflection of ethics but of a poor fit with the culture. Below are a few examples, though this is by no means an exhaustive list.

Body Art

Tattoos or other body modifications, such as facial or body piercings, may not fit in with every professional environment or corporate culture. However, these are becoming more commonplace in the current workforce. According to a 2012 Harris poll, 21% of adults in the USA report having at least one tattoo (Braverman, 2012). Having attended many conferences over the years, I can also personally attest that several of these are behavior analysts, including myself. There may be many reasons that people have such body modifications, both religious and personal, but the presence of body art alone is no longer the cultural indication of rebelliousness that it once was. It may, however, lead to problems when seeking employment or being comfortable in a work environment. Organizations which are predominantly religious may take issue with modifications for this reason, even if they provide services for children of all religious backgrounds and are equal opportunity employers. In addition, there are other considerations which are worthy of note:

Safety. For those practitioners working in direct service, it is best to be prepared for any eventuality. Those piercings which might be grabbed should be dutifully covered to prevent injury. Any recent piercings should be protected from infection.

Placement. A tattoo's placement often determines to some extent its level of appropriateness within a given work environment. Tattoos on the arms, legs, or torso often go unnoticed or tend to be deemed acceptable given the overall acceptance of body art within many fields. Tattoos on the face, neck, or head are more difficult to overlook or justify.

Content. It is difficult to make an argument that body art is a form of self-expression and should therefore be tolerated if this self-expression is offensive. If you are attempting to show someone who you are, be aware of the possibility that they will receive this message. If such art contains material that is violent or sexual in nature, including images of nudity, it is best covered up, especially when working with young children.

Dress

"Appropriate dress" is another description that may vary, and is often in the eyes of the beholder. The context is appropriate here. What is considered "appropriate" is often determined by the responsibilities of the job rather than by universal rules. There are, however, certain considerations to bear in mind.

Neatness. It is said that you never get a second chance to make a first impression. Neatness of attire indicates a level of attentiveness, which is often necessary in making that first impression. Working with young children, we often find that neatness is a fleeting state, often replaced by crayon marks, applesauce, and, the first author recounts, even on one occasion a full handprint of spaghetti sauce. However, a reasonable effort should be made to present such attentiveness and caring.

Formality. Among nurses and teachers, jobs with more administrative responsibilities are sometimes referred to as "pumps and pearls." This is precisely because such clothing may be appropriate only for office environments, where little fingers are less likely to break a string of pearls, and maneuvering around playground equipment is not a consideration. "Appropriate dress" for a behavior analyst, however, must be determined by the job responsibilities themselves as well as the general work culture.

Distraction. We cannot work effectively if we are continually readjusting straps or having difficulty finding a modest way to sit in a skirt or tight pants. Clothing in the workplace should allow us to do our work comfortably and without distraction. It is necessary here to define what is meant by the word "distraction" in this context. The reason we must be mindful of the fit and comfort of our clothing is that it may be distracting *to the person wearing it.* Tight fitting clothes are inappropriate because it may cause discomfort or necessitate continual adjusting throughout the day. Clothing with excessive cleavage will also require continued readjustment and ultimately interfere with the often-physical work of direct service. Distractibility to those observing the clothes is the responsibility of the observers. There is no style of dress that provides an adequate excuse for aggressive behavior or sexual harassment.

Cultural considerations. Although an appropriate level of dress should ultimately be decided by the judgment of the person wearing it, cultural considerations must also be kept in mind. In an environment where modesty is the cultural standard, some adjustments to one's own personal style can and should be made. It is important to dress in a manner that would not cause offense, as this could damage the professional relationship.

Grooming. Grooming is a deeply personal and surprisingly loaded topic. Styles of grooming which compromise vision or interfere with safety (e.g., longer hairstyles when working with young children with a history of hairpulling) should certainly be avoided. Beyond this, there are certain grooming behaviors that are often considered "unprofessional," often with little justification for the characterization. There are very few situations in which grooming may impact the ability to perform professional responsibilities. Many of these characterizations of "unprofessionalism" can in fact be problematic and even discriminatory.

Natural hair texture. Natural hair, particularly among black women, can often be accompanied by biases under the disguise of a focus on "grooming." In a study developed by the Perception Institute, biases in the definition of "good hair" were examined. In this study, white women were likely to show explicit bias against black women's natural hair, deeming it less professional (Johnson et al., 2017). Such bias, despite its irrelevance to professionalism, can also lead to discrimination. There is nothing about natural textured hair that precludes the responsible execution of the professional responsibilities of the behavior analyst.

Facial hair. For those few workplaces that have guidelines as to the proper grooming of facial hair, it is important to be aware of reasonable accommodations. There may be religious or cultural practices that influence the personal choice involved in grooming practices. Dreadlocks, sidelocks, or uncut beards may be a part of religious or cultural practices and should be afforded accommodation.

Hair color. The selection of hair color, unlike some other aspects of grooming, is a purely personal decision. While naturally textured hair or the facial hair characteristic of certain religions may lead to discrimination against a legally protected class, personal appearance is not protected under law. Many direct service providers "light it up blue" during Autism Acceptance month by dying their hair, and it is not unusual to see a veritable rainbow of hair colors at any professional event.

Concluding Thoughts

In our professional behavior, context is a deciding factor in determining "appropriateness." What works for one environment may not work for another. It may be helpful to understand what the conflict is that drives a particular issue – ethics, professionalism, or perhaps neither. There are many possible solutions to any conflict, including either changing our own behavior or changing the environment. There are as many ways to be a behavior analyst as there are behavior analysts. Not every environment is suitable for every person. A job is not the same as a career and you may find that there are certain jobs within this career that may not be a perfect fit. Though the field has some work to do in its effort to embrace diversity, there is great diversity in terms of skill sets, personality, and what we might refer to as "bedside manner."

Perhaps the best advice is this: "Be yourself, because whoever that is, there will be an environment that needs exactly that." In the following chapters, we will offer suggestions as to the professional behavioral expectation of the behavior analyst. We will explore the responsibilities of behavior analysts within several different roles they may play.

Works Cited

Baer, D. M., Wolf, M. M., & Risley, T. R. (1968). Some current dimensions of applied behavior analysis. *Journal of Applied Behavior Analysis, 1*(1), 91–97.

Braverman, S. (2012, February 23). One in five U.S. adults now has a tattoo. Harris Polls.

Glenn, S. S. (1988). Contingencies and metacontingencies: toward a synthesis of behavior analysis and cultural materialism. *The Behavior Analyst*, 11(2), 161–179.

Johnson, A. M., Godsil, R. D., MacFarlane, J., Tropp, L., & Goff, P. A. (2017). The "Good Hair" study: explicit and implicit attitudes toward black women's hair. The Perception Institute.

Stewart, J. (1964). 378 U.S. 184/378 U.S. at 197 (Stewart, J., concurring).

2.2   The Behavior Analyst as Service Provider

Service Provision and "Treatment"

A session in a clinic or home setting, particularly for young children, should look a great deal like playing. The clinician may sit on the floor with the child and engage them in activities that they enjoy. There should be smiling, noise, and, ideally, laughter. For the untrained eye, it may be difficult to discern precisely what, if anything, the clinician is actually teaching.

However, like the swan on the surface of the water, the elegance of what can be seen above the surface may mask the paddling that goes on underneath. A skilled clinician must be engaged in a number of behaviors at all times. There is indeed a great deal of teaching taking place. Whether our background is in education, psychology, social work, speech pathology, or any of the other human services professions, each of us is engaged in supporting learning, defined within our field as a durable change in behavior. If the client is learning, we are indeed teaching.

The Fifth Edition Task List offers some guidance on how we can provide high-quality teaching. In similar fashion to the Ethics Code®, it is a document written by and for behavior analysts. As is our habit in our clinical practice, it is written with an eye toward the *behaviors* that are expected. In this chapter we will review the relevant tasks within the Fifth Edition Task List and discuss how each of these relates to the responsibilities of the behavior analyst as a direct service provider.

It is often true that a skilled and ethical clinician must begin by meeting a client where they are. This, certainly, refers to acceptance of the client as a person worthy of dignity and respect regardless of their level of independence or ability to communicate. However, in the promotion of lasting meaningful behavior change, it also means conducting assessments in order to have a clear idea of "where they are" actually is.

F-4 Conduct assessments of relevant skill strengths and deficits.

Those of us who provide services often begin working with clients after a need has been established by another entity. This may be a doctor or independent evaluator with a background in education or developmental psychology. This may or may not include a medical diagnosis, but is likely to report on at least a general problem that must be addressed.

As mentioned in Part 1, some caution should be exercised in the overemphasis upon a specific diagnosis or on the description of applied behavior analysis programs as "a treatment for autism spectrum disorder." There are several reasons that such a description is problematic. The following is by no means an exhaustive list of these reasons, though they are some of the most relevant from this discussion:

Applied behavior analysis is a science, not a treatment. Applied behavior analysis, according to the defined provided in the text *Applied Behavior Analysis* by Cooper, Heron,

DOI: 10.4324/9781003190707-14

and Heward (2007), can be described as the science in which procedures that are derived from the principles of behavior as demonstrated scientifically are applied in order to improve socially significant behavior to a meaningful degree. Experimental analysis is then completed in order to demonstrate a functional relation between the procedure implemented and the improvement in behavior (Cooper, Heron, & Heward, 2007). There is nothing within this definition that restricts the potential impact of the science to the treatment of any one disorder. The science itself, in fact, can potentially expand to any human (or even nonhuman) behavior.

Autism spectrum disorder is behaviorally defined. The Diagnostic and Statistical Manual V defines autism spectrum disorder as a developmental disorder marked by deficits in social-emotional reciprocity, including joint attention and understanding of body language, communication, including speech and language development and the ability to create and sustain social relationships. Autism spectrum disorder is not diagnosed medically, through blood tests or other lab work. Rather, it is diagnosed through observation of behavioral deficits and behavioral excesses, which may manifest differently for different clients.

Autism, in and of itself, does not require treatment. Many of us who work with individuals with autism could be described as "neurotypical" or "allistic," meaning that they do not meet the diagnostic criteria, or do not identify as an individual with autism.

This commitment to neurodiversity becomes more complicated as insurance providers require that treatment meet the criteria of "medical necessity" and address the "core deficits" of autism spectrum disorder. In this case, it is important to remember that we must focus on aspects that are, in fact, disabling. In other words, "what aspects of the diagnosis interfere with this individual accessing what they need for health and happiness?" *Behavior analysts treat behaviors, not diagnoses and not people.* It has often been said, "If you've met one child with autism, you've met one child with autism." The diagnostic criteria for autism spectrum disorder are sufficiently broad that a "one size fits all" approach would not be appropriate.

F-1: Review records and available data (e.g., educational, medical, historical) at the outset of the case.

It is essential that we consider all data when performing assessments or developing behavior change programs. This being said, not all information that we are provided is of equal quality, and we are often faced with the choice of accepting information at face value or ignoring it entirely.

There is, however, another option. Data is essentially a more academic term meaning "information" and while the information we are given may appear at first glance to be worthless, it may indeed be redeemable. Behaviors that are reported in one setting and not under other conditions may not be absent, but require further teaching to bring them under stimulus control, for example. The information provided may be different than intended, but its value is still notable.

In Part 1, we discussed the responsibilities of the behavior analyst to seek our medical consultation when appropriate (BACB, 2020). This becomes both more complex and more necessary when medical issues, such as pain or fatigue, affect behavior. Even in cases where the behavior may have specific antecedents, there may be underlying medical or biological issues which can exacerbate maladaptive or dangerous behavior. If treatment focuses exclusively on these antecedents or on the behavior itself, without addressing the mitigating factors that affect an individual's response, the impact will clearly be limited.

Even the best behavioral program would be limited in scope if it fails to address these factors. It is natural, however, for behavior analysts to follow their training in the focus on observable measurable behavior. However, it is essential that we remember that the term "measurable" is not restricted to what the behavior analyst generally measures, but rather expansive to what can be measured by *any* instrument. Too often, behavior analysts limit their client's right to effective treatment to only that treatment that we ourselves can provide. Following the Law of the Instrument (Maslow, 1966), it is perhaps tempting to view everything as a possible nail when one's skills set is limited to the use of a hammer.

There are examples within the literature of a departure from the habit of viewing all behavior through the lens of what can be observed with the naked eye. In their study of the setting events of biological phenomena, Carr, Smith, Giacin, Whelan, and Pancari (2003) identified an increase in aggression and self-injury in women with developmental disabilities when they experienced pain during menstruation. Though the behavior also occurred at high rates in response to task demands, using a multicomponent strategy that addressed the biological needs as well formed a more effective strategy (Carr et al., 2003).

C-1: Establish operational definitions of behavior.

Equating behavior with character is a habit that is incredibly difficult to break for many students of behavior analysis. It is important to acknowledge here that behavior does not occur in a vacuum and that all behavior has an effect on the environment. Such effects may include a number of things, but among them is the possibility that the behavior will be annoying or offensive.

Particularly in the case of behavior that should be targeted for decrease, the risk is that behavior will be described by its effect on the environment rather than its observable and measurable characteristics. Describing behavior as "naughty" or "stubborn" are examples of interpreting behavior rather than defining it. Behavior itself is not "naughty" or "stubborn" without context. Screaming "no" may be considered naughty when being asked to clean up toys, but would it be interpreted the same way in response to watching someone about to accidentally ingest poison? Refusing to answer a question may be interpreted as "stubborn," but if the questions were extremely personal and asked by a stranger, this interpretation becomes less likely.

In defining behavior, the language that we use becomes crucially important. Being precise in our phrasing can avoid confusion and allow us to more closely adhere to the intention of this task list item.

Given that behavior is defined as anything that an organism *does*, our first effort at precision in our language should focus on this requirement. Behavior cannot be defined in descriptive terms, such as "stubborn" or "naughty." Adjectives of any kind describe the person and do not define the behavior itself. Behavior must be described in *action words*. If it is not something that can be done, it is not a behavior. Behaviors can only be verbs.

In addition to defining behavior by using verbs, we would also define the presence of behavior rather than its absence. Definitions of behavior must focus on what an individual does rather than what they do not do. A behavior may be targeted for increase or decrease but it is its presence rather than its absence that must be observed with this goal in mind. Appropriate behavior-analytic goals may include a 50% reduction in self-injurious biting, but this can only be detected by looking at occurrences of biting, rather than "not biting."

Just as we must focus on what can be directly observed when describing behavior, we must also maintain this standard when describing environmental conditions.

It is necessary here to review how behavior analysts define "environment." Behavior cannot occur in a vacuum. In behavioral philosophy, environmental conditions are essential to our analysis of behavior. "Environment" in this case might be considered synonymous with "context." Cooper, Heron, and Heward (2007) describe environment as "the conglomerate of real circumstances in which the organism or referenced part of the organism of the organism exists." Despite the clarity of this definition, many clinicians engage in "natural environment teaching" by simulating the same tasks performed in more intensive teaching but doing so on the floor rather than in a chair. "Environment" in the context of behavior analysis does not refer to a place but to a set of circumstances. These circumstances must be described in ways that can be easily understood and identified by an outside observer. Context must be objectively measured.

When describing the environmental conditions, we are often addressing the antecedent conditions. Those phenomena which occur before the behavior occurs also require objective observation. Again, precision in our language is essential. Any phrasing that describes what cannot be directly observed should be avoided. Phrases such as "when the client is sad" or "when frustrated" cannot be objectively observed and would therefore be an inadequate descriptions.

Our descriptions of these conditions must focus on two elements: the actions of the client and the actions of others. While "feeling sad" cannot be observed, crying or protests can be observed. While "disappointment" cannot be observed, the circumstances likely to induce disappointment, such as being denied a preferred item, can be observed. While "frustration" cannot be observed, a situation that may induce frustration, such as a peer's attempt to take their toy, can be observed. Describing those conditions as an observer may witness them increases clarity and objectivity, which directly increases our ability to be effective.

F-4: Conduct assessments of relevant skill strengths and deficits.

Part of our assessment procedures includes assessing those behaviors which are currently in the individual's repertoire. The focus of behavioral assessment is *what* an individual does and the rationale behind performing such an assessment is to determine the extent of behavioral deficits – what should an individual be able to do, and what skills must be taught in order for an individual to function independently.

There are several choices when it comes to behavioral assessments and several factors that must be considered when selecting the best assessment for a given situation. Certainly the requirements of any funding source (educational agencies as well as insurance companies) must be taken into consideration.

In addition, the characteristics of the assessment tools themselves must be considered. The target age range should be a good fit with the age of the client, and areas targeted by the assessment should be relevant to the client. The assessor must have the required training and qualifications. Popularity of a given assessment is of little practical value if the assessment results do not allow for a clear path forward to be developed.

Working in international environments, these guidelines can become somewhat problematic. Although behavior analysts rely upon scientifically validated techniques and advocate the use of evidence-based practice, the vast majority of this evidence originates from the United States. Many of the criterion referenced assessments commonly used have not been assessed for validity in other countries or validated in Czech or Bahasa Indonesia. Even within the United States, some assessment items may not reflect the values of the audience. Items that ask, for example, if a young child is able to walk to a destination alone may elicit more incredulous looks than affirmative answers.

Behavior analysts must use behavioral assessments, but must also be committed to doing so responsibly. It is essential to remember the rationale behind these assessments in order to fulfill this responsibility. An assessment is a picture of the client's current level of progress. We must ensure that such a picture accurately reflects the client's abilities and that this picture is reflective of the value that the client's culture places on the behaviors assessed.

F-7/F-8: Conduct a descriptive assessment of problem behavior/Conduct a functional analysis of problem behavior/Interpret functional assessment data.

A behavioral assessment focuses on *what* the individual does, or what behaviors the individual can be reasonably expected to do. A functional assessment, however, focuses on *why* an individual engages in behavior.

The underlying assumption of a functional analysis is that all behavior is maintained by reinforcement, and therefore all behavior that persists must be reinforced. At its core, a functional assessment is an acknowledgment of the scientific assumption of determinism, which Cooper, Heron, and Heward (2007) define as the assumption that the universe is lawful and orderly, with all phenomena occurring as a result of other events. There is no behavior that occurs "for no reason." Rather, all behavior occurs for some reason, even if it is one we have yet to figure out.

In the Guidelines for Responsible Conduct, the document which described our ethical obligations before the development of the Professional and Ethical Compliance Code or the Ethics Code, a functional assessment was described as "a variety of information gathering activities" (BACB). Although the Professional and Ethical Compliance Code is often acknowledged as an improvement upon the Guidelines, particularly since it is a more enforceable document, I do lament the loss of this phrasing. Functional assessment is essentially an investigative exercise, the goal of which is to determine the reinforcers maintaining behavior. Though there have been several behavior analysts who have developed specific protocols toward that end, functional assessment is far more than simply a bag of tricks or any one specific procedure.

One of these possible "information gathering activities" is descriptive analysis (Atwater & Morris, 1988). In this method, the behavior analyst observes and analyzes the natural conditions under which the target behavior occurs. This naturalistic observation includes collecting detailed information about the behavior as it occurs in the current environment, as well as detailed information regarding the antecedents and consequent conditions. The goal of a descriptive analysis is to identify those factors which affect the behavior, and it is often possible to develop a hypothesis regarding putative reinforcers from naturalistic observations, questionnaires, and interviews with those in the environment.

In those instances when a descriptive analysis does not provide enough information to determine function, other protocols have been developed that can provide the information needed if a hypothesis remains elusive. In their seminal article, Iwata, Dorsey, Slifer, Bauman, and Richman (1994) proposed a scientific approach to determining likely reinforcers that maintain dangerous or otherwise problematic behavior. In this functional analysis procedure, possible reinforcers within several general categories are tested in an alternating treatments design (Iwata et al., 1994). The motivating operations which control the effectiveness of these reinforcers are simulated in each condition (Iwata et al., 1994). When a confederate appears distracted or otherwise occupied, self-injury is met with contingent attention in the form of social disapproval (Iwata et al., 1994). When a boring or difficult task is presented, self-injurious responses are met with the removal of task demands (Iwata et al., 1994). An experimental condition with limited stimulation were also presented, in order to assess the effects of self-reinforcement through the act of self-injury (Iwata et al., 1994). A condition in which the subjects were allowed noncontingent access to play materials and attention was also presented to serve as a control for other variables (Iwata et al., 1994).

Often students of behavior analysis will grumble that the experimental conditions do not account for the variety of potential reinforcers, and that the list of commonly assessed reinforcers is not sufficient to allow for preferences within those categories. This point is well taken, and raises an interesting consideration in the evaluation of functional analysis as a tool for assessing behavior.

The essential point to remember about functional assessment and functional analysis specifically is that the protocol originated by Iwata et al. (1994) is not, and never was, intended to be a universally applied prescription or a definitive or exhaustive list of the controlling variables of behavior. In the 30 years since Iwata et al.'s article was published, many more studies have expanded the procedures employed by the original researchers (Beavers et al., 2013). Common modifications may include the addition of a tangible condition (Beavers et al., 2013), but the conditions may also be modified based on descriptive data and include suspected reinforcers unaccounted for in the original study (Hagopian, Rooker, Jessel, and DeLeon, 2013).

A functional assessment procedure can, and should, allow for a more straightforward interpretation of the controlling variables in order to facilitate the development of a hypothesis of the behavior's function. The goal is to develop an accurate and relevant picture of the target behavior and its controlling variables. As is the case with behavioral assessment, the relevance of the information to be gained should take precedence over any of the trappings of the procedures or methods themselves. Applied behavior analysis does not describe a treatment, treatment package, or set of procedures. Rather, it is the science from which such procedures are developed.

Prioritizing Goals

The power of the science of behavior to construct and support lasting meaningful behavior change cannot be overstated. Applied behavior analysis can, and has, been used to teach and maintain many behaviors of significance to clients. It has also, sadly, been used to teach behaviors that, with the benefit of hindsight and a greater knowledge of our responsibility to vulnerable populations, been used in ways that were potentially harmful. The procedures developed from this science are a tool that can be used in ways that are good, bad, or neutral.

It is important to demonstrate caution when selecting target behaviors. Using the techniques developed from the science of behavior, we can teach anything. However, the fact that we *could* teach *anything* should not be confused with the idea that we *should* teach *everything*. The behaviors that are increased in a behavior-analytic program must be relevant and socially significant to the client, rather than those behaviors that are taught due to our own preferences. Those behaviors which are targeted for decrease must be barriers to the client's successful accomplishment of their own goals rather than those which reflect our own values and inclinations, or those taught for our own convenience.

When determining the appropriateness of goals in a behavior-analytic program, a behavior analyst must be ever cognizant that the word "applied" comes before the words "behavior analysis." Our emphasis on socially significant behavior must not be an afterthought, but the cornerstone of our programming.

H-2: Identify potential interventions based on assessment results and the best available scientific evidence.

Within this task list item, there are two points of emphasis: assessment results and scientific evidence. It would be fitting in the examination of this obligation to consider the dimensions of behavior analysis as described by Baer, Wolf, and Risley (1968). A behavior-analytic program must be applied, behavioral, analytic, conceptually systematic, technological, effective, and promote generalization (Baer, Wolf, & Risley, 1968). For the purposes of this task list item, the focus is on two of these dimensions. A program that is *conceptually systematic* follows scientific evidence, and one that is *applied* reflects assessment results.

There is a common description of applied behavior analysis as "the only evidence-based intervention for individuals with autism" that I have found somewhat problematic. While it may be a shorthand description of our commitment to evidence-based practice, there is a misplacement of emphasis in referring it as science – something that one can *understand* – as an intervention – something that one *does*.

When I have been asked, "Are there any other evidence-based methods?" I have had to respond "yes and no." There are several evidence-based practices identified in reviews of the literature on (Wong, Odom, Hume, Cox, Fettig, Kucharczyk, Brock, Plavnick, Fleury, & Schultz, 2015). Many of these techniques are integral components of applied behavior analysis programs, including task analysis, prompting, modeling, and reinforcement (Wong et al., 2015). Other techniques, such as social skills training or visual supports, are implemented as needed for individual clients (Wong et al., 2015). Among these evidence-based practices, "applied behavior analysis" is not listed, though the techniques that are frequently the elements of a behavior-analytic program are (Wong et al., 2015).

There are those who believe that the overlap between the techniques commonly used in behavior analysis to be a reflection of bias toward applied behavior analysis. However, this overlap is not because of a lack of evidence for specific treatments or because clinicians and researchers have stopped looking for further evidence or future innovations in treatment. Rather, it is because applied behavior analysis follows the evidence rather than leading it. Over the past several decades, many techniques have been added to the body of evidence-based practices and to the repertoire of many behavior analysts. As evidence grows in support of specific procedures, behavior analysts implement them and add these procedures to their repertoire of practices.

Because those who practice applied behavior analysis recommend and implement only those procedures that have sufficient scientific support, applied behavior analysis will remain evidence-based. Because behavior analysts follow the evidence rather than leading it, a behavior-analytic program looks very different than it did 20 years ago and will likely look very different 20 years from now. As the evidence grows and evolves, so does the practice and the volume of behavioral technologies.

In addition to being conceptually systematic, a behavioral program must be *applied*. Applied refers to the social significance of the goals in question. What is the rationale for teaching this behavior to the client, and what would be the impact for the family, and for the greater community? Are the skills we endeavor to teach the skills that are needed and identified by the assessments performed?

Programming goals must reflect the strengths and needs of the individual client and the methods used to attain these goals must reflect the best practices of the science of behavior analysis.

H-3: Recommend intervention goals and strategies based on such factors as client preferences, supporting environments, *risks*, *constraints*, and social validity.

In teaching skills it is crucial that behavior analysts use "the right tool for the job." The procedures implemented must be a good match not only for the client's identified needs and the current body of research, but also for the task itself.

A behavior chain, though often described as the procedure used for teaching behaviors which have many component steps, has a different definition according to Cooper,

Heron, and Heward (2007). A behavior chain is defined as an arrangement of responses in which each behavior within the series signals the response that is to follow and reinforces the behavior that precedes it (Cooper, Heron, & Heward, 2007). As each step is completed, this completion reinforces the response, and results in a signal of the next task to be performed.

Essentially, a procedure that builds behavior should focus on the goal of creating behavior chains. The goal of a program should be to build the level of fluency where each component flows seamlessly to the next. It is this emphasis on fluency that should be a deciding factor in the selection of teaching procedures.

H-3: Recommend intervention goals and strategies based on such factors as *client preferences*, supporting environments, risks, constraints, and *social validity*.

These task list items refer to what is considered "applied." The social significance of goals must always be the cornerstone of our programming. Goals must be considered socially significant. A distinction that is often considered subjective. In Wolf's 1978 article, "Social validity: the case for subjective measurement or how applied behavior analysis is finding its heart," the author describes the importance of social validity. Whether or not a target behavior is applied is determined by the client and those in the client's environment rather than by outside forces.

H-3: Recommend intervention goals and strategies based on such factors as client preferences, supporting environments, risks, *constraints*, and social validity.

A responsible behavior analyst must develop programming based on the client's current repertoires. Programming must address whether the client has demonstrated the prerequisite skills necessary for identified targets. If these prerequisite skills are currently in place, the client may indeed be ready for more advanced skills and new responses can be taught. Prerequisite skills, as identified in skills assessments, must lay the foundation for later skill development.

The limitations of a client's current repertoire must be considered in the design of behavioral programming. While these limitations are malleable and constantly evolving, either through intervention or maturation, they must be adequately addressed.

There is, however, another important consideration in the assessment of a client's current behavioral repertoire: the importance of including programs that address a client's strengths rather than an exclusive focus on behavioral deficits. One of the benefits of the behavioral assessment process is identifying not only the needs or behavioral deficits, but also the clients' strengths. In their 2010 article, Bellini and McConnell make the case for programming that is based on client strengths. In their study of video self-modeling, Bellini and McConnell (2010) demonstrated an effective and strength-based intervention, hypothesizing that such interventions could positively impact overall growth and development, particularly for youth diagnosed with autism spectrum disorder. In this meta-analysis of video self-modeling approaches, an approach that portrayed these clients as capable of performing difficult tasks independently resulted in increased attention to task and improved performance. Improvement in their own assessment of competency was also noted.

There is nothing incompatible with applied behavior analysis programming and strengths-based programming. Indeed, as a science focused on behavior – what an organism *does* – we should be far more concerned with those behaviors that we observe than those that are absent.

**H-3: Recommend intervention goals and strategies based on such factors as client prefer-
ences, *supporting environments*, risks, constraints, and social validity.**

The dimensions of behavior analysis identified by Baer, Wolf, and Risley (1968) are considered the litmus test for programming to be considered "behavior-analytic." Although
originally intended to describe the requirements for publication, these dimensions have
been considered the standards for quality behavior-analytic programming outside of the
realm of research as well. These dimensions include the stipulation that programming
must be applied, behavioral, analytic, conceptually systematic, technological and demonstrate generalization (Baer, Wolf, & Risley, 1968). Also included in these dimensions is the
requirement that a behavior-analytic program be effective (Baer, Wolf, & Risley, 1968).
For publication in the *Journal of Applied Behavior Analysis*, the strategy for meeting this
requirement is clear: null results, or those treatments which do not produce significant
results, are not accepted for publication. For application of these dimensions to clinical
practice, a path forward becomes a bit more cloudy. There are times in clinical practice
when our first attempts at teaching a necessary skill or decreasing a behavior may not be
successful. This would not necessarily mean that the program is not behavior-analytic,
but that modifications are necessary before effectiveness can be achieved. The program
can still be behavior-analytic, although it is incomplete.

While the effectiveness of each behavior change program can certainly not be guaran-
teed, the environment must be arranged to promote effectiveness. This means a careful
examination of all available resources, and their limits. The materials needed to achieve
the goals of intervention must be considered, including the cost of these materials initially
as well as the subsequent cost if replacement is necessary. Relevant aspects of the physical
environment must also be considered and limitations to safe implementation of the recommended behavior plans must be addressed.

Perhaps the most difficult resource to assess is the human capital necessary to implement and evaluate the program and ensure effectiveness. Addressing needs in terms of
training and oversight and making the necessary adjustments of our expectations is a
fundamental step in program development. We must not allow perfection to be the en-
emy of good, or for that matter effectiveness. If compromises must be made in terms of
the simplicity of our program implementation or our data collection systems in order to
decrease the response effort or increase the level of reinforcement for those responsible
for implementing programs, this is not the "dumbing down" of our programs. Rather it is
"smartening up" by budgeting and spending our resources as wisely as possible.

Among our most precious resources in the work of human services is time. The
amount of time that we have to spend on training, program implementation, and making modifications is a finite and limited reserve. Using this resource wisely can be the
difference between safe and effective programming and long lists of unaccomplished
goals. Our allocation of time as an invaluable asset is perhaps the best assurance that
our other resources (materials, financial resources, and human capital) will be used
wisely as well.

H-9: Collaborate with others who support and/or provide services to clients.

Applied behavior analysis is a science and not a set of practices. It is the *science* of how
every organism learns, rather than the *practice* of using techniques developed from our
study of this science to teach individuals with autism. As such, it is a science that seeks
to understand and explain the behavior of all organisms, including the behavior of other
professionals that we work with.

Many behavior analysts have, at a minimum, a tacit understanding of this. Many will refer to themselves as radical behaviorists in both their personal philosophy and professional lives. And yet, many of these professionals overlook the opportunity to analyze behavior of relevant stakeholders.

Part of supporting the lasting effectiveness of behavior change programs is in the selection of behavioral cusps as goals of intervention. A behavioral cusp is defined by Rosales-Ruiz and Baer (1997) as "a behavior change that has implications beyond the change itself." Bosch and Fuqua (2001) further clarify this concept by outlining several criteria for referring to a recommended target behavior as a behavioral cusp. A behavioral cusp must increase a client's contact with new reinforcers and environments, must demonstrate social validity, must be a viable and competitive alternative to problem behavior, and must generate future behavior change as well (Bosch & Fuqua, 2001). This may seem like a concept with remarkable similarity to pivotal response training, in which pivotal areas are addressed in order to set a context for learning in inclusive settings and these pivotal areas have more widespread impact on a greater breadth of target behavior (Koegel, Koegel, Harrower, & Carter, 1999). However, the final criterion for evaluation of a behavioral cusp separates these two concepts. Whether or not a given target behavior can be considered a behavioral cusp depends on the number and relative importance of the people affected (Bosch & Fuqua, 2001).

Part of establishing the support for our services is to prioritize those goals which are already relevant to the important people in the client's community. We should be empowering others to work together toward a common goal, rather than a goal that is only important to an individual clinician. To translate the description of "low priority" into behavioral terms, we must ensure that reinforcers are adequate, not only for the work involved, but also for the accomplishment of the stated goals.

H-3: Recommend intervention goals and strategies based on such factors as client preferences, supporting environments, risks, constraints, and *social validity*.

These task items deal directly with our obligation to select goals and interventions based on their social validity. Social validity, as defined by Montrose Wolf (1978), addresses the social importance, or applied nature, of the intervention goals. Goals must be relevant to the clients' needs (Wolf, 1978). In addition, the social appropriateness of the procedures recommended and the social importance of the effects, both anticipated and unanticipated. One area where this issue is frequently raised is in the teaching of compliance to children with disabilities.

Many of us who work in the field of applied behavior analysis work with children, where there is a distinct imbalance of power. A certain degree of compliance is necessary when working with younger populations, whether or not these children have disabilities. Classrooms of 20 or more cannot function, and certainly cannot accomplish educational goals, without some sense of order to facilitate teaching.

The ethics of teaching compliance has, however, been questioned (McDonnell, 1993). In this article, the authors identify several questions to assist clinicians in identifying the necessity of teaching compliance to individuals with mental retardation. The author identifies the following as factors to consider when deciding if compliance should be taught:

> *Does the learner really have a compliance problem or is compliance being chosen as the cure-all for several more specific behavior problems?*
> *Is noncompliant behavior serious enough to significantly limit learning or participation in integrated environments?*

Is the criteria for expected performance related to normative standards or standards of perfection, i.e., is there really a problem?

Does the learner "own" the noncompliance problem or is the underlying problem a sterile environment? Lack of reinforcement? Excessive or unreasonable demands? Ineffective or punitive instructional or classroom management strategies? (i.e., who needs "treatment," the learner or the teacher?)

Will the learner significantly benefit from improved compliance, or is the real objective to make life easier for educators or caregivers? Is the real objective compliance with adult directives or appropriate behavior in response to a variety of environmental demands and contexts?

(McDonnell, 1993)

Noncompliance should not be taught merely for its own sake, or for the convenience of the clinicians. An ethical clinician must consider the question, "Is this for the client or is this for me?" In the case of teaching compliance, this means that compliance will have considerable benefit to the client, rather than merely being to the benefit of others.

Compliance is, of course, simply one of the target behaviors which may cause us to question the ethics of its selection. However, the issue of compliance as a target behavior, and of the process for determining its appropriateness, is one that must be taken seriously.

H-1: State intervention goals in observable and measurable terms.

It has been said that if you fail to plan, you simply plan to fail. In the practice of behavior analysis, our focused attention on the achievement of objective and measurable goals is the hallmark of a behavior change program.

It is essential that we not only develop an observable and measurable definition of the behavior that we are targeting for intervention, but also an observable and measurable definition of how we will know that this behavior change has been accomplished. Having a clear focus on the goals to be accomplished is of tremendous value.

Here again, however, we must be cautious and be mindful of the social validity of our interventions. For those of us working with individuals with disabilities, the social appropriateness of the goals of any program must be considered. If the goal is to assist on the inclusion of individuals with disabilities into society at large, we must ensure that these efforts will accomplish that goal. This often means carefully considering social skills and expectations.

Social rules are often learned through observation and, though many neurotypical people have an implicit understanding of them, their analysis can present a challenge. The boundaries of social competence for the neurotypical population must also be acknowledged. Those of us who consider ourselves adept at social navigation must concede that our performance of the skills we are teaching are often inconsistent and that no one is completely socially competent.

H-4: When a target behavior is to be decreased, select an acceptable alternative behavior to be established or increased.

Behavior analysts are frequently treated in a similar fashion to firefighters. Just as a firefighter is called upon to address a problem, make it go away, and then depart, behavior analysts are expected to decrease problem behaviors and then disappear. More often than not, behavior analysts are called upon to address behaviors targeted for decrease rather than those targeted for increase. The word "behavior" in many circles is synonymous with "maladaptive behavior," even to the extent that children who demonstrate problematic behavior are referred to as "behavior kids."

In reviewing the definition of "behavior" as anything that an organism does (Cooper, Heron, & Heward, 2007), it is evident that a characterization of all behavior as that which must be targeted for decrease would be, at the very least, inaccurate.

I will often caution supervisees against focusing on behaviors targeted for decrease to the exclusion of behaviors to be increased. To exaggerate this point for emphasis, I often add, "There should be a difference between a well-run classroom and a well-run morgue." There should be, at a minimum, an equal balance between those behaviors that are targeted for increase and those targeted for decrease.

G-21: Use procedures to promote stimulus and response generalization.

Generalization is acknowledged as a dimension of the science of behavior analysis. The necessity of behavior change programs to demonstrate generality is described in Baer, Wolf, and Risley's seminal article (Baer, Wolf, & Risley, 1968). According to Baer, Wolf, and Risley, generality is demonstrated in part of the behavior change can be observed across environments and spreads to other behaviors. This is an essential characteristic of effective teaching. Its importance cannot be overstated. In order for our clinical work to have a real-world impact, the skills taught in clinical settings must be demonstrated in those environments in which those skills are necessary and improve an individual's quality of life.

In their analysis of techniques that demonstrate and promote effective generalization in behavior-analytic literature, Stokes and Baer (1977) describe several that can be applied to both stimulus and response generalization.

Surprisingly in this analysis, one of the techniques that did lead to the generalization of behavior change was what the authors referred to as *Train and Hope* (Stokes and Baer, 1977). In this method of assessing generalization, performance of different behaviors or performance under different conditions was noted but not necessarily planned for. The use of Train and Hope was successful in 90% of those studies examined in this analysis (Stokes and Baer, 1977). One might be tempted toward overconfidence about the spontaneity of generalization. However, it is important to remember that this article's analysis included only those studies in which generalization of skills was demonstrated (Stokes & Baer, 1977). Given that null results are not generally published in the *Journal of Applied Behavior Analysis*, a lack of generalization may not be reported. While there is certainly room for optimism, a word of caution should be noted here: although spontaneous generalization is possible, one cannot presume that a Train and Hope method will be effective.

Several teaching procedures successfully led to the generalization of skills in the analysis by Stokes and Baer (1977). These procedures focus on the teaching conditions which promote mastery of skills as well as those procedures implemented after the skill has been taught under tightly controlled conditions. When Train and Hope methods for generalization were not successful, many of the studies examined utilized *sequential modification*. Using this strategy, conditions would be altered and the teaching procedure continued until the behavior change was evident under these new circumstances (Stokes and Baer, 1977). If a client masters the skill of trying new foods at home, the same procedures may not be employed at home. In addition to modifying the teaching conditions after the mastery of skills in one settings, Stokes and Baer (1977) found that successful generalization could be achieved by *training sufficient exemplars*. By teaching skills using a diverse set of stimuli, skills were often generalized (Stokes and Baer, 1977). Another technique used to promote generalization is one referred to as *training loosely*, and described by Stokes and Baer (1977) as "the negation of the discrimination techniques." Rather than using sequential modification to the environment or a diverse set of stimuli, this method focuses on the procedural elements of the teaching. Since the rigors of research would necessitate consistency in the teaching procedures, *training loosely* is a procedure rarely implemented in studies. However, this is a commonly used technique in clinical or educational settings. Rather than presenting tasks with only one scripted instruction, clinicians are often encouraged to vary the instructions given so that a client can learn to respond to varied instructions.

Response generalization, which can be observed when other responses beyond those initially taught are performed, was also targeted in many of the examined studies (Cooper, Heron, & Heward, 2007). In several studies that were examined a strategy referred to as *train to generalize* was employed (Stokes & Baer, 1977). In this procedure, variations of the response were targeted for increase and explicitly reinforced (Stokes & Baer, 1977). In such a method, generalization is built into the program as a target, rather than being merely an afterthought.

Applied behavior analysis, at its core, is a science, and the procedures based on this science can promote learning of almost anything. While we should not be indiscriminate in our application of behavior technologies, nor should we be excessively miserly or resistant to expanding the results we see. By carefully examining the training and conditions and conscientiously modifying these, stimulus and response generalization can be achieved.

G-22: Use procedures to promote maintenance.

Although generalization and maintenance are frequently described as two different concepts, there is no such distinction within the current dimensions described by Baer, Wolf, and Risley (1968). In this article generalization is described by stating that the results not only extend to other settings, circumstances, and behaviors but also last over time. In order to meet the dimension of behavior analysis, the behavior change must last beyond the teaching.

In addition to modifications to teaching techniques, Stokes and Baer (1977) also addressed the possibility of modifying goals themselves to promote generalization. Consequent conditions are one way to address the long-term benefit by promoting lasting behavior change. Among these is by introducing *indiscriminable contingencies* (Stokes and Baer, 1977). By providing reinforcers on a more intermittent schedule, the behavior is able to be maintained at high rates.

Another tactic utilized to promote lasting behavior change and the maintenance of results over time is to *mediate generalization* (Stokes & Baer, 1977). This method, helpful in promoting both generalization and maintenance, involves teaching a response that accompanies the target response (Stokes & Baer, 1977). Self-management techniques, including the use of self-instruction, have been used to maintain behavior change and generalize this change to other behaviors as well.

Data-Based Decision-Making

Data collection is one area in which there is a fair amount of flexibility. The definition of data in most circles is information gathered for analysis. The definition of "good" or "enough" data can therefore be adapted to mean data that is sufficient to make data-based decisions.

Beyond any preferences or habits surrounding the collection or display of data, data *must* be three things: data must be taken, looked at and analyzed, and used to modify behavior change programs.

Data must be taken. Collection systems that are too complicated may sacrifice accuracy. Those that require particular formats may be prohibitively burdensome for others to complete. Systems which can only be completed by the behavior analyst can be a challenge to promoting generalization to less structured settings. Often, this effort is made simpler by decreasing the expected response effort of those responsible for implementation so that accurate data can be collected. Creating data collection systems that make procedures easier is not "dumbing down" these systems, but rather ensuring that the data itself is taken and that it reflects the true values of the target behavior.

Data must be looked at and analyzed. It is essential that data be regularly analyzed. Programs should not continue for months without discernible progress. Baseline data on problem behavior, taken with the intention of an upcoming intervention, should not go on for months at a time without a plan being implemented, or even developed using this information. Too often this happens if the responsibility for analysis of the data remains unclear. Although the data is collected, it remains unread, while those who are responsible for documenting behavior continue to shout into the void.

Data in applied behavior analysis is essentially quantitative information communicated between clinicians. Like any form of communication, it must involve a listener. Someone must listen to what is being communicated so that action may be taken. Behavior analysts must ensure that data is not only collected, but looked at and analyzed.

Data must be used to modify behavior change programs. Once the data has been collected accurately and in sufficient amount, and has been reviewed by a behavior analyst and progress toward goals or emerging patterns have been noted, its true purpose must be employed. Data must be used to design, implement, and modify behavior change programs. This may appear to be what my high school history teacher would refer to as a "penetrating glimpse into the obvious." Given that we are all practitioners in the science and art of behavior change, certainly we would concede that this step is necessary. However, this obligation can be more difficult to meet than it initially appears. There must be some assurance that the data collected is not only accurate and frequently reviewed, but also a valid measure of the behavior in question and demonstrates the social significance of this goal. The primary obligation of data is to set a clear path forward in treating behavior. The data, therefore, must be sufficiently broad, detailed, and informative.

Beyond these three obligations – for data to be taken, looked at and analyzed, and used to modify behavior change programs – there is considerable room for variety in the application of data collection methods. Decisions regarding the systems of data collection can be made based on available resources, logistics, or even the personal and aesthetic preferences of the behavior analyst. These considerations can be taken into account at this point, but should not take precedence over the more pressing concerns of the obligations that we have when taking data.

Above all, these obligations must continually be revisited as data collection continues. In addition to analyzing the data itself, we must be constantly evaluating whether our systems are providing the information necessary to fulfill these obligations. Without such needs being met, it is of little use to the client, and it is their benefit that must always be our primary concern.

C-9: Select a measurement system to obtain representative data given the dimensions of behavior and the logistics of observing and recording.

In considering the logistics of recording behavior data, one is reminded of the philosophical question, "If a tree falls in the forest and no one is there to hear it, does it make a sound?" In behavior-analytic terms, this might easily be rephrased as, "If there is not a behavior analyst there to observe the behavior, did it occur?"

We must first ensure commitment to our first obligation in terms of data collection – *data must be taken*. There must be sufficient resources to collect the data necessary to set the stage for socially significant behavior change. Resources, in this context, refers to many environmental condition that are necessary to have in place. Material resources must be adequate to the task and in sufficient supply to continue data collection. Human resources are a consideration as well. Staff that are responsible for data collection must be adequately trained in the systems they are expected to implement and must have systems that allow them to collect accurate data without compromising safety or the fulfillment of their other responsibilities.

Our second obligation in terms of data collection is that *data must be looked at and analyzed*. In consideration of selecting both a measurement system and setting an appropriate schedule, this obligation must be taken into account. A schedule for the analysis of data must be created in conjunction with the creation of systems to collect data. The data that is collected but be sufficient, but not so overwhelming in volume that it makes analysis impossible.

Finally, *data must be used to modify behavior change programs*. When considering our obligation to select measurement systems and schedules that are most likely to capture the behavior, we must allow for these systems to adequately capture behavior change. These measures must be relevant to the behavior change we are hoping to see. Without the information needed to make data-based decisions that maximize the impact of programming, the data itself is meaningless.

C-10: Graph data to communicate.

Among our obligations as scientists is to communicate our findings. We would do well here to emphasize the use of the word, "communicate." In any communication, there must be both a speaker and a listener, and it is therefore our responsibility to make this communication as clear as possible to our audience.

Within our science, our area of focus is clinical significance rather than statistical significance. Single subject research is employed and the results are analyzed based on baseline performance. In this sense it is said that an individual acts as their own control. Effectiveness of a behavior change program is assessed based on the comparison of an individual's performance before and after the implementation of behavior change procedures. A visual analysis of this difference is how effectiveness is determined.

Our visual communication, therefore, is not only how we document results and determine the success of our interventions, which would certainly be adequate justification for a commitment to clarity and transparent communication. Our communication is how we assure the investment of community members, as well as how we advocate for services.

As engineer and management consultant W. Edwards Deming said, "In God we trust, all others show data." We must have the information needed to move a program forward and that information must allow programming to move forward.

Evaluation and Modification

It is common for writers to remark, "Writing is rewriting." Similarly, a well-constructed behavior plan is often a moving target. Once program implementation has begun, the effects of the behavior change plan must then be evaluated and, if necessary, changes must be made. Making these changes in a timely fashion is essential to effective programming

As Fred Keller once wrote, "the student is always right" (Keller, 1968). If we begin with this stance, allowing the client to guide programmatic changes, the data will indicate what a student needs and how to proceed, if we listen to the story that it tells and respond accordingly.

H-7: Make data-based decisions about the effectiveness of the intervention and the need for treatment revision.

As a clinician, we will undoubtedly be working with families who have no background in behavior analysis. As such, their goals for programming may be quite subjective and they may speak in terms of the client "doing better" without specific information as to what "better" means. While Wolf (1978) would certainly argue that there is a place for this level of subjectivity in our measures of success, our decisions cannot be made on the basis of social validity alone.

As a scientific field, we have the advantage of empiricism in our decision-making, and this advantage must not be wasted. We do not need to guess as to whether or not our goals have been achieved, we have evidence to support this view.

Our obligation once we have this evidence is to then act upon it. One of two scenarios will necessitate a change in a given program or revisiting a particular goal for programming: inadequate progress toward a given goal or the achievement of a goal or objective.

First we must determine what level of progress is "inadequate" and how such a determination can be made. Trends of data must be identified and programs must be immediately altered if a worsening trend is noted. Alteration of programs may mean introducing prompting hierarchies, or revisiting the task analysis or teaching procedures. In some cases, the program may be paused until prerequisite skills can be mastered. For those programs which target a behavior for decrease, the reinforcement schedule may be reconsidered.

If progress is noted, but insufficient, analysis of the antecedents and consequences is necessary. Determinations must be made as to what needs changing in order for the client to have practical results from the behavior change program.

Once a given goal has been achieved, it is necessary to evaluate the appropriate next steps. If this is a shorter-term objective toward a larger goal or a prerequisite skill, a new goal must be selected. If mastery of the ultimate goal has been met, plans must be formulated to ensure the maintenance of skills.

It is imperative that we remember one of the requirements of data collection: *data must be used to modify behavior change programs.* Data is meaningless if it is merely shouting into the void. We must use this data to identify the action to be taken and take it.

H-8: Make data-based decisions about the need for ongoing services.

It is often said that the behavior analyst's goal is to "work themselves out of a job." An essential part of the evaluation process in determining the effectiveness of our programming is determining the level of support necessary as we move forward. We must plan for behavior to be maintained by the environment rather than our intervention. Once that goal is achieved, we must be ready to allow the client to continue on their own.

The transition process should not be abrupt, and proper planning for this transition should be included in the final phases of a behavior plan. We should not fear what would be maintained in our absence, but rather plan for the transfer of stimulus control to the more natural environment.

Professional, Ethical, Uncomfortable

It is necessary in the practice of behavior analysis that we separate those factors which are unethical, unprofessional, and those which simply make us uncomfortable. Ethical behavior would involve adherence to the Ethics Code® as stipulated by the BACB®. Professional behavior relates to the accurate and efficient execution of job responsibilities. Those factors which simply make us uncomfortable, however, do not address the requirements of the BACB®, nor do they affect our ability to fulfill the obligations of our positions. These factors can be addressed with humility and flexibility.

Consent

Clara Claiborne Park also described the dangers inherent in this power of suggestion (Park, 1995). She recalls a story of visiting someone's home and encountering her child standing near a broken sundial (Park, 1995). After a long discussion of the importance of honesty, she and her child approached the homeowners with an apology, only to be told that the sundial had been broken for years (Park, 1995). Just as I was, her child was easily convinced.

For those of us who support clients and families directly, it is essential that we acknowledge the imbalance of power that is inherent in such a relationship. Such a dynamic is rife with opportunities for exploitation.

The necessity of consent is reiterated time and time again. Consent is required in performing an assessment, implementing a behavior plan, and making any changes as the data indicates. It is necessary that such consent be given freely and that this consent be informed. We cannot assume that clients or caregivers have an understanding of the risks and benefits of any proposed behavior change program, nor can we assume that they have an understanding of the risks of foregoing treatment of behavior problems. Clients must be afforded the information needed to make informed decisions and must be informed of all of their options.

Written consent is often considered the gold standard of ethical practice. However, it is important that we do not over-rely upon documentation as evidence of ongoing consent. A consent form is to consent as a photograph is to a person – it is the *evidence* of the thing, rather than the thing itself. A consent form indicates only that a conversation requesting consent has taken place, but is not an indication that consent is ongoing.

Consent is not one act of agreement, but a continuous process. If informed consent is to be considered valid, the individual must be able to withdraw consent at any point without penalty. One possible method to avoid even unintentional exploitation is to have frequent checks to assure that consent is maintained. Scheduling times for "consent checks" is as essential as scheduling times for program evaluation. This simple strategy can assure the incorporation of ongoing consent in programming.

A relationship with a client is a partnership, but that partnership is not necessarily equal. The clients' needs must be considered first and foremost, and take precedence over our own agendas as clinicians.

Evidence-Based Practice

Let us review here what is meant by the phrase "evidence-based." Several practices have been identified as "evidence-based" in addressing many of the behavioral excesses and deficits associated with a diagnosis of autism spectrum disorder (Wong et al., 2015). Several practices have been identified through reviews of peer-reviewed literature as being evidence-based practices. Such reviews have focused on those interventions which produced a change in behavior, and it should be no surprise that there is a great deal of overlap between the techniques generally used in applied behavior analysis programs and those repeatedly identified as effective in research studies (Wong et al., 2015). Among the evidence-based practices identified by Wong et al. (2015) are:

- Antecedent-based interventions
- Cognitive behavioral intervention
- Discrete trial teaching
- Exercise
- Extinction
- Functional behavior assessment
- Functional communication training
- Modeling
- Naturalistic intervention
- Parent-implemented intervention
- Peer-mediated intervention
- Use of the Picture Exchange Communication System (PECS)
- Pivotal Response Training
- Prompting
- Reinforcement
- Response interruption/redirection (RIR)
- Scripting
- Self-management
- Social narratives
- Social skills training
- Structured play groups
- Task analysis
- Technology-aided instruction and intervention
- Time-delay
- Video modeling
- Visual supports

Several of the tactics described here would certainly seem familiar to practitioners of applied behavior analysis in clinical settings. However, "applied behavior analysis" is not listed, even though many are fond of describing applied behavior analysis as "the only evidence-based treatment for autism spectrum disorder." This misplacement of emphasis can be problematic. As an evidence-based field of practice, applied behavior analysis does not *lead* the evidence, but rather *follows* it. A behavior analyst implements those techniques that have been demonstrated effective in peer-reviewed literature. As the science has evolved, so have the techniques commonly used. Practices are not evidence-based because they are used by behavior analysts, they are used by behavior analysts because they are supported by sufficient evidence.

There are several practices that would not be considered evidence-based but are often requested by clients. Restricted diets, sensory integration protocols, and psychodynamic therapies continue to be popular interventions, despite a lack of empirical support for their effectiveness. Often, the support for such interventions is anecdotal, and we may encounter clients or clients' families who insist that they have seen results from such therapies, despite our efforts to convince them otherwise.

It is important to consider here, not how another provider refers to their work, but the work itself. It may be helpful to analyze the antecedent and consequence conditions of particular methodologies, particularly if a client or client surrogate insists that they have seen positive results. It is possible that a client's behavior may improve using sensory integration techniques because the recommended sensory diet served as a noncontingent reinforcement schedule. It may also be possible that the use of rubber jewelry designed to "provide oral motor stimulation" may decrease mouthing of non-food items as a result of the differential reinforcement of an alternative response. It may even be possible that a weighted blanket may be so enjoyable that it offsets the setting event of physical discomfort and eliminates motivating operations in place increasing the value of escape. Taking an analytic view of methodologies and examining the practices themselves, rather than the way they are described, allows us to collaborate more effectively with clients without compromising our commitment to evidence-based practice.

It is not the client's responsibility to identify those practices which have been supported by scientific evidence. It is our responsibility.

Scope of Practice

Given that our field is the science of behavior, and that the definition of behavior is anything that an organism does, it might be easy to assume that behavior analysts are qualified to teach anything. Our understanding of learning processes surely does allow us a certain insight into the nature of learning in a more general sense. There is a, however, a wide berth between knowing a great deal and knowing everything.

While our knowledge of the science of learning may position us as generalists, we may still require the consultation of specialists in certain fields. It may be necessary to call upon the expertise of other team members of medical specialists, of practitioners of other fields. But above all, it is necessary to call upon the expertise of the client and the client's family. Behavior change programs must have social validity, defined by Wolf (1978) as the selection of socially important goals, the implementation of socially acceptable procedures, and the accomplishment of socially important results. We must be ready to respond if our recommendations if the goals we have prioritized lack social validity. If a client reports that a given procedure is unacceptable to them – if it is prohibitively difficult or if it simply makes them uncomfortable – we must be prepared to make accommodations. If the results of intervention are not what is hoped for or there are unintended results, we must be ready to make the modifications necessary.

Data-Based Decision-Making

It is our obligation as behavior analysts to employ data-based decision-making. As scientists, we do not guess as to what individuals think, feel, or know. Rather, we *observe* what individuals *do*. To some outside our field, this seems excessively fastidious. Restricting our contributions to those reflected by dots and lines on a graph may appear to preclude the inclusion of new targets or more holistic programming. For advocates within our science, this would certainly seem a fair point, and hardly a new one. Wolf (1978) urges us to consider the priorities of the client in planning programming and the social acceptability of both the procedures and results.

It is necessary here, however, to review that the meaning of "data" is simply "information gathered for analysis." If we expand our understanding of data as being all of the information we acquire in the process of our work, we create opportunities to work more holistically in the selection of goals and implementation of programs.

Any information that is gathered could present an opportunity for analysis. The presence of interferent behavior, the tendency to become drowsy at the end of a session, or even the difficulty of maintaining an organized system for storing materials are problems that can be solved. To use another example, if data fails to be collected, this fact is, in and of itself, data. If a client demonstrates a skill outside of the session but this is not reflected in the data, this also is, in and of itself, data. These also are problems to be solved. Analyzing the contingencies that govern these, rather than attempting to ignore them, may allow us to more efficiently solve the problems that they imply.

Relationship to Clients

For those of us in direct practice with children and families, it is a paradoxical experience in some ways, particularly in the practice of home services. One of these is the amount of direct contact with client or client surrogates is dramatically increased than when one is working in homes, and yet it can be very socially isolating.

For those of us who work with children with developmental disabilities or autism spectrum disorder specifically, we come into these family's lives at a time of crisis when uncertainty about their child's future is a cloud hanging over their lives. When we go into a family's home, it is important to remember that we are entering a private space. These are people who are entering a new phase in their lives with a tremendous amount of uncertainty as to what lies ahead. It is possible that we will be witness to what few are permitted to see. This is a tremendously intimate relationship, and is not to be entered into without understanding of the vulnerability of the families we serve. Above all, we must remember that the Professional and Ethical Compliance Code applies to our own behavior, not to the behavior of our clients or their families. We are held accountable for our ethics and professionalism. *Parents are not professionals.*

It is *our* responsibility, therefore, and not the family's, to maintain the boundaries of a professional relationship. Any expectation that family member will behave in a professional manner or prioritize adherence to our Professional Code in the same manner we might would be unreasonable. A relationship that may seem to us to maintain professional boundaries may appear to families to be simply unequal. Families may expect to expand this intimacy beyond what is considered "professional" for a behavior analyst to engage in. Analysis of the contingencies that control this behavior certainly may reveal that establishing intimacy is an attempt to gain favor. However, it may also reveal that the effect of this imbalance can be difficult for both clients and clinicians.

Behavior analysts are urged in the Professional and Ethical Compliance Code to avoid multiple relationships. A multiple relationship defined in the Professional and Ethical Compliance Code as, "one in which a behavior analyst is in both a behavior-analytic role and a non-behavior analytic role simultaneously with a client or someone closely associated with or related to the client." When accepting clients, this is of particular importance. A behavior analyst should not accept a client if there is currently a relationship. To treat relatives, friends, or their children would be unacceptable under this Code. A professional relationship should *not* be undertaken if the dominant relationship already exists.

Avoiding multiple relationships can be more complex than simply a criterion for the acceptance of clients, however. Those living in rural areas often find this difficult to navigate, since it may be impossible to serve clients in a small town without forming some sort of multiple relationship, such as client-pharmacist, client-mechanic, or client-grocery store owner.

When approached by a friend or relative to provide services, it should be made clear to them that this relationship is far from ideal. Certainly, if there is another professional without such a relationship available, this should be our first consideration. Telemedicine, where available, may also be a suitable alternative. As telehealth becomes more universally accepted as an option for parent training and support of parent-mediated intervention, supervision, and service delivery, the possibilities for finding qualified professional to work with individuals with autism spectrum disorder expands beyond the limits of an immediate geographic area. Every possibility should be explored in order to avoid a multiple relationship that may lead to exploitation or compromise effective treatment.

For those of us living in metropolitan areas in the U.S., this is often simply a matter of providing the information needed for a referral. In more remote areas, however, where services are more scarce, a solution can be more elusive. In some cases it may simply be a question of evaluating the nature of the initial relationship and assessing the probability of its impact on the quality of services. Although the relationship with someone with whom a behavior analyst has a long history, such as a close family member, carries definite established risk, a relationship with less history, such as a mechanic, may be less complex. This is not to say that such duality of relationships cannot bring with it its own set of complications. Simply seeing a client at a local park or buying groceries at the workplace of the client's parent may cause behavior analysts to question the appropriate ethical response. Saying hello risks violating confidentiality, refusing to do so may cause offense and damage the professional relationship. If the behavior analyst attempts to buy groceries, they may be offered groceries for free, which would be exploitation of the relationship. If they do not shop at that store any longer, this may be prohibitively difficult for the behavior analyst and their family and cost the store a customer.

However, the multiple relationship, like any relationship, may also evolve over time. Even when there is no multiple relationship at the start of services, the intimacy of direct services may cause another relationship to develop. What began as a strictly professional relationship may become more friendly as the clinician successfully pairs themselves with reinforcement and establishes the rapport necessary to work effectively. Those who work directly with clients may find that the boundaries of relationships can become blurred.

In both of these cases, the possibility of a multiple relationship presents a considerable amount of risk. In the Behavior Analyst Certification Board's October 2015, behavior analysts are urged to avoid "boundary stretching" (BACB, 2015). As the BACB states, the "ongoing monitoring of professional boundaries" (BACB, 2015) is a necessary component of ethical practice. Whether a multiple relationship develops because the seed of this complication was present from the beginning or because those involved simply enjoyed one another's company, such developments must be managed in order to preserve the primary relationship: that of clinician to client.

Because such relationships can become evident only when they have already become problematic, it is best to begin the clinical relationship by explaining what is meant by the term "multiple relationships" and describing the risks associated with them. Discuss scenarios which may cause difficulty ahead of time. Make it clear that, for example, you will not initiate a greeting with a client but are happy to respond to one if the client feels comfortable saying hello. Remind the client that providing goods or services for free would be considered exploitation and that you will happily pay for groceries. Assure the client that their information is confidential and will not be discussed in public spaces. A discussion at the outset of services will help to set expectations and is a necessary step in the process of this "ongoing monitoring."

As time progresses, however, we must be mindful of maintaining this "ongoing monitoring" process. One discussion at the start of the professional relationship is hardly sufficient to ensure that a multiple relationship can be avoided or that harm can be averted. Clinicians must be prepared to discuss the potential harm of multiple relationships at many points during a clinical relationship. For those clients we serve over a long-term period, one tactic may be to periodically discuss the importance of maintaining professional boundaries. Make it clear to clients that such boundaries are for the client's benefit, not for the personal comfort of the behavior analyst. Schedule a time every few months to revisit this conversation and check in with the client.

The requirement that we guard against multiple relationships is not out of callousness, it is to increase our focus on the client's benefit. When another relationship becomes evident, we must not allow that to eclipse our role as clinician. Scheduling time to discuss the nature of the clinical relationship with the client, as well as periodically asking ourselves, "Is this for the client or is this for me?" can avoid abuse. It is certainly worth the small amount of effort required.

Practical Considerations: Ethical, Professional, Uncomfortable

It is essential that those clinicians who work directly with vulnerable populations understand the distinction between truly unethical behavior and those behavior that simply make them uncomfortable. "Ethical" refers to the adherence to the Ethics Code, the set of regulations determined by the Behavior Analyst Certification Board®. This document clarifies the expectations for behavior analysts, which are enforceable by the Board.

In order to clarify this distinction, we must revisit an important point: *Parents are not professionals.* As such, they are not required to adhere to our professional ethical standards. The relationship is not one of colleagues, but one in which we provide services to them.

Culture Shock

When we speak of culture, many of us think of those descriptors that are aspects of our identity – our race, nationality, or language of origin. In behavior analysis, however, we define "culture" somewhat differently in comparison with its common usage. Culture, rather than referring to an ethnicity or country of origin, refers instead to a set of social contingencies that interlock (Glenn, 1988). By this definition, any group can be considered its own culture, with its own values, language, and customs.

Just as we may experience culture shock when we visit another country, so too we experience it when encountering any group that does things differently than we would prefer or expect. And, just as we must when visiting another country, we must be mindful that we are visitors here. This culture, like any other, prioritizes the comfort and security of its members.

Differences in parenting styles or in priorities for goal selection may be disconcerting at first, but these differences are often a matter of discomfort rather than ethical violations.

Works Cited

Atwater, J. B., Morris, E. K. (1998). Teachers' instructions and children's compliance in preschool classrooms: a descriptive analysis. *Journal of Applied Behavior Analysis*, *21*, 157–167.

Baer, D. M., Wolf, M. M., & Risley, T. R. (1968). Some current dimensions of applied behavior analysis. *Journal of Applied Behavior Analysis*, *1*(1), 91–97.

Beavers, G. A., Iwata, B. A., & Lerman, D. C. (2013). Thirty years of research on the functional analysis of problem behavior. *Journal of Applied Behavior Analysis*, *46*(1), 1–21.

Behavior Analyst Certification Board. (2020). *Ethics Code for Behavior Analysts*. Littleton, CO: Author.

Behavior Analyst Certification Board. (2015). October 2015 newsletter. Retrieved from www.bacb.com.

Bellini, S., & McConnell, L. L. (2010). Strength-based educational programming for students with autism spectrum disorders: a case for video self-modeling. *Preventing School Failure: Alternative Education for Children and Youth*, *54*(4), 220–227.

Bosch, S., & Fuqua, R. W. (2001). Behavioral cusps: a model for selecting target behaviors. *Journal of Applied Behavior Analysis*, *34*(1), 123–125.

Carr, E. G., Smith, C. E., Giacin, T. A., Whelan, B. M., & Pancari, J. (2003). Menstrual discomfort as a biological setting event for severe problem behavior: assessment and intervention. *American Journal on Mental Retardation*, *108*(2), 117–133.

Cooper, J. O., Heron, T. E., & Heward, W. L. (2007). *Applied behavior analysis*. Upper Saddle River, NJ: Pearson.

Glenn, S. S. (1988, Fall). Contingencies and metacontingencies: toward a synthesis of behavior analysis and cultural materialism. *The Behavior Analyst*, *11*(2), 161–179.

Hagopian, L. P., Rooker, G. W., Jessel, J., & DeLeon, I. G. (2013). Initial functional analysis outcomes and modifications in pursuit of differentiation: a summary of 176 inpatient cases. *Journal of Applied Behavior Analysis*, *46*(1), 88–100.

Iwata, B. A., Dorsey, M. F., Slifer, K. J., Bauman, K. E., & Richman, G. S. (1994). Toward a functional analysis of self-injury. *Journal of Applied Behavior Analysis*, *27*(2), 197–209.

Keller, F. S. (1968). Goodbye, teacher. *Journal of Behavior Analysis*, *1*, 79–89.

Koegel, L. K., Koegel, R. L., Harrower, J. K., & Carter, C. M. (1999). Pivotal response intervention I: overview of approach. *Journal of the Association for Persons with Severe Handicaps*, *24*(3), 174–185.

Maslow, A. H. (1966). The psychology of science: A reconnaissance (p. 15). Washington, DC: Gateway Editions.

McDonnell, A. P. (1993). Ethical considerations in teaching compliance to individuals with mental retardation. *Education and Training in Mental Retardation*, 3–12.

Park, C. C. (1995). *The siege: A family's journey into the world of an autistic child*. New York, NY: Little, Brown.

Rosales-Ruiz, J., & Baer, D. M. (1997). Behavioral cusps: a developmental and pragmatic concept for behavior analysis. *Journal of Applied Behavior Analysis*, *30*(3), 533–544.

Stokes, T. F., & Baer, D. M. (1977). An implicit technology of generalization 1. *Journal of Applied Behavior Analysis*, *10*(2), 349–367.

Wolf, M. M. (1978). Social validity: the case for subjective measurement or how applied behavior analysis is finding its heart 1. *Journal of Applied Behavior Analysis*, *11*(2), 203–214.

Wong, C., Odom, S. L., Hume, K. A., Cox, A. W., Fettig, A., Kucharczyk, S., ... & Schultz, T. R. (2015). Evidence-based practices for children, youth, and young adults with autism spectrum disorder: a comprehensive review. *Journal of Autism and Developmental Disorders*, *45*(7), 1951–1966.

2.3   Behavior Analysts and the Team

Many of us have served on interdisciplinary teams, and many more have been called upon to do so. Though it is a fairly common practice, particularly working with individuals with developmental disabilities, many behavior analysts do so begrudgingly, or with a significant amount of skepticism as to its value. Working with professionals from disparate philosophies can present significant challenges to the passionate behavior analyst, and many call into question the value or ethics of collaboration, particularly with colleagues from less scientifically rigorous disciplines.

Different philosophies of psychology are occasionally referred to as "churches," which appears to be an apt comparison. The level of fidelity to a philosophy such as behaviorism can involve zeal similar to that of a religion. This can make working with professionals in other fields challenging since we may be inclined to convert them from their sinful ways. Treating every interdisciplinary team as a missionary effort, however, will undoubtedly lead to compromises in our ability to effectively collaborate. It may also be argued that it would equally compromise our ability to effectively disseminate our own methodologies. More importantly, an overemphasis on conversion overlooks what colleagues from other fields offer in an interdisciplinary team. Although behavior analysts could fairly be described as generalists, concerned with anything an organism does, speech pathologists and physical and occupational therapists bring with them areas of expertise that are valuable and should be acknowledged and utilized.

Members and Their Roles

Professionals from several disciplines may participate in clinical teams, and each brings with them a background and expertise that may support the overall development of the client's skills.

Speech Therapists/Speech and Language Pathologists

According to the American Speech-Language Hearing association, a speech pathologist (sometimes referred to as a speech therapist) is a professional who can "work to prevent, assess, diagnose, and treat speech, language, social communication, cognitive-communication, and swallowing disorders in children and adults." Between speech pathologists and behavior analysts, there is perhaps the greatest extent of overlap. Because communication is observable and measurable, and because it is often taught and maintained through the use of reinforcers for specific communicative behaviors, behavior analysts and speech pathologists can often easily collaborate and work effectively with little conflict.

DOI: 10.4324/9781003190707-15

Speech pathologists have their own code of ethics as well, just as behavior analysts do. Just as our Code does, the Speech and Language Pathologist's Code of Ethics urges their adherence to standards of practice, including the fair and equitable treatment of clients and the necessity of highly qualified professionals.

Occupational Therapists

Occupational therapists are professionals whose role is to support clients in the pursuit of their occupation, or in the activities that the clients themselves prioritize as such. "Occupation" in this field is interpreted broadly as any activity of daily living that is a priority to the client, including daily living and leisure skills. The clinical work often focuses on acquisition of skills in the context of everyday activities. This support can be across the lifespan, including work with children with disabilities. In pediatric practice, the "occupation" of clients is often considered to be school and play, and occupational therapists will often engage in therapeutic activities in this context. One subspecialty of occupational therapy is sensory integration. This philosophy maintains that behavior can be maintained by sensory processing issues. "Sensory integration" refers to the neurological process of integrating visual, auditory, tactile, olfactory, taste, and proprioceptive information. Given that hyper- and hyposensitivities to sensory information are often characteristic of autism spectrum disorder, it is common for occupational therapists specializing in sensory integration to serve on clinical teams. Although there is substantial evidence that occupational therapy techniques can be helpful in the acquisition and maintenance of motor skills, there is not substantial evidence of the efficacy of sensory integration. "Sensory processing disorder" also is not established by evidence. There are certainly professionals who may argue that the absence of evidence should not be considered evidence for absence. It is within the realm of possibility that sensory processing disorder may be established in the future, just as chronic fatigue syndrome and fibromyalgia have been established. However, current evidence does not indicate either the presence of a stand-alone disorder or the efficacy of sensory integration techniques. A responsible behavior analyst must exercise caution in the application of such techniques. The phrase "exercise caution" need not be synonymous with "refuse to collaborate," however. Though specific challenges exist in the collaboration with disciplines who lack our commitment to evidence-based practice, these challenges can be met, and such a commitment can be maintained.

What is Meant by "Interdisciplinary"

When working in teams of professionals from other disciplines, any one of several philosophies of team dynamics can be in play. Many of the terms describing these philosophies are used interchangeably. There are, however, subtle differences that make a difference in how these teams interact.

Multidisciplinary

In a multidisciplinary team, professionals may draw upon knowledge from other professions, but remain firmly in their areas of expertise. There may be some communication regarding goals and the implementation of these goals, but this is not necessarily a defining feature of a team representing multiple disciplines. Rather, the participation of varied disciplines, rather than their full collaboration, is what defines such a team.

Interdisciplinary

Within an interdisciplinary team, different disciplines are synthesized and goals and treatment plans are aligned. Practitioners across disciplines are able to communicate and work on common goals, although they may describe these goals in different ways or add varied techniques. Greater time is needed to collaborate in an interdisciplinary model, and team members must be willing and able to share information and ideas. Collaboration in this model focuses primarily on shared information. Goals are developed by participants of individual disciplines and communicated to other members, but these goals are not necessarily aligned with one another. This communication can prevent contradictory goals or the development of multiple behavior plans that may be counterproductive to the client's well-being. However, the individual team members remain autonomous in their efforts to improve behavior.

Transdisciplinary

In a transdisciplinary team, the various disciplines are integrated. Not only goals but also the programming designed to meet them are planned and implemented in this team context. Assessment may be performed in an arena format, with each discipline contributing to the overall picture of the client's level of progress and programmatic needs. Choi and Pak (2006) describe this interaction by stating that, "Transdisciplinarity integrates the natural, social and health sciences in a humanities context, and in so doing transcends each of their traditional boundaries."

There are significant challenges to this model, particularly for those clients who rely on public funding for services. Communication and collaboration require significant investments of time and effort. The coordination of efforts to have face-to-face meetings becomes exponentially more difficult as more professionals with conflicting schedules become involved in a case. If funding is not provided for these meetings, the challenges become more pronounced, often forcing clients' families to serve as team coordinators responsible for all communication and collaboration. We may find we have little control over what team model is possible or what will be communicated and how. There are, however, several "team behaviors" that may facilitate effective collaboration that are well within our control.

What We Do: A Behavioral Description

F-1: Review records and available data (e.g. educational, medical, historical) at the outset of the case.

As behavior analysts, we are trained to focus our attention on observable and measurable behavior. However, we must be mindful that such observation may not be possible if we remain unaware of what to look for. We must be ever-mindful of Maslow's "Law of the Instrument" (Maslow, 1966), which provides us with a familiar metaphor: that, given only a hammer, we will be tempted to assume that everything is a nail. Other disciplines may be trained in areas which we are not. Speech pathologists may be able to offer insight on physical limitations to producing certain sounds effectively. They may also offer assistance in other areas, particularly those who specialize in feeding. Occupational therapists may have the training to discern aspects of motor development that offer information that allows us to assess these variables and program accordingly. Biological and medical needs must be addressed, and we cannot allow arrogance to mask itself as adherence to commitment to our focus on observable behavior.

Fifth Edition Task List H-2: Identify potential interventions based on assessment results and the best available scientific evidence.

Perhaps the most challenging aspect of working in interdisciplinary or transdisciplinary teams is maintaining a commitment to evidence-based practice when other fields of practice do not maintain such commitments. This is where we often come across the most resistance, and the response that we should be more open-minded is a common complaint. To make such interactions more challenging, we will often hear anecdotal reports that interventions which lack supporting evidence have been effective in the past with other clients or have even been successful in promoting socially significant behavior change with the current client. It is often tempting to ignore these anecdotal reports, remaining steadfast in our refusal to promote or participate in practices that lack scientific support. However, we must acknowledge that our science relies upon the evidence provided in single-subject design studies, and on the importance of data.

If professionals or families are reporting that a particular intervention has been effective in improving socially significant behavior, it would be not only foolish, but anti-scientific to ignore this. One tactic to promote both collaboration and evidence-based practice would be to analyze what caused the change in behavior. Others may state that, for example, self-biting may be decreased by offering a rubber necklace to chew because it "gives them input" or that a sensory diet that includes jumping on a trampoline "helps organize" a client and decreases disruptive behavior. However, acknowledgment of improvement of the behavior itself may not constitute acknowledgment of the explanation of why they were effective.

It is helpful here to review those practices in the treatment of autism which have been maintained by the current research. Among the evidence-based practices identified by Wong et al. (2015) are antecedent-based intervention, differential reinforcement of incompatible, alternative, or other behaviors, exercise, prompting, reinforcement, and naturalistic interventions. As behavior scientists we acknowledge that these are processes that promote behavior change regardless of how we refer to them. Behavior is learned through the use of reinforcement regardless of whether we do so deliberately, and certainly regardless of our use of the term. It is not only possible but likely that the use of a rubber necklace to chew decreases self-biting as the result of the differential reinforcement of an alternative behavior. It is not only possible but likely that jumping on a trampoline served as the exercise necessary to cause improvement in disruptive behavior.

If we analyze tactics with less evidence, we may find that these are simply similar techniques using unfamiliar materials. Though some caution must be exercised, and our commitment to evidence-based practice must be maintained, we must be equally cautious of dismissing techniques because of how they are described rather than how they are implemented. To acknowledge that a given tactic has been effective is not necessarily to agree on why it was effective. We must not ignore data, even if it comes from a source we may find questionable or is described in ways we find confusing or uncomfortable. And most importantly we must not limit our tactics to what we have habitually used rather than expanding our own repertoire of reinforcers and skills.

C-1: Establish operational definitions of behavior.

All members of a clinical team begin with the same goal in mind: all members hope to promote skill development and allow the client to reach their maximum potential. Our common commitment to that destination may be well understood, but the path can often be a confusing one. Clinicians from other disciplines will often use mentalistic terms, and many of these terms will be new to us, if not incredibly confusing. Often I have asked what it meant that a proposed treatment would "organize" a client, only to hear "they will be organized." Definitions of "sense of self" have been equally confounding for me, as for many behavior analysts; and the use of these terms can interfere with effective communication. It is often best to begin with an understanding of our common goal in mind, as well as an understanding that these terms do mean something, and may require more translation than outright dismissal. Rather than ending any possibility of dialogue by dismissing the concept of "being organized" or the existence of a "sense of self," it is best to find out precisely, in behavioral terms, what is meant by each of these terms.

A helpful tactic in finding common ground and to develop that translation is to ask questions. What would "being organized" look like? What would the client do to indicate that they had an adequate "sense of self?" We likely find, after asking for clear descriptions of these concepts, that they are attributed to specific behaviors. When non-behavioral colleagues are asked to describe these concepts by describing what the manifestations of their mastery would look like, it is often possible to understand these as observable and measurable behaviors. An "organized" client can be described as one who engages in on-task behavior, remains in their seat during classroom time, and gives consistent eye contact. A client who demonstrates an adequate "sense of self" may now be described as one who uses personal pronouns accurately, is able to answer personal questions, or engages in reciprocal conversations. Once such a definition of behavior is developed, we can more effectively collaborate and prioritize intervention goals. In many cases, the terms used to describe may be analogous to a photograph. Terminology may illustrate a concept, but terminology is not the concept itself. Differences in the way we describe phenomena are not necessarily differences in the existence of these phenomena, nor do they necessarily preclude working together toward our common goals. We cannot allow a breakdown in communication to lead to a breakdown in collaboration.

H-9: Collaborate with others who support and/or provide services to clients.

As behavior analysts, we often consider ourselves capable of understanding and analyzing the controlling variables of the behavior of any organism and the changes in behavior that we describe as the learning process. Understanding behavior as anything a given organism does should not be confused, however, with the capability of teaching anything to anyone. While we may have a general understanding of the mechanism of how behavior is learned, there may be gaps in our knowledge of what behavior should be learned. Appropriate sequences of communication skills or social behavior may not be an aspect of our training. This is where the input of other clinicians can be helpful in programming and goal development. The addition of knowledge of the structure of vocal sound production, the awareness of the mechanics of motor skills, and proficiency in the developmental appropriateness of goals should be a welcome addition to our programming. In order to provide socially significant programming to our clients, we must have clarity on the distinction between teaching well and good teaching. These two distinctions, while not mutually exclusive, are distinct. Certainly our knowledge of the science of behavior and our training in the use of that science to promote skill development would constitute teaching well. If we also include the contribution of other professionals in order to promote social significance, this is what distinguishes good teaching.

C-9: Select a measurement system to obtain representative data given the dimensions of behavior and the logistics of observing and recording.

In the day-to-day practices of their profession, behavior analysts may have a great deal of overlap with other disciplines. The boundaries of this overlap are very often seen in our commitment to consistent documentation and data collection. For many disciplines, it may be viewed as a cumbersome and unnecessary addition to the session to introduce data collection, and it may be argued that anecdotal information allows for greater flexibility and is sufficient for making programmatic decisions. It would be beneficial here to review the three requirements of data collection: Data must be taken. Data must be looked at and analyzed. Data must be used to modify behavior change programs.

Data must be taken.

Though the practice may not come naturally to practitioners from many disciplines, many of these professionals are receptive to the idea. It is important to create systems that are objective enough to collect meaningful data but simple enough for professionals with less proficiency in data collection to use while performing their primary responsibilities. Training in these systems should also be provided, and behavior analysts must be prepared to modify systems as needed.

Data must be looked at and analyzed.

Behavior analysts must be prepared to follow up with professionals and communicate clearly about what the data indicates about client progress.

Data must be used to modify behavior change programs.

Perhaps the biggest challenge for professionals may be the need to respond to the data. There must be an agreement in place to allow the data to guide decision-making, and this agreement must be made before data is collected. There may be situations when professionals are tempted to ignore results – a program that was begun with great enthusiasm may be proven ineffective or a program entered into with skepticism may force the clinician to reexamine preconceived notions. Regardless of what the results tell us, their message must be taken to heart. Data collection practices are an essential component of behavior-analytic programming and can be a component of any program designed to improve client outcomes. Incorporating this practice into other disciplines can be an asset to any discipline.

H-4: When a target behavior is to be decreased, select an acceptable alternative behavior to be established or increased.

It is often the case that behavior analysts are called upon to decrease behaviors. In some settings, "behavior" has become synonymous with "disruptive behavior" or "problematic behavior." As specialists in behavior, we know that "behavior" refers to anything that an organism does, and that this definition is not restricted to those behaviors that are targeted for decrease. However, this misunderstanding of the behavior analyst's role remains persistent in the human services field. Very often, behavior analysts are viewed in a similar way as firefighters are: their role is to intervene in emergencies, make a problem go away, and then leave. We must work tirelessly to combat this misunderstanding of a behavior analyst's role within a clinical team. The role of the behavior analyst is not akin to that of a firefighter. Rather, there are equal, if not greater opportunities for growth and skill acquisition. It is vital that behavior analysts be full participants in any discussion of what clients need to learn and that we are also full participants in the development of programming to meet these skill acquisition goals. We must be offering solutions at every possible opportunity, rather than waiting to be asked. In addition, we must be forthcoming about the goals that we have been able to accomplish, as well as information on how we have accomplished them. We must clarify the methodologies used, as well as the underlying principles behind them. When our skill set allows us to offer help, we should be vocal about our ability to do so. It is not the responsibility of those outside our field to grasp the breath of the possibilities of our methodologies. It is not their responsibility to fully understand the potential of our science. If we are not proactive in our dissemination of the potential of our work to support lasting, meaningful behavior change, we cannot expect others to receive that message.

H-9: Collaborate with others who support and/or provide services to clients.
I-6: Use a functional assessment approach (e.g., performance diagnostics) to identify variables affecting personnel performance.

I-7: Use function-based strategies to improve personnel performance.

All behavior is controlled by antecedents and consequences, and this is true for all organisms, including professionals from other fields. Analysis of these factors can allow us to work more effectively with professionals from all disciplines.

Antecedents. Behavior will often be selected for treatment based on its effect on the clinician. Those behaviors which are most disruptive or disturbing are the behaviors which are most likely to access treatment without delay. Assuming that behavior analysts are specialists in the reduction of problem behavior, this may be when our support is most actively sought out. It is important that behavior analysts make themselves available for the selection of treatment goals focused on skill acquisition as well. Essentially, we must ensure that our presence and participation become discriminative stimuli, signaling that reinforcement is available for seeking out our assistance.

Behavior. Implementation of behavior plans with others, particularly from other disciplines, can be challenging. It is often tempting to interpret a failure of others to follow our protocols or accept our suggestions as a personal attack. Worse, we may alienate them further by refusing to accept suggestions ourselves. It is equally possible, however, that we have failed to make the task simple enough to perform given the other responsibilities of these professionals. Reducing the effort of the response required, particularly in data collection, can often make a tremendous difference in the overall functioning of the team.

Consequence. In all of our interactions with other team members, it is crucial that we bear in mind our common ground. Each team member is driven by the same overall goal: we are all working for the benefit of our clients. How we interpret what is best for the client in either the long or short term may differ, however. When we discuss the level of "buy in," this refers to the reinforcer that increases teaching behavior. "Buy in," as all reinforcers are, often varies greatly from one individual to another. Behavior analysts must be prepared to answer why a particular skill is important and to ask that of others as well. Analysis of the factors that govern the behavior of others, as well as what may govern our own, is an essential skill for the behavior analyst.

Legal, Ethical, Moral

Legal

Team Coordination: Meetings

When serving on multidisciplinary teams, we are often working with professionals of different disciplines who may also have different funding sources. While team meetings may be mandated by some agencies, it may not be permitted by others. Every effort must be made to facilitate communication among disciplines, even if in-person meetings are not possible. Several paperless data collection companies have solutions to this by adding virtual "spaces" to send messages within their systems. Another tactic using far less advanced technology is simply a notebook that is shared by team members.

Confidentiality and Privacy

Sharing information also requires special consideration, and regulations concerning confidentiality must be clearly understood by all parties. In the USA, the regulations regarding the privacy of health information was established by the Health Insurance Portability and Accountability Act of 1996 (HIPAA). Patient or client confidentiality must be protected, particularly when sharing information. The convenience of sharing information must not blind us to the dangers of exposing health information. Communication is permitted so long as reasonable safeguards to protect the privacy of our clients in place. One should avoid sharing of video or pictures in any video which is not HIPAA compliant, including YouTube or many other video sharing sites. One simple step to take is to include a HIPAA statement in the signature of your email. This warning alerts the receiver that the information may be confidential and requests that they alert the sender if it is sent in error. This reasonable safeguard is simple and easy to implement. Perhaps the simplest of safeguards, however, is to exercise extreme caution in sharing of information in any medium other than standardized, HIPAA compliant systems designed for this purpose.

Insurance and Billing Procedures

The importance of accurate information being shared with an insurance company cannot be overstated. Treatment plans must be carefully followed and data collection systems kept up to date. Accuracy in accounting for our time and activities is essential. The repercussions of inaccuracies of this type can have devastating effects on agencies, individuals, and the families that we serve.

Ethical

The Behavior Analyst Certification Board's® (BACB's®) Ethical Code® is also integral to practicing as a "good behavior analyst." Code element 2.10 addresses our collaboration with colleagues, encouraging us to compromise when possible. When working with team members from different backgrounds, it is essential to remember that they do not have familiarity with this Code. Their own ethical practice, governed by different codes of conduct, may have significant overlap, but it is likely that there will be several differences as well. It is then that the second phrase becomes particularly relevant: "make others aware of this code." Explain that the BACB's Code may provide some insight or that certain practices may be considered questionable. Ask for evidence to support suggested practices and advocate for the use of practices that are evidence-based, even if their presentation may be novel. Given that "ethical" refers to the rules of a governing body, the ethics of our field apply only to behavior analysts. Be mindful that these practitioners may be acting within the ethical codes of their own professional organizations and refrain from accusations of impropriety or a lack of ethics if suggestions or programs are unethical only within the Ethical Code®. Our Code is not their code.

Moral

The moral principle which guides our work with multidisciplinary, interdisciplinary, or transdisciplinary teams is this: every client deserves our very best and the best chance at autonomy. Far from a simple flowery principle, this right is well established as one of our primary values in behavior analysis. Every client has the right to effective treatment as defined by Van Houten et al. (1988). Included in the description of what constitutes "effective treatment" is treatment by a skilled behavior analyst, effective treatment procedures, a program that addresses functional skills, and a therapeutic environment. Perhaps the most relevant of the aspects of what constitutes "effective treatment" is this: "an individual has a right to services whose overriding goal is personal welfare" (Van Houten et al., 1988). Behavior analysts are passionate individuals who believe wholeheartedly in the work that we do. That passion is perhaps our greatest asset, and should be spent wisely. We must not allow our ego to mislead us into thinking that our knowledge and skill set have no limits. Partnership and collaboration with other professionals is central to living this principle and practicing it in our vocation.

Ethical, Professional, Uncomfortable

It is also necessary to distinguish those aspects of our work life that would be considered "unprofessional" as opposed to those which simply make us uncomfortable. Just as not every work environment is a good match for every behavior analyst, so also the dynamics of a team may not be a good fit.

Determining the "Team Leader"

In a collaborative team, it can be difficult to discern where the proverbial buck must stop. Often the behavior analysts may feel the need to enter a situation as a leader rather than a collaborator. However, we must be ready to follow as much as we lead. There are certainly exceptions to this guideline, as in situation where we are hired on a consultancy basis to offer suggestions. When serving as a member of a team, however, we are not there to dictate recommendations, but we are participating as equal members. Whenever possible, consensus should be sought in the development of behavior plans. We may be part of that consensus, but we do not have the final word.

Discussing Behavior with Other Professionals

One common complaint of behavior analysts who serve on multidisciplinary, interdisciplinary, or transdisciplinary teams is that other professionals engage in mentalistic explanation, inappropriate use of behavioral procedures, and pseudoscientific practices. As behavior analysts, however, we are uniquely suited to address this. Analyzing the common reasons that professionals engage in such behaviors, it is easy to see that mentalistic explanations are part of their training. Although we may be uncomfortable with it, simply hearing mentalistic explanations is not unethical. Nor is their use unethical for professionals from other fields. This conflict can be easily resolved by simply asking questions rather than imposing our views. A conversation that begins with descriptions such as "seeking sensory input" or "sense of self" can be redirected into a discussion of objective descriptions of behavior. It is often effective to simply ask, "What would that look like? What would they do or not do if they demonstrated 'seeking sensory input' or 'sense of self'?" This discussion can lead to effective problem solving and collaboration. Though we may describe behavior in different ways, there is a common element in the philosophy of all human services professions: each of us fulfills our role for the benefit of the client. Beginning with that standpoint, matters of translation can be more easily overcome.

Evaluating Treatments Collaboratively

When serving on a collaborative team, the behavior analyst is often the lone voice advocating for data collection. The response effort of data collection is often seen as cumbersome and unnecessary when anecdotal data would suffice, or when we can just "know" how well a client is doing. There may be some resistance to collecting data, but these concerns can be easily offset by ensuring that data is both simple and relevant. The reinforcer for the behaviors involved in data collection is the information provided, and this reinforcer must be both pertinent and easily attained.

Evaluate Team Functioning

Part of evaluating the effectiveness of the team's programming must also be evaluating our own performance as team members. Are we working collaboratively? Are we listening to other team members? Are we advocating for best practices as established by scientific research, and more importantly, are we balancing this need with the need to be pleasant to work with? Just as we must be mindful of pairing ourselves with reinforcement and the importance of using reinforcement when working directly with clients, we must be mindful of these principles when working with team members. Pairing ourselves with reinforcement often makes a tremendous difference in our ability to work effectively.

Parsimony and Making Others Comfortable

The Law of Parsimony states that the simplest explanation for a phenomenon is most likely to be correct. While this refers specifically to assuming as little as possible in our explanations of phenomena or our explanations of behavior, we might also extend this to discussion of response effort and team functioning. If we find ourselves in a situation where the team fails to function and our many suggestions fall continually on deaf ears, it may be our instinct to assume that everyone else is wrong. Every other team member who refuses to work with us is too deeply entrenched in pseudoscience – all of them. It may be tempting to draw a line in the sand and refuse to work with these other practitioners. The simpler explanation, however, may address the common denominator in our failed attempts to work collaboratively: our own behavior. A commitment to working together often means putting aside our own ego, exercising patience, and demonstrating friendliness. The importance of being personable is integral to our work, and yet often forgotten or ignored. Though this advice may appear to be overly simplistic, it is too often the downfall of a clinician. Too many behavior analysts prioritize winning arguments over working collaboratively. Very rarely is this an effective way to disseminate behavior analysis. In fact, it is much more likely to alienate team members, and eventually clients. Digging in our heels may appear to be the most ethical stance, but the result often interferes with the client's right to effective treatment. I will often say that being nice follows the Law of Parsimony. It is often the simplest solution and the failure to do it is often the simplest explanation for the failure to function as a team.

The Behavior Analyst in Schools

There are few experiences more inspiring than watching a particularly skilled teacher. An outside observer may also have difficulty discerning what exactly I was teaching. It is often tempting to consider the art of teaching as secondary to the science of behavior analysis, to dismiss the artful nature of goal-directed teaching as "cute," or worse yet, "babysitting." Just as we may look at a swan and see only the grace on the surface, there is a great deal of paddling below the surface, that makes exceptionally good teaching. Though we may approach the same goal using different tactics, we have the same goal: for each student to succeed. Bearing this in mind, a school is essentially a community and therefore represents a culture of its own. Just as we must be mindful of the needs of a culture when working within a different country or within a family, we must be mindful of the cultural needs of the school as a community. Working in schools can be a personally rewarding and professionally enriching experience for the behavior analyst. As is true for many of our responsibilities, a conscientious approach increases the likelihood of success.

What We Do: A Behavioral Description

G-2: Use interventions based on motivating operations and discriminative stimuli.

G-6: Use instructions and rules.

Because of the nature of schools, and in particular the need for the establishment of instructional control in a large group, classrooms will often succeed or fail on the strength of their rules. The rules of a given classroom are often established on the first day of school, and every response is categorized as one that is either following or not following these rules. What is often considered rigidity is actually essential for the survival of the classroom. Having an orderly environment is a necessity to teaching, and communicating the expectations is vital to creating an effective learning environment. As behavior analysts, however, we are aware that the mere communication of rules is not sufficient to ensure that instructional control is maintained in all cases. Lamenting that students "know what they should be doing" is neither a wise expenditure of our time nor is it necessarily the case for all students. Verbal stimuli, such as the communication of rules, can control behavior in some cases; and this is a valuable first step in the establishment of classroom control. However, it is only the first step. For many students, rules themselves will be insufficient to establish the behavior that will allow them to learn and facilitate teaching, so that their classmates can learn as well. Behavior is far more likely to be shaped by contingencies than by rules, and we must not allow the mere existence of rule-governed behavior to lull us into a false sense of security regarding rules as a behavioral intervention. Other ways to communicate the expectations can also be part of classroom preparation, and the importance of these other forms of communication should be acknowledged as well. There should be clear visual cues as to the expectations of the classroom. For younger ages or those students who require more assistance and support, visual distractions should be eliminated whenever possible. The use of visual supports has been well established in the literature and should be incorporated into the classroom as an aspect of the environmental modifications that will set the classroom and the individual students up for success. Greater intervention will certainly be necessary beyond merely communicating expectation. There must be assurance that rules are followed and expectations met. These rules, however, represent the overlap between the work of the behavior analyst and that of a classroom teacher. The physical structure of the classroom, the establishment of rules, and the clear communication of these expectations are the first steps in a longer journey.

G-17: Use token economies.

G-18: Use group contingencies.

G-19: Use contingency contracting.

The use of group contingencies is very common in schools but must be used in ways that promote socially significant behavior for all participants in the system. These are often tied to token economy systems and often communicated as part of the classroom rules. The ethics of group contingencies must be considered before and during their implementation. An interdependent group contingency is one in which all participants must meet a performance or behavior criterion before members of a group gain access to a contingency. Such a method, while common in classrooms, carries with it significant risk. For those students who require greater motivation, the promise of a reward contingent upon completion of tasks or adherence to classroom rules may provide the necessary catalyst to improve performance. For those whose performance may already be satisfactory, or even exemplary, a reinforcer would now be dependent on the performance of other students. By compromising the rate of reinforcement for higher-performing students, we run the risk of punishing performance rather than reinforcing it. In a dependent group contingency, a reward for the whole group would be dependent upon the performance of a small group or an individual. Occasionally referred to as the "hero procedure" by Cooper, Heron, and Heward (2007), this may result in an increase in the target behavior by the individual or small group. However, the inverse may also be true: if a reinforcer for the whole group is not delivered, the individual is a pariah rather than a hero. If we anticipate the possibility of greater opportunities for inclusion, we must also be prepared for the risk of threats to inclusion. An independent group contingency, in contrast, is one in which all members of the group who achieve a given criterion have access to a given contingency or reward. Privileges are given based on one's own behavior and are not dependent on the behavior of others. Such a system has advantages for both higher-performing students and those who struggle with the demands of the classroom. There is little risk within this system that students would be left unmotivated or unnecessarily stigmatized. The creation of the system itself, however, is merely the beginning of the process. Once the system has been established, careful attention must be paid to the students who consistently surpass expectations as well as those who consistently fail to meet them. The needs of all students must be identified and addressed. In his article on social validity, Wolf (1978) urges us to be mindful not only of the intended results of intervention, but all results. Group contingencies can have effects that may not be intended, but can be anticipated, and every effort must be made for intervention to encourage full inclusion of all students into the greater school community.

C-1: Establish operational definitions of behavior.

H-1: State intervention goals in observable and measurable terms.

Addressing problem behavior in the classroom is often a task that teachers approach with dread. There are many demands on a teacher's time, and the needs can be as varied as the students themselves. Disruptive or even dangerous behavior threatens their ability to teach all of the children, not only the student who engages in this behavior. Treating, or even managing, these behaviors often seems like adding another item to an already overflowing plate. It is tempting, therefore, for a teacher to characterize the student themselves rather than the observed behavior. Rather than describing the topography of a given behavior, teachers may fall into the trap of describing the student themselves, referring to them as "stubborn," "naughty," or far worse labels.

There is a simple trick to prevent the practice of labeling students to eclipse the more effective one of describing behavior. Behavior, as behavior analysts understand it, refers to anything that an organism does. As such, any description of behavior *must be a verb*. It must be something that one is actively engaged in. A behavior is not something someone is, but something someone does. Encouraging teachers to use this criterion for behavioral definitions can eliminate confusion and provide a "gold standard" for our descriptions. In addition to its technical precision, however, this criterion has another advantage. If we are to use descriptions of children rather than descriptions of behavior, we are left with resignation rather than a way to move forward. We cannot possibly treat who someone is, and these labels are part of their identity. A child who is "naughty" or "stubborn" or a teenager who is a "thug" is one whom we have already given up on. A focus on behavior, however, carries with it an assumption of hope that the behavior can change, given the right supports. Behaviors such as "screaming," "running away when given a direction," or "cursing at authority figures" are behaviors and not aspects of character. Behavior can be treated and other behaviors encouraged. Prompting the use of this strategy often is a matter of continually asking questions, such as, "What did he do? What do you want her to do?" Like any behavior change, some patience will be required, and teachers will need to be patient with themselves as they build this new habit. The extra effort involved in changing this habit is an investment well worth making.

Fifth Edition Task List H-9: Collaborate with others who support and/or provide services to clients.

Those of us consulting in schools would also do well to eliminate the word "just" from our vocabulary. The tasks that we ask teachers to perform are often more complex than they initially appear, and the responsibilities that they are performing are often of great importance. Asking, or even demanding, that teachers "just" follow your suggestions is more likely to lead to increased resistance than increased compliance.

Suggestions made to improve classroom functioning or the performance of a specific student should be as easy to implement as possible. Decreasing the response effort increases the likelihood of follow-through and the accuracy of the data collected. It is important to address another commonly misunderstood aspect of classroom dynamics: there are no babysitters in a classroom. Regardless of the level of education of the instructor, they are there to perform an essential task in the education of the students. Every moment is a teachable moment and should be treated with the level of respect that is deserved. Teaching is taking place at all times. The role of the behavior analyst is to increase the efficiency of that teaching, but it has begun. Part of practicing within the limitations of our competence is acknowledging the areas of competence of others. Teachers at every grade level bring a skill set and level of expertise that is essential in the development of their student's academic skills. A bit of humility in the acknowledgment of those skills goes a long way toward effective intervention in schools.

C-9: Select a measurement system to obtain representative data given the dimensions of behavior and the logistics of observing and recording.

H-7: Make data-based decisions about the effectiveness of the intervention and the need for treatment revision.

Perhaps the most important turn of phrase in these task list items related to data collection is "given the dimensions of the behavior and the logistics of observing and recording." The greatest challenge for behavior analysts working in schools is often addressing this factor. Teachers are often overwhelmed with many responsibilities and adding one more is unlikely to be well received. While we may have preferences in terms of what data collection systems are in place, there are only three requirements for data collection in behavior analysis, and one of these is that data must be taken. A system that is too cumbersome or requires too much training is unlikely to yield accurate data even from the most enthusiastic teacher. Data collection systems that require specialized equipment may also be problematic, since they may cause distraction in a room full of curious children. Systems that require the use of a cell phone may be met with resistance if the use of cell phones is prohibited. Additionally, data must be looked at and analyzed. The behavior analyst must be on hand to monitor progress and make data-based decisions. Additionally, teachers should have clear criteria for when consultation is required. Analysis can be made on a regular basis, or the criteria for checking may be more or less conservative. Regardless of how time for this analysis is scheduled, it must be scheduled. It is easy for regular monitoring to fall by the wayside, and far more difficult to correct a persistent problem.

H-3: Recommend intervention goals and strategies based on such factors as client preferences, supporting environments, risks, constraints, and social validity.

H-4: When a target behavior is to be decreased, select an acceptable alternative behavior to be established or increased.

Behavior analysts often define behavior by using what we refer to as the "Dead Person's Test." Behavior is defined as anything that a dead person cannot do. For many in the education field, however, "behavior" is synonymous with "disruptive/dangerous/problematic behavior." We are often called upon to "deal with all these behaviors" or in some cases to address the needs of "behavior kids." This misunderstanding of the definition of behavior and the subsequent overemphasis on behaviors targeted for decrease presents us with a misunderstanding of the role of both the behavior analysts and the teacher. The behavior analyst is equally capable of supporting the acquisition of skills and assuming that our only role is to decrease behavior is an unnecessary limitation. Additionally, when teachers are focused on the acquisition of skills such as decoding, sentence construction, addition, or subtraction, this also is behavior. Learning is nothing more or less than a durable change in behavior. This takes place in classrooms every day, and requires the expertise of skilled teachers. Still, the frustration of dealing with interferent behavior in the classroom can often eclipse the conversation. Rather than discussing behaviors to increase, many teachers will say, "I just want them to stop running/calling out/talking/moving." If the only goal is to stop behavior, however, this would fail the dead person's test. A dead person is fully capable of not running, calling out, talking, or moving. It is often necessary to remind teachers of this, and explain that, although the current situation may be very frustrating, a class of completely silent, immobile children is not an appropriate goal. There should be a difference between a well-run classroom and a well-run morgue. Redirecting the conversation toward what would make an ideal classroom may be more helpful than focusing exclusively on the aspects that make the current situation less than ideal. Asking questions about what children should be doing is often the start of a more productive conversation. Behavior analysts may often be treated as firefighters, called upon to make a problem disappear and expected to depart as soon as the problem does. We must focus our efforts in equal measure on "construction work" – the work of supporting foundational skills and building upon them.

H-2: Identify potential interventions based on assessment results and the best available scientific evidence.

Although teachers are ultimately responsible for what goes on in the classroom, the day-to-day functioning of the class is often a case of several "cooks in the kitchen." Curricular decisions are often made by administrators or school board members. Many students may require specialized instruction, including those who are English language learners, those receiving special education services, and those with medical needs or disabilities that do not necessarily qualify for special education services. Beyond the educational needs of the students they serve, teachers must also be mindful of other needs for those children who may be food insecure or exposed to violence or poverty. Though we would hope that teacher education programs would emphasize those practices that have been established by research, we must understand that research can vary widely in quality and outlier studies can often be given more weight than is necessarily appropriate. This, in addition to the conflicting information provided by other professionals, can lead to confusion and the implementation of pseudoscientific procedures. This potentially ethical issue can be dealt with in two ways: by talking and by listening. We must talk about the research and what current scientific evidence indicates as best practice. It is our responsibility to be well versed in the current literature in behavior analysis and it is also our responsibility to share such findings with the professionals with whom we work. Explaining the research findings and how these procedures can reasonably be implemented in the classroom is therefore our responsibility as well. We must also listen, and observe how procedures are being implemented in the classroom. Many programs do not appear at first to implement behavior-analytic or evidence-based procedures. In preschool classroom, for example, sensory activities are commonplace. Holidays or birthdays may interfere with scheduling. Field trips may shut down our ability to provide adequate classroom time to discrete trial teaching. It may be tempting to dismiss each of these activities as a meaningless and frivolous waste of time. It may seem to be counterproductive to spend time on these activities when sensory activities and holiday celebrations are certainly not evidence-based interventions. If we are to examine those practices that have been supported by current research, however, we may see a different picture of what constitutes evidence-based practice. Among the practices that have been supported by analysis of research are reinforcement, prompting, redirection, differential reinforcement of incompatible, alternative, and other behaviors, and naturalistic teaching strategies (Wong et al., 2015). Rather than addressing our attention to how teachers and school staff describe these activities, it would be best to listen and observe what actually takes place. Often sensory activities use redirection, naturalistic teaching strategies, and differential reinforcement. Reinforcement and prompting is often utilized in play or art activities. Even school trips can be opportunities to implement strategies to promote generalization, such as training loosely, using sufficient exemplars, and training with common stimuli (Stokes & Baer, 1977). It is entirely possible that these activities do, in fact, use evidence-based strategies. Teachers may not need a lecture on the importance of evidence-based practice, nor a refusal to support their work if they insist on wasting our time. Simply encouraging them to use these practices conscientiously often makes the difference between teaching and high-quality teaching.

I-4: Train personnel to competently perform assessment and intervention procedures.

I-5: Use performance monitoring, feedback, and reinforcement systems.

Implementing behavior change procedures often requires significant behavior change on the part of teachers. As simple as we may attempt to make such procedures, we must understand that simple is very rarely the same as "easy," and practice will be required. Professional development often includes only a description of the procedure to be followed, and perhaps includes the rationale behind the use of such procedures. In some cases, some supplementary materials such as written checklists or data sheets may be provided. Although this may appear to be a cost-effective solution to staff training, it is very rarely effective.

It is far more effective in changing teacher behavior to provide behavioral skills training. This method of staff training includes an instruction phase, in which the trainee is provided with a task analysis of the procedure to be performed. The procedure would be reviewed and the trainee would be given an opportunity to ask questions. Following the delivery of instructions, a modeling phase would be implemented, in which the trainer would demonstrate the procedure and again give the trainee an opportunity to ask questions. The final phase of behavioral skills training is the rehearsal and feedback phase, in which participants in training practice the techniques and procedures described and are given feedback on their fidelity to the procedure. Feedback can be delivered by the trainer, or in some cases by a peer, and is based on the written description provided in the instruction phase. In addition to being an effective and efficient method of providing training in techniques, an advantage of the behavior skills training method is that the instruction phase allows us to develop clear and objective criteria for what constitutes "good teaching." Trainees who demonstrate proficiency in the accurate implementation of these procedures can be considered "competent" in these techniques. There is another factor to be considered, however, in the implementation of our training, and certainly in our criteria for mastery, and that is the development of fluency in these techniques.

Fluency is described by Binder (1996) as "that combination of accuracy plus speed of responding that enables competent individuals to function efficiently and effectively in their natural environments." The importance of this concept is widely acknowledged in our direct work, as developing fluency is certainly the goal of any well-designed behavior change program. In our training, we also ignore this to our peril. It is often a lack of fluency in a given technique that increases the cost in time and energy. Training must include a focus on fluency as well as accuracy, and supervision should provide support toward that goal. We must also be ready to adjust accordingly as we monitor the trainee's progress and support their behavior change.

I-6: Use a functional assessment approach (e.g., performance diagnostics) to identify variables affecting personnel performance.

I-7: Use function-based strategies to improve personnel performance.

Just as we would with our direct service clients, we must retain the philosophy that "the trainee is always right." Regardless of our hopes or preferences, we must be responsive to the needs and behavior of school staff in our recommendations and in the implementation of behavior change procedures and training in behavior-analytic techniques. In behavior analysis the question, "Why do they do that?" is not a rhetorical one, nor is it one that indicates resignation on our part. Rather, it is a question that deserves an answer, and we are in a unique position to investigate and develop hypotheses as to what the answer might be.

We also must be mindful of the meaning of the phrase "buy in." We will often use this phrase to describe the level of enthusiasm with which clients, families, or other professionals approach a given program or procedure. However, there is also a description that fits well within our science – reinforcer. The anticipated behavior change is often the reinforcer for the implementation of the procedure. We are often entering a situation in which the current condition has become unbearable, making the promise of a solution a potent reinforcer. We are often in the luxurious position of significant "buy in." There are times, however, when compliance with our suggestions may not be readily offered. In these cases, it is important to analyze the variables controlling the behavior of these other professionals, just as we would analyze the behavior of direct service clients. If the promised reinforcer of a change in the behavior of students is insufficient to produce behavior change for teachers and paraprofessionals, and if the behavior of these professionals is consistently different from our recommended procedures, an analysis of the factors that affect choices may be in order.

Matching Law illustrates how choices can be affected by factors of both the behavior and the reinforcers available (Reed & Kaplan, 2011). Given a choice between two responses, the rate of reinforcement is one factor that affects the likelihood of one such response. Those behaviors that are reinforced at a higher rate are more likely to be engaged in. Additionally, the delay of a given reinforcer may affect choices. Behavior is most likely to reoccur if a reinforcer is delivered quickly, as opposed to those behaviors where the reinforcer may only occur after some time. Both of these factors would appear to place us at a distinct disadvantage when encouraging behavior change among teachers and school personnel. Though we may have some degree of confidence in the suggestion of evidence-based techniques, we certainly cannot begin a program with certainty that it will be effective. The rate of reinforcement may not be as consistent as we would hope, particularly as the student learns new expectations and may engage in extinction burst or other acts of rebellion. One of the only guarantees that we can make is that behavior change does require an investment of time, making the delay of reinforcement another cause for concern. Other factors affecting choice can be used in our favor, however, in the encouragement of behavior change for teachers. In addition, the effort of the response is a factor that may affect a client's choices, and those behaviors that involve lower effort tend to occur more frequently than those for which a greater effort is required. This factor is, to some degree, within our control. The effort involved can be altered so that behavior change procedures are not prohibitively cumbersome to implement. A slight increase in our own effort could yield a significant decrease in the effort of the teachers, and thus significant gains to students.

Legal, Ethical, Moral

An important distinction in our work with schools is among those considerations that involve legal concerns, ethical concerns, and moral concerns. To review the distinction between these categories, legal concerns are those that involve governmental regulations. These may be determined by state or federal governments and there may be serious repercussions for failure to meet their requirements. Ethical concerns are addressed by governing bodies of various professionals. There is often a great deal of overlap between these two categories, but the overlap may not be complete. There may be requirements of our Ethical Code that are unaddressed in legal statutes. Moral concerns, in contrast, are individually determined. Influenced by our culture and upbringing, it is often our moral responses that we consider the defining features of a "good person." It is necessary to make this distinction of what constitutes "goodness" in our work with schools. If we become clouded in our perception of ethics, we may fall into the trap of making decisions based on what feels good rather than what is good. Our primary role is to serve the client – or in this case, the students – rather than our own ego.

Legal

In the USA, there are several laws governing the provision of education. A full analysis of this legislation is beyond the scope of this book, but there are several points that deserve review. For those whose training in behavior analysis is outside the field of education, a brief overview is provided here.

Individuals with Disabilities Education Act

The Individuals with Disabilities Education Act (IDEA), reinstated in 2004, establishes the right of all students to a "free and appropriate education," known within education circles as simply FAPE. Though there has been some significant debate over the meaning of the word "appropriate," there is certainly an understanding that this must exceed "de *minimis*" standards of progress. This legal standard indicates that the level of progress must be greater than what would be considered trivial or too minimal to be considered. This would be upheld by the phrasing of the IDEA statute, which states more precisely that students have "the right to a free and appropriate education designed to meet their unique needs." Each student has a right to an education that promotes individual progress and supports their achievement of higher education, employment, and independent living. The overlap between the purpose of IDEA and our own commitment to the right to effective treatment is considerable. Both the requirements of IDEA and the description of "effective treatment" first proposed by Van Houten et al. (1988) address the need for programming to address functional needs and to be provided by a competent professional. This is perhaps our greatest area of common ground.

Family Education Rights to Privacy Act and the Necessity of Consent

The Family Education Rights to Privacy Act (FERPA) also governs the practices of schools and the sharing of educational records. This statute mandates that parents, as well as students themselves, have access to all of their child's records and that these records be kept confidential. FERPA influences our work with schools in two ways: by addressing the need for consent and by addressing the needs for documentation systems that allow for transparency with all stakeholders. We may find that, as school personnel become more familiar with our work and its value to students and teachers alike, we may be called upon to serve more and more students. We must not rush into assessment or treatment plan development, however, no matter how tempting the behavior change or the flattery that comes with it. Before beginning any behavior assessment, consent must be obtained. It is also necessary to be aware that data from behavior change programs are considered "educational records." They must be maintained according to school policy and shared with parents or guardians upon request.

Mandates/Job Responsibilities and Union Requirements

As part of the stipulations of IDEA, each student requiring special education services also receives an Individualized Education Plan (IEP). This document includes a description of the student's current level of progress, as well as the services required and their level of intensity. In some cases, a behavior-intervention plan may also be included. The IEP is a legal document and all services must be met at the mandated frequency and duration. Any changes must be made in writing and involve a meeting with the IEP team, including the relevant interventionists and parents or guardians.

International Considerations

Though the laws mentioned here govern the delivery of special education services within the USA, the laws which address education may differ from country to country. There are many countries throughout the world where special education services are minimal or nonexistent. The absence of laws mandating the inclusion of children with disabilities in the education system vary widely from one country to another, and efforts at inclusion in the developing world may be particularly challenging (Srivastava, de Boer, & Pijl, 2015). In many countries, and even in many school districts within the USA, the inclusion of students with disabilities represents a cultural shift rather than advocacy for established rights. In some cases, a lack of clear policies on inclusion can cause confusion and difficulties with implementation (Mafa, 2012).

Ethical

Use of Punishment

The use of punishment is a common practice in schools across the USA. The use of corporal punishment, including "paddling" is a legal practice in many US states. This blatant use of punishment is certainly a cause for concern, but we must also guard against the use of more pernicious punishers – equally harmful, but more socially acceptable. Despite its acceptance legally, the use of punishment poses several ethical issues for behavior analysts. The Ethical Code® addresses many issues that arise in the use of punishment. Code element 2.15 states,

> "They recommend and implement restrictive or punishment-based procedures only after demonstrating that desired results have not been obtained using less intrusive means, or when it is determined by an existing intervention team that the risk of harm to the client outweighs the risk associated with the behavior-change intervention."

It is often those professionals who are quickest to use punishment who claim that learning should be its own reward and that reinforcers should not be delivered for those behaviors that students "should be doing anyway." The use of reinforcers may be confused with bribery or perceived as a waste of time that diverts attention for attention. Many schools proudly proclaim that the students there do not work for stickers or other tokens. What this proclamation appears to overlook is that, in those cases where learning is in fact its own reward, this is a reinforcer. If a student is motivated by a teacher's praise, this too is a reinforcer. What serves as a reinforcer, however, can be as varied as the students themselves. Teachers often need to be given permission, and grant themselves permission, to use extrinsic reinforcers. It is often necessary to explain that this is not an interruption of teaching, but is teaching itself. In fact, it may be the most important teaching that these teachers do. One tactic to encourage the use of reinforcers over punishers is to urge teachers to focus on the ideal classroom they hope to create rather than their current less-than-ideal reality. Remind teachers that not doing is not a behavior.

In schools, punishment, particularly in the form of reprimands, is often the first resort rather than the last. Reprimands may vary in severity and are perhaps even public humiliation in the form of public posting of behavior charts indicating "red/yellow/green" status. These systems are often intended to encourage cooperative classroom behavior, but their emphasis frequently shifts from increasing participation and attending to decreasing disruption. Rather than a system focused on reinforcement, it becomes one focused on punishment. This transition becomes far easier if the language used to describe such systems is not responsibly chosen. Rather than using the word "punishment," many teachers and other professionals choose to use the word "consequence" or "correction" to describe these procedures. A procedure in which a stimulus is added that is aversive enough to decrease the future likelihood of behavior is, by definition, punishment. Referring to this procedure as "correction" or "consequences" serves only to make the person delivering these aversive stimuli more comfortable. We must use such language responsibly. If we are unwilling to label punishment honestly, we should be more resistant still to implementing those procedures.

Scope of Competence: Social Skills

Behavior analysts are often lauded for their expertise, particularly in the treatment of autism spectrum disorder. This praise is deserved to some extent – we have a great deal of knowledge in the science of learning and this informs how to teach. However, there is a distinction between expertise in how to teach and expertise in what to teach, or how much of it to teach. In the development of program goals, we should be mindful of the social significance of the target behaviors, as well as the social significance of the criteria for mastery. If, for example, our goal is to increase compliance with directions, we must make sure that our criteria for mastery are on par with peers. A mastery criterion of 90% accuracy for a three-year-old student working on this goal may seem reasonable initially, but we may find that same-age peers only respond to directions at a rate of 50%. If our goal is to increase social initiation, teaching conversation scripts begins with an introduction and "Can I play with you?" may seem like a good place to start. Observation of same-age peers may reveal, however, that generalized imitation would be more successful in initiating and sustaining interaction. Far too often, students are taught to socialize with adults rather than with children. The requirement that goals be socially significant refers to the social community of the client – or in this case, the student. Students should not be taught excessive degrees of compliance or politeness, but should be given opportunities to socialize with peers as equals to the greatest extent possible. We must be prepared to teach a student to be a part of the student community.

Scope of Priority

It is often the case that when working in groups, there is a shift in priorities. This shift is a constant presence in classrooms and must be addressed. Classrooms often focus on those behaviors that affect the greatest number of students. This is often a more efficient classroom management strategy, but it carries with it considerable risk. It is possible that, just as the urgent may crowd out the important, the group's needs may crowd out the needs of the individual. It is commonplace for self-injury to be ignored or go untreated in classrooms. There are several reasons this may be the case; among them that the possibility of treating this behavior may not be raised by consultants or related service professionals. There may also be an assumption that a child will be able to refrain from serious self-harm. Without treating this behavior, however, we may risk shaping greater intensity of this behavior. It is unlikely that teachers are unconcerned or unfeeling. Rather, the likelihood is that teachers have many concerns, and self-injury is simply crowded out by many other priorities. Part of our role can be re-shifting this attention and assisting in the development of behavior plans to treat behaviors that must be addressed quickly (e.g., self-injurious behavior).

Moral

Given that morality is individually determined and culturally influenced, addressing issues of morality will certainly involve a bit of editorializing. However, the influences on the values of behavior analysis and the ethics of education cannot be overlooked. Where our moral and ethical practice may overlap is in the belief that all students deserve and are worthy of an education that meets their needs. These needs may be emotional as well as academic. Children deserve to be included in their community. Every opportunity to promote acceptance should be afforded, particularly for students with disabilities. Eliminating the barriers to inclusion should be the standard of social significance. This can also be somewhat extended in terms of how we define "inclusion" and "acceptance." To speak loosely rather than in behavioral terms, children have a right to be respected and accepted. A classroom should be a safe place to learn. Authoritarian rule and the security to take risks and make mistakes are mutually exclusive states. Teachers are there to teach all children – those who excel, those who struggle, and everyone in between. Classroom management can certainly emphasize discipline, but it should not be forgotten that "discipline" comes from the word "to teach." Behavioral interventions are the teacher's opportunity to be an educator. We would never scold a child for not knowing what has not been taught if the topic was mathematics or reading, and we must also acknowledge that functioning in a community must often be taught. Shame has no place in the curriculum. The role of all school staff is to help support each student to accomplish their dreams. Giving every child that opportunity should be the mission of every teacher.

Ethical, Professional, Uncomfortable

In considering the ethical issues that arise when working in a school, it is also necessary to determine what situations reflect ethical violations, what may be considered unprofessional, and what merely makes us uncomfortable. Here we provide descriptions of the uncomfortable situations that may arise, and how to avoid the ethical pitfalls that may result.

The Two Kinds of Teachers

When consulting in classrooms, it is often the case that there are two types of teachers. The first type of teacher prizes their independence. When we walk into this classroom and ask if there is any need for consultation, they will respond that everything is fine, there are no aberrant or problematic behaviors, and there is no need for behavior plans. We will then sit and observe, until we notice that it seems rather dark. "Why are the lights off?" we may ask. "Oh," the teacher responds, "We have to have the lights off. They are much calmer that way."

The second type of teacher does not wait for us to ask if there is any need for a behavior plan, nor do they wait for us to completely enter the room. They need no prompt to begin asking for our advice, but rather begin regaling us immediately with complaints and requests for behavior plans. This type of teacher may not be as friendly and the visits to their classroom may be far more tense. However, in many ways they are easier to work with. The needs of the classroom are clearly communicated and they are actively seeking out our help. Much less initial assessment is needed to determine the referral problems, and these problems can therefore be resolved with greater efficiency.

Although the first type of teacher is far more pleasant to work with, consultation is far more complex. A good deal of more observation is frequently required to determine what the needs of the classroom are. Behaviors may be managed, but teachers may not be aware that there are better options than sitting in the dark as if they are witnesses in a bank robbery. They may not ask for solutions, but this must not be confused with the nonexistence of problems. Taking the extra time to observe is essential in being able to offer solutions. No one can know your ability to help if you do not tell them.

Policies and Their Side Effects

There is universal acknowledgment that school consultation should include building independence for teachers and school staff. Just as we hope to "work ourselves out of a job" with our direct service clients, we hope to foster enough independence in teachers' application of behavioral procedures so that our services are no longer needed. Teachers should not rely on us too heavily, particularly for those tasks for which they have been trained to independently perform.

We must be careful, however, that our policies to foster independence do not inadvertently punish seeking out help or guidance. Policies that, for example, involve withholding assistance until baseline data is collected may be prohibitively difficult when asking for staff to collect data. Rather than encouraging data collection, it may in fact discourage seeking out help for fear of reprimand. Behavior change can be difficult, and this is equally true when we are dealing with the behavior of staff. When we hope to encourage behavior change, shaping approximations toward independence is not only kind, it is necessary.

Works Cited

Binder, C. (1996). Behavioral fluency: evolution of a new paradigm. *The Behavior Analyst, 19*(2), 163–197.

Choi, B. C. K., & Pak, A. W. P. (2006). Multidisciplinarity, interdisciplinarity and transdisciplinarity in health research, services, education and policy: definitions, objectives, and evidence of effectiveness. *Clinical and Investigative Medicine, 29*(6), 351–364.

Cooper, J. O., Heron, T. E., & Heward, W. L. (2007). *Applied behavior analysis.* Upper Saddle River, NJ: Pearson.

Mafa, O. (2012). Challenges of implementing inclusion in Zimbabwe's Education System. *Online Journal of Education Research, 1*(2), 14–22.

Maslow, A. H. (1966). *The psychology of science: A reconnaissance.* New York, NY: Google Scholar.

Reed, D. D., & Kaplan, B. A. (2011). The matching law: a tutorial for practitioners. *Behavior Analysis in Practice, 4*(2), 15–24.

Srivastava, M., de Boer, A., & Pijl, S. J. (2015). Inclusive education in developing countries: a closer look at its implementation in the last 10 years. *Educational Review, 67*(2), 179–195.

Stokes, T. F., & Baer, D. M. (1977). An implicit technology of generalization. *Journal of Applied Behavior Analysis, 10*(2), 349–367.

Van Houten, R., Axelrod, S., Bailey, J. S., Favell, J. E., Foxx, R. M., Iwata, B. A., & Lovaas, O. I. (1988). The right to effective behavioral treatment. *Journal of Applied Behavior Analysis, 21*(4), 381–384.

Wong, C., Odom, S. L., Hume, K. A., Cox, A. W., Fettig, A., Kucharczyk, S., Brock, M. E., Plavnick, J. B., Fleury, V. P, and Schultz, T. R. (2015). Evidence-based practices for children, youth, and young adults with autism spectrum disorder: a comprehensive review. *Journal of Autism and Developmental Disorders, 45*(7), 1951–1966.

2.4   The Behavior Analyst as Advocate

Behavior analysts are a passionate group. We believe deeply in the importance of evidence-based service and in the power of behavioral technologies to improve the lives of individuals. We are prepared to make the case for the services required to endure the "best outcomes" for our clients. When acting as advocates, however, we must be mindful of several factors: what should we advocate for and how should we do so? Is our vision for "best outcomes" compatible with what the client would consider the best outcome for them? More and more, as the rise of social media allows us to communicate on a larger scale than ever before, we are hearing the voices of those who have gone largely ignored – specifically, those of autistic self-advocates who call upon us to reexamine our ideas of what constitutes these "best outcomes." Rather than thinking of "best outcomes" as being "cured" of autism, we are challenged to encourage acceptance, to listen to the community and to embrace a philosophy of neurodiversity.

Applied behavior analysis, when practiced responsibly, need not be incompatible with the ideals of neurodiversity, but it does represent a challenge for professionals. In this chapter, we examine the possibility of a supportive model for applied behavior analysis programming and offer suggestions on advocacy that focus upon the "best outcome" for all concerned, in particular the client.

What We Do: A Behavioral Description

F-1: Review records and available data (e.g., educational, medical, historical) at the outset of the case.

As behavior analysts, we value objectivity. This is what separates the practice of behavior analysis from other fields of human services. We do not speculate as to what individuals think or feel, but we observe what they do. This commitment to explanations of behavior based on observable phenomena should not, however, be confused with an assumption that behavior analysts are capable of observing all factors controlling behavior. There are many equally valid controlling variables that cannot be observed with our own limited expertise. We must not fall prey to the "Law of the Instrument," which states that, if we are equipped with only a hammer, all things begin to look equally like a nail. There are several medical conditions that may be comorbidities of autism spectrum disorder (Zafeiriou, Ververi, & Vargiami, 2007). Among such comorbidities are seizure disorders and gastrointestinal disorders, either of which could affect behavior.

DOI: 10.4324/9781003190707-16

F-2: Determine the need for behavior-analytic services.

F-3: Identify and prioritize socially significant behavior-change goals.

H-7: Make data-based decisions about the effectiveness of the intervention and the need for treatment revision.

The overwhelming majority of behavior analysts are those who provide services, either directly or in supervision and administrative roles, to individuals with autism spectrum disorder. A diagnosis of autism spectrum disorder is the most common reason for referral to a behavior analyst. The reason for this is simple: it is a matter of history of reinforcement – the reinforcer in question being access to services. In order to have services funded by insurance providers, an official diagnosis is necessary. In addition, this diagnosis may be further categorized into "levels" indicating the level of functioning and the degree of need for intensive intervention. An individual given a diagnosis of "level 1 autism" would require some level of support, and would demonstrate difficulty with communication and social skills. Those individuals given a diagnosis of "level 2 autism" would demonstrate greater difficulty with verbal and nonverbal skills and would therefore require greater support. A diagnosis of "level 3 autism" would indicate that the client has significant and very noticeable difficulty in communication, with limited social interaction skills. A child with this diagnosis would require intensive services. Within the US education system as well, a diagnosis of autism spectrum disorder is necessary in order to qualify for certain services.

Under the Individuals with Disabilities Education Act, known as IDEA, school age children must be referred to services based on a specific disability category, one of which is autism. A diagnosis is an important step in advocating for services. However, there must be a distinction between our acceptance of the necessity of diagnosis in the process of advocating for services and viewing autism itself as a referral problem.

In a curative model of autism treatment, the behavior analyst or other treatment providers would design programming with the goal of being "indistinguishable from peers." This is often what is referred to as "best outcomes" or "recovery" from autism. An acceptance of this curative model presents several issues for the clinician concerned about ethical practice. One reason that a curative model may be considered problematic is that it offers a potentially inaccurate depiction of our work. Applied behavior analysis is often referred to "the most effective treatment for autism spectrum disorder," and effectiveness is among the dimensions of applied behavior analysis according to Baer, Wolf, and Risley (1968). However, "effective" is not intended to be curative. This refers only to the results of an individual behavior-change program and that program's capacity to produce "practical results" for the client (Baer et al., 1968). As behavior analysts, we might accurately be described as uninterested in diagnosis. Despite the fact that autism could be considered a medical diagnosis, the treatment is given within the framework of a medical model. We do not treat a diagnosis, we treat behavior. Because a diagnosis of autism spectrum disorder is based on behavioral deficits and behavioral excesses, consistent intervention may lead to improvement to the point that an individual no longer meets the diagnostic criteria for autism spectrum disorder. This is not necessarily a treatment goal, in and of itself, but the cumulative effects of the accomplishment of many treatment goals.

The appropriateness of being "indistinguishable from peers" as a goal is also suspect. Given that the work of the behavior analyst should be focused on the acquisition of socially significant behavior as well as the reduction of behavior that interferes with one's full inclusion into their community, a diagnosis is not equivalent to a problem. Specific behaviors that may interfere with an individual's ability to communicate their needs or remain safe would certainly require treatment. However, the determination of social significance should be made by the client rather than by the clinician. Not every behavior change would necessarily be considered socially significant to the client.

An additional concern for those of us who work with individuals with autism is whether or not autism should be regarded as a "problem" at all. There are those within the autistic self-advocacy community (as they refer to themselves) who maintain that, rather than a problem to be solved, autism should be regarded as a natural extension of the diversity of humanity. In his book *Neurotribes*, author Steve Silberman argues precisely this point. Eligibility for an autism diagnosis, in this view, could be described as "naturally occurring cognitive variations with distinctive strengths" (Silberman, 2015).

The requirement that goals in behavior analysis be socially significant would seem to be in perfect alignment with a neurodiversity approach. The goal of treatment must be focused on the priorities of the individual clients. A supportive model of treatment – one that optimizes the client's goals and the client's autonomy – would be preferable to one that attempts to make an individual "indistinguishable from peers." To adopt a view that embraces the neurodiversity movement is to commit fully to our obligation to promote social significance. The level of importance of a particular goal is determined by its significance to the individual, rather than its significance to the outside world.

C-1: Establish operational definitions of behavior.

If clients have a clear understanding of behavioral concepts, including the specific behaviors to be changed, it increases the likelihood that such programming will be successful in accomplishing lasting meaningful behavior change. One challenge in communicating our goals and describing recommended procedures is that the terminology we use may have different meanings when used more colloquially. The ubiquitous use of terms such as "reinforcement," "punishment," and even the term "behavior" or "behavioral" can cause confusion and compromise our ability to communicate clearly.

H-9: Collaborate with others who support and/or provide services to clients.

While the science of behavior analysis can be used to teach any skill, this should not be confused with our individual ability to teach every skill, nor with the ability to adequately perform any skill. Behavior analysts must seek the assistance, training, and guidance of those with greater expertise. In some cases, this may mean seeking the guidance of professional expertise in specialized fields of medicine or psychology. With adult or adolescent clients, we may find that the assistance of a sexologist or female-driven gynecological practice may increase the comfort and quality of life for our clients. In some cases, however, the expertise may be different, but of equal value. Consulting with outside experts can considerably expand the opportunities we are able to offer. Experts in comic book writing, game design, French cooking, or African drumming can be as valuable in contributing to the quality of life for our clients as more traditional programming.

Legal, Ethical, Moral

When acting as an advocate for our clients we must be mindful of our legal, ethical, and moral obligations. The obligations that are categorized as "legal" are those which are matters of law and of civil rights legislation. Those which are referred to as "ethical" are outlined by our Ethical Code®. Our moral responsibilities are those which we often equate with "goodness" – those which are driven by our upbringing and learning history, often described as our "sense of what is right and wrong."

Legal

Individuals with disabilities, including those with intellectual disabilities, have the same rights as other citizens. Among these are the right to practice the religion of their choice, the right to education, the right to petition their government, and the right to vote. Though accommodations may need to be made in order to allow access to these rights, they remain as consistent for those with disabilities as for their neurotypical or nondisabled peers. If our programming is to be considered "applied" in the sense of its social significance, the skills involved in accessing these rights would be appropriate targets for behavior change.

Ethical

The most essential theme within this chapter is the necessity of programming that is sufficiently *applied*. Applied behavior analysis must be applied, first, foremost, and above all. Some of the common criticisms of behavior-analytic programming can be addressed by prioritizing adherence to our core principles. Behavior goals must reflect the goals of the client, and must follow their determinations of social significance, and that significance must be determined by the client.

Moral

Finally, we must consider our moral obligations as professionals working with vulnerable populations. Many of us came into this field out of a strong desire to help people, and it is necessary to reflect on what sort of "help" is actually helpful. We must maintain goals that are designed to allow the individual to pursue their own goals. We may teach a client to engage in leisure activities, but we cannot coerce their choice to engage in them. We may teach a client how to make the bed, but they have as much right as we do to decline to do it. We may teach clients to communicate, but we cannot control what they say. Our moral obligation is to our client – to their quality of life, rather than to the society that can/should accommodate them. That, more than anything else, is our legacy.

Ethical, Professional, Uncomfortable

There are several aspects of advocacy for individuals with disabilities that may make neurotypical ABA professionals uncomfortable. Rather than allowing ourselves to become defensive in support of our viewpoints, it is helpful to analyze these and determine the legitimacy of the argument – we must determine if these criticisms do in fact address ethical concerns. An emphasis on high-quality programming need not run counter to a goal of self-determination. However, several aspects of our interaction with vulnerable populations and common programming deserve review.

Language and Our Audience

Many of us are neurotypical individuals working with children or adults with autism disorder. Many of us also have developed the habit of using person-first language, saying "person with autism" rather than "autistic person" and understood this to be the currently accepted lexicon. Those in the neurodiversity movement, however, disagree. Sinclair (2013) writes that the phrasing "person with autism" implies that personhood can be separated from autism, rather than reflecting an understanding that autism is an integral aspect to one's identity, just as gender or ethnicity is. They argue that such a central aspect cannot be separated from personhood and the attempt to do so further stigmatizes autistics by implying that such a separation should be advocated (Sinclair, 2015). They write,

> I know that autism is not a terrible thing, and that it does not make me any less a person. If other people have trouble remembering that autism doesn't make me any less a person, then that's their problem, not mine. Let them find a way to remind themselves that I'm a person, without trying to define an essential feature of my personhood as something bad. I am autistic because I accept and value myself the way I am.
>
> (Sinclair, 2013)

Within behavior analysis, it is commonly accepted that context is an essential component in the determination of "appropriateness." It is considered best practice to ask those who are members of a given marginalized group how this group should be referred to. This would lead to the conclusion that "autistic" as an adjective (e.g., "autistic people") or "autistic" as a noun would be preferable (e.g., "autistics"). Person-first language, however, remains the commonly accepted standard for writing and presentation. Just as we must when considering other aspects of ethical practice, we must consider the intention of the language that is used. The intention of the use of person-first language is to emphasize the personhood, and not to disregard autism. When speaking to neurotypical audiences, this phrasing is often considered best practice. The prevalence of this argument in the literature on self-advocacy and autism acceptance should certainly give us pause in making assumptions as to the "right" way to refer to this population. As explored in this volume, the argument is often more nuanced than a more binary, black-or-white interpretation.

Compliance as a Treatment Goal

Among the most controversial applications of applied behavior analysis is the use of behavioral technologies to teach compliance. The stereotype of the behavioral program in which compliance is emphasized above all else remains prevalent and is among the more pernicious of the arguments against applied behavior analysis. In considering compliance as a treatment goal, one must consider its appropriateness – its suitability within a framework that emphasizes social significance. Particularly when working with young children, there may be arguments in favor of a certain degree of compliance. Compliance may be necessary to maintain safety and ensure inclusion in a school environment in which some compliance with teacher instructions would provide access to greater opportunities. However, compliance as a more generalized behavior can come with significant risks. McDonnell (1993) writes, "To expect complete compliance in children, when thoughtful and selective noncompliance is valued in adults, does not appear to be particularly good preparation for future functioning within our society." The dangers of teaching compliance must also be considered in light of the vulnerability of individuals with autism spectrum disorder and their increased risk of sexual abuse (Westcott & Jones, 1999). The adoption of compliance as a treatment goal must be justified by its social significance. Compliance for its own sake and generalized to every situation must be avoided in favor of goals that would lead to greater autonomy.

Self-Advocacy as a Treatment Goal

It is essential that we remember that the goal of programming should be increased independence, and to have a clear idea of what "independence" means. Among those of us who are considered neurotypical, we do not question asking for directions, hiring cleaning help, or dining out as threats to our independence, raising the question, "How independent should we reasonably expect anyone to be?" Independence among neurotypical individuals is not necessarily the onus to do everything but rather the right to determine for oneself how these things will be done. Rather than a focus on self-sufficiency, individuals with disabilities must have opportunities for self-determination – the opportunity to make their own decisions and set their own priorities. Independence is not, in the final analysis, synonymous with skill development, nor do skills need to be demonstrated in all contexts. Rather, independence is the ability to make the choice about what skills we will use. Once we have helped a client to develop the skills to communicate, we must allow them to do so and we must be ready to listen to what they have to say. Providing these opportunities should be the goal of every well-designed program.

Works Cited

Baer, D. M., Wolf, M. M., & Risley, T. R. (1968). Some current dimensions of applied behavior analysis. *Journal of Applied Behavior Analysis*, *1*(1), 91–97.

McDonnell, A. P. (1993). Ethical considerations in teaching compliance to individuals with mental retardation. *Education and Training in Mental Retardation*, *28*, 3–12.

Silberman, S. (2015). *Neurotribes: The legacy of autism and the future of neurodiversity*. New York, NY: Penguin.

Sinclair, J. (2013). Why I dislike "person first" language. *Autonomy, the Critical Journal of Interdisciplinary Autism Studies*, *1*(2).

Westcott, H. L., & Jones, D. P. (1999). Annotation: the abuse of disabled children. *The Journal of Child Psychology and Psychiatry and Allied Disciplines*, *40*(4), 497–506.

Zafeiriou, D. I., Ververi, A., & Vargiami, E. (2007). Childhood autism and associated comorbidities. *Brain and Development*, *29*(5), 257–272.

2.5   The Behavior Analyst as Employee

As behavior analysts, we may find ourselves at different places of employment but often we are doing the same job, or perhaps very similar ones. The tasks of the employment are often similar, or even identical, from one employment site to another. Each will require us to assess client needs, develop behavior programs, collect data or oversee its collection, make data-based decisions, and train others in the implementation of programs. While there may be individual differences in the methods of training, data collection protocols, and the resources available, there is a great deal more overlap than contrast in the day-to-day activities of behavior analysts working for different employers. An overemphasis on the tasks of employment at the expense of consideration of the environment of employment would be a fallacy that would assuredly affect our performance, ultimately harming the clients we serve. Years ago, many of the agencies that provided applied behavior-analytic services or related services were originated by professionals or parents who saw the need for increased services and attempted to meet this need. In many cases, the challenges of running a business meant that there were long hours and, in some cases, months without compensation for those who established these agencies. In some cases, poor business practices meant that therapists were overextended or not paid for months. While this may not apply to the majority of agencies, the challenge of running a sustainable practice has had considerable impact. In recent years, it has become a common practice that investors or managers either buy out struggling agencies or create their own, hiring the behavior analysts as employees. When we enter the field of behavior analysis, we begin a journey that is often considered more than "just a job." The prevalence of this phrase when describing our career path is evidence that there are many aspects to happy and fulfilling employment beyond the job tasks we perform. Creating and nurturing a mutually agreeable relationship when serving as an employee directly affects our work performance and is a goal worth striving for.

What We Do: A Behavioral Description

H-9: Collaborate with others who support and/or provide services to clients.

In an employee-employer relationship, there is a power dynamic that often eclipses all other interactions. Ultimately the employer is the highest point in the hierarchy of a job environment and the last word in decision-making. The consensus building often associated with the term "collaboration" may not always be possible. As companies that provide applied behavior analysis services are more frequently being overseen by business people rather than by clinicians, the relationship to employers and their role in collaborative decision-making grows increasingly complex. The term "collaboration," however, does

DOI: 10.4324/9781003190707-17

not necessarily mean that such collaboration would lead to decision-making entirely by consensus or that all factors regarding such decisions would be the purview of each collaborator. There may be several factors that affect decisions that are outside the scope of the behavior analyst's responsibilities. Leaders of agencies may be beholden to the investors or donors who support their work in order to remain financially sustainable. The final decision must be in their hands. This is not to say, however, that collaboration is not possible. It is only to point out that the goal of such collaboration is not necessarily consensus building, but to advocate for what is necessary. The goal should also not be conversion, however. Rather, a behavior analyst should have a clear idea of what is essential, what is preferable, and what is "preferable to me."

C-9: Select a measurement system to obtain representative data, given the dimensions of behavior and the logistics of observing and recording.

As behavior analysts, our emphasis on the importance of data collection sets us apart from many other human services professions. It is often the case that an additional task in data collection must be performed – convincing others that it is necessary and valuable. However, this is one area where business professionals and behavior analysts have a great deal of overlap. It is common practice within the business world to make data-based decisions. Successful businesses rely on specific data measures, which are often referred to as "key performance indicators." These are defined as the measurable outcomes that help executives to evaluate the success of an organization in meeting its mission. Some key performance indicators might emphasize profit, the number of customers, or how many customers refer someone they know. These measures are an essential tool in the assessment of a company's success. Where this understanding falls short is in the amount of time required to make programmatic decisions, plan treatment, and analyze data. While we should have systems to allow efficient accomplishment of these goals, it is essential that data collection be implemented in a way that is realistic and focused on that efficiency. While the practice of collecting data may be intimidating, particularly to those starting out in the field, "data" is essentially a more academic word for "information." It is our obligation as behavior analysts to use this information to the benefit of our clients. Although there are many methods for data collection, the elemental task of data collection is threefold: data must be taken, data must be analyzed, and data must be used to modify behavior change programs. Though these requirements may seem simple, these obligations are substantial and require significant time. The requirement that data be taken means that adequate materials, support, and training must be provided, so that this responsibility is fulfilled by all clinicians. If paperless systems are used, there must be policies in place to ensure that these systems will be sustainable agency-wide and confidentiality will be maintained. All staff members must be trained in the proper use of these systems, and performance must be monitored so that competency can be assessed and maintained. While this may appear to be somewhat obvious, it is vital that all factors affecting the accuracy and consistency of data collection be considered so that data can then be appropriately used to modify behavior change programs. Perhaps the area of greatest conflict with employers or managers, however, is this: data must also be looked at and analyzed. This requires the expenditure of perhaps our greatest resource: time. The time that we spend looking at and analyzing data is a necessary component of a well-run program, and essential to our ability to provide high-quality services. The fact that these services are often classified as "non-billable" by funding sources in no way diminishes their necessity. Adequate time must be allotted for this purpose. It becomes the responsibility of the behavior analyst in this case to make clear that behavior data is our most important "key performance indicator." Without adequate time to analyze it, we cannot be effective in our work.

H-9: Collaborate with others who support and/or provide services to clients.

When we shift from a discussion of "customers" to a discussion of "clients" or "consumers," we must acknowledge that a business person's view of "successful" may be different from that of a behavior analyst, particularly when working with vulnerable populations. While the necessity of data collection may not be a source of disagreement, we may have to advocate for alternative measures of success. Business owners will naturally be more concerned with billable hours and rate of compensation from funding agencies, and we may need to advocate for a reasonable caseload. Understanding that the business owner has a different perspective is necessary in this case. Making your case firmly but patiently often goes a long way.

Legal, Ethical, Moral

In order to practice as "good" employees, "good" behavior analysts, and "good" people, we must consider that there are different aspects to "goodness." This is especially true as we perceive it in human services – being good involves not only following our conscience as influenced by our values and conscience, but meeting our legal obligations, practicing ethically as dictated by the governing body or bodies of our profession, and practicing morally as prescribed by our conscience.

Legal

Contracts (Noncompete, Nondisclosure/Intellectual Property)

"Contract negotiations" is a term rarely heard in behavior-analytic circles. More often than not, a behavior analyst or other human services professional is given a contract and they simply sign it, assuming that this written contract reflects the final word on the matter of their employment agreement. It is often assumed that employment contracts will be identical from one agency or employer to another. Given that the responsibilities are often remarkably similar, this may seem on its face to be somewhat reasonable assumptions. Although we often think of legality in terms of avoiding arrest, it is equally important to acknowledge that a contract is a legal agreement. It is our legal obligation to fulfill the responsibilities delineated in our contract to the greatest extent of our abilities. Review your contract carefully and be sure to ask questions about anything that is unclear. There should be no confusion as to what responsibilities you will perform.

In addition, you should have a clear sense of when and how you will be compensated. Compensation should be made very clear in the contract. This is often the aspect of employment that we are the least comfortable discussing, but it is an essential element to a mutually agreeable contract. Employers enter into contract negotiation with a clear idea of what salary they can offer, and they know full well that every behavior analyst they interview has expenses and financial obligations. Asking about compensation, and being clear about your needs and your value as a professional, is uncomfortable, but necessary. Behavior analysis is a career path and not a hobby to be dabbled in casually. Behavior analysts must be compensated for their work and you have every right to be able to support yourself and your family.

One aspect of contracts that causes a great deal of confusion for behavior analysts is a noncompete agreement. In such a contract clause, the employee agrees not to compete with the employer. Such clauses often include a period of time after the employment is terminated by either party as well. For example, a noncompete agreement might include a stipulation that the employee cannot engage in competition with the agency or employer for several years following termination. This is certainly an intimidating clause to many of us who are in specialized fields. Given that any future employment would almost certainly be in a similar (or perhaps the same) field, competition would seem to be inevitable. How enforceable such agreements are may vary from state to state, but there are certain stipulations that are commonly recognized. A noncompete agreement cannot unreasonably restrict the employee or former employee's ability to make a living. Such an agreement cannot cause undue hardship. In other words, a noncompete agreement is not indentured servitude, but it is merely an agreement that protects the business from direct competition.

It would behoove us to pause here and define what constitutes "competition" in this context. Behavior analysts will often say that there is "more work than we know what to do with" and certainly the prevalence of autism spectrum disorder indicates that the need for high-quality evidence-based services for this population far outweighs our ability as a field to provide services for all children who need it. Additionally, many other vulnerable populations benefit from behavioral services, and are equally deserving of high-quality treatment. Other behavior analysts are not necessarily our competitors – it would be more accurate to refer to them as colleagues, or even referral partners. To provide behavioral services to high-need clients would not necessarily be perceived as "competition" by an employer. What would, in most cases, be considered "competition" is taking on clients currently served by the employer. To encroach upon the client list of an employer or former employer would be considered a violation of a noncompete clause. Again, such an agreement may or may not be enforceable, and a legal analysis is beyond the scope of this text to provide. However, in a field where so many go without adequate services, it is often unnecessary.

Nondisclosure and intellectual property agreements should also be carefully reviewed during contract negotiations and should be clearly understood before signing. Understanding the requirement for any data sheets or training materials that you design is essential to fulfilling our legal obligations. Carefully note any requirements for the use of copyright or trademark symbols and make sure that all materials created maintain the appropriate copyright. Even if an employment contract does in fact represent the final word on matters such as compensation, responsibilities, and obligations to our employer, asking questions for clarification is expected. It is better to ask and gain clarity than to mistakenly violate this agreement.

Harassment and Discrimination

In 2006, Tarana Burke began a movement that gained sweeping recognition ten years later (Ohlheiser, 2017). Following the high-profile accusations of sexual assault and sexual misconduct by several celebrities and powerful media executives, women were encouraged to share their own stories of sexual harassment and assault on social media using the hashtag #metoo. The hashtag was shared over 500,000 times in 24 hours, leading many to reexamine how workplace sexual harassment and discrimination has historically been responded to, and what changes are needed (Elerding & Risam, 2018) In the #metoo era, one common complaint is that "the rules have changed." There are many people, across all fields, who see this as a cultural shift in which the rules have been obscured.

However, sexual harassment law has not changed, and in fact these laws have not changed for several decades. It is merely the public acknowledgment of sexual harassment that has been altered, along with an increased willingness to enforce the laws and regulations already in existence. Harassment in the workplace is not exclusive to women. Discrimination and harassment can be on the basis of race, age, ethnicity, disability, sexual orientation, or gender identity, including transgender or non-binary individuals. The protections for these groups have certainly evolved as we grow into a more accepting society and as case law in the USA establishes these rights under the law. The cultural shift of the #metoo movement, therefore, does not represent a change in the rules themselves, but in our acknowledgment of the necessity to enforce them and create safe work environments for all employees. In our ethical requirements as well, this is hardly a new idea. The Ethics Code® explicitly states, "Behavior analysts do not engage in behavior that is harassing or hostile toward others" (BACB, 2020).

For employees, it can be difficult to discern what an appropriate response might be. In addition to the power dynamic so often operating in these interactions, embarrassment or uncertainty can cloud one's judgment as to the appropriateness of making accusations. The Code offers some guidance, but also allows some room for personal judgment in these situations. In the Code section related to our relationship to colleagues, the Code states, "Behavior analysts should address concerns about the professional misconduct of others directly with them when, after assessing the situation, it seems possible that doing so will resolve the issue and not place the behavior analyst or others at undue risk." If it is possible that addressing concerns directly with those involved could improve the safety of the work environment, this is indeed an option. It is by no means a mandate, however.

The phrasing here allows considerable room for judgment. The determination of the appropriateness of this action should involve, at least in part, an assessment of whether or not such an informal resolution would be likely to be successful. If an offensive statement is made in a casual setting and under more social conditions, informing the individual of the offensiveness of the remark may be sufficient to shape the behavior. Their response to feedback may indicate that such an offense was unintentional, and will hopefully serve to change this behavior in the future. As suggested in this Code element, the behavior analyst should document this as well, so that the success of such efforts to increase the safety of the work environment can be evaluated, rather than simply trusting that this behavior will change. There are, however, situations in which the success of an informal resolution is unlikely. There are patterns of harassing and demeaning behavior that may be so entrenched that any attempt to resolve them will be met with resistance, both from the perpetrator and their supporters. One common defense of those who engage in repeated harassing and demeaning behavior is "that is just who they are." If this is the case, this only indicates a pattern of harassing and demeaning behavior, all of which should be documented. Sexual harassment law does not make the stipulation "except when that is who they are." Every employee has a right to a safe working environment free of discrimination. As behavior analysts, we should also be uneasy using mentalistic explanations, or those that assign an internal state of being as a behavior's cause. We must acknowledge that it is far more likely that this behavior has been maintained by the environment. The harassing and demeaning behavior demonstrated is reinforced time and again as it is repeatedly overlooked, and laws and policies go unenforced. Employees (as well as students, clinicians, and supervisees) should be aware that there is recourse available. Further, we must remember that behavior is taught not merely through the communication of rules, but through the enforcement of rules.

Ethical

Professional and Scientific Relationships/Integrity/Supervisory Volume Remuneration

One of the challenges of human services is the conflict between our values and our needs. Many of us who begin a career in human services do so with the goal of changing lives and making a difference in the world. It is common for behavior analysts, as well as other human services professionals, to say "I am not in it for the money" and to dismiss the importance of fair compensation. There should be a distinction, however, between "being in it for the money" and "being in it *just* for the money." It is true that financial reinforcers may not be the most potent reinforcers for our work. Many of us are much more highly motivated by the success of our clients, the respect of our colleagues, the relationships that we build as we pursue our career, and the knowledge that our work makes a profound difference to people with disabilities and their families. However, we also have debts, expenses, and families to support. It is a harsh reality that, though we may not be motivated exclusively by the acquisition of money, financial compensation allows us the freedom to do our jobs and to perform them well.

It may be necessary for the ethical behavior analyst to advocate for adequate compensation, and to do so is not a sign of greed or materialism. Accepting inadequate compensation causes many professionals to increase their caseload to offset lower pay. This leads them to take on more responsibilities than they can reasonably fulfill and compromises the quality of their work.

Environmental Conditions: Identify Support Systems

It is clear within the Ethics Code® that we must take on only those responsibilities that we can reasonably fulfill and commit to follow through with high-quality work. How to do so is often left to the discretion of the individual behavior analyst. It is possible that there will be systems already in place to increase productivity and accountability and that training in these systems will be provided by your employer. However, it is equally possible that you will be entirely responsible for managing your tasks in a timely fashion and that systems to document progress will be your responsibility. If we are in a more administrative or supervisory role, we will often find that we are pulled away from the tasks that maintain or grow the mission of the organization to handle emergencies. There are providers who need our advice, emails to be responded to, and dozens of tasks that usurp our time. If our responsibilities are primarily direct clinical services, the challenge is somewhat different but no less daunting. Discussions with parents or other providers can eclipse the session and threaten our ability to provide high-quality services as mandated by employers. In either case, we may find that we spend the majority, or perhaps all, of our time "putting out fires" – dealing with crises that come up rather than building on success or executing our duties responsibly. In Dwight Eisenhower's words, we must not allow the urgent to crowd out the important. Emergencies will certainly arise and these must be dealt with. However, we must allow the time to deal with them aside from the time allotted to our other responsibilities. There are several methods to increase productivity, but some of the simplest may also be the most effective.

Schedule your day. Create a calendar (digital or paper) of an ideal schedule, including tasks to be performed at specific times during the work day. Include scheduled times to complete paperwork, check email, return phone calls, eat meals, take breaks, and, if necessary, commute between cases. Every necessary task must be included.

Plan for the unexpected. Allow more time than is necessary for transitions between tasks and allot time for those tasks to complete "when you have a second." Do not depend on a calm commute or uninterrupted time. Assume that tasks will take longer than expected, and plan for this by adding extra time into your schedule.

Allot time for "when you have a minute" or urgent tasks. Time to complete urgent tasks that come up suddenly should be built into your calendar and schedule.

Plan for the next day before the end of the current day. Identify the priority tasks to be completed and, if you have not already done so, schedule the time to complete them.

Though these tactics are simple, it should be acknowledged here that "simple" is not synonymous with "easy." There may be considerable effort in arranging systems and, when time is a precious and finite resource, there may be some resistance to doing so. This behavior is, however, an investment of time and effort that can have significant returns.

Integrity and Supervisor Volume: Setting Limits with Employers and Prioritizing Self-care

It may be tempting to work without a break, to sacrifice one's own needs for the client, but it would be a mistake to do so. In the human services, it is common for many of us to take on too much and ask for too little. It may even be reinforced by our own romantic ideas of self-sacrifice – an image of ourselves as martyrs. This idealistic vision of suffering for the benefit of others is an example of what makes us feel good but allows us to fail at doing good. Vacations and sick time may be referred to as "benefits" but they are not niceties. They are not provided for their own sake. Allowing employees to take time off for illness also keeps work environments free of contagious diseases. For those of us working with children with disabilities or other vulnerable populations, this is of particular concern, since illness could cause a gap in services. Vacations also have benefits to employers – taking vacation time can increase productivity (Westman & Etzion, 2001). The essential point to remember here is this: your self-care is not the employer's top priority, nor is it their responsibility to advocate for it. Our commitment to professional integrity must also include a commitment to personal integrity. Our commitment to practicing within the boundaries of our competence must also include practicing within the boundaries of our physical and emotional health.

Ethical, Professional, Uncomfortable

"Corporate Culture" as Behaviorists Understand It

The term "culture" is one that is often used synonymously with ethnicity, religion, or nationality. It is often the intention that learning about a culture will lead to greater empathy, and by extension, a more empathetic work environment where different cultures are accepted and differences embraced. Unfortunately, the opposite effect often occurs. Rather than emphasizing our areas of commonality, learning about culture can overemphasize differences. More concerning, the implication can be that such differences are static – people of this particular group have these values, they are different from us, and there is little or nothing to be done to bridge the distance between us. Behavior analysts, however, have a different understanding of culture. Culture does not refer to ethnicity, religion, or country of origin, but rather a set of social contingencies (Glenn, 2004). Behavior analysts, rather than referring to the trappings of culture, refer to "culture" as a set of interlocking behavioral contingencies (Glenn, 2004). In other words, what we understand as "culture" evolves from the behaviors that are socially reinforced among a certain group. Any group of people, then, can be considered a "culture." As certain behaviors are reinforced, these behaviors increase among that group, creating what we may call a "culture."

Some of these site-specific practices may be obvious, such as proprietary software, data collection methods, or training procedures. Other "cultural practices" may take the form of collective habit, and may be subtler. Some of these habits may be idiosyncratic, and some may even be illogical. None of these are necessarily static and can be influenced by reinforcement and punishment, just as any other behavior may be. However, they have been established and maintained by consequences over time.

Starting a new job can, in many ways, be similar to moving to a new country. Every workplace environment has its own customs, its own way of speaking, and its own collective values. As is often the case when moving to a new country, there may be a period of adjustment. We may realize that the more familiar ways of fulfilling our responsibilities are themselves products of the culture in which we were originally trained. In these situations, we must be mindful of whether our suggestions or preferences are, in fact, an improvement. Behavior analysts must distinguish those practices that are essential, those which are preferable, and those that are "preferable to me." While a behavior analyst should be prepared to advocate for the dignity of clients, for evidence-based practice, and for limitation on their workload in order to provide quality services, not every battle is a battle worth fighting. The use of reinforcement would be an example of what would be considered essential – essential practices must be conducted in order to maintain the ethics of one's work. Those practices which would be considered preferable may increase efficiency, cut costs, or result in more adequate distribution of resources, but are not necessary to ethical practice. Those conventions that could be placed in the category "preferable to me" represent the habits of the individual practitioner. Understanding the differences among these categories is the key to effective performance for a behavior analyst and employee. Not every corporate culture is a good match for the values or personality of every behavior analyst, and there are certainly arguments to be made for a work environment where one can enjoy the day-to-day interactions of like-minded people. However, it is unnecessary for every difference of opinion or practice to be considered an insurmountable obstacle.

Transitions: When to Move On

In human services our dedication to clients is often conflated with our dedication to specific employers, and this dedication can, unfortunately, be exploited. However, as reviewed in our discussion of the importance of self-care, we cannot possibly do our best work if the conditions in place are causing undue stress. Many of us stay in jobs that make us miserable out of concern for the clients we serve. For those of us working with children, we often stay "for the kids." It is important to highlight something here: a job is not a marriage. There is no need to try to save it, attempt to work things out for someone else's sake, or grudgingly accept our own misery. The clients may need our care, but there are other clients whose cases are overseen by other potential employers whose needs also must be met. A safe working environment, being treated with respect, and adequate compensation relate directly to our effectiveness and the importance of these factors should not be overlooked. We began this section by stating that behavior analysts must be keenly aware of the difference between those environmental conditions that hamper implementation and those that preclude implementation. This is, of course, an important distinction. Often the determination of whether or not conditions preclude implementation can only be determined when these conditions are repeated, and our judgments are often subjective. We should, however, be aware that these subjective judgments that affect our ability to work productively and provide high-quality services are still relevant. There is a distinct difference between giving a new environment a chance and allowing ourselves to be exploited.

A first job need not be the last job. Behavior analysts are not trees that are forced to bloom where they are planted. Our contributions and expertise are desperately needed all over the world. Deciding to move on from an employment opportunity to another can be a difficult one, particularly if we are not lucky enough to find the perfect fit with our first job. There is, however, as the saying goes, a lid for every pot. If your current employer is not aligned with the values and principles of behavior analysis, as well as your own personal values, there is nothing unethical or unprofessional in moving on. There are as many corporate cultures as there are employers to support them, and it is possible to find one where you feel comfortable and respected. To paraphrase B.F. Skinner, the real mistake would be to stop trying.

Works Cited

Elerding, C., & Risam, R. (2018). Introduction: a gathering of feminist perspectives on digital labor. *First Monday, 23*(3).

Glenn, S. S. (2004). Individual behavior, culture, and social change. *The Behavior Analyst, 27*(2), 133–151.

Ohlheiser, A. (2017). The woman behind "Me Too" knew the power of the phrase when she created it – 10 years ago. *Washington Post.*

Westman, M., & Etzion, D. (2001). The impact of vacation and job stress on burnout and absenteeism. *Psychology & Health, 16*(5), 595–606.

2.6   The Behavior Analyst as Researcher

There is a certain level of excitement in participating in research. Adding to the breadth of knowledge in the field of behavior analysis is a thrilling undertaking. It should not, however, be entered into lightly. When engaged in the activities of research, the behavior analyst has certain responsibilities in relation to the Code. Whether or not we are engaged in formal research, the behavior analyst is a scientist. Applied behavior analysis is the science in which those procedures which have been demonstrated through the experimental analysis of behavior are put into use in the support of socially significant behavior change. In the application of these techniques, we also have the responsibility to ensure that the procedures themselves were the cause of the change in behavior. It is this evidence on which we rely as an evidence-based field. Before addressing the responsibilities of the researcher as a behavior analyst, it would be helpful to review the role of the researcher in more general terms.

Scientific research follows the scientific method, and as scientist-practitioners, we can use this method in our clinical work as well. This process can be described in the following way:

Identify a problem through observation. Before beginning any program for behavior change, the referral problem must be determined. Often this will be individually determined, but research may also address issues that reflect the more general needs of a given population or include multiple subjects. Some degree of external validity in a study is generally preferable, and the results should be applicable to other clients as well. For example, in a study that examines the effectiveness of techniques to increase variety in a client's community of reinforcers, several clients may be selected for participation and the results may inform treatment for clients who present with similar issues.

Research the relevant literature. It is often said in the sciences that we are taller because we stand on the shoulders of giants. It is the work of other scientists that builds the foundation for our own research. Given that we are a field that engages in evidence-based practice, these "giants" in the field of behavior analysis build the foundation for our clinical work as well. This is an essential step in developing research, and one that is often overlooked in the development of treatment plans. Before we begin to develop plans, we must familiarize ourselves with the work in this area that has already been done. In clinical work, we may want to attempt to replicate these results by implementing similar procedures, to the extent that logistics allow.

Develop a hypothesis. In the clinical work of behavior analysts, our hypothesis is generally a variation of "This treatment will have a socially significant impact on behavior, and will produce practical results for the client." A hypothesis is simply an idea that must be tested in the course of an experiment. In research, we take nothing for granted.

DOI: 10.4324/9781003190707-18

Test this hypothesis. A hypothesis is an excellent start, but the testing of this idea as part of an experiment must be implemented. Despite any desire we may have to treat behavior immediately, a sense of our starting point is a necessity. We must collect baseline data that is sufficient to make predictions as to the likely trend if we do not intervene. If a baseline shows an improving trend, it may not be possible to evaluate the effectiveness of our intervention. Testing of our hypothesis must also be ascertained by establishing a functional relation – determining if the behavior is truly dependent on the application of the treatment. This can be determined by comparing those phases with or without treatment, by comparing treatments to one another, or by comparing baseline performance to performance during treatment for different subjects. Regardless of how such comparisons are made, they are the basis of determining a functional relation.

Analyze the results. Whether our work is clinical or within the context of research, we must be prepared to analyze the data. More importantly, we must approach this analysis with the objectivity that is central to scientific discovery, accepting the conclusions indicated. There is no room for our own agenda or for ego. When the data reveals the story, it is our obligation to listen and respond accordingly.

Communicate the findings. For both the researcher and the direct service clinician, this is the final step. Once we have determined the effectiveness of our intervention, the results must be communicated. There are several avenues for this communication, including presentations at conferences in the form of talks or posters highlighting the findings. Of equal or greater importance, however, is communicating the finding of our clinical work to clients and those affected by our work in a clinical context. Regardless of whether or not our career path takes us into the realm of research, every behavior analyst is capable of being a scientist-practitioner and using the practices of research in their clinical practices. The practice of solving problems through the application of the scientific method is an essential skill set for the behavior analyst.

What We Do: A Behavioral Description

Though the behavior analyst could consider themself a "scientist-practitioner," there may be many aspects of the research process that are overlooked when our focus is exclusively on clinical work.

In this section, we will describe the process of engaging in research activities and how this process relates to the responsibilities of the Fifth Edition Task List published by the Behavior Analyst Certification Board® (BACB®).

H-3: Recommend intervention goals and strategies based on such factors as client preferences, supporting environments, risks, constraints, and social validity.

As clinicians, particularly those who work with specific populations, we may often fall into a bit of a rut, identifying similar behavioral deficits and excesses within this population and offering very similar solutions. This may, to some extent, be a reasonable approach, as there are behavioral deficits that are common among, for example, young children diagnosed with autism spectrum disorder. When beginning with a young child with limited language, we will often begin by teaching functional language, as guided by our understanding of the importance of this behavior in encouraging autonomy, its appropriateness from a developmental standpoint, and its relevance to the needs of both the client and their community. Rather than focus on the rationale behind teaching these skills, we take this rationale as a given and move immediately to the strategies necessary to teach them.

Fluency with the most logical general approaches, however, may have side effects when we begin engaging in research activities. We may be tempted to skip the first phase of the process of engaging in research activities: identifying the need for improvement in the status quo.

The first step in the planning and execution of research in any research study is the identification of the research problem. At the heart of the explanation of the research problem is the argument that this is a problem that must be addressed for these participants and a rationale behind addressing it. We must examine the current state of affairs and what needs to be improved, but we must also be able to explain why this needs to be improved. Before engaging in any research, we must first determine what can be improved and have a clear picture of the necessity of this improvement, as well as an idea of whether or not this behavior change should be considered a priority.

Part of the determination of the research problem is an assessment of the present state of affairs. This includes the analysis of the client's current repertoires. The current level of functioning of the client with respect to the proposed goal of intervention must be considered. An essential consideration is whether or not participants have the necessary prerequisite skills for the proposed change in behavior to take place. The task analysis of the given behavior must also be addressed. If a proposed behavior change is prohibitively complex, there may be other needs that must be accommodated.

The analysis and explanation of the research problem must also address any environmental and resource constraints and priorities and needs of supporting environments. Some of the aspects that may be addressed are the availability of support staff and the level of training required.

Finally, the research problem must address client preferences as well as the social validity of any proposed intervention. The problem must be one that is a priority among the *participants*, rather than merely a problem for the researcher. Given that we are so well trained in the ways that behavior can be treated, exploration of the research problem can be a challenge for behavior analysts. Providing a rationale for resolving a problem may appear to be an unnecessary step. In our enthusiasm, we may overlook *why* we are attempting to change behavior and focus our attention exclusively on *how* we plan to do it. It is essential however, that we remain steadfast in our commitment to the dimensions of applied behavior analysis. And that we remember that "applied" comes before "behavior."

A-5: Describe and define the dimensions of applied behavior analysis (Baer, Wolf, & Risley, 1968).

C-11: Interpret graphed data.

H-2: Identify potential interventions based on assessment results and the best available scientific evidence.

Science is a field that is not made up of many individuals working separately, but of many individuals whose works build upon the work of each other. In our scientific pursuit of explanations, we do not start from the beginning each time a study is done, but rather pick up where others have left off. The scientific pursuit of truth necessitates incorporating the previous discoveries of other scientists. It is not a sprint, or a marathon, but rather a relay. Once we have identified the research problem, a literature review is the next necessary step. The researcher is responsible for identifying what methods have been attempted in the past, and what has been successful. Gaps in the literature should also be identified. Every study has its limitations, and the researcher's efforts at controlling for confounding variables may lead to issues with external validity. A study performed with a limited population may not apply to all members of a larger group. This is why replication in other contexts and with other groups is necessary.

C-1: Establish operational definitions of behavior.

Once the research problem has been identified and the literature provides a clear path forward, we must identify the appropriate dependent variable – that which is measured during the course of the experiment. In our science, the dependent variable is always a behavior. Following the dimensions of applied behavior analysis, our science involves the study of socially significant behavior and any study within that science must be behavioral in nature. Studies within behavior analysis must be empirically based – the behaviors that are studied must be objectively observable and measurable. This emphasis on the quantitative study of behavior in single-case studies is not to diminish the value of large-group studies, nor of more qualitative studies, but rather to clarify the focus of our field.

A-5: Describe and define the dimensions of applied behavior analysis (Baer, Wolf, & Risley, 1968).

G-21: Use procedures to promote stimulus and response generalization.

Fifth Edition Task List G-22: Use procedures to promote maintenance.

The next necessary step in the development of research is to outline the research question. The research question identifies the dependent and independent variables within a given research study and describes how the goals of the study align with possible solutions to the research problem. The research problem identifies needs, as well as the gap between the status quo and our ideal picture of what is possible. The research question, however, asks whether or not a proposed treatment would be effective in addressing these needs and bringing us closer to that ideal. In order to address the needs identified in the research problem and ask a research question that properly addresses them, we must, as behavior analysts, ask ourselves about the practical application of any proposed behavior change and the proposed treatment that supports it. Within these two task elements we see an emphasis on two of the dimensions of behavior analysis as proposed by Baer, Wolf, and Risley (1968): behavior-analytic studies must be effective, demonstrate generalization, and, perhaps most importantly, be applied. Treatments that are implemented as part of a research study must be effective. This means, in part, that the *Journal of Applied Behavior Analysis* does not publish null results. Treatments that do not show an effect at all will be rejected for publication. However, the results of behavior-analytic study must also result in what Baer, Wolf, and Risley refer to as "practical results" (Baer et al., 1968). Results must demonstrate that the treatment was clinically significant. The treatment must have an effect on daily life. In addition, the treatment implemented must also result in generalization. This is commonly defined as the effect when the resulting behavior change lasts over time, expands to new responses, and is demonstrated in other stimulus conditions than those in the original teaching conditions. In order to meet the requirements of this dimension, researchers must plan for treatment whose effects are not limited to the study itself. The practical results demonstrated must not be limited to the study. Finally, the behavior change must be *applied*. Applied behavior analysis is not merely the science of behavior change, but of *socially significant behavior change*. The goals of a behavior change program, also known as the target behavior or the dependent variable within a research study, must be socially significant. They must be meaningful, not merely for academic purposes, but because the increase or decrease of these behaviors will have a significant impact on the participant's quality of life. These three dimensions are intimately connected. Those behaviors that are deemed important by the community – those which exhibit social validity – will produce effects that have a practical effect on the lives of participants and clients. Those behavior changes that have social validity will be maintained and expanded. This is essential in order for research to be a meaningful practice.

D-1: Distinguish between dependent and independent variables.

D-2: Distinguish between internal and external validity.

D-5: Use single-subject experimental designs (e.g., reversal, multiple baseline, multielement, changing criterion).

The next step, perhaps obviously, is to decide how the research question will be answered. Any study is an attempt to answer a question about how circumstances could be improved for those who share similarities with the participants and therefore are affected by the same problems. Once the research question is developed, the discussion shifts to how the researcher can best approach finding an answer to that question. The decision of which design to use is influenced by many factors, including the nature of the target behavior, the population served, and the ethics of various designs. Among the strongest designs in terms of demonstrating a functional relationship is the withdrawal design. In this type of study, the behavior of interest is measured in three phases. In the first phase, the behavior is examined without treatment being applied in order to establish an appropriate baseline against which to measure a treatment's effects. In the second phase, treatment is implemented and the effects are observed. In the third phase, the treatment is withdrawn in order to determine if any beneficial effects were the result of treatment, rather than some other factor, such as maturity, greater rapport with the clinicians, or even the weather (an unproven but nevertheless common explanation for behavior change). All things being equal, this design, given the strength of the evidence it provides, is preferable.

However, as we see so often in our clinical practice, it is very rare indeed that all things are equal. When considering how the research question will be answered, there are several factors that must be considered in selecting the experimental design, and among these are "Can this treatment be withdrawn?" and "Should this treatment be withdrawn?" To address the question of whether or not a treatment can be withdrawn, we must consider that there are treatments that do not lend themselves to withdrawal, and changes in behavior that cannot be undone, regardless of whether a treatment is stopped. In this case, a withdrawal design would not adequately measure the success of our program. The impact of the treatment would perhaps be better assessed by comparing that intervention with another in an alternating treatments design. Another option would be to compare baseline performance with treatment by using a multiple baseline design. For those behavior changes that may be irreversible, these experimental designs may be preferable. Such practical considerations are essential in planning research. The next question, whether or not a treatment should be withdrawn, brings us to ethical concerns rather than practical ones. There is certainly apprehension in the idea of withdrawing a treatment that has proven effective in the treatment of behavior, particularly if this behavior is harmful.

This is not to say that the use of a withdrawal design is necessarily out of the question, but that the safety of the participant or participants must be considered. There must be safety measures taken so that the participants' safety can be assured. The length of the withdrawal phase can also be modified so that an extended lack of treatment does not lead to ill effects. The Task List® items listed here address two of the obligations of the behavior analyst with respect to research: our obligation to participants and our obligation to the truth. The selection of an experimental design must adequately address the research question. However, our obligations to ensure the safety and dignity of our participants must be fulfilled as well.

C-10: Graph data to communicate relevant quantitative relations (e.g., equal-interval graphs, bar graphs, cumulative records).

C-11: Interpret graphed data.

In the Task List® items listed above, we see the importance of fulfilling the behavior analyst's obligations to the truth. Once the conditions of the research study have been arranged, it is our obligation to minimize interference and allow the data to tell its own story. It is in this stage that the data must be analyzed in order for conclusions to be drawn. In the field of psychology and other sciences, this step involves the assessment of statistical significance. Statistical significance is the goal of large-group studies, as this demonstrates the effects of a given treatment on the population studied. In behavior analysis, however, the vast majority of the research conducted is in single-subject designs. In single-subject designs, the results are not communicated in terms of their statistical significance, but in terms of clinical significance. It is the practical impact of the treatment that is measured in this case. The visual analysis of this data is what indicates that the treatment has been effective. It is the responsibility of the researcher, therefore, to ensure that not only are these data analyzed and interpreted, but that the visual presentation of the data makes the impact of interventions clear, without understatement or exaggeration. The impact of treatment must be clear and any potentially misleading presentations must be avoided.

Legal, Ethical, Moral

A researcher has three obligations: to participants, to one another, and to the truth. These obligations also align with our requirement to engage in "good behavior" as reflected by legal, ethical, and moral standards. As "good" behavior analysts, scientists, and researchers, we must uphold the standards of behavior within the law (legal) as well as upholding the standards as dictated by a governing body, in this case, the BACB®. Our moral obligations of "goodness," informed by our upbringing and history of reinforcement, involve the legacy that our research leaves behind.

Legal

Behavior analysts engaging in research activities must be mindful of their obligations under the law. To comply with the law is a necessary step in our ethical and "good" practice.

Obligations to Participants: Animals

There are few laws with regard to the treatment of animals in research. In the USA, the Animal Welfare Act applies to those facilities and institutions that engage in research using animals and legislates the standards for the housing and care of animals. Although the most common nonhuman subjects – birds, mice, and rats – are excluded from this legislation, it is essential that we be mindful of the treatment of our animal subjects.

Obligations to Participants: Human Subjects

There is considerably more legislation protecting human subjects compared to those statutes protecting animal welfare. The most commonly cited legislation deals with the protection of participants' health information – the Health Insurance Portability and Accountability Act of 1996. This statute ensures the confidentiality of health information. A distinction must be made here between confidentiality and privacy. Privacy refers to the right of each participant to share only what they choose. Privacy is, therefore, the responsibility of the participant. Confidentiality, on the other hand, refers to the obligation of the researchers to protect the information that is shared by participants. Confidentiality is the exclusive responsibility of researchers. It is not only a courtesy but also our legal obligation to ensure that any identifying information shared be protected.

Ethical

The BACB® outlines our obligations as behavior analysts with respect to research. In this volume, we have categorized these ethical requirements as related to the obligations of all researchers: our obligations to participants, to each other, and to the truth. Beyond our responsibilities under the law, these elements of the Compliance Code clarify our obligations to participants and each other.

Obligation to Participants: Protection of Dignity and Safety

The Ethical Code for Behavior Analysts® is abundantly clear on the subject of our obligation to protect the welfare of participants in behavior-analytic studies. The protection of dignity of those with whom we work is within our core principles. One way to ensure that the necessary steps are taken is by focusing our attention on one of the dimensions of applied behavior analysis – behavior-analytic studies must be *applied.*

It is often within the realm of an Institutional Review Board to determine if a given research study unnecessarily threatens the safety or dignity of participants. The Institutional Review Board is, ideally, the research safety net that prevents unethical research practices. However, the protection of dignity and safety of the study's participants is ultimately the responsibility of the behavior analyst.

Obligations to Each Other: Authorship

It is our obligation to acknowledge contributions in any research study and to ensure that this acknowledgment is commensurate with the level of contribution. Authorship must be based on the level of contribution, but minor contributions to the research can and should be acknowledged as well. A research study must also appropriately cite the previous work in their area of study. The importance of acknowledging contributors to the current study is certainly integral to ethical practice, but the proper use of citations is also essential. In the sciences, we "stand on the shoulders of giants." There is truly nothing in any science that can be, or has been, accomplished by only one person. Those who contribute to our work, and to the field as a whole, must be adequately acknowledged.

Moral

Obligations to the Truth: Communicating Our Findings

Research is certainly not a simple undertaking. It is an investment of years of effort, filled with numerous tasks that are simultaneously overwhelming and tedious. Research activities are not to be entered into lightly, nor with inadequate support or supervision. It might be assumed that ego or the desire for fame would drive the researcher's behavior and serve as a reinforcer for engaging in these activities. Many of us, however, find more potent reinforcers in the impact of our efforts on the lives of those we serve. Given that this science and its applications can be life-saving, the question then becomes: if you could save a life, or significantly improve one, simply by sharing information would you do it?

The moral underpinnings of our obligations when engaged in research activities of any kind are closely aligned with our obligations to the truth. The need to communicate our findings is a vital aspect of our obligations. This is where the contribution of science becomes a public service. Our responsibility is not merely to discover the truth, but also to communicate it. Many of us in the field of behavior analysis believe that behavioral technologies can have a direct and lasting impact on the quality of life for our clients, and in some cases to be potentially life-saving. It is our moral obligation, in this case, that drives our commitment to share research findings and add to the field of behavior analysis.

Ethical, Professional, Uncomfortable

In our judgment of what constitutes "unethical" behavior, we must also seek clarity regarding the distinction between those research activities that may be considered "unethical" and those that merely make us uncomfortable on a personal level. Ethics, as previously stated, refers to compliance with the regulations of a governing body. In our case, this would be our adherence to the Ethical Code® as published by the BACB®. There are several aspects of ethical research practice that should be examined, and many considerations that must be assessed in their importance. While some of the elements of research and our commitment to it may indeed be ethical, there are others that may be more accurately described as simply "uncomfortable." While not in direct violation of the Professional and Ethical Compliance Code®, those "uncomfortable" behaviors on the part of researchers may still raise concerns among behavior analysts, or those outside of the field – concerns that should be addressed.

Rats in Cages: The Appropriateness of Extrapolating from Animal Research

There are several criticisms that are made about behavior analysis as a treatment, particularly in addressing the needs of children with autism spectrum disorder. One common criticism is that such treatment is "dehumanizing," and that it too closely resembles "dog training." There are those who would argue that human beings are simply too complex, too separate from nonhumans, for our behavior to be analyzed in this way. Despite the famous title of B.F. Skinner's work, the idea of dismissing or minimizing the value of freedom and dignity can be troublesome. "We are not rats in cages, after all," many will claim. "Human beings are more complex than that." Even the commonly accepted functions of behavior may seem so limited that they lack any usefulness in addressing why individuals engage in behavior. Since so much of the foundation of our science is based on these experimental analyses of animal behavior, it is easy to see how this mischaracterization can be perpetuated. One obvious way to address such concerns is to point out that all of medical science also depends on studies of animals. In fact, the treatments derived from such studies are often delivered to humans with fewer modifications than those treatments derived from animal studies in the experimental analysis of behavior.

Still, there is an interesting point here: there is certainly no arguing that human beings have a more complex community of reinforcers than a rat or pigeon. The repertoire of behaviors is also more expansive. However, the factors that influence behavior may be, though by no means identical, similar across all species. Functions of behavior also can be viewed as general categories that do not limit the possibility of individual preference. While it may make us uncomfortable to notice the similarities between human and non-human animals, acknowledging this foundation of the study of behavior does not mean that we do not equally acknowledge the complexity of human behavior.

Deception in Research

Our comfort with deception in research is related to our comfort level with deception in general, and informed by the personal judgments of the moral level of what we consider "goodness." There is an adage about honesty; "Tell the truth but don't always be telling it." In our personal lives, we acknowledge that telling the truth is often the moral choice, but equally acknowledge that honesty must always be tempered with compassion. There are exceptions to the rule "always tell the truth." In psychological research activities, there is still some acknowledgment of the moral imperative to be honest. This also must be tempered. But rather than tempering honesty with kindness, we must temper it with the necessity to maintain the integrity of the research. Behavior analysts and psychologists occasionally use deception in research, which may be in the form of "lies of commission," meaning that the participant is deliberately misinformed. "Lies of omission" are also possible, meaning that the participant, while not directly misinformed, is not told the study's purpose or what specific behavior will be observed. The use of deception is not directly addressed in the current edition of the Ethical Code®. However, previous incarnations of these elements, as well as points within the Compliance Code itself, indicate that the use of deception is acceptable under certain conditions. The debriefing process is essential in the ethical implementation of research activities, and participants must be informed that it will take place at the conclusion of the study. This debriefing is the opportunity to correct any deception that occurred during the study. This is certainly an appropriate guideline to bear in mind once the deception has occurred, but does not address the decision of whether or not to implement deception as part of a study. Deception must be used only if the integrity of the study demands it. The use of deception must be essential to answering the research question. Such determinations, and other ethical issues raised by research study methodology, are not to be made exclusively by the researchers, but rather with the guidance of the Institutional Review Board. Just as we are mindful to "tell the truth but don't always be telling it," we must bear in mind that in research activities some level of deception may be justified by the greater good. The value of the information gained through research may allow us to become more comfortable as well as engage in ethical research.

What Constitutes a Research "Problem?"

Many of us in the field of behavior analysis believe that the technologies developed from this field of study can have life-changing impacts and significantly improve the quality of life for some of the most vulnerable populations. There is tremendous power in the application of the science of behavior analysis and using these technologies can be a force for good. With great power, however, comes perhaps an even greater responsibility. Using the technologies that have been made available by the study of behavior and its controlling variables we *can* teach anything, but this does not mean that we *should* teach *everything*. When considering the dimensions of applied behavior analysis, it is essential to remember that applied comes before behavior. In contrast to the experimental analysis of behavior, in which the basic principles of behavior are examined without regard for the social significance of the behavior change, applied behavior analysis depends on social significance. Any target behavior for intervention must be socially significant and the behavior change must improve the quality of life for the participant. This is equally as true of our research activities as it is for our more direct clinical work. The judgment of what would be considered "socially significant" can be subjective, and often changes as cultures shift. If it is true that, in Martin Luther King, Jr.'s words, "The arc of the moral universe is long, but it bends toward justice," research certainly reflects the moral universe as it exists at the time a study is conducted.

It is with good reason that an ethical behavior analyst may be uncomfortable with studies in which the behavior of interest is in conflict with full acceptance of marginalized groups. Studies which, for example, target traditionally feminine speech or mannerisms in biologically male children would be considered more objectionable now compared to when they were first published. To target such behaviors may be socially significant to those uncomfortable with a more fluid conception of gender as a social construct, but not to the participant. Additionally, studies that determine such targets to be "socially significant" strengthen systems of oppression for the LGBT (lesbian, gay, bisexual, transgender) community, which is an dangerous outcome for members of this community. Our responsibility to refrain from complicity in the marginalization of disenfranchised groups goes far beyond our own personal comfort, however. The Ethical Code® also admonishes us to be aware of implicit bias in our professional activities in Code element 1.10, which states: "Behavior analysts maintain awareness that their personal biases or challenges … may interfere with the effectiveness of their professional work. Behavior analysts take appropriate steps to resolve interference, ensure that their professional work is not compromised…" If the target behavior addressed in a study reflects a personal or cultural bias on the part of the researcher, this may be considered a violation of this Code element.

These cultural biases are not exclusive to the marginalization of LGBT community, but should also be considered in our research addressing the needs of individuals with autism. Many of the single-subject studies address the needs of individuals with autism with a focus on: increasing communicative and social behavior, decreasing those behaviors that may be dangerous, and upholding the commitment to social significance. However, we must ensure that research has social relevance to the participant. Curative models of behavior-analytic services – those programs that focus on the goal of being "indistinguishable from peers" – may be more socially significant to others than to the participants themselves. A supportive model of treatment on the other hand – one which focuses on the needs and desires of the participant/client – focuses on applied research and treatment. The requirement that the dependent variables be socially significant is a vital component to ethical programming. Beyond our personal discomfort, it is an ethical requirement.

Works Cited

Baer, D. M., Wolf, M. M., & Risley, T. R. (1968). Some current dimensions of applied behavior analysis. *Journal of Applied Behavior Analysis, 1*(1), 91–97.

Part 3

Voices from the Field

3.1   A Reflection on Integrity

Nasiah Cirincione-Ulezi and Scott Herbst

In May 2020, after the killing of George Floyd, the world catapulted into a frenzy of disruption around racial injustice. This was largely brought on by a global awakening to the reality of anti-Black racism in the United States. Despite decades of effort to pass legislation that protects the rights of Black citizens, in broad daylight, a Black man was publicly brutalized, at the hands of law enforcement – whose sworn duty it is to serve and protect. Section I of Amendment XIV of the United States' Constitution states:

> All persons born or naturalized in the United States and subject to the jurisdiction thereof, are citizens of the United States and of the State wherein they reside. No State shall make or enforce any law which shall abridge the privileges or immunities of citizens of the United States; nor shall any State deprive any person of life, liberty, or property, without due process of law; nor deny to any person within its jurisdiction the equal protection of the laws.

From a common understanding of integrity, in which word and actions align and doing so is considered "good" and not doing so is "bad" or "wrong," this act clearly lacked any. George Floyd was not given due process of the law before being deprived of his life. And the lack of integrity goes far beyond this single incident. For example, the fact that Black people are more likely to serve prison time for minor drug offenses than White people, despite similar rates of usage (Drug Policy Alliance, 2018), indicates a breakdown regarding "equal protection of the laws."

Unfortunately, this common understanding of integrity leads to dealing with breakdowns in integrity ineffectively. We assert we (human beings) have a tendency to relate to integrity as a moral phenomenon and hold that people *should* act with integrity. Again, acting with integrity is good, and not doing so is bad. From this view, when we uncover any lack of integrity, it's natural to look for who is at fault, finding that person or group, and punish them. Further, it's just as natural to avoid being seen as having any lack of integrity, and to locate the lack of integrity with other people or due to outside circumstances. In other words, we blame or justify.

This was plainly obvious during the trial of Derek Chauvin for the murder of George Floyd. As the prosecution made its case, they brought numerous witnesses from within the police department, including the Chief of Police, to testify that Chauvin's actions were not in accordance with department policy and training. In other words, this breach of integrity was his fault. Then, as the defense made its case, their argument focused on that Chauvin claimed that he was afraid for his life. The prosecution blamed. The defense justified.

We propose a different view of integrity, however, in which integrity is not a moral or ethical phenomena and rather approached simply as the state of being whole and complete

DOI: 10.4324/9781003190707-20

(Erhard, Jensen, & Zafffron, 2016). From this view, a system such as a government would be considered to have integrity when its actions, practices, policies, etc. are in alignment with its founding documents. That is, it has integrity when it does what it says it is going to do and treats its citizens as it says it will treat them. From there, when any lack of integrity is uncovered, the next action becomes to locate the source and then to restore integrity by dealing with the consequences and putting in what's necessary such that the lapse is not repeated.

Taking this view opens up a very different conversation. Instead of finding the person whose "fault" it is, the question becomes, "Systemically, what allowed for this lapse in integrity?" While Derek Chauvin was the officer who had his knee on George Floyd's neck, there were three other officers present who didn't intervene. There's a legal system in which officers justify the use of deadly force by pointing to fear, and which is more punitive toward Black people. There's a system of police training that, if officers are going beyond their training, the outcome is poorly trained officers. Further, there's a citizenry that tolerates breaches of integrity by dealing with them ineffectively. Both data and direct video-evidence show the lapse in integrity by an individual or a "few bad apples." Rather, the system lacks integrity.

Which leads us to the question: what is the system? Again, if we look at the system as having something "wrong" with it, that directs attention to finding individuals to blame and punish. Dealing with integrity purely as the state of being whole and complete, we can then ask: How do I participate in this system? Where does my action (or inaction) contribute to the structural integrity (or lack thereof). And what can I do, with integrity (that is, consistent with how we say the system works and what we, as participants, value) to strengthen that foundation? That is, how can I bring workability to the system and do so in a way that works?

We believe behavior science has a lot to contribute to this restoration. We are specially situated to deal with "what's so," which is where an authentic inquiry into integrity begins. As we do so, it will require deep reflection and constant realignment to our values in order to make the difference of which we know we are capable of doing.

Works Cited

Drug Policy Alliance. (2018, January). *The Drug War*. Retrieved from Mass Incarceration of Race: https://drugpolicy.org/resource/drug-war-mass-incarceration-and-race-englishspanish.

Erhard, W., Jensen, M. C., & Zafffron, S. (2016). Integrity: a positive model that incorporates the normative phenomena of morality, ethics, and legality-abridged (English language version). Harvard Business School NOM Unit Working Paper No.10–01.

3.2 Reflections on the BCBA® as a Researcher

An Interview with Yulema Cruz

Yulema Cruz

ANN BEIRNE: What do you think is the biggest challenge for behavior analysts when they first start doing research?

YULEMA CRUZ: I think that it's coming up with a question. I think a lot of us see a lot of need in specific areas that we're interested in – where we practice, where we had our practice – but it's that research question that's harder, I think, for a lot of the newly minted BCBAs® to sort of develop, I think. Beyond that, I think is the conceptualization of the research. So, it's research question to begin with. It's trying to conceptualize a problem as "How can I ask a question in a way that I can measure it? And quantify it?" If that's the type of question that you are asking because the research design obviously depends on the research question that you have, right? Not all questions are going to be answered by a single subject or a group design. So, it depends. So, I think that's a big deal and, again, it leads you to choosing the type of research – the proper research – to answer that question. And, of course, beyond that is conceptualization, as I mentioned.

AB: Could you describe that a bit?

YC: For my specific study – which is the one that I have the most experience in – it was conceptualizing the idea of teaching supervisors how to be supervisors. How do we get to do this systematically? And so, it took a lot of researching the literature, of course, which is one of the first things that you to do, and also reaching out to other behavior analysts who were supervisors and observing the type of supervision that they did. So, it was a lot of video data collection, a lot of research, and also surveys. I sent out surveys to other behavior analysts to see if what I was in the process of conceptualizing made sense to *them*. And it was indeed an area in which they had identified, does that answer your question?

And of course, mentoring. Having the right mentor makes a big difference. You have mentors who help you every step along the way and give you deadlines so that you are not lost in limbo research or "research limbo." And then you have other advisors who just sort of let you be. In my experience, you want the type of advisor who's going to stay up on top of you and help you along and give you deadlines for work products.

AB: As someone who's done research, what are some of your biggest concerns when you do research or when you start to develop a research project?

YC: Getting subjects. Recruitment is big, very big. That was my biggest problem with this research, recruitment and treatment integrity. Those are the two that I've probably personally experienced. Trying to set up the environment in a way that you know you're going to have treatment and integrity, as the researcher is a big deal. Making

DOI: 10.4324/9781003190707-21

sure that you do everything that was written, the way in the way that it was conceptualized. That's a big deal. Making sure that you're sticking to your criteria. And not go crazy with [saying], "I have to finish this research, so I'll accept whoever." No, no, no. You have specific criteria and, so sticking to those criteria is important.

AB: How did you make the challenge of recruitment in particular?

YC: I went all over the place. I broadened my search area to outside of my city. So currently, I'm traveling an hour and a half to get my research completed. And [another challenge is] time management. It's a lot of time management, a lot of following up with people, a lot of, sort of being flexible. I have to be very flexible. And broadening your area where you want to do your research. Perhaps I can't find subjects in Miami and other parts of Dade County but I can find them in Palm Beach and other parts of Palm Beach County and that's what I'm doing.

AB: Is there anything that you did to manage your commitment to the treatment integrity?

YC: I have a treatment integrity checklist and I also completed a pilot study. So, I did a pilot study prior to my dissertation study where I learned a lot about my own research and my own way of doing my research. And I recommend that everyone does a pilot study if they can, if it's feasible. That would be my recommendation. Do a pilot, learn from the pilot, make a lot of mistakes during the pilot. Learn and then you can make adjustments to your proposal and after that, after you get it approved, then do the actual study.

AB: So, the pilot study was before any IRB approval?

YC: Yes, the pilot study was before any IRB approval.

AB: So, what was the IRB process like, was it helpful for you or did it represent a challenge in terms of your vision for the study that you were going to do and their vision of the kind of study that you should do?

YC: No, my IRB process was pretty comparable I believe to the norm. I believe I submitted everything in January and I got a response in March. An IRB at my university typically meets about once a month. They meet about once a month or once every two months or something like that. So, because I had completed my IRB Form in a way that did not pose a threat to participants. And even though I [was] collecting video data during the DDT Sessions – which include children with developmental disabilities between the ages of two and ten – I am not collecting specific data on the child's performance. So, I think that was one of the biggest things. And because for the rest of the time I'm using adults – the supervisors are adults, the therapists are adults – they are consenting adults. So that made it easier I think. And again, my process I think was expedited for that reason – because I excluded the data from the child participants. But I was very clear in my IRB that I was only going to use video to look up the behaviors of the therapists, while they're working together with the child. So being very clear and using language – the language that they teach you during the CITI training that you take, about your participants and how you have to protect your participants and all of that – use some of that language to draft your IRB Form. Because that's what they're going to be looking at, right? It's "How does your research pose a threat to the participants?" And also, something that we already do in the field that I think is really helpful is your "risk versus benefit ratio analysis." So, if you can also include that as part of your IRB – and they have a section for that anyway – but just as you're drafting it, continue to think about "what are the benefits of this research versus the risks?" If that makes sense.

AB: As a professor what have you taught students about research and its importance?

YC: Well, because I'm only teaching undergraduate students I'm a little limited to as to what research [and] how much research I can teach them. Because then you can learn about all this new terminology that has nothing to do with research before they get into it. But I do emphasize the differences between group and single case design. I have to change my language on my proposal because it's not single subject, it's single case now. I've had to really highlight the differences between those two, highlight the fact that single case research means that *everybody* gets the same treatment that's one of the features of single case research, so, highlight that. And also highlight the differences within a research design, which is what we do, right? Single case. Highlight the differences among, for example, a reversal design where you probably don't want to use an IV [independent variable] that's some sort of training because you can't untrain people. So, you can't do a true reversal with that type of design, if your IV is a training. If you're using some type of reinforcement-based intervention, then obviously you can reverse that. And also highlighting the features of multiple baseline design, and how it focuses on the individual, like we all know, from single case design. And how the multiple baselines lets you rule out maturation – that confounding variable that you may find sometimes in research. And those are the primary two ones, I haven't really delved into changing criterion in any of these, again because I'm teaching undergraduate students. So, they get a little bit of a taste of research but they're not there yet.

AB: So, one of the things that I have been saying in this book is that researchers have an obligation to participants – in terms of maintaining safety and dignity, responsibilities to colleagues – in terms of authorship and avoiding plagiarism and also a responsibility to the truth – in terms of the accuracy of data and misleading results. So how do you fulfill those obligations as the researcher?

YC: Checks and balances are good. With respect to my participants, I make sure I'm always protecting confidentiality. So, I don't talk about anyone else's scores with anybody else unless I have their permission. So, if I am collecting data, for example, on a therapist and I need to share those data research purposes with a supervisor – you know because treatment is coming and I need to share this particular video – then I specifically ask for their consent. In my consent form I have a section that says that I will not disclose any information that may affect their job, right? Because let's say they get low scores. So that may paint a picture to their supervisor different from the purpose of the research. And it may not represent their skills because I'm just narrowing down my research to an area. So, it's not necessarily – it's not really fair to them. So, I don't share any of that. I protect confidentiality at all times. I also, if there's a child, for example, who is engaging in problem behaviors with the therapist, before I bring it to the supervisor and then I immediately call the supervisor [and say], "Hey, they need you. We have a problem." We stop the recording. And so, everything is about trying to deescalate the behaviors with that child. And then perhaps we can continue, perhaps not. I've had times where I have said, "The child is tired. He's had it for the day. I am not gonna put him through a 20-minute recording for my purposes – for the purposes of my research. I can wait another week and we can come back again and collect data again." And in that way, I've been very mindful of protecting the child. I collect data during their sessions and if anything happens, I stop the recordings. And we take care of that and forget about the research. So, things like that. As far as colleagues, my colleagues are my checks and balances. I attend a biweekly meeting at FSU with my mentor where I talk about my research. Every other week and I have to have product. I have to have something produced, whether it's data, or whether it's things I've done or recruitment or whatever it is. And so, when I present my data and some of the concerns and discoveries as I am conducting the research and then my peers and my mentor give me feedback and tell me, "Oh, okay well look at this in this way. And what about that other thing? And have you thought about this?" And so that's why I think having that structure of continuing – having to check in with someone who is also checking in on your research and making sure that they're doing everything by the book – is good. And as far as the truth, I don't code my own data. I only record it. And without watching it, I sent it off to my coders. And I've trained my coders to reliability, so they're reliable. I trust them – I train them, I train them on reliability. I trust their data and their judgment, and I don't watch my own videos. So, I do not touch my own data. All of this is put into clouds that are encrypted and password protected and all of that. So, nobody gets to see the videos but my coders, myself, and my mentor. And again: I only record it. They get to score it.

AB: So what are some things for behavior analysts to keep in mind when they're designing a study, in terms of ethical practice? What do you think are the most important things?

YC: Well, I know that we owe it to our field to produce good research but I think always having the most vulnerable person in my mind. And one of the first things that Jon Bailey told me was "do no harm" so always have that in mind. In what way can I fulfill my research that poses the least amount of risks and harm to my participants? Especially children. So you always to make sure that you're protecting *them*. Protecting *their* identity, protecting *their* participation. Nobody needs to know that these people are participating in research. Nobody needs to know their names, nobody needs to know any of that. So always protecting the most vulnerable ones I guess would be the conclusion.

AB: So you teach in both English and Spanish and you lead a program in the Dominican Republic. So, what do you see as the biggest challenge in expanding research in other countries?

YC: There isn't research in their language that they can draw from. And get ideas from. We need to, not only translate their research from the lab to application, but we also need to translate it into other languages. So that other people can benefit from that research. Also, a lot of the research that's done in the United States is done with a specific population. So, drawing conclusions from research done in one population may not apply to a population in another country and in another language. And, so, I think it's the lack of resources that limits their ideas that they have, limits the questions that they may want to answer and the support that they may get for doing this type of research. Or just engaging in research altogether.

Works Cited

Baer, D. M., Wolf, M. M., & Risley, T. R. (1968). Some current dimensions of applied behavior analysis 1. *Journal of Applied Behavior Analysis*, *1*(1), 91–97.

Behavior Analyst Certification Board (2014). Professional and Ethical Compliance Code. Retrieved December 22, 2017 from www.bacb.com.

3.3 Ethics and Functional Analysis

Michael Dorsey and Mary Jane Weiss

Functional assessment and functional analysis technologies have been extant in the field for decades, and the mandate to use these tools has also been clear for decades. One of the historic defining differences between the field of behavior modification and the field of Applied Behavior Analysis (ABA) has been the advent of the functional analysis age. Instead of focusing solely on behavior reduction, as was the case in the "B Mod" era, interventionists seek to understand the maintaining variables and develop function-based treatments to address them. This was a monumental shift in the way in which challenging behaviors were construed and treated. Clinicians sought to identify the communicative function of behaviors and to create more comprehensive approaches to behavioral intervention. Support plans contained both preventative/antecedent strategies, to reduce the likelihood of the behaviors, and replacement skills, which enable the person to meet their needs in a prosocial and appropriate alternative manner.

Introduction

Functional assessment and functional analysis technologies have been extant in the field for decades, and the mandate to use these tools has also been clear for decades. One of the historic defining differences between the field of behavior modification and the field of Applied Behavior Analysis (ABA) has been the advent of the functional analysis. Instead of focusing solely on behavior reduction, as was the case in the "B Mod" era, interventionists now seek to understand the maintaining variables and develop function-based treatments to address them. This was a monumental shift in the way in which challenging behaviors were construed and treated. Clinicians sought to identify the communicative function of behaviors and to create more comprehensive approaches to behavioral intervention. Support plans now routinely contain both preventative/antecedent strategies, to reduce the likelihood of the behaviors, and replacement skills, which enable the person to meet their needs in a prosocial and appropriate alternative manner. In general, there is a focus within the field on ensuring that intervention programs are individualized, humane, and effective.

Reviewing the existing literature for the support of functional analysis technology is beyond the scope of this paper. However, suffice it to say, FA is an evidence-based practice that has been shown to be highly effective in identifying and treating many complex challenging behaviors. There is substantial evidence that functional analysis procedures are more accurate and reliable than (early questionnaire forms of) functional assessment procedures, and that they can be systematically taught to others. While there has been some criticism of the methods (e.g., based on time efficiency, need for training, risk of

DOI: 10.4324/9781003190707-22

implementation), there has been strong consensus that FA methods should be used to increase the efficiency and effectiveness of behavioral intervention.

A number of variations of the Standard FA procedure have been developed (e.g., brief FA, latency-based FA, precursor FA, trial-based FA), and several of them have accumulated substantial evidence. Some of these variations address the logistical and safety concerns raised about the Standard FA. The Standard FA remains the most tested and empirically supported format, and is the basis for the variations that have been explored. A more recent intervention approach developed by Hanley and colleagues (e.g., IISCA/ Practical Functional Assessment) has demonstrated effectiveness, efficiency, and application to the natural environment.

While the field has embraced function-based treatment and the need for assessments to guide such individualized interventions, there is still a lack of consensus about how these procedures should be trained and implemented. There are also a myriad of examples on conduct around these matters that might be described as unethical, or at least as clinically questionable. In this piece, we will explore the ethical challenges that may arise in the context of functional assessment/analysis and provide some guidelines for adherence to ethical conduct guidelines in this regard.

The Ethical Mandates

The BACB Ethics Code (2020), which goes into effect in 2022, reflects the increased focus on humane care. The Code now contains core principles that serve as a framework and as a guide for assessment and intervention. The four Core Principles are: Benefit Others; Treat Others with Compassion, Respect, and Dignity; Behave with Integrity; and Ensure Competence. These principles obligate the practitioner to implement humane and effective treatment, and to behave in a compassionate and professional manner. While these values have always been at the forefront of the science of ABA, they were not explicitly outlined in prior versions of the Ethics Code. This represents a major advance in the field, and aligns behavior analysis with other allied health professions, who also operate in a framework of overarching ethical obligations.

In terms of information specifically aimed at assessment, the subcode section 2.13 Selecting, Designing, and Implementing Assessments states,

> Before selecting or designing behavior-change interventions behavior analysts select and design assessments that are conceptually consistent with behavioral principles; that are based on scientific evidence; and that best meet the diverse needs, context, and resources of the client and stakeholders. They select, design, and implement assessments with a focus on maximizing benefits and minimizing risk of harm to the client and stakeholders.

This reflects many of the core principles noted (e.g., benefit, dignity, integrity, choice). It also reflects movement within the field to ensure that the practitioner is aware of the evidence-based methods that exist for the assessment/intervention, and selects one based on individual needs and contextual factors.

Other Code sections that ensure professionalism in the context of functional analysis include sections citing the need to uphold the best interests of the client (3.01), to practice only within one's scope of competence (1.05), to be aware of one's personal biases (1.10), and to provide effective treatment (2.01). A notable addition to the information on informed consent (subsection 2.11) is a reference to also attaining assent from the individual themselves. This denotes an increased focus on and support for self-determination of clients.

In addition, the Task List, which outlines all of the skills, abilities, and knowledge objectives associated with mastery of the field's content, also specifies specific content relevant to functional assessment/functional analysis. According to the 5th edition (2020), clinicians need to conduct a functional analysis and interpret FA data (F-8 and F-9). Furthermore, there is an expectation that the FA technology could be extended to assessing performance problems in staff (I-6).

Gap in Practice

Given these strong data, and given the professional consensus and ethical mandate, one would assume that FAs are highly valued and routinely used by practicing behavior analysts. Sadly, this is not the case. Oliver et al. (2015) found that close to half of behavior analysts surveyed reported that they did not use FA procedures. There appears to be a gap between what the professional literature and the governing professional organizations have concluded about the need for using this technology and the skill set of the everyday behavior analyst in practice.

Furthermore, the ways in which FA are used may have associated ethical risks. The following hypothetical cases reflect some areas of concern/danger that clinicians may encounter.

Scenarios

Joe is a behavior analyst working in a residential setting who oversees 54 cases. He often is scrambling to get his work done and spends many days "putting out fires." One day he receives a call about Anna, a 54-year-old woman with developmental disabilities who is refusing to go to program. For the third day in a row, this woman has stayed in bed instead of going to program. The behavior is new and unusual. Joe recalls that Anna has a history of escape motivated behavior, and tells the staff member to prompt Anna to get out of bed and to get to program. Fast forward a month. Anna has continued to refuse to go many places, has lost weight, and had begun sleeping excessively. After a thorough medical evaluation, Joe and staff learn that Anna has a serious illness that has impacted her energy.

Joe has violated several ethical codes here, and has violated best practices. Providing recommendations in the absence of direct observation or a new assessment is not appropriate, especially since the behavior is new. Behavior analysts do not provide plans in the absence of assessments (2.13). In addition, the omission of a medical consultation is a notable problem. Overwhelmed clinicians are still accountable to provide the highest quality interventions, to operate in the best interests of the client, and to ensure effective treatment.

Bob is involved in supervised independent fieldwork. His supervisor has suggested he do a latency-based FA to assess severe aggression. Bob has never done a latency-based FA, and expresses trepidation. His supervisor hands him a couple of articles and a review paper, and tells him to give it a whirl.

Bob's supervisor has engaged in inappropriate delegation of tasks, assigning Bob tasks he is not qualified to do and failing to provide adequate preparation and competency-based training (4.09 and 4.06). This is likely to result in ineffective treatment (2.01). It is also a violation of all of the core principles: benefit others; treat others with compassion, dignity, and respect; behave with integrity; and ensure competence.

Tyler is a 23-year-old man with autism who exhibits severe self-injury. The behavior analyst (Jeanine) notes that it has been some time since his last FA, and decides to conduct a new one, thinking it may shed new light on function. Jeanine plans a standard FA, despite the voiced concerns of several team members concerned about the level of SIB. Jeanine also does not consult with the nursing team about the FA, about how and whether protective equipment should be used in the FA, and does not invite them to the sessions to provide medical monitoring.

Jeanine has failed to include medical personnel in important elements of this high-risk assessment (2.12). She has also failed to consider the most appropriate format for the assessment, given the characteristics of the learner and the dangers involved, failing to act in the best interests of the client (3.01).

Research Questions

There are many unanswered questions about FA methodologies, as it is an evolving evidence-based practice. It would be interesting to develop the means to identify the function of a challenging behavior and an effective function-based treatment in the absence of an FA. Identifying and training a nuanced skill set in this regard could greatly increase the efficiency of assessment and intervention, leading to significant outcomes sooner. More refined methodologies need to be extended to several continuing challenges, including the identification of functionally equivalent replacement behaviors and the interpretation of confounding FA results. More research on FA interviews, including component analyses and validation studies, is needed. Replication methodologies and extensions are also needed, as well as methods for examining the impact of setting, the sequence of settings used in a phased assessment, and the role of cultural and language issues in FA.

What is a clinician to do?

It is important to consider ethical practice at every stage of assessment and intervention, especially in the realm of challenging behaviors.

1. Obtain written and informed consent for all assessments and all treatments
2. Ensure medical rule-outs, clearance, and monitoring as appropriate
3. Consider the range of FA alternatives and choose the best procedure for the clinical presentation context
4. In training and in supervision, remember the delegation obligations, and ensure that trainees and supervisees are not asked to do procedures that they have not demonstrated competence in. Ensure competence and comfort before expecting independent implementation
5. Stay abreast of research results and developments in clinical guidelines as they relate to the evolving technology of FA. Read the research literature and attend trainings on this topic
6. Ensure that consent is truly informed and that assent is obtained whenever possible
7. Consider the wide range of factors related to decisions in assessment and intervention, including the evidence behind the procedure, contextual factors, and individual needs

Take Home Messages

As delineated in the above section on research questions, the FA technology is impressive, but many elements of its use require skill, training, and analysis. The need for training and supervision in the context of FA is crucial to developing clinicians who can use this powerful technology safely, humanely, effectively, and in a conceptually systematic manner that aligns with the core principles of ABA.

The ethical obligations include the need to assure that clinicians considering its use evaluate whether they possess the skill set or need assistance in planning and implementing the procedures. It is also imperative that medical and safety concerns are considered in planning and in consent/assent, and that a risk-benefit assessment is part of every decision to conduct an FA. Behavior analysts are encouraged to stay abreast of developments in the research literature and in the ethical guidelines that surround the application of these procedures. On individual and organizational levels, behavior analysts must strive to create, nurture, and maintain an ethical culture of assessment and intervention, and to make individualized decisions in the best interest of each and every client.

Works Cited

Allen, K. A., Hart, B., Buell, J. S., Harris, F. R., & Wolf, M. M. (1964). Effects of social reinforcement on isolate behavior of a nursery school child. *Child Development*, *35*, 511–518.

Allyon, T. & Michael, J. (1959). The psychiatric nurse as a behavioral engineer. *Journal of the Experimental Analysis of Behavior*, *2*, 323–334.

Bailey, J. S., & Burch, M. R. (2005). *Ethics for behavior analysts: A practical guide to the Behavior Analyst Certification Board guidelines for responsible conduct.* Mahwah, NJ: Lawrence Erlbaum Associates.

Beaulieu, L., Van Nostrand, M. E., Williams, A. L., & Herscovitch, B. (2018). Incorporating interview-informed functional analyses into practice. *Behavior Analysis in Practice*, *11*, 385–389. https://doi. org/10.1007/s40617-018-0247-7.

Behavior Analyst Certification Board. (2020). *Ethics Code for Behavior Analysts.* Littleton, CO: Behavior Analyst Certification Board.

Behavior Analyst Certification Board (2017). *BCBA/BCaBA 5th Edition Task List.* Littleton, CO: Behavior Analyst Certification Board.

Bijou, S.W., Peterson, R.F., & Ault, M.H. (1968). A method to integrate descriptive and experimental field studies at the level of data and empirical concepts. *Journal of Applied Behavior Analysis*, *1*, 175–191.

Bloom, S. E., Iwata, B. A., Fritz, J. N., Roscoe, E. M., & Carreau, A. B. (2011). Classroom application of a trial-based functional analysis. *Journal of Applied Behavior Analysis*, *44*, 19–31. https://doi.org/10. 1901/jaba.2011.44-19.

Carr, E. G., Newsom, C. D., & Binkoff, J. A. (1976). Escape as a factor in the aggressive behavior of two retarded children. *Journal of Applied Behavior Analysis*, *13*, 101–117.

Carr, E. G. (1994). Emerging themes in the functional analysis of problem behavior. *Journal of Applied Behavior Analysis*, *27*, 393–399.

Cooper, J. O., Heron, T. E., & Heward, W. L. (2007). *Applied behavior analysis.* Upper Saddle River, NJ: Pearson.

Dixon, D.R., Vogel, T., & Tarbox, J. A brief history of functional analysis and applied behavior analysis. In J. L. Matson (ed.), *Functional assessment for challenging behaviors*, pp. 3–24. New York, NY: Springer.

Hanley, G. P. (2010). Prevention and treatment of severe problem behavior. In E. Mayville & J. Mulick (Eds.), *Behavioral foundations of autism intervention* (pp. 233–256). New York, NY: Sloan Publishing.

Hanley, G. P. (2011). Functional analysis. In J. Luiselli (Ed.), *Teaching and behavior support for children and adults with autism spectrum disorder: A "how to" practitioner's guide.* New York, NY: Oxford University Press.

Hanley, G. P., Iwata, B. A., & McCord, B. E. (2003). Functional analysis of problem behavior: a review. *Journal of Applied Behavior Analysis*, *36*(2), 147–185. DOI: 10.1901/jaba.2003.36-147.

Hanley, G.P., Jin, C. S., Vanselow, N.R., & Hanratty, L.A. (2014). Producing meaningful improvements in problem behavior of children with autism via synthesized analyses and treatments. *Journal of Applied Behavior Analysis*, *47*(1), 16–36. https://doi.org/10.1002/jaba.106.

Iwata, B. A., Dorsey, M. F., Slifer, K. J., Bauman, K. E., & Richman, G. S. (1994). Toward a functional analysis of self injury. *Journal of Applied Behavior Analysis, 27*, 197–209. (Reprinted from *Analysis and Intervention in Developmental Disabilities, 2*, 3–20, 1982.)

Iwata, B. A., & Dozier, C. L. (2008). Clinical application of functional analysis methodology. *Functional Analysis Methodology, 1*(1), 3–8.

Jessel, J., Hanley, G. P., & Ghaemmaghami, M. (2020). On the standardization of functional analysis. *Behavior Analysis in Practice, 13*, 205–216.

Lovaas, O. I., & Simmons, J. Q. (1969). Manipulation of self-destructive in three retarded children. *Journal of Applied Behavior Analysis, 2*, 143–157.

Maslow, A. H. (1966). *The psychology of science.* Washington, DC: Gateway Editions.

McCord, B. E., & Neef, N. A. (2005). Leisure items as controls in the attention condition of functional analyses. *Journal of Applied Behavior Analysis, 38*, 417–426. https://doi.org/10.1901/jaba.2005. 116-04.

Najdowski, A. C., Wallace, M. D., Ellsworth, C. L., MacAleese, A. N., & Cleveland, J. M. (2008). Functional analyses and treatment of precursor behavior. *Journal of Applied Behavior Analysis, 41*, 97–105. https://doi.org/10.1901/jaba.2008.41-97.

Northup, J., Wacker, D., Sasso, G., Steege, M., Cigrand, K., Cook, J., & DeRaad, A. (1991). A brief functional analysis of aggressive and alternative behavior in an outclinic setting. *Journal of Applied Behavior Analysis, 24*(3), 509–522.

Oliver, A.C., Pratt, L.A., & Normand, M.P. (2015). A survey of functional behavior assessment methods used by behavior analysts in practice. *Journal of Applied Behavior Analysis, 48*, 817–829. DOI:10.1002/jaba.256.

Skinner B. F. (1965). *Science and human behavior.* New York, NY: Free Press.

Tarbox, J., Wallace, M. D., Tarbox, R. S. F., Landaburu, H. J., & Williams, L. W. (2004). Functional analysis and treatment of low rate behavior in individuals with developmental disabilities. *Behavioral Interventions, 19*, 187–204.

Thomas, D.R., Becker, W.C., & Armstrong, M. (1968). Production and elimination of disruptive classroom behavior by systematically varying teacher behavior. *Journal of Applied Behavior Analysis, 1*, 35–45.

Zarcone, J. R., Rodgers, T. A., Iwata, B. A., Rourke, D. A., & Dorsey, M. F. (1991). Reliability analysis of the Motivation Assessment Scale: a failure to replicate. *Research in Developmental Disabilities, 12*, 349–362.

3.4   "One of the Good NTs"

An Interview with Dr. Peter Gerhardt

Peter Gerhardt

In presentations and workshops, Peter Gerhardt will often explain the meaning of the word "NT" within the autism community, particularly among self-advocates. This abbreviation for "neurotypical" is often considered a tongue-in cheek insult to the neurotypical community, and particular to those who serve individuals with autism. As a behavior analyst with over 30 years of experience working with adolescents and adults with autism spectrum disorder, Dr. Gerhardt has also formed relationships with several adults with autism and proudly says that some have referred to him as "one of the good NTs." In the following interview, we discuss how attempting to be "one of the good NTs" can influence goal selection, shift priorities, and allow for more socially significant and ethical practice.

ANN BEIRNE: So, I want to start off with one question. You have some friends in the self-advocacy community who've referred to you as "one of the good NTs." So, could you explain that description a little bit?

PETER GERHARDT: I think it's because, working with adults for a long period of time, you learn that it's their life. You know, and that it's not about me establishing control. It's about me helping them control their own life. And, you know, respecting that and understanding that. You know, it becomes a partnership when you work with other individuals. Little kids like, you're their teacher. You're the behavior analyst. Me, I have to be, like, one part of their life. You know – help them achieve *their* goals – whether they're high verbal or not verbal at all. I still have to help them figure out their goals. And then my job too, my job to is to put myself out of a job.

AB: Right.

PG: You know, it has to be their life. It has to be what they want. And I think that if you adopt that posture, I think it becomes easy to be one of the "good NTs."

AB: That's the whole secret.

PG: Yeah, it really is. It's not about me. You know, it's about this person. And if you look at the behavior of typical people, it's incredibly crazy. Seriously, I mean just the diversity of behavioral expression of typical people and what we do in private and what we do, like... And then I worry about this person hand flapping? When I need to get him to use the public bathroom? I'd rather get him to use a public bathroom and not worry about hand flapping right now, you know?

AB: Right.

PG: And what's also nice is, I think, at least I know in this area of the country, people know autism. So they don't think, they don't see a kid engaging in stereotypy and think "oh what's that weird kid doing?" They think "oh, he's got autism." And then it's "Oh and he's shopping!"

DOI: 10.4324/9781003190707-23

AB: And you've also talked about – deviating from my written questions here – but you've also talked about how your goal isn't necessarily to have someone indistinguishable from peers but to get them 80% of where they want to be and then society picks up the other 20%. So I guess my question is – what if someone *did* think "hey that kid is weird," are we just going to say that's not the 20% we're going to worry about. We're going to seek out more...

PG: Normally, that's what I do. I think 25% of the typical world out there is great. Wants to help us, in understanding, is supportive. Sometimes they try to help too much. They become almost, like, enablers you know? Fifty percent *wants* to help us but just doesn't know what to do. So they're the ones that we, as professionals, behavior analysts, whatever our role is, have to give them some encouragement and support – we have to shape their behavior in the right way. Twenty-five percent I think are just untrainable, and I just walk away from them. I don't have the time to worry about them. And that still gives me 75% of the population.

AB: And also is this the best use of your time and resources to be an advocate for people who are not willing to meet you part of the way?

PG: Right. Now I've always thought that if the autism community ever got its political act together. You know, take this one out of 54 number or whatever it is, multiply that by two parents, four grandparents, aunts, uncles, teachers, you know, all of us in the field... we're bigger than the NRA.

AB: That's a good point!

PG: We're bigger than the AARP! We would be the biggest advocacy group in the country. You know, we would be the ones who would set the agenda! You know, but we don't do that.

AB: What do you think prevents it?

PG: In the autism world, whether you're a parent or a professional, I think we agree on 90% of the issues, disagree on 10% and then spend 90% of the time fighting about the 10%.

AB: That's actually an incredibly good point.

PG: Yeah, I think we're like, "Well, they're a VB person." Well, they're a behavior analyst. You know? Or "Well, they're a speech path." Like, Skinner never wrote about iPads. So, you need somebody who understands augmentative systems. You know I can find commonality among all these groups. Again it's what I love about – and I've only come kind of recently in effect to this realization – that's what I love about behavior analysis. Because I think it truly is a field that is not about me at all. It is just about this student, this adult, and their data. That's all. You know, Keller said: the student's always right. Skinner said, "The rat's always right,' Keller said, "The student is always right." That's what it is. I don't get to say I'm right or not. He or she will tell me if I'm right.

AB: That's what I say all the time, I say, "Well, they'll tell us if it works."

PG: Yeah, so my ego is out of it. So if I think the fastest way to get this kid to the goal that he or she needs to accomplish is to coordinate with these people who I might disagree with, I'm gonna coordinate with them. Because it's not about my ego. It's just about what this kid needs.

AB: That's so important and one of the questions that I encourage people to ask in this book is, "Is this for the client or is it for me?" That's really the essential question is that you're thinking about is the responsibilities of clients, because it really isn't about us.

PG: No, it's really not. We're a tool. We're a well-researched, highly educated, professional tool but we're still just a tool.

AB: So, another thing that I like to say is that in ABA the "applied" comes before anything else, comes before "behavior," before "analysis"...

PG: Yes, 100%.

AB: So, how do you ensure that your recommendations are socially significant? I know that's a huge interest of yours.

PG: Umm, I don't always. I would love to be able to, but it's very hard because it's time consuming to do it. Some of it is built just on experience. But there are times where we will actually do social validity studies. You know, there's a great article, Montrose Wolf, about social validity, "How behavior analysis found its heart again." You know, and it's not... we're so enamored with *how* we teach that we've forgotten that *what* we teach is equally, is more important. One of my slides in one of my talks is "Independent of how evidence-based your interventions are, teaching the wrong skills well is no better than teaching the right skills poorly." So you could have the most beautifully, clinically appropriate, well-designed intervention, and if you're teaching stupid stuff, who cares?

AB: Right. When I think of all the years that I wasted teaching preschoolers conversational scripts that began with an introduction. And then I realized, not only do my neurotypical kids not do that, but *I never do that.* I never start off meeting someone by saying, "Hi. My name is Ann." I start with some sort of commonality.

PG: There was a study, where they asked employers in terms of social skills what were really important social skills. And then they looked at a large group of IEPS for transitioning kids with autism. And, like, none of them matched. And as a matter of fact, one of the things that employers said is that, you know how we will often teach kids who use an augmentative system to tap someone to get attention? *Don't do that.* In today's society, touching another person without consent is not a good thing. So, if you're walking around and you're tapping people? Like, have a button on their augmentative system that says, "Excuse me?" You know? There are hundreds of other ways, but that's become our sort of "default." And if you look at social validity, that's a really bad skill. So, that's kind of what we need. And I've talked about, when I was working in Manhattan and we asked people at the supermarket, "What's the most important skill for us to teach?" And they basically told us, "Teaching kids to pay quickly." That they didn't care if he was talking to himself, they didn't care if he was engaging in stereotypy, there were some boundaries, but if he paid slowly it screwed up their lives. It slowed them down. The rest, they were like, "Eh, that's just him." I mean of course, this is New York. The definition of appropriate behavior is kind of broad.

AB: If I had a dime for everyone that talked to themselves at the grocery store!

PG: But it was really eye-opening. And so one of the things that we did, we changed the task analysis. Instead of waiting for the cashier to say, "That's 14 dollars," and then take out your debit card, as soon as you put your stuff on the conveyor belt, take out your debit card, and get it ready. And now we're moving into ApplePay with everybody. Because it's easier, it's what everybody's going to be doing. I've spent 20 years of my life teaching kids to swipe their debit cards and then they put chips on them! So now we go to ApplePay, because it's easier, it's consistent, you know? The world is changing in our favor. And so I've spent years on travel training. Well, now we have Uber and we're gonna have self-driving cars. This kid can just, can access, can get an Uber and take it to work, or ten years from now there'll be a car available that's a self-driving car. That sort of stuff is changing and it's hard to keep up with all of the changes that are coming in technology that I think are going to benefit us. That sort of drives them crazy because I always think I'm missing something.

AB: But it is kind of a "champagne problem" because things are going to be so much easier but then the issue is how to we adapt to these...

PG: Right. And it's a different skill set you're gonna need. So how do I figure out how to do these things? Especially now, working out of a school. The one thing that I keep coming back to is the one resource that we don't have enough of. We have BCBAs, we have – you can't swing a cat without hitting a BCBA in New Jersey – we have great special educators, we have speech and language pathologists, we have dedicated parents. We don't have time. Six hours a day for 240 days. Take out a lunch, take out time to use the bathroom, wound down to four and a half hours? It's not a lot of time. To teach you everything they need you know for the rest of your life. You know, that's why our mission now is not – like, I hate – I'm going off on a tangent here but – when schools have missions like "allow our students to achieve their highest potential." Because it's a cop-out. It's like, no matter where the kid goes we say "that's their highest potential." It's like, no... Ours is very operationally defined. Our kids have to graduate, not employable, but employed, 20 hours a week. And our kids have to graduate not just with social skills, but as a member of a social community. Our kids have to graduate, not under *my* stimulus control but under stimulus control of the environment. My kids have to graduate, not with me controlling their behaviors but them being able to manage their behavior across environments. Very clear, very concrete, very operational: *those* are the goals. Not, "he'll achieve his highest potential." Like, what the fuck does that mean?

AB: And it's also so subjective. What I might think that someone's highest potential is not necessarily what *they* think their highest potential is.

PG: So that's the idea, how do I do that? That's the... that's what keeps me up at night now, is how do I do that? Especially when we look at the adult service system, which – resources are significantly less. Personnel tend to be less trained. They also tend to be somewhat more transient. There's much higher turnover ratio in the adult service world. So how do I make sure that this *kid* has all those skills independently and doesn't have to rely on this person being properly trained.

AB: What I've noticed is that – I haven't had a lot of experience in adult services but the experience I do have – that those who work in adult services is very fear-oriented in a lot of ways, like safety. Their own safety is the biggest part of their job that they are concerned about.

PG: Right, as that's a big thing, in terms of the ethics of what we do that our field doesn't talk about. We talk about professional liability issues. But with independence comes risk. And we do five-year plans for parents about their kids starting at the ages of 12, So, okay, 12. At 17 what's he doing? So we have something for them to shoot for. But also at that meeting we have them define what they mean by independence. Because they may think independence means grocery shopping when the staff is ten feet behind them. I think independence means we wait in the van. But if that's what independence is then what are the risks associated with that? And, it's interesting, some of the risks that people come up with that are not – I mean the most common one is, "He's not going to get everything on his shopping list." Well, neither do I.

AB: I almost never do.

PG: Right. Or, "Well, he takes stuff off of the shelves that's not on his list." Right, and that's called a reinforcer selection. He's doing a big preference assessment and that's okay. "Oh, he might open a bag of Doritos and eat them first." Like one out of ten people. As long as you pay for the bag when it's empty, I don't really care. Because independence has to be... we get so hung up on these little things that aren't really risks that we don't even look at the big risks.

AB: What do you think are the big risks in that example?

PG: The big risk in that example is that the individual would go out a door that we don't know about, would wander off the premises without us being aware. That would be the biggest. So now again, how do we address that? Do we address it because is his iPhone now has a tracker on it so that we can sort of see where he is at all these times? There's other ways around it. But I think we really need to have that discussion as professionals, we need to have that discussion with parents. And to extent possible we need to have that discussion with clients. You know, I was just at a meeting this morning and it was "he knows he's not supposed to do that." And I always think, "the best times in my life are when I knew I wasn't supposed to do it." Seriously. What I think of all the stuff that I did that that I knew if I got caught, those were the best. And then we wonder why our kids will do things like that – it's like, because it's fun. Because the reinforcer in the moment is *doing that*. It is not this delayed reinforcer or the knowledge of "I'm not supposed to do it." But we expect them, we hold them to higher standards than we hold ourselves. And we do it all the time. So that's I think a big transition between certainly raising a child and moving more into adolescence – allowing them that kind of freedom. And as a stepmom of neurotypical kids, I was always felt like I had a job to do. If my stepdaughter didn't do her homework, I had to say, "You have to do your homework." She was expected to lie to me about whether or not it was done. Everybody kind of did their jobs. So, but when there is such a clear difference in the amount of power and agency that someone has, are there ways that you can navigate it where that there are still the logically accepted consequences of, "Well, you should've done your homework?"

PG: Well, I think that it's an ongoing process, I really do. And the example that I often use is typical four-year-olds. If people are visiting and one of them goes to the bathroom, it's not unusual that four-year-old to run to the bathroom and see what they're doing. It's curiosity, it's funny, but now we have to think, if a four-year-old on the spectrum does it, "Can we let this become a habit?" Your typical four-year-old will sort of developmentally get out of on their own but I can't allow [this behavior]. So where do I draw this line between saying, "That's typical behavior of a four-year-old but I really shouldn't allow it because I don't want that to be a habit that's going to be much harder to change five years from now."

AB: Also, the typical four-year-old is still going to encounter the consequences of the behaviors that will be, while more casually, targeted for decrease in some way. So grandma will say, "You have to get out of the bathroom and give me some privacy."

PG: I think it's always, "What are the implications of what we are doing?" And then, also for me and this five-year-old that I just sort of made up work with. But it is, it like, how does this play five years from now? And what does he or she need to know five years from now? That's got to be, that's foremost in what we should be doing. And I think that there's also a contradiction there because I think that good behavior analysts are kind of very zen. Because we should be very "in the moment" and we should be analyzing contingencies *as they occur*, you know? And making clinically based evidence-based decisions based upon those data points as they are occurring. But at the same time we have to think long term. So we have this inherent – I think – challenge between doing what's good right now and doing what's good for five years from now. And tying that in with, "But I want to put myself out of a job and I want to do it as soon as possible. And I want him to be happy. And I want him to be employed." And I also have to say, "Well, am I wanting something that he doesn't want?" I keep myself up at night with this stuff because I get tied into knots. Thinking about what is really in the best interest of this person – and not because of me because I want to say "we got all these kids employed." I can do that. I consider contingencies to get all of these kids employed. But if he doesn't want to work there, I haven't improved his life. You know? So, it's really freaking hard is what I'm trying to say.

AB: It is. So, how do you navigate the client preferences, particularly in terms of employment? What sort of considerations do you think about when trying to find the right employment for a particular individual?

PG: I think when we're looking at employment the big question is, "What type of environment and when would this person like to work? In which type of environment would this person like to work?" Secondarily, is then "Doing what?" I think we tend to focus on the "doing what." So we look for the job where he can assemble something, or where he can fold clothes at REI or she can bus tables, or that kind of stuff. For individuals with more challenges, and then for people who are higher verbal, but still it's that "*What* do you do?" The fact is the "where" and "when" are probably more important. We've all had, I've had jobs in behavior analysis for 38 years now. When I would change jobs, it's not because I didn't like *what I did*. I was bored with *where* I was. And so, "Do I like working in the morning? Do I like working at night? Do I like standing up? Do I like sitting down? Do I like music on in the background? If I do like music in the background, what kind of music do I like in the background? Do I like being able to, on my break, buy something there? Do I like having a lot of communication with people? Or do I like kind of being left alone?" Then it's, "Well what am I doing then?" So when we start at 16 bringing kids out, those are the variables that we really start to look at. The work task itself is the easiest freaking thing to teach. Yet we put 90% of our effort there. And folks on the autism spectrum, across the ability spectrum rarely lose jobs because of inabilities to do the work tasks. They lose them for all the social and navigational stuff. That's where they state they're in trouble. But we don't look at those or we look at it in a very checklist sort of way. And I think we've taken a very simplistic approach to social competencies in our field. And I don't think there's a set of skills that are more context-based than social skills. And so if I'm trying to teach you work skills in a classroom, I'm not teaching the right skills, I guarantee it. Like in the old days, when people tried to teach grocery shopping at the fake grocery store in the classroom? Didn't generalize? Shocker. Because none of the skills are even close to what you really have to use. But we do the same thing with social skills without going out and going to REI or some other employer and spending an hour or so there and watching what people actually do. And seeing what the social norms are there. And then coming back and saying, "these are the things we've gotta really work on." So, while she's there we can practice those things but then also when we come back. We've got to get some practice to doing these things so that they become part of our repertoire. But we don't think in those terms. And it always comes back to – I also have to look at their co-workers and how much of the slack are they gonna pick up. Because I'm never – in the time I have – I'm never going to get this kid to be 100% socially competent in this environment.

AB: Do you think that anyone is 100% socially competent in any environment?

PG: No. No. I know I'm not. Are you kidding? Absolutely not! No!

AB: I always say that having children really made it very clear to me the boundaries of my social competence. Particularly initiating social interactions. I still struggle with it.

PG: Right, I talk about myself sometimes. When I do workshops or presentations, people expect me to present in a certain way now. And I have had people come up to me when I didn't curse during a talk and ask me why I didn't. Because that's become expected. But if I was a new professional I could not get away with that. But it's because over the years it's become, my behavior's been shaped in that direction so it's appropriate for me to do it and it's not appropriate for other people to do it. But that's how complex social skills are.

AB: I went to one conference where you talked about the social skills involved in riding an elevator. And all of the rules that you mentioned: putting your back to the back, walking to the back of the elevator, pressing the button and moving to the back of the elevator, and you could only speak to somebody who you would have some sort of common experience with. And this was a conference and – I have to tell you, I'm sure that other people have told you this – the lunch break was right after your talk. And that was the most awkward elevator ride I have ever been on. Because everyone was so hyper-conscious of whether or not we were following those rules.

PG: Right. And on the flipside, because I often do the "urinal rules."

AB: About which urinal to stand in.

PG: I've learned that I do it now every much towards the end of the day when I am not going to have to be in the men's room. Because if I do it earlier, I'll be in the men's room at a urinal and some other guy will come in and take the urinal next to me and start talking to me just to break the rules. And it freaks me out.

AB: That just seems so deliberately combative.

PG: Well, I see, they're trying to be funny, and I get it. So I'm appreciative that they were listening to it. But at the same time, it so violates the norms that it bothers me. I'm like, "there's like four other urinals."

But it's interesting. Those rules really are, to some extent, universal but we don't think about them. I remember that I was an adjunct professor at the time and I recommended the urinal game to one of my students. And, just as a test of social validity, I spoke to my dad, who does not work with this populations and I said, "Try this game out." And he got every answer correct. He was like, "This is fascinating but yeah, there are definitely rules."

Yeah and I think that our non-verbal social repertoire is more important than our verbal repertoire. And that we don't concentrate on at all. Knowing where to sit on your break. Eating neatly. Waiting in line appropriately in the cafeteria. All of those things – and what I mean by "appropriate" you can't cut the line. Those sort of things are the ones that really piss the typical world off. If you violate those *non-verbal* rules. But in our field we tend to focus on social skills as verbal – the greeting skills. They're "Excuse me," they're "Can I help you?" They're those things. They're part of it and they're important but it's much a bigger universe than that.

AB: And the universe is not really generally as polite as we teach – particularly children – to behave. I'm always very suspicious that we're teaching kids to socialize with adults rather than other kids.

PG: 100%. You know, one of the fun things that I have done with the five-year plans with the 12-year-olds is with this one family – his twin sister – fraternal twins, obviously. And we were talking about greeting skills. And I said, "So like 12-year-old boys, do they high-five?" And she went, "Oh, please, no." And I said, "What, do they fist-bump?" and she said, "No." I said, "What do they do?" And she said, "They say hi and they grunt. They punch each other." That's the typical interaction. And the I have to sort this thing about five years down the road.

AB: How do you navigate the context of who you can punch and who you cannot punch?

PG: I think – I always think about five years down the road and I think at some point DSM 6 – I guess or whatever – I think giving a high-five is going to be diagnostically autism/ on the autism spectrum. Because they're the only kids who are taught to do a high fives anymore, are kids with autism. We can pick them out of a crowd, because we can greet people with a high-five. And it's kind of an awkward high-five. Nobody else does it anymore but we continue to do it. That's where we screw up. Well, it's not a screw up. It's just, is this really what we should be doing, that's all.

AB: We talked a little bit about incorporating client preferences and making sure that they have a place, particularly in employment where they really feel comfortable. So how do you incorporate client preferences when the client has a little bit more difficulty communicating? Like clients who may not be vocally verbal?

PG: There's always behavioral indicators that we can look at. Whether it's affect that we can look at, time on task, the rate of production. Even – we have one student right now who we can look at data – willingness to go to work. We have two students who have significant behavior challenges. Both of them, when they're working at actual jobs, have fewer behavioral challenges than when they're with us.

And I think it's because they know they're doing "real stuff." I can't get in their heads, it's all private event stuff. But I can make assumptions that the environment is set up to support this, other people are doing it. They feel like they're part of something real, as opposed to another make-work thing. I think all those things really play into it.

AB: And all the things do affect your productivity.

PG: Yes. In the world of supported employment, if you really get into the SE world. It's like the four Fs: Flowers, Food, Filth, and Filing. Those are supposed to be the "low-hanging" bad jobs. Fast food, horticulture, recycling is filth and cleaning, and filing is office-related stuff, but first of all I'm a believer that none of us – our first jobs, all of our first jobs sucked. That's why you land another job. So, we try that sort of stuff but also if I have someone who loves walking around, you know what? Delivering the mail or collecting the garbage in an office is probably going to be something that they're going to like to do. And is that what I'm trying to do anyway, give them a job that they like to do? And that they find desirable. So, there's this segment of our field that gets kind of elitist. And again, it's not about them, it's about him. And I fully agree. And I fully understand that we've often gone for the low-hanging fruit. And we haven't looked at what real jobs people can do. But I also don't want to discount anything that someone might want to do because, again, it's not about me, it's about him. And if I can find something that he wants to do, my job is done. You know, I don't have to worry about the token system, I don't have to worry about anything. Because he wants to do it.

AB: So, do you think the environment affects that? I'm thinking of one individual I know who does mostly custodial work, which he didn't love, but one of his jobs is at a zoo, which was way more fun because there's all these animals.

PG: And yes, can it be less about the job tasks and more about what you're doing it, and that can be the fun thing. Or just that you work with people who like you and appreciate you, and treat you with respect. And that can be enough for you to keep doing what might typically be a shitty job. But, you know, that's a valuable resource when you can find that sort of stuff. And increasingly we find that. People really want to help, you know. We had a meeting recently with a medical center in the area – I won't say the name – because we want to start having some kids doing job training and internships there. We had the president, we had the director of human resources, we had five VPs of this major medical center, who were meeting with me and our SLE Coordinator. Their combined salaries for this one-hour meeting was probably a year's salary for one of my staff. But that's how important they saw this. And how important do they saw their contribution to the communities. Like being able to offer jobs to our students and then our adults when they graduate out. That's what's been the biggest change that's been enabling us to do a lot of stuff. They can do this and then hiring someone with autism is not just a good PR thing, it's good for your business. You know, you get another reliable employee – I'm going off on another tangent here. But that's where we see change in what we do here. That people reach out to us as often as we reach out to them about the possibilities.

AB: That's amazing. I do want to talk a little about leisure skills and I came here with a bit of an agenda. It's hard to pick my favorite of the stories I've seen you present. But if I had to I would say the one about your client, you worked with a client who only watched *Sesame Street*. Would you mind telling that story a bit?

PG: Well, first of all I think that teaching functional leisure skills is one of the hardest if not the hardest things we do. Because leisure skills by definition have to work for the person. And I think we often end up teaching things that look like leisure but are not leisure. So trying to find stuff that really relaxes the person, that the person enjoys is incredibly, incredibly difficult. But we had an individual who loved – his favorite thing in the world – *Sesame Street* videos. And we tried to pair it with other stuff that was more age appropriate and all these things, and failed miserably. Because he loved [*Sesame Street*]. And we finally – you know dawn comes to Marblehead after a while – we realized that, you know, worst case scenario, this makes him happy. And, good, bad, or indifferent, I sort of equated it to like – it's like his pornography. And we said, "If you're at work and you want to take a break and watch Sesame Street, that's great but watch it on your iPod with your headphones, so it's like a private thing. Don't put it on a big screen." And, once you sort of came to that realization, that we can adapt it so his life is still good, he can have access to what he wants. We don't have to worry about taking – all of a sudden life became so much easier for everybody. You know, do his co-workers know? He works independently. Do his co-workers know? Yeah. But do they care? No. But he also does it in a way that just works for him. I am a comic book geek. Not necessarily the most age-inappropriate behavior, quite honestly. You know, if you look at from a very typical point of view. I read comic books. You'd think I'd have grown beyond that. But you know, don't take it away from me. Because it worked for me.

AB: Yeah, and I think that sort of a privilege of being neurotypical as we get to choose our own leisure skills. I tell that story about the individual who watched *Sesame Street* and your ultimate decision to just say this what he likes.

PG: It's his life.

AB: But I always add to it that there is a museum near where I live, the Museum of Moving Image with a permanent Jim Henson exhibit. It's like a 20minute walk from my house, my family and my children go there all the time and my children are in the minority. It is mostly adults walking around this exhibit. And enjoying, and they may add a level of pretension about like how "I'm really interested in this early avant garde stuff." But we're all there looking at Muppets.

PG: Yes, and you know what I think is interesting? I think culturally the leisure skills of – millennials? I guess what it is now. And I don't mean this negatively but they've regressed. Because, like, they have like these kickball leagues that they play in. And they are really social things. So they like play a game and they drink. But I can get a lot of my students who play kickball involved in that league. And they're going to kick ass because they're going to be sober the whole time. And the example I use is Connect Four. I have never met a person that I worked with who saw Connect Four as a leisure skill. But they are all taught to play it. They never go, "Damn! I want to play Connect Four!" You know, it's just this stupid work task we talked about. Dave and Buster's – this restaurant, the one in Times Square – one entire wall is a Connect Four game. And they have leagues of Connect Four. So, now again, those sorts of things are becoming more and more accessible again because culture is allowing – society is allowing – these things to happen. There is a thing called Foot Golf. There are 289 Foot Golf Courses around the country. They are associated with golf courses. There are only nine holes. But the hole is, like, three feet across and you use a soccer ball. So it's like Frisbee Golf. But it was designed for families to be able to go out and play.

Now, every kid I know can kick a ball. But if I can now get him to kick the ball there but I can also have him drive the golf cart, which would be a lot of fun. While he has a Diet Coke. And I can add all of these things so that – maybe this kicking the ball, which isn't an all that exciting thing but that whole event now becomes fun and it's a low-skill, fun event now. And like I said, there's an American Foot Golf Association. Do you know – this has nothing to do with anything – I was flipping through the channels, two weeks ago and on ESPN there was the United States Invitational Cornhole Tournament. There are people who actually do this professionally. They cross bean-bags at wooden boards with holes in them. So, all of that stuff is out there if I really wanted to try and access it. That's because that's moved down, it's no longer a kids' game anymore. All of this stuff that was kids' games, now adults do them. So, I can try and integrate those sorts of things now. But society's changing in ways that, again, help us and don't hurt us, which is good.

AB: What advice would you give to a clinician who wanted to be "one of the good NTs?"

PG: I think, I would go back first of all to what you said earlier. That ABA is a three-term contingency. And I think that we've become enamored with behavior analysis part and not the applied part. And it's all about applied. And if you look at the seven dimensions: the number one is socially significant behavior change. And then the last one is interventions designed to continue it after intervention has terminated, so we're looking at generalization and maintenance. If you want to want to one of "the good NTs," look at socially significant behavior change, based upon that person's environment, that person's culture, that person's goals. And then come up with ways to get yourself out of the picture. You know, of the seven things that we're supposed to do, we're not really good at least two of them.

So I think if you can do that, that's the movement to the right direction. The other thing that I think – and it took me a really, really long time to get more comfortable with this. Don't be afraid to fail. A lot of the stuff that we try to teach, that we develop interventions for, there is nothing in the literature about. We just got some grant money to do a protocol and to study, we're working on sort of a manual, on women's health care issues and in autism. Because there's nothing out there and so our role is really to teach girls with classic autism to have a gynecological exam. There's nothing out there about this. And this is something that I think is so important for typical women, but nobody has thought about this for people on the spectrum? You know, why is that? You know that we work with kids, with our young adults who buy their own clothes. We don't somebody pick them out for them. Because, you know, that's how life should be. You've probably heard me say it when I do the sexuality talk. The one thing I know about women, for sure, is that when it comes to feminine hygiene products everyone has a very particular choice. And if it's on the shopping list and I get sent to the grocery store, that is a no-substitution thing on that list. If it says Tampax Pearls, I cannot come back with OB. That's a choice that so important to typical women. Do we ever think about it for women on the spectrum? I don't even know how we would do it. I have no idea. I have no claim to knowledge there. But those are the questions that we need start asking. If we really want, at the end of the day, if we want our goal to be quality of life. It is why *can't* we do this for him? Why can't we do this for her? And I think we use the terminology correctly. I like the word "client." Because I work for them. I'm the hired gun. And I think that, if you realize that, it's very humbling. But you also get overwhelmed by the importance of what we really want to do.

AB: I usually describe it as – I sang opera for many years – and so I'll describe the relationship to people by saying: "In operas – like when the Met hires a director – the director comes in and says, 'I want horses going down the stage, I want flames coming out here or I want white, red whatever.' And the stage hands sit down and say, 'Okay. How are we going to do that?'" Then I clarify like, "You're the director, and I'm the stage hand."

PG: Right, I think that's a great way to put it. I really do. It is *his* life. And how do I do it so that when he or she is 21, it's a good life. But this process keeps going on until his 70s, 80s, and 90s. And we know nothing about that. And that's where I think we need to – we have a truly amazing field of behavior analysis that it is incredibly broad and incredibly rich in resources and evidence. But we've only scratched the surface as to how we apply it to folks on the spectrum. There's so much more to figure out and that's the beauty of the field. You know, you're ever done. In this field, you are never, ever, ever done. It's really annoying. But it's what keeps me coming back. There's always a next step, there's always a next step.

Works Cited

Ahrens, E. N., Lerman, D. C., Kodak, T., Worsdell, A. S., Keegan, C. (2011). Further evaluation of response interruption and redirection as treatment for stereotypic behavior. *Journal of Applied Behavior Analysis, 44*, 95–108.

Alwell, M., Hunt, P., Goetz, L., & Sailor, W. (1989). Teaching generalized communicative behaviors within interrupted behavior chain contexts. *Journal of the Association for Persons with Severe Handicaps, 14*(2), 91–100.

Artoni, S., Bastiani, L., Buzzi, M. C., et al. (2018). Technology-enhanced ABA intervention in children with autism: a pilot study. *Universal Access in the Information Society, 17*, 191.

Baer, D. M., Wolf, M. M., & Risley, T. R. (1968). Some current dimensions of applied behavior analysis 1. *Journal of Applied Behavior Analysis, 1*(1), 91–97.

Bannerman, D. J., Sheldon, J. B., Sherman, J. A., & Harchik, A. E. (1990). Balancing the right to habilitation with the right to personal liberties: the rights of people with developmental disabilities to eat too many doughnuts and take a nap. *Journal of Applied Behavior Analysis, 23*(1), 79–89.

Baron-Cohen, S. (2017). Editorial Perspective: Neurodiversity – a revolutionary concept for autism and psychiatry. *Journal of Child Psychology and Psychiatry, 58*(6), 744–747.

Cassella, M. D., Sidener, T. M., Sidener, D. W., & Progar, P. R. (2011). Response interruption and redirection for vocal stereotypy in children with autism: a systematic replication. *Journal of Applied Behavior Analysis, 44*(1), 169–173.

Cooper, J. O., Heron, T. E., & Heward, W. L. (2007). *Applied behavior analysis.* Upper Saddle River, NJ: Pearson.

Devlin, S., Healy, O., Leader, G., & Hughes, B. M. (2011). Comparison of behavioral intervention and sensory-integration therapy in the treatment of challenging behavior. *Journal of Autism and Developmental Disorders, 41*(10), 1303–1320.

Frost, L., & Bondy, A. (2002). *The picture exchange communication system training manual.* Newark, DE: Pyramid Educational Products, Incorporated.

Lovaas, O. I. (1987). Behavioral treatment and normal educational and intellectual functioning in young autistic children. *Journal of Consulting and Clinical Psychology, 55*(1), 3.

Morgan, R. L. (1989). Judgments of restrictiveness, social acceptability, and usage: review of research on procedures to decrease behavior. *American Journal of Mental Retardation, 94*, 121.

O'Neil, J., & Conzemius, A. (2006). *The power of SMART goals: using goals to improve student learning.* Bloomington, IN: Solution Tree Press.

Parsons, M. B., Reid, D. H., Bentley, E., et al. (2012). Identifying indices of happiness and unhappiness among adults with autism: potential targets for behavioral assessment and intervention. *Behavior Analysis in Practice, 5*, 15.

Wolf, M. M. (1978). Social validity: the case for subjective measurement or how applied behavior analysis is finding its heart. *Journal of Applied Behavior Analysis, 11*(2), 203–214.

3.5 Ethics and Social Validity
Considering Neurodiversity in Intervention is Essential

Joy Johnson

Personal Experience

I am Autistic. As a child, my Autistic identity and relative neurodiversity were wholly ignored and not addressed in my therapeutic experience. This left me initially ignorant and unequipped to navigate society as my authentic self. All behavior change programs that are ethical, culturally responsive, and effective must also address Autistic culture and neurodiversity. I had to rely on trial-and-error and punishment contingencies in my environment to learn that my social and behavioral differences often serve as the first introduction and means of analysis that the public has of me. Inevitably the explicit and implicit biases largely present in current society shape the subsequent responses I am likely to receive from others. Ignoring this is culturally unresponsive and dismissive of how neurodiversity impacts social experiences in current society. Not understanding what being Autistic in society meant for me not only put my safety at risk, but robbed me of self-awareness, an ability to be authentic, and delayed realization of my potential. In neglecting to consider neurodiversity, my differences were equated to inferiority to the neurotypical population based on norms and a flawed, biased concept of social significance. The unintended but still present promotion of suppressed/ignored autistic self-identity led to internalized ableism, low self-esteem, masking (acting allistic to contact social reinforcement), mastering inauthenticity, and a lack of self-awareness. The outcome of my interventions resulted in trauma and emotional harm, which ironically required the pursuit of recovery as an adult. To insinuate Autistic people need to be recovered is an ableist notion that being different equates to being inferior. We are not stricken with an illness or disease; we are simply different. This also goes against neurodiversity, implying that neurodivergent norms are inferior to neurotypical norms.

The psychological conditioning of Autistic people to believe they are inferior and need to mimic neurotypical standards results in masking or camouflaging not "recovery." Masking and camouflaging is simply a life of pretending to be what you are not. Research has proven that long term masking and camouflaging results in severe negative consequences affecting individuals' mental health, self-perception, access to support, thwarted belongingness, and/or lifetime suicidality (Cage et al., 2018; Cassidy et al., 2020; Hull et al., 2017; Lawson et al., 2020; Nordyke et al., 1977). What we (Autistics) need is support in learning how to navigate the world as our authentic selves while learning how to address our challenges and access our strengths.

My personal experiences have taught me that Autistic people should not be held to neurotypical norms but rather to those of their own community. Our behavioral differences should not always automatically be pathologized or presumed as social deficits, as this dismisses our Autistic identity and neurodiversity. Our behaviors need to be assessed in a manner that respects, considers, and includes neurodiversity as a part of society and over time this will generalize and promote acceptance within societal norms. Although noncompliant

DOI: 10.4324/9781003190707-24

to neurotypical norms, certain behaviors we engage in may simply represent an adaptive form of compensatory communication, biological needs, or regulation that is essential to our well-being and identity. Furthermore, if these behaviors are not harmful, do not interfere with our quality of life, and in fact, benefit us from our perspective, they should not be targeted for reduction or replacement. It is essential that BCBAs consider neurodiversity and ensure that they work collaboratively with the parents and the clients that they serve. We (Autistic people) should not be passive recipients but rather active leads in our therapeutic experiences. Not only is this more likely to decrease any harm but it also exemplifies ideal measures of social validity and limits treatment biases from a learning history that is based on the experiences of a neurotypical ABA practitioner. By allowing us, Autistic people, the consumers directly impacted by interventions, to be valued as the primary stakeholder, the outcome will be a behavior change program that is culturally responsive, socially significant, and promotes autistic self-worth and autonomy by having the client guide intervention.

Social Validity

Social validity is an essential component of applied behavior analysis that denotes social importance of the intervention and social significance of behaviors to be targeted for intervention for stakeholders impacted directly (the individual) and indirectly (Callahan et al., 2017; Carter & Wheeler, 2019; Snodgrass et al., 2018; Wolf, 1978). Social significance is measured both objectively and subjectively by the social acceptability of the behavior (Callahan et al., 2017; Carter & Wheeler, 2019; Leko, 2014; Snodgrass et al., 2018). Historically, behaviors innate to Autistic community members have been deemed socially significant and thus targeted for behavior reduction due to nonconformity to neurotypical norms. This is typically due to: unusual appearance, perceived disruption, discomfort by others, potential interference with social engagement due to stigmas associated with these behaviors, and other perceived adverse repercussions on the individual's social integration (Chebli et al., 2016; Cunningham & Schreibman, 2009; McLaughlin & Fleury, 2018). Social validity is often taken via questionnaire or an alternative indirect assessment based on the views of caregivers, family members, clinicians, and societal norms. However, involving the actual client receiving services is essential in achieving effective, ethical, and culturally sound practices and having informed social validity data (Ness et al., 2018). The individual receiving services is always the primary stakeholder; however, a client's age (a child) or magnitude of their disability (cognitive impairment or non-vocal) may render them unable to provide feedback (Chebli et al., 2016; McLaughlin & Fleury, 2018). Frequently this results in the objective and subjective assessments relative to social validity left to the views of others (Chebli et al., 2016; McLaughlin & Fleury, 2018). This is why meaningful engagement with clients and the consideration of neurodiversity is essential to ensure that there are effective, ethical, and socially valid intervention outcomes (Ness et al., 2018). Meaningful engagement of the target population (e.g., Autistics) representing the consumer and stakeholders may not only serve to represent those that are unable to represent themselves (due to age or disability), but also serve as a vital resource and vehicle to transferring necessary knowledge into practice (Ness et al., 2018). For BCBAs, this is also a crucial component needed to enable more ethical practices and policies relative to effective implementation of interventions (Ness et al., 2018).

The Autistic Community

The general consensus amongst Autistic adults is that targeting non-harmful atypical behaviors is ableist and dismisses neurodiversity (Hull et al., 2017; Kapp et al., 2019). Specifically, the Autistic community largely reports perceptions of being disregarded as key stakeholders (Hull et al., 2017; Kapp et al., 2019). This negatively impacts buy-in within the Autistic community resulting in the population largely objecting to ABA, reporting experiences of perceived abuse/trauma in treatment settings, perceived forced allistic (neurotypical) dominance, and unethical disregard for the Autistic community (Hull et al., 2017; Kapp et al., 2019).

Neurodiversity

The promotion of neurodiversity is becoming an increasingly relevant concern in today's society (Pantazakos, 2019; Pellicano, Dinsmore, & Charman, 2014). The promotion of neurodiversity dictates that not only are social norms changing but research is also required to serve as an agent for further change (Pantazakos, 2019; Pellicano et al., 2014). Ultimately, in order to successfully achieve and support an inclusive society, BCBAs need to refer to and researchers need to pursue empirically valued undertakings that will both facilitate and support such in treatment settings and society in general (Pellicano et al., 2014).

Interventions and Research Moving Forward

In addition to BCBAs ensuring that they work collaboratively with parents and clients which they serve, existing and future qualitative research can be used to effectively explore and gain a comprehensive understanding of phenomena surrounding opinions, perspectives, and/or values (Edmonds & Kennedy, 2016; Leko, 2014; Regnault et al., 2018). Furthermore, quantitative research can be used to quantify answers to research problems through data analysis and statistical validation of the results (Campbell & Stanley, 1963; Edmonds & Kennedy, 2016; Regnault et al., 2018). Mixed methods research represents an experiment which utilizes both quantitative and qualitative methods (Lopez-Fernandez & Molina-Azorin, 2011; Schoonenboom & Johnson, 2017). Moreover, it is this author's opinion that given the nature of neurodiversity, mixed methods research provides an access to meaningfully engage Autistic community members; ensuring that the findings are both grounded in experiences, authentic, with both social and statistical validity. Although additional research is needed, existing qualitative methods coupled with descriptive and inferential statistics provided by quantitative methods already systematically, comprehensively, and affirmatively support that neurodiversity is relevant to inform interventions (Heydarian, 2016; Leko, 2014; Regnault et al., 2018).

Conclusion

It is essential that interventionists who work with the Autistic population listen to members of the Autistic community in an effort to overcome implicit bias related to ableism. If not, the practitioner runs the risk of providing a program that is ill-informed, socially invalid, and unethical, which may result in a focus on behavior change initiatives that are inconsequential to the client at the expense of targets that could be of greater intrinsic or social value to the client (Hull et al., 2017; Kapp et al., 2019; Pantazakos, 2019; Pellicano et al., 2014). The overall lack of consideration negatively impacts assent, autistic autonomy, and social validity (Callahan et al., 2017). The consideration of neurodiversity is and should remain a primary ethical concern to BCBAs and should be a focus in research and intervention along with efforts towards the potential reframing of social validity that promotes neurodiversity, inclusion, and self-determination (Callahan et al., 2017; Hull et al., 2017; Kapp et al., 2019). Finally, in framing these efforts, BCBAs must acknowledge that considering neurodiversity is essential to effective, ethical, and socially valid interventions.

Works Cited

Boyd, B. A., McDonough, S. G., & Bodfish, J. W. (2012). Evidence-based behavioral interventions for repetitive behaviors in autism. *Journal of Autism and Developmental Disorders, 42*(6), 1236–1248.

Cage, E., Di Monaco, J., & Newell, V. (2018). Experiences of autism acceptance and mental health in autistic adults. *Journal of Autism and Developmental Disorders, 48*(2), 473–484.

Callahan, K., Hughes, H. L., Mehta, S., Toussaint, K. A., Nichols, S. M., Ma, P. S., Kutlu, M., & Wang, H.-T. (2017). Social validity of evidence-based practices and emerging interventions in autism. *Focus on Autism and Other Developmental Disabilities, 32*(3), 188–197. https://doi.org/10.1177/1088357616632446.

Campbell, D. T., & Stanley, J. C. (1963). *Experimental and quasi-experimental designs for research.* New York: Houghton Mifflin Co.

Carter, S. L., & Wheeler, J. J. (2019). *The social validity manual: Subjective evaluation of interventions* (2nd ed.). London: Academic Press.

Cassidy, S. A., Gould, K., Townsend, E., Pelton, M., Robertson, A. E., & Rodgers, J. (2020). Is camouflaging autistic traits associated with suicidal thoughts and behaviours? Expanding the interpersonal psychological theory of suicide in an undergraduate student sample. *Journal of autism and developmental disorders, 50*(10), 3638–3648.

Chebli, S. S., Martin, V., & Lanovaz, M. J. (2016). Prevalence of stereotypy in individuals with developmental disabilities: a systematic review. *Review Journal of Autism and Developmental Disorders, 3*(2), 107–118.

Cunningham, A. B., & Schreibman, L. (2008). Stereotypy in autism: the importance of function. *Research in Autism Spectrum Disorders, 2*(3), 469–479. https://doi.org/10.1016/j.rasd.2007.09.006.

Edmonds, W. A., & Kennedy, T. D. (2016). *An applied guide to research designs: Quantitative, qualitative, and mixed methods.* New York, NY: Sage.

Heydarian, N. (2016). Developing theory with the grounded-theory approach and thematic analysis. *Observer, 29*(4), 38–39.

Hull, L., Petrides, K. V., Allison, C., Smith, P., Baron-Cohen, S., Lai, M., & Mandy, W. (2017). Putting on my best normal: social camouflaging in adults with autism spectrum conditions. *Journal of Autism and Developmental Disorders, 47*(8), 2519–2534. doi:10.1007/s10803-017-3166-5.

Kapp, S. K., Steward, R., Crane, L., Elliott, D., Elphick, C., Pellicano, E., & Russell, G. (2019). People should be allowed to do what they like: autistic adults' views and experiences of stimming. *Autism, 23*(7), 1782–1792. doi:10.1177/1362361319829628.

Lawson, W. B. (2020). Adaptive morphing and coping with social threat in autism: an autistic perspective. *Journal of Intellectual Disability-Diagnosis and Treatment, 8*(3), 519–526.

Leko, M. M. (2014). The value of qualitative methods in social validity research. *Remedial and Special Education, 35*(5), 275–286. doi:10.1177/074193251452400.

Lopez-Fernandez, O., & Molina-Azorin, J. F. (2011). The use of mixed methods research in the field of behavioural sciences. *Quality & Quantity, 45*(6), 1459–1472. https://doi.org/10.1007/s11135-011-9543-9.

McLaughlin, A., & Fleury, V. P. (2018). Flapping, spinning, rocking, and other repetitive behaviors: intervening with young children who engage in stereotypy. *Young Exceptional Children,* 1096250618798338.

Ness, E., Arne, G., Asperanden, E., & Kyrrestad, R. (2018). Meaningful stakeholder involvement: lessons learned from cross-disciplinary and cross sectional intervention research. *European Journal of Public Health, 28.*

Nordyke, N. S., Baer, D. M., Etzel, B. C., & LeBlanc, J. M. (1977). Implications of the stereotyping and modification of sex role. *Journal of Applied Behavior Analysis, 10*(3), 553– 557. https://doi.org/10.1901/jaba.1977.10-553.

Pantazakos, T. (2019). Treatment for whom? Towards a phenomenological resolution of controversy within autism treatment. Studies in History and Philosophy of Science Part C: *Studies in History and Philosophy of Biological and Biomedical Sciences, 77,* 101–176.

Pellicano, E., Dinsmore, A., & Charman, T. (2014). What should autism research focus upon? Community views and priorities from the United Kingdom. *Autism, 18*(7), 756–770. https://doi.org/10.1177/1362361314529627.

Regnault, A., Willgoss, T., & Barbic, S. (2018). Towards the use of mixed methods inquiry as best practice in health outcomes research. *Journal of Patient-reported Outcomes, 2*(1), 1–4.

Schoonenboom, J., & Johnson, R. B. (2017). How to construct a mixed methods research design. *Kolner Zeitschrift fur Soziologie und Sozialpsychologie, 69*(Suppl 2), 107–131. https://doi.org/10.1007/s11577-017-0454-1.

Snodgrass, M. R., Chung, M. Y., Meadan, H., & Halle, J. W. (2018). Social validity in single-case research: a systematic literature review of prevalence and application. *Research in Developmental Disabilities, 74*, 160–173. doi:10.1016/j.ridd.2018.01.007.

Wolf, M. M. (1978). Social validity: the case for subjective measurement or how applied behavior analysis is finding its heart. *Journal of Applied Behavior Analysis, 11*, 203–214.

3.6 The New Professional and Ethical Compliance Code for Behavior Analysts

An Opportunity for Renewed Commitment to Promoting Functional Communication

Tamara S. Kasper

"This is the perfect link between what speech-language pathologists recognize is essential for children with autism... capturing motivation and using it to establish functional communication... and the precise teaching procedures that children with autism require in order to learn and to learn relatively quickly."

This was the thought that inspired me the first time I attended a lecture by Dr. Vincent J. Carbone, BCBA-D. I clearly remember the surge of adrenaline that I experienced when I witnessed the solutions and strategies that the field of applied behavior analysis (ABA) provides to overcome many of the barriers that are encountered in teaching functional communication to children with autism spectrum disorders. I was incredulous that these procedures were not routinely included in the preparation to become a speech-language pathologist – the profession with a primary goal of establishing and improving communication. Since attending that lecture 25 years ago, I have devoted my life to being a "code switcher" between the fields of speech-language pathology and applied behavior analysis. I strive to educate other speech-language pathologists (SLPs) using terminology and examples that will resonate and inspire them to incorporate these elegant procedures into their daily practice. Further, I endeavor to educate behavior analysts about the unique knowledge and skills that speech-language pathologists bring to the instructional table. Initially, I was confident that my role as "code switcher" would be short-lived. The use of these ABA-based procedures was so clearly the ethical and evidence-based practice that both the Professional and Ethical Compliance Code for Behavior Analysts and the American Speech-Language-Hearing Association (ASHA) Code of Ethics mandate, that I assumed the teaching procedures would be routinely adopted in both fields within a few years. This, however, was not the case. My role continues and the New Code for BCBAs and the advent of ethics credit requirements for speech-language pathologists have provided a new platform to renew the mutual commitment in both fields to promote functional communication.

As a dually certified SLP and BCBA, I have had the unique opportunity to consult on challenging cases all over the world. In Ethiopia, I witnessed first-hand, in an environment free of confounding variables, the life-changing effect that teaching procedures from our field could achieve in 10 days. Children who had no form of communication at the beginning of our stay were vocally requesting at the end of our visit. Witnessing this

DOI: 10.4324/9781003190707-25

transformation from children who had no method to communicate wants and needs to children who could mand – ask for water, popcorn, a plate to spin, a rock to throw in a puddle, or a hug from their mother was incredible and inspiring! One would think that these situations in which children have received no instruction in functional communication would be limited to countries that have such limited access to ABA services, but unfortunately, this is not so. I recently encountered a teenager who, according to records review, had received years of intensive ABA programming, but had no functional communication system. I am happy to say that this client now mands vocally with three- to five-word utterances. I hope that these situations are few and far between, but with the recent dramatic growth of our field, I am uncertain. I remain incredibly gratified and honored when BCBAs or SLPs seek my assistance when experiencing barriers in establishing a functional communication system. This is, in fact, the ethical behavior directed by both ethical codes – consulting appropriate professionals when assistance is needed. It is especially relevant when the skill to be remedied is one that enhances the life of the client and his family. The right to convey basic wants and needs and refuse undesired objects, actions and events is a fundamental form of self-advocacy. It is a core principle upon which the Code of Ethics for Behavior Analysts was formed: respecting and actively promoting clients' self-determination. Every individual with an autism spectrum disorder or other developmental disability has a right to instruction in a functional communication system that is carefully selected and taught with technological precision and sufficient frequency that data collection reveals effectiveness. The functional communication system must be maintained and generalized across all the relevant individuals and environments within which the individual operates in order to fulfill our obligation as behavior analysts to provide socially significant change. Further, functional communication training (FCT) is one of the most common and effective interventions for severe behavior problems. (This topic is beyond the scope of this essay.) For the purpose of this essay, I will focus on the BCBA's ethical obligation to establish a functional communication system for all clients. The challenges to establishing a functional communication system share some common themes and the solutions are often available within the field of behavior analysis. I will highlight some of these issues and potential responses based on our ethical codes.

"He doesn't really need to communicate"

This statement usually indicates that a child has a very limited reinforcer pool and that he has free access to those items most of the time. It may also indicate that instructors are afraid to remove those reinforcers due to problem behavior or that the individual was too large to motivate to do anything outside of their usual routine. It also conveys little belief in the ability of the client to attain any independence. It is often related to the next concern.

"He doesn't have any/enough reinforcers"

Careful examination of situations in which the two previous statements are made may indicate that the client has no method of declaring motivation (I've had clients with autism who were blind and didn't ambulate toward preferred items). The client may have a limited number of preferences or appear to have a limited number of preferences due to a skill deficit in choosing between items. It is possible that the instructor or teaching environment signals worsening conditions (Conditioned Motivating Operation Reflexive CMO-R) and the client avoids instructors or engages in problem behavior when an attempt is made to teach a communication system. It is possible that reinforcers were killed by increase in response effort or overuse of a small number of (usually edible) reinforcers. Physical touch by the instructor may also be a conditioned aversive.

Teaching procedures to minimize these barriers exist within the field of ABA. ABA shaping and prompting procedures can be used to shape subtle declarations of MO and increase their frequency. Additional reinforcers can be identified through sensory matching or shaped from behaviors maintained by automatic reinforcement. For example, spitting on the family picture window can be replaced with spraying water on the window and then placing foam puzzle pieces on the window. Gradually the activity is shifted to a mirror next to the window and the puzzle pieces are being selected from the puzzle and replaced in the puzzle after the activity is complete. New reinforcing toys/activities can be conditioned through stimulus-stimulus pairing and direct reinforcement, created by using and interrupting behavioral chains, and conditioned or identified by providing direct instruction in manipulation of novel toys and activities. Instructors can be paired with reinforcement, so that clients will readily approach them to receive reinforcers. Environments can be contrived in which reinforcers are initially readily available via adults and then response effort systematically increased to maintain the value of a reinforcer to ensure that prompting of a communication system is feasible. Physical touch can be paired with reinforcement so that prompts to use a communication system can be tolerated. Use of these procedures is essential to our ethical responsibility to our clients to support their rights, maximize benefits, and do no harm.

"He is prompt dependent" aka "He can talk, but he just refuses"

Prompt dependency is an instructional problem rather than a learner problem. It is related to failure to fade prompts, lack of sufficient training trials and/or failure to contrive sufficient motivation. If we address these variables by identifying additional reinforcers and contriving more training trials, independent manding is possible. Further, careful analysis of the type and topography of prompts is needed so that unnecessary verbal prompts or an arbitrary number of prompts at each level are not being utilized unnecessarily. Pat McGreevy, Vince Carbone, and others strongly advocate against the use of arbitrary prompting hierarchies and suggest that prompts be faded as quickly as possible. Analysis of variables that may be impeding progress is inherent in our continual evaluation of behavior-change intervention and appropriate modification dictated by the ethical code.

"He used to communicate vocally/with sign language, but he's gotten really sloppy and no one can understand him"

When staff come to me with this concern, I usually say "Who's gotten sloppy?" Behavior analysts have the technology to differentially reinforce and maintain intelligible topographies for verbal vocal communicators and those who communicate with sign language or sign plus vocalization. It is essential that all the members of a child's team have knowledge of the target vocal or sign approximation and a prompt that reliably evokes that approximation so that it can be prompted consistently, reinforced differentially, and maintained. This can be accomplished with digital photos, digital movies of teaching procedures/topographies or audio bytes of the best approximations and calibration of team members in terms of prompting and fading of prompts. Often with clients with speech production issues, behavior analysts can provide technically precise teaching strategies and SLPs can be consulted or relied upon to shape initial vocal targets and specify appropriate sound and syllable sequences for instruction. The SLP can provide or facilitate strategies to improve and maintain correct articulation. Together, behavior analysts and SLPs have the technology to shape and maintain these vital skills. We have an ethical obligation to work together to achieve this goal.

"He used to communicate with his speech generating device, but he doesn't use it anymore"

"She uses an app on her iPad for her structured teaching, but she doesn't use it to communicate"

"His parents don't let him use his speech generating device at home because they are afraid he will break it again"

"I'm not sure if his parents know how to use the system"

"He uses PECs at school, sign language during therapy, and I'm not sure how he communicates at home"

One foundational principle of the Ethical Code is that BCBAs work to collaborate with others effectively and respectfully in the best interest of our client. In the actual quotes above, one can easily identify the need to adhere to subsection 2.09 involving clients and stakeholders in selecting and designing interventions. A communication system must be selected in collaboration with parents and other relevant parties to identify a communication response topography that takes into account current evidence of effectiveness, social recognition of the response, likely speed of response acquisition, and the ability to promote generalization beyond the initial teaching conditions. When barriers to generalization arise, we have an obligation to address conditions that interfere with service delivery or generalization (2.14).

As a dually certified speech-language pathologist and behavior analyst, I am often called upon to consult on cases in which promoting a functional communication system is clearly challenging, but is essential in positively impacting the lives of the client and stakeholders. The Ethics Code for Behavior Analysts, in effect January 1, 2022, provides ample reiteration of our obligation as behavior analysts to meet this most essential need. The ethical decision-making processes in meeting the communicative needs of our clients are interspersed throughout the Ethics Code for Behavior Analysts, including the core principles upon which the Ethics Code was established. As the new Ethics Code comes into effect, let's take advantage of the opportunity to renew our commitment to collaborate and cooperate to ensure an effective and sustainable communication system for every client we treat.

3.7 The "Good" Life

An Interview with Dr. Todd May

Todd May

ANN BEIRNE: Thank you so much for meeting with me.

TODD MAY: Thanks for inviting me. I know that you wrote an ethics textbook relative to working with autism and Asperger's.

AB: Yes.

TM: When I was 16 and 17 and 18 I counselored at a camp for kids with autism, this is many decades ago. I worked with kids who were severely autistic. It was one of the few camps that did this. It was a sleep away camp. it was called Camp Ramapo.

AB: I was going to ask you if it was Ramapo. I worked at a day camp.

TM: I worked at Ramapo for three years as a counselor and I was in psychology, but I started to read critiques of psychology. And I thought, "You know I'm winding up putting people back into a system that I want to question." So I sort of veered off into philosophy and I do political organizing and things like that.

AB: That's amazing! So that kind of brings me – that's a great jumping off point. For people in the helping professions, and particularly for people in my field, in behavior analysis, we have a very strict – it's written by behavior analysts, it's very behavior specific, is what I'm trying to say. It's an [Ethics Code]. And it's very rules-oriented, there's a lot about what we're supposed to do, what we're not supposed to do. And navigating that within our own moral framework can be a little bit challenging. So for people within helping fields in general, what do you think is a school of philosophy that helps us to navigate what we're supposed to do according to the rules, but also all these contextual variables that get in the way of sometimes doing the right thing, but also within the rules, does that make sense?

TM: Yeah. Let me offer, I guess, four different ways of looking. Some of which may be more relevant and some will be less. There are three main schools of thought in Western ethics. One of them comes from Aristotle, it's called virtue ethics. The idea is that you develop certain characteristics or qualities that you then express. So moral development is a matter of becoming a certain kind of person. Now, modern moral philosophy, before the return of virtue ethics, which now has become very big. But for several hundred years, that was neglected. And in modern moral philosophy there were two competing views. One was utilitarianism, and that was the view that you ought to act to cause the best overall outcome.

AB: For others, you mean? Because I remember in one of your videos you explained how it's pleasure vs pain. So when we're talking about utilitarian outcomes is it good for others?

TM: I would say it's "good" all around. It's not altruistic. You don't have to sacrifice yourself. But you also don't count any more than anybody else.

AB: But no less.

DOI: 10.4324/9781003190707-26

TM: No more and no less. But different utilitarians will have different views of what the "good" is that you're supposed to promote the most of. And we get into that if you like. But the other main strain of moral thought was deontology, particularly Kant. And it has to do, not with consequence but with intentions. And so you act in such a way, as Kant put it, act in such a way that if everybody acted that way, that would be a good world. So it has to do with your intentions rather than the outcomes. But there's another view. And the reason I bring this up – although it's not one of the standard three – I think it might be more relevant for you. A development of care ethics. As a psychologist you probably know Carol Gilligan's work.

AB: I'm not familiar with Carol Gilligan's work.

TM: She did a book, *In A Different Voice*. The psychological theory of moral development, one of the main ones early on was Lawrence Colburn. Colburn's view was that people develop through six stages up through abstract moral principles. Gilligan challenged that on the basis of her work with women and said that for women, their experience of morality has less to do with abstract principles and more to do with the kind of caring relationships they have with those around them. So a recent theory or set of theories have emerged called care ethics. And in care ethics the idea is to work less on principles. So if you think for Kant there's a certain principle you work on, for utilitarian the principle is "cause the most good." As to try to develop a relationship of caring that can then be extended in a broader way. So out of feminist thought care ethics has become more significant. Although, again, it's not a leading theory. But when we talk about issues of the helping profession it's probably one that's worth looking at.

AB: So you mentioned that virtue ethics is becoming more talked about. Why do you suppose that is?

TM: Well, the main two modern moral theories focused on how one should act. So as a utilitarian you're saying, "What is the best thing to do in this situation? What's going to cause the best consequence?" If you're a Kantian, you're focusing on, "What's the right intention to act with in this situation?" Whereas what Aristotle did, he asked a different question. He wasn't asking so much, "How shall I act in this situation?" as "What kind of person should I try to become?" And so what happened was, people got disaffected with the act by act views. They thought they also separated our moral lives from other aspects of our lives. And so what the virtue ethicists offered was a way of looking at the full person and their moral development and saying, "The way they act should be expressions of the kinds characteristics they've developed for themselves." Aristotle has I think about 12 of them. Courage, temperance, and friendliness and things like that. If you went to the internet, "Aristotle's virtues" – they just pop up. But that's the idea. Now, there are weaknesses to the Aristotelian theory that people have pointed out. Which are that it's harder if you're simply talking about people's personalities to ask, "Okay, what do I do in this dilemma?" Whereas the utilitarian and the Kantian deontologist because they're focusing on specific situations can help navigate dilemmas. But a number of theorists thinning about morality became concerned that the wrong question was being asked. And that the right question would be, "What kind of person should I become?"

AB: More generally speaking. So rather than think about situation like the trolley problem, "What should I do in this particular instance?" It's more about, generally speaking, what kind of person do I want to be?

TM: Right. And so my acts become expressions of who I am. So I'm acting the right way because I'm expressing aspects of myself that are morally worthwhile.

AB: So the four main theories would be Aristotle's, care ethics, utilitarianism...

TM: Kantian deontology's the third. And I wouldn't say care ethics is a main theory. It's a theory that's getting increasing amounts of play. But it's very recent. And, standardly, in *The Good Place*, remember when Chidi's making that stew? "There's been three main Western theories of ethics. They're Aristotle, utilitarianism, and deontology." By the way, that scene, when they sent me the scene to review they said, "Did we get this right?" and they said that there have been over the last 2,500 years three main theories of ethics. And I said, "You guys really need to say, 'three main *Western* theories of ethics. Because there's Confucian traditions and there are other traditions here, and you're gonna get dinged.'"

AB: Another question I have for you. I know that you also have done some work teaching in prisons.

TM: Yeah.

AB: I looked at little bit [of information about philosopher] Foucault, who I know is influential in your work and when I was reading about structure of power and knowledge I was like, "that sounds like we would describe in 2020 as privilege." So do you approach these ideas of moral development differently when working with such a marginalized group? What sort of different responses do you have when you're teaching in a college setting which would be – I'm guessing – where you're teaching students in relative positions of privilege versus in a prison system? Is it different the way that they respond to and in the way that you convey it?

TM: There's certain insignificant differences. So for instance I give more and more difficult reading to the college student than I give to the incarcerated men. But as far as the discussion goes – they certainly have different experiences – but as far as the discussion itself, I don't direct it differently. What will generally happen is that the college students will be a little bit more focused abstractly. And the incarcerated men are much more likely to bounce it against their experience. Which is interesting because I get very interesting examples that they will generate – sometimes from their lives, but sometimes not – among the incarcerated men. For example, at one point I was talking about something that I did in my own work about what makes life meaningful and we were talking about the idea, a theme of a life being adventurous. And I said something about, "Well look if a person goes to the mall all the time they may think of that as an adventure but they're not really being adventurous." So one of my students said, "Well, suppose it's some who is an outlier in some marginal place and this is completely different, wouldn't that be an adventure for them?" I said, "Yeah, that would be an adventure but it wouldn't be a theme of adventurousness unless they were being adventurous a lot." So this person then said, "Well, how about if they went to all kinds of mall a lot." And then another one of my students said, "Yeah but you know people at the malls they're all the same, you can go to different malls and get the same people." And then he said, "Well, suppose he went to malls in different countries?" And they're generating examples, they're thinking it through in ways that my students probably wouldn't as much. They're concerned with the abstract character of the thought.

AB: That's interesting.

TM: And I don't ask my students in the prison for biographies. But they offer them. Not full biographies, but they'll talk about experiences that they've had in their lives and how that relates to the issues. Because the theories that I'm telling you about I teach in my moral philosophy class and I teach with them. In that sense it's the same topics.

AB: That's very interesting. And it's great that they're able to be so open with you also.

TM: Well, I like the discussion. I like to throw challenges out, but I don't like to challenge them in the deep way. I had an interview [titled] "How does an atheist approach death?" And one of the things I said is when I teach in a prison I'm not challenging their religious views, because that helps keep them together. But they're willing to go most places to discuss things. And I think part of it is they're intellectually starved. And they get – the classes they get are often "Here's how to be less brutal" or something. And we're just putting up theories and discussing them and they – they'll run with them.

AB: It's interesting that so much inner work of morality and how it affects others can be a relief. That that's less intense than what be, like, anger management or whatever, what they might be doing otherwise.

TM: Well, I think it could be less intense but it's also a chance – it's less judgmental. The idea is that their ideas – they're not being told, "here's what you should do" but their ideas are being welcomed in. And I'm trying to get their thoughts. One person put it – and this is not only in my class – but he said in my class he feels like an adult. Because we're taking one another's ideas seriously and discussing them.

AB: You've also done a lot of political activism, I was surprised to see it's even listed on your university page, which is amazing. So what makes a meaningful life? You're mentioning adventure. But you also are very much focused on your personal work on justice and helping marginalized communities so what do you think makes a good life?

TM: There's a term "a good life" and there's a term "a meaningful life" and they aren't necessarily the same. When we think of a good life we think of a person who contributes a lot morally. Bit when I wrote about a meaningful life I was taking off from another philosopher, Susan Wolf. And she's a philosopher in North Carolina and Susan writes that we have this category of morally good and we have this idea of "happy." But she thinks there's a third category at least. And she says, "I'm going to use the term 'meaningfulness.'" And her slogan for it is: "A meaningful life is when subjective engagement meets objective worthwhileness." So you have to be taken up, feel like you're participating, you're in the flow, of something that's worthwhile. But the worthwhile thing doesn't have to be something morally good. It's just objectively worthwhile. And when she was asked about this she said, "Well, objectively worthwhile, there's so many things." So I wrote a book suggesting, okay, so here's one way to think about objective worthwhileness which is the certain themes that characterize your life. I call them "narrative values." Not necessarily moral, but the theme of a life. So some lives we think of as adventurous, and some as intense and some as curious and some as spontaneous. And these can be themes characterizing a life. So if we think of a meaningful life as one where subjective engagement is meeting objective worthwhileness, one way to think about that is, you take the person who is adventurous, or curious, or spiritual, and that theme characterizes their life and they're caught up in that. And that can be a way of thinking about meaningfulness that doesn't reduce it just to moral goodness.

AB: How much overlap do you think there is among the good life, the happy life, and the meaningful life?

TM: I think it's various and it's going to depend on context. So for instance, there can be people who are loyal and also exhibit, say, a certain kind of justice. That would be meaningfulness overlapping with morality. But imagine this – imagine the rock star who is really intense. And their intensity is part of what people are drawn to about them. But they leave bodies in their wake. So now we would say there's a meaningfulness there that we can see and admire but at the same time there's a certain moral deficiency there. And I think that's often why with certain people we feel ambivalent. Because we admire the theme but don't necessarily admire the morality. Or we could go the other way around. You could have a person who's very good, but just alienated from themselves. They are just constantly having to be a good person. And so I think there can be overlap, but I think there are three distinct categories.

AB: So the category of the person who is always the good person but they are disconnected from themselves would be, like the utilitarian "happiness pump."

TM: Right. They're good, but their life isn't meaningful in the way that Wolf is describing it and they're clearly not happy.

AB: And if everything about that person is about giving to other people then there's nothing to that person in a lot of ways.

TM: Yes.

AB: So what do you think the secrets are to being in a caring profession and, first of all, avoiding being that "happiness pump" and also can you have a life in the overlap?

TM: I think it's possible. If we're thinking in the helping professions. And by the way my wife's a licensed professional counselor. I think, it seems to me that one of the tricks is not to get overwhelmed. To have things that are outside of the work you do. And those things can be things that make you happy or they can be meaningful. But things that you are caught up in that matter to you above and beyond the work that you do. In some sense, I suppose, one might say – although I think this is a little inaccurate – that you're able to walk away. The reason I think that's a little inaccurate is that there may be times when it's good to sort of turn over in your head an issue that's going with somebody that you're working with. But I think that's different from getting overwhelmed. In that sense I would say, if we think of the helping professions in moral categories, then we have to move away from those kinds of moral considerations and parts of our lives so that the rest of our lives aren't being colonized by those moral considerations, but we have other aspects to our lives.

AB: Is that where the morally good would compromise the meaningfulness? So meaningfulness doesn't mean you are defined by one aspect of your life necessarily, it just means that there's a theme?

TM: Or a set of themes. A person can be, say, adventurous and intellectually curious. They aren't exclusive of one another. Now I have an article in the *New York Times* a few years ago about this and then the book I wrote called *The Significant Life* is trying to sort all that out. And the relationships between meaning and morality and things like that.

3.8 The Compassionate and Curious Behavior Analyst

Navigating Criticism of Behavior Analysis

Megan M. Miller

Criticisms of behaviorism and the field of behavior analysis are not a new phenomenon. Popular critiques include failure to account comprehensively for the human experience, early research focused on animal behavior not human behavior (McLeod, 2017), and the infamous debates between Noam Chomsky and B.F. Skinner on language development (Ibbotson & Tomasello, 2016). As evidenced by the widely used Cooper et al. (2007, 2020) textbooks, it should be fairly common for behavior analysts to discuss these criticisms in their coursework and to learn how to navigate these discussions by dispelling misconceptions or justifying their necessity from a behaviorist worldview.

Over the past 20 years, widespread criticism has grown relating to applied behavior analysis (ABA) as a therapy for autism being abusive (Kirkham, 2017; Kupferstein, 2018; Leadbitter et al., 2021; McGill & Robinson, 2020; Pyne, 2020; Robinson et al., 2020; Sandoval-Norton & Shkedy, 2019; Sandoval-Norton et al., 2021; Wilkenfeld & McCarthy, 2020). The arguments that surround this criticism are often seen in online forums and on social media. Based on the content in Cooper et al. (2007), it is unlikely that behavior analysts are receiving training on how to address these criticisms. It is also likely the training provided on supporting and promoting the science may run counter to making progress forward in lessening the divide between behavior analysts and those who oppose ABA. The discourse modeled for behavior analysts in conference presentations, journal articles, online discourse, social media, and the Professional and Ethical Compliance Code (BACB, 2014) is defensive in nature and fails to take into account research on how to navigate discourse with marginalized groups or people who are in disagreement (e.g., Dore, 2017; Klimecki, 2019; LaFrance, et al., 2019; Museux et al., 2016; Rubak et al., 2005; Tschaepe, 2018) or recent literature in behavior analysis on cultural humility, diversity, equity, and inclusion (e.g., Beaulieu et al., 2019; Miller et al., 2019; Pritchett et al., 2020; Taylor et al., 2019; Wright, 2019).

The purpose of this chapter is (1) to briefly summarize the points being made by those who claim ABA as abusive and unethical, (2) to explore the responsibility of Board Certified Behavior Analysts (BCBAs) and Board Certified Assistant Behavior Analysts (BCaBAs) in responding to or addressing these criticisms based on the Ethics Code for Behavior Analysts (BACB, 2021), and (3) to provide recommendations how behavior analysts can be compassionate and curious when responding to criticisms of ABA.

ABA is Abusive and Unethical

Criticisms of abuse and ethical concerns surrounding ABA are also not a recent development (e.g., Bailey & Burch, 2016). In the past few years, several articles published in peer-reviewed journals have either studied the impact of ABA therapy on autistics or outlined historical perspectives and justifications as to why ABA should be considered abusive and unethical.

DOI: 10.4324/9781003190707-27

A highly controversial article claiming autistics who receive ABA therapy have an increased risk of PTSD symptoms was published by Kupferstein (2018). This research is cited frequently in the papers that follow as support that ABA is abusive or at least concerning. Leaf et al. (2018) published an evaluation of Kupferstein's study and identified several methodological concerns: the hypothesis was focused on proving ABA was harmful, participant selection, framing of the questions in the survey, and interpretation of the results. Chown et al. (2019) respond to this evaluation in a letter to the editor. They express three concerns with the evaluation: Kupferstein's study may have methodological weaknesses but it was the first of its kind and was undertaken without funding, Leaf et al. received funding from a special interest group and a donor who supports ABA interventions thus bringing into question their objectivity in writing an evaluation, and despite the methodological weaknesses of Kupferstein's study, it provides enough information to justify a possible link and this should be explored further.

Sandoval-Norton and Shkedy (2019) express their concerns with ABA therapy as applied to non-verbal autistics. They argue that ABA is unethical and abusive, promotes prompt dependency, only works for specific characteristics of autism, uses methodologies that are ineffective and "out of date," and has no data showing long-term effectiveness. Gorycki et al. (2019) provide a response to this article and Sandoval-Norton et al. (2021) provide a response where they continue to assert that ABA is abusive and they primarily argue the Gorycki et al. (2019) response was not specific to non-verbal autistics and ignored research from neuroscience relating to autism even though the authors identified autism as a neurological diagnosis. Readers are encouraged to access each of these articles for free online to fully evaluate the points made in each article.

It is important to note that in both of the examples provided above, the response articles from behavior analysts provide thorough rebuttals and defenses of the science of behavior analysis but there is a failure to fully demonstrate curiosity, compassion, empathy, or any of the other behaviors recommended within the research on resolving conflict (e.g., Dore, 2017; Klimecki, 2019; LaFrance et al., 2019; Museux et al., 2016; Rubak et al., 2005; Tschaepe, 2018).

Wilkenfeld and McCarthy (2020) provide a bioethics analysis of ABA therapy. Their paper lays out arguments for why ABA is unethical and accounts for potential objections to their claims. The authors posit the dominant form of ABA therapy is unethical because it infringes on the autonomy of children and potentially their parents as well. They also argue ABA therapy is unjust because it puts the burden on autistics to fit into society as opposed to society accepting and accommodating autistics. Lastly, they express concerns ABA therapy violates nonmaleficence due to the exorbitant cost and the real-world impact of ABA therapy. Most notably, the authors state: "Our central point in most of our arguments is that ABA alters behavior without engaging the patient as the person he is right now" (p. 59). Based on their analysis, they make the following recommendations: use measures of success of ABA therapy that focus on the well-being of the individual instead of how well they function within a societal structure, develop a deeper understanding of what aspects of a personality is essential versus accidental, and to change society to accept neurodiversity instead of insisting people change or act like someone they are not.

Two publications provide a historical account of early research in applications of behavior analysis and express similar concerns (Kirkham, 2017; Pyne, 2020). Examples of abusive behavior analytic practices identified in these papers include: locking an autistic child in a room by himself daily for a year and ignoring him during tantrums (Ferster, 1964); striking an autistic girl who was self-injurious and admitting to being willing to strike her so hard she would die (Chance, 1974); the discourse from Lovaas about the treatment he had designed and how he was "building a person"; the "Feminine Boy Project" that aimed to cure male children from "becoming" gay or trans; the consideration of autism as a deficit instead of a way of being; suppressing self-stimulatory behavior; and the overall dehumanization of autistics perpetuated by the field of behavior analysis.

Leadbitter et al. (2021) argue all stakeholders involved in autism intervention and research should understand neurodiversity and the views of autistic people. Their paper provides recommendations based on a balanced view of neurodiversity. The authors identify three implications for intervention: refrain from attempting to "cure" or "normalize"; focus on improving physical or socio-emotional environments for autistics and address extrinsic factors that contribute to a negative experience or a disadvantage; depathologize characteristics of autism unless they are causing harm or discomfort to the individual or violating the rights of others. They also recommend interventionists and researchers reframe how they measure the effectiveness of their interventions to focus on outcomes that are most important to autonomy and well-being of the child, use outcome measures that assess goodness of fit between the environment and the child, and to develop relationships with autistic people to develop a better understanding of autistic culture. This publication provides a much-needed starting point for behavior analysts in navigating the neurodiversity movement while also adhering to our ethical responsibilities.

The Ethics Code for Behavior Analysts

There are several sections of the Code (BACB, 2021) that should guide how behavior analysts respond to criticism of behavior analysis as described above. This section briefly highlights these sections. First, we must consider the Core Principles that apply: (1) Benefit others, (2) Treat others with compassion, dignity and respect, and (3) Ensure their competence. The publications discussed in the previous section indicate for at least some of society, there are concerns that ABA is abusive and harmful. Based on these Core Principles, behavior analysts should be familiar with this research to ensure they are engaging in practices that truly protect the welfare and rights of their clients, they do so in respectful ways that provide space and opportunity for personal choice, and they remain knowledgeable of interventions that are culturally responsive, to include autism as its own culture.

In reviewing the Code, I identified at least 18 Code items that inform how to engage with these criticisms of ABA. It is beyond the scope of this chapter to provide a detailed analysis of each Code item. The reader is encouraged to review the Code and analyze the interaction between the Code items listed here and the information provided in the previous section. Determine how your practices uphold each of these Code items, while also being responsive to the concerns of the public at large about abusive ABA practices. For example, we can analyze Code 1.10 Awareness of Personal Biases and Challenges with a focus on "personal biases." Given the learning history most behavior analysts have relating to the beneficial aspects of behavior analysis and the presence of ableism inherent in our society (e.g., Bottema-Beutel et al., 2021), it is highly likely our own personal biases will influence intervention development in ways that are deficit-focused and dehumanizing to autistics and other differing abilities. Because of this, behavior analysts are encouraged to actively engage with the literature regarding ableism, autistic culture, disability studies, and disability justice, to regularly interrogate how their own biases could potentially influence treatment, and develop actionable steps to take to ensure their personal biases are not interfering with their professional work.

Readers are encouraged to analyze at least the following Code items in a similar manner: 1.05, 1.06, 1.07, 1.08, 1.09, 1.10, 1.13, 2.01, 2.09, 2.11, 2.12, 2.13, 2.14, 2.15, 2.16, 3.01, 3.13, and 6.03.

Compassionate and Curious

Research within and outside of the field of behavior analysis provides a framework for behavior analysts to follow in responding to criticisms of ABA (Beaulieu et al., 2019; Dore, 2017; Klimecki, 2019; LaFrance et al., 2019; Museux et al., 2016; Rubak et al., 2005; LeBlanc et al., 2019; Miller et al., 2019; Pritchett et al., 2020; Tschaepe, 2018; Wright, 2019). Based on this research and the criticisms detailed in this chapter, behavior analysts can demonstrate compassionate and curious practices in the following ways.

Be humble. Robinson et al. (2020) evaluated the practitioner experience after receiving training on person-centered therapy (PCT). The authors conclude when practitioners see themselves as the "expert" or "fixer," they see problems that need to be corrected and lose sense of the person. This research points both to the necessity of staying humble and receiving training in person-centered approaches in order to work with clients and maintain their humanity.

Listen to learn. Research demonstrates the effectiveness of empathy and compassion in improving outcomes and/or resolving conflicts (e.g., Klimecki, 2019; LaFrance et al., 2019; Museux et al., 2016). Listening to learn involves maintaining curiosity, which most behavior analysts would understand as philosophical doubt. Compassionate listening involves five steps and is demonstrated to work effectively in resolving conflicts between groups. The five steps are: (1) cultivating compassion, (2) developing the fair witness, (3) respecting self and others, (4) listening with the heart, and (5) speaking from the heart (Furman, 2009).

Kirkham (2017) states: "This lack of meaningful dialogue between supports and detractors of ABA means these controversies are unlikely to end soon" (p. 117). Leadbitter et al. (2021) provide a similar conclusion:

> With close attention to the needs, preferences and priorities of autistic people, we can move beyond historical divides, misunderstandings and wrongdoings to a place where we value the expertise of autistic people, embrace practices that respect and accept individual neurotypes, and ensure our interventions address the things that matter most to the recipients.

The time has come where behavior analysts can no longer operate in their own bubble and worldview. Will we continue to choose to respond to criticisms defensively and with a strong, rigid adherence to defending the science in the same ineffective way as behavior analysts who came before us (e.g. Critchfield et al., 2017) or will we heed the advice provided above and take note of the research on conflict resolution to show the world that behavior analysts can do better and are compassionate and curious practitioners?

Works Cited

Bailey, J., & Burch, M. (2016). *Ethics for behavior analysts.* London: Routledge.

Beaulieu, L., Addington, J., & Almeida, D. (2019). Behavior analysts' training and practices regarding cultural diversity: the case for culturally competent care. *Behavior Analysis in Practice, 12*(3), 557–575.

Bevill-Davis, A., Clees, T. J., & Gast, D. L. (2004). Correspondence training: a review of the literature. *Journal of Early and Intensive Behavior Intervention, 1*(1), 13.

Behavior Analyst Certification Board. (2014). *Professional and Ethical Compliance Code for Behavior Analysts.* Littleton, CO: Author.

Behavior Analyst Certification Board. (2020). *Ethics Code for Behavior Analysts.* Littleton, CO: Author.

Bottema-Beutel, K., Kapp, S. K., Lester, J. N., Sasson, N. J., & Hand, B. N. (2021). Avoiding ableist language: suggestions for autism researchers. *Autism in Adulthood*, *3*(1), 18–29.

Chance, P. (1974). After you hit a child, you can't just get up and leave him; you are hooked to that kid. O. Ivar Lovaas interview. *Psychology Today*, *7*(8), 76–84.

Chown, N., Hughes, E., Leatherland, J., & Davison, S. (2019). Response to Leaf et al.'s critique of Kupferstein's finding of a possible link between applied behaviour analysis and post-traumatic stress disorder. *Advances in Autism*, *5*(4), 318–318. https://doi.org/10.1108/aia-01-2019-0002.

Cooper, J. O., Heron, T. E., & Heward, W. L. (2007). *Applied behavior analysis*. Upper Saddle River, NJ: Pearson.

Cooper, J. O., Heron, T. E., & Heward, W. L. (2020). *Applied behavior analysis* (3rd edn.). Upper Saddle River, NJ: Pearson.

Critchfield, T. S., Doepke, K. J., Epting, L. K., Becirevic, A., Reed, D. D., Fienup, D. M., Kremsreiter, J.L., & Ecott, C. L. (2017). Normative emotional responses to behavior analysis jargon or how not to use words to win friends and influence people. *Behavior Analysis in Practice*, *10*(2), 97–106.

Dore, J. (2017). The four processes of motivational interviewing. *Psych Central*. Retrieved on September 17, 2020, from https://pro.psychcentral.com/the-four-processes-of-motivational-interviewing.

Ferster, C. B. (1964). Positive reinforcement and behavioral deficits of autistic children. In *Conditioning techniques in clinical practice and research* (pp. 255–274). Berlin: Springer.

Furman, F. K. (2009). Compassionate listening as a path to conflict resolution. *Journal for the Study of Peace and Conflict*, 24.

Gorycki, K. A., Ruppel, P. R., & Zane, T. (2020). Is long-term ABA therapy abusive: a response to Sandoval-Norton and Shkedy. *Cogent Psychology*, *7*(1), 1823615.

Ibbotson, P., & Tomasello, M. (2016). Language in a new key. *Scientific American*, *315*(5), 70–75.

Kirkham, P. (2017). "The line between intervention and abuse": autism and applied behaviour analysis. *History of the human sciences*, *30*(2), 107–126.

Klimecki, O. M. (2019). The role of empathy and compassion in conflict resolution. *Emotion Review*, *11*(4), 310–325.

Kupferstein, H. (2018). Evidence of increased PTSD symptoms in autistics exposed to applied behavior analysis. *Advances in Autism*, *4*(1), 19–29.

LaFrance, D. L., Weiss, M. J., Kazemi, E., Gerenser, J., & Dobres, J. (2019). Multidisciplinary teaming: enhancing collaboration through increased understanding. *Behavior Analysis in Practice*, *12*(3), 709–726.

Leadbitter, K., Buckle, K. L., Ellis, C., & Dekker, M. (2021). Autistic self-advocacy and the Neurodiversity movement: implications for autism early intervention research and practice. *Frontiers in Psychology*, *12*. https://doi.org/10.3389/fpsyg.2021.635690.

Leaf, J. B., Ross, R. K., Cihon, J. H., & Weiss, M. J. (2018). Evaluating Kupferstein's claims of the relationship of behavioral intervention to PTSS for individuals with autism. *Advances in Autism*, *4*(3), 122–129.

McGill, O., & Robinson, A. (2020). "Recalling hidden harms": Autistic experiences of childhood applied behavioural analysis (ABA). *Advances in Autism*. https://doi.org/10.1108/aia-04-2020-0025.

McLeod, S. A. (2017, February 5). *Behaviorist approach*. Simply Psychology. www.simplypsychology.org/behaviorism.html.

Miller, K. L., Cruz, A. R., & Ala'i-Rosales, S. (2019). Inherent tensions and possibilities: Behavior analysis and cultural responsiveness. *Behavior and Social Issues*, *28*(1), 16–36.

Museux, A. C., Dumont, S., Careau, E., & Milot, É. (2016). Improving interprofessional collaboration: the effect of training in nonviolent communication. *Social Work in Health Care*, *55*(6), 427–439.

Pritchett, M., Ala'i, S., Re Cruz, A., & Cihon, T. (2020). Social justice is the spirit and aim of an applied science of human behavior: moving from colonial to participatory research practices. https://doi.org/10.31234/osf.io/t87p4.

Pyne, J. (2020). "Building a person": legal and clinical personhood for autistic and trans children in Ontario. *Canadian Journal of Law and Society*, *35*(2), 341–365.

Robinson, A., Galbraith, I., & Carrick, L. (2020). Practitioner experience of the impact of humanistic methods on autism practice: a preliminary study. *Advances in Autism*, 7(2), 114–128. https://doi.org/10.1108/aia-05-2020-0033.

Rubak, S., Sandbaek, A., Lauritzen, T., & Christensen, B. (2005). Motivational interviewing: a systematic review and meta-analysis. *British Journal of General Practice*, 55(513), 305–312.

Sandoval-Norton, A. H., & Shkedy, G. (2019). How much compliance is too much compliance: is long-term ABA therapy abuse? *Cogent Psychology*, 6(1), 1641258.

Sandoval-Norton, A. H., Shkedy, G., & Shkedy, D. (2021). Long-term ABA therapy is abusive: a response to Gorycki, Ruppel, and Zane. *Advances in Neurodevelopmental Disorders*, 1–9.

Taylor, B. A., LeBlanc, L. A., & Nosik, M. R. (2019). Compassionate care in behavior analytic treatment: can outcomes be enhanced by attending to relationships with caregivers? *Behavior Analysis in Practice*, 12(3), 654–666.

Tschaepe, M. (2018). Cultural humility and Dewey's pattern of inquiry: developing good attitudes and overcoming bad habits. *Contemporary Pragmatism*, 15(1), 152–164.

Wilkenfeld, D. A., & McCarthy, A. M. (2020). Ethical concerns with applied behavior analysis for autism spectrum "disorder." *Kennedy Institute of Ethics Journal*, 30(1), 31–69.

Wright, P. I. (2019). Cultural humility in the practice of applied behavior analysis. *Behavior Analysis in Practice*, 12(4), 805–809.

3.9   An Updated Ethics Code?
Why Is that Necessary?

Bobby Newman

At first blush, the idea of an updated Ethics Code seems superfluous at best. After all, didn't the human species figure out proper conduct thousands of years ago?

- "That which is hateful to you, do not do to your neighbor. That is the whole Torah; the rest is commentary. Go and study it." (Rabbi Hillel)
- "Therefore all things whatsoever ye would that men should do to you, do ye even so to them: for this is the law and the prophets." (Jesus of Nazareth, Matthew, 7:12)
- "What you do not want done to yourself, do not do to others." (Confucius)

Of course, these are great generalities, and the proverbial devil is in the details (with apologies to Lucifer Morningstar). More importantly, social conditions change dramatically, and this necessitates alterations in professional and personal behavior. In the following essay, I will highlight three developments in the last several years that have caused dramatic shifts in our personal and professional behavior. These three areas are:

1. The newly widespread availability of third party (private insurance) payments for applied behavior analytic services.
2. The explosion of social media.
3. A much greater societal and professional concern with cultural competency and sensitivity.

I will provide just a couple of examples for each area. Each could have their own chapter of considerations.

Third Party Payments for ABA Services

I began my own clinical career in the mid-1980s, and continued to form my thinking during the explosion of interest in ABA that followed the publication of Catherine Maurice's *Let Me Hear Your Voice* in the early 1990s. I received my certification by going to Florida and getting the certification as a behavior analyst in the years before there actually was a Behavior Analysis Certification Board. I joke that while I am recognized as the first BCBA in NY, that is not a tribute to my abilities but rather to my poor planning, getting a certification that would not be recognized in my own home state for many years. Certification itself came into being for a variety of reasons, chief among them consumer protection in those days was in great demand and there was little regulation/understanding of what made a competent behavior analyst.

For all this, third party insurance payment for ABA was not even a consideration for decades to follow. It is here now, however. As is always the case, there are unintended

DOI: 10.4324/9781003190707-28

consequences of each significant development (see Henry Drummond's courtroom speech in *Inherit the Wind* for a more eloquent discussion of the tradeoffs of "progress" than I could ever muster). Let me provide just a few examples.

"Growing up" as a clinician supporting people diagnosed with autism spectrum disorder, I gradually evolved the phrase "we are in this for all day." That meant that we would be responsible for addressing behavior in nearly all areas of our clients' lives (upon request). Activities of daily living such as showering and toothbrushing, etc. were commonly targeted activities and formed the basis of training in shaping and chaining for new staff, etc. In recent years, however, many insurance companies have insisted that clinicians should only address the "core" deficits of autism spectrum disorder. In other words, addressing anything other than language and socialization is iffy in the approval process. (And, by the way, when did an "approval process" enter into it?) Working on "ADL skills" went from being a standard in behavioral programming to a point of contention. One now finds oneself embroiled in philosophical arguments in order to gain approval for the goals. To take another example, I had a lengthy debate regarding what I considered a "no brainer" travel training goal. My client had to be able to read the street signs. That was kicked back to me as an educational goal rather than a "medically necessary" goal addressing one of the core deficits of ASD. My argument that my client could not socialize if he could not find his way to the socialization setting took more energy and time than I care to describe. I will admit that I lost a similar round trying to explain that my client could not easily socialize if his personal hygiene was not what was expected and this then required another approach.

The above example highlights a key difficulty. Who is the client? Whose concerns do I need to address and satisfy in our discussions? Obviously, the learner is the person whose personal welfare and personal desires are what I need to be concerned with. The reality, however, is that I need to do this within the parameters that a third party may approve. The new reality is that we are forced to consider this balancing act and portions of the new ethics guidelines are meant to have us consider those new realities.

Social Media

I will admit that I joined Facebook kicking and screaming, totally under protest. I was under the impression that it was people posting "Okay, I'm going to the bathroom now" and narrating their days. When some of the special interest groups that I was involved with through professional organizations moved over to Facebook from Yahoo Groups, however, I had to make the switch. I can admit that I was totally wrong. The social media platform is wonderful for keeping up with friends from all over the world that I would never otherwise see, except at professional conferences, and *can* be a wonderful tool for giving support to friends and generally keeping in touch. There can also be hazards for professionals, however. Let's consider a few common issues.

In desperation, or just for further ideas, people often post clinical scenarios online and ask for assistance. "Why do you think he is doing this and what should I do?" This is done by both parents and clinicians. If I may repeat one of my mantras that people are likely sick of hearing, "Anyone who wants to tell you that they can give you a treatment plan without first doing a functional behavior assessment/analysis is selling something." A behavior analyst answering and making suggestions on social media is violating at least five different ethical guidelines regarding appropriate and effective practice that I could mention off the top of my head, and there are probably more if I looked more closely. A clinician posting looking for help is likely adding a violation of confidentiality into the mix (i.e., some of us live and work in areas where there are so few programs that any identifying information about the situation likely also creates opportunities for the client to accidentally be identified). In at least one real-life scenario I knew of, a clinician posted about having a tough day (and how the clinician was going to cope!) and it was in a situation where a client could relatively easily be identified. Obviously, this is a serious error in judgment.

Social media also allows for inadvertent violations, or at least gray areas. To take one example, in a different consideration of this area, I spoke of donations to charity. Every year, I do two big fundraisers. I bother everyone in the ABA world to either join me in the activity or to at least financially support the activity (the two activities being running the marathon in Nashville to support St. Jude Children's Research Hospital and the Long Beach Polar Bear Swim on Superbowl Sunday, swimming in the frigid Atlantic Ocean in February to support the Make a Wish Foundation). Now, while I bother everyone in the ABA world to participate or support, I never solicit from clients or supervisees. I would never want to *even appear* to "pressure" anyone to support the cause. Social media posting about such things can be tricky. What if a friend of a friend makes a post about their donation on their own page, or shares your fundraiser without your knowledge, and then your supervisee or client sees it (small world!) and decides to donate? Should I actively call every such person when I first set up my fundraising and tell them not to donate? Should I give the money back from my own pocket? Should I tell St. Jude or Make a Wish not to accept the money? Obviously, we can see that there can be accidental issues that arise through the use of social media.

Some people have taken such considerations even further, into highly questionable territory. During the 2020 Presidential Election, which was obviously extremely contentious, I saw some behavior analysts making what I personally regarded as absurd commentary that one could not be a good behavior analyst and support one of the other; namely, candidates. I am also a homebrewer and enjoy the occasional cigar. I have gotten (unsolicited, I may add!) feedback that posting photos of my homebrewed beers and evenings at a cigar lounge with friends/colleagues creates "a bad image" for ABA. Please understand that these were not drunken debauchery photos, but rather bottling beer with my family and sitting in business attire with a cigar in a lounge. Then, of course, there are the photos of me covered in mud with no shirt on and tattoos on full display from obstacle course races or road races. I have received commentary that this is not very professional. Well, to be honest, it is my *personal* and not my *professional* page. Is that distinction good enough? I don't have sufficient space to analyze that here but again I just wish to point out where a potential pitfall can occur and why social media has become such a ubiquitous part of life, with all its potential benefits and pitfalls.

Cultural Competence/Sensitivity

Obviously, cultural competence and sensitivity refers to a great deal more than making potentially offensive jokes, language or statements. For the purposes of this essay, however, I wish to stay close to this topic area so as to focus the discussion.

Joke #1: A local station advertised that they would be showing *Blazing Saddles* on television. They had to edit out all the portions that would be considered offensive by modern standards. The showing of the movie took six and one half minutes, including one commercial break.

Legendary story #1: Danny Thomas (founder of the previously mentioned St. Jude Children's Hospital) wanted to join a country club that was populated primarily by Jewish celebrities who had been excluded from other clubs due to their religion/ethnicity.

Speaking of Danny, who was actually Lebanese by birth, Groucho Marx famously quipped, "I don't mind having a non-Jew, but do we have to have one who looks so Jewish?"

Stand up commentary #1: Comedian Steve Hughes has a routine that has gone viral on the internet, easily searched for under "Steve Hughes" and "I was offended." It includes lines such as:

1. "What happens if you say that and someone gets offended?" and Steve replies "Then they can be offended... when did sticks and stones may break my bones stop being relevant? ... nothing happens! ... (it isn't like) I was offended and when I woke up, I had leprosy!"
2. "I want to live in a democracy but I never want to be offended again!" "Then you're an idiot!"

The first point about *Blazing Saddles* is a joke, the second may be more story than fact but is part of the legends of both Danny and Groucho. I threw them in because I expect even reading these two quips would make many people uncomfortable. *Blazing Saddles* was written by a team that featured Mel Brooks (a Jewish man) and Richard Pryor (an African American man). It is positively loaded with Jewish and African American stereotype jokes, and even includes inside jokes that are lost on most viewers (google the translation of Madeline Kahn's character's name, for you non-Yiddish speakers in the audience). You could not begin to get away with that in this day and age.

Now let's consider Steve Hughes' standup routine. The point that he hammers home again and again is that what offends one may not offend another, depending on their own life experiences and values, etc. and thus the difficulty in legislating such matters. He concludes, however, with a sentiment with which I hope we can all agree: "I'm offended when I see Boy Bands! But what am I going to do, call the cops...?"

Now, even my last joke here may be offensive to some. In keeping with Steve's point, though, let's examine *my* perspective. I was born in 1967, growing up in Queens, NY in a highly integrated area where over 25% of the population was on public assistance at any given time. We had the full socioeconomic and demographic range in Rockaway Beach. I grew up in an apartment complex that was very diverse. You would go to Alan's Bar Mitvzah one weekend, and Maria's Quinceanera the next. We ate each other's foods. We participated in each other's holidays. At the basketball and paddleball courts across the street, The Charlie Daniels Band or Motown might be coming through the radios at any given moment. Did we ever make fun of each other? Of course. The key point is that we were laughing *with* each other, rather than *at* each other. A joking story about one of my African American friends desperately trying to figure a way to keep a yarmulke in his afro during my Bar Mitzvah might be followed up by a joke about the stereotyped lack of dancing rhythm among my people at that same event. That's okay, we all grew up together and you knew who your friends were and good-natured joking was allowed and even encouraged. It was nearly impossible to offend us due to our conditions growing up. And to quote Jason Aldin, "We just figured that's how it was, and everybody else was just like us... That's the only way I know."

Let's look at other perspectives, however. Not everyone grew up the same way and that is *not* the only way they know. My family will tell the stories of grandparents with co-workers who were not allowed into certain eateries because of the color of their skin. The solution was to tell the restaurant owner to get bent, that if everyone could not come in then no one was coming in, and to invite everyone home to eat. My father was a Military Police officer in World War II, probably one of the shortest ones ever. He told me a story of a big guy who confronted him: "Are you one of them HEE brews?" My dad braced for a fight and claimed it. There was a moment of silence and the reply came, "I played hockey in high school with a guy who was a Jew. Good guy." The situation was defused. And a follow-up question, "His name was Goldberg, maybe you know him?" led to an explanation that no, in fact, not all Jews know each other. But my dad could not be mad at someone who just did not have the necessary background and had been taught odd things about our people. Carl Reiner tells an elaborate and informative similar story as part of his memoirs of army life. As the military desegregated, exposure was forced, for some for the first time in their lives. That enforced exposure led to mutual respect.

Why do I give these contrasting personal backgrounds? As noted above, different experiences shape different sensibilities and sensitivities. Music during the marathon provides an interesting example. I had fun during a running of the Disney Marathon teaching runners from a Brazilian team I was pacing near to fully participate in *Sweet Caroline* as a band played it on the course. Then, during a running of the NYC Marathon, I had one of those "one in a billion" events that only seem to happen to me. I was pacing alongside some runners from Tokyo, and we came across a band playing the 1980s one hit wonder song, *Turning Japanese*. Muttering under my breath the full version of "FFS," I was surprised that my new friends got all excited rather than offended. Was I too sensitive on their behalf?

The Warriors is a 1979 movie about a street gang, stranded miles from home and falsely accused of a murder and needing to fight their way home. They are one of only a very small percentage of racially integrated gangs in the movie. For that, anti-gay slurs are in common usage. An interesting character is Rembrandt, the gang's graffiti artist. He is physically slight, rarely partakes in the fights in a meaningful way, and is not interested in the female gang that seeks to seduce other Warriors. It is never stated, but it is intimated and generally understood that Rembrandt is stereotypically gay. For all the anti-gay slurs, individual Warriors pull Rembrandt aside and privately tell him to stick close to them if there is a fight, they will take care of him and make sure he doesn't get hurt. They show a genuine concern and affection for him, despite the insensitive or even abusive language they use in general (although interestingly never directed at him). Uncle Paul Newman once famously stated,

> I'm a supporter of gay rights. And not a closet supporter either. From the time I was a kid, I have never been able to understand attacks upon the gay community. There are so many qualities that make up a human being... by the time I get through with all the things that I really admire about people, what they do with their private parts is probably so low on the list that it is irrelevant.

The Warriors seem to live this sentiment as regards Rembrandt, but their verbal behavior does not match their other, much more accepting and protective behavior. Were they not sensitive enough to Rembrandt in their language? It is never stated, but we can guess how he might have felt.

Why do I provide these examinations? As Steve Hughes pointed out, offense is very subjective. What may offend you may not offend me. But Steve is a standup comedian and social commentator. He has no ethical responsibility, and in fact it has often been the role of the comedian to make people uncomfortable by pointing out uncomfortable social truths.

In contrast, I am a BCBA. It is not my job to make people feel uncomfortable, in fact quite the opposite. I cannot assume that, just because I find something inoffensive, everyone else will feel the same way and, in contrast to Steve, I *do* need to care about what others find offensive. The BACB Ethics Code reminds me that I need to be aware of my own biases, and that not everyone will share my perspective.

I have an ethical duty towards "cultural competence" and to take all necessary steps to ensure that my behavioral work does not clash with the values of my clients or staff in terms of goal selection, language, priorities, and a myriad of other areas. If I am not knowledgeable about a given culture, I seek consultation and training. If it is not possible to make myself competent within the necessary time period, I might have to consider a referral. I certainly never engage in any discriminatory practices and attempt to ensure that I never offend anyone. Again, forgive me for belaboring my and my family's history above. The point that I hope I made clear was that while I myself may not find something offensive, for example, that is irrelevant. I have to always consider the perspectives of everyone that I am working with, client or staff, and be sure to behave accordingly. And if I don't know, I ask.

Again, whole books can be written on this topic. I only wish to give a flavor of topics that might need to be considered.

Final Summary Note

We have a new Ethics Code to consider. In contrast to the common sense idea that ethics should be the same across time, we need to acknowledge that social factors such as described above change and our Ethics Code therefore needs to change with it.

3.10   Ethics in Supervision

Dana Reinecke and Cheryl Davis

To obtain the Board Certified Behavior Analyst (BCBA) credential, one must complete a Verified Course Sequence (VCS) as well as required supervised fieldwork (BACB, 2020a). Finally, the candidate needs to pass the BACB exam, meeting competency in each task list area (BACB, 2020a). Supervision is the certification requirement that has the most fluctuation in format, content, and criteria, yet is arguably the most important component to develop competent, caring, and effective behavior analysts because these topics are not explicitly included in the task list. Supervisory practices impact trainees, consumers, and the field at large as the trainees become the future supervisors (Sellers et al., 2016). As supervisors provide supervision to trainees, they in turn model supervision practices, which is likely how the trainee will also conduct future supervision. It is important to keep this cycle clean by modeling ethical supervision practices.

Ethics is clearly taught as a standalone course in all VCS programs, with many such programs using the past atrocities of our field such as Sunland as well as current everyday applied examples to convey ethical principles. Examples and scenarios are crucial for teaching ethics, which is not black and white, but instead a decision-making process. This process is not always fully understood in the context of coursework, and also needs to be taught in the context of supervision of real-life experiences. Supervisors need to move beyond the verbatim aspect of the Ethics Code (BACB, 2020b) or *Ethics for Behavior Analysts* (Bailey & Burch, 2016) to develop trainees' skills in making ethical decisions through problem-solving, evaluating all possible scenarios and solutions, and being able to predict the outcome of each potential solution.

Each supervision interaction has the potential to develop trainees' ethical behavior in an applied context. This is particularly important as the supervisor is developing the trainee to not only make ethical decisions within their daily practice, but to also represent the field of behavior analysis in a positive manner. To do this, it is paramount that the supervisor work to develop the trainee's ability to be compassionate along with their soft skills. As a field, we are adding emphasis to both of these priorities late in our development, with neither being taught in coursework (LeBlanc et al., 2020) or assessed on the board exam. Instead, the development of these skills is left to the supervisor with the ultimate and nearly universal aim for any behavior analyst to embody compassion and present with effective soft skills in all interactions.

Soft skills are often difficult to operationally define and teach. These require ongoing development and assessment during each supervision interaction. With the new Ethics Code there is an emphasis on both affirming principles and disseminating behavior analysis (BACB, 2020b). Additionally, the personnel supervision and management content area in the fifth edition task list (BACB, 2017) includes both professionalism and soft skills. Encouragingly, Sellers et al. (2019) reported that more than two-thirds of supervision-providing BCBAs directly measured their trainees' interpersonal and communication

DOI: 10.4324/9781003190707-29

skills. Using an applied approach with teaching opportunities employing real-life examples enhances supervisors' ability to improve trainees' skills to interact with clients and consumers.

There is no general agreement as to what soft skills are needed as a behavior analyst. Andzik and Kranak (2020) discussed social skills and interpersonal skills in broad terms. Conversely, Callahan et al. (2019) identified specific skills such as "liking others," "having thick skin," and "being optimistic" (p. 3558). It is imperative that supervisors assess soft skills needed for the trainee to be successful in disseminating behavior analysis in their particular area of practice, and ensuring these are addressed within each supervision session. In general, these skills should come from a place of compassion toward clients, caregivers, stakeholders, colleagues, and the community at large.

As behavior analysts, we are naturally most comfortable with objective descriptions of behavior, so a concept like compassion might be difficult to operationalize for the purposes of training. One solution is to identify clear and observable responses that are usually associated with compassion. Using a definition of compassion that relies on perspective-taking as a skill set, Taylor and colleagues (2018) developed a list of behavioral indicators and surveyed parents of children receiving ABA services about their perceptions of the empathy and compassion shown by behavior analysts in the therapeutic relationship. Supervisors may choose to use these or other behavioral indicators to assess their own practice as well as the practices of trainees to determine areas for improvement. For example, many of the parents who responded to the survey developed by Taylor et al. (2018) reported that their behavior analysts were strong in acknowledging and celebrating the child's accomplishments, but less likely to ask the parent how they are doing on a regular basis. These data present an opportunity to discuss the notion of who the client is with a trainee, and to explore the impact of behavioral interventions across the family unit. Trainees are taught to consider the client to be the person in need of behavioral interventions, and that the Ethics Code requires the behavior analyst to keep the client's needs at the forefront of intervention. This emphasis may inadvertently distract behavior analysts from the impact of the behavioral intervention on the whole family, and thus result in a less than compassionate response to parents, which has a negative impact on the behavior analyst's effectiveness and on the parents' perceptions of the field as a whole. Supervision is a perfect context for discussing this balance, and for providing trainees with clear and concrete ways to ensure that they are demonstrating compassion to both clients and family members.

Another solution to the problem of compassion as a concept rather than a skill set is to identify and develop a set of meta-skills that can be applied to any situation. While the indicators provided by Taylor et al. (2018) are extremely useful within the context of interventions with children that closely involve family members, not all behavior-analytic applications fall within this framework. Compassion is an important skill for behavior analysts in all settings, therefore a broader set of behavioral goals should be addressed with trainees. Compassionate action requires three steps, no matter the setting or the task: first, to actively listen to the person who is in need of help; second, to at least attempt to take on the perspective of the person you are listening to; and third, to take action to alleviate their concerns. By teaching trainees to engage in these three steps as part of all of their behavior-analytic work, we can ensure that all of their practice will be approached with compassion.

Supervisors have the valuable opportunity to embed instruction and feedback on compassion and other soft skills throughout all of the training they provide. As supervisors, we are both models and teachers, and just as we use behavior analysis to teach behavior analysis, we can also use compassion to teach compassion. A starting recommendation is to take the time to listen to trainees. Ask them to honestly reflect on their own strengths and weaknesses, and attempt to understand their self-perceptions. Conducting regular assessment of trainee skills and inviting trainees to self-assess is a compassionate and meaningful way to ensure that the supervision experience is meeting the trainee's needs.

Next, supervisors should use effective training practices such as behavioral skills training and performance feedback to teach trainees what they need to know. Just as we should not assume that trainees have the behavioral intervention skills that they will need to be great behavior analysts, we should not assume that they have the know-how to be compassionate, professional, and comfortable in their therapeutic relationships. These are skills that need to be assessed and then taught, and then assessed again. Behavior analysts are hopefully great at providing positive reinforcement for behavior that we want to see more of, so let's remember to reinforce compassion and other soft skills in our trainees. Additionally, we need to be willing to compassionately point out and provide support when these skills are lacking, giving our trainees the instruction needed to develop and hone their skills.

Finally, supervisors need to remember that compassion and other soft skills are going to shift and change over time and with experience. Trainees will benefit from regular, frequent, and ongoing discussions, assessments, and learning opportunities in these areas. We can teach trainees to interact with others in ways that will improve their effectiveness and satisfaction just as well as we can teach them to design functional assessments, collect data, and read and analyze research literature.

Supervision is an opportunity to mold and develop a new generation of behavior analysts, which is a responsibility that must be taken seriously. BACB guidelines for supervision have become more stringent and clear (BACB, 2020c), indicating an appreciation for the importance of supervision experiences as being more than "getting hours" or even worse, "getting a signature." Not only does addressing compassion in supervision result in better behavior analysis for clients and their families, but it also results in happier, more satisfied and fulfilled new behavior analysts who have a healthy respect for the vast importance of the work they are doing. Finally, supervision that takes into account compassion and soft skills provides a service to the field in general, which continues to suffer from negative public opinion (Freedman, 2016). This may be an assumption, but we think it is safe to say that the vast majority of people who become behavior analysts do so because they want to help others. Supervisors can help to ensure that not only do future and new behavior analysts know how to use behavioral assessments and interventions effectively, but that they also know how to express and demonstrate their care for others.

Works Cited

Andzik, N. R., & Kranak, M. P. (2020). The softer side of supervision: recommendations when teaching and evaluating behavior-analytic professionalism. *Behavior Analysis: Research and Practice*. Advance online publication. <ds>https://doi.org/10.1037/bar0000194.</ds>

Bailey, J., & Burch, M. (2016). *Ethics for behavior analysts* (3rd ed.). London: Routledge.

Behavior Analyst Certification Board. (2017). *BCBA Task List* (5th ed.).

Behavior Analyst Certification Board. (2020a). *BACB 2022 Eligibility Requirements*.

Behavior Analyst Certification Board. (2020b). *Ethics Code for Behavior Analysts*.

Behavior Analyst Certification Board. (2020c). *Experience Standards*.

Callahan, K., Foxx, R. M., Swierczynski, A., Aerts, X., Mehta, S., McComb, M. E., Nichols, S., Segal, G., Donald, A., & Sharma, R. (2019). Behavioral artistry: examining the relationship between the interpersonal skills and effective practice repertoires of applied behavior analysis practitioners. *Journal of Autism and Developmental Disorders*, 49(9), 3557–3570.

Freedman, D. H. (2016). Improving public perception of behavior analysis. *The Behavior Analyst, 39*(1), 89–95.

LeBlanc, L. A., Taylor, B. A., & Marchese, N. V. (2020). The training experiences of behavior analysts: compassionate care and therapeutic relationships with caregivers. *Behavior Analysis in Practice, 13*, 387–393.

Sellers, T. P., Alai-Rosales, S., & MacDonald, R. P. (2016). Taking full responsibility: the ethics of supervision in behavior analytic practice. *Behavior Analysis in Practice, 9*(4), 299–308.

Sellers, T. P., Valentino, A. L., Landon, T. J., & Aiello, S. (2019). Board certified behavior analysts' supervisory practices of trainees: survey results and recommendations. *Behavior Analysis in Practice, 12*(3), 536–546.

Taylor, B. A., LeBlanc, L. A., & Nosik, M. R. (2018). Compassionate care in behavior analytic treatment: can outcomes be enhanced by attending to relationships with caregivers? *Behavior Analysis in Practice, 12*(3), 654–666.

3.11   The Importance of Self-care
An Interview with Dr. Shane Spiker

Shane Spiker

ANN BEIRNE: I am so glad that I'm getting a chance to interview you for our second edition, because in our first edition we talked a lot about self-care and the importance of self-care. But in the first edition that felt kind of rebellious.

SHANE SPIKER: Yeah.

AB: And now one of the things that I'm really excited about in the new Ethics Code is that self-care is specifically mentioned in the introduction.

SS: Yes.

AB: So I wanted to talk to you about that because I know that it's a research interest of yours. So could you talk to me a little bit about how you got interested in self-care and burnout prevention, where that started and where it's led you?

SS: Yeah. So the whole thing with self-care – I come from a psychology background, so there's a lot of discussion about self-care within psychology – and I don't know that I ever really attended to it until I started paying attention to burnout in our field. And watching, kind of, the unique things that were happening to behavior analysts. So I could specifically mention that I worked at a place for a little bit. I had a supervisor at this place – won't mention any names, won't mention anything like that – but whenever things would go kind of horribly wrong, that person would just really have a really hard time with whatever dilemma was going on. Whether it was an audit, whether it was hiring new staff, or losing staff, whatever it was it was, it just became this unique problem. So I kind of started looking at, "Well maybe this is just a culture issue."

AB: You mean sort of personally, like she was taking it on, on a personal level?

SS: Yeah, yeah, exactly. So like, high levels of stress, high levels of anxiety, no self-management skills, no coping skills. I mean, it just really became this significant personal problem for this person. And so I took a step back and was like, "Well, maybe it's just this person." And then I would go to conferences and just kind of sit back. And you know we can't help but people watch while we're at conferences. And so sitting back and just watching people [drinking] drink after drink after drink, just burning the candle at both ends, you know. Really spending all this time at these conferences. And that's our "play." And then just watching people burn out from that too. And so you kind of start hearing this conversation about burnout, and you kind of of hear about all the side effects that go along with self-care deficits. And I just started exploring that. And then really looking at the literature on data in our field and found that there were maybe two articles in self-care. And I want to say both of them were on toothbrushing, they weren't even on self-care. And one of them was from 1992. So it was really interesting to see how we totally missed the mark on that. So that's kind of of where it started. And you know, just kind of expanded from there. Just started

DOI: 10.4324/9781003190707-30

looking at what we're doing, what our culture looks like. It's just been a fascinating journey. Like how little we know about it in our field.

AB: And I think as the field moves more toward compassionate service, it's such a delicate balance. Because our emotional involvement with our clients, honestly that's our most potent reinforcer. It's that moment of "yes! They've got it!"

SS: Yeah!

AB: I remember very early in my career hearing a child's first word and I've been chasing that high.

[both laugh]

SS: Yeah, right?

AB: That's often our most potent reinforcer so we do get emotionally involved in our work. I know so many people on the field and also in special education have heard somebody say, "You care too much." And the usual response is, "Screw you, there's no such thing as caring too much."

SS: Like "how dare you."

AB: But when people say that what they mean is "your emotional involvement has over-taken your work, it's not informing your work anymore, it's overwhelming your work."

SS: Yeah.

AB: It's such a delicate balance to allow it to inform your work and reinforce your work without allowing it to overwhelm your work. Which is kind of what you're describing with that supervisor.

SS: Yeah.

AB: She got so emotionally involved she couldn't take the next step in what was the appropriate care.

SS: Right, and so I think that to take that point and expand upon it – to neglect that idea that we are emotional human beings or that we care about our clients, to neglect that is a disservice. That's actually probably one of the biggest criticisms of our field is that we don't care enough or that we're robotic or clinical. And it's like, that's not the case at all. I mean, how many times do we talk about behavior analysts who stay up at night, who are losing sleep over their clients who are pulling their hair out, who leave the field because they cannot handle the stressors that go along with some of the stuff that we do? And so, you know, this whole idea of self-care, it becomes this mul-ti-fold set of repertoires this set of behaviors that you go, okay it's preventive in that it's gonna prevent burnout, it's gonna prevent stressors, its gonna prevent this issue that comes along with not contacting enough reinforcers. And then it's gonna become a management strategy for when things start going wrong. Because I have good self-care management strategies then I can start recognizing, "Hey, when things are start-ing to go bad, then I can engage in these behaviors." But the problem is that we neglect that piece where we go well, it's just behavior, it's just behavior, it's just behavior. Well it's not just behavior, we're working with human beings in complex situations that are difficult, very emotional. I mean every one of us, every one of us has a moment in our career – I call them "critical incidents" – where you always remember that moment. Whether it was a significant behavioral event, whether it was a family that really got to you, whether it was a situation that really got to you. We all keep that and remember those things and we never forget those things. And I've found that to be interesting because in the discussion of trauma when you get into people being traumatized and when you get into counseling, counseling talks about vicarious traumatization where you hear about these traumas from somebody and you empathize and you have that kind of experience with that person, and it's very tough to hear about these scenarios.

And then I started thinking about that in relation to behavior analysis. And it was kind of like, "Well, aren't we just traumatized?" We're not there with the event in counseling. In counseling you are not there at the event that it's happening, you're not seeing that directly, unless the event happens to you. But for the most part in counseling you're not there for that person's event, you're working through that event in the aftermath. We're there. We're often – sometimes – the target of an event. So there is this level of traumatization that behavior analysts experience that we pretend doesn't even exist. So this whole idea of self-care becomes even more potent, and even more powerful and even more important when we consider that aspect of our field too. Because we spend so much time with families, so much time in intervention and usually are directly observing that event happening.

AB: There's such a level of intimacy, especially because a lot of our responsibility is observing those behaviors and trying to treat behaviors in the environments in which they naturally occur so we're in homes.

SS: Yeah.

AB: We're in residences, we're in the environments where these clients are most at home so to speak, whether it be their literal home or their school or the places where they are at most themselves. So the level of intimacy there, it really connects us to people. We see people at their most vulnerable.

SS: Yeah, absolutely. And it's got to be vulnerable to ask for help and ask for somebody to step into your home. You have to be vulnerable to ask somebody to care for your kid. That's a lot of responsibility. I mean so much responsibility. They don't really teach you that in grad school. It's like, "Okay so you're going to learn how to do these procedures, you're going to learn how to collect data." Some programs do kind of emphasize that, but you don't realize to what degree that level of care is in place. So on top of providing good intervention, on top of providing quality services, you've got somebody's life on your hands. And I don't even say that from a perspective of "we are life-savers and we can save the world." Because that type of hubris is a problem for our field too. That's not even what I'm saying. What I'm saying is that, legitimately, when we work with some learners – some learners have problem behavior that is their life. It only takes one episode of elopement that that person is not gonna make it. It only takes only swallowing of some poison or chemical and now we've got a significant problem. So when I say that I say that from a most literal sense because I've worked in those situations and it is not easy. And if I didn't have good self-care repertoires or at least some kind of semblance of it, I don't know that I would still be in the field.

AB: What I find so interesting about talking to you Shane – and I don't think I've EVER talked to anyone about self-care who highlights this also – is that you also really took notice of this tendency to work with a tremendous amount of intensity and then party with a tremendous amount of intensity. So that the so-called self-care was also mismanaged.

SS: Yeah.

AB: And I think that part of that is that, given 2020 and lockdown, I really noticed – with all the quarantines and the lockdowns and everything and everybody trapped in their house – I really noticed a marked increase in jokes about wine.

SS: [laughs] Yeah.

AB: And I made them too. Especially as a mom. There were liquor stores that put up signs that said, "Homeschooling? We've got your school supplies!" And it's genuinely funny and I reposted those pictures too.

SS: Yeah.

AB: And I laughed and I thought it was funny, but there was an aspect to it – that it was so increased. And you are the only person I've ever heard to point out that aspect to it. That there is self-care that is healing and there's self-care that is at the same intensity and still burning the candle at both ends.

SS: Yeah!

AB: And I've never heard anyone else really highlight that piece of it.

SS: Yeah, you now we were just talking about this the other day and I thought this was a really interesting way to frame it. You know I love my job, being a behavior analyst is the coolest job in the world. When I was a kid I used to tell people "I want to be an astronaut." I loved science. I was a marine biology major, I was all about science. So to get to be a scientist for a living, that's the coolest job in the world. So with that, with loving your job comes a whole set of reinforcers. Why would you want to give those things up? I love reading research, I love reading new books on our field. I love doing that, I love staying in contact with that. Because knowledge is also one of my primary reinforcers you could say. But within that, there is that point where how much self-care is too much self-care? And it becomes, I don't make time for other aspects that are also required of self-care, of me to engage in self-caring behavior. There's emotional self-care and social self-care and spiritual self-care that you kind of wrap it all up into this. But it is really so much more than just, you know, a glass of wine. You know, the jokes are funny. I always laugh at the one where it's like the biggest glass of wine and it says "The doctor said just one." That always makes me laugh. Because it is so silly. It is, I get it. But that's so superficial compared to the day that you've gone a week and half without taking a shower because you're just too stressed and you can't even motivate yourself to do something that simple. So you know taking a shower, brushing your teeth, going to the doctor when you need to. Those things are also self-care. And while they might not contact immediate reinforcers, and they might be preventative in that they're avoiding something harmful in the future, that's exactly what they are. I think about how I've had friends who wouldn't go to the dentist for years. They're like, "I hate the dentist, I can't stand it" and now they have to go back because now they need root canals.

AB: And now you really hate the dentist.

SS: Now you really hate it! Exactly! You did that to yourself because you avoided the situation that was really tough. And so some self-caring is not necessarily contacting reinforcers. Sometimes self-caring is maintenance. It's keeping yourself at homeostasis, right? It's keeping yourself at baseline so you can get through to the other side and contact those higher reinforcers. And I don't think that people realize that part of it, you know? They think self-care is about reinforcers and it's not just about that. It's about maintenance so you can make it to the reinforcers that you really want.

AB: Yeah, that's an excellent point. I find also that one of the challenges for self-care, especially for people who are new in the field is that there is this kind of competition between this really incredible drive to help people and taking care of themselves. So it's very hard – especially for new and passionate clinicians – to say, "No I don't want to work that extra day a week." Or "No, I'll take that holiday." Or "I'm taking that vacation or that day off." It's so hard for clinicians to do that, especially knowing that a client or a family is really in need of services.

SS: Yeah.

AB: That is the toughest. So how do you advise people on how to say "No"?

SS: Practice. You know, it's something that I still struggle with. I think Jonathan Tarbox said this really great. It was in a podcast and I can't remember where he said it, but he was basically collecting data on times he said "no." And he started reframing it like,

"Well I'm honored that I would even be asked to do these things." So I take that as a reinforcer in itself.

AB: That's great.

SS: I get asked to speak at conferences all the time so I had to learn to say no and set a boundary. So I think the first thing is practicing to say no. And the other thing is setting very clear boundaries about what you're going to say no to so that you have a rule for when that situation presents itself, right? Let's talk supervisory volume for a second, right? So when you're like, I love supervising and I love teaching, and I love building up budding behavior analysts. But there are tens of thousands of students in grad programs and there are only so many supervisors and so you can't take them all on. I mean you legitimately physically can't take them all on. I mean, I can barely manage the ones that I have myself so I have had to set a boundary of "This is my cap." And so then if somebody does ask, even if I like them, even if I want to, even if they have a really cool research idea I'm like, "This is so cool and it's very difficult for me to say no but I have to because have to set a boundary and I have to set a rule for myself and adherent it." And while that might not be immediately reinforcing and that conversation might be difficult it's also necessary as a preventative measure. I think of it like that: saying no is a prevention. It's not a management strategy, it's literally a prevention measure to prevent you from burning out later, to prevent you from taking on too much and filling your plate so that you have to get second and third and fourth plate just to manage the road. I think that's the first thing: practice, set boundaries, and if you do those two things consistently I think that'll help with easing the "nos" for people.

AB: Yeah. I think another good tip is not to give a reason. Because sometimes if you give a reason people will try and solve that reason. I remember once I had a supervisor who was wonderful and we were also very good friends. So I said, "Oh, I can't do that because of XYZ." And then I said to her, "By the way, I'm not stupid. I know that if I tell you why I can't do something you're going to solve the problem. So if you can solve this problem, I am open to doing it."

SS: Yeah [laughs] You know what's funny is that students will do that too. And I don't know if this is something that's pervasive in our entire culture, I would imagine that it is. But in helping professions, people don't normalize saying no and they don't reinforce saying no. So a way of making that easier for somebody else is reinforcing when they do tell you no. And especially when they don't give an excuse. This is one of the most bizarre things. I've seen this with students where they'll say, "I'm gonna miss this deadline because," and they'll like, they'll give me their whole medical record. Or they'll be like, "I've had 15 family members die and..." And I'm like, "You don't have to tell me all that, you can just say 'I can't do it' and I will be okay with that." I mean, I get that some professors are not compassionate when it comes to that stuff. And that is a different problem, right? We're trying to engage in a set of behaviors that are, like, helping behaviors in a culture that values productivity over mental health or well-being. So that becomes a unique set of contingencies that you battle against. But too many times – I just had a student the other day who was like, "I have Covid, I had an uncle and a great uncle die from Covid recently so I'm not going to be able to make this deadline." And I'm like, "It *is* okay that you don't make this deadline. Please, go handle your family stuff." And I just think part of it is we already exist in a culture that values productivity, so self-care does not become a valued commodity or a valued set of behavior repertoires, it's not reinforced across the board. Now put that into a behavior analytic community and behavior analytic lens where there's many people to help, there's not enough behavior analysts. And we have this culture of "work hard, play hard" but we never play hard. We just work hard.

AB: And sometimes we play so hard that we're working harder at playing hard.

SS: Yes!

AB: Your example of going to conferences and drinking heavily and making it this whole culture of partying at conferences – you're still at work! This is a conference. You're not at Disneyland.

SS: I think people forget that because conferences, especially FABA [Florida Association for Behavior Analysis] – FABA's a blast. I love my state conference. But it is a lot of work. I think of it like this. So I'm paying to go to this conference to listen to these experts speak. If I walk into a talk hung over, why did I even pay to be there? What's the point? How am I gonna get information from this brilliant mind in our field if I'm nursing a headache and trying to hydrate and trying to find the closest bottle of Gatorade so I can get my electrolytes back up, right? So you know I think that you're right, when we have conferences it is a "play hard" situation. But also I would make the argument that we don't ever get ourselves into a space where we can actually take time off. Think about going on vacation. Vacation in our field has become so aversive because you come back to more work. Because we don't set boundaries and we still have families that call or text you while you're on vacation. Because you have RBTs that need you on vacation because we are expected to be almost an emergency response team. And that's not what behavior analysts do. Your general practitioner is not an emergency response team. Your dentist is not an emergency response team. You would not call them at 8, 9, 10 o'clock at night and be like, "Hey I chipped my tooth." You wouldn't do that. So there's this expectation in behavior analysis that there are no boundaries. Ad so because there's this expectation that there are no boundaries – or we haven't set that – now it produces "If I take time off, I can't even enjoy it because I'm either going to come back to more work or I'm working when I'm on vacation." And I'm guilty of it too. I'm not even gonna sit there and say, "Everybody needs to do better." I need to do better about that myself. But you know it is something that is pretty consistent – I mean I would make the argument to say – plight in our field.

AB: And I think there's a little bit of ego involved there too. I know that the thought that comes into my head – my covert behavior – if I get a text is, "This person needs me." And it either, "This person needs me because I need to do something or they'll be mad and I'll get in trouble" or "This person needs me because I'm so good at my job, I'm gonna come in and save the day." And either one involves some level of ego. Which – it becomes about me and not about the client. And that's how I describe when your emotions start to overwhelm your work. It also becomes about you and not about the client. I always give the example of self-care – I have a cousin who did Doctors Without Borders and he went to Darfur. It was a really rough situation, there was an active genocide going on, really terrible public health situation, at the end he got evacuated by UN helicopter in the middle of the night.

SS: Wow.

AB: It was a rough scene. And some of the advice he got when he first went was, it's really tempting in that situation to skip your breaks, to skip your malaria prophylaxis. And the advice he got was, "Don't do that." Because if you pass out from exhaustion, the bed that was supposed to go to that mother who has been walking for two days to get to the only clinic nearby goes to you. If you get dehydrated, the IV that was supposed to go to that malnourished kid goes to you. If you get malaria, that malaria medicine that is supposed to go to that two-year-old goes to you.

SS: Right.

AB: So what I'll sometimes tell people, if they seem like they're not the type to take care of themselves for themselves, I'll say, "Remember it's worse for the kids, because you take the resources that are really for them."

SS: Yeah, yeah, absolutely. And when you think about this in behavior analysis absolutely. Okay, so you're burning the candle at both ends and you're running into the ground, running into the ground. Now what happens? Now you're sick. Now you can't make it. And all of the signs of burnout are very objective and measurable. When people talk about the idea of self-care and burnout being like, "Oh it's fluffy and it's like—" cancellations. Turning in documentation late. Not answering the phone when caregivers call you. Snapping at people. You can see these indicators of burnout across the board. And so you're absolutely, when you're pouring from an empty vessel, what ends up happening is, eventually you're gonna have nothing left to give. And that is gonna be a resource drain and actually hurt the learners that you're working with and the families you work with more. I always use the example too of – when you're in an airplane. And the airplane's going down and the masks drop. And everybody immediately tells you: you put the mask on yourself first before you put it on anybody else. And the reason being is that you can't help anybody until you help yourself. Like, imagine this scenario for a second: so all the masks drop and you run around and you're putting the masks on everybody else. "Okay, I got, I got you, I got you." And then eventually you don't have enough energy or you don't even have enough oxygen to make it back to your mask to put it on. That's what would happen if you did that. So they tell us to put the mask on first so that we can actively help other people. We engage in self-care so that we can continue the work and do it consistently. And to your point about the egos thing, yeah. I had a mentor of mine who describes it as "Savior behavior." So once I reframed it like that, I'm like, "I am not that important in this person's life, that I am gonna be their savior and save their life." Have there been moments where, if it hadn't been me being there – that this person is probably alive today? Yes, there have been those moments, legitimately. Pulling somebody out of traffic. I've been there for that. But am I the reason this family thrives? No. And we gotta let that go. They will be okay, I promise you. They got to this point, years before without you. They will get to this point and they will have these moments years after you're gone. They'll be okay. And you've just gotta be okay with setting a boundary. It's really more of setting a boundary than anything.

AB: And that doesn't diminish the gifts that you've given them.

SS: No.

AB: You don't have to be their savior to contribute.

SS: Right.

AB: You can contribute in smaller ways and that's valuable too. And that's amazing.

SS: Absolutely. Absolutely.

AB: But if you don't take care of yourself, you can't even contribute in those ways.

SS: Right, right. Going back to what you said, those small moments, of where you're chasing that high of somebody's first word or something like that. How can you even appreciate that when you're so tired and burnt out that you can't even attend to it in a meaningful way? I think of it like that, that's what it comes down to. If I'm working, and I want to be there for that person, and I want to be ever-present for that person, then I have to make sure that I am at my baseline. And I joke when I say that I'm at baseline when I have had at least one cup of coffee. That gets me to baseline, you know? That's good for me. And I think the other side too is – it's a process. It's not something people do consistently. It's not something that people do perfectly. We all slip up, I slip up. I'm not going to sit here and pretend to be like some self-care guru and be like "Follow my lead" because I'm probably not a great example for self-care sometimes, right? I mean people tell me all the time, "You look like you're doing all these things. You're so busy." I'm like, "You're right, I am busy." But people don't know in the background I have a very strict schedule. I don't work on Saturdays. It is blocked out. On Sundays I do just catch-up and planning for the week. I have a very very strict schedule that, if somebody asks me to do something, I'm like, "Sorry, can't do it." I've learned to do that. It's taken some time. That's the part that – I am busy – but I do have this boundary setting.

AB: And it takes a lot of work to arrange a schedule where you can preserve those times.

SS: Yes! It really is. And also it's hard to say no. It goes back to that, "Hey can you do this?" "Oh it sounds like a really cool opportunity." And for a long time I said yes because I was padding my resume. Like, "Yeah I'll do that, yeah I'll do that, yeah I'll do that." Like, "Sure, that looks great." I need to have the experience if I want to like go somewhere and be a professor one day, you know? But now I'm like "I don't have bandwidth" is what I'll say, "I don't have the bandwidth for that anymore." And I don't need to explain it and people appreciate it. But what I do too that's actually helped me with my guilt with has been, "I can't do that but here are some people who might be able to." And so, like, opening up the space for somebody who can do it and probably better than I can but in a way that gives them the opportunity and makes those connections. So for me that has been helpful. Like, not just saying "no," right? Because sometimes being told no or saying no is just kind of a problem, like that's the endpoint. So I have a problem with endpoints. I'm like, "No, but" – that's my diversion. "No, but here's this resource."

AB: That also lets go of the ego and that sort of opens up – you know we don't refer to each other enough in this field. We don't make recommendations for each other enough. This field has a lot of really wonderful, intelligent, compassionate, and talented people.

SS: Yeah! And I think you're absolutely right. And being able to leverage that support system. I mean, why not, right? I mean, I talk to people all the time at my job where people want to do more. They want to present, they want to get out there, they want to do these projects and they want to do these passion projects which… passion projects in themselves are a type of occupational self-care. So do the passion projects. Do the things that make you happy if you have the time to do them. But sometimes the people who want to do those things never have an opportunity. Like research. I get people asking me to do research all the time. You can go do research. You don't have to have a doctorate to do research. Which is beautiful. I have an RBT right now who's doing this really cool research project. You can do research right now. There's an RBT that published in JABA that did a really cool study on orcas. The actual subject was orcas!

AB: Wow, that's fantastic.

SS: So it's just a matter of setting it up so it's like, "Here's the pathway." I'm very solution-focused. If I see a problem, it's never gonna be a "no" and that's it, it's a "yes, here's how," or "no, but you can do this." But the same thing with self-care: I'm seeing a problem. And when I saw the problem of self-care come up in our field, or when I started to notice it, it became like a solution-focused thing for me. How do I solve this? Or how do I at least come up with some answers to give people so that they can solve this on their own. That's where – going back to your first question – that's really where that came from. I tend to be solution-oriented. So, I saw a problem, wanted to study it, wanted to fix it, and now I'm realizing it's a network of serious issues.

AB: So basically you looked at this from a function-based point of view.

ss: Yeah.

ab: And you're even looking at saying "no" from a function-based point of view. You're like, "You're asking me for something, so what's your motivating operation here, let's resolve that. Because you don't really need me. You need the problem solved. So let's resolve that issue."

ss: [laughing] Right. Yeah.

ab: So if we really think about problems to solve the way we're trained to think about problems to solve we'll have a lot fewer problems.

ss: Right! Absolutely. Or at least a better path for solution. I describe myself – I did my degree in psychology and all that – and I've been lately describing myself as "pathologically behaviorist." I have such a hard time looking at any other theoretical orientation. I understand the disciplinary practices and evidence-based practices but lie from a theory standpoint I cannot help but see the world through a behavioral lens. And it is a purely behavioral lens. So when I look at this problem, absolutely. It's not me. I am not the conduit to your problem being solved. I am not your solution. Your solution lies in the outcome, right? So maybe I'm a means to your solution, maybe I'm a resource towards your solution, but I am not the solution. And I am never gonna pretend to be. But at least let's get connected with the right pathways and the right resources in the right moment, and at least maybe a network of people can help solve this particular problem. And that has been incredibly liberating. That has taken so much pressure off of me. I don't have to be the self-care person. I don't have to be that person. My talks on self-care are simply just, if you zoom in a little but, here is the topic and here is the problem. But here are solutions that are out there – I didn't create these. As a matter of fact, the self-care theory came from nursing, it's Dorothea Orem. So like, that happened in the 50s. That's not a new thing. So I'm not discovering anything, I'm not producing anything. I'm not the savior of self-care in behavior analysis, it's nothing like that. It's simply, "Hey, here's a problem, here's some solutions." Now you have a resource and there's a function-based outcome exactly like you said. It's a skill deficit, there's a function related to self-care. We look at it from a prevent-teach-manage strategy. Most of self-care is prevention.

ab: So I'm gonna ask you one more wrap-up question.

ss: Let's do it!

ab: I'm curious: what is your self-care? What do you do, what are your self-care behaviors?

ss: Oh, you know it's funny, if I'm gonna go with things that are purely reinforcing, I make a point to read books that are not behavior analytic. I love reading Kurt Vonnegut. He is probably my favorite. I just love, he's got such a great perspective on the world. I guess like – comically cynical? I feel like that fits my world view a little bit. Tom Robbins is kind of the same way. So I do spend some time reading books that are not behavior analytic. For me, also, I play music so that's really helpful for me. Things that are not part of my job because I kind of always ask myself, "Who am I if I'm not a behavior analyst?" And I think that's where a lot of my other self-caring behaviors come in. Like, I'm a parent, I'm a husband, I'm a son. Spending time with my family, all of that stuff is really part of my self-caring routine. And that comes from identifying my values, right? My values are the people I care about, the people I love. Specifically spending time with the people that matter to me. Part of self-caring for me is helping others so I do get a lot of reinforcers out of that. I also, as somebody who has severe anxiety, I get treated for that. So that's a self-caring behavior. Actually getting treatment for a mental health diagnosis I have. That in itself is self-caring too. So I think when you ask the question "what are my self-caring behaviors?" There are some fun ones, but there are some definite necessary ones to keep me on homeostasis. Now, the last one I'll say is, like, coffee. Coffee is 100%...

AB: [laughing] Same here.

SS: Give me that cold brew, I will go... a roaster... send me anywhere. Which is funny because I was never a coffee guy until I started working at Starbucks. And then I was like, "Oh wait, there's a whole world out there." As much as I know about self-care, I know just as much about coffee. Which is kind of wild.

3.12 The Pressing Need for Ethical, Effective Supervision

Noor Y. Syed, Ksenia Gatzunis, and Nasiah Cirincione-Ulezi

The number of behavior analyst certificants continues to increase at exponential rates. As of March 2021, data collected from the Behavior Analyst Certification Board (BACB®) suggest approximately 20,000 Board Certified Behavior Analysts (BCBAs) have successfully obtained certification in 2016 or later (BACB, n.d.), a number that represents half of the total BCBAs currently certified. In addition, the number of Registered Behavior Technicians (RBTs) has increased nearly 300% since 2014 when the certification was first introduced; there are currently 89,000 RBTs worldwide. These data do not include behavior analysts in the United States who have chosen licensure exclusively, rather than state licensure and BACB certification, or through organizations such as the Qualified Applied Behavior Analysis Credentialing Board (QABA®) or the International Behavior Analyst Organization™ (IBAO). With the increase in certifying and licensure bodies, changes in BACB supervision requirements, and the growing number of newly certified BCBAs, many of whom will become supervisors of both trainees (e.g., licensure and certificant candidates) and RBTs, it is incumbent upon the field to continue refining strong supervisory practices.

While many behavior analysts turn to the BACB Task List (2012; 2017) for guidance in developing a scope and sequence of supervision for trainees, we argue that effective, ethical supervision must go beyond the task list. Turner and colleagues (2016) describe additional areas for supervision as critical, including clinical decision-making skills, professionalism, delivery and acceptance of feedback, and evaluation of performance expectations. Recent texts have also begun to explore supervision from the trainee, supervisor, and mentor perspectives, such as those published by Kazemi, Rice, and Adzhyan (2018) and LeBlanc, Sellers, and Ala'i (2020). The below will highlight what we believe are some of the most areas in supervision: critical thinking and problem solving, humility, and the importance of bidirectionality in supervision; however, the authors recommend reviewing the references texts for an in-depth investigation of supervision and mentorship tools.

A Few Key Repertoires in the Development of Behavior Analysts

Critical Thinking and Problem Solving

It is vital for behavior analysts to engage not only in "first level" decision-making, such as deciding to continue with a skill acquisition program when observing an ascending data trend, but also to engage in continuous problem solving regarding all aspects of their practice. These may include, but are not limited to, choosing an appropriate assessment, creating goals, deciding when to offer novel items as reinforcers within session, and how to deliver feedback in a compassionate, culturally humble manner.

DOI: 10.4324/9781003190707-31

Let us take choosing an appropriate assessment and goal creation as examples. When asked to conduct an assessment for a client to receive services, the behavior analyst must consider not only which assessment would be age and developmentally appropriate, but also what language the assessment should be conducted in. If the assessment has been normed with individuals for whom English is their primary language, has this assessment been validated for those who identify primarily with a language other than English? Does another assessment exist that would better fit the language of the client? If not, how does the behavior analyst engage in ways to promote the integrity of assessment results and client dignity throughout the process? As assessments drive many of our goals and interventions, is imperative that we engage in assessment implementation in a manner that is compassionate and humble or, in other words, is driven by our clients' cultural, linguistic, age, and developmental identifications rather than chosen for convenience.

This same precedent must be set for goal development. Far too often, the authors have heard that goals are chosen "because they are next on the (insert assessment here)." Instead, goals must be chosen compassionately and humbly (see Figure 1). They must be chosen in conjunction with the client whenever possible (e.g., person-centered planning, Holburn & Vietze, 2000) and caregivers such that goals of the highest social and cultural significance are chosen. The behavior analyst should consider which goals contextually match the environment, are feasible financially, and of the highest priority. Engaging in this continuous critical thinking increases social validity of programming, leading to strong compassionate care.

Engaging in behaviors such as those described here, along with the myriad of other ethical, clinical decisions behavior analysts make continuously throughout their work, must be treated as a cusp (Rosales-Ruiz & Baer, 1997). It should be taught to trainees through constant discussion surrounding rationale for decision-making with both positive and corrective feedback and via behavioral skills training (BST) (Parsons et al., 2012) until the behaviors become automatic. It is recommended that supervisors encourage behavior analysts to consider all contingencies surrounding each situation, including available data, review of literature, reinforcer strength and availability, clarity in instructional delivery, social and cultural significance, social validity, instructional history of clients and caregivers, and phylogenetic variables. Once the behavior analyst readily engages in such questions when making clinical and ethical decisions, ability to lead others in these behaviors should be assessed.

Bidirectionality and Power in the Supervisory Relationship

In this section, we will move from compassion and humility in client-behavior analyst relations to supervisee-trainee relationships within the supervision dynamic, which is paramount for success. Leblanc, Sellers and Ala'i (2020) describe supervision as an opportunity to establish and maintain a meaningful, rewarding, and sustained relationship that enhances the professional growth of *both* parties. In this description, the supervisor and supervisee co-create a mutually beneficial professional exchange. Because the word supervisor is often used synonymously with words like *boss, manager,* or *head,* many mistakenly enter the supervisory relationship operating from the paradigm that the supervisor has more to offer than the supervisee. This belief is further reinforced because the supervisory relationship has a built-in power differential which is a result of the accountability process (Kaiser, 1997). Supervisors have power over supervisees primarily because of the need to evaluate the quality of their work (Kaiser, 1997), potentially making power and authority two of the most salient features of the supervisory relationship. Therefore, supervisors and supervisees are encouraged to each assume partial responsibility for the health of the

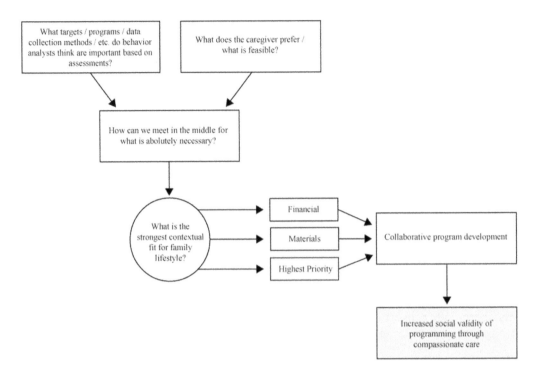

Figure 1 Compassionate care and cultural humility in goal development.

relationship (LeBlanc et al., 2020). One way this can be achieved is by supervisors and supervisees committing to a collaborative supervisory relationship, characterized by routine and consistent bidirectional feedback, and open discussion about supervisory interaction.

Bidirectional feedback, unlike unidirectional feedback, flows in two directions between the supervisor and supervisee. When working within this framework, the supervisor shares directional feedback with the supervisee and receives their perspectives on effective supervisory practices. This bidirectionality is one way to manage power differentials in the supervisory relationship. Stakeholders within the supervisory relationship are invited to continuously identify and seek to understand the role of power and the differentials in power that may manifest in the supervisory relationship.

VeneKlasen and Miller (2007) describe four different expressions of power that may be useful for individuals within the context of a supervisory relationship: *power over, power with, power to*, and *power within*. A *power within* expression has to do with a person's sense of self-worth and self-knowledge; it includes an ability to recognize individual differences while respecting others (VeneKlasen & Miller, 2007). *Power within* has the broadest reach, is most sustainable, and leads to the greatest compassion and humility within supervision.

Cultural Considerations and Humility within Supervision

Just as clinicians must consider cultural variables and factors within their assessment and treatment of behavior for their clients (e.g., Fong et al., 2016), behavior analysts have also identified culturally responsive supervision and mentorship as crucial components for a successful supervision experience for behavior analytic practitioners (Fong, 2020; LeBlanc et al., 2020). Education, training, and continuing education opportunities on culturally responsive practices have been limited (Beaulieu et al., 2019; Conners et al., 2019). Behavior analysts have called for an increase in educational and training opportunities, as well as increased guidance, accountability, and transparency for behavior analytic practitioners. Guidance is needed in this area; LeBlanc and colleagues (2020) stated that culturally responsive supervisors:

> Assess and understand their own culture, learn from and appreciate the culture of others, tailor systems to meet the unique cultural and linguistic needs to diverse people in their organizations, acknowledge and response to inequities related to identity, work towards educational justice, embrace diversity and inclusion as an organizational strength, understand that cultural responsiveness is a lifelong endeavor, and are humble.
>
> (p. 46)

The authors provided readers with a variety of activities to help work toward these goals, such as cultural awareness interviews and reflections on own levels of privilege within a supervisory relationship (e.g., race, sex, gender, religion, socioeconomic status, education, health, languages spoken, age).

Fong (2020) broke down how providing effective cross-cultural supervision directly relates to the Behavior Analyst Certification Board's® (BACB®) Professional and Ethical Compliance Code. For example, according to code 3.04, behavior analysts must explain the results of an assessment in a manner that is understandable to the consumer/client (BACB®, 2014); in terms of cross-cultural supervision, Fong pointed out that this may require the use of an interpreter and/or documents that are translated in the language most comfortable to the client. Additionally, Fong provided a flowchart titled the Assessment of Culturally Sensitive Practice in Behavior Analysis Algorithm, which can aid the behavior analyst in how to best proceed when working with clients from different backgrounds.

Recent changes within the field of behavior analysis provide hope for the future, such as the expansion of the BACB®'s Professional and Ethical Compliance Code (2014, 2020) to include additional cultural considerations. The existing version of the Professional and Ethical Compliance Code (BACB®, 2014) had one main code that prohibited discriminatory practices (code 1.05); however, the Ethics Code for Behavior Analysts (BACB®, 2020), effective January 2022, also includes several additional relevant codes (e.g., see codes 1.07, 1.08, 4.07) and core principles (e.g., see core principles 1, 2, and 4) surrounding this topic. It is important to note that while some codes and core principles specifically mention terms like cultural responsiveness and diversity, the need to address cultural considerations is relevant to a much wider set of codes. For example, code 4.08 discusses the need to provide supervisees with performance feedback (BACB®, 2020). Supervisors must consider the differences that may exist in cultural norms between the supervisor's and supervisee's cultures in terms of both what is acceptable while giving and/or receiving feedback. Additionally, the BACB® began collecting and sharing demographic data of BACB® certificants in 2020 (e.g., RBTs®, BCBAs®, and BCBA-Ds® which allow increased understanding of any discrepancies between the demographics of supervisors and direct service workers, as well as the demographics of certificates and the consumers of their services (BACB®, 2020).

Additionally, more journal articles and books have focused on this important issue. Conners et al. (2019) specifically discussed gaps in graduate school training, supervision/fieldwork, and professional development opportunities. Other authors discussed topics such as the importance of cultural humility within the field (Wright, 2019), a review of existing literature on multilingualism within ABA and ideas for future directions (Wang et al., 2019), and the introduction of a self-assessment tool that can be utilized to ensure the use of affirming practices with a variety of individuals (e.g., supervisees, clients, workers) who are transgender and gender-nonconforming (Leland & Stockwell, 2019). Additionally, a special designation has been developed for the annual Association for Behavior Analysis International convention featuring talks about issues related to diversity, equity, and inclusion (DEI).

Despite these moves in a positive direction, behavior analysts will continue to require more guidance at both individual and organizational levels (e.g., Miller et al., 2019). As previously mentioned, the BACB® should increase its certification criteria to include coursework and continuing education requirements on DEI topics, similar to its ethics and supervision requirements. For example, to become a licensed behavior analyst of a certified behavior analyst assistant in New York State, applicants are required to have had coursework surrounding issues of cultural and ethnic diversity (New York State Education Department, n.d.); in Tennessee, continuing education in cultural diversity is required (Tennessee Department of Health, n.d.). While other states could adopt similar rules, a BACB® requirement would cover all BCBA®/BCBA-Ds® regardless of their location. On the individual level, behavior analysts must continue to seek out additional education and training when available, follow the recommendations that exist in current literature, and advocate for social justice changes within our field for both clients and practitioners.

Conclusion

It is critical for supervisors and professors to teach effective, ethical supervision practices, as newly certified supervisors undertake the responsibility of educating behavior analysts of our future. The emergence of supervision curricula and literature, particularly surrounding diversity, equity, and inclusion, is heartening, but we must continue this work. We have highlighted a few pivotal behaviors our supervisors must possess, but this list is by no means exhaustive. Too, we must be cognizant of the continuity between supervision and mentorship. What are skills an effective mentor must have and impart upon their mentees and how do we begin to delineate pure supervision from effective mentorship? We continue to encourage our colleagues to systematically evaluate our supervisory practices while asking ourselves, our trainees, behavior technicians, and most importantly, our clients – how are we doing? And how can we do better?

Works Cited

Beaulieu, L., Addington, J., & Almeida, D. (2019). Behavior analysts' training and practices regarding cultural diversity: the case for culturally competent care. *Behavior Analysis in Practice*, *12*(3), 557–575. doi: 10.1007/s40617-018-00313-6.

Behavior Analyst Certification Board (n.d.). *BACB Certificant Data*. Retrieved from <ds>www.bacb.com/BACB-certificant-data.</ds>

Behavior Analyst Certification Board (2012). *BCBA Task List* (4th ed.). Littleton, CO: Author.

Behavior Analyst Certification Board (2017). *BCBA Task List* (5th ed.). Littleton, CO: Author.

Behavior Analyst Certification Board. (2021). *BCBA® 2022 Eligibility Requirements*. Retrieved from <ds>www.bacb.com/wp-content/uploads/2020/11/BCBA-2022EligibilityRequirements_210212-2.pdf.</ds>

Behavior Analyst Certification Board. (2014). *Professional and Ethical Compliance Code for Behavior Analysts*. <ds>www.bacb.com/wp-content/uploads/2020/05/BACB-Compliance-Code-english_190318.pdf.</ds>

Behavior Analyst Certification Board. (2020b). *Ethics Code for Behavior Analysts*. <ds>www.bacb.com/wp-content/uploads/2020/11/Ethics-Code-for-Behavior-Analysts-210106.pdf.</ds>

Conners, B., Johnson, A., Duarte, J., Murriky, R., & Marks, K. (2019). Future directions of training and fieldwork in diversity issues in applied behavior analysis. *Behavior Analysis in Practice, 12*(4), 767–776. doi:10.1007/s40617-019-00349-2.

Fong, E. H. (2020). Examining cross-cultural supervision in applied behavior analysis. In B. M. Conners & S. T. Capell (eds.), *Multiculturalism and diversity in applied behavior analysis: Bridging theory and application.* (pp. 181–193). London: Routledge.

Fong, E. H., Catagnus, R. M., Brodhead, M. T., Quigley, S., & Field, S. (2016). Developing the cultural awareness skills of behavior analysts. *Behavior Analysis in Practice, 9*(1), 84–94. doi:10.1007/ s40617-016-0111-6.

Holburn, S. & Vietze, P. (2000). Person-centered planning and cultural inertia in applied behavior analysis. *Behavior and Social Issues, 10*, 39–70.

Kaiser, T. L. (1997). *Supervisory relationships exploring the human element.* Pacific Grove, CA: Brooks/Cole Publishing Company.

Kazemi, E., Rice, B., & Adzhyan, P. (2018). *Fieldwork and supervision for behavior analysts: A handbook.* New York, NY: Springer.

LeBlanc, L. A., Sellers, T. P., & Ala'i, S. (2020). *Building and sustaining meaningful and effective relationships as a supervisor and mentor.* Cornwall on Hudson, NY: Sloan Publishing.

Leland, W., & Stockwell, A. (2019). A self-assessment tool for cultivating affirming practices with transgender and gender-nonconforming (TGNC) clients, supervisees, students, and colleagues. *Behavior Analysis in Practice, 12*(4), 816–825. doi:10.1007/s40617-019-00375-0.

Miller, K. L., Re Cruz, A., & Ala'i-Rosales, S. (2019). Inherent tensions and possibilities: behavior analysis and cultural responsiveness. *Behavior and Social Issues, 28*(1), 16–36. doi:10.1007/ s42822-019-00010-1.

New York State Education Department. (2021, March 16). *Applied behavior analysis.* <ds>www. op.nysed.gov/prof/aba.</ds>

Parsons, M.B., Rollyson, J.H., & Reid, D.H. (2012). Evidence-based staff training: a guide for practitioners. *Behavior Analysis in Practice, 5*(2), 2–11. doi:10.1007/BF03391819.

Rosales-Ruiz, J. & Baer, D.M. (1997). Behavioral cusps: a developmental and pragmatic concept of behavior analysis. *Journal of Applied Behavior Analysis, 30*(3), 533–544.

Tennessee Department of Health (n.d.). *About the applied behavior analyst.* <ds>www.tn.gov/health/ health-program-areas/health-professional-boards/applied-behavior-analyst/applied-behavior-analyst/about-applied-behavior-analyst.html.</ds>

Turner, L.B., Fischer, A.J., & Luiselli, J.K. (2016). Towards a competency-based, ethical, and socially valid approach to the supervision of applied behavior analytic trainees. *Behavior Analysis in Practice, 9*, 287–298. doi:10.1007/s40617-016-0121-4.

Wang, Y., Kang, S., Ramirez, J., & Tarbox, J. (2019). Multilingual diversity in the field of applied behavior analysis and autism: a brief review and discussion of future directions. *Behavior Analysis in Practice, 12*(4), 795–804. doi:10.1007/s40617-019-00382-1.

Wright, P. I. (2019). Cultural humility in the practice of applied behavior analysis. *Behavior Analysis in Practice, 12*(4), 805–809. doi:10.1007/s40617-019-00343-8.

VeneKlasen, L., & Miller, V. (2007). *A new weave of power, people and politics.* Sterling, VA: Stylus.

3.13 Bringing Challenge to Coercion and the Status Quo

Alexandria L. Thomas and Matthew T. Brodhead

Sidman (2000) defined acts of *coercion* as instances in which a person is "compelled under duress or threat to do something" that is against their will (p. 36). Sidman explains the use of positive reinforcement is noncoercive. Instead, behavior change through negative reinforcement, avoidance, and punishment may very well align with the definition of coercion.

Nature is, by its own design, coercive. For example, touching a hot stove prevents the occurrence of similar behavior in the future, and eating a poison berry that results in stomach discomfort presents future consumption of harmful fruit. In these cases, and many others, coercion is likely of great biological benefit to the organism. But again, in these cases, coercion is a matter of design by nature itself, and to the benefit of its inhabitants.

Like nature, many cultural systems (see Skinner, 1981) of coercion exist today. For example, governments rely on financial penalties and incarceration to control behavior. Teachers penalize students for tardiness, and banks seize assets when mortgages go unpaid. It would be nearly impossible to list every coercive system that has been built through human action. But the reality is that despite the robust technology of positive reinforcement and its effectiveness in changing behavior, society has largely defaulted to creating coercive systems to further its own benefit and, in many cases, at the cost of its inhabitants.

The practice of Applied Behavior Analysis (ABA) is no different in terms of its construction being a matter of cultural design. ABA is a cultural system (Glenn, 1993), including its ethics codes and values, and members of that cultural system are constantly faced with an important choice between using positive reinforcement or coercion to change behavior. In some cases, the use of coercion may be obvious, such as the use of overcorrection as a consequence for inappropriate behavior. In other cases, coercion may very well manifest in the form of an often used behavior change strategy, such as escape extinction, that may appear commonplace and occurs without question.

Every single clinical behavior or decision in ABA practice occurs within a choice context, and ethical behavior is no different (Brodhead et al., 2018; Cox & Brodhead, in press). And as we mentioned above, countless times a day, the behavior analyst is faced with the decision of whether to use positive reinforcement or coercion to change behavior. The selection of positive reinforcement, we argue, is generally the more ethically justifiable topography.[1] And even though that response may require more effort, time, and financial and physical resource (amongst others) to result in effective behavior change, we argue this is a small response cost compared to the fallout of coercive practices and the dangers they present to our field and its reputation and, most importantly, its consumers.

The purpose of this paper is to briefly examine clinical practices through the lens of coercion. We argue that context determines whether or not a certain behavioral practice

DOI: 10.4324/9781003190707-32

is coercive. By describing examples of potential coercive contexts in clinical practice, we hope to illustrate the nuance and prevalence of coercion, in order to help the reader identify and resolve coercive practices in their own areas of work. Finally, we provide some general recommendations to begin to eliminate coercive practices from treatment, in an effort to engage in better and more ethically justifiable practice decisions, and to continue to reform the way ABA interventions are delivered to ensure delivery occurs in a manner that supports the ultimate protection and dignity of its consumers.

Examples of Coercion in ABA Practice

Below, we provide examples of potentially coercive practices in ABA service delivery. Each and every one of the below examples represents an outcome of a choice a behavior analyst made: to use positive reinforcement or coercion. We argue the ethically justifiable decision, in a vast majority of cases, is to adopt strategies of positive reinforcement, even if such strategies require more response effort to effectively execute. Therefore, the examples described below likely represent ethical decisions that are incongruent with what we would define as ABA that is free from coercive practices.

It is possible that the reader may review the below examples and dismiss them as examples of "behavior analysts behaving in unethical ways" that do not represent "best practice" in the field. Though we can appreciate this feeling and recognize the below descriptions do not represent the high standards of the profession and scientific discipline, this dismissive narrative is one that our field has been repeating for quite some time, and unfortunately, this narrative has brought little success in changing consumer perceptions of ABA. So instead of attributing the below examples to "bad actors," we ask the reader to consider these examples in the context in which they deliver ABA services, and look at their current model of service delivery to identify the coercive practices that are present, and to replace those coercive practices with interventions rooted in positive reinforcement. The reader should consider the elimination of coercion (and therefore the "total adoption" of reinforcement-only interventions) as a process, never an endpoint; because changes and shifts in systems of practice and care will continue to raise new issues and problems that require resolution.

Example #1: Escape Extinction

Escape extinction involves withholding access to a reinforcer, when a response occurs that has previously produced access to that reinforcer. Unlike extinction of positively reinforced behavior (where a response no longer produces the reinforcer), escape extinction involves continued presentation of an aversive stimulus, even in the presence of the escape response that once produced the removal of that aversive stimulus (negative reinforcer) (see Catania, 2013).

The use of escape extinction, we argue, is coercive in many cases. Consider the following example of an 18-year-old person with autism and anemia who refuses to eat foods that are green. A behavior analyst may begin a feeding program, and in that program, place green foods in front of that client, insisting those foods are consumed before any additional activities take place, despite continued refusal from the client. This practice is coercive because it involves the continued presentation of an aversive stimulus (green food), even if the response that once resulted in its removal occurs. Though eating green foods is likely very important, the medical condition of anemia could very well supersede the need for "compliance" in food consumption in exchange for ensuring healthy red blood cell levels.

Example #2: Intensive Stereotypy Reduction Programs

Intensive stereotypy reduction programs may resemble another example of coercive practices. Response interruption and redirection (RIRD), for example, involves interrupting a target response and redirecting the person to engage in another behavior or activity. One of the reasons RIRD is thought to be effective in reducing stereotypy is because the response interruption component may function as positive punishment. Further, by engaging in non-stereotypic behavior in the presence of people who deliver the RIRD intervention, that person is likely under the control of an avoidance contingency whereas non-stereotypic behaviors result in the prevention of onset of an aversive stimulus (in this case, response interruption).

Consider an example where a three-year-old child engages in stereotypy in the form of hand flapping and fast running back and forth. The behavior analyst introduced an intensive RIRD intervention to reduce the stereotypy in order to help reduce stigma from their peers in general education classrooms, even though the child's stereotypy does not interfere with the child's learning. In this case, the use of RIRD involves the unnecessary introduction of aversive stimuli into the child's environment and, as a result, the use of RIRD is likely coercive in this case.

Example #3: Time Out

Time out involves putting someone in a situation they find less enjoyable than the one they are currently in, in an effort to reduce the frequency of that behavior. Through this negative punishment contingency, the person is less likely to engage in the target behavior in the future, and likely begins to engage in "appropriate" and "alternative" behaviors in an effort to avoid the negative punishment contingency. Therefore, the use of time out to change behavior is coercive.

Consider an example of a four-year-old child from a single-parent household, who often screams at home in order to gain access to attention from his very busy mom. In this case, the mother reports to her behavior analyst that the child's screaming often occurs when they are alone. At the behavior analyst's clinic, the child often screams in large group settings due to the low frequency of attention that is provided to them. As a result of screaming, the child is removed from large group instruction, taken into a separate room where even less attention is provided, so they can "calm down" and to reduce the disruption of the other children in the large group setting. In this case, the use of timeout involves moving someone to a less desirable situation than they were currently in. And this application of timeout likely meets the definition of coercion.

Additional Examples

The above three examples of escape extinction, RIRD, and time out represent only three situations in which a behavior analyst made a choice to use a coercive behavior-change practice instead of using positive reinforcement. But these examples illustrate a mere fraction of the types of coercive interventions that can occur during daily practice. Additional examples include using aggressive tones of voice towards consumers, physical prompting, overcorrection, withholding access to basic needs, denying access to free time, and so on.

Moving Beyond Coercion in ABA Practice

Above, we described examples of coercive practice in ABA service delivery. Next, we briefly describe a framework for creating systems that foster positive reinforcement-only interventions and ensure that behavior analysts continue to operate in a manner that is consumer focused while upholding the high ethical standards and values of the profession. We recommend taking a behavioral systems approach to promoting ethical employee behavior in the workplace, including noncoercive employee behavior. For more information about behavioral systems analysis in the workplace, see Brodhead and Higbee (2012), Brodhead et al. (2018), and Brodhead (2020).

We recommend behavior analysts construct an organizational definition of coercion. This definition may align with that described by Sidman (2000), or the definition may be modified to reflect the values of their consumers, community, employees, and profession. Next, behavior analysts should specify goals for reducing coercive practices, describe measurement techniques for evaluating the reduction of coercive practices over time, and indicate how those data will be reviewed to inform future systems revision.

Behavior analysts should identify interventions to help reduce the occurrence of coercive practices in the workplace.[2] Examples include, but are not limited to, systems of employee oversight and supervision that ensure reinforcement-only interventions are used, direct training that highlights what coercion is and how it can be harmful to consumers, and incentives for employees who increase their use of reinforcement-only interventions. Additional examples include incorporating consumers into treatment decision-making as much as possible (e.g., through concurrent operant preference assessments), frequent use of preference assessments, and reducing physical prompting procedures to the greatest extent possible.

In addition, we encourage organizations to invest heavily in systems of employee monitoring that (1) prevent coercive practices from occurring when supervisors are not present, and (2) can serve as documented evidence in the event coercive practices are suspected. Consider a recent example where two employees were caught on video physically abusing children with autism who could not speak (Hannah, 2018). Though it is difficult to project if these horrific practices could have been prevented with proper training and supervision, without video surveillance systems, this abuse might have gone unnoticed. Given the increase in funding in many popular sectors of ABA treatment (e.g., autism), we believe the costs associated with such systems are drops in the bucket compared to the longstanding damages to consumers that arise from intervention practices that go unmonitored.

For any intervention or change a behavior analyst makes with the intention to reduce coercive practices, we recommend they closely monitor intervention progress. A lack of behavior change would be cause for intervention revision. Also, in the hopeful event that an intervention is successful, it remains quite possible that intervention may drift into mediocracy, either quite quickly or slowly and without notice. Therefore, we strongly encourage continued monitoring of intervention progress along with an ironclad commitment to revising interventions to help to achieve the ultimate objective of reducing coercive practices in ABA treatment.

Conclusion

In this paper, we described Sidman's (2000) definition of coercion and identified potentially coercive practices in ABA treatment. Then, we briefly described a framework for how behavior analysts may reduce the occurrence of coercive practices in the workplace. Though it is difficult to fully list or address every type of coercive act, we hope this paper serves as a framework for igniting improvements in the way ABA practices are delivered.

We recognize that some may be critical of our position, especially since many of the interventions we have described (e.g., RIRD) have been shown to be successful in changing behavior. We do not dispute the efficacy of behavioral interventions such as RIRD.

Instead, we dispute the default use of coercive interventions when alternatives rooted in positive reinforcement are readily available. We dispute the widespread acceptance of adopting and implementing interventions without thought to whether or not those interventions may be coercive.

In the end, we recognize that readers of this text, regardless of their agreement with our position, want the same thing, which is to see a world comprised of humane and effective application of behavioral interventions. We challenge readers to pursue this goal by questioning the status quo and becoming critical of the use of coercive practices in ABA treatment. Though coercion may likely never be fully removed from the environment, if we put our minds to it, we can come awfully close to doing so.

Notes

1 Certainly, there are exceptions to this statement and the use of coercion could be ethically justifiable.
2 If a behavior analyst is unsure as to what intervention strategy to pursue when trying to reduce coercive employee behavior, we strongly encourage them to review the Performance Diagnostic Checklist – Human Services, described by Carr et al. (2013).

Works Cited

Brodhead, M. T. (2020). A workbook in behavioral systems analysis and ethical behavior. BetterABA.

Brodhead, M. T., & Higbee, T. S. (2012). Teaching and maintaining ethical behavior in a professional organization. Behavior Analysis in Practice, 5, 86–92. https://dx.doi.org/10.1007%2FBF03391827.

Brodhead, M. T., Cox, D. J., & Quigley, S. P. (2018). Practical ethics for effective treatment of autism spectrum disorder. Cambridge, MA: Academic Press.

Catania, A. C. (2013). Learning (5th edition). Cornwall on Hudson, NY: Sloan Publishing.

Carr, J. E., Wilder, D. A., Majdalany, L., Mathisen, D., & Strain, L. A. (2013). An assessment-based solution to a human-service employee performance problem: an initial evaluation of the Performance Diagnostic Checklist – Human Services. Behavior Analysis in Practice, 6, 16–32. doi:10.1007/BF03391789.

Cox, D. J., & Brodhead, M. T. (in press). A proof of concept analysis of decision-making with time-series data. The Psychological Record. Advanced online publication. https://doi.org/10.1007/s40732-020-00451-w.

Glenn, S. S. (1993). Windows on the 21st century. The Behavior Analyst, 16, 133–151. doi:10.1007/BF03392619.

Hannah, J. (2018, April 16). Three families speak on abuse at ProMedica's autism center at Bixby Hospital. NBC24News. https://nbc24.com/news/local/three-families-speak-on-abuse-at-promedicas-autism-center-at-bixby-hospital.

Sidman, M. (2000). Coercion and its fallout (revised ed.). Authors Cooperative.

Skinner, B. F. (1981). Selection by consequence. Science, 213, 501–504. https://doi.org/10.1126/science.7244649.

3.14 Confidentiality in the Age of Social Media

Mary Jane Weiss and Samantha Russo

As behavior analysts, we often come across situations where the Ethics Code for Behavior Analysts serves as a compass for decision making. It can guide the way, and it can right us when we are off course. In the context of confidentiality, we are very much in need of a compass. The risks and considerations have intensified as a result of the ways in which technology now intersects with our personal and professional lives.

Historically, confidentiality has always been an emphasis in the provision of human services and in the field of applied behavior analysis. Effort has also been made to maintain confidentiality, to disguise the identity of clients, and to refrain from using descriptors that could potentially lead to identifiability of the client. However, as behavior analysts, we may need to realize that "identifiable" may not be as clear cut as we think.

A lack of identifiable information is commonly an emphasis during staff training, with a focus on sensitizing staff to unintentional violations. Typically, we think of this to mean discussions of the client's first name, the client's surname, and posting information in and around schools, clinics, or centers. Behavior analysts have also been instructed to censor conversations in the community, to be cautious when discussing clients at dinner with colleagues, and to be aware of chance meetings with clients outside of the clinical setting. All of these behaviors could lead to unintentional violations of confidentiality.

A behavior analyst might shy away from using the client's name or revealing their age; however, one must consider other information that may make the client identifiable. If two behavior analysts are talking about a specific client's challenging behavior, and someone close to the client overhears, might that yield enough information for the client to be identified? Might a family member reading a description of a behavioral episode knowingly identify their own child?

These have been historic issues, and are not new concerns. However, as technology has evolved, the risk has changed. Social media is now a way of life, and is used for both professional and personal functions. Facebook, Instagram, Snapchat, and Twitter are all common for professionals to use to network with other professionals. There are study groups, online forums, and chat boards. All of them are easily accessible for professionals to pose a question, share an article, or just talk to other professionals. In addition, most individuals in modern society also use such platforms to socially engage personally. They may use these platforms as a way to stay in touch with friends and family, to find others with shared interests, or to expand their personal social network. Increasingly, checking in on electronic devices and platforms, as well as on social media outlets, has become normative. Sharing information about one's personal and professional life in electronic arenas is ubiquitous, and society views it as acceptable and essential. However, with constant access, there is an increased risk of virtually crossing paths with someone that is connected to the client or can identify them by descriptors.

DOI: 10.4324/9781003190707-33

This is a real-world problem with severe consequences. In the Ethics Code for Behavior Analysts (2020), sections 2.03 and 2.04 are devoted entirely to maintaining client confidentiality. Not only does the code specify that confidentiality must be maintained, it also outlines how information about the client may be used. Additionally, this section emphasizes that information must only be discussed for scientific and/or professional purposes. Furthermore, in section 5.10, behavior analysts are specifically prohibited from sharing any identifying information about clients or supervisees within a social media context.

Behavior analysts' assessment of the risk associated with sharing information on social media may often be inaccurate, increasing the risk posed by use of social media platforms. Although information on sanctions is publicly posted on the Board Analyst Certification Board's website, this information is not reliably accessed by behavior analysts. Therefore, the risk factor, and the reality of the potential consequences, may not be salient to most behavior analysts. In other disciplines, the potential risk of posting on social media has been more publicized. Mostaghimi and Crotty (2011) compared the social media world to the new generation's elevator. In other words, conversations may be heard, even when presumed or intended to be private. Even if something is said without making specific reference to a client, the tone of the conversation may be enough to raise alarms. In 2011, a medical professional, Dr. Alexandra Thran, was terminated from a Rhode Island hospital after she posted information online about a patient. Even though she did not post the patient's name or other obviously identifying information, she wrote enough information on the posting that members of the community could identify the patient. This issue of what is "identifiable" information is one that many professionals may overlook or underestimate. And our assessments of the adequacy of disguise, sadly, are often lacking.

Mostaghimi and Crotty (2011) make several recommendations for physicians who are active on social media, which are still highly relevant to behavior analysts. The first and foremost is that all posted content should be considered public and permanent. An additional guideline to follow is not to post anything that would not be said or physically posted in the office. The authors also stress that no identifiable vignettes should be posted. While these guidelines may be in place for medical professionals, each one is a sound recommendation for behavior analysts as well. In public presentations, some behavior analysts now post disclaimers about vignettes, and many have begun to use the names of fictional characters rather than actual names that might be perceived as referencing an actual individual.

There are also guidelines posted specifically for behavior analysts and social media use. O'Leary et al. (2017) use some of the same guiding principles from the medical profession, with the addition of a few that pertain more to behavior analysts and the code. For example, an important guideline in the age of instant advice is to avoid making treatment recommendations in an online forum. Advice giving seems to be turning into a common place behavior in Facebook groups specifically dedicated to the field of applied behavior analysis. Every day, there are new posts asking for advice on a client's challenging behavior, or even on what skills should be targeted next. Advising on clients through a snapshot of the individual posted on social media could lead to an ethical violation of sections 2.01: Providing Effective Treatment, 2.13: Selecting, Designing and Implementing Assessments, and 2.14: Selecting, Designing and Implementing Behavior Change Interventions (BACB, 2020). However, behavior analysts are posting back with treatment recommendations at an alarmingly high rate. O'Leary et al. also recommend referring readers of social media posts, blogs, or chat boards back to the extant literature. This recommendation may help behavior analysts to stay in compliance with 1.05: Practicing within Scope of Competence, and 1.06: Maintaining Competence (BACB, 2020). Finally, a good guiding principle is the recommendation for ongoing training. In order to stay current with best practices within the field, professionals must maintain competency through professional development (BACB, 2020).

Behavior analysts should also be aware of mishaps unrelated to the actual client served. Frustrations about work conditions, frustration with co-workers, administration, or other employees could all be situations in which confidentiality is breached. When an employee posts something in this context, there may be a situation in which six degrees of separation lead to the information falling into the wrong hands. This could be something as careless as tagging the organization in the post, or as seemingly benign as being affiliated with the organization as an employee listed on Facebook. All of the information could easily find its way back into the hands of the organization. This could lead to a potential violation of the core principles, in which behavior analysts are tasked with upholding the values, ethics, and principles of the field and behaving with integrity (BACB, 2020).

Students of behavior analysis should also be cautious with what they post online. Although not yet bound to the same ethical code as a board certified behavior analyst, students should practice conducting themselves in a manner consistent with the ethical rigor expected of a behavior analyst. There are a multitude of online forums specifically targeting students, which may lure some into thinking that this is a safe place to seek advice. However, students must be careful not to engage in behavior that would violate their college's academic dishonesty policy. Some examples of inappropriate forum posting could be soliciting advice on homework, attempting to secure scholarly articles without conducting proper research, or asking for help with case studies. All of these behaviors are inappropriate for a new professional about to enter the field of applied behavior analysis.

Scenarios

A behavior analytic organization uses Instagram and Facebook to post pictures of their clients. The organization never posts pictures with the client's name; however, they often post pictures from school dances, programs, and other events. Once the pictures are posted, parents will often comment on the pictures and talk about their child. Is this a concern if the behavior analyst comments on the pictures? What if they share the pictures in other contexts?

Yes, there is an enormous amount of identifiable information on the post. Once the client's picture is posted, there is already personal information identified. Then, if the parent starts to comment on the post, the client's last name (assuming it is the same as the parent's) is now publicly posted to the picture. If the behavior analyst then comments on the picture, he or she may have inadvertently shared confidential information. And sharing the pictures in other contexts literally expands the risk exponentially, and makes an inadvertent identification more likely.

A parent of a current student sends a behavior analyst a "friend request" on Facebook. Is the behavior analyst able to accept the request, and is this permissible?

While the ethical code may not explicitly have a statement in this area, this is a dangerous and slippery slope. The most conservative interpretation of the code would explicitly prohibit this. The parent of the student could potentially gain access to personal information about the behavior analyst that could lead to blurred lines between the two. And the behavior analyst could end up mixing personal and professional worlds in a way that fails to protect the confidentiality of clients served. This could also lead to a multiple relationship or conflict of interest.

A behavior analyst who runs a small consultation service has a chat board in which she encourages parents to post success stories of their child as a way to network with the local community and other parents. The parents find comfort and share in each other's successes as their children make progress on various skills. Is this okay?

Under 5.07: Soliciting Testimonials from Current Clients for Advertising, this would be prohibited if the client is currently receiving services from the behavior analyst. Even if the information was from a former client, there must be a disclaimer announcing how the information was obtained (solicited or unsolicited) as well as a statement including information on the relationship between the behavior analyst and the client. Additionally, under the Ethics Code (BACB, 2020), behavior analysts must consider the possibility that former clients may re-enter services.

Furthermore, it may be that the behavior analyst is participating in public sharing of confidential information in a manner that exposes the individual to a violation of their privacy.

Guidelines for Navigating Social Media Risk

Individuals and organizations need to address the issues of social media risk in multiple ways. It is important to tackle the issue in a direct and clear way. It is a difficult task, in part because it is counter-cultural, especially for younger workers who are comfortable with and present on social media in many contexts of their lives. They need to be coached and instructed to have a different set of rules for themselves professionally and personally. Rationales should be provided to both clients and staff members about why social media interactions must be avoided and how engaging in social media contact may place clients at risk for violations of their privacy and confidentiality. Policies can assist staff members in adhering to the code. Supervisors can support staff, and staff members can support one another, by revisiting the issue frequently, by providing feedback when violations are noted or raised by others, by examining potential drift from policy, and by strengthening the organization's overall commitment to the protection of confidential client information.

In public discussions within the field, behavior analysts must take care to ensure that they are not providing advice inappropriately, disguising confidential information adequately, and using disclaimers to indicate that the information shared is not reflective of an actual or a particular context. With these safeguards in place, the unintended violations of confidentiality should be minimized. Behavior analysts are urged to be vigilant about the ways in which technology presents unique challenges, and to be mindful of the obligations to protect the privacy and confidentiality of the vulnerable individuals we serve.

In addition, behavior analysts should behave professionally, and treat others with compassion and respect. When disagreements arise among professionals and are discussed in professional forums, it is important to maintain decorum, to convey respect, and to refrain from accusation and defamation. The context of speaking in online formats may embolden individuals to speak in harsh or extreme terms; this should be avoided. Efforts to ensure professional interactions must extend to online venues, and the criteria for professionalism should be enforced in these contexts, just as they are in face-to-face interactions.

Top Ten List of Strategies for Staying on Course

1. Train others in the risks associated with social media use
2. Share real-world examples of social media mishaps to sensitize individuals to the risks
3. Create social media policies within organizations
4. Inform clients about social media policy and about why staff members are prohibited from social media connections with clients
5. Address confidentiality and related policies up front with clients and periodically
6. Address confidentiality and related policies with staff when hired and at least annually thereafter

7. Develop drift patrol strategies to ensure all staff are following policies and behaving appropriately
8. Ensure that any online participation (in chats and list serves) follows best practice guidelines (e.g., do not give professional advice, direct individuals to the research literature)
9. Use disclaimers when presenting scenarios in training or professional contexts
10. Create an ethical culture around social media and other risks (encourage frequent discussions and evaluations of adherence to policy, empower all staff to raise issues and concerns in this regard). Ensure that violations noted are brought up to the individual who erred, and that organizational solutions are enacted to prevent recurrence.

Summary

Online interaction has brought the science of ABA to much broader audiences and has helped disseminate the field's potential and successes. It has also come with risks, especially for violations of confidentiality. It is important for behavior analysts to be mindful of identifiability, not just in obviously defining ways, but in terms of behavioral descriptors. It is also important to ensure that one exudes professionalism in all interactions and comments, whether discussing clinical issues or organizational matters. Specific clinical advice should be restricted to contexts in which the individual has a clinical role and direct knowledge of the situation. Vigilance is important in evaluating our own behavior and that of our colleagues; it is important to provide feedback and to enact prevention strategies in response to social media mistakes. Finally, it is important to treat one another, inside and outside of our field, with respect and courtesy, even when our opinions differ. Committing to the appropriate and professional use of social media can augment the impact of our work, and can minimize any negative potential issues associated with its misuse.

Works Cited

Behavior Analyst Certification Board (2020). *Ethics Code for Behavior Analysts.* Littleton, CO: Author.

Mostaghimi, A., & Crotty, B. H. (2011). Professionalism in the digital age. *Annals of Internal Medicine, 154*(8), 560–562.

O'Leary, P. N., Miller, M. M., Olive, M. L., & Kelly, A. N. (2017). Blurred lines: ethical implications of social media for behavior analysts. *Behavior Analysis in Practice, 10,* 45–51.

3.15 Reflections: Crisis Stabilization and Treatment

Confusing Short-term Behavior Reduction with Lasting Treatment Gains

Merrill Winston

The Problem

Everyone knows that one of the main goals of applied behavior analysis is the reduction of problem behavior, but it is *only one of the goals*. Granted, even if behavioral reduction were the only outcome, for example, in the case of severe self-injury, then clearly the intervention was successful in terms of this single goal. Forty years ago, methodological behaviorism used to be the norm, in which the primary concern was with the reduction of behavior problems through the application of standard procedures. These procedures could often produce good outcomes irrespective of behavioral function as they were often very powerful procedures. High magnitude reinforcers and punishers fall into this category, as do DRO (differential reinforcement of other behavior) procedures. Regardless of the procedures used, there was little analysis of the behavior problem and no conceptualizing of problem behavior in terms of function.

That was more like "your father's behavior analysis." Today's behavior analysis goes much further and has the goals of the acquisition of new functional skills that will make the problem behavior unnecessary (replacement behaviors). Furthermore, the clinician typically gains a good understanding of the individual's current skill level in a variety of areas, and their likes and dislikes (aversives and reinforcers) to gain a more complete picture of the variables that contribute to the behavior problem. It is quite common to see multiple goals in a clinical intervention including behavior reduction, behavioral acquisition, improving the individual's overall quality of life, creating plans for generalization and maintenance of behavior change, providing training to parents and caregivers so that they may carry out treatment goals, and helping prepare the individual to be as independent as possible.

Part of today's clinical treatment is to use the information gained about clients not only to better understand the individual's likes and dislikes, but to rapidly decelerate problem behavior, even before the acquisition of any new skills. This rapid behavioral reduction is typically based on both antecedent manipulations (eliminating or modifying antecedent conditions to prevent problem behavior), and the de-escalation of those precursor behaviors that may be predictive of crisis behaviors (self-injury, aggression, destroying the environment). These antecedent manipulations can be quite broad in scope and may involve changes to the physical environment, changes in the sequence or duration of tasks/events, alterations of academic curricula or treatment goals, modification of the delivery of demands/instructions, and the creation of "static" physical and social environments (the chair can't ever be out of position, the teacher can't ever take off her glasses). In many instances, as this is easiest, a variety of things identified as aversive to the individual are simply eliminated. On the other end of the spectrum, the individual may be "flooded"

DOI: 10.4324/9781003190707-34

with (alleged) reinforcers. In the most extreme case, this means no demands and iPad during all waking hours.

Now, as my mentor Dr. Jim Johnston likes to point out, quite correctly, not all behavior problems require "replacement behaviors" and the acquisition of new skills. Sometimes problems are more a matter of motivation than skill deficits. People don't speed (problem behavior) because they don't have the skills of reading the speedometer, scanning for speed limit signs, or because they lack a basic understanding of the function of gas and brake pedals. Similarly, some of our students and clients may not show their problems because of a lack of skill but because they live and learn in "unreasonable environments." That is, there are things that truly need to be changed or eliminated. There may be unreasonable social interactions (angry teachers/parents, teasing/aggressive peers), there may be unreasonable academic/treatment goals (attempting to teach traditional academics before the individual has any communication/social skills) and there may be unreasonable schedules in terms of the number of demands placed on the individual and the duration of events with respect to developmental level. That is, sometimes the individual simply needs "reasonable accommodations." There is nothing wrong with this notion and these reasonable accommodations (he prefers to type instead of handwriting, noises bother him, so he wears headphones in the cafeteria) are very often part of a well-thought-out behavior plan. A problem arises, however, when long-term accommodations become *unreasonable* and become confused with or are used in place of *treatment*. Later, in the discussion section, some guidelines will be offered to help determine what constitutes "reasonable" or "unreasonable."

Crisis Stabilization: "It's a Good Thing!"

The phrase "crisis stabilization" will be defined here as the use of procedures that can be implemented almost instantly with only a minimal understanding of the individual's big reinforcers and aversives and a focus on the immediate de-escalation of precursor behaviors (those that reliably predict problem behavior). In some clinical cases, behavior problems may be less dangerous, and they may be better understood, because they are more common and less complex. In these simpler cases, behavioral interventions can be probed, a functional assessment performed, and a simple plan written quickly and implemented. Certain cases, on the other hand, involve very dangerous behavior that is less-well understood, less common and more complex requiring more data collection, probes, and analysis. These more complex cases may also require significant skill acquisition (not to mention behavior reduction) on the parts of parents/teachers/direct care staff. In short, these more complex cases involving severe behavior problems typically require more time for the development of a treatment plan, but their dangerous nature demands rapid reduction. This is where crisis stabilization is so valuable. This is when it may be considered "reasonable" to make "unreasonable" accommodations. The student pokes his finger in his eye when academic demands are made? Then stop all academic demands. The child starts to self-injure whenever mom makes a left-hand turn in the car? Then no more left-hand turns on the way home from school. The student who escalates to a crisis when staff utter her name, so mom tells staff to say, "Hey gorgeous?" Then staff say, "Hey gorgeous!" (yes, this really happened).

Not only can one simply eliminate aversive events, but it is also a simple matter to just give individuals whatever they want when their behavior escalates so that problem behavior may be avoided. These two strategies together are often known as "walking on eggshells." This too may rapidly reduce problem behavior to zero levels. True, one may by necessity reinforce those behaviors that lead to a behavioral crisis, but at least the crisis does not occur. Allowing free access to alleged reinforcers is another stabilization strategy that can work rapidly. One could easily argue that it is reasonable to make *unreasonable* accommodations to obtain a rapid initial reduction of dangerous behavior, but to *continue to do so* under the guise of treatment and to claim treatment gains is not only in itself unreasonable but *could also be construed as unethical*. In most cases, one would hope, this practice is not knowingly unethical. In fact, most individuals probably feel that they are doing the right thing, and in one sense they are. They are reducing dangerous behavior. However, all too often this crisis stabilization becomes the "new normal" and not only will it fail to constitute treatment, it will *actually prevent treatment from happening* as it will appear that there is no longer a behavior problem.

The Data Show He's Doing Better!

Who doesn't love a nice decreasing trend? Yes, data showing fewer restraints and/or fewer instances of problem behavior are always encouraging but these data don't always reflect good clinical treatment. Once it has been established that the behavior is less frequent (or at zero) the important question is "Why?" If the answer is "We simply created the perfect world for the individual!" Then there is a big problem. The biggest problem with this problem is that few people recognize it as a problem. Example:

MERRILL: "How's Bobby doing?"
TEACHER: "He's doing great! He's had no crisis for two weeks!"
MERRILL: "That's great, but just out of curiosity, how many times did he *almost* go into crisis?"
TEACHER: "Oh, that's pretty much every day all through the day."
MERRILL: [facepalm]

This child did not reach the end of his clinical path where he would become a well-adjusted individual ready to enter society. This child was at the beginning of that path. The child in this example (Bobby) is someone whose behavior has been *stabilized* and the teachers did a very good job of stabilizing him. What they did was very valuable and important, and it should not be demeaned or overlooked, but it must be recognized for what it is and not confused with treatment. Bobby's stability was "brittle" like so many individuals who are subjected to excessive, extended antecedent manipulations. "Brittle" simply means that he was stable under a very narrow range of conditions. If he were to stray outside of those conditions his behavior would most likely "reappear" in full force. This kind of error can result in statements like this: "He did great last year in Ms. Robertson's class, but now in Mr. Thompson's class he is having problems again!"

What Happens After Stabilization?

Now that the individual is stable most of the time, which can be considered part of treatment, it's time to move forward into skill acquisition (for both students/clients and staff/parents/teachers) and slowly change the accommodations to become, well, a little less accommodating as new skills are acquired. As an example, if all tasks have been eliminated it is now time to start introducing easy tasks, teaching appropriate escape responses or choice-making, teaching skills that will make task completion easier, etc. Most individuals with behavior problems don't handle a variety of aversives very "gracefully" and this might include having to wait, complying with reasonable requests, giving up a reinforcer, accepting an alternate when a preferred item is unavailable, being disappointed and getting teased to name a few. Moving forward, how does one determine what is reasonable and unreasonable? This is something that requires an understanding of what causes problems for the individual and if these causes are common and if the individual could be taught an approximation to what most people do when confronted with similar problems. It's also important to ask, "Would the average typically developing child or adult also have difficulty with this problem?" As an example, one student would engage in severe eye gouging when he heard another student coughing. Would it be reasonable to ensure that the child is *never* around anyone who might cough? Maybe for stabilization (which would still be difficult), but not for the long-term. Eventually the child would have to learn to stay relaxed when hearing coughing, habituate to it or engage in behaviors to minimize the effects (cover his ears, put on headphones with music, remove himself from the room). What if a child *only* becomes aggressive when other children attack him? Anyone might become aggressive when attacked. Here is a little grid that may help when attempting to think things out as all situations are not so straightforward.

The Grid of Acceptability!

Behavior\Situation	Unacceptable	Unreasonable	Reasonable
Reasonable	1		
Unreasonable		2	
Unacceptable			3

Table 1 Categorizing scenarios across three situation levels and three behavior levels to assess appropriateness of intervention.

Behavior of the individual may be reasonable or unreasonable (based on age/developmental level) or unacceptable (dangerous). The situation (the environment, both physical and social) can also be reasonable, unreasonable or unacceptable (abuse/neglect/danger). The most problematic behaviors fall in Category 3, an unacceptable response to a reasonable situation. That is, the individual is told "Sorry, but we ran out of orange juice" and the individual destroys the kitchen (see Table 1).

Category 1 shows a scenario in which perhaps antecedent manipulations are *all that is needed.* For example, an individual with special needs bites their housemate, *but only when attacked by their housemate!* The client is living in a dangerous condition where they may become attacked by their peers. Under those circumstances it may be considered a reasonable behavior. This is why our laws use phrases like "reasonable force" to determine if a citizen acted in a prudent manner. The most pressing problem in the realm of crisis stabilization and treatment is that individuals with behaviors in Category 3, unacceptable responses to reasonable situations, may *stay in Category 3 forever.*

In most cases, the way that we move individuals forward in their treatment is by teaching them what to do (and what not to do) when confronted with the same sorts of problems that we all encounter. One analogy to help explain this concept is the old adage, "If you *give a man a fish* he eats for a day, if you *teach a man how to fish* he eats for the rest of his life." Of course, he'll probably have very high blood-levels of mercury too, but at least he won't starve. Crisis stabilization is the "giving the fish" part and treatment is the "teaching to fish" part. Treatment takes more time, patience, dedication, and expertise and, like any worthwhile endeavor, there may be some failure along the way, but it is vitally important and should not be confused with crisis stabilization.

3.16   On Heroes and Villains

An Interview with Philip Zimbardo

Philip Zimbardo

Philip Zimbardo is best known as the lead researcher of the Stanford Prison Experiment, a social psychology experiment which attempted to discover the psychological and social effects of perceived power and the lack thereof. After only six days, the experiment had to be discontinued due to the egregious abuse of "prisoners" by those randomly assigned to play the role of "guards." Although an investigation immediately following this experiment found no direct ethical violations, it is often considered one of the more unethical experiments and has been the subject of several documentaries and a feature film. Informed by the Stanford Prison experiment, Dr. Zimbardo's work focuses on the situational and societal influences of behavior that is considered "evil," as well as the psychology of heroism.

In the following interview we discuss research ethics, the obligations of researchers, the challenge of communicating findings and correcting misinformation, the researcher's obligation to the truth and the positive effects made possible by the Stanford Prison experiment.

ANN BEIRNE: Thank you so much for agreeing to talk to me. I have a few questions. The first is: you have described the Stanford Prison Experiment as being both ethical and unethical. Could you talk a little bit about that description?

PHILIP ZIMBARDO: Yeah, so in *The Lucifer Effect*, which I wrote and published in 2007 or 2008, I have a whole chapter on the ethics of the Stanford Prison Experiment. And obviously, it's a very controversial experiment. I did mention that as part of the examination for psychologists there's always a question about "Which of the following is an unethical experiment?" It's always Zimbardo and Milgram. Within our system it's evaluated as unethical. What makes it unethical is that participants suffered seriously over five days and were in a setting where it was not clear how to leave other than go to the parole board, which rejected everybody, or to have an emotional breakdown. Or a medical problem, which five of the participants did. And just the fact that even a single participant experienced so much stress that he had to be... that he ended up screaming and out of control and has said subsequently that this was the only time in his life he was totally out of control of his emotions and of the situation. That was Prisoner 8612. That alone is more prolonged stress than in any other experiment. In Milgram's study the participants experienced stress for at most half an hour and then at the end Milgram said, "Hey, in fact you're not really shocking your student. He was a confederate." But they... some of them still felt the guilt of knowing that they blindly obeyed the authority to go against, to commit actions that went against their moral conscience. To knowingly, continue to shock well beyond any reasonable level. In Milgram's study, two out of every three adult males and one group of women went all the way to 450 volts.

DOI: 10.4324/9781003190707-35

AB: Yes.

PZ: Now, in Milgram's study, the reason it was judged unethical immediately was because he made a film called *Obedience*. Milgram wanted to be a filmmaker, in fact he made a number of films. And in the film you see the incredible stress and incredible ambivalence where the experimenter is saying, "You must go on," and they're saying, "I don't want to harm anybody." And the confederate, pretending to be the student, is saying, "I have a heart condition, I want to quit." So Milgram's experiment, even though it was intense, it was a very short time. In the Stanford Prison Study, there were three guard shifts who worked eight hours each. The prisoners lived in the prison for 24 hours, 24/7. And within 36 hours the first prisoner, the prisoner demonstrated an emotional breakdown. Then that became, in a sense, a model for how to exit the prison. And each day, every single day thereafter another prisoner had an emotional breakdown. and one of them, that was 8612, and four others. And one of them had a medical problem, broke out in hives and had to be released to get his medicine. So that's what makes it unethical. I mean, you can't create a situation where people suffer. Now, what makes it ethical – and that's the interesting contrast – is that even though it's 1971, Stanford University had recently just instituted a Human Subjects Research Committee, which included several townspeople who were not personally connected to the university to make the judgment. And I presented the study with as much detail as we imagined. And they helped me prepare an informed consent statement that every participant read, and it said, "If I am assigned to be a prisoner I will live in this place for 24 hours [for as long as] the experiment will go, for perhaps a week or up to two weeks. There will be minimum adequate diet," I think we said there will be some stress, some deprivation, etc. I think it said, "but there would be medical services available," which there always were. So what's ethical about it is, the Human Subjects Research Committee approved of what we were doing: randomly assigning college students to these two conditions, putting them in a cramped cell. I think somebody from the Subject Research Committee actually visited the location, which was the basement of the Stanford Psychology Department. And they approved it. So, that's the definition of ethical, is that the Human Subjects Committee evaluated the protocol, prepares an informed consent statement along with the researcher, which is me, and every participant reads that statement and then signs on. So, I'm saying paradoxically it is an example of both one of the most unethical studies, or maybe the most unethical study ever done and also a very ethical one.

AB: And it's so fascinating that you can follow all of the rules and still have this... you based the informed consent on the other thing that you anticipated. But it seems from reading in *The Lucifer Effect* that there were a lot of aspects of this experiment that weren't anticipated...

PZ: The bottom line is we went out of our way to pick participants who were [as] normal and healthy as possible. That is... we gave him a battery of six personality tests, a clinical interview, a personal interview. And so when they started, these are normal, healthy American college students who knew what they were getting into, knew the role that they were playing. And so we, the staff – me and my graduate student staff – could never anticipate that anybody would have a, quote, "an emotional or nervous breakdown." And nor could they. And, in fact. To back up, on Day 1... Now I should say it's 1971, it's the middle of the civil rights era, the middle of the anti-Vietnam War student protests, the middle of women's lib, it's an era in which college students were rebelling against authority. Again, if you remember, many students in many colleges in the United States protested the Vietnam War, often the administration would call police onto campus, police often beat up the students who were protesting. In some cases, the police actually killed, or National Guard actually killed students. So nobody wanted to be a guard in my study. We asked, "Do you want to be a prison guard?" and nobody. Actually, in the movie *The Stanford Prison Experiment* it really opens with the simulated staff asking the students, asking the actors playing participants, "Do you want to be a prison guard?" Everybody said, "No, I don't want to be a guard. Nobody wants to be a guard. Nobody likes guards." And that was true. But we told them, "I'm sorry. You're randomly assigned, you have to do it." And on Day 1, nothing was happening, meaning that you could hear the video we made, which included excerpts from the video, we had 12 hours of videos made at various times throughout the study, at what we saw were key points. Where guards were giving the prisoners rules, a little bit on each of the three guards' shifts, which were eight hours, morning, afternoon, and night. A little bit of visiting times, a bit of the parole board hearings. We couldn't afford to have around the clock videos, because in those days video recording was very expensive and we had a very modest budget. But, again, if you look at these first day videos you see the guards say, "Come on guys, let's take it seriously." The guard were telling the prisoners, "Let's take it seriously." And the guards are giggling. At the end of the first day I said, "Okay, look, this is not working. We wasted a lot of time with this big setup, you know." And, in fact one of the three guards on that first shift, he was sitting in a corner. And David Jaffe, who was an undergraduate student who had performed a simulated prison in his dormitory as part of my class exercise... I'll back up, that's the reason we did the study. So I gave him the role of warden. And he says, to this guard who is doing nothing, he says, "Really, you're getting paid to be a guard. You've gotta act like a guard, you've gotta get, quote 'on the yard.'" And then he says, "you have to be firm and you have to act tough like a guard does." And I'll get back to that because that's been a big critique. David Jaffe said to one guard on one shift, nothing beyond, "You have to be tough, you know, like real guards do." But if you're a college student you have no idea of what real guards do. And then on the second morning, the experiment started on Sunday August 14th, on Monday morning, August 15th, something happened that changed the entire complexion of the study: the prisoners rebelled. The prisoners in two of the three cells locked themselves in the cells, ripped off their numbers, shouting, "I don't want to be a number, I don't want to be dehumanized." And then guards came to me and said, "What are you going to do?" And I said, "It's your prison. What do you want to do?" And they said, "Okay, we have to call in all the guards on all the guard shifts to confront these prisoners." And there were two guards on each of three shifts, plus there were three backup guards, so they had 12 guards come down and they broke down the doors that were being barricaded, stripped the prisoners naked, there was actual physical confrontation, fighting between the prisoners and the guards. And the guards actually, obviously won. It was 12 guards against prisoners. Because prisoners in one cell, cell number one which was, quote, "the good cell" did not want to participate in the rebellion. So that changed everything, because one of the guards said, "These are dangerous prisoners." And from that moment, nobody used the word "experiment." It was a prison run by psychologists. So that was the transformative experience, which essentially gave this experiment a new level of reality. So, boys knowingly playing the role of guards became guards. Boys knowingly playing the roles of prisoners became prisoners. See, the fascinating thing is, everybody knew this was an experiment. Everybody knew they were role playing. Everybody knew it wasn't a real prison but the basement of the Psychology Department, so that's one level of reality. Another level of reality is the guards now say, "We have to show them who's boss, who's in charge. We have to dominate them." And for some part, "We not only have to dominate them, we have to break any potential future of these rebellions." And from that moment on, the situation got worse and worse. Now I describe in *Lucifer*, although the study is a demonstration – really it should not be called an experiment, it should be called the Stanford Prison Demonstration. It's a demonstration of how situational forces, social situational forces can overwhelm individual resistance, individual personalities, individual dispositions. And what happens is some of the guards on some of the shifts got meaner and meaner over time. Each day more mean than the previous day, each day beginning to be what I call "creatively evil" or "sadistic." Some guards were tough guards but never went really beyond their roles' demands. They were tough with their prisoners and made them do pushups and sit-ups, obey them. Other guards were good guards who never challenged the bad guards but who never abused them. So there were individual differences. And we could not – we had personality data – the personality data that we analyzed could not predict who would be the tough guards, I mean the mean guards, the tough guards, and the nice guards. So the conclusion is not that when put in a powerful social situation, everyone caves in and becomes what the situation demands. The fact that some of them – normal and intelligent psychologically healthy college students – began to do unimaginably cruel, creatively evil things. That's the legacy of the Stanford Prison Study.

AB: So, I talk a lot about researchers having obligations to participants, in terms of maintaining safety, and to colleagues, in terms of authorship and providing citations, and also to the truth in terms of making sure that our data is accurate and that our results are clearly communicated to the public at the large. Do you think that – that sort of insight into the human condition and the capacity of ordinary people to do extraordinarily cruel things – do you think we would have this level of knowledge without the Stanford Prison Experiment?

PZ: Not in the same way. I mean, we've seen this throughout, we've seen this with the guards in Nazi concentration camps. These are ordinary people, there's been pictures released of male and female guards having a picnic, singing and dancing. We have evidence that Dr. Mengele, who was Dr. Death, every Sunday night would have a musical soireé with Jewish musicians and dancers would perform for him. And, so again it's only when they went into that about the concentration camp – Auschwitz, Birkenau, any of them. And their job was not only to maintain law and order but to make these Jewish prisoners realize that they are nothing, they are vermin. But again we saw this coming up now 40 years later, in Jonestown. Ordinary people from San Francisco, for Los Angeles. who are following a leader, Jim Jones, who said he was going to lead them to a new kind of freedom, away from a terrible life in the ghetto of Los Angeles or San Francisco. And they go to Jonestown, and suddenly they are in a concentration camp. And ultimately he gets them to commit to willingly die for their father, for God. So we didn't need this research to demonstrate this, there's been a lot of real world demonstration. However, in all of those we have no evidence to demonstrate who they were before they took the job, before they joined Jonestown, before they became Nazi guards. Here we know on Day 1 every single one of the 24 participants was psychologically normal, as judged by their performance on six personality tests, normal in terms of what we psychologists could assess in interviews. So, we have a baseline of normality from which we could see the progression, which, over time – and you could see the increment... day by day got worse the meanness, the evil got worse and worse day by day over those five days. And as I said, we thought we'd run the study for two weeks. And I had to end it after five days because it was literally out of control. We couldn't predict what the guards would do next. After I decided on Thursday night – we prepared to end the study the next day, at the persuasion of my girlfriend, Christina Maslach – I went down, back to the prison cell. And I was not telling anybody about ending the study because the next morning on Friday a public defender was coming in to talk to all of them about release. And so I was going to wait till after he did that on Friday. I come in and I look at the video that had just been taken, and the guards on the night shifts got the prisoners to simulate sodomy. And so here's what happened in Abu Ghraib. The guards in Abu Ghraib were getting the prisoners to simulate fellatio. And here in a study at a college – in a study where everybody knew it was a study, in a basement, which is not a real prison, playing the role, they know that the other students are college students like them and not prisoners. Nevertheless, they're saying, "You bend over, you're female camels. You get behind them, you're male camels. Now hump them." And they were simulating sodomy. And all three guards kept yelling and screaming and laughing.

AB: After only five days.

PZ: Five days, right. But the point is, I had already determined to end it. Surely as soon as I saw that, I would have ended it at that moment. Now that scene in *The Stanford Prison Experiment* movie, I don't know if you've seen that.

AB: I have.

PZ: That's the final scene. In the movie, there is the confrontation between my girlfriend and me. In the movie. But in the movie, they didn't have me say, "You're right. You're going to end this study." Because at that moment, it's a peak and then it's over. You can't do anything after that. So they had the confrontation and then I go back down, I look, I see what's happening. But every single thing showed in that scene was verbatim of what happened in the real study. Here again, it goes so far beyond anything in Milgram, anything imaginable. You can't imagine this. But in 2004, we had videos and photos of American prison guards in Abu Ghraib doing similar things, getting prisoners to say, "Okay, you get down on your knees, you take your penis out," and to have them simulating sodomy, simulating fellatio.

AB: One thing also that struck me, watching the movie and reading *The Lucifer Effect* as well, there's one contrast that I thought was very interesting and I wanted to ask you about that. You've been very, very clear every time you've spoken about the Stanford Prison Experiment, about this is really a story of how ordinary people were situationally influenced.

PZ: Right.

AB: And particularly, you've been 100% consistent in trying to get that point across. But especially in public response to Guard Eshelman who was also called John Wayne and was one of the more creative of his guards in his cruelty. I was surprised reading *The Lucifer Effect* how much remorse he seemed to have during the debriefing. Because none of the other TV news magazine shows that I've seen that interviewed him really gave me that impression. And the movie didn't either. So one of the most important parts of research is communicating our results and our obligation to make sure that those results are clear. How have you tried to kind of get that point across? And it has been frustrating for you that the public still really wants to believe that there was something dispositional, especially about Guard Eshelman?

PZ: Yeah, but again, he is a phenomenon and still is. The problem is that over time the stories that each guard tells will change – memory distortion. Immediately after the study… okay, let me back up. The study ended on August 20th and on August 21st there was an alleged escape attempt at San Quentin State Prison where George Jackson, a black activist prisoner, was killed and the prisoners in solitary confinement were released and killed, others killed a guard, and that was the day after the prison study. And then three weeks later was Attica. And so those two events made this little demonstration suddenly nationally famous. Because I had involved a local TV station in the study in order to film the arrest, in order to, I think, persuade the Palo Alto Police Department to participate in making the arrest look very real, in a real police car and bringing prisoners to a real jail. So that when the thing happened at San Quentin, the Associate Warden, his name was Warden Parks, had a press conference. And one of the people at the press conference was from station KGO who had been involved in filming the prison arrest, the week before. And he said to Warden Parks, "Does this have anything to do with the way guards dehumanize prisoners, as was shown in the study at Stanford?" And Warden Parks went ballistic, you know, "They don't know what they're talking about." And so a TV station the next day invited me to have a debate with Warden Parks, which I did. And then somebody from NBC – some media person who was part of what was called *Chronologue* then, which was the forerunner of *60 Minutes* – heard that debate, called me and said, "Can I talk to you?" came to my home, said, "Do you have any videos?" I said, "Yeah." I showed him what we had. He said, "Okay, we want to make a TV special of this." So they made a special and it was called *Prisoner 819 Did a Bad Thing.*

AB: I was going to ask if it was going to be *Prisoner 819 Did a Bad Thing.*

PZ: What that means is that, within a month of having done that study, before we even analyzed all the data to prepare a write-up, it was now on national media. And then, in preparation for that movie, they asked me to have some of the prisoners and guards come down to be interviewed. And in one of those interviews they had Eshelman talking with Prisoner 416. Prisoner 416 is the guy who went on a hunger strike, the skinny kid. And 416 was now confronting him, because now they are now equals, they are not in their prison uniforms. And he said, "You know, he said if I was a guard. I would be a guard." I forget the word... "It would not be such a masterpiece." That's the word he used. And so he said, "You went way beyond anything you had to do." And then Eshelman says something like, "You put on your uniform. And then you put on your glasses, you get a nightstick, and you become a guard. That's your job. That's what I did." And then he [Prisoner 416] says, "No, you did more than that." "Yes, I was doing some little experiments of my own." And then 416 says sarcastically, "Tell me about your little experiments?" he said, "I wanted to see how cruel I could be," or I don't know what word he used, "to get the prisoners to do horrible things until they refused. But they never refused. They never stopped me." So he's saying he was play-acting, he wanted the prisoners to rebel, and they didn't. And because of that he just got meaner and meaner and meaner. Now, ten years later he's interviewed and he says – he's been interviewed a number of times – it's got to be ten years later and he says, "You know, in my role, I was like a puppeteer. And the prisoners were like puppets. And I could make them do anything." Now that's the ultimate dehumanization, that statement. A puppeteer means he's controlling them, he is pulling the string. Now again, more recently he has said, "No I was just acting, I was playing a role, I was not as bad as they make me out to seem." We have a video of the sodomy thing. We have the video of him, the prisoner is doing sit-ups and he is stepping on them and so forth. Over time the prisoners and guards, their story has changed. The reality of the video is what you see on the video of that time. Now are you aware of the recent controversy, all of the bloggers attacking me?

AB: I am. Although to tell you the truth, it doesn't seem like there is anything uncovered that you can't read in *The Lucifer Effect.*

PZ: You're right.

AB: So it seemed to me... well, we could talk a little about science communication and how it can be misconstrued and certainly that's a very big issue. But...

PZ: I had to respond and I spent the last ten days every day talking to colleagues, preparing a response, and getting feedback. I wrote a 27-page rebuttal, point by point, with all the evidence in contrast. In addition to me we've got Craig Haney, who was my assistant, Christina Maslach, who is the one who came down and intervened. We have a person who made the video of Doug Korpi describing his real breakdown. Because again the bloggers say he told them now, almost 40 years later, more than, 47 years later, that he was faking. But we have his word, and I use him in *The Lucifer Effect* as one of the prime positive outcomes of the study, because he said originally, "Because I was so ashamed that I lost control of myself, I went into clinical psychology to understand my unconscious so it wouldn't happen again." And then instead of becoming a therapist, he becomes a forensic psychologist, and he's working for 20 years in a San Francisco County Jail, which is where we made that movie, *Quiet Rage*. The segment is Doug Korpi in the San Francisco County Jail talking about that experiment 14 years later, saying, "I totally lost control of my emotions, of the situation." We have it on record. And we also have a student who made that movie that I didn't even know about. He's not a psychologist, he was in communication and decide to make a movie and he tracked down Doug Korpi. I had no idea where Doug Korpi was. He has a statement saying, "I tracked him down, we had lunch together, I asked him, 'Would you be willing to recount your experience?' and he said yes." there was no coercion, not even question and answer, somebody [asks] "tell me about your experience." And so we have that statement. Scott Plous, who was a former graduate student of mine, he is the creator of this social psychology network, which is really a critical thing for you to look at. It's a brilliant center for everything happening in social psychology. He is the one who invited me to have a subsection of his website called prisonexp.org. Everything in the prison study had been deposited there – all the videos, all the slides, etc., etc. So Scott Plous took the lead in helping me answer the rebuttal. So he's created a whole new website, it's prisonerexp.org/response, and if you click on that up comes my 27-page rebuttal and then on the side, you click on that and it has additional commentary and then all of the critiques in detail from Medium, from Fox, from LiveScience. And then after that, it has a full page of every single thing, every article, every movie, everything ever written about the movie, about the prison study. So it's a new resource which is remarkable. I've used the occasion to go beyond simply "Let me debunk these bloggers." It's like "Let me reiterate that this is a unique demonstration of situational power." Now again one of the things that the bloggers did, I don't read blogs, I don't pay attention to any of that stuff, but the way you get attention is, "The story of a lie. The Stanford Prison Study is a sham. It's a sham, it's a lie, it's a fraud. Zimbardo's a liar, it's dishonest. The study should be removed from scientific literature, etc., etc." And it's this really extreme hostile thing. And not only did none of them send it to me in advance, those resources, Medium didn't say, "Do you want to reply?" Which is really unacceptable. I wrote them recently, I said, "This is horrific. You put some stuff out." I didn't even know that stuff was out until I started getting letters – I do a lot of work in Hungary, Poland, China, Japan and Brazil. Now I'm getting media from all of those five countries saying, "We're so sorry that your study is now disreputable and you're disreputable." And so that's when I got alerted, when people I knew in those countries said, "Oh my God, how are you handling this?" In two weeks, I have been preparing this reply, so I know it's important for you to look at.

AB: So it hasn't just been a matter of you communicating your findings, but communicating your findings then communicating your findings on a much larger scale than most people do and then communicating them over and over and over again for 40-plus years.

PZ: Again, I'm the first one, I've always said, "Of course the study has flaws. It isn't a perfect study." On the other hand, it's unique in the history of virtually all research – that it went for more than 120 hours, not one hour. There were endless things happening. Nobody [that was in the experiment] was in control of things, prisoners were having breakdowns, parents are coming, the Catholic priests are coming, the public defender is coming, the parole board, students playing the role of prisoners are having emotional breakdowns in the parole board because the parole board leader, Carl Prescott, who is an ex-con, is berating them, is telling them that they're worthless, that they're never gonna get out. So again, it was… things are happening all the time. Again the thing we underestimated, it's me, two graduate students, one undergraduate. So at any point any one of us is sleepy because there's only three. The last day, Craig Haney, who's a senior graduate student, had a family emergency, so it's now just me and two other students. One of the students who lived on campus, he had a child who was sick. So again, I am working sometimes 18 to 20-hour shifts, so we're all under extreme stress. Obviously, I should have ended the study when the second prisoner broke down. When the first one broke down, Korpi, I was suspicious, I said "Yeah, he could be faking it." Because I didn't hear the final screams, etc., etc. But when the second one broke down, there was no question it was real. And the third one – again, I say that for me the biggest indication of the power of this situation was the impact it had on me. I became the superintendent of the San Francisco County Jail. And in that capacity, I did not allow physical punishment, but I allowed psychological punishment. Because I could see, I could see what was happening. I didn't see the sodomy, but guards getting prisoners to spit in each other's face, to step on them, to do horrific things. So I should have ended it, and I say that. I should have ended it much earlier. But I got trapped in my own experiment.

AB: I think sometimes the research environment itself can lend itself to dehumanization and also deindividuation. And you referred earlier to Guard Eshelman talking about his "little experiments." There was one story that I was very curious about from *The Lucifer Effect*, when you described Dr. B meeting you in a hallway when there was a threatened rebellion and you had changed the location of the experiment. Dr. B's question for you, seeing the prisoners, was, "What is the independent variable?" I remember thinking that's a very academic question, he wasn't asking, "Are these boys okay?" So I guess how do we strike a balance between excessive involvement, like you mentioned getting wrapped up in your experiment, and too much distance?

PZ: He and I were college roommates at Yale, we were graduate students together. I was the best man at his wedding, so always we've been really close. He's a very formal guy. For him, before he even wraps his head around what's happening, he wanted to know, if this is an experiment, what's the independent variable? So again I'm laughing to myself, saying, "Oh my God, I've got a prison rebellion and this guy is asking reasonable questions, but in the wrong context."

Now even later on he says, 'cause he's seen that, he says, "No, I was just kidding." Well, I'm not sure he was just kidding, that's a question he would ask if somebody describes an experiment, "I could see all of these things but what's the independent variable?" I said, "random assignment of prison guards" and, essentially, "now get out." I didn't say that, "I'm dealing with rebellion."

Again, I say in *The Lucifer Effect*, when there was the rumor of the break-in – in my class at Stanford, my social psychology class, one of the main topics is the psychology of rumor and every student in that class for years would do would do demonstrations of rumor transmission and on distortion. So I'm interested in rumors. So, had I not been so involved I would have sat back and said, "I am going to crack this. Let's begin to break this. Who heard it first? What did you hear?" [I would] make a note of it. I simply assume it's going to happen. There's going to be a big confrontation and people could get really hurt. My job was to prevent any physical confrontation. And I call up the Palo Alto Police sergeant who arranged for the squad cars to do the arrests. And I knew there was an old jail which was not being used because they just built a new jail. And I persuaded him to let me move the prisoners to the old jail for one night. And then he called and said, "I'm sorry we can't do it because the city manager said there would be a problem with insurance, say, if somebody got hurt." And I went down and I confronted him. And I again, I said – he must have thought I was a lunatic – he knows that it's a fucking experiment! And I'm saying, "You know, I've got a prison break on my hands, and there could be bloodshed." I'm now totally losing it. But again that's – if you want to say what is the power of the situation, it's the impact it had on me. That I'm beginning to believe that the rumor of a prison break is not a rumor, it's a reality that's gonna happen. And now I'm in charge. I have to prevent disaster. And just totally losing it.

AB: Because of your involvement, and because you were the superintendent?

PZ: I'm the grown-up in charge of this whole play. So I have to make it happen. I have to prevent the rebellion. And then the next thing we did is when he says, "You know, we take all the prisoners we take them to a fifth floor storage room." Which later, people tell me later, "Hey, it turns out there was asbestos in the ceiling in that room." The effects could have been terrible. And then we kept them there for hours. Then we literally – we have in the film – we took the prison doors off and put them down. The scenario was, when you break in, say, "Haha you're too late. Nothing was happening in the study, we ended it. All the prisoners have gone home. All the guards have gone home. Get outta here." And then once they left, then we would have time to get the technician in the psychology department to put in more powerful doors. So we were going to continue. I'm using this as a way to prevent physical confrontation and then for me to buy time to rebuild the prison to make it able to resist a break-in.

AB: So you at that point were very deep in the role of the prison superintendent.

PZ: But I was not "in the role of." I *was the superintendent*. Again, the first major thing I wrote about the prison study – so again, the critiques, breaking them down, say, "You didn't publish in a peer-reviewed journal because you knew it would be rejected." That's nonsense. The first publication was in the *Naval Research Reviews* because I had used some money left over from a previous grant from the ONR to fund the salaries for everybody, buying the beds, paying the technician to set up, etc. And they insisted that I reported that. The other thing I did is I took my graduate students to be the senior authors and I was the junior author. The next thing was the *International Journal of Criminology and Penology* because the editors of the journals heard about that study and invited us to do it. So we didn't have to wait for a year to get peer-reviewed and rejected. The major publication for me was in 1973, two years later in the *New York Times Magazine*, which is not easy to get an article in. I wrote a long article called "The Pirandellian Prison" about how the study was really like Pirandello – Luigi Pirandello. I'm Sicilian, so he's always been a hero. He wrote this, *Six Characters in Search of an Author*. So here now we have characters, we have a set, we have costumes, and we don't have a script. And there's really no director. So they're going to have to make up the show. So that's really what we did, we put people in costumes and we said, "Here's your role, you're going to do this, you are going to do that." But we don't give them a script. So the prison study is a study in improvisation. Everybody's improvising what they imagine guards do, what prison staff do, or what prisoners do.

AB: I hadn't thought of that in terms of the improvisation aspect. I did also want to ask you about the work that you're involved in now with the Heroic Imagination Project and how the Stanford Prison Experiment has informed that.

PZ: So, again, at the end of my rebuttal, I say, "I want to end on my positive note." I want to talk about three interesting domains that I personally have created which were engendered by my involvement with the Stanford Prison Study. The first thing was the psychology of shyness. That is, immediately after their prison study in talking to my students at Stanford, I asked how many students who intend to be prison guards? Nobody. "How many of you imagine being a prisoner?" Nobody. I said, "Why do you care about this study?" They look around. I said, "How many of you think of yourselves as shy?" And a lot of hands go up. And I said, "How many of you are too shy to even raise your hand?" And everybody laughed. I said, "Now isn't shyness a self-imposed psychological prison?" The prison is a place – now, it's a physical place but it's also a, as well as a psychological place. When you say someone is in prison, I mean you limit their freedom of speech, their freedom of association, their freedom of movement – you can't move out. And it's self-imposed because nobody one ever accuses you of being shy. Shyness is unique because people put that label on themselves. They say, "I'm a shy person, therefore I can't raise my hand to answer the question that I know the answer of, I can't ask my boss for a raise, I can't ask a girl for a date, etc." So you become your own guard, limiting your freedom and you're the prisoner, obviously, who's the victim of this. I use that metaphor and then students came up afterwards and said say, "Gee we're really shy. Could you tell us more?" And I said, "No, I'm not shy, I never thought about it." And I said – this is 1972, the year after the study – I said, "Okay, go to the library, get me a reference list and I'll prepare a lecture." And the come back and they say, "There's nothing at all on shyness. Shyness does not exist. There's no research ever done on the psychology of shyness for adolescents or adults." And I couldn't believe it. You know in those days you had to go to the library and I looked and there was... so I said, "Okay. I'm going to have a noncredit shyness seminar for shy students. And we're gonna start the Stanford Shyness Project, we named it up front. We're gonna find out what shyness is, what people think it is, what percentage of people are shy." And that started the first scientific study of shyness. And then after four or five years, my students said, "Hey we know enough about shyness to help other kids at Stanford who are shy." So we set up the Stanford Shyness Clinic, the first clinic ever – and it's still the first clinic with that name, "Shyness Clinic" – and we were able to cure literally everybody that we work with. And then a clinical psychologist heard about this and said, "I would like to move this into the community, not just for Stanford students." And the Shyness Clinic is still in existence at Palo Alto University almost 50 years later. And also, I wrote several books: *Shyness: What It Is, What to Do About It*. Which helped millions of people who have read that book, and also, *The Shy Child*.

The next thing is the psychology of time perspective, a whole area which I started. Because again, during our prison study, all of our sense of time was distorted. There were no windows, there were no clocks. Each guard shifts became almost like a day. When the shifts were more cruel, it seemed like time was never-ending.

AB: And their sleep was disrupted too, which affects your time perception.

PZ: Yeah, yeah. So you get to think about time. And I created the first precise valid measure of time perspective, Zimbardo's Time Perspective Inventory. I wrote several articles in peer-reviewed journals. And now time perspective is an international phenomenon.

> There's international conferences on Zimbardo's Time Perspective every two years in different countries around the world. So that's another thing that came.

And then the third thing that came is the Hero Project. So in Chapter 16, I believe, of *Lucifer* [*The Lucifer Effect*], is where I introduced the notion that in all of this research by Milgram, by Asch, by Zimbardo, there's always a small number – a minority – who do not conform, do not comply, are not obedient. And the interesting thing is we know nothing about them. Because we've always focused on the drama of the evil. We always focus on the devil within. And then I said – well I speculated – "What attributes would these people have that enabled them to resist these situational forces that make the majority of people go off?" And I said, "Could be this, could be this, could be that." And then I said, "You know, we could think of them as heroes." And then I began to think about the nature of heroism. And again, even in 2007 there was not a single psychology textbook that had any mention of heroes. The word "hero" is not on the index of any psychology text. It's not in the positive psychology movement started by Marty Seligman. And they have a huge book, *Human Strengths and Virtues*. Compassion, yes. Empathy, yes. Altruism, yes. Heroism, no. And I confronted Mary Seligman, who is a buddy. And he said, "Compassion and empathy are the highest private virtues. Heroism is a civic virtue." But I'm saying, "What good is empathy and compassion if it's not translated into behavior?" Heroism is a behavior. It's behavior that changes the world. Attitudes, values, feeling don't change the world. They put you in a position to appreciate the need for action, but it doesn't always lead to action. So that's my program, is teaching people how to act wisely and well to make a difference. That was the foundation of, coming out of this, creating what I call the Heroic Imagination Project. The idea is heroism starts in the mind. We're talking about a new kind of hero, not a military hero, not a political hero, not a religious hero but ordinary people who are willing to stand up, speak out and take action in a wise and effective way to make somebody feel special and make the world better in some way every day. So that's the foundation of the Hero Project experiment. And now what we do is, we do some research on heroism. We have been doing some research on heroism. But in addition, the last thing is – what we do is – I have created a series of lessons or interventions which provide a foundation of how to be a wise and effective hero. One of them is "The Psychology of Mindset," how to develop a dynamic, growth mindset in place of a narrow, fixed, static mindset. [This is] from the work of Carol Dweck. How to become, how to transform passive bystanders into backup heroes. How to change prejudice and discrimination into understanding and acceptance of others. So we have these lessons which I developed. Each of these lessons are two to three hours long. They're in great detail with videos and provocative questions. And what happens is schools, businesses, school systems license the lessons and then I, or one of my team goes and does a training for up to 20 people – 20 teachers or we train trainers. And the program now is in a dozen countries around the world. It's all over Hungary, it's all over Poland, it's in Sicily, many many places. I have a list, I think somewhere on the website of all these countries. So for me, those three things are the legacy of the Stanford Prison Study. That three really positive things came out of that week of suffering. Out of that week of evil came three very positive transformative things. It transformed me and all the people connected with those projects.

3.17 Behavior Consultation in Schools

Michelle Zube

Behavior analysts are called upon for school consultations for various behavioral concerns to service a wide variety of student populations. Each school bears its own culture and climate, even if the schools are within the same district. There are even disparities from classroom to classroom within the same school. The behavior analyst is required to adapt to each setting and its unique dynamic while maintaining the integrity and principles of the science.

Here are a few best practice suggestions for a successful classroom experience:

1. **Survey the scene:** Take note of the classroom environment, the resources currently available, the number of children and any foreseeable obstacles (e.g., arrangement of furniture). Objectively observe the mechanics of the classroom (e.g., how the teacher interacts with students, the number of interruptions within the class, other logistical considerations such as schedules and routines). This will help you to get an understanding of how the classroom functions.
2. **Listen:** Upon speaking with the teacher and/or staff, notice the language used to describe the behaviors (whether the information is objective or subjective), and if the staff highlights positive attributes along with the challenges.
3. **Pair yourself as a reinforcer:** Pairing yourself with a teacher and/or staff can make or break a consultation. The pairing process here is just as important as it is with pairing with a student. One must gain trust, buy in, and be seen as a source of support. Pairing yourself means being collegial – not getting personal or becoming new best friends. Suggestions for pairing include asking questions, responding with empathetic statements (e.g., "That must be challenging when the student disrupts the entire class"), having a positive presence (e.g., smile, greeting people), discussing generic topics (e.g., weather, traffic), giving compliments (e.g., "This art project is so creative") and, when possible, stopping by to say hello or check in outside of scheduled meeting times.

While the point of the consultation is generally to modify the student's behavior in some way, it is often necessary to change the behavior of the staff as well. Speaking as a former paraprofessional *and* teacher, I understand how this works from all angles. Now, don't get me wrong, teachers have a lot on their plates and dealing with another professional (you!) who comes with a behavior plan, a system of reinforcement, and data sheets is no easy task! That being said, let's look at some consultation scenarios.

1. **The teacher who has tried everything:** In some cases, you may come into a situation as a "last resort." Often, a teacher is given a variety of strategies and interventions from other professionals (e.g., school psychologist, social worker, learning disabilities

DOI: 10.4324/9781003190707-36

teacher consultant – LDTC). Teachers may have implemented some or all the suggestions given to them to no avail. The behaviorist is often perceived as the end of the line – if the behaviorist can't fix it, no one can. This attitude may increase the pressure on the consultant while concurrently creating more stress for the teacher. Needless to say, the teacher is likely feeling frustrated, overwhelmed, and hopeless. This teacher may present as unwilling or resistant to change, perhaps seeming unaccepting of your suggestions or unmotivated. While it may be easy to take this personally, don't. For this teacher, the pairing process is critical. You will need to set the teacher and the intervention up for success so that the student in question can benefit. This situation may warrant having the teacher implement small changes so that the teacher and student alike experience success and build behavioral momentum. Behavioral momentum increases the likelihood that they will follow through on increased demands (e.g., implementing schedules of reinforcement, or behavior interventions such as Differential Reinforcement of Other Behavior – DRO).

2. **The classroom with no management:** While many BCBAs go into the field not expecting to practice in the realm of Organizational Behavior Management (OBM) they will quickly learn that the basics of OBM will be helpful in their classroom consultations, especially in a classroom in which organization is lacking. As behaviorists, we manage behavior and we manage environments. The behavior and environments that require the most management are often beyond the target client. Upon an initial observation of a target student, it is important to note structural and logistical constraints within a classroom and school environment. Some critical components to consider may include the following:

    a. Landscape of the classroom: While it is not necessary to feng shui the classroom, it may be of benefit to organize furniture and materials in a way that is functional for the student(s). For example, shelves can be used to create barriers and/or section off areas to create centers. Materials can be designated for particular centers, which lends itself to the classroom having a place for everything and a flow across activities.

    b. Schedule: Does the classroom have a schedule? Do they follow the schedule? How often is the schedule disrupted? What are the disruptions? Can the disruptions be minimized? Does everyone know what's going on at any given point throughout the day? These questions are critical for building capacity within the classroom. The more consistency and continuity that can be created and extended throughout the day, the greater the likelihood that students and staff will remain on course. This can be achieved by creating a schedule that details the expectations for the day, including routines, procedures, and transitions and regularly scheduled activities. Once a classroom is in proper working order with systems in place, it is more conducive for learning, management of challenging behavior, and implementation of interventions. At times, the shaping of classroom management alone is sufficient in decreasing problem behavior because students (and staff) are aware of expectations and transitions.

3. **Unmotivated staff:** This may be the one of the more challenging situations to resolve because there are variables outside of the control of the consultant that could ultimately have a positive impact on the motivation of staff. Some factors that are beyond the scope of the behaviorist include: we cannot increase pay for school staff, we cannot hand out extra vacation days, and in most cases we are unable to reward school staff with tangible reinforcers. There are, however, a number of factors that we can control which can have a positive impact on staff motivation.

a. Training: An issue for some staff is that they have not received proper training and/ or have not contacted reinforcement associated with success for their students. When people are unsure of what they are doing or have not made an impact, they may lose motivation. Providing staff with adequate training and feedback will build their skill set, leading to more opportunities for positive interactions with their students. Building skills may lead to staff taking on different roles within the classroom, which may be reinforcing for some individuals.

b. Positive reinforcement: In general, there is not nearly enough positive reinforcement going on in the workplace. Providing staff with positive reinforcement for proper implementation of procedures, giving praise for appropriately handling a situation, and acknowledging the hard work everyone does at the end of the day with a "thank you" can go a long way. It is possible to use behavior charts with staff. Goals can be determined and measured, and based on performance staff may earn reinforcers. In some cases, school administration will approve reinforcers such as a gift cards, school swag (e.g., t-shirt), or a special lunch. If reinforcers are going to be utilized, it is best to conduct a preference assessment with staff to discern which items may function as a reinforcer for each individual.

4. **Can't we all just get along?** Consultants are generally part of a multidisciplinary team. Collaboration with teachers, parents, child study team members, administration, and related services (e.g., speech, occupational therapy, physical therapy) is all part of the consultative process. As behavior analysts, we abide by a strict ethical Code which averts us from practicing pseudoscience or endorsing interventions that are not empirically based or validated. So how can we collaborate with other disciplines or be involved in situations in which our ethical Code is compromised? Let's look at some examples:

a. Weighted vest: It is recommended that a student wears a weighted vest for a prescribed amount of time per day to regulate his/her body and decrease target behavior. This is outside of the practice of applied behavior analysis. What to do? Collect baseline data of target behavior prior to weighted vest intervention. Collect data throughout the day to measure target behavior with the vest on and off and compare to baseline.

b. A behavior plan is created; however, the team collectively decides to have aspects of the plan removed. This plan was created based on a functional behavior assessment and all parts of the plan are critical components based on the findings of the assessment. What do you do? Consider the following:

   i.) Review the team's concerns and address points as needed to clarify or modify the plan in an effort to come to a resolution that is agreed upon by all members.

   ii.) If an agreement cannot be reached, and as often is the case, your signature is required for the intervention to be implemented; include a statement regarding your recommendations and opposition to elements of the plan being removed. This caveat allows for the plan to move forward while maintaining the integrity of your concerns.

Working in schools can be a rewarding experience. It allows for collaboration with a number of professionals and a variety of clients. This is not an exhaustive list of challenges or ethical conundrums; however, these are situations that are common when practicing in schools. It is recommended to seek the advice of colleagues when ethical concerns are raised in an effort to determine the most practical and ethical way to resolve a situation.

Works Cited

Binder, C. (1996). Behavioral fluency: evolution of a new paradigm. *The Behavior Analyst, 19*(2), 163–197.

Choi, B. C. K., & Pak, A. W. P. (2006). Multidisciplinarity, interdisciplinarity and transdisciplinarity in health research, services, education and policy: 1. definitions, objectives, and evidence of effectiveness. *Clinical and Investigative Medicine, 29*(6), 351–64.

Mafa, O. (2012). Challenges of implementing inclusion in Zimbabwe's Education System. *Online Journal of Education Research, 1*(2), 14–22.

Reed, D. D., & Kaplan, B. A. (2011). The matching law: a tutorial for practitioners. *Behavior Analysis in Practice, 4*(2), 15–24.

Srivastava, M., de Boer, A., & Pijl, S. J. (2015). Inclusive education in developing countries: a closer look at its implementation in the last 10 years. *Educational Review, 67*(2), 179–195.

Stokes, T. F., & Baer, D. M. (1977). An implicit technology of generalization 1. *Journal of Applied Behavior Analysis, 10*(2), 349–367.

Van Houten, R., Axelrod, S., Bailey, J. S., Favell, J. E., Foxx, R. M., Iwata, B. A., & Lovaas, O. I. (1988). The right to effective behavioral treatment. *Journal of Applied Behavior Analysis, 21*(4), 381–384.

Wolf, M. M. (1978). Social validity: the case for subjective measurement or how applied behavior analysis is finding its heart. *Journal of Applied Behavior Analysis, 11*(2), 203–214.

Wong, C., Odom, S. L., Hume, K. A., Cox, A. W., Fettig, A., Kucharczyk, S. ... & Schultz, T. R. (2015). Evidence-based practices for children, youth, and young adults with autism spectrum disorder: a comprehensive review. *Journal of Autism and Developmental Disorders, 45*(7), 1951–1966.

Appendix A
Ethics Code for Behavior Analysts

Introduction

As a diverse group of professionals who work in a variety of practice areas, behavior analysts deliver applied behavior analysis (ABA) services to positively impact lives. The Behavior Analyst Certification Board® (BACB®) exists to meet the credentialing needs of these professionals and relevant stakeholders (e.g., licensure boards, funders) while protecting ABA consumers by establishing, disseminating, and managing professional standards. The BACB facilitates ethical behavior in the profession through its certification eligibility and maintenance requirements, by issuing the ethics standards described in this document, and by operating a system for addressing professional misconduct.

The Ethics Code for Behavior Analysts (Code) guides the professional activities of behavior analysts over whom the BACB has jurisdiction (see *Scope of the Code* below). The Code also provides a means for behavior analysts to evaluate their own behavior and for others to assess whether a behavior analyst has violated their ethical obligations. An **introduction** section describes the scope and application of the Code, its core principles, and considerations for ethical decision making. The core principles are foundational concepts that should guide all aspects of a behavior analyst's work. The introduction is followed by a **glossary** that includes definitions of technical terms used in the Code. The final section includes the **ethics standards**, which are informed by the core principles. The standards are organized into six sections: (1) Responsibility as a Professional, (2) Responsibility in Practice, (3) Responsibility to Clients and Stakeholders, (4) Responsibility to Supervisees and Trainees, (5) Responsibility in Public Statements, and (6) Responsibility in Research.

Scope of the Code

The Code applies to all individuals who hold Board Certified Behavior Analyst® (BCBA®) or Board Certified Assistant Behavior Analyst® (BCaBA®) certification and all individuals who have completed an application for BCBA or BCaBA certification. For the sake of efficiency, the term "behavior analyst" is used throughout this document to refer to those who must act in accordance with the Code. The BACB does not have separate jurisdiction over organizations or corporations.

The Code applies to behavior analysts in all of their professional activities, including direct service delivery, consultation, supervision, training, management, editorial and peer-review activities, research, and any other activity within the ABA profession. The Code applies to behavior analysts' professional activities across settings and delivery modes (e.g., in person; in writing; via phone, email, text message, video conferencing). Application of the Code does not extend to behavior analysts' personal behavior unless it is determined that the behavior clearly poses a potential risk to the health and safety of clients, stakeholders, supervisees, or trainees.

Specific terms are defined in the <u>Glossary</u> section; however, two definitions are provided here because they are frequently used in the Core Principles section.

Client: The direct recipient of the behavior analyst's services. At various times during service provision, one or more stakeholders may simultaneously meet the definition of client (e.g., the point at which they receive direct training or consultation). In some contexts, the client might be a group of individuals (e.g., with organizational behavior management services).

Stakeholder: An individual, other than the client, who is impacted by and invested in the behavior analyst's services (e.g., parent, caregiver, relative, legally authorized representative, collaborator, employer, agency or institutional representative, licensure board, funder, third-party contractor for services).

Core Principles

Four foundational principles, which all behavior analysts should strive to embody, serve as the framework for the ethics standards. Behavior analysts should use these principles to interpret and apply the standards in the Code. The four core principles are that behavior analysts should: benefit others; treat others with compassion, dignity, and respect; behave with integrity; and ensure their own competence.

1. **Benefit Others.** Behavior analysts work to maximize benefits and do no harm by:
   - Protecting the welfare and rights of clients above all others
   - Protecting the welfare and rights of other individuals with whom they interact in a professional capacity
   - Focusing on the short- and long-term effects of their professional activities
   - Actively identifying and addressing the potential negative impacts of their own physical and mental health on their professional activities
   - Actively identifying potential and actual conflicts of interest and working to resolve them in a manner that avoids or minimizes harm
   - Actively identifying and addressing factors (e.g., personal, financial, institutional, political, religious, cultural) that might lead to conflicts of interest, misuse of their position, or negative impacts on their professional activities
   - Effectively and respectfully collaborating with others in the best interest of those with whom they work and always placing clients' interests first

2. **Treat Others with Compassion, Dignity, and Respect.** Behavior analysts behave toward others with compassion, dignity, and respect by:
   - Treating others equitably, regardless of factors such as age, disability, ethnicity, gender expression/identity, immigration status, marital/ relationship status, national origin, race, religion, sexual orientation, socioeconomic status, or any other basis proscribed by law
   - Respecting others' privacy and confidentiality
   - Respecting and actively promoting clients' self-determination to the best of their abilities, particularly when providing services to vulnerable populations
   - Acknowledging that personal choice in service delivery is important by providing clients and stakeholders with needed information to make informed choices about services

3. **Behave with Integrity.** Behavior analysts fulfill responsibilities to their scientific and professional communities, to society in general, and to the communities they serve by:
   - Behaving in an honest and trustworthy manner
   - Not misrepresenting themselves, misrepresenting their work or others' work, or engaging in fraud
   - Following through on obligations
   - Holding themselves accountable for their work and the work of their supervisees and trainees, and correcting errors in a timely manner
   - Being knowledgeable about and upholding BACB and other regulatory requirements
   - Actively working to create professional environments that uphold the core principles and standards of the Code
   - Respectfully educating others about the ethics requirements of behavior analysts and the mechanisms for addressing professional misconduct
4. **Ensure their Competence.** Behavior analysts ensure their competence by:
   - Remaining within the profession's scope of practice
   - Remaining current and increasing their knowledge of best practices and advances in ABA and participating in professional development activities
   - Remaining knowledgeable and current about interventions (including pseudoscience) that may exist in their practice areas and pose a risk of harm to clients
   - Being aware of, working within, and continually evaluating the boundaries of their competence
   - Working to continually increase their knowledge and skills related to cultural responsiveness and service delivery to diverse groups

Application of the Code

Behavior analysts are expected to be knowledgeable about and comply with the Code and Code-Enforcement Procedures. Lack of awareness or misunderstanding of an ethics standard is not a defense against an alleged ethics violation. When appropriate, behavior analysts should inform others about the Code and Code-Enforcement Procedures and create conditions that foster adherence to the Code. When addressing potential code violations by themselves or others, behavior analysts document the steps taken and the resulting outcomes. Behavior analysts should address concerns about the professional misconduct of others directly with them when, after assessing the situation, it seems possible that doing so will resolve the issue and not place the behavior analyst or others at undue risk.

The BACB recognizes that behavior analysts may have different professional roles. As such, behavior analysts are required to comply with all applicable laws, licensure requirements, codes of conduct/ethics, reporting requirements (e.g., mandated reporting, reporting to funding sources or licensure board, self-reporting to the BACB, reporting instances of misrepresentation by others), and professional practice requirements related to their various roles. In some instances, behavior analysts may need to report serious concerns to relevant authorities or agencies that can provide more immediate relief or protection before reporting to the BACB (e.g., criminal activity or behavior that places clients or others at risk for direct and immediate harm should immediately be reported to the relevant authorities before reporting to the BACB or a licensure board).

The standards included in the Code are not meant to be exhaustive, as it is impossible to predict every situation that might constitute an ethics violation. Therefore, the absence of a particular behavior or type of conduct from the Code standards does not indicate that such behavior or conduct is ethical or unethical. When interpreting and applying a standard, it is critical to attend to its specific wording and function, as well as the core principles. Additionally, standards must be applied to a situation using a functional, contextualized approach that accounts for factors relevant to that situation, such as variables related to diversity (e.g., age, disability, ethnicity, gender expression/identity, immigration status, marital/relationship status, national origin, race, religion, sexual orientation, socioeconomic status) and possible imbalances in power. In all instances of interpreting and applying the Code, behavior analysts should put compliance with the law and clients' interests first by actively working to maximize desired outcomes and minimize risk.

Ethical decision making. Behavior analysts will likely encounter complex and multifaceted ethical dilemmas. When faced with such a dilemma, behavior analysts should identify problems and solutions with care and deliberation. In resolving an ethical dilemma, behavior analysts should follow the spirit and letter of the Code's core principles and specific standards. Behavior analysts should address ethical dilemmas through a structured decision-making process that considers the full context of the situation and the function of relevant ethics standards. Although no single ethical decision-making process will be equally effective in all situations, the process below illustrates a systematic approach behavior analysts can take to document and address potential ethical concerns.

Throughout all of the following steps, document information that may be essential to decision making or for communicating the steps taken and outcomes (e.g., to the BACB, licensure boards, or other governing agencies). For example, consider documenting: dates, times, locations, and relevant individuals; summaries of observations, meetings, or information reported by others. Take care to protect confidentiality in the preparation and storage of all documentation.

---

1. Clearly define the issue and consider potential risk of harm to relevant individuals.
2. Identify all relevant individuals.
3. Gather relevant supporting documentation and follow-up on second-hand information to confirm that there is an actual ethical concern.
4. Consider your personal learning history and biases in the context of the relevant individuals.
5. Identify the relevant core principles and Code standards.
6. Consult available resources (e.g., research, decision-making models, trusted colleagues).
7. Develop several possible actions to reduce or remove risk of harm, prioritizing the best interests of clients in accordance with the Code and applicable laws.
8. Critically evaluate each possible action by considering its alignment with the "letter and spirit" of the Code, its potential impact on the client and stakeholders, the likelihood of it immediately resolving the ethical concern, as well as variables such as client preference, social acceptability, degree of restrictiveness, and likelihood of maintenance.
9. Select the action that seems most likely to resolve the specific ethical concern and reduce the likelihood of similar issues arising in the future.
10. Take the selected action in collaboration with relevant individuals affected by the issue and document specific actions taken, agreed-upon next steps, names of relevant individuals, and due dates.
11. Evaluate the outcomes to ensure that the action successfully addressed the issue.

Enforcement of the Code

The BACB enforces the Code to protect clients and stakeholders, BCBA and BCaBA certificants and applicants, and the ABA profession. Complaints are received and processed according to the processes outlined in the BACB's <u>Code-Enforcement Procedures</u> document.

Glossary

Behavior Analyst

An individual who holds BCBA or BCaBA certification or who has submitted a complete application for BCBA or BCaBA certification.

Behavior-Change Intervention

The full set of behavioral procedures designed to improve the client's wellbeing.

Behavioral Services

Services that are explicitly based on the principles and procedures of behavior analysis and are designed to change behavior in meaningful ways. These services include, but are not limited to, assessment, behavior-change interventions, training, consultation, managing and supervising others, and delivering continuing education.

Client

The direct recipient of the behavior analyst's services. At various times during service provision, one or more stakeholders may simultaneously meet the definition of client (e.g., the point at which they receive direct training or consultation). In some contexts, the client might be a group of individuals (e.g., with organizational behavior management services).

Clients' Rights

Human rights, legal rights, rights codified within behavior analysis, and organization rules designed to benefit the client.

Conflict of Interest

An incompatibility between a behavior analyst's private and professional interests resulting in risk or potential risk to services provided to, or the professional relationship with, a client, stakeholder, supervisee, trainee, or research participant. Conflicts may result in a situation in which personal, financial, or professional considerations have the potential to influence or compromise professional judgment in the delivery of behavioral services, research, consultation, supervision, training, or any other professional activity.

Digital Content

Information that is made available for online consumption, downloading, or distribution through an electronic medium (e.g., television, radio, ebook, website, social media, videogame, application, computer, smart device). Common digital content includes documents, pictures, videos, and audio files.

Informed Consent

The permission given by an individual with the legal right to consent before participating in services or research, or allowing their information to be used or shared.

> *Service/Research*: Providing the opportunity for an individual to give informed consent for services or research involves communicating about and taking appropriate steps to confirm understanding of: (1) the purpose of the services or research; (2) the expected time commitment and procedures involved; (3) the right to decline to participate or withdraw at any time without adverse consequences; (4) potential benefits, risks, discomfort, or adverse effects; (5) any limits to confidentiality or privacy; (6) any incentives for research participation; (7) whom to contact for questions or concerns at any time; and (8) the opportunity to ask questions and receive answers.
>
> *Information Use/Sharing*: Providing the opportunity for an individual to give informed consent to share or use their information involves communicating about: (1) the purpose and intended use; (2) the audience; (3) the expected duration; (4) the right to decline or withdraw consent at any time; (5) potential risks or benefits; (6) any limitations to confidentiality or privacy; (7) whom to contact for questions or concerns at any time; and (8) the opportunity to ask questions and receive answers.

Legally Authorized Representative

Any individual authorized under law to provide consent on behalf of an individual who cannot provide consent to receive services or participate in research.

Multiple Relationship

A comingling of two or more of a behavior analyst's roles (e.g., behavioral and personal) with a client, stakeholder, supervisee, trainee, research participant, or someone closely associated with or related to the client.

Public Statements

Delivery of information (digital or otherwise) in a public forum for the purpose of either better informing that audience or providing a call-to-action. This includes paid or unpaid advertising, brochures, printed material, directory listings, personal resumes or curriculum vitae, interviews, or comments for use in media (e.g., print, statements in legal proceedings, lectures and public presentations, social media, published materials).

Research

Any data-based activity, including analysis of preexisting data, designed to generate generalizable knowledge for the discipline. The use of an experimental design does not by itself constitute research.

Research Participant

Any individual participating in a defined research study for whom informed consent has been obtained.

Research Review Committee

A group of professionals whose stated purpose is to review research proposals to ensure the ethical treatment of human research participants. This committee might be an official entity of a government or university (e.g., Institutional Review Board, Research Ethics Board), an independent committee within a service organization, or an independent organization created for this purpose.

Scope of Competence

The professional activities a behavior analyst can consistently perform with proficiency.

Social Media Channel

A digital platform, either found through a web browser or through an application, where users (individuals and/or businesses) can consume, create, copy, download, share, or comment on posts or advertisements. Both posts and advertisements would be considered digital content.

Stakeholder

An individual, other than the client, who is impacted by and invested in the behavior analyst's services (e.g., parent, caregiver, relative, legally authorized representative, collaborator, employer, agency or institutional representatives, licensure board, funder, third-party contractor for services).

Supervisee

Any individual whose behavioral service delivery is overseen by a behavior analyst within the context of a defined, agreed- upon relationship. Supervisees may include RBTs, BCaBAs, and BCBAs, as well as other professionals carrying out supervised behavioral services.

Testimonial

Any solicited or unsolicited recommendation, in any form, from a client, stakeholder, supervisee, or trainee affirming the benefits received from a behavior analyst's product or service. From the point at which a behavior analyst asks an individual for a recommendation it is considered solicited.

Third Party

Any individual, group of individuals, or entity, other than the direct recipient of services, the primary caregiver, the legally authorized representative, or the behavior analyst, who requests and funds services on behalf of a client or group of clients. Some examples include a school district, governmental entity, mental health agency, among others.

Trainee

Any individual accruing fieldwork/experience toward fulfilling eligibility requirements for BCaBA or BCBA certification.

Website

A digital platform found through a web browser where an entity (individual and/or organization) produces and distributes digital content for the consumption of users online. Depending on the functionality, users can consume, create, copy, download, share, or comment on the provided digital content.

Note: Terms defined in the glossary are *italicized* the first time they appear in a standard in each section of the Code.

Ethics Standards

Section 1: Responsibility as a Professional

1.01   **Being Truthful**
Behavior analysts are truthful and arrange the professional environment to promote truthful behavior in others. They do not create professional situations that result in others engaging in behavior that is fraudulent or illegal or that violates the Code. They also provide truthful and accurate information to all required entities (e.g., BACB, licensure boards, funders) and individuals (e.g., clients, stakeholders, supervisees, trainees), and they correct instances of untruthful or inaccurate submissions as soon as they become aware of them.

1.02   **Conforming with Legal and Professional Requirements**
Behavior analysts follow the law and the requirements of their professional community (e.g., BACB, licensure board).

1.03   **Accountability**
Behavior analysts are accountable for their actions and professional services and follow through on work commitments. When errors occur or commitments cannot be met, behavior analysts take all appropriate actions to directly address them, first in the best interest of *clients*, and then in the best interest of relevant parties.

1.04   **Practicing within a Defined Role**
Behavior analysts provide services only after defining and documenting their professional role with relevant parties in writing.

1.05   **Practicing within Scope of Competence**
Behavior analysts practice only within their identified *scope of competence*. They engage in professional activities in new areas (e.g., populations, procedures) only after accessing and documenting appropriate study, training, supervised experience, consultation, and/or co-treatment from professionals competent in the new area. Otherwise, they refer or transition services to an appropriate professional.

1.06   **Maintaining Competence**
Behavior analysts actively engage in professional development activities to maintain and further their professional competence. Professional development activities include reading relevant literature; attending conferences and conventions; participating in workshops and other training opportunities; obtaining additional coursework; receiving coaching, consultation, supervision, or mentorship; and obtaining and maintaining appropriate professional credentials.

1.07   **Cultural Responsiveness and Diversity**
Behavior analysts actively engage in professional development activities to acquire knowledge and skills related to cultural responsiveness and diversity. They evaluate their own biases and ability to address the needs of individuals with diverse needs/backgrounds (e.g., age, disability, ethnicity, gender expression/identity, immigration

status, marital/relationship status, national origin, race, religion, sexual orientation, socioeconomic status). Behavior analysts also evaluate biases of their *supervisees* and *trainees*, as well as their supervisees' and trainees' ability to address the needs of individuals with diverse needs/backgrounds.

1.08 Nondiscrimination

Behavior analysts do not discriminate against others. They behave toward others in an equitable and inclusive manner regardless of age, disability, ethnicity, gender expression/identity, immigration status, marital/relationship status, national origin, race, religion, sexual orientation, socioeconomic status, or any other basis proscribed by law.

1.09 Nonharassment

Behavior analysts do not engage in behavior that is harassing or hostile toward others.

1.10 Awareness of Personal Biases and Challenges

Behavior analysts maintain awareness that their personal biases or challenges (e.g., mental or physical health conditions; legal, financial, marital/relationship challenges) may interfere with the effectiveness of their professional work. Behavior analysts take appropriate steps to resolve interference, ensure that their professional work is not compromised, and document all actions taken in this circumstance and the eventual outcomes.

1.11 Multiple Relationships

Because *multiple relationships* may result in a *conflict of interest* that might harm one or more parties, behavior analysts avoid entering into or creating multiple relationships, including professional, personal, and familial relationships with clients and colleagues. Behavior analysts communicate the risks of multiple relationships to relevant individuals and continually monitor for the development of multiple relationships. If multiple relationships arise, behavior analysts take appropriate steps to resolve them. When immediately resolving a multiple relationship is not possible, behavior analysts develop appropriate safeguards to identify and avoid conflicts of interest in compliance with the Code and develop a plan to eventually resolve the multiple relationship. Behavior analysts document all actions taken in this circumstance and the eventual outcomes.

1.12 Giving and Receiving Gifts

Because the exchange of gifts can invite conflicts of interest and multiple relationships, behavior analysts do not give gifts to or accept gifts from clients, *stakeholders*, supervisees, or trainees with a monetary value of more than $10 US dollars (or the equivalent purchasing power in another currency). Behavior analysts make clients and stakeholders aware of this requirement at the onset of the professional relationship. A gift is acceptable if it functions as an infrequent expression of gratitude and does not result in financial benefit to the recipient. Instances of giving or accepting ongoing or cumulative gifts may rise to the level of a violation of this standard if the gifts become a regularly expected source of income or value to the recipient.

1.13 Coercive and Exploitative Relationships

Behavior analysts do not abuse their power or authority by coercing or exploiting persons over whom they have authority (e.g., evaluative, supervisory).

1.14 Romantic and Sexual Relationships

Behavior analysts do not engage in romantic or sexual relationships with current clients, stakeholders, trainees, or supervisees because such relationships pose a substantial risk of conflicts of interest and impaired judgment. Behavior analysts do not engage in romantic or sexual relationships with former clients or stakeholders for a minimum of two years from the date the professional relationship ended. Behavior analysts do not engage in romantic or sexual relationships with former supervisees or trainees until the parties can document that the professional relationship has ended (i.e., completion of all professional duties). Behavior analysts do not accept as supervisees or trainees individuals with whom they have had a past romantic or sexual relationship until at least six months after the relationship has ended.

1.15 Responding to Requests

Behavior analysts make appropriate efforts to respond to requests for information from and comply with deadlines of relevant individuals (e.g., clients, stakeholders, supervisees, trainees) and entities (e.g., BACB, licensure boards, funders). They also comply with practice requirements (e.g., attestations, criminal background checks) imposed by the BACB, employers, or governmental entities.

1.16 Self-Reporting Critical Information

Behavior analysts remain knowledgeable about and comply with all self-reporting requirements of relevant entities (e.g., BACB, licensure boards, funders).

Section 2: Responsibility in Practice

2.01 Providing Effective Treatment

Behavior analysts prioritize *clients' rights* and needs in service delivery. They provide services that are conceptually consistent with behavioral principles, based on scientific evidence, and designed to maximize desired outcomes for and protect all *clients, stakeholders, supervisees, trainees,* and *research participants* from harm. Behavior analysts implement nonbehavioral services with clients only if they have the required education, formal training, and professional credentials to deliver such services.

2.02 Timeliness

Behavior analysts deliver services and carry out necessary service-related administrative responsibilities in a timely manner.

2.03 Protecting Confidential Information

Behavior analysts take appropriate steps to protect the confidentiality of clients, stakeholders, supervisees, trainees, and research participants; prevent the accidental or inadvertent sharing of confidential information; and comply with applicable confidentiality requirements (e.g., laws, regulations, organization policies). The scope of confidentiality includes service delivery (e.g., live, teleservices, recorded sessions); documentation and data; and verbal, written, or electronic communication.

2.04 Disclosing Confidential Information

Behavior analysts only share confidential information about clients, stakeholders, supervisees, trainees, or research participants: (1) when *informed consent* is obtained; (2) when attempting to protect the client or others from harm; (3) when attempting to resolve contractual issues; (4) when attempting to prevent a crime that is reasonably likely to cause physical, mental, or financial harm to another; or (5) when compelled to do so by law or court order. When behavior analysts are authorized to discuss confidential information with a *third party*, they only share information critical to the purpose of the communication.

2.05 Documentation Protection and Retention

Behavior analysts are knowledgeable about and comply with all applicable requirements (e.g., BACB rules, laws, regulations, contracts, funder and organization requirements) for storing, transporting, retaining, and destroying physical and electronic documentation related to their professional activities. They destroy physical documentation after making electronic copies or summaries of data (e.g., reports and graphs) only when allowed by applicable requirements. When a behavior analyst leaves an organization these responsibilities remain with the organization.

2.06 Accuracy in Service Billing and Reporting

Behavior analysts identify their services accurately and include all required information on reports, bills, invoices, requests for reimbursement, and receipts. They do not implement or bill nonbehavioral services under an authorization or contract for *behavioral services*. If inaccuracies in reporting or billing are discovered, they inform all relevant parties (e.g., organizations,

licensure boards, funders), correct the inaccuracy in a timely manner, and document all actions taken in this circumstance and the eventual outcomes.

2.07 Fees

Behavior analysts implement fee practices and share fee information in compliance with applicable laws and regulations. They do not misrepresent their fees. In situations where behavior analysts are not directly responsible for fees, they must communicate these requirements to the responsible party and take steps to resolve any inaccuracy or conflict. They document all actions taken in this circumstance and the eventual outcomes.

2.08 Communicating About Services

Behavior analysts use understandable language in, and ensure comprehension of, all communications with clients, stakeholders, supervisees, trainees, and research participants. Before providing services, they clearly describe the scope of services and specify the conditions under which services will end. They explain all assessment and *behavior-change intervention* procedures before implementing them and explain assessment and intervention results when they are available. They provide an accurate and current set of their credentials and a description of their area of competence upon request.

2.09 Involving Clients and Stakeholders

Behavior analysts make appropriate efforts to involve clients and relevant stakeholders throughout the service relationship, including selecting goals, selecting and designing assessments and behavior-change interventions, and conducting continual progress monitoring.

2.10 Collaborating with Colleagues

Behavior analysts collaborate with colleagues from their own and other professions in the best interest of clients and stakeholders. Behavior analysts address conflicts by compromising when possible and always prioritizing the best interest of the client. Behavior analysts document all actions taken in these circumstances and their eventual outcomes.

2.11 Obtaining Informed Consent

Behavior analysts are responsible for knowing about and complying with all conditions under which they are required to obtain informed consent from clients, stakeholders, and research participants (e.g., before initial implementation of assessments or behavior-change interventions, when making substantial changes to interventions, when exchanging or releasing confidential information or records). They are responsible for explaining, obtaining, reobtaining, and documenting required informed consent. They are responsible for obtaining assent from clients when applicable.

2.12 Considering Medical Needs

Behavior analysts ensure, to the best of their ability, that medical needs are assessed and addressed if there is any reasonable likelihood that a referred behavior is influenced by medical or biological variables. They document referrals made to a medical professional and follow up with the client after making the referral.

2.13   Selecting, Designing, and Implementing Assessments

Before selecting or designing behavior-change interventions behavior analysts select and design assessments that are conceptually consistent with behavioral principles; that are based on scientific evidence; and that best meet the diverse needs, context, and resources of the client and stakeholders. They select, design, and implement assessments with a focus on maximizing benefits and minimizing risk of harm to the client and stakeholders. They summarize the procedures and results in writing.

2.14   Selecting, Designing, and Implementing Behavior-Change Interventions

Behavior analysts select, design, and implement behavior-change interventions that: (1) are conceptually consistent with behavioral principles; (2) are based on scientific evidence; (3) are based on assessment results; (4) prioritize positive reinforcement procedures; and (5) best meet the diverse needs, context, and resources of the client and stakeholders. Behavior analysts also consider relevant factors (e.g., risks, benefits, and side effects; client and stakeholder preference; implementation efficiency; cost effectiveness) and design and implement behavior-change interventions to produce outcomes likely to maintain under naturalistic conditions. They summarize the behavior-change intervention procedures in writing (e.g., a behavior plan).

2.15   Minimizing Risk of Behavior-Change Interventions

Behavior analysts select, design, and implement behavior-change interventions (including the selection and use of consequences) with a focus on minimizing risk of harm to the client and stakeholders. They recommend and implement restrictive or punishment-based procedures only after demonstrating that desired results have not been obtained using less intrusive means, or when it is determined by an existing intervention team that the risk of harm to the client outweighs the risk associated with the behavior-change intervention. When recommending and implementing restrictive or punishment-based procedures, behavior analysts comply with any required review processes (e.g., a human rights review committee). Behavior analysts must continually evaluate and document the effectiveness of restrictive or punishment-based procedures and modify or discontinue the behavior-change intervention in a timely manner if it is ineffective.

2.16   Describing Behavior-Change Interventions Before Implementation

Before implementation, behavior analysts describe in writing the objectives and procedures of the behavior-change intervention, any projected timelines, and the schedule of ongoing review. They provide this information and explain the environmental conditions necessary for effective implementation of the behavior-change intervention to the stakeholders and client (when appropriate). They also provide explanations when modifying existing or introducing new behavior-change interventions and obtain informed consent when appropriate.

2.17   Collecting and Using Data

Behavior analysts actively ensure the appropriate selection and correct implementation of data collection procedures. They graphically display, summarize, and use the data to make decisions about continuing, modifying, or terminating services.

2.18   Continual Evaluation of the Behavior-Change Intervention

Behavior analysts engage in continual monitoring and evaluation of behavior-change interventions. If data indicate that desired outcomes are not being realized, they actively assess the situation and take appropriate corrective action. When a behavior analyst is concerned that services concurrently delivered by another professional are negatively impacting the behavior-change intervention, the behavior analyst takes appropriate steps to review and address the issue with the other professional.

2.19 Addressing Conditions Interfering with Service Delivery

Behavior analysts actively identify and address environmental conditions (e.g., the behavior of others, hazards to the client or staff, disruptions) that may interfere with or prevent service delivery. In such situations, behavior analysts remove or minimize the conditions, identify effective modifications to the intervention, and/or consider obtaining or recommending assistance from other professionals. Behavior analysts document the conditions, all actions taken, and the eventual outcomes.

Section 3: Responsibility to Clients and Stakeholders

3.01 Responsibility to Clients (see 1.03, 2.01)

Behavior analysts act in the best interest of *clients*, taking appropriate steps to support *clients' rights*, maximize benefits, and do no harm. They are also knowledgeable about and comply with applicable laws and regulations related to mandated reporting requirements.

3.02 Identifying Stakeholders

Behavior analysts identify *stakeholders* when providing services. When multiple stakeholders (e.g., parent or *legally authorized representative*, teacher, principal) are involved, the behavior analyst identifies their relative obligations to each stakeholder. They document and communicate those obligations to stakeholders at the outset of the professional relationship.

3.03 Accepting Clients (see 1.05, 1.06)

Behavior analysts only accept clients whose requested services are within their identified *scope of competence* and available resources (e.g., time and capacity for case supervision, staffing). When behavior analysts are directed to accept clients outside of their identified scope of competence and available resources, they take appropriate steps to discuss and resolve the concern with relevant parties. Behavior analysts document all actions taken in this circumstance and the eventual outcomes.

3.04 Service Agreement (see 1.04)

Before implementing services, behavior analysts ensure that there is a signed service agreement with the client and/ or relevant stakeholders outlining the responsibilities of all parties, the scope of *behavioral services* to be provided, the behavior analyst's obligations under the Code, and procedures for submitting complaints about a behavior analyst's professional practices to relevant entities (e.g., BACB, service organization, licensure board, funder). They update service agreements as needed or as required by relevant parties (e.g., service organizations, licensure boards, funders). Updated service agreements must be reviewed with and signed by the client and/or relevant stakeholders.

3.05 Financial Agreements (see 1.04, 2.07)

Before beginning services, behavior analysts document agreed-upon compensation and billing practices with their clients, relevant stakeholders, and/or funders. When funding circumstances change, they must be revisited with these parties. Pro bono and bartered services are only provided under a specific service agreement and in compliance with the Code.

3.06 Consulting with Other Providers (see 1.05, 2.04, 2.10, 2.11, 2.12)

Behavior analysts arrange for appropriate consultation with and referrals to other providers in the best interests of their clients, with appropriate *informed consent*, and in compliance with applicable requirements (e.g., laws, regulations, contracts, organization and funder policies).

3.07   Third-Party Contracts for Services (see 1.04, 1.11, 2.04, 2.07)

When behavior analysts enter into a signed contract to provide services to a client at the request of a *third party* (e.g., school district, governmental entity), they clarify the nature of the relationship with each party and assess any potential conflicts before services begin. They ensure that the contract outlines (1) the responsibilities of all parties, (2) the scope of behavioral services to be provided, (3) the likely use of the information obtained, (4) the behavior analysts' obligations under the Code, and (5) any limits about maintaining confidentiality. Behavior analysts are responsible for amending contracts as needed and reviewing them with the relevant parties at that time.

3.08   Responsibility to the Client with Third-Party Contracts for Services (see 1.05, 1.11, 2.01)

Behavior analysts place the client's care and welfare above all others. If the third party requests services from the behavior analyst that are incompatible with the behavior analyst's recommendations, that are outside of the behavior analyst's scope of competence, or that could result in a *multiple relationship*, behavior analysts resolve such conflicts in the best interest of the client. If a conflict cannot be resolved, the behavior analyst may obtain additional training or consultation, discontinue services following appropriate transition measures, or refer the client to another behavior analyst. Behavior analysts document all actions taken in this circumstance and the eventual outcomes.

3.09   Communicating with Stakeholders About Third-Party Contracted Services (2.04, 2.08, 2.09, 2.11)

When providing services at the request of a third party to a minor or individual who does not have the legal right to make personal decisions, behavior analysts ensure that the parent or legally authorized representative is informed of the rationale for and scope of services to be provided, as well as their right to receive copies of all service documentation and data, Behavior analysts are knowledgeable about and comply with all requirements related to informed consent, regardless of who requested the services.

3.10   Limitations of Confidentiality (see 1.02, 2.03, 2.04)

Behavior analysts inform clients and stakeholders of the limitations of confidentiality at the outset of the professional relationship and when information disclosures are required.

3.11   Documenting Professional Activity (see 1.04, 2.03, 2.05, 2.06, 2.10)

Throughout the service relationship, behavior analysts create and maintain detailed and high-quality documentation of their professional activities to facilitate provision of services by them or by other professionals, to ensure accountability, and to meet applicable requirements (e.g., laws, regulations, funder and organization policies). Documentation must be created and maintained in a manner that allows for timely communication and transition of services, should the need arise.

3.12   Advocating for Appropriate Services (1.04, 1.05, 2.01, 2.08)

Behavior analysts advocate for and educate clients and stakeholders about evidence-based assessment and *behavior- change intervention* procedures. They also advocate for the appropriate amount and level of behavioral service provision and oversight required to meet defined client goals.

3.13   Referrals (see 1.05, 1.11, 2.01, 2.04, 2.10)

Behavior analysts make referrals based on the needs of the client and/or relevant stakeholders and include multiple providers when available. Behavior analysts disclose to the client and relevant stakeholders any relationships they have with potential providers and any fees or incentives they may receive for the referrals. They document any referrals made, including relevant relationships and fees or incentives received, and make appropriate efforts to follow up with the client and/ or relevant stakeholders.

3.14 Facilitating Continuity of Services (see 1.03, 2.02, 2.05, 2,08, 2.10)

Behavior analysts act in the best interests of the client to avoid interruption or disruption of services. They make appropriate and timely efforts to facilitate the continuation of behavioral services in the event of planned interruptions (e.g., relocation, temporary leave of absence) and unplanned interruptions (e.g., illness, funding disruption, parent request, emergencies). They ensure that service agreements or contracts include a general plan of action for service interruptions. When a service interruption occurs, they communicate to all relevant parties the steps being taken to facilitate continuity of services. Behavior analysts document all actions taken in this circumstance and the eventual outcomes.

3.15 Appropriately Discontinuing Services (see 1.03, 2.02, 2.05. 2.10, 2.19)

Behavior analysts include the circumstances for discontinuing services in their service agreement. They consider discontinuing services when: (1) the client has met all behavior-change goals, (2) the client is not benefiting from the service, (3) the behavior analyst and/or their *supervisees* or *trainees* are exposed to potentially harmful conditions that cannot be reasonably resolved, (4) the client and/or relevant stakeholder requests discontinuation, (5) the relevant stakeholders are not complying with the behavior-change intervention despite appropriate efforts to address barriers, or (6) services are no longer funded. Behavior analysts provide the client and/ or relevant stakeholders with a written plan for discontinuing services, document acknowledgment of the plan, review the plan throughout the discharge process, and document all steps taken.

3.16 Appropriately Transitioning Services (see 1.03, 2.02, 2.05. 2.10)

Behavior analysts include in their service agreement the circumstances for transitioning the client to another behavior analyst within or outside of their organization. They make appropriate efforts to effectively manage transitions; provide a written plan that includes target dates, transition activities, and responsible parties; and review the plan throughout the transition. When relevant, they take appropriate steps to minimize disruptions to services during the transition by collaborating with relevant service providers.

Section 4: Responsibility to Supervisees and Trainees

4.01 Compliance with Supervision Requirements (see 1.02)

Behavior analysts are knowledgeable about and comply with all applicable supervisory requirements (e.g., BACB rules, licensure requirements, funder and organization policies), including those related to supervision modalities and structure (e.g., in person, video conference, individual, group).

4.02 Supervisory Competence (see 1.05, 1.06)

Behavior analysts supervise and train others only within their identified *scope of competence*. They provide supervision only after obtaining knowledge and skills in effective supervisory practices, and they continually evaluate and improve their supervisory repertoires through professional development.

4.03 Supervisory Volume (see 1.02, 1.05, 2.01)

Behavior analysts take on only the number of *supervisees* or *trainees* that allows them to provide effective supervision and training. They are knowledgeable about and comply with any relevant requirements (e.g., BACB rules, licensure requirements, funder and organization policies). They consider relevant factors (e.g., their current client demands, their current supervisee or trainee caseload, time and logistical resources) on an ongoing basis and when deciding to add a supervisee or trainee. When behavior analysts determine that they have met their threshold volume for providing effective supervision, they document this self-assessment and communicate the results to their employer or other relevant parties.

4.04 Accountability in Supervision (see 1.03)

Behavior analysts are accountable for their supervisory practices. They are also accountable for the professional activities (e.g., client services, supervision, training, research activity, public statements) of their supervisees or trainees that occur as part of the supervisory relationship.

4.05 Maintaining Supervision Documentation (1.01, 1.02, 1.04, 2.03, 2.05, 3.11)

Behavior analysts create, update, store, and dispose of documentation related to their supervisees or trainees by following all applicable requirements (e.g., BACB rules, licensure requirements, funder and organization policies), including those relating to confidentiality. They ensure that their documentation, and the documentation of their supervisees or trainees, is accurate and complete. They maintain documentation in a manner that allows for the effective transition of supervisory oversight if necessary. They retain their supervision documentation for at least 7 years and as otherwise required by law and other relevant parties and instruct their supervisees or trainees to do the same.

4.06 Providing Supervision and Training (see 1.02, 1.13 2.01)

Behavior analysts deliver supervision and training in compliance with applicable requirements (e.g., BACB rules, licensure requirements, funder and organization policies). They design and implement supervision and training procedures that are evidence based, focus on positive reinforcement, and are individualized for each supervisee or trainee and their circumstances.

4.07 Incorporating and Addressing Diversity (see 1.05, 1.06, 1.07, 1.10)

During supervision and training, behavior analysts actively incorporate and address topics related to diversity (e.g., age, disability, ethnicity, gender expression/identity, immigration status, marital/relationship status, national origin, race, religion, sexual orientation, socioeconomic status).

4.08 Performance Monitoring and Feedback (see 2.02, 2.05, 2.17, 2.18)

Behavior analysts engage in and document ongoing, evidence-based data collection and performance monitoring (e.g., observations, structured evaluations) of supervisees or trainees. They provide timely informal and formal praise and feedback designed to improve performance and document formal feedback delivered. When performance problems arise, behavior analysts develop, communicate, implement, and evaluate an improvement plan with clearly identified procedures for addressing the problem.

4.09 Delegation of Tasks (see 1.03)

Behavior analysts delegate tasks to their supervisees or trainees only after confirming that they can competently perform the tasks and that the delegation complies with applicable requirements (e.g., BACB rules, licensure requirements, funder and organization policies).

4.10 Evaluating Effects of Supervision and Training (see 1.03, 2.17, 2.18)

Behavior analysts actively engage in continual evaluation of their own supervisory practices using feedback from others and *client* and supervisee or trainee outcomes.

Behavior analysts document those self-evaluations and make timely adjustments to their supervisory and training practices as indicated.

4.11 Facilitating Continuity of Supervision (see 1.03, 2.02, 3.14)
Behavior analysts minimize interruption or disruption of supervision and make appropriate and timely efforts to facilitate the continuation of supervision in the event of planned interruptions (e.g., temporary leave) or unplanned interruptions (e.g., illness, emergencies). When an interruption or disruption occurs, they communicate to all relevant parties the steps being taken to facilitate continuity of supervision.

4.12 Appropriately Terminating Supervision (see 1.03, 2.02, 3.15)
When behavior analysts determine, for any reason, to terminate supervision or other services that include supervision, they work with all relevant parties to develop a plan for terminating supervision that minimizes negative impacts to the supervisee or trainee. They document all actions taken in this circumstance and the eventual outcomes.

Section 5: Responsibility in Public Statements

5.01 Protecting the Rights of Clients, Stakeholders, Supervisees, and Trainees (see 1.03, 3.01)
Behavior analysts take appropriate steps to protect the *rights* of their *clients, stakeholders, supervisees,* and *trainees* in all *public statements.* Behavior analysts prioritize the rights of their clients in all public statements.

5.02 Confidentiality in Public Statements (see 2.03, 2.04, 3.10)
In all public statements, behavior analysts protect the confidentiality of their clients, supervisees, and trainees, except when allowed. They make appropriate efforts to prevent accidental or inadvertent sharing of confidential or identifying information.

5.03 Public Statements by Behavior Analysts (see 1.01, 1.02)
When providing public statements about their professional activities, or those of others with whom they are affiliated, behavior analysts take reasonable precautions to ensure that the statements are truthful and do not mislead or exaggerate either because of what they state, convey, suggest, or omit; and are based on existing research and a behavioral conceptualization. Behavior analysts do not provide specific advice related to a client's needs in public forums.

5.04 Public Statements by Others (see 1.03)
Behavior analysts are responsible for public statements that promote their professional activities or products, regardless of who creates or publishes the statements. Behavior analysts make reasonable efforts to prevent others (e.g., employers, marketers, clients, stakeholders) from making deceptive statements concerning their professional activities or products. If behavior analysts learn of such statements, they make reasonable efforts to correct them. Behavior analysts document all actions taken in this circumstance and the eventual outcomes.

5.05 Use of Intellectual Property (see 1.01, 1.02, 1.03)
Behavior analysts are knowledgeable about and comply with intellectual property laws, including obtaining permission to use materials that have been trademarked or copyrighted or can otherwise be claimed as another's intellectual property as defined by law. Appropriate use of such materials includes providing citations, attributions, and/or trademark or copyright symbols. Behavior analysts do not unlawfully obtain or disclose proprietary information, regardless of how it became known to them.

5.06 Advertising Nonbehavioral Services (see 1.01, 1.02, 2.01)
Behavior analysts do not advertise nonbehavioral services as *behavioral services.* If behavior analysts provide nonbehavioral services, those services must be clearly

distinguished from their behavioral services and BACB certification with the following disclaimer: "These interventions are not behavioral in nature and are not covered by my BACB certification." This disclaimer is placed alongside the names and descriptions of all nonbehavioral interventions. If a behavior analyst is employed by an organization that violates this Code standard, the behavior analyst makes reasonable efforts to remediate the situation, documenting all actions taken and the eventual outcomes.

5.07 Soliciting Testimonials from Current Clients for Advertising (see 1.11, 1.13, 2.11, 3.01, 3.10)
Because of the possibility of undue influence and implicit coercion, behavior analysts do not solicit *testimonials* from current clients or stakeholders for use in advertisements designed to obtain new clients. This does not include unsolicited reviews on *websites* where behavior analysts cannot control content, but such content should not be used or shared by the behavior analyst. If a behavior analyst is employed by an organization that violates this Code standard, the behavior analyst makes reasonable efforts to remediate the situation, documenting all actions taken and the eventual outcomes.

5.08 Using Testimonials from Former Clients for Advertising (see 2.03, 2.04, 2.11, 3.01, 3.10)
When soliciting testimonials from former clients or stakeholders for use in advertisements designed to obtain new clients, behavior analysts consider the possibility that former clients may re-enter services. These testimonials must be identified as solicited or unsolicited, include an accurate statement of the relationship between the behavior analyst and the testimonial author, and comply with all applicable privacy and confidentiality laws. When soliciting testimonials from former clients or stakeholders, behavior analysts provide them with clear and thorough descriptions about where and how the testimonial will appear, make them aware of any risks associated with the disclosure of their private information, and inform them that they can rescind the testimonial at any time. If a behavior analyst is employed by an organization that violates this Code standard, the behavior analyst makes reasonable efforts to remediate the situation, documenting all actions taken and the eventual outcomes.

5.09 Using Testimonials for Nonadvertising Purposes (see 1.02, 2.03. 2.04, 2.11, 3.01, 3.10)
Behavior analysts may use testimonials from former or current clients and stakeholders for nonadvertising purposes (e.g., fundraising, grant applications, dissemination of information about ABA) in accordance with applicable laws. If a behavior analyst is employed by an organization that violates this Code standard, the behavior analyst makes reasonable efforts to remediate the situation, documenting all actions taken and the eventual outcomes.

5.10 Social Media Channels and Websites (see 1.02, 2.03, 2.04, 2.11, 3.01, 3.10)
Behavior analysts are knowledgeable about the risks to privacy and confidentiality associated with the use of *social media channels* and websites and they use their respective professional and personal accounts accordingly. They do not publish information and/or *digital content* of clients on their **personal** social media accounts and websites. When publishing information and/or digital content of clients on their **professional** social media accounts and websites, behavior analysts ensure that for each publication they (1) obtain *informed consent* before publishing, (2) include a disclaimer that informed consent was obtained and that the information should not be captured and reused without express permission, (3) publish on social media channels in a manner that reduces the potential for sharing, and (4) make appropriate efforts to prevent and correct misuse of the shared information, documenting all actions taken and the eventual outcomes. Behavior analysts frequently monitor their

social media accounts and websites to ensure the accuracy and appropriateness of shared information.

5.11 **Using Digital Content** in **Public Statements** (see 1.02, 1.03, 2.03, 2.04, 2.11, 3.01, 3.10)
Before publicly sharing information about clients using digital content, behavior analysts ensure confidentiality, obtain informed consent before sharing, and only use the content for the intended purpose and audience. They ensure that all shared media is accompanied by a disclaimer indicating that informed consent was obtained. If a behavior analyst is employed by an organization that violates this Code standard, the behavior analyst makes reasonable efforts to remediate the situation, documenting all actions taken and the eventual outcomes.

Section 6: Responsibility in Research

6.01 **Conforming with Laws and Regulations in Research** (see 1.02)
Behavior analysts plan and conduct *research* in a manner consistent with all applicable laws and regulations, as well as requirements by organizations and institutions governing research activity.

6.02 **Research Review** (see 1.02, 1.04, 3.01)
Behavior analysts conduct research, whether independent of or in the context of service delivery, only after approval by a formal *research review committee.*

6.03 **Research in Service Delivery** (see 1.02, 1.04, 2.01, 3.01)
Behavior analysts conducting research in the context of service delivery must arrange research activities such that *client* services and client welfare are prioritized. In these situations, behavior analysts must comply with all ethics requirements for both service delivery and research within the Code. When professional services are offered as an incentive for research participation, behavior analysts clarify the nature of the services, and any potential risks, obligations, and limitations for all parties.

6.04 **Informed Consent in Research** (see 1.04, 2.08, 2.11)
Behavior analysts are responsible for obtaining *informed consent* (and assent when relevant) from potential *research participants* under the conditions required by the research review committee. When behavior analysts become aware that data obtained from past or current clients, *stakeholders, supervisees,* and/or *trainees* during typical service delivery might be disseminated to the scientific community, they obtain informed consent for use of the data before dissemination, specify that services will not be impacted by providing or withholding consent, and make available the right to withdraw consent at any time without penalty.

6.05 **Confidentiality in Research** (see 2.03, 2.04, 2.05)
Behavior analysts prioritize the confidentiality of their research participants except under conditions where it may not be possible. They make appropriate efforts to prevent accidental or inadvertent sharing of confidential or identifying information while conducting research and in any dissemination activity related to the research (e.g., disguising or removing confidential or identifying information).

6.06 **Competence in Conducting Research** (see 1.04, 1.05, 1.06, 3.01)
Behavior analysts only conduct research independently after they have successfully conducted research under a supervisor in a defined relationship (e.g., thesis, dissertation, mentored research project). Behavior analysts and their assistants are permitted to perform only those research activities for which they are appropriately trained and prepared. Before engaging in research activities for which a behavior analyst has not received training, they seek the appropriate training and become

demonstrably competent or they collaborate with other professionals who have the required competence. Behavior analysts are responsible for the ethical conduct of all personnel assigned to the research project.

6.07 Conflict of Interest in Research and Publication (see 1.01, 1.11, 1.13)

When conducting research, behavior analysts identify, disclose, and address *conflicts of interest* (e.g., personal, financial, organization related, service related). They also identify, disclose, and address conflicts of interest in their publication and editorial activities.

6.08 Appropriate Credit (see 1.01, 1.11, 1.13)

Behavior analysts give appropriate credit (e.g., authorship, author-note acknowledgment) to research contributors in all dissemination activities. Authorship and other publication acknowledgments accurately reflect the relative scientific or professional contributions of the individuals involved, regardless of their professional status (e.g., professor, student).

6.09 Plagiarism (see 1.01)

Behavior analysts do not present portions or elements of another's work or data as their own. Behavior analysts only republish their previously published data or text when accompanied by proper disclosure.

6.10 Documentation and Data Retention in Research (see 2.03, 2.05, 3.11, 4.05)

Behavior analysts must be knowledgeable about and comply with all applicable standards (e.g., BACB rules, laws, research review committee requirements) for storing, transporting, retaining, and destroying physical and electronic documentation related to research. They retain identifying documentation and data for the longest required duration. Behavior analysts destroy physical documentation after making deidentified digital copies or summaries of data (e.g., reports and graphs) when permitted by relevant entities.

6.11 Accuracy and Use of Data (see 1.01, 2.17, 5.03)

Behavior analysts do not fabricate data or falsify results in their research, publications, and presentations. They plan and carry out their research and describe their procedures and findings to minimize the possibility that their research and results will be misleading or misinterpreted. If they discover errors in their published data they take steps to correct them by following publisher policy. Data from research projects are presented to the public and scientific community in their entirety whenever possible. When that is not possible, behavior analysts take caution and explain the exclusion of data (whether single data points, or partial or whole data sets) from presentations or manuscripts submitted for publication by providing a rationale and description of what was excluded.

Appendix B
BCBA Fifth Edition Task List

Introduction

The BCBA Task List includes the knowledge and skills that serve as the foundation for the BCBA examination.

Structure

The BCBA Task List is organized in two major sections, Foundations, which includes basic skills and underlying principles and knowledge, and Applications, which includes more practice-oriented skills.

Section 1: Foundations

A   Philosophical Underpinnings
B   Concepts and Principles
C   Measurement, Data Display, and Interpretation
D   Experimental Design

Section 2: Applications

E   Ethics (Ethics Code for Behavior Analysts)
F   Behavior Assessment
G   Behavior-Change Procedures
H   Selecting and Implementing Interventions
I   Personnel Supervision and Management

Section 1: Foundations

Philosophical Underpinnings

Identify the goals of behavior analysis as a science (i.e., description, prediction, control).
A-2 Explain the philosophical assumptions underlying the science of behavior analysis (e.g., selectionism, determinism, empiricism, parsimony, pragmatism).
A-3 Describe and explain behavior from the perspective of radical behaviorism.
A-4 Distinguish among behaviorism, the experimental analysis of behavior, applied behavior analysis, and professional practice guided by the science of behavior analysis.
A-5 Describe and define the dimensions of applied behavior analysis (Baer, Wolf, & Risley, 1968).

Concepts and Principles

B-1 Define and provide examples of behavior, response, and response class.

B-2 Define and provide examples of stimulus and stimulus class.

B-3 Define and provide examples of respondent and operant conditioning.

B-4 Define and provide examples of positive and negative reinforcement contingencies.

B-5 Define and provide examples of schedules of reinforcement.

B-6 Define and provide examples of positive and negative punishment contingencies.

B-7 Define and provide examples of automatic and socially mediated contingencies.

B-8 Define and provide examples of unconditioned, conditioned, and generalized reinforcers and punishers.

B-9 Define and provide examples of operant extinction.

B-10 Define and provide examples of stimulus control.

B-11 Define and provide examples of discrimination, generalization, and maintenance.

B-12 Define and provide examples of motivating operations.

B-13 Define and provide examples of rule-governed and contingency-shaped behavior.

B-14 Define and provide examples of the verbal operants.

B-15 Define and provide examples of derived stimulus relations.

Measurement, Data Display, and Interpretation

C-1 Establish operational definitions of behavior.

C-2 Distinguish among direct, indirect, and product measures of behavior.

C-3 Measure occurrence (e.g., count, frequency, rate, percentage).

C-4 Measure temporal dimensions of behavior (e.g., duration, latency, interresponse time)

C-5 Measure form and strength of behavior (e.g., topography, magnitude).

C-6 Measure trials to criterion.

C-7 Design and implement sampling procedures (i.e., interval recording, time sampling).

C-8 Evaluate the validity and reliability of measurement procedures.

C-9 Select a measurement system to obtain representative data given the dimensions of behavior and the logistics of observing and recording.

C-10 Graph data to communicate relevant quantitative relations (e.g., equal-interval graphs, bar graphs, cumulative records).

C-11 Interpret graphed data.

Experimental Design

D-1 Distinguish between dependent and independent variables.

D-2 Distinguish between internal and external validity.

D-3 Identify the defining features of single-subject experimental designs (e.g., individuals serve as their own controls, repeated measures, prediction, verification, replication).

D-4 Describe the advantages of single-subject experimental designs compared to group designs.

D-5 Use single-subject experimental designs (e.g., reversal, multiple baseline, multielement, changing criterion).

D-6 Describe rationales for conducting comparative, component, and parametric analyses.

Section 2: Applications

Ethics

Behave in accordance with the Ethics Code for Behavior Analysts

E-1 Introduction

E-2 Responsibility as a Professional

E-3 Responsibility in Practice

E-4 Responsibility to Clients and Stakeholders

E-5 Responsibility to Supervisees and Trainees

E-6 Responsibility in Public Statements

E-7 Responsibility in Research

Behavior Assessment

F-1 Review records and available data (e.g., educational, medical, historical) at the outset of the case.

F-2 Determine the need for behavior-analytic services.

F-3 Identify and prioritize socially significant behavior-change goals.

F-4 Conduct assessments of relevant skill strengths and deficits.

F-5 Conduct preference assessments.

F-6 Describe the common functions of problem behavior.

F-7 Conduct a descriptive assessment of problem behavior.

F-8 Conduct a functional analysis of problem behavior.

F-9 Interpret functional assessment data.

Behavior-Change Procedures

G-1 Use positive and negative reinforcement procedures to strengthen behavior.

G-2 Use interventions based on motivating operations and discriminative stimuli.

G-3 Establish and use conditioned reinforcers.

G-4 Use stimulus and response prompts and fading (e.g., errorless, most-to-least, least-to-most, prompt delay, stimulus fading).

G-5 Use modeling and imitation training.

G-6 Use instructions and rules.

G-7 Use shaping.

G-8 Use chaining.

G-9 Use discrete-trial, free-operant, and naturalistic teaching arrangements.

G-10 Teach simple and conditional discriminations.

G-11 Use Skinner's analysis to teach verbal behavior.

G-12 Use equivalence-based instruction.

G-13 Use the high-probability instructional sequence.

G-14 Use reinforcement procedures to weaken behavior (e.g., DRA, FCT, DRO, DRL, NCR).

G-15 Use extinction.

G-16 Use positive and negative punishment (e.g., time-out, response cost, overcorrection).

G-17 Use token economies.

G-18 Use group contingencies

G-19 Use contingency contracting.

G-20 Use self-management strategies.

G-21 Use procedures to promote stimulus and response generalization.

G-22 Use procedures to promote maintenance.

Selecting and Implementing Interventions

H-1 State intervention goals in observable and measurable terms.

H-2 Identify potential interventions based on assessment results and the best available scientific evidence.

H-3 Recommend intervention goals and strategies based on such factors as client preferences, supporting environments, risks, constraints, and social validity.

H-4 When a target behavior is to be decreased, select an acceptable alternative behavior to be established or increased.

H-5 Plan for possible unwanted effects when using reinforcement, extinction, and punishment procedures.

H-6 Monitor client progress and treatment integrity.

H-7 Make data-based decisions about the effectiveness of the intervention and the need for treatment revision.

H-8 Make data-based decisions about the need for ongoing services.

H-9 Collaborate with others who support and/or provide services to clients.

Personnel Supervision and Management

I-1 State the reasons for using behavior-analytic supervision and the potential risks of ineffective supervision (e.g., poor client outcomes, poor supervisee performance).

I-2 Establish clear performance expectations for the supervisor and supervisee.

I-3 Select supervision goals based on an assessment of the supervisee's skills.

I-4 Train personnel to competently perform assessment and intervention procedures.

I-5 Use performance monitoring, feedback, and reinforcement systems.

I-6 Use a functional assessment approach (e.g., performance diagnostics) to identify variables affecting personnel performance.

I-7 Use function-based strategies to improve personnel performance.

I-8 Evaluate the effects of supervision (e.g., on client outcomes, on supervisee repertoires).

Appendix C
Code-Enforcement Procedures

SECTION A. Preamble

The Behavior Analyst Certification Board is charged with promoting and maintaining standards of professional conduct in the practice of behavior analysis. To protect the public from practitioners who do not meet these standards, the BACB has adopted the Professional and Ethical Compliance Code for Behavior Analysts (Code) and the RBT Code of Ethics (RBT Code). The term "ethics requirements" is used to refer to the content in both documents. The purpose of the BACB's ethics standards and Code-Enforcement System is to protect the public by accepting and processing a Notice of Alleged Violation (Notice) submitted against an applicant or certificant.

The BACB provides due process to applicants and certificants who have allegedly violated one or more ethics requirements. Due process includes the BACB giving the Subject notice of the allegation(s) and an opportunity to respond, having the case decided by a neutral party, and providing an opportunity to appeal. BACB Ethics Department staff who are trained in code-enforcement review and process each Notice received.

SECTION B. Procedural Actions

1. **Revocation of Eligibility or Invalidation of Certification:** The BACB reserves the right to bar any individual from sitting for any BACB examination, or to invalidate any certification (immediately making the certification null and void), in the event the BACB finds that the individual submitted falsified, forged, or untrue information to the BACB. The BACB reserves this right regardless of when the BACB becomes aware of the falsified, forged, or untrue information. The BACB will revoke an individual's eligibility to apply to sit for any BACB examination for a minimum of 5 years, after which time the individual must meet the requirements applicable at the time they reapply. For individuals already certified, the BACB will invalidate the certification and revoke the individual's eligibility to apply to sit for any other BACB certification for a minimum of 5 years. After the revocation or ineligibility period ends, the individual must recomplete all experience hours (as applicable), meet the requirements applicable at the time they reapply, complete appropriate additional coursework in ethics, and submit to a full audit of experience hours (as applicable) at the time of application. Any invalidation or revocation of eligibility will be published in the individual's Registry record on the BACB website. Any eligibility revocation or certification invalidation may be applied prior to additional future sanctions that may be imposed on the individual's eligibility for BACB certification. An individual retains the right to appeal the hold or invalidation if they can submit evidence demonstrating that the information in question was submitted accurately and truthfully.

2. **Procedural Inactivation:** The BACB reserves the right to apply a preliminary inactive status to any applicant or certificant for whom the BACB has information indicating that the individual:

   a) is incarcerated or in any form of inpatient care;
   b) is unable to completely and competently provide client services; or
   c) poses an immediate risk of harm to a client or other relevant individual (e.g., trainee, supervisee).

Note: During a period of preliminary inactive status, the BACB will make every reasonable attempt to expedite the deadlines identified in the Code-Enforcement Procedures in order to minimize the duration of the preliminary inactive status period.

3. **Summary Suspension of Eligibility or Certification:** The BACB reserves the right to summarily suspend an applicant or certificant for failure to respond to requests from the BACB Ethics Department by the date indicated in the correspondence, or for failure to comply with the consequences in a Disciplinary or Appeal Determination. This is an automatic suspension of certification, application eligibility, or other status with the BACB that is published in the individual's Registry record on the BACB website. During the period of suspension, the individual may not represent themselves as certified by the BACB and may not practice or bill under a BACB certification. Certificants suspended under this provision may include their relevant certification designation in communications, but they must accurately identify their status as suspended or inactive (e.g., John Doe, BCBA (inactive) or Jane Doe, BCBA (suspended)). Failure to respond to the BACB during the suspension period may result in revocation. The individual may be reinstated during the suspension period if they:

   a) request reinstatement in writing by identifying the reason for the nonresponse and an action plan to ensure timely responding moving forward;
   b) complete any recertification requirements (BCBA, BCaBA, RBT) or renewal requirements (ACE);
   c) comply with all requirements during the educational or disciplinary process, including response to the Notice; and
   d) demonstrate appropriate reporting to, and from, third parties and licensure board(s), if applicable.

Note: Reinstatement, if approved, does not occur until the individual meets the conditions outlined in subsections a-d, complies with any other indicated actions (e.g., consequences in a Disciplinary or Appeal Determination or some other required action, such as providing documentation or other information), and the Ethics Department makes the determination to clear the suspension. If the suspension is converted to a revocation for continued failure to respond, the individual will be required to apply for consideration for re-entry.

SECTION C. Basis for Action

An accepted Notice serves as the basis for processing within the Code-Enforcement System. The individual submitting the Notice is referred to as the Notifier, and the individual alleged to have violated ethics requirements is referred to as the Subject. Because RBTs and BCaBAs are required to practice under the supervision of a BACB authorized supervisor, the BACB reserves the right to correspond and share information directly with their supervisors of record. Notices of Alleged Violation and supporting documentation,

Disciplinary Determinations, and Appeal Determinations will be shared directly with supervisors of record; other documentation may be shared if determined necessary for consumer protection.

SECTION D. Intake and Routing of a Notice

Jurisdiction of a Notice: The BACB has jurisdiction over any individual certified as a Board Certified Behavior Analyst- Doctoral (BCBA-D), Board Certified Behavior Analyst (BCBA), Board Certified Assistant Behavior Analyst (BCaBA), or Registered Behavior Technician (RBT), those with a complete application for examination, as well as prior applicants and certificants who are on inactive status, suspended, or revoked. The BACB also has jurisdiction over those who have applied to be, or are, Authorized Continuing Education (ACE) providers. The BACB does not have jurisdiction over non- certified individuals, trainees, or organizations/agencies.

1. **Intake of a Notice**
   a) Evaluating *a Notice:* The BACB evaluates each Notice upon receipt to ensure that it:
      i. is submitted against an individual over whom the BACB has jurisdiction; is submitted within 6 months of the alleged violation or of the Notifier becoming aware of the alleged violation (BACB staff have the discretion to extend this deadline in exceptional circumstances);
      ii. does not appear to be retaliatory in nature. Complaints by certificants that appear to be submitted in bad faith or in retaliation may be viewed as an abuse of process and a potential violation of the Code;
      iii. has a valid signature; and
      iv. includes clear documentation supporting each alleged violation of a specific ethics requirement (i.e., a specific element in the Code or RBT Code). Supporting documentation should not be speculative or composed of unsubstantiated suspicions. All supporting documentation must be properly redacted (confidential identifying information removed or covered) and must not exceed 20 pages. If the supporting documentation is not properly redacted or exceeds the page-limit, the BACB may return it to the Notifier with a request to correct and resubmit.

Note: For Notices of Publicly-Documented Alleged Violation the documentation must be freely and currently available (i.e., not behind a paywall or login requirement) and must substantiate an alleged violation of the ethics requirements by an individual over whom the BACB has jurisdiction.

   b) *Declining a* Notice: When a Notice does not meet the criteria above (or it is otherwise not actionable as determined by the BACB), the BACB declines the Notice and informs the Notifier.

Note: For Notices against an RBT: When the alleged violation does not relate to one of the following requirements: 1) abuse/neglect of a client, 2) charged/convicted of violation of law, or 3) violation of obligations to BACB or 1.10, 1.11, 1.12, or 3.01 of the RBT Code, the Notice may be declined and the Notifier is directed to take appropriate actions (e.g., address the issue directly, address the issue with the RBT Requirements Coordinator or Supervisor).

   c) *Deferring a Notice:* When a Notice is related to a complaint that has been submitted to an agency with investigative powers (e.g., law enforcement, licensure board, third-party payer), the BACB may, but is not required to, postpone processing the Notice until a final determination has been issued by the investigatory agency. In such cases, the BACB informs the Notifier of the next steps regarding the notice submitted.

d) *Accepting a Notice*: After accepting a Notice for processing, the BACB informs the Notifier. The BACB then informs the Subject of the Notice by sending 1) the Notice document, 2) the supporting documentation, and 3) a response form with instructions for submitting the form and any supporting documentation. If the Subject is an RBT they will also receive a BACB Required Supervisor Acknowledgment of Notice form that must be completed and returned.

2. **Routing of a Notice:** At least two BACB staff collaborate to make an appropriate routing decision for each accepted Notice. The Notice may be declined, deferred, or routed to one of the following systems:

    1) Disciplinary Review or 2) Educational Review.

3. **Failure to Respond to a Notice:** Failure to respond to the BACB by the date indicated in the correspondence results in automatic suspension of certification, application eligibility, or other status with the BACB, which is published on the BACB website in the individual's Registry record. See section B, subsection 3 of this document for more information about summary suspensions and the required steps for initiating reinstatement of certification, application eligibility, or other status with the BACB.

SECTION E. Code-Enforcement Systems

Accepted Notices are routed to one of the following systems:

1. **Educational:** This system focuses on providing the Subject with guidance and support to reduce the likelihood that future violations may occur. Activities within this system may include sending an educational memorandum or notice of required action or offering voluntary coaching (an educational and professional development process) to the Subject.

2. **Disciplinary Review:** This system focuses on determining whether the submitted documentation substantiates the alleged violation and, if so, what consequences should be applied to the case. The BACB takes disciplinary action against a Subject when a preponderance of the documentation supports the alleged violation(s). In other words, the documentation must support a finding that it is more likely than not that the violation occurred. Neither the Subject nor the Notifier are allowed to be present at, or to participate in, the Disciplinary Review meeting. There are two possible outcomes of a Disciplinary Review:

    1) no further action or
    2) consequences are prescribed. The review committee considers the submitted documentation for a case, makes a decision regarding the alleged violation(s), and, if applicable, issues one or more consequences based on precedent.

Typically, within 30 days of the review commitee's decision the BACB staff notifies the Subject of the Disciplinary Determination. The Subject has 30 days to notify the BACB Ethics Department whether they accept the Disciplinary Determination (i.e., intend to comply with the indicated consequences) or request an appeal.

a) If the Subject declines an appeal, they may begin fulfilling the requirements of the Disciplinary Determination on that date. The BACB informs the Notifier of the Disciplinary Determination.

b) The Disciplinary Determination becomes final and unappealable if the Subject fails to accept the Disciplinary Determination OR request an appeal within 30 days. The BACB informs the Notifier of the Disciplinary Determination.

SECTION F. Possible Consequences

There are two categories of consequences that may be applied in a Disciplinary Determination: (1) corrective actions and (2) sanctions. Corrective actions include steps the Subject must take to address the violation and reduce the likelihood that future violations may occur. Sanctions include actions that place a restriction on the Subject.

1. **Corrective Actions:** These consequences are not published on the website. This list is not exhaustive, as other relevant actions may be determined during the Disciplinary Review process.

   a) *Professional Development:* The Subject must engage in relevant professional development activities (e.g., earn continuing education credits or University course credits on a topic relevant to the violation).

   b) *Mentorship:* The Subject is required to receive mentorship from an approved individual for the indicated duration to address professional development related to the specific violations and any other areas identified.

   c) *Verification of Competency:* This may be requested when the Subject has disclosed a condition that may impact their ability to practice or when evidence has been submitted which suggests this circumstance. Examples include, but are not limited to: reports of a mental health condition (or treatment for a condition) that prevents or significantly impacts work for a period of time, physical injuries that prevent work, or criminal offenses like repeated instances of drinking and driving that raise questions about the Subject's competency to practice.

   d) *Paper or Product Submission:* The Subject must read one or more relevant articles and submit a paper related to the relevant code violation, and/or create and submit other related products (e.g., policies, procedures, tracking systems, handbooks).

2. **Sanctions:** These consequences are published on the BACB website in the Subject's Registry record until the sanction requirements are completed, with the exceptions of revocation and invalidation, which remain in the individual's Registry record permanently.

   a) *Certification Invalidation:* The Subject's certification is invalidated because the eligibility requirements were not met. The Subject whose certification is invalidated was, in effect, never legitimately certified.

   b) *Revocation:* The Subject's certification is terminated. After the duration of the revocation period the Subject must apply for post-revocation re-entry to be reviewed by a committee that will make a decision to approve or deny.

   c) *Certification Suspension:* The Subject's certification may not be used for a specified period of time. *Eligibility Suspension:* The Subject is not eligible to apply for BACB certification for a specified period of time.

   d) *Practice Restriction:* The Subject's ability to practice behavior analysis using BACB certification is limited.

e) *Mandatory Supervision:* The Subject is required to receive supervision from an approved individual for the indicated duration to address concerns related to the specific violations and any other areas identified.

Note: Violating the terms of a consequence issued in a Disciplinary or Appeal Determination will result in immediate certification or eligibility suspension or revocation. See section *B*, subsection 3 of this document for more information about summary actions and the required steps for initiating reinstatement of certification, application eligibility, or other status with the BACB.

SECTION G. Appeal Process

Procedures for Appeal Process: If the Subject is issued consequences as a part of Disciplinary Review, the Subject has 30 days to submit a written request for appeal. Once the subject requests an appeal they will receive instructions and information about the appeal process. The Notifier does not have the right to request an appeal. The Disciplinary Appeal Committee – consisting of a minimum of three current or former members of the BACB Board of Directors – hears the appeal. Members of the Review Committee that issued the Disciplinary Determination in the matter may not serve on the Appeal Committee. Formal rules of evidence do not apply to BACB appeal processes.

1. **Cases with Sanctions (i.e., Published Consequences):** In addition to submitting the required appeal document, the Subject has the right to be present during the appeal, via video conference. The Subject may submit written or verbal documentation in support of their appeal, may choose to be represented by counsel, and may have witnesses present during the video conference. The Subject must submit all additional documentation and a list of all individuals who will be present at the meeting to the BACB Ethics Department by the date required.
2. **Cases with Corrective Actions (i.e., Non-published Consequences):** In cases that only include Corrective Actions, the Subject must submit a written appeal document and may not be present during the appeal. The Subject may include additional documentation in support of their appeal, statements from witnesses, and appeal documents prepared by an attorney by the date required by the BACB Ethics Department.
3. **Disciplinary Appeal Committee Decision:** The Committee may issue one of three outcomes in the Appeal Determination, in part or in whole: (1) uphold, (2) modify (but not in a manner more adverse to the Subject), or (3) overturn.
4. **Notification of Outcome:** Typically, BACB staff send the Subject the Appeal Determination within 15 days of the Committee's decision. Any additional documentation the Subject submits after the conclusion of the appeal will not be considered. The BACB also sends the Appeal Determination to the Notifier.

SECTION H. Release of Documentation

Upon formal request (e.g., subpoena or court order) by a governmental agency or court of law, or at the discretion of the Chief Executive Officer, the BACB may release all documentation (i.e., Notice, documents relevant to violation, Subject's response and related documents, and relevant correspondence) to the requesting party.

SECTION I. Amendment to Procedures

The BACB reserves the right to amend these procedures at any time.

Appendix D

Considerations for Self-Reporting

Use this checklist to help determine if you should make a self-report to the BACB Ethics Department. Always refer to the BACB website to access and review the most current version of the RBT Ethics Code or the Professional and Ethical Compliance Code for Behavior Analysts. More guidance on self-reporting requirements and considerations can be found in the November 2016 and April 2017 BACB Newsletters. If you are a certificant with a BACB required supervisor, consider consulting with them before submitting your self-report.

This checklist is based on sections 10.02(a), (b), (c) of the Professional and Ethical Compliance Code for Behavior Analysts (Compliance Code), as well as the Preamble of the RBT Ethics Code.

Timely reporting requires the individual to self-report within 30 days of becoming aware of any of the conditions listed in the Preamble of the RBT Ethics Code or 10.02 of the Professional and Ethical Compliance Code for Behavior Analysts.

If you answer **yes** *to any of the questions, you should self-report to the BACB Ethics Department.*

Related Ethics Requirement Element	Question to consider	Yes	No
RBT Ethics Code Preamble Professional and Ethical Compliance Code for Behavior Analysts 10.02(a)	Have you violated an ethics requirement?	❏	❏
	Have you been the subject of any criminal legal actions, including filing of criminal charges, arrest, plea of guilty or no contest, presentencing agreements, diversion agreements, convictions, and any period of custody in a jail, prison, or community corrections setting such as a "halfway house"?	❏	❏
	Have you been the subject of any civil legal actions, including filing of lawsuits, or any legal actions in which you have been named or identified (even if not a direct party to the suit)?	❏	❏
	Have you been the subject of any regulatory actions, including investigations, consent agreements, administrative law proceedings, mediation, arbitration, etc.?	❏	❏

Related Ethics Requirement Element	Question to consider	Yes	No
	Have you been the subject of any healthcare agency and employer actions, including investigations and sanctions for incompetent or neglectful service delivery?	❏	❏
	Have you been issued a public health- and safety-related ticket or fine related to an incident that may indicate a physical or mental condition that could impact the competent delivery of services?	❏	❏
RBT Ethics Code Preamble Professional and Ethical Compliance Code for Behavior Analysts 10.02(b)	Have you been issued a public health- and safety-related ticket or fine related to an incident that is evidence of another Compliance Code violation (e.g., a citation for negligently leaving a client unattended)?	❏	❏
	Have you been issued a public health- and safety-related ticket or fine related to an incident where a client was present (regardless of the amount of the fine)?	❏	❏
	Have you been issued a public health- and safety-related ticket or fine related to an incident that involved the operation of a motor vehicle and the fine was greater than $750?	❏	❏
	Have you been issued a public health- and safety-related ticket or fine related to an incident that you were required to report to your professional liability insurance provider?	❏	❏
RBT Ethics Code Preamble Professional and Ethical Compliance Code for Behavior Analysts 10.02(b) cont.	Have you been issued a public health- and safety-related ticket or fine related to an incident that you were required to report to a client's third-party payer?	❏	❏
	Have you been issued a public health- and safety-related ticket or fine related to an incident that you were required to report to a governmental regulatory board?	❏	❏
	Have you been the subject of any investigation, charge, allegation, or sanction that could have placed the client at risk for harm or impacted the competent delivery of services?	❏	❏
RBT Handbook (pg. 19) BCaBA Handbook (pg. 34) Professional and Ethical Compliance Code for Behavior Analysts 10.02	Have you failed to meet the relevant requirements (e.g., number of contacts, % supervision) when providing supervision* to an RBT or BCaBA?	❏	❏
	Have you failed to maintain documentation meeting the relevant requirements when providing supervision* to an RBT or BCaBA?	❏	❏
	Are you an RBT or BCaBA who provided services without a qualified supervisor overseeing your work?	❏	❏
	Are you an RBT or BCaBA who did not meet the relevant supervision requirements (e.g., number of contacts, % supervision)?	❏	❏
	Are you an RBT or BCaBA who did not maintain documentation meeting the relevant supervision requirements?	❏	❏
RBT Ethics Code Preamble Professional and Ethical Compliance Code for Behavior Analysts 10.02(c)	Have you been diagnosed, treated, or hospitalized for any mental or physical condition that could put clients at risk for harm?	❏	❏
	Have you been diagnosed, treated, or hospitalized for any mental or physical condition that could impair the competent delivery of services?	❏	❏

* If you did not meet the relevant supervision or documentation requirements for a trainee make sure you address the issue with the trainee and adjust relevant records for the experience hours meeting the requirements.

Gather and Prepare all Supporting Documentation

- Any documentation that includes protected or identifying information (e.g., client name, address, date of birth) must be redacted. This can be done by removing the information from an electronic document and replacing it with generic terms (e.g., NAME, GENDER, XX/XX/XX). This can also be done in electronic documents by highlighting the sensitive information in black or placing a black box over the information (e.g., name, date of birth, photographs). For hard copies of documents this can be done by using a marker or correction ink or tape to cover the sensitive information before scanning or taking a photo.
- All documents with sensitive information must be converted to PDFs.
- When taking screenshots of websites, emails, or text messages, it is best to validate the date/time of the screen shot by capturing the date/time on the screen.
- When taking screenshots of text messages, it must be clear when the text messages occurred and with whom the conversation occurred (e.g., the name of the individual should appear at the top of the screenshots).
- It is best to combine all supporting documentation into one PDF with page numbers and a table of contents, if possible. It is also best to name each separate piece of supporting documentation and link it to an alleged code violation.

Self-Report Checklist

Use this checklist to verify that you have completed all of the necessary steps for self-reporting and have compiled the relevant documentation for submitting and documenting your self-report.

- ❏ RBT or BCaBA – disclose matter to supervisor (keep record of disclosure)
- ❏ Self-report to the BACB within 30 days of the incident
- ❏ Cover letter (see Considerations for Self-Report Cover Letter) Provide documentation where applicable
- ❏ Initial documentation related to self-report (e.g., ticket, letter from investigative body, letter from physician, supervision tracker)
- ❏ Concluding documentation related to self-report (e.g., court documentation, letter from investigative body, letter from physician)
- ❏ Copy of correspondence with supervisor/supervisee
- ❏ Continue to provide the BACB with updates on pending matters (every six months or earlier if information becomes available)

Note: If documentation is unavailable, please provide an explanation in your cover letter.

Considerations for Self-Reporting Cover Letter

The purpose of providing a cover letter when self-reporting is to provide the BACB with context that might not be available, or readily apparent, from simply reviewing the documentation. Essentially, the cover letter allows you to tell your story and explain additional information that can help the BACB in reviewing your self-report. This document lists things you should consider including in your cover letter.

Standard Information

- Your full name
- Your BACB ID
- Your application/certification level and certification number (if applicable)
- The name of your BACB required supervisor (if applicable)
- The date you are reporting
- The date of the incident, and the date you became aware (if relevant)
- An explanation if you are reporting past the 30 day requirement
- An explanation of the incident. Specify the following:
  - if clients were involved or present
  - if the incident occurred in the work context
  - if other vulnerable individuals (e.g., children, elderly) were involved or present
  - if drugs/and or alcohol were involved
  - if you notified anyone (e.g., supervisor, employer, regulatory body)
- A description of the documents provided (If documentation is unavailable, please provide an explanation)
- A description of any actions you have taken to address the situation (if applicable)

If Incident Is Related to an Investigation or Disciplinary Action (as applicable)

- Describe who conducted the investigation
- Describe the specific focus of the investigation
  - Indicate if the investigation was related to abuse (e.g., physical, sexual), neglect, harassment, or other action that did or could cause harm to an individual
  - Indicate if the investigation was related to fraud or theft
- Provide the status of the investigation (e.g., pending, concluded, ongoing)
- Describe the specific disciplinary action/s taken, if any (e.g., terminated, monetary penalty, restitution)
- Provide the status of any disciplinary actions, corrective actions, penalties (e.g., completed and date, currently completing and anticipated completion date)

If the Incident Is Related to a Violation of the Law (e.g., driving offense, assault, theft, public health and safety ticket)

- Specify if the charges were misdemeanors or felonies
- Specify if the charges were related to, or resulted in, harm to an individual (e.g., manslaughter, aggravated assault)
- Describe the status of the matter (e.g., pending, concluded, ongoing)
- Describe any outcomes or consequences (e.g., fines paid, completion of probation, completion of substance abuse courses or diversion programs)
- Provide the status of any outcomes or consequences (e.g., completed and date, currently completing and anticipated completion date)

If the Incident Is Related to a Physical or Mental Health Condition that Impairs Your Ability to Competently Practice

- Describe how the physical or mental health condition impairs your ability to practice
- Provide the status of the matter (e.g., hospitalized, receiving outpatient care, cleared by physician or mental health professional)

- Specify if you are currently practicing
- Specify if you have a treatment plan in place
- Specify if you are currently under the care of a physician or a mental health professional (e.g., Psychiatrist, Psychologist, Medical Doctor, Therapist, Addiction Counselor)

Index